"I'd like to congratulate the both of you for a very impressive work! Not only did I find your book to be an enjoyable and rewarding read ... I was astounded by the accuracy both in terms of technical correctness and use of the language ... I believe that you have attained a level of craftsmanship that is simply outstanding."

Bjorn Karlsson
Editorial Board, C/C++ Users Journal

"This book is a tremendous achievement. You owe it to yourself to have a copy on your shelf."

Al Stevens
Contributing Editor, Doctor Dobbs Journal

"Eckel's book is the only one to so clearly explain how to rethink program construction for object orientation. That the book is also an excellent tutorial on the ins and outs of C++ is an added bonus."

Andrew Binstock
Editor, Unix Review

"Bruce continues to amaze me with his insight into C++, and *Thinking in C++* is his best collection of ideas yet. If you want clear answers to difficult questions about C++, buy this outstanding book."

Gary Entsminger
Author, *The Tao of Objects*

"*Thinking in C++* patiently and methodically explores the issues of when and how to use inlines, references, operator overloading, inheritance and dynamic objects, as well as advanced topics such as the proper use of templates, exceptions and multiple inheritance. The entire effort is woven in a fabric that includes Eckel's own philosophy of object and program design. A must for every C++ developer's bookshelf, *Thinking in C++* is the one C++ book you must have if you're doing serious development with C++."

Richard Hale Shaw
Contributing Editor, PC Magazine

Duke stat 2015

Sean Chang   Nov 2014

D0609728

Thinking

In

C++

Volume 2:
Practical Programming

Bruce Eckel, President, MindView, Inc.
Chuck Allison, Utah Valley State College

PEARSON

Prentice
Hall

Upper Saddle River, New Jersey 07458

Library of Congress Cataloging-in-Publication Data

CIP DATA AVAILABLE

Vice President and Editorial Director, ECS: *Marcia J. Horton*
Publisher: *Alan R. Apt*
Associate Editor: *Toni Dianne Holm*
Editorial Assistant: *Patrick Lindner*
Vice President and Director of Production and Manufacturing, ESM: *David W. Riccardi*
Executive Managing Editor: *Vince O'Brien*
Managing Editor: *Camille Trentacoste*
Production Editor: *Irwin Zucker*
Director of Creative Services: *Paul Belfanti*
Creative Director: *Carole Anson*
Cover and Interior Designer: *Daniel Will-Harris*
Cover Illustrations: *Tina Jensen*
Manufacturing Manager: *Trudy Pisciotti*
Manufacturing Buyer: *Lisa McDowell*
Marketing Manager: *Pamela Shaffer*

©2004 MindView, Inc.
Published by Pearson Prentice Hall
Pearson Education, Inc.
Upper Saddle River, NJ 07458

Printed in the United States of America

10 9 8 7 6 5 4 3 2

ISBN   0-13-035313-2

Pearson Education Ltd., *London*
Pearson Education Australia Pty. Ltd., *Sydney*
Pearson Education Singapore, Pte. Ltd.
Pearson Education North Asia Ltd., *Hong Kong*
Pearson Education Canada, Inc., *Toronto*
Pearson Educación de Mexico, S.A. de C.V.
Pearson Education-Japan, *Tokyo*
Pearson Education Malaysia, Pte. Ltd.
Pearson Education, Inc., *Upper Saddle River, New Jersey*

DID THE BOOK YOU'RE HOLDING
GET YOU THINKING? THEN TRY...

WINNER:

Software Development
Magazine Jolt Award for
Best book of 2002

JavaWorld Editor's Choice
Award for Best Book, 2001

JavaWorld Reader's Choice
Award for Best Book, 2001

Software Development
Magazine Productivity
Award, 1999

Java Developer's Journal
Editor's Choice Award for
Best Book, 1998, 2003

Dedication

To all those who have worked tirelessly
to develop the C++ language

What's inside...

2: Defensive Programming   63

II: The Standard C++ Library 101

3: Strings in Depth 103

4: Iostreams 151

5: Templates in Depth   227

Contents   xv

III: Special Topics   549

8: Runtime Type Identification   551

9: Multiple Inheritance   573

10: Design Patterns   613

11 : Concurrency   691

A: Recommended Reading   777

B: Etc   783

Index   791

Introduction

In Volume 1 of this book, you learned the fundamentals of C and C++. In this volume, we look at more advanced features, with an eye towards developing techniques and ideas that produce robust C++ programs.

We assume you are familiar with the material presented in Volume 1.

Goals

Our goals in this book are to:

1. Present the material a simple step at a time, so the reader can easily digest each concept before moving on.

2. Teach "practical programming" techniques that you can use on a day-to-day basis.

3. Give you what we think is important for you to understand about the language, rather than everything we know. We believe there is an "information importance hierarchy," and there are some facts that 95% of programmers will never need to know, but that would just confuse people and add to their perception of the complexity of the language. To take an example from C, if you memorize the operator precedence table (we never did) you can write clever code. But if *you* must think about it, it will confuse the reader/maintainer of that code. So forget about precedence and use parentheses when things aren't clear. This same attitude will be taken with some information in the C++ language, which is more important for compiler writers than for programmers.

4. Keep each section focused enough so the lecture time—and the time between exercise periods—is small. Not only does this keep the audience' minds more active and involved during a hands-on seminar, but it gives the reader a greater sense of accomplishment.

5. We have endeavored not to use any particular vendor's version of C++. We have tested the code on all the implementations we could (described later in this introduction), and when one implementation absolutely refused to work because it doesn't conform to the C++ Standard, we've flagged that fact in the example (you'll see the flags in the source code) to exclude it from the build process.

6. Automate the compiling and testing of the code in the book. We have discovered that code that isn't compiled and tested is probably broken, so in this volume we've instrumented the examples with test code. In addition, the code that you can download from http://www.MindView.net has been extracted directly from the text of the book using programs that automatically create makefiles to compile and run the tests. This way we know that the code in the book is correct.

Chapters

Here is a brief description of the chapters contained in this book:

Part 1: Building Stable Systems

1. Exception handling. Error handling has always been a problem in programming. Even if you dutifully return error information or set a flag, the function caller may simply ignore it. Exception handling is a primary feature in C++ that solves this problem by allowing you to "throw" an object out of your function when a critical error happens. You throw different types of objects for different errors, and the function caller "catches" these objects in separate error handling routines. If you throw an exception, it cannot be ignored, so you can guarantee that *something* will happen in response to your error. The decision to use exceptions affects code design in positive, fundamental ways.

2. Defensive Programming. Many software problems can be prevented. To program defensively is to craft code in such a way that bugs are found and fixed early before they can damage in the field. Using assertions is the single most important way to validate your code during development, while at the same time leaving an executable documentation trail in your code that reveals your thoughts while you wrote the code in the first place. Rigorously test your code before you let out of your hands. An automated unit testing framework is an indispensable tool for successful, everyday software development.

Part 2: The Standard C++ Library

3. Strings in Depth. The most common programming activity is text processing. The C++ string class relieves the programmer from memory management issues, while at the same time delivering a powerhouse of text processing capability. C++ also supports the use of wide characters and locales for internationalized applications.

 4. Iostreams. One of the original C++ libraries—the one that provides the essential I/O facility—is called iostreams. Iostreams is intended to replace C's **stdio.h** with an I/O library that is easier to use, more flexible, and extensible—you can adapt it to work with your new classes. This chapter teaches you how to make the best use of the existing iostream library for standard I/O, file I/O, and in-memory formatting.

5. Templates in Depth. The distinguishing feature of "modern C++" is the broad power of templates. Templates do more than just create generic containers. They support development of robust, generic, high-performance libraries. There is a lot to know about templates—they constitute, as it were, a sub-language within the C++ language, and give the programmer an impressive degree of control over the compilation process. It is not an overstatement to say that templates have revolutionized C++ programming.

6. Generic Algorithms. Algorithms are at the core of computing, and C++, through its template facility, supports an impressive entourage of powerful, efficient, and easy-to-use generic algorithms. The standard algorithms are also customizable through function objects. This chapter looks at every algorithm in the library. (Chapters 6 and 7 cover that portion of the Standard C++ library commonly known as the Standard Template Library, or STL.)

7. Generic Containers & Iterators. C++ supports all the common data structures in a type-safe manner. You never need to worry about what such a container holds. The homogeneity of its objects is guaranteed. Separating the traversing of a container from the container itself, another accomplishment of templates, is made possible through iterators. This ingenious arrangement allows a flexible application of algorithms to containers using the simplest of designs.

Part 3: Special Topics

8. Runtime type identification. Runtime type identification (RTTI) finds the exact type of an object when you only have a pointer or reference to the base type. Normally, you'll want to intentionally ignore the exact type of an object and let the virtual function mechanism implement the correct behavior for that type. But occasionally (like when writing software tools such as debuggers) it is helpful to know the exact type of an object—with this information, you can often perform a special-case operation more efficiently. This chapter explains what RTTI is for and how to use it.

9. Multiple inheritance. This sounds simple at first: A new class is inherited from more than one existing class. However, you can end up with ambiguities and multiple copies of base-class objects. That problem is solved with virtual base classes, but the bigger issue remains: When do you use it? Multiple inheritance is only essential when you need to manipulate an object through more than one common base class. This chapter explains the syntax for multiple inheritance and shows alternative approaches—in particular, how templates solve one typical problem. Using multiple inheritance to repair a "damaged" class interface is demonstrated as a valuable use of this feature.

10. Design Patterns. The most revolutionary advance in programming since objects is the introduction of *design patterns*. A design pattern is a language-independent codification of a solution to a common programming problem, expressed in such a way that it can apply to many contexts. Patterns such as Singleton, Factory Method, and Visitor now find their way into daily discussions around the keyboard. This chapter shows how to implement and use some of the more useful design patterns in C++.

11. Concurrent Programming. People have come to expect responsive user interfaces that (seem to) process multiple tasks simultaneously. Modern operating systems allow processes to have multiple threads that share the process address space. Multithreaded programming requires a different mindset, however, and comes with its own set of difficulties. This chapter uses a freely available library (the ZThread library by Eric Crahen of IBM) to show how to effectively manage multithreaded applications in C++.

Exercises

We have discovered that simple exercises are exceptionally useful during a seminar to complete a student's understanding. You'll find a set at the end of each chapter.

These are fairly simple, so they can be finished in a reasonable amount of time in a classroom situation while the instructor observes, making sure all the students are absorbing the material. Some exercises are a bit more challenging to keep advanced students entertained. They're all designed to be solved in a short time and are only there to test and polish your knowledge rather than present major challenges (presumably, you'll find those on your own—or more likely they'll find you).

Exercise solutions

Solutions to exercises can be found in the electronic document *The C++ Annotated Solution Guide*, Volume 2, available for a nominal fee from http://www.MindView.net.

Source code

The source code for this book is copyrighted freeware, distributed via the web site http://www.MindView.net. The copyright prevents you from republishing the code in print media without permission.

In the starting directory where you unpack the code you will find the following copyright notice:

```
//:! :CopyRight.txt
(c) 1995-2004 MindView, Inc.  All rights reserved.
Source code file from the book
"Thinking in C++, 2nd Edition, Volume 2."

The following permissions are granted respecting the
computer source code, which is contained in this file:

Permission is granted to classroom educators to use this
file as part of instructional materials prepared for
classes personally taught or supervised by the educator who
uses this permission, provided that (a) the book "Thinking
```

```
In no event will the authors or the publisher be liable for
any lost revenue, savings, or data, or for direct,
indirect, special, consequential, incidental, exemplary or
punitive damages, however caused and regardless of any
related theory of liability, arising out of this license
and/or the use of or inability to use this software, even
if the vendors and/or the publisher have been advised of
the possibility of such damages. Should the software prove
defective, you assume the cost of all necessary servicing,
repair, or correction.

If you think you have a correction for an error in the
software, please submit the correction to www.MindView.net.
(Please use the same process for non-code errors found in
the book.)

If you have a need for permissions not granted above,
please inquire of MindView, Inc., at www.MindView.net or
send a request by email to Bruce@EckelObjects.com.
///:~
```

You may use the code in your projects and in the classroom as long as the
copyright notice is retained.

Compilers

Your compiler may not support all the features discussed in this book,
especially if you don't have the newest version of your compiler.
Implementing a language like C++ is a Herculean task, and you can expect
that the features will appear in pieces rather than all at once. But if you
attempt one of the examples in the book and get a lot of errors from the
compiler, it's not necessarily a bug in the code or the compiler—it may simply
not be implemented in your particular compiler yet.

We used a number of compilers to test the code in this book, in an attempt to
ensure that our code conforms to the C++ Standard and will work with as
many compilers as possible. Unfortunately, not all compilers conform to the
C++ Standard, and so we have a way of excluding certain files from building
with those compilers. These exclusions are reflected in the makefiles
automatically created for the package of code for this book that you can
download from www.MindView.net. You can see the exclusion tags
embedded in the comments at the beginning of each listing, so you will know

whether to expect a particular compiler to work on that code (in a few cases, the compiler will actually compile the code but the execution behavior is wrong, and we exclude those as well).

Here are the tags and the compilers that they exclude from the build:

- **{-dmc}** Walter Bright's Digital Mars compiler for Windows, freely downloadable at www.DigitalMars.com. This compiler is very conformant and so you will see almost none of these tags throughout the book.

- **{-g++}** The free Gnu C++ 3.3.1, which comes pre-installed in most Linux packages and Macintosh OSX. It is also part of Cygwin for Windows (see below). It is available for most other platforms from gcc.gnu.org.

- **{-msc}** Microsoft Version 7 with Visual C++ .NET (only comes with Visual Studio .NET; not freely downloadable).

- **{-bor}** Borland C++ Version 6 (not the free download; this one is more up to date).

- **{-edg}** Edison Design Group (EDG) C++. This is the benchmark compiler for standards conformance. This tag occurs only because of library issues, and because we were using a complimentary copy of the EDG front end with a complimentary library implementation from Dinkumware, Ltd. No compile errors occurred because of the compiler alone.

- **{-mwcc}** Metrowerks Code Warrior for Macintosh OS X. Note that OS X comes with Gnu C++ pre-installed, as well.

If you download and unpack the code package for this book from www.MindView.net, you'll find the makefiles to build the code for the above compilers. We used the freely-available GNU-**make**, which comes with Linux, Cygwin (a free Unix shell that runs on top of Windows; see www.Cygwin.com), or can be installed on your platform—see www.gnu.org/software/make. (Other **make**s may or may not work with these files, but are not supported.) Once you install **make**, if you type **make** at the command line you'll get instructions on how to build the book's code for the above compilers.

Note that the placement of these tags on the files in this book indicates the state of the particular version of the compiler at the time we tried it. It's possible and likely that the compiler vendor has improved the compiler since the publication of this book. It's also possible that while building the book with so many compilers, we may have misconfigured a particular compiler that would otherwise have compiled the code correctly. Thus, you should try the code yourself on your compiler, and also check the code downloaded from www.MindView.net to see what is current.

Language standards

Throughout this book, when referring to conformance to the ANSI/ISO C standard, we will be referring to the 1989 standard, and will generally just say '**C**.' Only if it is necessary to distinguish between Standard 1989 C and older, pre-Standard versions of C will we make the distinction. We do not reference C99 in this book.

The ANSI/ISO C++ Committee long ago finished working on the first C++ Standard, commonly known as C++98. We will use the term *Standard C++* to refer to this standardized language. If we simply refer to C++, assume we mean "Standard C++." The C++ Standards Committee continues to address issues important to the C++ community that will become C++0x, a future C++ Standard not likely to be available for many years.

Seminars, CD–ROMs & consulting

Bruce Eckel's company, MindView, Inc., provides public hands-on training seminars based on the material in this book, and also for advanced topics. Selected material from each chapter represents a lesson, which is followed by a monitored exercise period so each student receives personal attention. We also provide on-site training, consulting, mentoring, and design & code walkthroughs. Information and sign-up forms for upcoming seminars and other contact information is found at **http://www.MindView.net**.

Errors

No matter how many tricks writers use to detect errors, some always creep in and these often leap off the page for a fresh reader. If you discover anything you believe to be an error, please use the feedback system built into the electronic version of this book, which you will find at **http://www.MindView.net**. Your help is appreciated.

About the cover

The cover artwork was painted by Larry O'Brien's wife, Tina Jensen (yes, the Larry O'Brien who was the editor of Software Development Magazine for so many years). Not only are the pictures beautiful, they are also excellent suggestions of polymorphism. The idea for using these images came from Daniel Will-Harris, the cover designer (www.Will-Harris.com), working with Bruce.

Acknowledgements

Volume 2 of this book languished in a half-completed state for a long time while Bruce got distracted with other things, notably Java, Design Patterns and especially Python (see www.Python.org). If Chuck hadn't been willing (foolishly, he has sometimes thought) to finish the other half and bring things up-to-date, this book almost certainly wouldn't have happened. There aren't that many people whom Bruce would have felt comfortable entrusting this book to. Chuck's penchant for precision, correctness and clear explanation is what has made this book as good as it is.

Jamie King acted as an intern under Chuck's direction during the completion of this book. He was an essential part of making sure the book got finished, not only by providing feedback for Chuck, but especially because of his relentless questioning and picking of every single possible nit that he didn't completely understand. If your questions are answered by this book, it's probably because Jamie asked them first. Jamie also enhanced a number of the sample programs and created many of the exercises at the end of each chapter. Scott Baker, another of Chuck's interns funded by MindView, Inc., helped with the exercises for Chapter 3.

Eric Crahen of IBM was instrumental in the completion of Chapter 11 (Concurrency). When we were looking for a threads package, we sought out one that was intuitive and easy to use, while being sufficiently robust to do the job. With Eric we got that and then some—he was extremely cooperative and has used our feedback to enhance his library, while we have benefited from his insights as well.

We are grateful to Pete Becker for being our technical editor. Few people are as articulate and discriminating as Pete, not to mention as expert in C++ and software development in general. We also thank Bjorn Karlsson for his gracious and timely technical assistance as he reviewed the entire manuscript with short notice.

Walter Bright made Herculean efforts to make sure that his Digital Mars C++ compiler would compile the examples in this book. He makes the compiler available for free downloads at http://www.DigitalMars.com. Thanks, Walter!

The ideas and understanding in this book have come from many other sources, as well: friends like Andrea Provaglio, Dan Saks, Scott Meyers, Charles Petzold, and Michael Wilk; pioneers of the language like Bjarne Stroustrup, Andrew Koenig, and Rob Murray; members of the C++ Standards Committee like Nathan Myers (who was particularly helpful and generous with his insights), Herb Sutter, PJ Plauger, Kevlin Henney, David Abrahams, Tom Plum, Reg Charney, Tom Penello, Sam Druker, Uwe Steinmueller, John Spicer, Steve Adamczyk, and Daveed Vandevoorde; people who have spoken in the C++ track at the Software Development Conference (which Bruce created and developed, and Chuck spoke in); Colleagues of Chuck like Michael Seaver, Huston Franklin, David Wagstaff, and often students in seminars, who ask the questions we need to hear to make the material clearer.

The book design, typeface selection, cover design, and cover photo were created by Bruce's friend Daniel Will-Harris, noted author and designer, who used to play with rub-on letters in junior high school while he awaited the invention of computers and desktop publishing. However, we produced the camera-ready pages ourselves, so the typesetting errors are ours. Microsoft® Word XP was used to write the book and to create camera-ready pages. The body typeface is Georgia and the headlines are in Verdana. The code type face is Andale Mono.

We also wish to thank the generous professionals at the Edison Design Group and Dinkumware, Ltd., for giving us complimentary copies of their compiler and library (respectively). Without their expert assistance, graciously given, some of the examples in this book could not have been tested. We also wish to thank Howard Hinnant and the folks at Metrowerks for a copy of their compiler, and Sandy Smith and the folks at SlickEdit for keeping Chuck supplied with a world-class editing environment for so many years. Greg Comeau also provided a copy of his successful EDG-based compiler, Comeau C++.

A special thanks to all our teachers, and all our students (who are our teachers as well).

Evan Cofsky (Evan@TheUnixMan.com) provided all sorts of assistance on the server as well as development of programs in his now-favorite language, Python. Sharlynn Cobaugh and Paula Steuer were instrumental assistants, preventing Bruce from being washed away in a flood of projects.

Bruce's sweetie Dawn McGee provided much-appreciated inspiration and enthusiasm during this project. The supporting cast of friends includes, but is not limited to: Mark Western, Gen Kiyooka, Kraig Brockschmidt, Zack Urlocker, Andrew Binstock, Neil Rubenking, Steve Sinofsky, JD Hildebrandt, Brian McElhinney, Brinkley Barr, Bill Gates at Midnight Engineering Magazine, Larry Constantine & Lucy Lockwood, Tom Keffer, Greg Perry, Dan Putterman, Christi Westphal, Gene Wang, Dave Mayer, David Intersimone, Claire Sawyers, The Italians (Andrea Provaglio, Laura Fallai, Marco Cantu, Corrado, Ilsa and Christina Giustozzi), Chris & Laura Strand, The Almquists, Brad Jerbic, John Kruth & Marilyn Cvitanic, Holly Payne (yes, the famous novelist!), Mark Mabry, The Robbins Families, The Moelter Families (& the McMillans), The Wilks, Dave Stoner, Laurie Adams, The Cranstons, Larry Fogg, Mike & Karen Sequeira, Gary Entsminger & Allison Brody, Chester Andersen, Joe Lordi, Dave & Brenda Bartlett, The Rentschlers, The Sudeks, Lynn & Todd, and their families. And of course, Mom & Dad, Sandy, James & Natalie, Kim& Jared, Isaac, and Abbi.

Part 1

Building Stable Systems

Software engineers spend about as much time validating code as they do creating it. Quality is or should be the goal of every programmer, and one can go a long way towards that goal by eliminating problems before they happen. In addition, software systems should be robust enough to behave reasonably in the presence of unforeseen environmental problems.

Exceptions were introduced into C++ to support sophisticated error handling without cluttering code with an inordinate amount of error-handling logic. Chapter 1 shows how proper use of exceptions can make for well-behaved software, and also introduces the design principles that underlie exception-safe code. In Chapter 2 we cover unit testing and debugging techniques intended to maximize code quality long before it's released. The use of assertions to express and enforce program invariants is a sure sign of an experienced software engineer. We also introduce a simple framework to support unit testing.

1: Exception Handling

Improving error recovery is one of the most powerful ways you can increase the robustness of your code.

Unfortunately, it's almost accepted practice to ignore error conditions, as if we're in a state of denial about errors. One reason, no doubt, is the tediousness and code bloat of checking for many errors. For example, **printf( )** returns the number of characters that were successfully printed, but virtually no one checks this value. The proliferation of code alone would be disgusting, not to mention the difficulty it would add in reading the code.

The problem with C's approach to error handling could be thought of as coupling—the user of a function must tie the error-handling code so closely to that function that it becomes too ungainly and awkward to use.

One of the major features in C++ is *exception handling*, which is a better way of thinking about and handling errors. With exception handling:

1.   Error-handling code is not nearly so tedious to write, and it doesn't become mixed up with your "normal" code. You write the code you *want* to happen; later in a separate section you write the code to cope with the problems. If you make multiple calls to a function, you handle the errors from that function once, in one place.

2.   Errors cannot be ignored. If a function needs to send an error message to the caller of that function, it "throws" an object representing that error out of the function. If the caller doesn't "catch" the error and handle it, it goes to the next enclosing dynamic scope, and so on until the error is either caught or the program terminates because there was no handler to catch that type of exception.

This chapter examines C's approach to error handling (such as it is), discusses why it did not work well for C, and explains why it won't work at all for C++. This chapter also covers **try**, **throw**, and **catch**, the C++ keywords that support exception handling.

Traditional error handling

In most of the examples in these volumes, we use **assert( )** as it was intended: for debugging during development with code that can be disabled with **#define NDEBUG** for the shipping product. Runtime error checking uses the **require.h** functions (**assure( )** and **require( )**) developed in Chapter 9 in Volume 1 and repeated here in Appendix B. These functions are a convenient way to say, "There's a problem here you'll probably want to handle with some more sophisticated code, but you don't need to be distracted by it in this example." The **require.h** functions might be enough for small programs, but for complicated products you'll want to write more sophisticated error-handling code.

Error handling is quite straightforward when you know exactly what to do, because you have all the necessary information in that context. You can just handle the error at that point.

The problem occurs when you *don't* have enough information in that context, and you need to pass the error information into a different context where that information does exist. In C, you can handle this situation using three approaches:

1.   Return error information from the function or, if the return value cannot be used this way, set a global error condition flag. (Standard C provides **errno** and **perror( )** to support this.) As mentioned earlier, the programmer is likely to ignore the error information because tedious and obfuscating error checking must occur with each function call. In addition, returning from a function that hits an exceptional condition might not make sense.

2.   Use the little-known Standard C library signal-handling system, implemented with the **signal( )** function (to determine what happens when the event occurs) and **raise( )** (to generate an event). Again, this approach involves high coupling because it requires the user of any library that generates signals to understand and install the appropriate signal-handling mechanism. In large projects the signal numbers from different libraries might clash.

3.   Use the *nonlocal goto* functions in the Standard C library: **setjmp( )** and **longjmp( )**. With **setjmp( )** you save a known good state in the program, and if you get into trouble, **longjmp( )** will restore that

---

state. Again, there is high coupling between the place where the state is stored and the place where the error occurs.

When considering error-handling schemes with C++, there's an additional critical problem: The C techniques of signals and **setjmp( )/longjmp( )** do not call destructors, so objects aren't properly cleaned up. (In fact, if **longjmp( )** jumps past the end of a scope where destructors should be called, the behavior of the program is undefined.) This makes it virtually impossible to effectively recover from an exceptional condition because you'll always leave objects behind that haven't been cleaned up and that can no longer be accessed. The following example demonstrates this with **setjmp/longjmp**:

```
//: C01:Nonlocal.cpp
// setjmp() & longjmp().
#include <iostream>
#include <csetjmp>
using namespace std;

class Rainbow {
public:
  Rainbow() { cout << "Rainbow()" << endl; }
  ~Rainbow() { cout << "~Rainbow()" << endl; }
};

jmp_buf kansas;

void oz() {
  Rainbow rb;
  for(int i = 0; i < 3; i++)
    cout << "there's no place like home" << endl;
  longjmp(kansas, 47);
}

int main() {
  if(setjmp(kansas) == 0) {
    cout << "tornado, witch, munchkins..." << endl;
    oz();
  } else {
    cout << "Auntie Em! "
         << "I had the strangest dream..."
         << endl;
  }
```

```
} ///:~
```

The **setjmp( )** function is odd because if you call it directly, it stores all the relevant information about the current processor state (such as the contents of the instruction pointer and runtime stack pointer) in the **jmp_buf** and returns zero. In this case it behaves like an ordinary function. However, if you call **longjmp( )** using the same **jmp_buf**, it's as if you're returning from **setjmp( )** again—you pop right out the back end of the **setjmp( )**. This time, the value returned is the second argument to **longjmp( )**, so you can detect that you're actually coming back from a **longjmp( )**. You can imagine that with many different **jmp_buf**s, you could pop around to many different places in the program. The difference between a local **goto** (with a label) and this nonlocal goto is that you can return to any pre-determined location higher up in the runtime stack with **setjmp( )/longjmp( )** (wherever you've placed a call to **setjmp( )**).

The problem in C++ is that **longjmp( )** doesn't respect objects; in particular it doesn't call destructors when it jumps out of a scope.[1] Destructor calls are essential, so this approach won't work with C++. In fact, the C++ Standard states that branching into a scope with **goto** (effectively bypassing constructor calls), or branching out of a scope with **longjmp( )** where an object on the stack has a destructor, constitutes undefined behavior.

Throwing an exception

If you encounter an exceptional situation in your code—that is, if you don't have enough information in the current context to decide what to do—you can send information about the error into a larger context by creating an object that contains that information and "throwing" it out of your current context. This is called *throwing an exception*. Here's what it looks like:

```
//: C01:MyError.cpp {RunByHand}

class MyError {
  const char* const data;
```

---

[1] You might be surprised when you run the example—some C++ compilers have extended **longjmp( )** to clean up objects on the stack. This behavior is not portable.

```
public:
  MyError(const char* const msg = 0) : data(msg) {}
};

void f() {
  // Here we "throw" an exception object:
  throw MyError("something bad happened");
}

int main() {
  // As you'll see shortly, we'll want a "try block" here:
  f();
} ///:~
```

MyError is an ordinary class, which in this case takes a **char*** as a constructor argument. You can use any type when you throw (including built-in types), but usually you'll create special classes for throwing exceptions.

The keyword **throw** causes a number of relatively magical things to happen. First, it creates a copy of the object you're throwing and, in effect, "returns" it from the function containing the throw expression, even though that object type isn't normally what the function is designed to return. A naive way to think about exception handling is as an alternate return mechanism (although you'll find you can get into trouble if you take that analogy too far). You can also exit from ordinary scopes by throwing an exception. In any case, a value is returned, and the function or scope exits.

Any similarity to a **return** statement ends there because *where* you return is some place completely different from where a normal function call returns. (You end up in an appropriate part of the code—called an exception handler— that might be far removed from where the exception was thrown.) In addition, any local objects created by the time the exception occurs are destroyed. This automatic cleanup of local objects is often called "stack unwinding."

In addition, you can throw as many different types of objects as you want. Typically, you'll throw a different type for each category of error. The idea is to store the information in the object and in the *name* of its class so that someone in a calling context can figure out what to do with your exception.

Catching an exception

As mentioned earlier, one of the advantages of C++ exception handling is that you can concentrate on the problem you're trying to solve in one place, and then deal with the errors from that code in another place.

The try block

If you're inside a function and you throw an exception (or a called function throws an exception), the function exits because of the thrown exception. If you don't want a **throw** to leave a function, you can set up a special block within the function where you try to solve your actual programming problem (and potentially generate exceptions). This block is called the *try block* because you try your various function calls there. The try block is an ordinary scope, preceded by the keyword **try**:

```
try {
  // Code that may generate exceptions
}
```

If you check for errors by carefully examining the return codes from the functions you use, you need to surround every function call with setup and test code, even if you call the same function several times. With exception handling, you put everything in a **try** block and handle exceptions after the **try** block. Thus, your code is a lot easier to write and to read because the goal of the code is not confused with the error handling.

Exception handlers

Of course, the thrown exception must end up some place. This place is the *exception handler*, and you need one exception handler for every exception type you want to catch. However, polymorphism also works for exceptions, so one exception handler can work with an exception type and classes derived from that type.

Exception handlers immediately follow the **try** block and are denoted by the keyword **catch**:

```
try {
  // Code that may generate exceptions
} catch(type1 id1) {
  // Handle exceptions of type1
```

```
} catch(type2 id2) {
  // Handle exceptions of type2
} catch(type3 id3)
  // Etc...
} catch(typeN idN)
  // Handle exceptions of typeN
}
// Normal execution resumes here...
```

The syntax of a **catch** clause resembles functions that take a single argument.
The identifier (**id1**, **id2**, and so on) can be used inside the handler, just like a
function argument, although you can omit the identifier if it's not needed in
the handler. The exception type usually gives you enough information to deal
with it.

The handlers must appear directly after the **try** block. If an exception is
thrown, the exception-handling mechanism goes hunting for the first handler
with an argument that matches the type of the exception. It then enters that
catch clause, and the exception is considered handled. (The search for
handlers stops once the **catch** clause is found.) Only the matching **catch**
clause executes; control then resumes after the last handler associated with
that try block.

Notice that, within the **try** block, a number of different function calls might
generate the same type of exception, but you need only one handler.

To illustrate **try** and **catch**, the following variation of **Nonlocal.cpp**
replaces the call to **setjmp( )** with a **try** block and replaces the call to
longjmp( ) with a **throw** statement:

```
//: C01:Nonlocal2.cpp
// Illustrates exceptions.
#include <iostream>
using namespace std;

class Rainbow {
public:
  Rainbow() { cout << "Rainbow()" << endl; }
  ~Rainbow() { cout << "~Rainbow()" << endl; }
};

void oz() {
  Rainbow rb;
```

```
  for(int i = 0; i < 3; i++)
    cout << "there's no place like home" << endl;
  throw 47;
}

int main() {
  try {
    cout << "tornado, witch, munchkins..." << endl;
    oz();
  } catch(int) {
    cout << "Auntie Em! I had the strangest dream..."
        << endl;
  }
} ///:~
```

When the **throw** statement in **oz( )** executes, program control backtracks until it finds the **catch** clause that takes an **int** parameter. Execution resumes with the body of that **catch** clause. The most important difference between this program and **Nonlocal.cpp** is that the destructor for the object **rb** is called when the **throw** statement causes execution to leave the function **oz( )**.

Termination and resumption

There are two basic models in exception-handling theory: termination and resumption. In *termination* (which is what C++ supports), you assume the error is so critical that there's no way to automatically resume execution at the point where the exception occurred. In other words, whoever threw the exception decided there was no way to salvage the situation, and they don't *want* to come back.

The alternative error-handling model is called *resumption*, first introduced with the PL/I language in the 1960s.[2] Using resumption semantics means that the exception handler is expected to do something to rectify the situation, and then the faulting code is automatically retried, presuming success the second time. If you want resumption in C++, you must explicitly transfer execution back to the code where the error occurred, usually by repeating the function call that sent you there in the first place. It is not

---

[2] The BASIC language has long supported a limited form of resumptive exception handling with its ON ERROR facility.

unusual to place your **try** block inside a **while** loop that keeps reentering the **try** block until the result is satisfactory.

Historically, programmers using operating systems that supported resumptive exception handling eventually ended up using termination-like code and skipping resumption. Although resumption sounds attractive at first, it seems it isn't quite so useful in practice. One reason may be the distance that can occur between the exception and its handler. It is one thing to terminate to a handler that's far away, but to jump to that handler and then back again may be too conceptually difficult for large systems where the exception is generated from many points.

Exception matching

When an exception is thrown, the exception-handling system looks through the "nearest" handlers in the order they appear in the source code. When it finds a match, the exception is considered handled and no further searching occurs.

Matching an exception doesn't require a perfect correlation between the exception and its handler. An object or reference to a derived-class object will match a handler for the base class. (However, if the handler is for an object rather than a reference, the exception object is "sliced"—truncated to the base type—as it is passed to the handler. This does no damage, but loses all the derived-type information.) For this reason, as well as to avoid making yet another copy of the exception object, it is always better to catch an exception by *reference* instead of by value.[3] If a pointer is thrown, the usual standard pointer conversions are used to match the exception. However, no automatic type conversions are used to convert from one exception type to another in the process of matching. For example:

```
//: C01:Autoexcp.cpp
// No matching conversions.
#include <iostream>
using namespace std;
```

---

[3] You might always want to specify exception objects by **const** reference in exception handlers. (It's rare to modify and rethrow an exception.) However, we are not dogmatic about this practice.

```
class Except1 {};

class Except2 {
public:
  Except2(const Except1&) {}
};

void f() { throw Except1(); }

int main() {
  try { f();
  } catch(Except2&) {
    cout << "inside catch(Except2)" << endl;
  } catch(Except1&) {
    cout << "inside catch(Except1)" << endl;
  }
} ///:~
```

Even though you might think the first handler could be matched by
converting an **Except1** object into an **Except2** using the converting
constructor, the system will not perform such a conversion during exception
handling, and you'll end up at the **Except1** handler.

The following example shows how a base-class handler can catch a derived-
class exception:

```
//: C01:Basexcpt.cpp
// Exception hierarchies.
#include <iostream>
using namespace std;

class X {
public:
  class Trouble {};
  class Small : public Trouble {};
  class Big : public Trouble {};
  void f() { throw Big(); }
};

int main() {
  X x;
  try {
    x.f();
```

```
  } catch(X::Trouble&) {
    cout << "caught Trouble" << endl;
  // Hidden by previous handler:
  } catch(X::Small&) {
    cout << "caught Small Trouble" << endl;
  } catch(X::Big&) {
    cout << "caught Big Trouble" << endl;
  }
} ///:~
```

Here, the exception-handling mechanism will always match a **Trouble**
object, *or anything that is a* **Trouble** (through public inheritance),[4] to the
first handler. That means the second and third handlers are never called
because the first one captures them all. It makes more sense to catch the
derived types first and put the base type at the end to catch anything less
specific.

Notice that these examples catch exceptions by reference, although for these
classes it isn't important because there are no additional members in the
derived classes, and there are no argument identifiers in the handlers
anyway. You'll usually want to use reference arguments rather than value
arguments in your handlers to avoid slicing off information.

Catching any exception

Sometimes you want to create a handler that catches *any* type of exception.
You do this using the ellipsis in the argument list:

```
catch(...) {
  cout << "an exception was thrown" << endl;
}
```

Because an ellipsis catches any exception, you'll want to put it at the *end* of
your list of handlers to avoid pre-empting any that follow it.

---

[4] Only *unambiguous, accessible base classes* can catch derived exceptions.
This rule minimizes the runtime overhead needed to validate exceptions.
Remember that exceptions are checked at runtime, not at compile time,
and therefore the extensive information available at compile time is not
available during exception handling.

The ellipsis gives you no possibility to have an argument, so you can't know anything about the exception or its type. It's a "catchall." Such a **catch** clause is often used to clean up some resources and then rethrow the exception.

Rethrowing an exception

You usually want to rethrow an exception when you have some resource that needs to be released, such as a network connection or heap memory that needs to be deallocated. (See the section "Resource Management" later in this chapter for more detail). If an exception occurs, you don't necessarily care what error caused the exception—you just want to close the connection you opened previously. After that, you'll want to let some other context closer to the user (that is, higher up in the call chain) handle the exception. In this case the ellipsis specification is just what you want. You want to catch *any* exception, clean up your resource, and then rethrow the exception for handling elsewhere. You rethrow an exception by using **throw** with no argument inside a handler:

```
catch(...) {
  cout << "an exception was thrown" << endl;
  // Deallocate your resource here, and then rethrow
  throw;
}
```

Any further **catch** clauses for the same **try** block are still ignored—the **throw** causes the exception to go to the exception handlers in the next-higher context. In addition, everything about the exception object is preserved, so the handler at the higher context that catches the specific exception type can extract any information the object may contain.

Uncaught exceptions

As we explained in the beginning of this chapter, exception handling is considered better than the traditional return-an-error-code technique because exceptions can't be ignored, and because the error handling logic is separated from the problem at hand. If none of the exception handlers following a particular **try** block matches an exception, that exception moves to the next-higher context, that is, the function or **try** block surrounding the **try** block that did not catch the exception. (The location of this **try** block is not always obvious at first glance, since it's higher up in the call chain.) This process continues until, at some level, a handler matches the exception. At that point, the exception is considered "caught," and no further searching occurs.

The terminate( ) function

If no handler at any level catches the exception, the special library function **terminate( )** (declared in the **<exception>** header) is automatically called. By default, **terminate( )** calls the Standard C library function **abort( )** , which abruptly exits the program. On Unix systems, **abort( )** also causes a core dump. When **abort( )** is called, no calls to normal program termination functions occur, which means that destructors for global and static objects do not execute. The **terminate( )** function also executes if a destructor for a local object throws an exception while the stack is unwinding (interrupting the exception that was in progress) or if a global or static object's constructor or destructor throws an exception. (In general, do not allow a destructor to throw an exception.)

The set_terminate( ) function

You can install your own **terminate( )** function using the standard **set_terminate( )** function, which returns a pointer to the **terminate( )** function you are replacing (which will be the default library version the first time you call it), so you can restore it later if you want. Your custom **terminate( )** must take no arguments and have a **void** return value. In addition, any **terminate( )** handler you install must not return or throw an exception, but instead must execute some sort of program-termination logic. If **terminate( )** is called, the problem is unrecoverable.

The following example shows the use of **set_terminate( )**. Here, the return value is saved and restored so that the **terminate( )** function can be used to help isolate the section of code where the uncaught exception occurs:

```
//: C01:Terminator.cpp
// Use of set_terminate(). Also shows uncaught exceptions.
#include <exception>
#include <iostream>
using namespace std;

void terminator() {
  cout << "I'll be back!" << endl;
  exit(0);
}
```

```
void (*old_terminate)() = set_terminate(terminator);

class Botch {
public:
  class Fruit {};
  void f() {
    cout << "Botch::f()" << endl;
    throw Fruit();
  }
  ~Botch() { throw 'c'; }
};

int main() {
  try {
    Botch b;
    b.f();
  } catch(...) {
    cout << "inside catch(...)" << endl;
  }
} ///:~
```

The definition of **old_terminate** looks a bit confusing at first: it not only creates a pointer to a function, but it initializes that pointer to the return value of **set_terminate( )**. Even though you might be familiar with seeing a semicolon right after a pointer-to-function declaration, here it's just another kind of variable and can be initialized when it is defined.

The class **Botch** not only throws an exception inside **f( )**, but also in its destructor. This causes a call to **terminate( )**, as you can see in **main( )**. Even though the exception handler says **catch(...)**, which would seem to catch everything and leave no cause for **terminate( )** to be called, **terminate( )** is called anyway. In the process of cleaning up the objects on the stack to handle one exception, the **Botch** destructor is called, and that generates a second exception, forcing a call to **terminate( )**. Thus, a destructor that throws an exception or causes one to be thrown is usually a sign of poor design or sloppy coding.

Cleaning up

Part of the magic of exception handling is that you can pop from normal program flow into the appropriate exception handler. Doing so wouldn't be useful, however, if things weren't cleaned up properly as the exception was

---

thrown. C++ exception handling guarantees that as you leave a scope, all objects in that scope *whose constructors have been completed* will have their destructors called.

Here's an example that demonstrates that constructors that aren't completed don't have the associated destructors called. It also shows what happens when an exception is thrown in the middle of the creation of an array of objects:

```
//: C01:Cleanup.cpp
// Exceptions clean up complete objects only.
#include <iostream>
using namespace std;

class Trace {
  static int counter;
  int objid;
public:
  Trace() {
    objid = counter++;
    cout << "constructing Trace #" << objid << endl;
    if(objid == 3) throw 3;
  }
  ~Trace() {
    cout << "destructing Trace #" << objid << endl;
  }
};

int Trace::counter = 0;

int main() {
  try {
    Trace n1;
    // Throws exception:
    Trace array[5];
    Trace n2;  // Won't get here.
  } catch(int i) {
    cout << "caught " << i << endl;
  }
} ///:~
```

The class **Trace** keeps track of objects so that you can trace program progress. It keeps a count of the number of objects created with a **static** data member **counter** and tracks the number of the particular object with **objid**.

The main program creates a single object, **n1** (**objid** 0), and then attempts to create an array of five **Trace** objects, but an exception is thrown before the fourth object (#3) is fully created. The object **n2** is never created. You can see the results in the output of the program:

```
constructing Trace #0
constructing Trace #1
constructing Trace #2
constructing Trace #3
destructing Trace #2
destructing Trace #1
destructing Trace #0
caught 3
```

Three array elements are successfully created, but in the middle of the constructor for the fourth element, an exception is thrown. Because the fourth construction in **main( )** (for **array[2]**) never completes, only the destructors for objects **array[1]** and **array[0]** are called. Finally, object **n1** is destroyed, but not object **n2**, because it was never created.

Resource management

When writing code with exceptions, it's particularly important that you always ask, "If an exception occurs, will my resources be properly cleaned up?" Most of the time you're fairly safe, but in constructors there's a particular problem: if an exception is thrown before a constructor is completed, the associated destructor will not be called for that object. Thus, you must be especially diligent while writing your constructor.

The difficulty is in allocating resources in constructors. If an exception occurs in the constructor, the destructor doesn't get a chance to deallocate the resource. This problem occurs most often with "naked" pointers. For example:

```
//: C01:Rawp.cpp
// Naked pointers.
#include <iostream>
#include <cstddef>
using namespace std;

class Cat {
public:
  Cat() { cout << "Cat()" << endl; }
```

```
    ~Cat() { cout << "~Cat()" << endl; }
};

class Dog {
public:
  void* operator new(size_t sz) {
    cout << "allocating a Dog" << endl;
    throw 47;
  }
  void operator delete(void* p) {
    cout << "deallocating a Dog" << endl;
    ::operator delete(p);
  }
};

class UseResources {
  Cat* bp;
  Dog* op;
public:
  UseResources(int count = 1) {
    cout << "UseResources()" << endl;
    bp = new Cat[count];
    op = new Dog;
  }
  ~UseResources() {
    cout << "~UseResources()" << endl;
    delete [] bp; // Array delete
    delete op;
  }
};

int main() {
  try {
    UseResources ur(3);
  } catch(int) {
    cout << "inside handler" << endl;
  }
} ///:~
```

The output is

```
UseResources()
Cat()
Cat()
Cat()
```

```
allocating a Dog
inside handler
```

The **UseResources** constructor is entered, and the **Cat** constructor is successfully completed for the three array objects. However, inside **Dog::operator new( )**, an exception is thrown (to simulate an out-of-memory error). Suddenly, you end up inside the handler, *without* the **UseResources** destructor being called. This is correct because the **UseResources** constructor was unable to finish, but it also means the **Cat** objects that were successfully created on the heap were never destroyed.

Making everything an object

To prevent such resource leaks, you must guard against these "raw" resource allocations in one of two ways:

- You can catch exceptions inside the constructor and then release the resource.

- You can place the allocations inside an object's constructor, and you can place the deallocations inside an object's destructor.

Using the latter approach, each allocation becomes atomic, by virtue of being part of the lifetime of a local object, and if it fails, the other resource allocation objects are properly cleaned up during stack unwinding. This technique is called Resource Acquisition Is Initialization (RAII for short) because it equates resource control with object lifetime. Using templates is an excellent way to modify the previous example to achieve this:

```
//: C01:Wrapped.cpp
// Safe, atomic pointers.
#include <iostream>
#include <cstddef>
using namespace std;

// Simplified. Yours may have other arguments.
template<class T, int sz = 1> class PWrap {
  T* ptr;
public:
  class RangeError {}; // Exception class
  PWrap() {
    ptr = new T[sz];
```

```
      cout << "PWrap constructor" << endl;
  }
  ~PWrap() {
    delete[] ptr;
    cout << "PWrap destructor" << endl;
  }
  T& operator[](int i) throw(RangeError) {
    if(i >= 0 && i < sz) return ptr[i];
    throw RangeError();
  }
};

class Cat {
public:
  Cat() { cout << "Cat()" << endl; }
  ~Cat() { cout << "~Cat()" << endl; }
  void g() {}
};

class Dog {
public:
  void* operator new[](size_t) {
    cout << "Allocating a Dog" << endl;
    throw 47;
  }
  void operator delete[](void* p) {
    cout << "Deallocating a Dog" << endl;
    ::operator delete[](p);
  }
};

class UseResources {
  PWrap<Cat, 3> cats;
  PWrap<Dog> dog;
public:
  UseResources() { cout << "UseResources()" << endl; }
  ~UseResources() { cout << "~UseResources()" << endl; }
  void f() { cats[1].g(); }
};

int main() {
  try {
    UseResources ur;
  } catch(int) {
    cout << "inside handler" << endl;
```

```
  } catch(...) {
    cout << "inside catch(...)" << endl;
  }
} ///:~
```

The difference is the use of the template to wrap the pointers and make them into objects. The constructors for these objects are called *before* the body of the **UseResources** constructor, and any of these constructors that complete before an exception is thrown will have their associated destructors called during stack unwinding.

The **PWrap** template shows a more typical use of exceptions than you've seen so far: A nested class called **RangeError** is created to use in **operator[ ]** if its argument is out of range. Because **operator[ ]** returns a reference, it cannot return zero. (There are no null references.) This is a true exceptional condition—you don't know what to do in the current context and you can't return an improbable value. In this example, **RangeError**[5] is simple and assumes all the necessary information is in the class name, but you might also want to add a member that contains the value of the index, if that is useful.

Now the output is

```
Cat()
Cat()
Cat()
PWrap constructor
allocating a Dog
~Cat()
~Cat()
~Cat()
PWrap destructor
inside handler
```

Again, the storage allocation for **Dog** throws an exception, but this time the array of **Cat** objects is properly cleaned up, so there is no memory leak.

---

[5] Note that there's an exception class called **std::out_of_range** in the C++ Standard Library, intended to be used in situations such as this.

auto_ptr

Since dynamic memory is the most frequent resource used in a typical C++ program, the standard provides an RAII wrapper for pointers to heap memory that automatically frees the memory. The **auto_ptr** class template, defined in the **<memory>** header, has a constructor that takes a pointer to its generic type (whatever you use in your code). The **auto_ptr** class template also overloads the pointer operators * and -> to forward these operations to the original pointer the **auto_ptr** object is holding. So you can use the **auto_ptr** object as if it were a raw pointer. Here's how it works:

```
//: C01:Auto_ptr.cpp
// Illustrates the RAII nature of auto_ptr.
#include <memory>
#include <iostream>
#include <cstddef>
using namespace std;

class TraceHeap {
  int i;
public:
  static void* operator new(size_t siz) {
    void* p = ::operator new(siz);
    cout << "Allocating TraceHeap object on the heap "
         << "at address " << p << endl;
    return p;
  }
  static void operator delete(void* p) {
    cout << "Deleting TraceHeap object at address "
         << p << endl;
    ::operator delete(p);
  }
  TraceHeap(int i) : i(i) {}
  int getVal() const { return i; }
};

int main() {
  auto_ptr<TraceHeap> pMyObject(new TraceHeap(5));
  cout << pMyObject->getVal() << endl;  // Prints 5
} ///:~
```

The **TraceHeap** class overloads the **operator new** and **operator delete** so you can see exactly what's happening. Notice that, like any other class template, you specify the type you're going to use in a template parameter.

You don't say **TraceHeap***, however—**auto_ptr** already knows that it will be storing a pointer to your type. The second line of **main( )** verifies that **auto_ptr**'s **operator->( )** function applies the indirection to the original, underlying pointer. Most important, even though we didn't explicitly delete the original pointer, **pMyObject**'s destructor deletes the original pointer during stack unwinding, as the following output verifies:

```
Allocating TraceHeap object on the heap at address 8930040
5
Deleting TraceHeap object at address 8930040
```

The auto_ptr class template is also handy for pointer data members. Since class objects contained by value are always destructed, **auto_ptr** members always delete the raw pointer they wrap when the containing object is destructed.[6]

Function–level try blocks

Since constructors can routinely throw exceptions, you might want to handle exceptions that occur when an object's member or base subobjects are initialized. To do this, you can place the initialization of such subobjects in a *function-level try block*. In a departure from the usual syntax, the **try** block for constructor initializers is the constructor body, and the associated **catch** block follows the body of the constructor, as in the following example:

```
//: C01:InitExcept.cpp {-bor}
// Handles exceptions from subobjects.
#include <iostream>
using namespace std;

class Base {
  int i;
public:
  class BaseExcept {};
  Base(int i) : i(i) { throw BaseExcept(); }
};
```

---

[6] For more detail on **auto_ptr**, see Herb Sutter's article entitled, "Using auto_ptr Effectively" in the October 1999 issue of the *C/C++ Users Journal*, pp. 63–67.

```cpp
class Derived : public Base {
public:
  class DerivedExcept {
    const char* msg;
  public:
    DerivedExcept(const char* msg) : msg(msg) {}
    const char* what() const { return msg; }
  };
  Derived(int j) try : Base(j) {
    // Constructor body
    cout << "This won't print" << endl;
  } catch(BaseExcept&) {
    throw DerivedExcept("Base subobject threw");;
  }
};

int main() {
  try {
    Derived d(3);
  } catch(Derived::DerivedExcept& d) {
    cout << d.what() << endl;  // "Base subobject threw"
  }
} ///:~
```

Notice that the initializer list in the constructor for **Derived** goes after the **try** keyword but before the constructor body. If an exception does occur, the contained object is not constructed, so it makes no sense to return to the code that created it. For this reason, the only sensible thing to do is to throw an exception in the function-level **catch** clause.

Although it is not terribly useful, C++ also allows function-level **try** blocks for *any* function, as the following example illustrates:

```cpp
//: C01:FunctionTryBlock.cpp {-bor}
// Function-level try blocks.
// {RunByHand} (Don't run automatically by the makefile)
#include <iostream>
using namespace std;

int main() try {
  throw "main";
} catch(const char* msg) {
  cout << msg << endl;
  return 1;
```

```
} ///:~
```

In this case, the **catch** block can return in the same manner that the function body normally returns. Using this type of function-level **try** block isn't much different from inserting a **try-catch** around the code inside of the function body.

Standard exceptions

The exceptions used with the Standard C++ library are also available for your use. Generally it's easier and faster to start with a standard exception class than to try to define your own. If the standard class doesn't do exactly what you need, you can derive from it.

All standard exception classes derive ultimately from the class **exception**, defined in the header **<exception>**. The two main derived classes are **logic_error** and **runtime_error**, which are found in **<stdexcept>** (which itself includes **<exception>**). The class **logic_error** represents errors in programming logic, such as passing an invalid argument. Runtime errors are those that occur as the result of unforeseen forces such as hardware failure or memory exhaustion. Both **runtime_error** and **logic_error** provide a constructor that takes a **std::string** argument so that you can store a message in the exception object and extract it later with **exception::what( )**, as the following program illustrates:

```
//: C01:StdExcept.cpp
// Derives an exception class from std::runtime_error.
#include <stdexcept>
#include <iostream>
using namespace std;

class MyError : public runtime_error {
public:
  MyError(const string& msg = "") : runtime_error(msg) {}
};

int main() {
  try {
    throw MyError("my message");
  } catch(MyError& x) {
    cout << x.what() << endl;
  }
```

```
} ///:~
```

Although the **runtime_error** constructor inserts the message into its **std::exception** subobject, **std::exception** does not provide a constructor that takes a **std::string** argument. You'll usually want to derive your exception classes from either **runtime_error** or **logic_error** (or one of their derivatives), and not from **std::exception**.

The following tables describe the standard exception classes:

exception	The base class for all the exceptions thrown by the C++ Standard library. You can ask **what( )** and retrieve the optional string with which the exception was initialized.
logic_error	Derived from **exception**. Reports program logic errors, which could presumably be detected by inspection.
runtime_error	Derived from **exception**. Reports runtime errors, which can presumably be detected only when the program executes.

The iostream exception class **ios::failure** is also derived from **exception**, but it has no further subclasses.

You can use the classes in both of the following tables as they are, or you can use them as base classes from which to derive your own more specific types of exceptions.

Exception classes derived from logic_error

domain_error	Reports violations of a precondition.
invalid_argument	Indicates an invalid argument to the function from which it is thrown.

Exception classes derived from logic_error

length_error	Indicates an attempt to produce an object whose length is greater than or equal to **npos** (the largest representable value of context's size type, usually **std::size_t**).
out_of_range	Reports an out-of-range argument.
bad_cast	Thrown for executing an invalid **dynamic_cast** expression in runtime type identification (see Chapter 8).
bad_typeid	Reports a null pointer **p** in an expression **typeid(*p)**. (Again, a runtime type identification feature in Chapter 8).

Exception classes derived from runtime_error

range_error	Reports violation of a postcondition.
overflow_error	Reports an arithmetic overflow.
bad_alloc	Reports a failure to allocate storage.

Exception specifications

You're not required to inform the people using your function what exceptions you might throw. However, failure to do so can be considered uncivilized because it means that users cannot be sure what code to write to catch all potential exceptions. If they have your source code, they can hunt through and look for **throw** statements, but often a library doesn't come with sources. Good documentation can help alleviate this problem, but how many software projects are well documented? C++ provides syntax to tell the user the exceptions that are thrown by this function, so the user can handle them. This is the optional *exception specification*, which adorns a function's declaration, appearing after the argument list.

The exception specification reuses the keyword **throw**, followed by a parenthesized list of all the types of potential exceptions that the function can throw. Your function declaration might look like this:

```
void f() throw(toobig, toosmall, divzero);
```

As far as exceptions are concerned, the traditional function declaration

```
void f();
```

means that *any* type of exception can be thrown from the function. If you say

```
void f() throw();
```

no exceptions whatsoever will be thrown from the function (so you'd better be sure that no functions farther down in the call chain let any exceptions propagate up!).

For good coding policy, good documentation, and ease-of-use for the function caller, consider using exception specifications when you write functions that throw exceptions. (Variations on this guideline are discussed later in this chapter.)

The unexpected( ) function

If your exception specification claims you're going to throw a certain set of exceptions and then you throw something that isn't in that set, what's the penalty? The special function **unexpected( )** is called when you throw something other than what appears in the exception specification. Should this unfortunate situation occur, the default **unexpected( )** calls the **terminate( )** function described earlier in this chapter.

The set_unexpected( ) function

Like **terminate( )**, the **unexpected( )** mechanism installs your own function to respond to unexpected exceptions. You do so with a function called **set_unexpected( )**, which, like **set_terminate( )**, takes the address of a function with no arguments and **void** return value. Also, because it returns the previous value of the **unexpected( )** pointer, you can save it and

restore it later. To use **set_unexpected( )**, include the header file
<exception>. Here's an example that shows a simple use of the features
discussed so far in this section:

```
//: C01:Unexpected.cpp
// Exception specifications & unexpected(),
//{-msc} (Doesn't terminate properly)
#include <exception>
#include <iostream>
using namespace std;

class Up {};
class Fit {};
void g();

void f(int i) throw(Up, Fit) {
  switch(i) {
    case 1: throw Up();
    case 2: throw Fit();
  }
  g();
}

// void g() {}          // Version 1
void g() { throw 47; } // Version 2

void my_unexpected() {
  cout << "unexpected exception thrown" << endl;
  exit(0);
}

int main() {
  set_unexpected(my_unexpected); // (Ignores return value)
  for(int i = 1; i <=3; i++)
    try {
      f(i);
    } catch(Up) {
      cout << "Up caught" << endl;
    } catch(Fit) {
      cout << "Fit caught" << endl;
    }
} ///:~
```

The classes **Up** and **Fit** are created solely to throw as exceptions. Often exception classes will be small, but they can certainly hold additional information so that the handlers can query for it.

The **f( )** function promises in its exception specification to throw only exceptions of type **Up** and **Fit**, and from looking at the function definition, this seems plausible. Version one of **g( )**, called by **f( )**, doesn't throw any exceptions, so this is true. But if someone changes **g( )** so that it throws a different type of exception (like the second version in this example, which throws an **int**), the exception specification for **f( )** is violated.

The **my_unexpected( )** function has no arguments or return value, following the proper form for a custom **unexpected( )** function. It simply displays a message so that you can see that it was called, and then exits the program (**exit(0)** is used here so that the book's **make** process is not aborted). Your new **unexpected( )** function should not have a **return** statement.

In **main( )**, the **try** block is within a **for** loop, so all the possibilities are exercised. In this way, you can achieve something like resumption. Nest the **try** block inside a **for**, **while**, **do**, or **if** and cause any exceptions to attempt to repair the problem; then attempt the **try** block again.

Only the **Up** and **Fit** exceptions are caught because those are the only exceptions that the programmer of **f( )** said would be thrown. Version two of **g( )** causes **my_unexpected( )** to be called because **f( )** then throws an **int**.

In the call to **set_unexpected( )**, the return value is ignored, but it can also be saved in a pointer to function and be restored later, as we did in the **set_terminate( )** example earlier in this chapter.

A typical **unexpected** handler logs the error and terminates the program by calling **exit( )**. It can, however, throw another exception (or rethrow the same exception) or call **abort( )**. If it throws an exception of a type allowed by the function whose specification was originally violated, the search resumes at the *call* of the function with this exception specification. (This behavior is unique to **unexpected( )**.)

If the exception thrown from your **unexpected** handler is not allowed by the original function's specification, one of the following occurs:

---

1. If **std::bad_exception** (defined in **<exception>**) was in the function's exception specification, the exception thrown from the unexpected handler is replaced with a **std::bad_exception** object, and the search resumes from the function as before.

2. If the original function's specification did not include **std::bad_exception**, **terminate( )** is called.

The following program illustrates this behavior:

```
//: C01:BadException.cpp {-bor}
#include <exception>    // For std::bad_exception
#include <iostream>
#include <cstdio>
using namespace std;

// Exception classes:
class A {};
class B {};

// terminate() handler
void my_thandler() {
  cout << "terminate called" << endl;
  exit(0);
}

// unexpected() handlers
void my_uhandler1() { throw A(); }
void my_uhandler2() { throw; }

// If we embed this throw statement in f or g,
// the compiler detects the violation and reports
// an error, so we put it in its own function.
void t() { throw B(); }

void f() throw(A) { t(); }
void g() throw(A, bad_exception) { t(); }

int main() {
  set_terminate(my_thandler);
  set_unexpected(my_uhandler1);
  try {
    f();
  } catch(A&) {
```

```
      cout << "caught an A from f" << endl;
   }
   set_unexpected(my_uhandler2);
   try {
      g();
   } catch(bad_exception&) {
      cout << "caught a bad_exception from g" << endl;
   }
   try {
      f();
   } catch(...) {
      cout << "This will never print" << endl;
   }
} ///:~
```

The **my_uhandler1( )** handler throws an acceptable exception (**A**), so
execution resumes at the first catch, which succeeds. The **my_uhandler2( )**
handler does not throw a valid exception (**B**), but since **g** specifies
bad_exception, the **B** exception is replaced by a **bad_exception** object,
and the second catch also succeeds. Since **f** does not include **bad_exception**
in its specification, **my_thandler( )** is called as a terminate handler. Here's
the output:

```
caught an A from f
caught a bad_exception from g
terminate called
```


Better exception specifications?

You may feel that the existing exception specification rules aren't very safe,
and that

```
void f();
```

should mean that no exceptions are thrown from this function. If the
programmer wants to throw any type of exception, you might think he or she
should have to say

```
void f() throw(...); // Not in C++
```

This would surely be an improvement because function declarations would be
more explicit. Unfortunately, you can't always know by looking at the code in

---

a function whether an exception will be thrown—it could happen because of a memory allocation, for example. Worse, existing functions written before exception handling was introduced into the language may find themselves inadvertently throwing exceptions because of the functions they call (which might be linked into new, exception-throwing versions). Hence, the uninformative situation whereby

```
void f();
```

means, "Maybe I'll throw an exception, maybe I won't." This ambiguity is necessary to avoid hindering code evolution. If you want to specify that **f** throws no exceptions, use the empty list, as in:

```
void f() throw();
```

Exception specifications and inheritance

Each public function in a class essentially forms a contract with the user; if you pass it certain arguments, it will perform certain operations and/or return a result. The same contract must hold true in derived classes; otherwise the expected "is-a" relationship between derived and base classes is violated. Since exception specifications are logically part of a function's declaration, they too must remain consistent across an inheritance hierarchy. For example, if a member function in a base class says it will only throw an exception of type **A**, an override of that function in a derived class must not add any other exception types to the specification list because that would break any programs that adhere to the base class interface. You can, however, specify *fewer* exceptions or *none at all*, since that doesn't require the user to do anything differently. You can also specify anything that "is-a" **A** in place of **A** in the derived function's specification. Here's an example.

```
//: C01:Covariance.cpp {-xo}
// Should cause compile error. {-mwcc}{-msc}
#include <iostream>
using namespace std;

class Base {
public:
  class BaseException {};
  class DerivedException : public BaseException {};
  virtual void f() throw(DerivedException) {
    throw DerivedException();
```

```
    }
    virtual void g() throw(BaseException) {
      throw BaseException();
    }
};

class Derived : public Base {
public:
  void f() throw(BaseException) {
    throw BaseException();
  }
  virtual void g() throw(DerivedException) {
    throw DerivedException();
  }
}; ///:~
```

A compiler should flag the override of **Derived::f( )** with an error (or at least a warning) since it changes its exception specification in a way that violates the specification of **Base::f( )**. The specification for **Derived::g( )** is acceptable because **DerivedException** "is-a" **BaseException** (not the other way around). You can think of **Base/Derived** and **BaseException/DerivedException** as parallel class hierarchies; when you are in **Derived**, you can replace references to **BaseException** in exception specifications and return values with **DerivedException**. This behavior is called *covariance* (since both sets of classes vary down their respective hierarchies together). (Reminder from Volume 1: parameter types are *not* covariant—you are not allowed to change the signature of an overridden virtual function.)

When not to use exception specifications

If you peruse the function declarations throughout the Standard C++ library, you'll find that not a single exception specification occurs anywhere! Although this might seem strange, there is a good reason for this seeming incongruity: the library consists mainly of templates, and you never know what a generic type or function might do. For example, suppose you are developing a generic stack template and attempt to affix an exception specification to your pop function, like this:

```
T pop() throw(logic_error);
```

Since the only error you anticipate is a stack underflow, you might think it's safe to specify a **logic_error** or some other appropriate exception type. But type **T**'s copy constructor could throw an exception. Then **unexpected( )** would be called, and your program would terminate. You can't make unsupportable guarantees. If you don't know what exceptions might occur, don't use exception specifications. That's why template classes, which constitute the majority of the Standard C++ library, do not use exception specifications—they specify the exceptions they know about in *documentation* and leave the rest to you. Exception specifications are mainly for non-template classes.

Exception safety

In Chapter 7 we'll take an in-depth look at the containers in the Standard C++ library, including the **stack** container. One thing you'll notice is that the declaration of the **pop( )** member function looks like this:

```
void pop();
```

You might think it strange that **pop( )** doesn't return a value. Instead, it just removes the element at the top of the stack. To retrieve the top value, call **top( )** before you call **pop( )**. There is an important reason for this behavior, and it has to do with *exception safety*, a crucial consideration in library design. There are different levels of exception safety, but most importantly, and just as the name implies, exception safety is about correct semantics in the face of exceptions.

Suppose you are implementing a stack with a dynamic array (we'll call it **data** and the counter integer **count**), and you try to write **pop( )** so that it returns a value. The code for such a **pop( )** might look something like this:

```
template<class T> T stack<T>::pop() {
  if(count == 0)
    throw logic_error("stack underflow");
  else
    return data[--count];
}
```

What happens if the copy constructor that is called for the return value in the last line throws an exception when the value is returned? The popped element is not returned because of the exception, and yet **count** has already been decremented, so the top element you wanted is lost forever! The problem is that this function attempts to do two things at once: (1) return a value, and (2) change the state of the stack. It is better to separate these two actions into two separate member functions, which is exactly what the standard **stack** class does. (In other words, follow the design practice of *cohesion*—every function should do *one thing well*.) Exception-safe code leaves objects in a consistent state and does not leak resources.

You also need to be careful writing custom assignment operators. In Chapter 12 of Volume 1, you saw that **operator=** should adhere to the following pattern:

1. Make sure you're not assigning to self. If you are, go to step 6. (This is strictly an optimization.)

2. Allocate new memory required by pointer data members.

3. Copy data from the old memory to the new.

4. Delete the old memory.

5. Update the object's state by assigning the new heap pointers to the pointer data members.

6. Return ***this**.

It's important to not change the state of your object until all the new pieces have been safely allocated and initialized. A good technique is to move steps 2 and 3 into a separate function, often called **clone( )**. The following example does this for a class that has two pointer members, **theString** and **theInts**:

```
//: C01:SafeAssign.cpp
// An Exception-safe operator=.
#include <iostream>
#include <new>          // For std::bad_alloc
#include <cstring>
#include <cstddef>
using namespace std;

// A class that has two pointer members using the heap
class HasPointers {
  // A Handle class to hold the data
```

```
  struct MyData {
    const char* theString;
    const int* theInts;
    size_t numInts;
    MyData(const char* pString, const int* pInts,
      size_t nInts)
    : theString(pString), theInts(pInts), numInts(nInts) {}
  } *theData;  // The handle
  // Clone and cleanup functions:
  static MyData* clone(const char* otherString,
      const int* otherInts, size_t nInts) {
    char* newChars = new char[strlen(otherString)+1];
    int* newInts;
    try {
      newInts = new int[nInts];
    } catch(bad_alloc&) {
      delete [] newChars;
      throw;
    }
    try {
      // This example uses built-in types, so it won't
      // throw, but for class types it could throw, so we
      // use a try block for illustration. (This is the
      // point of the example!)
      strcpy(newChars, otherString);
      for(size_t i = 0; i < nInts; ++i)
        newInts[i] = otherInts[i];
    } catch(...) {
      delete [] newInts;
      delete [] newChars;
      throw;
    }
    return new MyData(newChars, newInts, nInts);
  }
  static MyData* clone(const MyData* otherData) {
    return clone(otherData->theString, otherData->theInts,
                 otherData->numInts);
  }
  static void cleanup(const MyData* theData) {
    delete [] theData->theString;
    delete [] theData->theInts;
    delete theData;
  }
public:
  HasPointers(const char* someString, const int* someInts,
```

```
                  size_t numInts) {
    theData = clone(someString, someInts, numInts);
  }
  HasPointers(const HasPointers& source) {
    theData = clone(source.theData);
  }
  HasPointers& operator=(const HasPointers& rhs) {
    if(this != &rhs) {
      MyData* newData = clone(rhs.theData->theString,
        rhs.theData->theInts, rhs.theData->numInts);
      cleanup(theData);
      theData = newData;
    }
    return *this;
  }
  ~HasPointers() { cleanup(theData); }
  friend ostream&
  operator<<(ostream& os, const HasPointers& obj) {
    os << obj.theData->theString << ": ";
    for(size_t i = 0; i < obj.theData->numInts; ++i)
      os << obj.theData->theInts[i] << ' ';
    return os;
  }
};

int main() {
  int someNums[] = { 1, 2, 3, 4 };
  size_t someCount = sizeof someNums / sizeof someNums[0];
  int someMoreNums[] = { 5, 6, 7 };
  size_t someMoreCount =
  sizeof someMoreNums / sizeof someMoreNums[0];
  HasPointers h1("Hello", someNums, someCount);
  HasPointers h2("Goodbye", someMoreNums, someMoreCount);
  cout << h1 << endl;   // Hello: 1 2 3 4
  h1 = h2;
  cout << h1 << endl;   // Goodbye: 5 6 7
} ///:~
```

For convenience, **HasPointers** uses the **MyData** class as a handle to the
two pointers. Whenever it's time to allocate more memory, whether during
construction or assignment, the first **clone** function is ultimately called to do
the job. If memory fails for the first call to the **new** operator, a **bad_alloc**
exception is thrown automatically. If it happens on the second allocation (for
theInts), we must clean up the memory for **theString**—hence the first **try**

---

block that catches a **bad_alloc** exception. The second **try** block isn't crucial here because we're just copying **int**s and pointers (so no exceptions will occur), but whenever you copy objects, their assignment operators can possibly cause an exception, so everything needs to be cleaned up. In both exception handlers, notice that we *rethrow* the exception. That's because we're just managing resources here; the user still needs to know that something went wrong, so we let the exception propagate up the dynamic chain. Software libraries that don't silently swallow exceptions are called *exception neutral*. Always strive to write libraries that are both exception safe and exception neutral.[7]

If you inspect the previous code closely, you'll notice that none of the **delete** operations will throw an exception. This code depends on that fact. Recall that when you call **delete** on an object, the object's destructor is called. It turns out to be practically impossible to design exception-safe code without assuming that destructors don't throw exceptions. Don't let destructors throw exceptions. (We're going to remind you about this once more before this chapter is done).[8]

Programming with exceptions

For most programmers, especially C programmers, exceptions are not available in their existing language and require some adjustment. Here are guidelines for programming with exceptions.

When to avoid exceptions

Exceptions aren't the answer to all problems; overuse can cause trouble. The following sections point out situations where exceptions are *not* warranted.

---

[7] If you're interested in a more in-depth analysis of exception safety issues, the definitive reference is Herb Sutter's *Exceptional C++*, Addison-Wesley, 2000.

[8] The library function **uncaught_exception( )** returns **true** in the middle of stack unwinding, so technically you can test **uncaught_exception( )** for **false** and let an exception escape from a destructor. We've never seen a situation in which this constituted good design, however, so we only mention it in this footnote.

The best advice for deciding when to use exceptions is to throw exceptions only when a function fails to meet its specification.

Not for asynchronous events
The Standard C **signal( )** system and any similar system handle asynchronous events: events that happen outside the flow of a program, and thus events the program cannot anticipate. You cannot use C++ exceptions to handle asynchronous events because the exception and its handler are on the same call stack. That is, exceptions rely on the dynamic chain of function calls on the program's runtime stack (they have "dynamic scope"), whereas asynchronous events must be handled by completely separate code that is not part of the normal program flow (typically, interrupt service routines or event loops). Don't throw exceptions from interrupt handlers.

This is not to say that asynchronous events cannot be *associated* with exceptions. But the interrupt handler should do its job as quickly as possible and then return. The typical way to handle this situation is to set a flag in the interrupt handler, and check it synchronously in the mainline code.

Not for benign error conditions
If you have enough information to handle an error, it's not an exception. Take care of it in the current context rather than throwing an exception to a larger context.

Also, C++ exceptions are not thrown for machine-level events such as divide-by-zero.[9] It's assumed that some other mechanism, such as the operating system or hardware, deals with these events. In this way, C++ exceptions can be reasonably efficient, and their use is isolated to program-level exceptional conditions.

Not for flow–of–control
An exception looks somewhat like an alternate return mechanism and somewhat like a **switch** statement, so you might be tempted to use an exception instead of these ordinary language mechanisms. This is a bad idea, partly because the exception-handling system is significantly less efficient than normal program execution. Exceptions are a rare event, so the normal

---

[9] Some compilers do throw exceptions in these cases, but they usually provide a compiler option to disable this (unusual) behavior.

program shouldn't pay for them. Also, exceptions from anything other than error conditions are quite confusing to the user of your class or function.

You're not forced to use exceptions

Some programs are quite simple (small utilities, for example). You might only need to take input and perform some processing. In these programs, you might attempt to allocate memory and fail, try to open a file and fail, and so on. It is acceptable in these programs to display a message and exit the program, allowing the system to clean up the mess, rather than to work hard to catch all exceptions and recover all the resources yourself. Basically, if you don't need exceptions, you're not forced to use them.

New exceptions, old code

Another situation that arises is the modification of an existing program that doesn't use exceptions. You might introduce a library that *does* use exceptions and wonder if you need to modify all your code throughout the program. Assuming you have an acceptable error-handling scheme already in place, the most straightforward thing to do is surround the largest block that uses the new library (this might be all the code in **main( )**) with a **try** block, followed by a **catch(...)** and basic error message). You can refine this to whatever degree necessary by adding more specific handlers, but, in any case, the code you must add can be minimal. It's even better to isolate your exception-generating code in a **try** block and write handlers to convert the exceptions into your existing error-handling scheme.

It's truly important to think about exceptions when you're creating a library for someone else to use, especially if you can't know how they need to respond to critical error conditions (recall the earlier discussions on exception safety and why there are no exception specifications in the Standard C++ Library).

Typical uses of exceptions

Do use exceptions to do the following:

- Fix the problem and retry the function that caused the exception.

- Patch things up and continue without retrying the function.

- Do whatever you can in the current context and rethrow the *same* exception to a higher context.

- Do whatever you can in the current context and throw a *different* exception to a higher context.

- Terminate the program.

- Wrap functions (especially C library functions) that use ordinary error schemes so they produce exceptions instead.

- Simplify. If your error handling scheme makes things more complicated, it is painful and annoying to use. Exceptions can be used to make error handling simpler and more effective.

- Make your library and program safer. This is a short-term investment (for debugging) and a long-term investment (for application robustness).

When to use exception specifications

The exception specification is like a function prototype: it tells the user to write exception-handling code and what exceptions to handle. It tells the compiler the exceptions that might come out of this function so that it can detect violations at runtime.

You can't always look at the code and anticipate which exceptions will arise from a particular function. Sometimes, the functions it calls produce an unexpected exception, and sometimes an old function that didn't throw an exception is replaced with a new one that does, and you get a call to **unexpected( )**. Any time you use exception specifications or call functions that do, consider creating your own **unexpected( )** function that logs a message and then either throws an exception or aborts the program.

As we explained earlier, you should avoid using exception specifications in template classes, since you can't anticipate what types of exceptions the template parameter classes might throw.

Start with standard exceptions

Check out the Standard C++ library exceptions before creating your own. If a standard exception does what you need, chances are it's a lot easier for your user to understand and handle.

If the exception type you want isn't part of the standard library, try to inherit one from an existing standard exception. It's nice if your users can always write their code to expect the **what( )** function defined in the **exception( )** class interface.

Nest your own exceptions

If you create exceptions for your particular class, it's a good idea to nest the exception classes either inside your class or inside a namespace containing your class, to provide a clear message to the reader that this exception is only for your class. In addition, it prevents pollution of the global namespace.

You can nest your exceptions even if you're deriving them from C++ Standard exceptions.

Use exception hierarchies

Using exception hierarchies is a valuable way to classify the types of critical errors that might be encountered with your class or library. This gives helpful information to users, assists them in organizing their code, and gives them the option of ignoring all the specific types of exceptions and just catching the base-class type. Also, any exceptions added later by inheriting from the same base class will not force all existing code to be rewritten—the base-class handler will catch the new exception.

The Standard C++ exceptions are a good example of an exception hierarchy. Build your exceptions on top of it if you can.

Multiple inheritance (MI)

As you'll read in Chapter 9, the only *essential* place for MI is if you need to upcast an object pointer to two different base classes—that is, if you need polymorphic behavior with both of those base classes. It turns out that exception hierarchies are useful places for multiple inheritance because a base-class handler from any of the roots of the multiply inherited exception class can handle the exception.

Catch by reference, not by value

As you saw in the section "Exception matching," you should catch exceptions by reference for two reasons:

- To avoid making a needless copy of the exception object when it is passed to the handler.

- To avoid object slicing when catching a derived exception as a base class object.

Although you can also throw and catch pointers, by doing so you introduce more coupling—the thrower and the catcher must agree on how the exception object is allocated and cleaned up. This is a problem because the exception itself might have occurred from heap exhaustion. If you throw exception objects, the exception-handling system takes care of all storage.

Throw exceptions in constructors

Because a constructor has no return value, you've previously had two ways to report an error during construction:

- Set a nonlocal flag and hope the user checks it.

- Return an incompletely created object and hope the user checks it.

This problem is serious because C programmers expect that object creation is always successful, which is not unreasonable in C because the types are so primitive. But continuing execution after construction fails in a C++ program is a guaranteed disaster, so constructors are one of the most important places to throw exceptions—now you have a safe, effective way to handle constructor errors. However, you must also pay attention to pointers inside objects and the way cleanup occurs when an exception is thrown inside a constructor.

Don't cause exceptions in destructors

Because destructors are called in the process of throwing other exceptions, you'll never want to throw an exception in a destructor or cause another exception to be thrown by some action you perform in the destructor. If this happens, a new exception can be thrown *before* the catch-clause for an existing exception is reached, which will cause a call to **terminate( )**.

If you call any functions inside a destructor that can throw exceptions, those calls should be within a **try** block in the destructor, and the destructor must handle all exceptions itself. None must escape from the destructor.

Avoid naked pointers

See **Wrapped.cpp** earlier in this chapter. A naked pointer usually means vulnerability in the constructor if resources are allocated for that pointer. A pointer doesn't have a destructor, so those resources aren't released if an exception is thrown in the constructor. Use **auto_ptr** or other smart pointer types[10] for pointers that reference heap memory.

Overhead

When an exception is thrown, there's considerable runtime overhead (but it's *good* overhead, since objects are cleaned up automatically!). For this reason, you never want to use exceptions as part of your normal flow-of-control, no matter how tempting and clever it may seem. Exceptions should occur only rarely, so the overhead is piled on the exception and not on the normally executing code. One of the important design goals for exception handling was that it could be implemented with no impact on execution speed when it *wasn't* used; that is, as long as you don't throw an exception, your code runs as fast as it would without exception handling. Whether this is true depends on the particular compiler implementation you're using. (See the description of the "zero-cost model" later in this section.)

You can think of a **throw** expression as a call to a special system function that takes the exception object as an argument and backtracks up the chain of execution. For this to work, extra information needs to be put on the stack by the compiler, to aid in stack unwinding. To understand this, you need to know about the runtime stack.

Whenever a function is called, information about that function is pushed onto the runtime stack in an *activation record instance* (ARI), also called a *stack frame.* A typical stack frame contains the address of the calling function (so execution can return to it), a pointer to the ARI of the function's static parent (the scope that lexically contains the called function, so variables global to the function can be accessed), and a pointer to the function that called it (its *dynamic parent*). The path that logically results from repetitively following the dynamic parent links is the *dynamic chain*, or *call chain*, that we've mentioned previously in this chapter. This is how execution can backtrack when an exception is thrown, and it is the mechanism that makes it possible

---

[10] Check out the Boost smart pointer types at http://www.boost.org/libs/smart_ptr/index.htm. Some of these are being considered for inclusion in the next revision of Standard C++.

for components developed without knowledge of one another to communicate errors at runtime.

To enable stack unwinding for exception handling, extra exception-related information about each function needs to be available for each stack frame. This information describes which destructors need to be called (so that local objects can be cleaned up), indicates whether the current function has a **try** block, and lists which exceptions the associated catch clauses can handle. There is space penalty for this extra information, so programs that support exception handling can be somewhat larger than those that don't.[11] Even the compile-time size of programs using exception handling is greater, since the logic of how to generate the expanded stack frames during runtime must be generated by the compiler.

To illustrate this, we compiled the following program both with and without exception-handling support in Borland C++ Builder and Microsoft Visual C++:[12]

```
//: C01:HasDestructor.cpp {O}
class HasDestructor {
public:
  ~HasDestructor() {}
};

void g(); // For all we know, g may throw.

void f() {
  HasDestructor h;
  g();
} ///:~
```

If exception handling is enabled, the compiler must keep information about **~HasDestructor( )** available at runtime in the ARI for **f( )** (so it can destroy **h** properly should **g( )** throw an exception). The following table

---

[11] This depends on how much return code checking you would have to insert if you weren't using exceptions.

[12] Borland enables exceptions by default; to disable exceptions use the −x− compiler option. Microsoft disables support by default; to turn it on, use the −GX option. With both compilers use the −c option to compile only.

summarizes the result of the compilations in terms of the size of the compiled (.obj) files (in bytes).

Compiler\Mode	With Exception Support	Without Exception Support
Borland	616	234
Microsoft	1162	680

Don't take the percentage differences between the two modes too seriously. Remember that exceptions (should) typically constitute a small part of a program, so the space overhead tends to be much smaller (usually between 5 and 15 percent).

This extra housekeeping slows down execution, but a clever compiler implementation avoids this. Since information about exception-handling code and the offsets of local objects can be computed once at compile time, such information can be kept in a single place associated with each function, but not in each ARI. You essentially remove exception overhead from each ARI and thus avoid the extra time to push them onto the stack. This approach is called the *zero-cost* model[13] of exception handling, and the optimized storage mentioned earlier is known as the *shadow stack*.[14]

Summary

Error recovery is a fundamental concern for every program you write. It's especially important in C++ when creating program components for others to use. To create a robust system, each component must be robust.

---

[13] The GNU C++ compiler uses the zero–cost model by default. Metrowerks Code Warrior for C++ also has an option to use the zero–cost model.

[14] Thanks to Scott Meyers and Josee Lajoie for their insights on the zero–cost model. You can find more information on how exceptions work in Josee's excellent article, "Exception Handling: Behind the Scenes," *C++ Gems*, SIGS, 1996.

The goals for exception handling in C++ are to simplify the creation of large, reliable programs using less code than currently possible, with more confidence that your application doesn't have an unhandled error. This is accomplished with little or no performance penalty and with low impact on existing code.

Basic exceptions are not terribly difficult to learn; begin using them in your programs as soon as you can. Exceptions are one of those features that provide immediate and significant benefits to your project.

Exercises

Solutions to selected exercises can be found in the electronic document *The Thinking in C++ Volume 2 Annotated Solution Guide*, available for a small fee from *www.MindView.net*.

1. Write three functions, one that returns an error value to indicate an error condition, one that sets **errno**, and one that uses **signal( )**. Write code that calls these functions and responds to the errors. Now write a fourth function that throws an exception. Call this function and catch the exception. Describe the differences between these four approaches, and why exception handling is an improvement.
2. Create a class with member functions that throw exceptions. Within this class, make a nested class to use as an exception object. It takes a single **const char*** as its argument; this represents a description string. Create a member function that throws this exception. (State this in the function's exception specification.) Write a **try** block that calls this function and a **catch** clause that handles the exception by displaying its description string.
3. Rewrite the **Stash** class from Chapter 13 of Volume 1 so that it throws **out_of_range** exceptions for **operator[ ]**.
4. Write a generic **main( )** that takes all exceptions and reports them as errors.
5. Create a class with its own **operator new**. This operator should allocate ten objects, and on the eleventh object "run out of memory" and throw an exception. Also add a **static** member function that reclaims this memory. Now create a **main( )** with a **try** block and a **catch** clause that calls the memory-restoration routine. Put these inside a **while** loop, to demonstrate recovering from an exception and continuing execution.

6. Create a destructor that throws an exception, and write code to prove to yourself that this is a bad idea by showing that if a new exception is thrown before the handler for the existing one is reached, **terminate( )** is called.

7. Prove to yourself that all exception objects (the ones that are thrown) are properly destroyed.

8. Prove to yourself that if you create an exception object on the heap and throw the pointer to that object, it will not be cleaned up.

9. Write a function with an exception specification that can throw four exception types: a **char**, an **int**, a **bool**, and your own exception class. Catch each in **main( )** and verify the catch. Derive your exception class from a standard exception. Write the function in such a way that the system recovers and tries to execute it again.

10. Modify your solution to the previous exercise to throw a **double** from the function, violating the exception specification. Catch the violation with your own unexpected handler that displays a message and exits the program gracefully (meaning **abort( )** is not called).

11. Write a **Garage** class that has a **Car** that is having troubles with its **Motor**. Use a function-level **try** block in the **Garage** class constructor to catch an exception (thrown from the **Motor** class) when its **Car** object is initialized. Throw a different exception from the body of the **Garage** constructor's handler and catch it in **main( )**.

2: Defensive Programming

Writing "perfect software" may be an elusive goal for developers, but a few defensive techniques, routinely applied, can go a long way toward improving the quality of your code.

Although the complexity of typical production software guarantees that testers will always have a job, we hope you still yearn to produce defect-free software. Object-oriented design techniques do much to corral the difficulty of large projects, but eventually you must write loops and functions. These details of "programming in the small" become the building blocks of the larger components needed for your designs. If your loops are off by one or your functions calculate the correct values only "most" of the time, you're in trouble no matter how fancy your overall methodology. In this chapter, you'll see practices that help create robust code regardless of the size of your project.

Your code is, among other things, an expression of your attempt to solve a problem. It should be clear to the reader (including yourself) exactly what you were thinking when you designed that loop. At certain points in your program, you should be able to make bold statements that some condition or other holds. (If you can't, you really haven't yet solved the problem.) Such statements are called *invariants*, since they should invariably be true at the point where they appear in the code; if not, either your design is faulty, or your code does not accurately reflect your design.

Consider a program that plays the guessing game of Hi-Lo. One person thinks of a number between 1 and 100, and the other person guesses the number. (We'll let the computer do the guessing.) The person who holds the number tells the guesser whether their guess is high, low or correct. The best strategy for the guesser is a *binary search*, which chooses the midpoint of the range of numbers where the sought-after number resides. The high-low response tells the guesser which half of the list holds the number, and the process repeats, halving the size of the active search range on each iteration. So how do you write a loop to drive the repetition properly? It's not sufficient to just say

```
bool guessed = false;
while(!guessed) {
  ...
}
```

because a malicious user might respond deceitfully, and you could spend all day guessing. What assumption, however simple, are you making each time you guess? In other words, what condition should hold *by design* on each loop iteration?

The simple assumption is that the secret number is within the current active range of unguessed numbers: [1, 100]. Suppose we label the endpoints of the range with the variables *low* and *high*. Each time you pass through the loop you need to make sure that if the number was in the range [**low**, **high**] at the beginning of the loop, you calculate the new range so that it still contains the number at the end of the current loop iteration.

The goal is to express the loop invariant in code so that a violation can be detected at runtime. Unfortunately, since the computer doesn't know the secret number, you can't express this condition directly in code, but you can at least make a comment to that effect:

```
while(!guessed) {
  // INVARIANT: the number is in the range [low, high]
  ...
}
```

What happens when the user says that a guess is too high or too low when it isn't? The deception will exclude the secret number from the new subrange. Because one lie always leads to another, eventually your range will diminish to nothing (since you shrink it by half each time and the secret number isn't in there). We can express this condition in the following program:

```
//: C02:HiLo.cpp {RunByHand}
// Plays the game of Hi-Lo to illustrate a loop invariant.
#include <cstdlib>
#include <iostream>
#include <string>
using namespace std;

int main() {
  cout << "Think of a number between 1 and 100" << endl
       << "I will make a guess; "
```

```
       << "tell me if I'm (H)igh or (L)ow" << endl;
  int low = 1, high = 100;
  bool guessed = false;
  while(!guessed) {
    // Invariant: the number is in the range [low, high]
    if(low > high) {  // Invariant violation
      cout << "You cheated! I quit" << endl;
      return EXIT_FAILURE;
    }
    int guess = (low + high) / 2;
    cout << "My guess is " << guess << ". ";
    cout << "(H)igh, (L)ow, or (E)qual? ";
    string response;
    cin >> response;
    switch(toupper(response[0])) {
      case 'H':
        high = guess - 1;
        break;
      case 'L':
        low = guess + 1;
        break;
      case 'E':
        guessed = true;
        break;
      default:
        cout << "Invalid response" << endl;
        continue;
    }
  }
  cout << "I got it!" << endl;
  return EXIT_SUCCESS;
} ///:~
```

The violation of the invariant is detected with the condition **if(low > high)**, because if the user always tells the truth, we will always find the secret number before we run out of guesses.

We also use a standard C technique for reporting program status to the calling context by returning different values from **main( )**. It is portable to use the statement **return 0;** to indicate success, but there is no portable value to indicate failure. For this reason we use the macro declared for this purpose in **<cstdlib>**: **EXIT_FAILURE**. For consistency, whenever we use **EXIT_FAILURE** we also use **EXIT_SUCCESS**, even though the latter is always defined as zero.

Assertions

The condition in the Hi-Lo program depends on user input, so you can't prevent a violation of the invariant. However, invariants usually depend only on the code you write, so they will always hold if you've implemented your design correctly. In this case, it is clearer to make an *assertion*, which is a positive statement that reveals your design decisions.

Suppose you are implementing a vector of integers: an expandable array that grows on demand. The function that adds an element to the vector must first verify that there is an open slot in the underlying array that holds the elements; otherwise, it needs to request more heap space and copy the existing elements to the new space before adding the new element (and deleting the old array). Such a function might look like the following:

```
void MyVector::push_back(int x) {
  if(nextSlot == capacity)
    grow();
  assert(nextSlot < capacity);
  data[nextSlot++] = x;
}
```

In this example, **data** is a dynamic array of **int**s with **capacity** slots and **nextSlot** slots in use. The purpose of **grow( )** is to expand the size of **data** so that the new value of **capacity** is strictly greater than **nextSlot**. Proper behavior of **MyVector** depends on this design decision, and it will never fail if the rest of the supporting code is correct. We *assert* the condition with the **assert( )** macro, which is defined in the header **<cassert>**.

The Standard C library **assert( )** macro is brief, to the point, and portable. If the condition in its parameter evaluates to non-zero, execution continues uninterrupted; if it doesn't, a message containing the text of the offending expression along with its source file name and line number is printed to the standard error channel and the program aborts. Is that too drastic? In practice, it is much more drastic to let execution continue when a basic design assumption has failed. Your program needs to be fixed.

If all goes well, you will thoroughly test your code with all assertions intact by the time the final product is deployed. (We'll say more about testing later.) Depending on the nature of your application, the machine cycles needed to test all assertions at runtime might be too much of a performance hit in the field. If that's the case, you can remove all the assertion code automatically by defining the macro **NDEBUG** and rebuilding the application.

To see how this works, note that a typical implementation of **assert( )** looks something like this:

```
#ifdef NDEBUG
  #define assert(cond) ((void)0)
#else
  void assertImpl(const char*, const char*, long);
  #define assert(cond) \
    ((cond) ? (void)0 : assertImpl(???))
#endif
```

When the macro **NDEBUG** is defined, the code decays to the expression **(void) 0**, so all that's left in the compilation stream is an essentially empty statement as a result of the semicolon you appended to each **assert( )** invocation. If **NDEBUG** is not defined, **assert(cond)** expands to a conditional statement that, when **cond** is zero, calls a compiler-dependent function (which we named **assertImpl( )**) with a string argument representing the text of **cond**, along with the file name and line number where the assertion appeared. (We used "???" as a place holder in the example, but the string mentioned is actually computed there, along with the file name and the line number where the macro occurs in that file. How these values are obtained is immaterial to our discussion.) If you want to turn assertions on and off at different points in your program, you must not only **#define** or **#undef NDEBUG**, but you must also re-include **<cassert>**. Macros are evaluated as the preprocessor encounters them and thus use whatever **NDEBUG** state applies at the point of inclusion. The most common way to define **NDEBUG** once for an entire program is as a compiler option, whether through project settings in your visual environment or via the command line, as in:

```
mycc -DNDEBUG myfile.cpp
```

Most compilers use the **−D** flag to define macro names. (Substitute the name of your compiler's executable for **mycc** above.) The advantage of this approach is that you can leave your assertions in the source code as an invaluable bit of documentation, and yet there is no runtime penalty. Because the code in an assertion disappears when **NDEBUG** is defined, it is important that you *never do work in an assertion*. Only test conditions that do not change the state of your program.

Whether using **NDEBUG** for released code is a good idea remains a subject of debate. Tony Hoare, one of the most influential computer scientists of all time,[1] has suggested that turning off runtime checks such as assertions is similar to a sailing enthusiast who wears a life jacket while training on land and then discards it when he goes to sea.[2] If an assertion fails in production, you have a problem much worse than degradation in performance, so choose wisely.

Not all conditions should be enforced by assertions. User errors and runtime resource failures should be signaled by throwing exceptions, as we explained in detail in Chapter 1. It is tempting to use assertions for most error conditions while roughing out code, with the intent to replace many of them later with robust exception handling. Like any other temptation, use caution, since you might forget to make all the necessary changes later. Remember: assertions are intended to verify design decisions that will only fail because of faulty programmer logic. The ideal is to solve all assertion violations during development. Don't use assertions for conditions that aren't totally in your control (for example, conditions that depend on user input). In particular, you wouldn't want to use assertions to validate function arguments; throw a **logic_error** instead.

The use of assertions as a tool to ensure program correctness was formalized by Bertrand Meyer in his *Design by Contract* methodology.[3] Every function has an implicit contract with clients that, given certain *preconditions*, guarantees certain *postconditions*. In other words, the preconditions are the requirements for using the function, such as supplying arguments within certain ranges, and the postconditions are the results delivered by the function, either by return value or by side-effect.

When client programs fail to give you valid input, you must tell them they have broken the contract. This is not the best time to abort the program (although you're justified in doing so since the contract was violated), but an exception is certainly appropriate. This is why the Standard C++ library

---

[1] He invented Quicksort, among other things.

[2] As quoted in *Programming Language Pragmatics*, by Michael L. Scott, Morgan–Kaufmann, 2000.

[3] See his book, *Object–Oriented Software Construction*, Prentice–Hall, 1994.

throws exceptions derived from **logic_error**, such as **out_of_range**.[4] If there are functions that only you call, however, such as private functions in a class of your own design, the **assert( )** macro is appropriate, since you have total control over the situation and you certainly want to debug your code before shipping.

A postcondition failure indicates a program error, and it is appropriate to use assertions for *any invariant at any time*, including the postcondition test at the end of a function. This applies in particular to class member functions that maintain the state of an object. In the **MyVector** example earlier, for instance, a reasonable invariant for all public member functions would be:

```
assert(0 <= nextSlot && nextSlot <= capacity);
```

or, if **nextSlot** is an unsigned integer, simply

```
assert(nextSlot <= capacity);
```

Such an invariant is called a *class invariant* and can reasonably be enforced by an assertion. Subclasses play the role of *subcontractor* to their base classes because they must maintain the original contract between the base class and its clients. For this reason, the preconditions in derived classes must impose no extra requirements beyond those in the base contract, and the postconditions must deliver at least as much.[5]

Validating results returned to the client, however, is nothing more or less than *testing*, so using post-condition assertions in this case would be duplicating work. Yes, it's good documentation, but more than one developer has been fooled into improperly using post-condition assertions as a substitute for unit testing.

---

[4] This is still an assertion *conceptually*, but since we don't want to halt execution, the **assert( )** macro is not appropriate. Java 1.4, for example, throws an exception when an assertion fails.

[5] There is a nice phrase to help remember this phenomenon: "Require no more; promise no less," first coined in *C++ FAQs*, by Marshall Cline and Greg Lomow (Addison–Wesley, 1994). Since pre–conditions can weaken in derived classes, we say that they are *contravariant*, and, conversely, post–conditions are *covariant* (which explains why we mentioned the covariance of exception specifications in Chapter 1).

A simple unit test framework

Writing software is all about meeting requirements.[6] Creating these
requirements is difficult, and they can change from day to day; you might
discover at a weekly project meeting that what you just spent the week doing
is not exactly what the users really want.

People cannot articulate software requirements without sampling an
evolving, working system. It's much better to specify a little, design a little,
code a little, and test a little. Then, after evaluating the outcome, do it all over
again. The ability to develop in such an iterative fashion is one of the great
advances of the object-oriented approach, but it requires nimble
programmers who can craft resilient code. Change is hard.

Another impetus for change comes from you, the programmer. The
craftsperson in you wants to continually improve the design of your code.
What maintenance programmer hasn't cursed the aging, flagship company
product as a convoluted, unmodifiable patchwork of spaghetti?
Management's reluctance to let you tamper with a functioning system robs
code of the resilience it needs to endure. "If it's not broken, don't fix it"
eventually gives way to, "We can't fix it—rewrite it." Change is necessary.

Fortunately, our industry is growing accustomed to the discipline of
refactoring, the art of internally restructuring code to improve its design,
without changing its behavior.[7] Such improvements include extracting a new
function from another, or inversely, combining member functions; replacing
a member function with an object; parameterizing a member function or
class; and replacing conditionals with polymorphism. Refactoring helps code
evolve.

---

[6] This section is based on Chuck's article, "The Simplest Automated Unit
Test Framework That Could Possibly Work," *C/C++ Users Journal*, Sept.
2000.

[7] A good book on this subject is Martin Fowler's *Refactoring: Improving
the Design of Existing Code* (Addison–Wesley, 2000). See also
http://www.refactoring.com. Refactoring is a crucial practice of Extreme
Programming (XP).

Whether the force for change comes from users or programmers, changes today may break what worked yesterday. We need a way to build code that withstands change and improves over time.

Extreme Programming (XP)[8] is only one of many practices that support a quick-on-your-feet motif. In this section we explore what we think is the key to making flexible, incremental development succeed: an easy-to-use automated unit test framework. (Note that *testers*, software professionals who test others' code for a living, are still indispensable. Here, we are merely describing a way to help developers write better code.)

Developers write *unit tests* to gain the confidence to say the two most important things that any developer can say:

1.   I understand the requirements.

2.   My code meets those requirements (to the best of my knowledge).

There is no better way to ensure that you know what the code you're about to write should do than to write the unit tests first. This simple exercise helps focus the mind on the task ahead and will likely lead to working code faster than just jumping into coding. Or, to express it in XP terms:

> *Testing + programming is faster than just programming.*

Writing tests first also guards you against boundary conditions that might break your code, so your code is more robust.

When your code passes all your tests, you know that if the system isn't working, your code is probably not the problem. The statement "All my tests pass" is a powerful argument.

Automated testing

So what does a unit test look like? Too often developers just use some well-behaved input to produce some expected output, which they inspect visually.

---

[8] See *Extreme Programming Explained: Embrace Change* by Kent Beck, Addison Wesley 1999. Lightweight methodologies such as XP have "joined forces" in the Agile Alliance (see http://www.agilealliance.org/home).

Two dangers exist in this approach. First, programs don't always receive only well-behaved input. We all know that we should test the boundaries of program input, but it's hard to think about this when you're trying to just get things working. If you write the test for a function first before you start coding, you can wear your "tester hat" and ask yourself, "What could possibly make this break?" Code a test that will prove the function you'll write isn't broken, and then put on your developer hat and make it happen. You'll write better code than if you hadn't written the test first.

The second danger is that inspecting output visually is tedious and error prone. Most any such thing a human can do a computer can do, but without human error. It's better to formulate tests as collections of *Boolean expressions* and have a test program report any failures.

For example, suppose you need to build a **Date** class that has the following properties:

- A date can be initialized with a string (YYYYMMDD), three integers (Y, M, D), or nothing (giving today's date).

- A date object can yield its year, month, and day or a string of the form "YYYYMMDD".

- All relational comparisons are available, as well as computing the duration between two dates (in years, months, and days).

- Dates to be compared need to be able to span an arbitrary number of centuries (for example, 1600–2200).

Your class can store three integers representing the year, month, and day. (Just be sure the year is at least 16 bits in size to satisfy the last bulleted item.) The interface for your **Date** class might look like this:

```
//: C02:Date1.h
// A first pass at Date.h.
#ifndef DATE1_H
#define DATE1_H
#include <string>

class Date {
public:
```

```
    // A struct to hold elapsed time:
    struct Duration {
      int years;
      int months;
      int days;
      Duration(int y, int m, int d)
      : years(y), months(m), days(d) {}
    };
    Date();
    Date(int year, int month, int day);
    Date(const std::string&);
    int getYear() const;
    int getMonth() const;
    int getDay() const;
    std::string toString() const;
    friend bool operator<(const Date&, const Date&);
    friend bool operator>(const Date&, const Date&);
    friend bool operator<=(const Date&, const Date&);
    friend bool operator>=(const Date&, const Date&);
    friend bool operator==(const Date&, const Date&);
    friend bool operator!=(const Date&, const Date&);
    friend Duration duration(const Date&, const Date&);
};
#endif // DATE1_H ///:~
```

Before you implement this class, you can solidify your grasp of the
requirements by writing the beginnings of a test program. You might come up
with something like the following:

```
//: C02:SimpleDateTest.cpp
//{L} Date
#include <iostream>
#include "Date.h" // From Appendix B
using namespace std;

// Test machinery
int nPass = 0, nFail = 0;
void test(bool t) { if(t) nPass++; else nFail++; }

int main() {
  Date mybday(1951, 10, 1);
  test(mybday.getYear() == 1951);
  test(mybday.getMonth() == 10);
  test(mybday.getDay() == 1);
```

```
    cout << "Passed: " << nPass << ", Failed: "
        << nFail << endl;
}
/* Expected output:
Passed: 3, Failed: 0
*/ ///:~
```

In this trivial case, the function **test( )** maintains the global variables **nPass** and **nFail**. The only visual inspection you do is to read the final score. If a test failed, a more sophisticated **test( )** displays an appropriate message. The framework described later in this chapter has such a test function, among other things.

You can now implement enough of the **Date** class to get these tests to pass, and then you can proceed iteratively until all the requirements are met. By writing tests first, you are more likely to think of corner cases that might break your upcoming implementation, and you're more likely to write the code correctly the first time. Such an exercise might produce the following version of a test for the **Date** class:

```
//: C02:SimpleDateTest2.cpp
//{L} Date
#include <iostream>
#include "Date.h"
using namespace std;

// Test machinery
int nPass = 0, nFail = 0;
void test(bool t) { if(t) ++nPass; else ++nFail; }

int main() {
  Date mybday(1951, 10, 1);
  Date today;
  Date myevebday("19510930");

  // Test the operators
  test(mybday < today);
  test(mybday <= today);
  test(mybday != today);
  test(mybday == mybday);
  test(mybday >= mybday);
  test(mybday <= mybday);
  test(myevebday < mybday);
```

```
test(mybday > myevebday);
test(mybday >= myevebday);
test(mybday != myevebday);

// Test the functions
test(mybday.getYear() == 1951);
test(mybday.getMonth() == 10);
test(mybday.getDay() == 1);
test(myevebday.getYear() == 1951);
test(myevebday.getMonth() == 9);
test(myevebday.getDay() == 30);
test(mybday.toString() == "19511001");
test(myevebday.toString() == "19510930");

// Test duration
Date d2(2003, 7, 4);
Date::Duration dur = duration(mybday, d2);
test(dur.years == 51);
test(dur.months == 9);
test(dur.days == 3);

// Report results:
cout << "Passed: " << nPass << ", Failed: "
     << nFail << endl;
} ///:~
```

This test can be more fully developed. For example, we haven't tested that long durations are handled correctly. We'll stop here, but you get the idea. The full implementation for the **Date** class is available in the files **Date.h** and **Date.cpp** in the appendix.[9]

The TestSuite Framework

Some automated C++ unit test tools are available on the World Wide Web for download, such as **CppUnit**.[10] Our purpose here is not only to present a test mechanism that is easy to use, but also easy to understand internally and even modify if necessary. So, in the spirit of "Do The Simplest Thing That

---

[9] Our Date class is also "internationalized," in that it supports wide character sets. This is introduced at the end of the next chapter.

[10] See http://sourceforge.net/projects/cppunit for more information.

Could Possibly Work,"[11] we have developed the *TestSuite Framework*, a namespace named **TestSuite** that contains two key classes: **Test** and **Suite**.

The **Test** class is an abstract base class from which you derive a test object. It keeps track of the number of passes and failures and displays the text of any test condition that fails. You simply to override the **run( )** member function, which should in turn call the **test_( )** macro for each Boolean test condition you define.

To define a test for the **Date** class using the framework, you can inherit from **Test** as shown in the following program:

```
//: C02:DateTest.h
#ifndef DATETEST_H
#define DATETEST_H
#include "Date.h"
#include "../TestSuite/Test.h"

class DateTest : public TestSuite::Test {
  Date mybday;
  Date today;
  Date myevebday;
public:
  DateTest(): mybday(1951, 10, 1), myevebday("19510930") {}
  void run() {
    testOps();
    testFunctions();
    testDuration();
  }
  void testOps() {
    test_(mybday < today);
    test_(mybday <= today);
    test_(mybday != today);
    test_(mybday == mybday);
    test_(mybday >= mybday);
    test_(mybday <= mybday);
    test_(myevebday < mybday);
    test_(mybday > myevebday);
    test_(mybday >= myevebday);
    test_(mybday != myevebday);
```

---

[11] This is a key principle of Extreme Programming.

```
  }
  void testFunctions() {
    test_(mybday.getYear() == 1951);
    test_(mybday.getMonth() == 10);
    test_(mybday.getDay() == 1);
    test_(myevebday.getYear() == 1951);
    test_(myevebday.getMonth() == 9);
    test_(myevebday.getDay() == 30);
    test_(mybday.toString() == "19511001");
    test_(myevebday.toString() == "19510930");
  }
  void testDuration() {
    Date d2(2003, 7, 4);
    Date::Duration dur = duration(mybday, d2);
    test_(dur.years == 51);
    test_(dur.months == 9);
    test_(dur.days == 3);
  }
};
#endif // DATETEST_H ///:~
```

Running the test is a simple matter of instantiating a **DateTest** object and calling its **run( )** member function:

```
//: C02:DateTest.cpp
// Automated testing (with a framework).
//{L} Date ../TestSuite/Test
#include <iostream>
#include "DateTest.h"
using namespace std;

int main() {
  DateTest test;
  test.run();
  return test.report();
}
/* Output:
Test "DateTest":
        Passed: 21,     Failed: 0
*/ ///:~
```

The **Test::report( )** function displays the previous output and returns the number of failures, so it is suitable to use as a return value from **main( )**.

The **Test** class uses RTTI[12] to get the name of your class (for example, **DateTest**) for the report. There is also a **setStream( )** member function if you want the test results sent to a file instead of to the standard output (the default). You'll see the **Test** class implementation later in this chapter.

The **test_( )** macro can extract the text of the Boolean condition that fails, along with its file name and line number.[13] To see what happens when a failure occurs, you can introduce an intentional error in the code, for example by reversing the condition in the first call to **test_( )** in **DateTest::testOps( )** in the previous example code. The output indicates exactly what test was in error and where it happened:

```
DateTest failure: (mybday > today) , DateTest.h (line 31)
Test "DateTest":
        Passed: 20      Failed: 1
```

In addition to **test_( )**, the framework includes the functions **succeed_( )** and **fail_( )**, for cases where a Boolean test won't do. These functions apply when the class you're testing might throw exceptions. During testing, create an input set that will cause the exception to occur. If it doesn't, it's an error and you call **fail_( )** explicitly to display a message and update the failure count. If it does throw the exception as expected, you call **succeed_( )** to update the success count.

To illustrate, suppose we modify the specification of the two non-default **Date** constructors to throw a **DateError** exception (a type nested inside **Date** and derived from **std::logic_error**) if the input parameters do not represent a valid date:

```
Date(const string& s) throw(DateError);
Date(int year, int month, int day) throw(DateError);
```

---

[12] "Runtime Type Identification," discussed in chapter 9. Specifically, we use the **name( )** member function of the **typeinfo** class. If you're using Microsoft Visual C++, you need to specify the compile option **/GR**. If you don't, you'll get an access violation at runtime.
[13] In particular, we use *stringizing* (via the # preprocessing operator) and the predefined macros **__FILE__** and **__LINE__**. See the code later in the chapter.

The **DateTest::run( )** member function can now call the following function to test the exception handling:

```
void testExceptions() {
  try {
    Date d(0,0,0);  // Invalid
    fail_("Invalid date undetected in Date int ctor");
  } catch(Date::DateError&) {
    succeed_();
  }
  try {
    Date d("");  // Invalid
    fail_("Invalid date undetected in Date string ctor");
  } catch(Date::DateError&) {
    succeed_();
  }
}
```

In both cases, if an exception is not thrown, it is an error. Notice that you must manually pass a message to **fail_( )**, since no Boolean expression is being evaluated.

Test suites

Real projects usually contain many classes, so you need a way to group tests so that you can just push a single button to test the entire project.[14] The **Suite** class collects tests into a functional unit. You add **Test** objects to a **Suite** with the **addTest( )** member function, or you can include an entire existing suite with **addSuite( )**. To illustrate, the following example collects the programs in Chapter 3 that use the **Test** class into a single suite. Note that this file will appear in the Chapter 3 subdirectory:

```
//: C03:StringSuite.cpp
//{L} ../TestSuite/Test ../TestSuite/Suite
//{L} TrimTest
// Illustrates a test suite for code from Chapter 3
#include <iostream>
#include "../TestSuite/Suite.h"
#include "StringStorage.h"
```

---

[14] Batch files and shell scripts work well for this. The **Suite** class is a C++-based way of organizing related tests.

```
#include "Sieve.h"
#include "Find.h"
#include "Rparse.h"
#include "TrimTest.h"
#include "CompStr.h"
using namespace std;
using namespace TestSuite;

int main() {
    Suite suite("String Tests");
    suite.addTest(new StringStorageTest);
    suite.addTest(new SieveTest);
    suite.addTest(new FindTest);
    suite.addTest(new RparseTest);
    suite.addTest(new TrimTest);
    suite.addTest(new CompStrTest);
    suite.run();
    long nFail = suite.report();
    suite.free();
    return nFail;
}
/* Output:
s1 = 62345
s2 = 12345
Suite "String Tests"
====================
Test "StringStorageTest":
   Passed: 2   Failed: 0
Test "SieveTest":
   Passed: 50  Failed: 0
Test "FindTest":
   Passed: 9   Failed: 0
Test "RparseTest":
   Passed: 8   Failed: 0
Test "TrimTest":
   Passed: 11  Failed: 0
Test "CompStrTest":
   Passed: 8   Failed: 0
*/ ///:~
```

Five of the above tests are completely contained in header files. **TrimTest** is not, because it contains static data that must be defined in an implementation file. The two first two output lines are trace lines from the **StringStorage** test. You must give the suite a name as a constructor argument. The

Suite::run( ) member function calls **Test::run( )** for each of its contained tests. Much the same thing happens for **Suite::report( )**, except that you can send the individual test reports to a different destination stream than that of the suite report. If the test passed to **addSuite( )** already has a stream pointer assigned, it keeps it. Otherwise, it gets its stream from the **Suite** object. (As with **Test**, there is an optional second argument to the suite constructor that defaults to **std::cout**.) The destructor for **Suite** does not automatically delete the contained **Test** pointers because they don't need to reside on the heap; that's the job of **Suite::free( )**.

The test framework code

The test framework code is in a subdirectory called **TestSuite** in the code distribution available at www.MindView.net. To use it, include the search path for the **TestSuite** subdirectory in your header, link the object files, and include the **TestSuite** subdirectory in the library search path. Here is the header for **Test.h**:

```
//: TestSuite:Test.h
#ifndef TEST_H
#define TEST_H
#include <string>
#include <iostream>
#include <cassert>
using std::string;
using std::ostream;
using std::cout;

// fail_() has an underscore to prevent collision with
// ios::fail(). For consistency, test_() and succeed_()
// also have underscores.

#define test_(cond) \
  do_test(cond, #cond, __FILE__, __LINE__)
#define fail_(str) \
  do_fail(str, __FILE__, __LINE__)

namespace TestSuite {

class Test {
  ostream* osptr;
  long nPass;
  long nFail;
```

```
  // Disallowed:
  Test(const Test&);
  Test& operator=(const Test&);
protected:
  void do_test(bool cond, const string& lbl,
    const char* fname, long lineno);
  void do_fail(const string& lbl,
    const char* fname, long lineno);
public:
  Test(ostream* osptr = &cout) {
    this->osptr = osptr;
    nPass = nFail = 0;
  }
  virtual ~Test() {}
  virtual void run() = 0;
  long getNumPassed() const { return nPass; }
  long getNumFailed() const { return nFail; }
  const ostream* getStream() const { return osptr; }
  void setStream(ostream* osptr) { this->osptr = osptr; }
  void succeed_() { ++nPass; }
  long report() const;
  virtual void reset() { nPass = nFail = 0; }
};

} // namespace TestSuite
#endif // TEST_H ///:~
```

There are three virtual functions in the **Test** class:

- A virtual destructor

- The function **reset( )**

- The pure virtual function **run( )**

As explained in Volume 1, it is an error to delete a derived heap object through a base pointer unless the base class has a virtual destructor. Any class intended to be a base class (usually evidenced by the presence of at least one other virtual function) should have a virtual destructor. The default implementation of the **Test::reset( )** resets the success and failure counters to zero. You might want to override this function to reset the state of the data in your derived test object; just be sure to call **Test::reset( )** explicitly in your override so that the counters are reset. The **Test::run( )** member function is pure virtual since you are required to override it in your derived class.

The **test_( )** and **fail_( )** macros can include file name and line number information available from the preprocessor. We originally omitted the trailing underscores in the names, but the **fail( )** macro then collided with **ios::fail( )**, causing compiler errors.

Here is the implementation of the remainder of the **Test** functions:

```
//: TestSuite:Test.cpp {0}
#include "Test.h"
#include <iostream>
#include <typeinfo>
using namespace std;
using namespace TestSuite;

void Test::do_test(bool cond, const std::string& lbl,
  const char* fname, long lineno) {
  if(!cond)
    do_fail(lbl, fname, lineno);
  else
    succeed_();
}

void Test::do_fail(const std::string& lbl,
  const char* fname, long lineno) {
  ++nFail;
  if(osptr) {
    *osptr << typeid(*this).name()
           << "failure: (" << lbl << ") , " << fname
           << " (line " << lineno << ")" << endl;
  }
}

long Test::report() const {
  if(osptr) {
    *osptr << "Test \"" << typeid(*this).name()
           << "\":\n\tPassed: " << nPass
           << "\tFailed: " << nFail
           << endl;
  }
  return nFail;
} ///:~
```

The **Test** class keeps track of the number of successes and failures as well as the stream where you want **Test::report( )** to display the results. The **test_( )** and **fail_( )** macros extract the current file name and line number information from the preprocessor and pass the file name to **do_test( )** and the line number to **do_fail( )**, which do the actual work of displaying a message and updating the appropriate counter. We can't think of a good reason to allow copy and assignment of test objects, so we have disallowed these operations by making their prototypes private and omitting their respective function bodies.

Here is the header file for **Suite**:

```
//: TestSuite:Suite.h
#ifndef SUITE_H
#define SUITE_H
#include <vector>
#include <stdexcept>
#include "../TestSuite/Test.h"
using std::vector;
using std::logic_error;

namespace TestSuite {

class TestSuiteError : public logic_error {
public:
  TestSuiteError(const string& s = "")
  : logic_error(s) {}
};

class Suite {
  string name;
  ostream* osptr;
  vector<Test*> tests;
  void reset();
  // Disallowed ops:
  Suite(const Suite&);
  Suite& operator=(const Suite&);
public:
  Suite(const string& name, ostream* osptr = &cout)
  : name(name) { this->osptr = osptr; }
  string getName() const { return name; }
  long getNumPassed() const;
  long getNumFailed() const;
```

```
    const ostream* getStream() const { return osptr; }
    void setStream(ostream* osptr) { this->osptr = osptr; }
    void addTest(Test* t) throw(TestSuiteError);
    void addSuite(const Suite&);
    void run();  // Calls Test::run() repeatedly
    long report() const;
    void free();  // Deletes tests
};

} // namespace TestSuite
#endif // SUITE_H ///:~
```

The **Suite** class holds pointers to its **Test** objects in a **vector**. Notice the exception specification on the **addTest( )** member function. When you add a test to a suite, **Suite::addTest( )** verifies that the pointer you pass is not null; if it is null, it throws a **TestSuiteError** exception. Since this makes it impossible to add a null pointer to a suite, **addSuite( )** asserts this condition on each of its tests, as do the other functions that traverse the **vector** of tests (see the following implementation). Copy and assignment are disallowed as they are in the **Test** class.

```
//: TestSuite:Suite.cpp {O}
#include "Suite.h"
#include <iostream>
#include <cassert>
#include <cstddef>
using namespace std;
using namespace TestSuite;

void Suite::addTest(Test* t) throw(TestSuiteError) {
  // Verify test is valid and has a stream:
  if(t == 0)
    throw TestSuiteError("Null test in Suite::addTest");
  else if(osptr && !t->getStream())
    t->setStream(osptr);
  tests.push_back(t);
  t->reset();
}

void Suite::addSuite(const Suite& s) {
  for(size_t i = 0; i < s.tests.size(); ++i) {
    assert(tests[i]);
    addTest(s.tests[i]);
  }
```

```
}

void Suite::free() {
  for(size_t i = 0; i < tests.size(); ++i) {
    delete tests[i];
    tests[i] = 0;
  }
}

void Suite::run() {
  reset();
  for(size_t i = 0; i < tests.size(); ++i) {
    assert(tests[i]);
    tests[i]->run();
  }
}

long Suite::report() const {
  if(osptr) {
    long totFail = 0;
    *osptr << "Suite \"" << name
           << "\"\n=======";
    size_t i;
    for(i = 0; i < name.size(); ++i)
      *osptr << '=';
    *osptr << "=" << endl;
    for(i = 0; i < tests.size(); ++i) {
      assert(tests[i]);
      totFail += tests[i]->report();
    }
    *osptr << "=======";
    for(i = 0; i < name.size(); ++i)
      *osptr << '=';
    *osptr << "=" << endl;
    return totFail;
  }
  else
    return getNumFailed();
}

long Suite::getNumPassed() const {
  long totPass = 0;
  for(size_t i = 0; i < tests.size(); ++i) {
    assert(tests[i]);
    totPass += tests[i]->getNumPassed();
```

```
    }
    return totPass;
}

long Suite::getNumFailed() const {
  long totFail = 0;
  for(size_t i = 0; i < tests.size(); ++i) {
    assert(tests[i]);
    totFail += tests[i]->getNumFailed();
  }
  return totFail;
}

void Suite::reset() {
  for(size_t i = 0; i < tests.size(); ++i) {
    assert(tests[i]);
    tests[i]->reset();
  }
} ///:~
```

We will be using the **TestSuite** framework wherever it applies throughout the rest of this book.

Debugging techniques

The best debugging habit is to use assertions as explained in the beginning of this chapter; by doing so you'll help find logic errors before they cause real trouble. This section contains some other tips and techniques that might help during debugging.

Trace macros

Sometimes it's useful to print the code of each statement as it is executed, either to **cout** or to a trace file. Here's a preprocessor macro to accomplish this:

```
#define TRACE(ARG) cout << #ARG << endl; ARG
```

Now you can go through and surround the statements you trace with this macro. However, this can introduce problems. For example, if you take the statement:

```
for(int i = 0; i < 100; i++)
  cout << i << endl;
```

and put both lines inside **TRACE( )** macros, you get this:

```
TRACE(for(int i = 0; i < 100; i++))
TRACE(  cout << i << endl;)
```

which expands to this:

```
cout << "for(int i = 0; i < 100; i++)" << endl;
for(int i = 0; i < 100; i++)
  cout << "cout << i << endl;" << endl;
cout << i << endl;
```

which isn't exactly what you want. Thus, you must use this technique carefully.

The following is a variation on the **TRACE( )** macro:

```
#define D(a) cout << #a "=[" << a << "]" << endl;
```

If you want to display an expression, you simply put it inside a call to **D( )**. The expression is displayed, followed by its value (assuming there's an overloaded operator **<<** for the result type). For example, you can say **D(a + b)**. You can use this macro any time you want to check an intermediate value.

These two macros represent the two most fundamental things you do with a debugger: trace through the code execution and display values. A good debugger is an excellent productivity tool, but sometimes debuggers are not available, or it's not convenient to use them. These techniques always work, regardless of the situation.

Trace file

DISCLAIMER: This section and the next contain code which is officially unsanctioned by the C++ Standard. In particular, we redefine **cout** and **new** via macros, which can cause surprising results if you're not careful. Our examples work on all the compilers we use, however, and provide useful information. This is the only place in this book where we will depart from the sanctity of standard-compliant coding practice. Use at your own risk! Note that in order for this to work, a using-declaration must be used, so that **cout** isn't prefixed by its namespace, i.e. **std::cout** will not work.

The following code easily creates a trace file and sends all the output that would normally go to **cout** into that file. All you must do is **#define** TRACEON and include the header file (of course, it's fairly easy just to write the two key lines right into your file):

```
//: C03:Trace.h
// Creating a trace file.
#ifndef TRACE_H
#define TRACE_H
#include <fstream>

#ifdef TRACEON
std::ofstream TRACEFILE__("TRACE.OUT");
#define cout TRACEFILE__
#endif

#endif // TRACE_H ///:~
```

Here's a simple test of the previous file:

```
//: C03:Tracetst.cpp {-bor}
#include <iostream>
#include <fstream>
#include "../require.h"
using namespace std;

#define TRACEON
#include "Trace.h"

int main() {
  ifstream f("Tracetst.cpp");
  assure(f, "Tracetst.cpp");
  cout << f.rdbuf(); // Dumps file contents to file
} ///:~
```

Because **cout** has been textually turned into something else by **Trace.h**, all the **cout** statements in your program now send information to the trace file. This is a convenient way of capturing your output into a file, in case your operating system doesn't make output redirection easy.

Finding memory leaks

The following straightforward debugging techniques are explained in Volume 1:

1. For array bounds checking, use the **Array** template in **C16:Array3.cpp** of Volume 1 for all arrays. You can turn off the checking and increase efficiency when you're ready to ship. (Although this doesn't deal with the case of taking a pointer to an array.)

2. Check for non-virtual destructors in base classes.

Tracking new/delete and malloc/free

Common problems with memory allocation include mistakenly calling **delete** for memory that's not on the free store, deleting the free store more than once, and, most often, forgetting to delete a pointer. This section discusses a system that can help you track down these kinds of problems.

As an *additional disclaimer* beyond that of the preceding section: because of the way we overload **new**, the following technique may not work on all platforms, and will only work for programs that do not call the *function* **operator new( )** explicitly. We have been quite careful in this book to only present code that fully conforms to the C++ Standard, but in this one instance we're making an exception for the following reasons:

1. Even though it's technically illegal, it works on many compilers.[15]
2. We illustrate some useful thinking along the way.

To use the memory checking system, you simply include the header file **MemCheck.h**, link the **MemCheck.obj** file into your application to intercept all the calls to **new** and **delete**, and call the macro **MEM_ON( )** (explained later in this section) to initiate memory tracing. A trace of all

---

[15] Our key technical reviewer, Pete Becker of Dinkumware. Ltd., brought to our attention that it is illegal to use macros to replace C++ keywords. His take on this technique was as follows: "This is a dirty trick. Dirty tricks are sometimes necessary to figure out why code isn't working, so you may want to keep this in your toolbox, but don't ship any code with it." Caveat programmer.

---

allocations and deallocations is printed to the standard output (via **stdout**). When you use this system, all calls to **new** store information about the file and line where they were called. This is accomplished by using the *placement syntax* for **operator new**.[16] Although you typically use the placement syntax when you need to place objects at a specific point in memory, it can also create an **operator new( )** with any number of arguments. This is used in the following example to store the results of the __**FILE**__ and __**LINE**__ macros whenever **new** is called:

```
//: C02:MemCheck.h
#ifndef MEMCHECK_H
#define MEMCHECK_H
#include <cstddef>  // For size_t

// Usurp the new operator (both scalar and array versions)
void* operator new(std::size_t, const char*, long);
void* operator new[](std::size_t, const char*, long);
#define new new (__FILE__, __LINE__)

extern bool traceFlag;
#define TRACE_ON() traceFlag = true
#define TRACE_OFF() traceFlag = false

extern bool activeFlag;
#define MEM_ON() activeFlag = true
#define MEM_OFF() activeFlag = false

#endif // MEMCHECK_H ///:~
```

It is important to include this file in any source file in which you want to track free store activity, but include it *last* (after your other **#include** directives). Most headers in the standard library are templates, and since most compilers use the *inclusion model* of template compilation (meaning all source code is in the headers), the macro that replaces **new** in **MemCheck.h** would usurp all instances of the **new** operator in the library source code (and would likely result in compile errors). Besides, you are only interested in tracking your own memory errors, not the library's.

---

[16] Thanks to Reg Charney of the C++ Standards Committee for suggesting this trick.

In the following file, which contains the memory tracking implementation, everything is done with C standard I/O rather than with C++ iostreams. It shouldn't make a difference, since we're not interfering with iostreams' use of the free store, but when we tried it, some compilers complained. All compilers were happy with the **<cstdio>** version.

```cpp
//: C02:MemCheck.cpp {O}
#include <cstdio>
#include <cstdlib>
#include <cassert>
#include <cstddef>
using namespace std;
#undef new

// Global flags set by macros in MemCheck.h
bool traceFlag = true;
bool activeFlag = false;

namespace {

// Memory map entry type
struct Info {
  void* ptr;
  const char* file;
  long line;
};

// Memory map data
const size_t MAXPTRS = 10000u;
Info memMap[MAXPTRS];
size_t nptrs = 0;

// Searches the map for an address
int findPtr(void* p) {
  for(size_t i = 0; i < nptrs; ++i)
    if(memMap[i].ptr == p)
      return i;
  return -1;
}

void delPtr(void* p) {
  int pos = findPtr(p);
  assert(pos >= 0);
  // Remove pointer from map
```

```cpp
    for(size_t i = pos; i < nptrs-1; ++i)
      memMap[i] = memMap[i+1];
    --nptrs;
}

// Dummy type for static destructor
struct Sentinel {
  ~Sentinel() {
    if(nptrs > 0) {
      printf("Leaked memory at:\n");
      for(size_t i = 0; i < nptrs; ++i)
        printf("\t%p (file: %s, line %ld)\n",
          memMap[i].ptr, memMap[i].file, memMap[i].line);
    }
    else
      printf("No user memory leaks!\n");
  }
};

// Static dummy object
Sentinel s;

} // End anonymous namespace

// Overload scalar new
void*
operator new(size_t siz, const char* file, long line) {
  void* p = malloc(siz);
  if(activeFlag) {
    if(nptrs == MAXPTRS) {
      printf("memory map too small (increase MAXPTRS)\n");
      exit(1);
    }
    memMap[nptrs].ptr = p;
    memMap[nptrs].file = file;
    memMap[nptrs].line = line;
    ++nptrs;
  }
  if(traceFlag) {
    printf("Allocated %u bytes at address %p ", siz, p);
    printf("(file: %s, line: %ld)\n", file, line);
  }
  return p;
}
```

```
// Overload array new
void*
operator new[](size_t siz, const char* file, long line) {
  return operator new(siz, file, line);
}

// Override scalar delete
void operator delete(void* p) {
  if(findPtr(p) >= 0) {
    free(p);
    assert(nptrs > 0);
    delPtr(p);
    if(traceFlag)
      printf("Deleted memory at address %p\n", p);
  }
  else if(!p && activeFlag)
    printf("Attempt to delete unknown pointer: %p\n", p);
}

// Override array delete
void operator delete[](void* p) {
  operator delete(p);
} ///:~
```

The Boolean flags **traceFlag** and **activeFlag** are global, so they can be modified in your code by the macros **TRACE_ON( )**, **TRACE_OFF( )**, **MEM_ON( )**, and **MEM_OFF( )**. In general, enclose all the code in your **main( )** within a **MEM_ON( )**-**MEM_OFF( )** pair so that memory is always tracked. Tracing, which echoes the activity of the replacement functions for **operator new( )** and **operator delete( )**, is on by default, but you can turn it off with **TRACE_OFF( )**. In any case, the final results are always printed (see the test runs later in this chapter).

The **MemCheck** facility tracks memory by keeping all addresses allocated by **operator new( )** in an array of **Info** structures, which also holds the file name and line number where the call to **new** occurred. To prevent collision with any names you have placed in the global namespace, as much information as possible is kept inside the anonymous namespace. The **Sentinel** class exists solely to call a static object destructor as the program shuts down. This destructor inspects **memMap** to see if any pointers are waiting to be deleted (indicating a memory leak).

Our **operator new( )** uses **malloc( )** to get memory, and then adds the pointer and its associated file information to **memMap**. The **operator delete( )** function undoes all that work by calling **free( )** and decrementing **nptrs**, but first it checks to see if the pointer in question is in the map in the first place. If it isn't, either you're trying to delete an address that isn't on the free store, or you're trying to delete one that's already been deleted and removed from the map. The **activeFlag** variable is important here because we don't want to process any deallocations from any system shutdown activity. By calling **MEM_OFF( )** at the end of your code, **activeFlag** will be set to **false**, and such subsequent calls to **delete** will be ignored. (That's bad in a real program, but our purpose here is to find *your* leaks; we're not debugging the library.) For simplicity, we forward all work for array **new** and **delete** to their scalar counterparts.

The following is a simple test using the **MemCheck** facility:

```
//: C02:MemTest.cpp
//{L} MemCheck
// Test of MemCheck system.
#include <iostream>
#include <vector>
#include <cstring>
#include "MemCheck.h"    // Must appear last!
using namespace std;

class Foo {
  char* s;
public:
  Foo(const char*s ) {
    this->s = new char[strlen(s) + 1];
    strcpy(this->s, s);
  }
  ~Foo() { delete [] s; }
};

int main() {
  MEM_ON();
  cout << "hello" << endl;
  int* p = new int;
  delete p;
  int* q = new int[3];
  delete [] q;
  int* r;
```

```
    delete r;
    vector<int> v;
    v.push_back(1);
    Foo s("goodbye");
    MEM_OFF();
} ///:~
```

This example verifies that you can use **MemCheck** in the presence of
streams, standard containers, and classes that allocate memory in
constructors. The pointers **p** and **q** are allocated and deallocated without any
problem, but **r** is not a valid heap pointer, so the output indicates the error as
an attempt to delete an unknown pointer:

```
hello
Allocated 4 bytes at address 0xa010778 (file: memtest.cpp,
line: 25)
Deleted memory at address 0xa010778
Allocated 12 bytes at address 0xa010778 (file: memtest.cpp,
line: 27)
Deleted memory at address 0xa010778
Attempt to delete unknown pointer: 0x1
Allocated 8 bytes at address 0xa0108c0 (file: memtest.cpp,
line: 14)
Deleted memory at address 0xa0108c0
No user memory leaks!
```

Because of the call to **MEM_OFF( )**, no subsequent calls to **operator
delete( )** by **vector** or **ostream** are processed. You still might get some
calls to **delete** from reallocations performed by the containers.

If you call **TRACE_OFF( )** at the beginning of the program, the output is

```
hello
Attempt to delete unknown pointer: 0x1
No user memory leaks!
```

Summary

Much of the headache of software engineering can be avoided by being
deliberate about what you're doing. You've probably been using mental
assertions as you've crafted your loops and functions, even if you haven't
routinely used the **assert( )** macro. If you'll use **assert( )**, you'll find logic

errors sooner and end up with more readable code as well. Remember to only use assertions for invariants, though, and not for runtime error handling.

Nothing will give you more peace of mind than thoroughly tested code. If it's been a hassle for you in the past, use an automated framework, such as the one we've presented here, to integrate routine testing into your daily work. You (and your users!) will be glad you did.

Exercises

Solutions to selected exercises can be found in the electronic document *The Thinking in C++ Volume 2 Annotated Solution Guide*, available for a small fee from *www.MindView.net*.

1. Write a test program using the **TestSuite** Framework for the standard **vector** class that thoroughly tests the following member functions with a **vector** of integers: **push_back( )** (appends an element to the end of the **vector**), **front( )** (returns the first element in the **vector**), **back( )** (returns the last element in the **vector**), **pop_back( )** (removes the last element without returning it), **at( )** (returns the element in a specified index position), and **size( )** (returns the number of elements). Be sure to verify that **vector::at( )** throws a **std::out_of_range** exception if the supplied index is out of range.

2. Suppose you are asked to develop a class named **Rational** that supports rational numbers (fractions). The fraction in a **Rational** object should always be stored in lowest terms, and a denominator of zero is an error. Here is a sample interface for such a **Rational** class:

```
//: C02:Rational.h {-xo}
#ifndef RATIONAL_H
#define RATIONAL_H
#include <iosfwd>

class Rational {
public:
  Rational(int numerator = 0, int denominator = 1);
  Rational operator-() const;
  friend Rational operator+(const Rational&,
                            const Rational&);
  friend Rational operator-(const Rational&,
                            const Rational&);
  friend Rational operator*(const Rational&,
                            const Rational&);
```

```
        friend Rational operator/(const Rational&,
                                    const Rational&);
        friend std::ostream&
        operator<<(std::ostream&, const Rational&);
        friend std::istream&
        operator>>(std::istream&, Rational&);
        Rational& operator+=(const Rational&);
        Rational& operator-=(const Rational&);
        Rational& operator*=(const Rational&);
        Rational& operator/=(const Rational&);
        friend bool operator<(const Rational&,
                                const Rational&);
        friend bool operator>(const Rational&,
                                const Rational&);
        friend bool operator<=(const Rational&,
                                 const Rational&);
        friend bool operator>=(const Rational&,
                                 const Rational&);
        friend bool operator==(const Rational&,
                                 const Rational&);
        friend bool operator!=(const Rational&,
                                 const Rational&);
    };
    #endif // RATIONAL_H ///:~
```

Write a complete specification for this class, including preconditions, postconditions, and exception specifications.

3. Write a test using the **TestSuite** framework that thoroughly tests all the specifications from the previous exercise, including testing exceptions.

4. Implement the **Rational** class so that all the tests from the previous exercise pass. Use assertions only for invariants.

5. The file **BuggedSearch.cpp** below contains a binary search function that searches the range **[beg, end)** for **what**. There are some bugs in the algorithm. Use the trace techniques from this chapter to debug the search function.

```
//: C02:BuggedSearch.cpp {-xo}
//{L} ../TestSuite/Test
#include <cstdlib>
#include <ctime>
#include <cassert>
#include <fstream>
#include "../TestSuite/Test.h"
```

```cpp
using namespace std;

// This function is only one with bugs
int* binarySearch(int* beg, int* end, int what) {
  while(end - beg != 1) {
    if(*beg == what) return beg;
    int mid = (end - beg) / 2;
    if(what <= beg[mid]) end = beg + mid;
    else beg = beg + mid;
  }
  return 0;
}

class BinarySearchTest : public TestSuite::Test {
  enum { SZ = 10 };
  int* data;
  int max; // Track largest number
  int current; // Current non-contained number
               // Used in notContained()
  // Find the next number not contained in the array
  int notContained() {
    while(data[current] + 1 == data[current + 1])
      ++current;
    if(current >= SZ) return max + 1;
    int retValue = data[current++] + 1;
    return retValue;
  }
  void setData() {
    data = new int[SZ];
    assert(!max);
    // Input values with increments of one.  Leave
    // out some values on both odd and even indexes.
    for(int i = 0; i < SZ;
        rand() % 2 == 0 ? max += 1 : max += 2)
      data[i++] = max;
  }
  void testInBound() {
    // Test locations both odd and even
    // not contained and contained
    for(int i = SZ; --i >=0;)
      test_(binarySearch(data, data + SZ, data[i]));
    for(int i = notContained(); i < max;
        i = notContained())
      test_(!binarySearch(data, data + SZ, i));
  }
```

```
      void testOutBounds() {
        // Test lower values
        for(int i = data[0]; --i > data[0] - 100;)
          test_(!binarySearch(data, data + SZ, i));
        // Test higher values
        for(int i = data[SZ - 1];
            ++i < data[SZ -1] + 100;)
          test_(!binarySearch(data, data + SZ, i));
      }
    public:
      BinarySearchTest() { max = current = 0; }
      void run() {
        setData();
        testInBound();
        testOutBounds();
        delete [] data;
      }
    };

    int main() {
      srand(time(0));
      BinarySearchTest t;
      t.run();
      return t.report();
    } ///:~
```

Part 2

The Standard C++ Library

Standard C++ not only incorporates all the Standard C libraries (with small additions and changes to support type safety), it also adds libraries of its own. These libraries are far more powerful than those in Standard C; the leverage you get from them is analogous to the leverage you get from changing from C to C++.

This section of the book gives you an in-depth introduction to key portions of the Standard C++ library.

The most complete and also the most obscure reference to the full libraries is the Standard itself. Bjarne Stroustrup's *The C++ Programming Language, Third Edition* (Addison Wesley, 2000) remains a reliable reference for both the language and the library. The most celebrated library-only reference is *The C++ Standard Library: A Tutorial and Reference*, by Nicolai Josuttis (Addison Wesley, 1999). The goal of the chapters in this part of the book is to provide you with an encyclopedia of descriptions and examples so that you'll have a good starting point for solving any problem that requires the use of the Standard libraries. However, some techniques and topics are rarely used and are not covered here. If you can't find it in these chapters, reach for the other two books; this book is not intended to replace those books but rather to complement them. In particular, we hope that after going through the material in the following chapters you'll have a much easier time understanding those books.

You will notice that these chapters do not contain exhaustive documentation describing every function and class in the Standard C++ library. We've left the full descriptions to others; in particular to P.J. Plauger's *Dinkumware C/C++ Library Reference* at http://www.dinkumware.com. This is an excellent online source of standard library documentation in HTML format that you can keep resident on your computer and view with a Web browser whenever you need to look something up. You can view this online or purchase it for local viewing. It contains complete reference pages for the both the C and C++ libraries (so it's good to use for all your Standard C/C++ programming questions). Electronic documentation is effective not only because you can always have it with you, but also because you can do an electronic search.

When you're actively programming, these resources should satisfy your reference needs (and you can use them to look up anything in this chapter that isn't clear to you). Appendix A lists additional references.

The first chapter in this section introduces the Standard C++ **string** class, which is a powerful tool that simplifies most of the text-processing chores you might have. Chances are, anything you've done to character strings with lines of code in C can be done with a member function call in the **string** class.

Chapter 4 covers the **iostreams** library, which contains classes for processing input and output with files, string targets, and the system console.

Although Chapter 5, "Templates in Depth," is not explicitly a library chapter, it is necessary preparation for the two chapters that follow. In Chapter 6 we examine the generic algorithms offered by the Standard C++ library. Because they are implemented with templates, these algorithms can be applied to any *sequence* of objects. Chapter 7 covers the standard containers and their associated iterators. We cover algorithms first because they can be fully explored by using only arrays and the **vector** container (which we have been using since early in Volume 1). It is also natural to use the standard algorithms in connection with containers, so it's good to be familiar with the algorithms before studying the containers.

3: Strings in Depth

String processing with character arrays is one of the biggest time–wasters in C. Character arrays require the programmer to keep track of the difference between static quoted strings and arrays created on the stack and the heap, and the fact that sometimes you're passing around a **char*** and sometimes you must copy the whole array.

Especially because string manipulation is so common, character arrays are a great source of misunderstandings and bugs. Despite this, creating string classes remained a common exercise for beginning C++ programmers for many years. The Standard C++ library **string** class solves the problem of character array manipulation once and for all, keeping track of memory even during assignments and copy-constructions. You simply don't need to think about it.

This chapter[1] examines the Standard C++ **string** class, beginning with a look at what constitutes a C++ string and how the C++ version differs from a traditional C character array. You'll learn about operations and manipulations using **string** objects, and you'll see how C++ **string**s accommodate variation in character sets and string data conversion.

Handling text is one of the oldest programming applications, so it's not surprising that the C++ **string** draws heavily on the ideas and terminology that have long been used in C and other languages. As you begin to acquaint yourself with C++ **string**s, this fact should be reassuring. No matter which programming idiom you choose, there are three common things you want to do with a **string**:

- Create or modify the sequence of characters stored in the **string**.

---

[1] Some of the material in this chapter was originally created by Nancy Nicolaisen.

- Detect the presence or absence of elements within the **string**.

- Translate between various schemes for representing **string** characters.

You'll see how each of these jobs is accomplished using C++ **string** objects.

What's in a string?

In C, a string is simply an array of characters that always includes a binary zero (often called the *null terminator*) as its final array element. There are significant differences between C++ **string**s and their C progenitors. First, and most important, C++ **string**s hide the physical representation of the sequence of characters they contain. You don't need to be concerned about array dimensions or null terminators. A **string** also contains certain "housekeeping" information about the size and storage location of its data. Specifically, a C++ **string** object knows its starting location in memory, its content, its length in characters, and the length in characters to which it can grow before the **string** object must resize its internal data buffer. C++ strings thus greatly reduce the likelihood of making three of the most common and destructive C programming errors: overwriting array bounds, trying to access arrays through uninitialized or incorrectly valued pointers, and leaving pointers "dangling" after an array ceases to occupy the storage that was once allocated to it.

The exact implementation of memory layout for the string class is not defined by the C++ Standard. This architecture is intended to be flexible enough to allow differing implementations by compiler vendors, yet guarantee predictable behavior for users. In particular, the exact conditions under which storage is allocated to hold data for a string object are not defined. String allocation rules were formulated to allow but not require a reference-counted implementation, but whether or not the implementation uses reference counting, the semantics must be the same. To put this a bit differently, in C, every **char** array occupies a unique physical region of memory. In C++, individual **string** objects may or may not occupy unique physical regions of memory, but if reference counting avoids storing duplicate copies of data, the individual objects must look and act as though they exclusively own unique regions of storage. For example:

```
//: C03:StringStorage.h
```

```
#ifndef STRINGSTORAGE_H
#define STRINGSTORAGE_H
#include <iostream>
#include <string>
#include "../TestSuite/Test.h"
using std::cout;
using std::endl;
using std::string;

class StringStorageTest : public TestSuite::Test {
public:
  void run() {
    string s1("12345");
    // This may copy the first to the second or
    // use reference counting to simulate a copy:
    string s2 = s1;
    test_(s1 == s2);
    // Either way, this statement must ONLY modify s1:
    s1[0] = '6';
    cout << "s1 = " << s1 << endl;  // 62345
    cout << "s2 = " << s2 << endl;  // 12345
    test_(s1 != s2);
  }
};
#endif // STRINGSTORAGE_H ///:~

//: C03:StringStorage.cpp
//{L} ../TestSuite/Test
#include "StringStorage.h"

int main() {
  StringStorageTest t;
  t.run();
  return t.report();
} ///:~
```

We say that an implementation that only makes unique copies when a string is modified uses a *copy-on-write* strategy. This approach saves time and space when strings are used only as value parameters or in other read-only situations.

Whether a library implementation uses reference counting or not should be transparent to users of the **string** class. Unfortunately, this is not always the case. In multithreaded programs, it is practically impossible to use a reference-counting implementation safely.[2]

Creating and initializing C++ strings

Creating and initializing strings is a straightforward proposition and fairly flexible. In the **SmallString.cpp** example below, the first **string**, **imBlank**, is declared but contains no initial value. Unlike a C **char** array, which would contain a random and meaningless bit pattern until initialization, **imBlank** does contain meaningful information. This **string** object is initialized to hold "no characters" and can properly report its zero length and absence of data elements using class member functions.

The next string, **heyMom**, is initialized by the literal argument "Where are my socks?" This form of initialization uses a quoted character array as a parameter to the **string** constructor. By contrast, **standardReply** is simply initialized with an assignment. The last string of the group, **useThisOneAgain**, is initialized using an existing C++ **string** object. Put another way, this example illustrates that **string** objects let you do the following:

- Create an empty **string** and defer initializing it with character data.

- Initialize a **string** by passing a literal, quoted character array as an argument to the constructor.

- Initialize a **string** using the equal sign (=).

- Use one **string** to initialize another.

```
//: C03:SmallString.cpp
#include <string>
using namespace std;

int main() {
```

---

[2] It's difficult to make reference–counting implementations thread safe. (See Herb Sutter, *More Exceptional C++*, pp. 104–14). See Chapter 10 for more on programming with multiple threads.

```
  string imBlank;
  string heyMom("Where are my socks?");
  string standardReply = "Beamed into deep "
    "space on wide angle dispersion?";
  string useThisOneAgain(standardReply);
} ///:~
```

These are the simplest forms of **string** initialization, but variations offer more flexibility and control. You can do the following:

- Use a portion of either a C **char** array or a C++ **string**.

- Combine different sources of initialization data using **operator+**.

- Use the **string** object's **substr( )** member function to create a substring.

Here's a program that illustrates these features:

```
//: C03:SmallString2.cpp
#include <string>
#include <iostream>
using namespace std;

int main() {
  string s1("What is the sound of one clam napping?");
  string s2("Anything worth doing is worth overdoing.");
  string s3("I saw Elvis in a UFO");
  // Copy the first 8 chars:
  string s4(s1, 0, 8);
  cout << s4 << endl;
  // Copy 6 chars from the middle of the source:
  string s5(s2, 15, 6);
  cout << s5 << endl;
  // Copy from middle to end:
  string s6(s3, 6, 15);
  cout << s6 << endl;
  // Copy many different things:
  string quoteMe = s4 + "that" +
  // substr() copies 10 chars at element 20
  s1.substr(20, 10) + s5 +
  // substr() copies up to either 100 char
  // or eos starting at element 5
  "with" + s3.substr(5, 100) +
  // OK to copy a single char this way
```

```
    s1.substr(37, 1);
    cout << quoteMe << endl;
} ///:~
```

The **string** member function **substr( )** takes a starting position as its first argument and the number of characters to select as the second argument. Both arguments have default values. If you say **substr( )** with an empty argument list, you produce a copy of the entire **string**, so this is a convenient way to duplicate a **string**.

Here's the output from the program:

```
What is
doing
Elvis in a UFO
What is that one clam doing with Elvis in a UFO?
```

Notice the final line of the example. C++ allows **string** initialization techniques to be mixed in a single statement, a flexible and convenient feature. Also notice that the last initializer copies *just one character* from the source **string**.

Another slightly more subtle initialization technique involves the use of the **string** iterators **string::begin( )** and **string::end( )**. This technique treats a **string** like a *container* object (which you've seen primarily in the form of **vector** so far—you'll see many more containers in Chapter 7), which uses *iterators* to indicate the start and end of a sequence of characters. In this way you can hand a **string** constructor two iterators, and it copies from one to the other into the new **string**:

```
//: C03:StringIterators.cpp
#include <string>
#include <iostream>
#include <cassert>
using namespace std;

int main() {
  string source("xxx");
  string s(source.begin(), source.end());
  assert(s == source);
} ///:~
```

The iterators are not restricted to **begin( )** and **end( )**; you can increment, decrement, and add integer offsets to them, allowing you to extract a subset of characters from the source **string**.

C++ strings may *not* be initialized with single characters or with ASCII or other integer values. You can initialize a string with a number of copies of a single character, however:

```
//: C03:UhOh.cpp
#include <string>
#include <cassert>
using namespace std;

int main() {
  // Error: no single char inits
  //! string nothingDoing1('a');
  // Error: no integer inits
  //! string nothingDoing2(0x37);
  // The following is legal:
  string okay(5, 'a');
  assert(okay == string("aaaaa"));
} ///:~
```

The first argument indicates the number of copies of the second argument to place in the string. The second argument can only be a single **char**, not a **char** array.

Operating on strings

If you've programmed in C, you are accustomed to the family of functions that write, search, modify, and copy **char** arrays. There are two unfortunate aspects of the Standard C library functions for handling **char** arrays. First, there are two loosely organized families of them: the "plain" group, and the ones that require you to supply a count of the number of characters to be considered in the operation at hand. The roster of functions in the C **char** array library shocks the unsuspecting user with a long list of cryptic, mostly unpronounceable names. Although the type and number of arguments to the functions are somewhat consistent, to use them properly you must be attentive to details of function naming and parameter passing.

The second inherent trap of the standard C **char** array tools is that they all rely explicitly on the assumption that the character array includes a null terminator. If by oversight or error the null is omitted or overwritten, there's little to keep the C **char** array functions from manipulating the memory beyond the limits of the allocated space, sometimes with disastrous results.

C++ provides a vast improvement in the convenience and safety of **string** objects. For purposes of actual string handling operations, there are about the same number of distinct member function names in the **string** class as there are functions in the C library, but because of overloading the functionality is much greater. Coupled with sensible naming practices and the judicious use of default arguments, these features combine to make the **string** class much easier to use than the C library **char** array functions.

Appending, inserting, and concatenating strings

One of the most valuable and convenient aspects of C++ strings is that they grow as needed, without intervention on the part of the programmer. Not only does this make string-handling code inherently more trustworthy, it also almost entirely eliminates a tedious "housekeeping" chore—keeping track of the bounds of the storage where your strings live. For example, if you create a string object and initialize it with a string of 50 copies of 'X', and later store in it 50 copies of "Zowie", the object itself will reallocate sufficient storage to accommodate the growth of the data. Perhaps nowhere is this property more appreciated than when the strings manipulated in your code change size and you don't know how big the change is. The string member functions **append( )** and **insert( )** transparently reallocate storage when a string grows:

```
//: C03:StrSize.cpp
#include <string>
#include <iostream>
using namespace std;

int main() {
  string bigNews("I saw Elvis in a UFO. ");
  cout << bigNews << endl;
  // How much data have we actually got?
  cout << "Size = " << bigNews.size() << endl;
  // How much can we store without reallocating?
```

```
    cout << "Capacity = " << bigNews.capacity() << endl;
    // Insert this string in bigNews immediately
    // before bigNews[1]:
    bigNews.insert(1, " thought I");
    cout << bigNews << endl;
    cout << "Size = " << bigNews.size() << endl;
    cout << "Capacity = " << bigNews.capacity() << endl;
    // Make sure that there will be this much space
    bigNews.reserve(500);
    // Add this to the end of the string:
    bigNews.append("I've been working too hard.");
    cout << bigNews << endl;
    cout << "Size = " << bigNews.size() << endl;
    cout << "Capacity = " << bigNews.capacity() << endl;
} ///:~
```

Here is the output from one particular compiler:

```
I saw Elvis in a UFO.
Size = 22
Capacity = 31
I thought I saw Elvis in a UFO.
Size = 32
Capacity = 47
I thought I saw Elvis in a UFO. I've been
working too hard.
Size = 59
Capacity = 511
```

This example demonstrates that even though you can safely relinquish much of the responsibility for allocating and managing the memory your **string**s occupy, C++ **string**s provide you with several tools to monitor and manage their size. Notice the ease with which we changed the size of the storage allocated to the string. The **size( )** function returns the number of characters currently stored in the string and is identical to the **length( )** member function. The **capacity( )** function returns the size of the current underlying allocation, meaning the number of characters the string can hold without requesting more storage. The **reserve( )** function is an optimization mechanism that indicates your intention to specify a certain amount of storage for future use; **capacity( )** always returns a value at least as large as the most recent call to **reserve( )**. A **resize( )** function appends spaces if the new size is greater than the current string size or truncates the string

---

otherwise. (An overload of **resize( )** can specify a different character to append.)

The exact fashion that the **string** member functions allocate space for your data depends on the implementation of the library. When we tested one implementation with the previous example, it appeared that reallocations occurred on even word (that is, full-integer) boundaries, with one byte held back. The architects of the **string** class have endeavored to make it possible to mix the use of C **char** arrays and C++ string objects, so it is likely that figures reported by **StrSize.cpp** for capacity reflect that, in this particular implementation, a byte is set aside to easily accommodate the insertion of a null terminator.

Replacing string characters

The **insert( )** function is particularly nice because it absolves you from making sure the insertion of characters in a string won't overrun the storage space or overwrite the characters immediately following the insertion point. Space grows, and existing characters politely move over to accommodate the new elements. Sometimes this might not be what you want. If you want the size of the string to remain unchanged, use the **replace( )** function to overwrite characters. There are a number of overloaded versions of **replace( )**, but the simplest one takes three arguments: an integer indicating where to start in the string, an integer indicating how many characters to eliminate from the original string, and the replacement string (which can be a different number of characters than the eliminated quantity). Here's a simple example:

```
//: C03:StringReplace.cpp
// Simple find-and-replace in strings.
#include <cassert>
#include <string>
using namespace std;

int main() {
  string s("A piece of text");
  string tag("$tag$");
  s.insert(8, tag + ' ');
  assert(s == "A piece $tag$ of text");
  int start = s.find(tag);
  assert(start == 8);
  assert(tag.size() == 5);
```

```
    s.replace(start, tag.size(), "hello there");
    assert(s == "A piece hello there of text");
} ///:~
```

The **tag** is first inserted into **s** (notice that the insert happens *before* the value indicating the insert point and that an extra space was added after **tag**), and then it is found and replaced.

You should check to see if you've found anything before you perform a **replace( )**. The previous example replaces with a **char***, but there's an overloaded version that replaces with a **string**. Here's a more complete demonstration **replace( ):**

```
//: C03:Replace.cpp
#include <cassert>
#include <cstddef>  // For size_t
#include <string>
using namespace std;

void replaceChars(string& modifyMe,
  const string& findMe, const string& newChars) {
    // Look in modifyMe for the "find string"
    // starting at position 0:
    size_t i = modifyMe.find(findMe, 0);
    // Did we find the string to replace?
    if(i != string::npos)
      // Replace the find string with newChars:
      modifyMe.replace(i, findMe.size(), newChars);
}

int main() {
  string bigNews = "I thought I saw Elvis in a UFO. "
                   "I have been working too hard.";
  string replacement("wig");
  string findMe("UFO");
  // Find "UFO" in bigNews and overwrite it:
  replaceChars(bigNews, findMe, replacement);
  assert(bigNews == "I thought I saw Elvis in a "
         "wig. I have been working too hard.");
} ///:~
```

If **replace** doesn't find the search string, it returns **string::npos**. The **npos** data member is a static constant member of the **string** class that represents a nonexistent character position.[3]

Unlike **insert( )**, **replace( )** won't grow the **string**'s storage space if you copy new characters into the middle of an existing series of array elements. However, it *will* grow the storage space if needed, for example, when you make a "replacement" that would expand the original string beyond the end of the current allocation. Here's an example:

```
//: C03:ReplaceAndGrow.cpp
#include <cassert>
#include <string>
using namespace std;

int main() {
  string bigNews("I have been working the grave.");
  string replacement("yard shift.");
  // The first argument says "replace chars
  // beyond the end of the existing string":
  bigNews.replace(bigNews.size() - 1,
    replacement.size(), replacement);
  assert(bigNews == "I have been working the "
         "graveyard shift.");
} ///:~
```

The call to **replace( )** begins "replacing" beyond the end of the existing array, which is equivalent to an append operation. Notice that in this example **replace( )** expands the array accordingly.

You may have been hunting through this chapter trying to do something relatively simple such as replace all the instances of one character with a different character. Upon finding the previous material on replacing, you thought you found the answer, but then you started seeing groups of characters and counts and other things that looked a bit too complex. Doesn't **string** have a way to just replace one character with another everywhere?

---

[3] It is an abbreviation for "no position," and is the largest value that can be represented by the string allocator's **size_type** (**std::size_t** by default).

You can easily write such a function using the **find( )** and **replace( )** member functions as follows:

```
//: C03:ReplaceAll.h
#ifndef REPLACEALL_H
#define REPLACEALL_H
#include <string>

std::string& replaceAll(std::string& context,
  const std::string& from, const std::string& to);
#endif // REPLACEALL_H ///:~
```

```
//: C03:ReplaceAll.cpp {O}
#include <cstddef>
#include "ReplaceAll.h"
using namespace std;

string& replaceAll(string& context, const string& from,
  const string& to) {
  size_t lookHere = 0;
  size_t foundHere;
  while((foundHere = context.find(from, lookHere))
    != string::npos) {
    context.replace(foundHere, from.size(), to);
    lookHere = foundHere + to.size();
  }
  return context;
} ///:~
```

The version of **find( )** used here takes as a second argument the position to start looking in and returns **string::npos** if it doesn't find it. It is important to advance the position held in the variable **lookHere** past the replacement string, in case **from** is a substring of **to**. The following program tests the **replaceAll** function:

```
//: C03:ReplaceAllTest.cpp
//{L} ReplaceAll
#include <cassert>
#include <iostream>
#include <string>
#include "ReplaceAll.h"
using namespace std;

int main() {
```

```
  string text = "a man, a plan, a canal, Panama";
  replaceAll(text, "an", "XXX");
  assert(text == "a mXXX, a plXXX, a cXXXal, PXXXama");
} ///:~
```

As you can see, the **string** class by itself doesn't solve all possible problems. Many solutions have been left to the algorithms in the Standard library[4] because the **string** class can look just like an STL sequence (by virtue of the iterators discussed earlier). All the generic algorithms work on a "range" of elements within a container. Usually that range is just "from the beginning of the container to the end." A **string** object looks like a container of characters: to get the beginning of the range you use **string::begin( )**, and to get the end of the range you use **string::end( )**. The following example shows the use of the **replace( )** algorithm to replace all the instances of the single character 'X' with 'Y':

```
//: C03:StringCharReplace.cpp
#include <algorithm>
#include <cassert>
#include <string>
using namespace std;

int main() {
  string s("aaaXaaaXXaaXXXaXXXXaaa");
  replace(s.begin(), s.end(), 'X', 'Y');
  assert(s == "aaaYaaaYYaaYYYaYYYYaaa");
} ///:~
```

Notice that this **replace( )** is *not* called as a member function of **string**. Also, unlike the **string::replace( )** functions that only perform one replacement, the **replace( )** algorithm replaces *all instances* of one character with another.

The **replace( )** algorithm only works with single objects (in this case, **char** objects) and will not replace quoted **char** arrays or **string** objects. Since a **string** behaves like an STL sequence, a number of other algorithms can be applied to it, which might solve other problems that are not directly addressed by the **string** member functions.

---

[4] Discussed in depth in Chapter 6.

Concatenation using nonmember overloaded operators

One of the most delightful discoveries awaiting a C programmer learning about C++ **string** handling is how simply **string**s can be combined and appended using **operator+** and **operator+=**. These operators make combining **string**s syntactically similar to adding numeric data:

```
//: C03:AddStrings.cpp
#include <string>
#include <cassert>
using namespace std;

int main() {
  string s1("This ");
  string s2("That ");
  string s3("The other ");
  // operator+ concatenates strings
  s1 = s1 + s2;
  assert(s1 == "This That ");
  // Another way to concatenates strings
  s1 += s3;
  assert(s1 == "This That The other ");
  // You can index the string on the right
  s1 += s3 + s3[4] + "ooh lala";
  assert(s1 == "This That The other The other oooh lala");
} ///:~
```

Using the **operator+** and **operator+=** operators is a flexible and convenient way to combine **string** data. On the right side of the statement, you can use almost any type that evaluates to a group of one or more characters.

Searching in strings

The **find** family of **string** member functions locates a character or group of characters within a given string. Here are the members of the **find** family and their general usage :

string find member function	What/how it finds
find( )	Searches a string for a specified character or group of characters and returns the starting position of the first occurrence found or **npos** if no match is found.
find_first_of( )	Searches a target string and returns the position of the first match of *any* character in a specified group. If no match is found, it returns **npos**.
find_last_of( )	Searches a target string and returns the position of the last match of *any* character in a specified group. If no match is found, it returns **npos**.
find_first_not_of( )	Searches a target string and returns the position of the first element that *doesn't* match *any* character in a specified group. If no such element is found, it returns **npos**.
find_last_not_of( )	Searches a target string and returns the position of the element with the largest subscript that *doesn't* match *any* character in a specified group. If no such element is found, it returns **npos**.
rfind( )	Searches a string from end to beginning for a specified character or group of characters and returns the starting position of the match if one is found. If no match is found, it returns **npos**.

The simplest use of **find( )** searches for one or more characters in a **string**. This overloaded version of **find( )** takes a parameter that specifies the character(s) for which to search and optionally a parameter that tells it where in the string to begin searching for the occurrence of a substring. (The default position at which to begin searching is 0.) By setting the call to **find** inside a loop, you can easily move through a string, repeating a search to find all the occurrences of a given character or group of characters within the string.

The following program uses the method of *The Sieve of Eratosthenes* to find prime numbers less than 50. This method starts with the number 2, marks all subsequent multiples of 2 as not prime, and repeats the process for the next prime candidate. The **SieveTest** constructor initializes **sieveChars** by setting the initial size of the character array and writing the value 'P' to each of its members.

```cpp
//: C03:Sieve.h
#ifndef SIEVE_H
#define SIEVE_H
#include <cmath>
#include <cstddef>
#include <string>
#include "../TestSuite/Test.h"
using std::size_t;
using std::sqrt;
using std::string;

class SieveTest : public TestSuite::Test {
  string sieveChars;
public:
  // Create a 50 char string and set each
  // element to 'P' for Prime:
  SieveTest() : sieveChars(50, 'P') {}
  void run() {
    findPrimes();
    testPrimes();
  }
  bool isPrime(int p) {
    if(p == 0 || p == 1) return false;
    int root = int(sqrt(double(p)));
    for(int i = 2; i <= root; ++i)
      if(p % i == 0) return false;
    return true;
  }
  void findPrimes() {
    // By definition neither 0 nor 1 is prime.
```

```
    // Change these elements to "N" for Not Prime:
    sieveChars.replace(0, 2, "NN");
    // Walk through the array:
    size_t sieveSize = sieveChars.size();
    int root = int(sqrt(double(sieveSize)));
    for(int i = 2; i <= root; ++i)
      // Find all the multiples:
      for(size_t factor = 2; factor * i < sieveSize;
          ++factor)
        sieveChars[factor * i] = 'N';
  }
  void testPrimes() {
    size_t i = sieveChars.find('P');
    while(i != string::npos) {
      test_(isPrime(i++));
      i = sieveChars.find('P', i);
    }
    i = sieveChars.find_first_not_of('P');
    while(i != string::npos) {
      test_(!isPrime(i++));
      i = sieveChars.find_first_not_of('P', i);
    }
  }
};
#endif // SIEVE_H ///:~

//: C03:Sieve.cpp
//{L} ../TestSuite/Test
#include "Sieve.h"

int main() {
  SieveTest t;
  t.run();
  return t.report();
} ///:~
```

The **find( )** function can walk forward through a **string**, detecting multiple occurrences of a character or a group of characters, and **find_first_not_of( )** finds other characters or substrings.

There are no functions in the **string** class to change the case of a string, but you can easily create these functions using the Standard C library functions **toupper( )** and **tolower( )**, which change the case of one character at a time. The following example illustrates a case-insensitive search:

```
//: C03:Find.h
#ifndef FIND_H
#define FIND_H
#include <cctype>
#include <cstddef>
#include <string>
#include "../TestSuite/Test.h"
using std::size_t;
using std::string;
using std::tolower;
using std::toupper;

// Make an uppercase copy of s
inline string upperCase(const string& s) {
  string upper(s);
  for(size_t i = 0; i < s.length(); ++i)
    upper[i] = toupper(upper[i]);
  return upper;
}

// Make a lowercase copy of s
inline string lowerCase(const string& s) {
  string lower(s);
  for(size_t i = 0; i < s.length(); ++i)
    lower[i] = tolower(lower[i]);
  return lower;
}

class FindTest : public TestSuite::Test {
  string chooseOne;
public:
  FindTest() : chooseOne("Eenie, Meenie, Miney, Mo") {}
  void testUpper() {
    string upper = upperCase(chooseOne);
    const string LOWER = "abcdefghijklmnopqrstuvwxyz";
    test_(upper.find_first_of(LOWER) == string::npos);
  }
  void testLower() {
    string lower = lowerCase(chooseOne);
    const string UPPER = "ABCDEFGHIJKLMNOPQRSTUVWXYZ";
    test_(lower.find_first_of(UPPER) == string::npos);
  }
  void testSearch() {
    // Case sensitive search
    size_t i = chooseOne.find("een");
```

```
    test_(i == 8);
    // Search lowercase:
    string test = lowerCase(chooseOne);
    i = test.find("een");
    test_(i == 0);
    i = test.find("een", ++i);
    test_(i == 8);
    i = test.find("een", ++i);
    test_(i == string::npos);
    // Search uppercase:
    test = upperCase(chooseOne);
    i = test.find("EEN");
    test_(i == 0);
    i = test.find("EEN", ++i);
    test_(i == 8);
    i = test.find("EEN", ++i);
    test_(i == string::npos);
  }
  void run() {
    testUpper();
    testLower();
    testSearch();
  }
};
#endif // FIND_H ///:~

//: C03:Find.cpp
//{L} ../TestSuite/Test
#include "Find.h"
#include "../TestSuite/Test.h"

int main() {
  FindTest t;
  t.run();
  return t.report();
} ///:~
```

Both the **upperCase( )** and **lowerCase( )** functions follow the same form:
they make a copy of the argument **string** and change the case. The **Find.cpp**
program isn't the best solution to the case-sensitivity problem, so we'll revisit
it when we examine **string** comparisons.

Finding in reverse

If you need to search through a **string** from end to beginning (to find the data in "last in / first out" order), you can use the string member function **rfind( )**:

```
//: C03:Rparse.h
#ifndef RPARSE_H
#define RPARSE_H
#include <cstddef>
#include <string>
#include <vector>
#include "../TestSuite/Test.h"
using std::size_t;
using std::string;
using std::vector;

class RparseTest : public TestSuite::Test {
  // To store the words:
  vector<string> strings;
public:
  void parseForData() {
    // The ';' characters will be delimiters
    string s("now.;sense;make;to;going;is;This");
    // The last element of the string:
    int last = s.size();
    // The beginning of the current word:
    size_t current = s.rfind(';');
    // Walk backward through the string:
    while(current != string::npos) {
      // Push each word into the vector.
      // Current is incremented before copying
      // to avoid copying the delimiter:
      ++current;
      strings.push_back(s.substr(current, last - current));
      // Back over the delimiter we just found,
      // and set last to the end of the next word:
      current -= 2;
      last = current + 1;
      // Find the next delimiter:
      current = s.rfind(';', current);
    }
    // Pick up the first word -- it's not
    // preceded by a delimiter:
    strings.push_back(s.substr(0, last));
```

```
    }
  void testData() {
    // Test them in the new order:
    test_(strings[0] == "This");
    test_(strings[1] == "is");
    test_(strings[2] == "going");
    test_(strings[3] == "to");
    test_(strings[4] == "make");
    test_(strings[5] == "sense");
    test_(strings[6] == "now.");
    string sentence;
    for(size_t i = 0; i < strings.size() - 1; i++)
      sentence += strings[i] += " ";
    // Manually put last word in to avoid an extra space:
    sentence += strings[strings.size() - 1];
    test_(sentence == "This is going to make sense now.");
  }
  void run() {
    parseForData();
    testData();
  }
};
#endif // RPARSE_H ///:~

//: C03:Rparse.cpp
//{L} ../TestSuite/Test
#include "Rparse.h"

int main() {
  RparseTest t;
  t.run();
  return t.report();
} ///:~
```

The string member function **rfind( )** backs through the string looking for
tokens and reports the array index of matching characters or **string::npos** if
it is unsuccessful.

Finding first/last of a set of characters

The **find_first_of( )** and **find_last_of( )** member functions can be
conveniently put to work to create a little utility that will strip whitespace
characters from both ends of a string. Notice that it doesn't touch the original
string, but instead returns a new string:

```
//: C03:Trim.h
// General tool to strip spaces from both ends.
#ifndef TRIM_H
#define TRIM_H
#include <string>
#include <cstddef>

inline std::string trim(const std::string& s) {
  if(s.length() == 0)
    return s;
  std::size_t beg = s.find_first_not_of(" \a\b\f\n\r\t\v");
  std::size_t end = s.find_last_not_of(" \a\b\f\n\r\t\v");
  if(beg == std::string::npos) // No non-spaces
    return "";
  return std::string(s, beg, end - beg + 1);
}
#endif // TRIM_H ///:~
```

The first test checks for an empty **string**; in that case, no tests are made, and a copy is returned. Notice that once the end points are found, the **string** constructor builds a new **string** from the old one, giving the starting count and the length.

Testing such a general-purpose tool needs to be thorough:

```
//: C03:TrimTest.h
#ifndef TRIMTEST_H
#define TRIMTEST_H
#include "Trim.h"
#include "../TestSuite/Test.h"

class TrimTest : public TestSuite::Test {
  enum {NTESTS = 11};
  static std::string s[NTESTS];
public:
  void testTrim() {
    test_(trim(s[0]) == "abcdefghijklmnop");
    test_(trim(s[1]) == "abcdefghijklmnop");
    test_(trim(s[2]) == "abcdefghijklmnop");
    test_(trim(s[3]) == "a");
    test_(trim(s[4]) == "ab");
    test_(trim(s[5]) == "abc");
    test_(trim(s[6]) == "a b c");
    test_(trim(s[7]) == "a b c");
```

```
      test_(trim(s[8]) == "a \t b \t c");
      test_(trim(s[9]) == "");
      test_(trim(s[10]) == "");
    }
    void run() {
      testTrim();
    }
};
#endif // TRIMTEST_H ///:~
```

```
//: C03:TrimTest.cpp {O}
#include "TrimTest.h"

// Initialize static data
std::string TrimTest::s[TrimTest::NTESTS] = {
  " \t abcdefghijklmnop \t ",
  "abcdefghijklmnop \t ",
  " \t abcdefghijklmnop",
  "a", "ab", "abc", "a b c",
  " \t a b c \t ", " \t a \t b \t c \t ",
  "\t \n \r \v \f",
  "" // Must also test the empty string
}; ///:~
```

```
//: C03:TrimTestMain.cpp
//{L} ../TestSuite/Test TrimTest
#include "TrimTest.h"

int main() {
  TrimTest t;
  t.run();
  return t.report();
} ///:~
```

In the array of **strings**, you can see that the character arrays are automatically converted to **string** objects. This array provides cases to check the removal of spaces and tabs from both ends, as well as ensuring that spaces and tabs are not removed from the middle of a **string**.

Removing characters from strings

Removing characters is easy and efficient with the **erase( )** member function, which takes two arguments: where to start removing characters (which defaults to **0**), and how many to remove (which defaults to

string::npos). If you specify more characters than remain in the string, the remaining characters are all erased anyway (so calling **erase( )** without any arguments removes all characters from a string). Sometimes it's useful to take an HTML file and strip its tags and special characters so that you have something approximating the text that would be displayed in the Web browser, only as a plain text file. The following example uses **erase( )** to do the job:

```
//: C03:HTMLStripper.cpp {RunByHand}
//{L} ReplaceAll
// Filter to remove html tags and markers.
#include <cassert>
#include <cmath>
#include <cstddef>
#include <fstream>
#include <iostream>
#include <string>
#include "ReplaceAll.h"
#include "../require.h"
using namespace std;

string& stripHTMLTags(string& s) {
  static bool inTag = false;
  bool done = false;
  while(!done) {
    if(inTag) {
      // The previous line started an HTML tag
      // but didn't finish. Must search for '>'.
      size_t rightPos = s.find('>');
      if(rightPos != string::npos) {
        inTag = false;
        s.erase(0, rightPos + 1);
      }
      else {
        done = true;
        s.erase();
      }
    }
    else {
      // Look for start of tag:
      size_t leftPos = s.find('<');
      if(leftPos != string::npos) {
        // See if tag close is in this line:
        size_t rightPos = s.find('>');
```

```
        if(rightPos == string::npos) {
          inTag = done = true;
          s.erase(leftPos);
        }
        else
          s.erase(leftPos, rightPos - leftPos + 1);
      }
      else
        done = true;
    }
  }
  // Remove all special HTML characters
  replaceAll(s, "&lt;", "<");
  replaceAll(s, "&gt;", ">");
  replaceAll(s, "&amp;", "&");
  replaceAll(s, " ", " ");
  // Etc...
  return s;
}

int main(int argc, char* argv[]) {
  requireArgs(argc, 1,
    "usage: HTMLStripper InputFile");
  ifstream in(argv[1]);
  assure(in, argv[1]);
  string s;
  while(getline(in, s))
    if(!stripHTMLTags(s).empty())
      cout << s << endl;
} ///:~
```

This example will even strip HTML tags that span multiple lines.[5] This is accomplished with the static flag, **inTag**, which is **true** whenever the start of a tag is found, but the accompanying tag end is not found in the same line. All forms of **erase( )** appear in the **stripHTMLFlags( )** function.[6] The version

---

[5] To keep the exposition simple, this version does not handle nested tags, such as comments.

[6] It is tempting to use mathematics here to factor out some of these calls to **erase( )**, but since in some cases one of the operands is **string::npos** (the largest unsigned integer available), integer overflow occurs and wrecks the algorithm.

---

of **getline( )** we use here is a (global) function declared in the **<string>** header and is handy because it stores an arbitrarily long line in its **string** argument. You don't need to worry about the dimension of a character array as you do with **istream::getline( )**. Notice that this program uses the **replaceAll( )** function from earlier in this chapter. In the next chapter, we'll use string streams to create a more elegant solution.

Comparing strings

Comparing strings is inherently different from comparing numbers. Numbers have constant, universally meaningful values. To evaluate the relationship between the magnitudes of two strings, you must make a *lexical comparison*. Lexical comparison means that when you test a character to see if it is "greater than" or "less than" another character, you are actually comparing the numeric representation of those characters as specified in the collating sequence of the character set being used. Most often this will be the ASCII collating sequence, which assigns the printable characters for the English language numbers in the range 32 through 127 decimal. In the ASCII collating sequence, the first "character" in the list is the space, followed by several common punctuation marks, and then uppercase and lowercase letters. With respect to the alphabet, this means that the letters nearer the front have lower ASCII values than those nearer the end. With these details in mind, it becomes easier to remember that when a lexical comparison that reports **s1** is "greater than" **s2**, it simply means that when the two were compared, the first differing character in **s1** came later in the alphabet than the character in that same position in **s2**.

C++ provides several ways to compare strings, and each has advantages. The simplest to use are the nonmember, overloaded operator functions: **operator ==, operator != operator >, operator <, operator >=**, and **operator <=**.

```
//: C03:CompStr.h
#ifndef COMPSTR_H
#define COMPSTR_H
#include <string>
#include "../TestSuite/Test.h"
using std::string;

class CompStrTest : public TestSuite::Test {
public:
```

```
  void run() {
    // Strings to compare
    string s1("This");
    string s2("That");
    test_(s1 == s1);
    test_(s1 != s2);
    test_(s1 > s2);
    test_(s1 >= s2);
    test_(s1 >= s1);
    test_(s2 < s1);
    test_(s2 <= s1);
    test_(s1 <= s1);
  }
};
#endif // COMPSTR_H ///:~

//: C03:CompStr.cpp
//{L} ../TestSuite/Test
#include "CompStr.h"

int main() {
  CompStrTest t;
  t.run();
  return t.report();
} ///:~
```

The overloaded comparison operators are useful for comparing both full strings and individual string character elements.

Notice in the following example the flexibility of argument types on both the left and right side of the comparison operators. For efficiency, the **string** class provides overloaded operators for the direct comparison of string objects, quoted literals, and pointers to C-style strings without having to create temporary **string** objects.

```
//: C03:Equivalence.cpp
#include <iostream>
#include <string>
using namespace std;

int main() {
  string s2("That"), s1("This");
  // The lvalue is a quoted literal
  // and the rvalue is a string:
```

```
    if("That" == s2)
      cout << "A match" << endl;
    // The left operand is a string and the right is
    // a pointer to a C-style null terminated string:
    if(s1 != s2.c_str())
      cout << "No match" << endl;
} ///:~
```

The **c_str( )** function returns a **const char*** that points to a C-style, null-terminated string equivalent to the contents of the **string** object. This comes in handy when you want to pass a string to a standard C function, such as **atoi( )** or any of the functions defined in the **<cstring>** header. It is an error to use the value returned by **c_str( )** as non-**const** argument to any function.

You won't find the logical not (**!**) or the logical comparison operators (**&&** and **||**) among operators for a string. (Neither will you find overloaded versions of the bitwise C operators **&**, **|**, **^**, or **~**.) The overloaded nonmember comparison operators for the string class are limited to the subset that has clear, unambiguous application to single characters or groups of characters.

The **compare( )** member function offers you a great deal more sophisticated and precise comparison than the nonmember operator set. It provides overloaded versions to compare:

- Two complete strings.

- Part of either string to a complete string.

- Subsets of two strings.

The following example compares complete strings:

```
//: C03:Compare.cpp
// Demonstrates compare() and swap().
#include <cassert>
#include <string>
using namespace std;

int main() {
  string first("This");
  string second("That");
  assert(first.compare(first) == 0);
  assert(second.compare(second) == 0);
```

```
  // Which is lexically greater?
  assert(first.compare(second) > 0);
  assert(second.compare(first) < 0);
  first.swap(second);
  assert(first.compare(second) < 0);
  assert(second.compare(first) > 0);
} ///:~
```

The **swap( )** function in this example does what its name implies: it exchanges the contents of its object and argument. To compare a subset of the characters in one or both strings, you add arguments that define where to start the comparison and how many characters to consider. For example, we can use the following overloaded version of **compare( )**:

s1.compare(s1StartPos, s1NumberChars, s2, s2StartPos,
               s2NumberChars);

Here's an example:

```
//: C03:Compare2.cpp
// Illustrate overloaded compare().
#include <cassert>
#include <string>
using namespace std;

int main() {
  string first("This is a day that will live in infamy");
  string second("I don't believe that this is what "
                "I signed up for");
  // Compare "his is" in both strings:
  assert(first.compare(1, 7, second, 22, 7) == 0);
  // Compare "his is a" to "his is w":
  assert(first.compare(1, 9, second, 22, 9) < 0);
} ///:~
```

In the examples so far, we have used C-style array indexing syntax to refer to an individual character in a string. C++ strings provide an alternative to the **s[n]** notation: the **at( )** member. These two indexing mechanisms produce the same result in C++ if all goes well:

```
//: C03:StringIndexing.cpp
#include <cassert>
#include <string>
using namespace std;
```

```
int main() {
  string s("1234");
  assert(s[1] == '2');
  assert(s.at(1) == '2');
} ///:~
```

There is one important difference, however, between **[ ]** and **at( )**. When you try to reference an array element that is out of bounds, **at( )** will do you the kindness of throwing an exception, while ordinary **[ ]** subscripting syntax will leave you to your own devices:

```
//: C03:BadStringIndexing.cpp
#include <exception>
#include <iostream>
#include <string>
using namespace std;

int main() {
  string s("1234");
  // at() saves you by throwing an exception:
  try {
    s.at(5);
  } catch(exception& e) {
    cerr << e.what() << endl;
  }
} ///:~
```

Responsible programmers will not use errant indexes, but should you want to benefits of automatic index checking, using **at( )** in place of **[ ]** will give you a chance to gracefully recover from references to array elements that don't exist. Execution of this program on one of our test compilers gave the following output:

```
invalid string position
```

The **at( )** member throws an object of class **out_of_range**, which derives (ultimately) from **std::exception**. By catching this object in an exception handler, you can take appropriate remedial actions such as recalculating the offending subscript or growing the array. Using **string::operator[ ]( )** gives no such protection and is as dangerous as **char** array processing in C.[7]

Strings and character traits

The program **Find.cpp** earlier in this chapter leads us to ask the obvious question: Why isn't case-insensitive comparison part of the standard **string** class? The answer provides interesting background on the true nature of C++ string objects.

Consider what it means for a character to have "case." Written Hebrew, Farsi, and Kanji don't use the concept of upper- and lowercase, so for those languages this idea has no meaning. It would seem that if there were a way to designate some languages as "all uppercase" or "all lowercase," we could design a generalized solution. However, some languages that employ the concept of "case" *also* change the meaning of particular characters with diacritical marks, for example: the cedilla in Spanish, the circumflex in French, and the umlaut in German. For this reason, any case-sensitive collating scheme that attempts to be comprehensive will be nightmarishly complex to use.

Although we usually treat the C++ **string** as a class, this is really not the case. The **string** type is a specialization of a more general constituent, the **basic_string< >** template. Observe how **string** is declared in the Standard C++ header file:[8]

```
typedef basic_string<char> string;
```

To understand the nature of the string class, look at the **basic_string< >** template:

```
template<class charT, class traits = char_traits<charT>,
  class allocator = allocator<charT> > class basic_string;
```

---

[7] For the safety reasons mentioned, the C++ Standards Committee is considering a proposal to redefine **string::operator[]** to behave identically to **string::at( )** for C++0x.

[8] Your implementation can define all three template arguments here. Because the last two template parameters have default arguments, such a declaration is equivalent to what we show here.

In Chapter 5, we examine templates in great detail (much more than in Chapter 16 of Volume 1). For now, just notice that the **string** type is created when the **basic_string** template is instantiated with **char**. Inside the **basic_string< >** template declaration, the line:

```
class traits = char_traits<charT>,
```

tells us that the behavior of the class made from the **basic_string< >** template is specified by a class based on the template **char_traits< >**. Thus, the **basic_string< >** template produces string-oriented classes that manipulate types other than **char** (wide characters, for example). To do this, the **char_traits< >** template controls the content and collating behaviors of a variety of character sets using the character comparison functions **eq( )** (equal), **ne( )** (not equal), and **lt( )** (less than). The **basic_string< >** string comparison functions rely on these.

This is why the string class doesn't include case-insensitive member functions: that's not in its job description. To change the way the string class treats character comparison, you must supply a different **char_traits< >** template because that defines the behavior of the individual character comparison member functions.

You can use this information to make a new type of **string** class that ignores case. First, we'll define a new case-insensitive **char_traits< >** template that inherits from the existing template. Next, we'll override only the members we need to change to make character-by-character comparison case insensitive. (In addition to the three lexical character comparison members mentioned earlier, we'll also supply a new implementation for the **char_traits** functions **find( )** and **compare( ))** . Finally, we'll **typedef** a new class based on **basic_string**, but using the case-insensitive **ichar_traits** template for its second argument:

```
//: C03:ichar_traits.h
// Creating your own character traits.
#ifndef ICHAR_TRAITS_H
#define ICHAR_TRAITS_H
#include <cassert>
#include <cctype>
#include <cmath>
#include <cstddef>
#include <ostream>
#include <string>
```

```cpp
using std::allocator;
using std::basic_string;
using std::char_traits;
using std::ostream;
using std::size_t;
using std::string;
using std::toupper;
using std::tolower;

struct ichar_traits : char_traits<char> {
  // We'll only change character-by-
  // character comparison functions
  static bool eq(char c1st, char c2nd) {
    return toupper(c1st) == toupper(c2nd);
  }
  static bool ne(char c1st, char c2nd) {
    return !eq(c1st, c2nd);
  }
  static bool lt(char c1st, char c2nd) {
    return toupper(c1st) < toupper(c2nd);
  }
  static int
  compare(const char* str1, const char* str2, size_t n) {
    for(size_t i = 0; i < n; ++i) {
      if(str1 == 0)
        return -1;
      else if(str2 == 0)
        return 1;
      else if(tolower(*str1) < tolower(*str2))
        return -1;
      else if(tolower(*str1) > tolower(*str2))
        return 1;
      assert(tolower(*str1) == tolower(*str2));
      ++str1; ++str2; // Compare the other chars
    }
    return 0;
  }
  static const char*
  find(const char* s1, size_t n, char c) {
    while(n-- > 0)
      if(toupper(*s1) == toupper(c))
        return s1;
      else
        ++s1;
    return 0;
```

```
    }
};

typedef basic_string<char, ichar_traits> istring;

inline ostream& operator<<(ostream& os, const istring& s) {
  return os << string(s.c_str(), s.length());
}
#endif // ICHAR_TRAITS_H ///:~
```

We provide a **typedef** named **istring** so that our class will act like an ordinary **string** in every way, except that it will make all comparisons without respect to case. For convenience, we've also provided an overloaded **operator<<( )** so that you can print **istring**s. Here's an example:

```
//: C03:ICompare.cpp
#include <cassert>
#include <iostream>
#include "ichar_traits.h"
using namespace std;

int main() {
  // The same letters except for case:
  istring first = "tHis";
  istring second = "ThIS";
  cout << first << endl;
  cout << second << endl;
  assert(first.compare(second) == 0);
  assert(first.find('h') == 1);
  assert(first.find('I') == 2);
  assert(first.find('x') == string::npos);
} ///:~
```

This is just a toy example. To make **istring** fully equivalent to **string**, we'd have to create the other functions necessary to support the new **istring** type.

The **<string>** header provides a wide string class via the following **typedef**:

```
typedef basic_string<wchar_t> wstring;
```

Wide string support also reveals itself in *wide streams* (**wostream** in place of **ostream**, also defined in **<iostream>**) and in the header **<cwctype>**, a wide-character version of **<cctype>**. This along with the **wchar_t** specialization of **char_traits** in the standard library allows us to do a wide-character version of **ichar_traits**:

```
//: C03:iwchar_traits.h {-g++}
// Creating your own wide-character traits.
#ifndef IWCHAR_TRAITS_H
#define IWCHAR_TRAITS_H
#include <cassert>
#include <cmath>
#include <cstddef>
#include <cwctype>
#include <ostream>
#include <string>

using std::allocator;
using std::basic_string;
using std::char_traits;
using std::size_t;
using std::towlower;
using std::towupper;
using std::wostream;
using std::wstring;

struct iwchar_traits : char_traits<wchar_t> {
  // We'll only change character-by-
  // character comparison functions
  static bool eq(wchar_t c1st, wchar_t c2nd) {
    return towupper(c1st) == towupper(c2nd);
  }
  static bool ne(wchar_t c1st, wchar_t c2nd) {
    return towupper(c1st) != towupper(c2nd);
  }
  static bool lt(wchar_t c1st, wchar_t c2nd) {
    return towupper(c1st) < towupper(c2nd);
  }
  static int compare(
    const wchar_t* str1, const wchar_t* str2, size_t n) {
    for(size_t i = 0; i < n; i++) {
      if(str1 == 0)
        return -1;
      else if(str2 == 0)
        return 1;
      else if(towlower(*str1) < towlower(*str2))
        return -1;
```

```
      else if(towlower(*str1) > towlower(*str2))
        return 1;
      assert(towlower(*str1) == towlower(*str2));
      ++str1; ++str2; // Compare the other wchar_ts
    }
    return 0;
  }
  static const wchar_t*
  find(const wchar_t* s1, size_t n, wchar_t c) {
    while(n-- > 0)
      if(towupper(*s1) == towupper(c))
        return s1;
      else
        ++s1;
    return 0;
  }
};

typedef basic_string<wchar_t, iwchar_traits> iwstring;

inline wostream& operator<<(wostream& os,
  const iwstring& s) {
  return os << wstring(s.c_str(), s.length());
}
#endif // IWCHAR_TRAITS_H  ///:~
```

As you can see, this is mostly an exercise in placing a 'w' in the appropriate place in the source code. The test program looks like this:

```
//: C03:IWCompare.cpp {-g++}
#include <cassert>
#include <iostream>
#include "iwchar_traits.h"
using namespace std;

int main() {
  // The same letters except for case:
  iwstring wfirst = L"tHis";
  iwstring wsecond = L"ThIS";
  wcout << wfirst << endl;
  wcout << wsecond << endl;
  assert(wfirst.compare(wsecond) == 0);
  assert(wfirst.find('h') == 1);
  assert(wfirst.find('I') == 2);
  assert(wfirst.find('x') == wstring::npos);
```

```
} ///:~
```

Unfortunately, some compilers still do not provide robust support for wide characters.

A string application

If you've looked at the sample code in this book closely, you've noticed that certain tokens in the comments surround the code. These are used by a Python program that Bruce wrote to extract the code into files and set up makefiles for building the code. For example, a double-slash followed by a colon at the beginning of a line denotes the first line of a source file. The rest of the line contains information describing the file's name and location and whether it should be only compiled rather than fully built into an executable file. For example, the first line in the previous program above contains the string **C03:IWCompare.cpp**, indicating that the file **IWCompare.cpp** should be extracted into the directory **C03**.

The last line of a source file contains a triple-slash followed by a colon and a tilde. If the first line has an exclamation point immediately after the colon, the first and last lines of the source code are not to be output to the file (this is for data-only files). (If you're wondering why we're avoiding showing you these tokens, it's because we don't want to break the code extractor when applied to the text of the book!)

Bruce's Python program does a lot more than just extract code. If the token **"{O}"** follows the file name, its makefile entry will only be set up to compile the file and not to link it into an executable. (The Test Framework in Chapter 2 is built this way.) To link such a file with another source example, the target executable's source file will contain an **"{L}"** directive, as in:

```
//{L} ../TestSuite/Test
```

This section will present a program to just extract all the code so that you can compile and inspect it manually. You can use this program to extract all the code in this book by saving the document file as a text file[9] (let's call it

---

[9] Beware that some versions of Microsoft Word erroneously replace single quote characters with an extended ASCII character when you save a

TICV2.txt) and by executing something like the following on a shell command line:

```
C:> extractCode TICV2.txt /TheCode
```

This command reads the text file **TICV2.txt** and writes all the source code files in subdirectories under the top-level directory **/TheCode**. The directory tree will look like the following:

```
TheCode/
    C0B/
    C01/
    C02/
    C03/
    C04/
    C05/
    C06/
    C07/
    C08/
    C09/
    C10/
    C11/
    TestSuite/
```

The source files containing the examples from each chapter will be in the corresponding directory.

Here's the program:

```cpp
//: C03:ExtractCode.cpp {-edg} {RunByHand}
// Extracts code from text.
#include <cassert>
#include <cstddef>
#include <cstdio>
#include <cstdlib>
#include <fstream>
#include <iostream>
#include <string>
using namespace std;
```

document as text, which causes a compile error. We have no idea why this happens. Just replace the character manually with an apostrophe.

```
// Legacy non-standard C header for mkdir()
#if defined(__GNUC__) || defined(__MWERKS__)
#include <sys/stat.h>
#elif defined(__BORLANDC__) || defined(_MSC_VER) \
   || defined(__DMC__)
#include <direct.h>
#else
#error Compiler not supported
#endif

// Check to see if directory exists
// by attempting to open a new file
// for output within it.
bool exists(string fname) {
  size_t len = fname.length();
  if(fname[len-1] != '/' && fname[len-1] != '\\')
    fname.append("/");
  fname.append("000.tmp");
  ofstream outf(fname.c_str());
  bool existFlag = outf;
  if(outf) {
    outf.close();
    remove(fname.c_str());
  }
  return existFlag;
}

int main(int argc, char* argv[]) {
  // See if input file name provided
  if(argc == 1) {
    cerr << "usage: extractCode file [dir]" << endl;
    exit(EXIT_FAILURE);
  }
  // See if input file exists
  ifstream inf(argv[1]);
  if(!inf) {
    cerr << "error opening file: " << argv[1] << endl;
    exit(EXIT_FAILURE);
  }
  // Check for optional output directory
  string root("./");  // current is default
  if(argc == 3) {
    // See if output directory exists
    root = argv[2];
    if(!exists(root)) {
```

```cpp
      cerr << "no such directory: " << root << endl;
      exit(EXIT_FAILURE);
    }
    size_t rootLen = root.length();
    if(root[rootLen-1] != '/' && root[rootLen-1] != '\\')
      root.append("/");
  }
  // Read input file line by line
  // checking for code delimiters
  string line;
  bool inCode = false;
  bool printDelims = true;
  ofstream outf;
  while(getline(inf, line)) {
    size_t findDelim = line.find("//" "/:~");
    if(findDelim != string::npos) {
      // Output last line and close file
      if(!inCode) {
        cerr << "Lines out of order" << endl;
        exit(EXIT_FAILURE);
      }
      assert(outf);
      if(printDelims)
        outf << line << endl;
      outf.close();
      inCode = false;
      printDelims = true;
    } else {
      findDelim = line.find("//" ":");
      if(findDelim == 0) {
        // Check for '!' directive
        if(line[3] == '!') {
          printDelims = false;
          ++findDelim;  // To skip '!' for next search
        }
        // Extract subdirectory name, if any
        size_t startOfSubdir =
          line.find_first_not_of(" \t", findDelim+3);
        findDelim = line.find(':', startOfSubdir);
        if(findDelim == string::npos) {
          cerr << "missing filename information\n" << endl;
          exit(EXIT_FAILURE);
        }
        string subdir;
        if(findDelim > startOfSubdir)
```

```
        subdir = line.substr(startOfSubdir,
                          findDelim - startOfSubdir);
      // Extract file name (better be one!)
      size_t startOfFile = findDelim + 1;
      size_t endOfFile =
        line.find_first_of(" \t", startOfFile);
      if(endOfFile == startOfFile) {
        cerr << "missing filename" << endl;
        exit(EXIT_FAILURE);
      }
      // We have all the pieces; build fullPath name
      string fullPath(root);
      if(subdir.length() > 0)
        fullPath.append(subdir).append("/");
      assert(fullPath[fullPath.length()-1] == '/');
      if(!exists(fullPath))
#if defined(__GNUC__) || defined(__MWERKS__)
        mkdir(fullPath.c_str(), 0);  // Create subdir
#else
        mkdir(fullPath.c_str());  // Create subdir
#endif
      fullPath.append(line.substr(startOfFile,
                    endOfFile - startOfFile));
      outf.open(fullPath.c_str());
      if(!outf) {
        cerr << "error opening " << fullPath
             << " for output" << endl;
        exit(EXIT_FAILURE);
      }
      inCode = true;
      cout << "Processing " << fullPath << endl;
      if(printDelims)
        outf << line << endl;
    }
    else if(inCode) {
      assert(outf);
      outf << line << endl;  // Output middle code line
    }
  }
}
exit(EXIT_SUCCESS);
} ///:~
```

First, you'll notice some conditional compilation directives. The **mkdir( )**
function, which creates a directory in the file system, is defined by the

POSIX[10] standard in the header **<sys/stat.h>**. Unfortunately, many compilers still use a different header (**<direct.h>**). The respective signatures for **mkdir( )** also differ: POSIX specifies two arguments, the older versions just one. For this reason, there is more conditional compilation later in the program to choose the right call to **mkdir( )**. We normally don't use conditional compilation in the examples in this book, but this particular program is too useful not to put a little extra work into, since you can use it to extract all the code with it.

The **exists( )** function in **ExtractCode.cpp** tests whether a directory exists by opening a temporary file in it. If the open fails, the directory doesn't exist. You remove a file by sending its name as a **char*** to **std::remove( )**.

The main program validates the command-line arguments and then reads the input file a line at a time, looking for the special source code delimiters. The Boolean flag **inCode** indicates that the program is in the middle of a source file, so lines should be output. The **printDelims** flag will be true if the opening token is not followed by an exclamation point; otherwise the first and last lines are not written. It is important to check for the closing delimiter first, because the start token is a subset, and searching for the start token first would return a successful find for both cases. If we encounter the closing token, we verify that we are in the middle of processing a source file; otherwise, something is wrong with the way the delimiters are laid out in the text file. If **inCode** is true, all is well, and we (optionally) write the last line and close the file. When the opening token is found, we parse the directory and file name components and open the file. The following **string**-related functions were used in this example: **length( )**, **append( )**, **getline( )**, **find( )** (two versions), **find_first_not_of( )**, **substr( )**, **find_first_of( )**, **c_str( )**, and, of course, **operator<<( )**.

Summary

C++ **string** objects provide developers with a number of great advantages over their C counterparts. For the most part, the **string** class makes referring

---

[10] POSIX, an IEEE standard, stands for "Portable Operating System Interface" and is a generalization of many of the low-level system calls found in UNIX systems.

---

to strings with character pointers unnecessary. This eliminates an entire class of software defects that arise from the use of uninitialized and incorrectly valued pointers.

C++ strings dynamically and transparently grow their internal data storage space to accommodate increases in the size of the string data. When the data in a string grows beyond the limits of the memory initially allocated to it, the string object will make the memory management calls that take space from and return space to the heap. Consistent allocation schemes prevent memory leaks and have the potential to be much more efficient than "roll your own" memory management.

The **string** class member functions provide a fairly comprehensive set of tools for creating, modifying, and searching in strings. String comparisons are always case sensitive, but you can work around this by copying string data to C-style null-terminated strings and using case-insensitive string comparison functions, temporarily converting the data held in string objects to a single case, or by creating a case-insensitive string class that overrides the character traits used to create the **basic_string** object.

Exercises

Solutions to selected exercises can be found in the electronic document *The Thinking in C++ Volume 2 Annotated Solution Guide*, available for a small fee from *www.MindView.net*.

1. Write and test a function that reverses the order of the characters in a string.
2. A palindrome is a word or group of words that read the same forward and backward. For example "madam" or "wow." Write a program that takes a string argument from the command line and, using the function from the previous exercise, prints whether the string was a palindrome or not.
3. Make your program from Exercise 2 return **true** even if symmetric letters differ in case. For example, "Civic" would still return **true** although the first letter is capitalized.
4. Change your program from Exercise 3 to ignore punctuation and spaces as well. For example "Able was I, ere I saw Elba." would report **true**.
5. Using the following string declarations and only **char**s (no string literals or magic numbers):

```
string one("I walked down the canyon with the moving
mountain bikers.");
string two("The bikers passed by me too close for
comfort.");
string three("I went hiking instead.");
```

produce the following sentence:

```
I moved down the canyon with the mountain bikers. The
mountain bikers passed by me too close for comfort. So
I went hiking instead.
```

6. Write a program named **replace** that takes three command-line arguments representing an input text file, a string to replace (call it **from**), and a replacement string (call it **to**). The program should write a new file to standard output with all occurrences of **from** replaced by **to**.

7. Repeat the previous exercise but replace all instances of **from** regardless of case.

8. Make your program from Exercise 3 take a filename from the command-line, and then display all words that are palindromes (ignoring case) in the file. Do not display duplicates (even if their case differs). Do not try to look for palindromes that are larger than a word (unlike in Exercise 4).

9. Modify **HTMLStripper.cpp** so that when it encounters a tag, it displays the tag's name, then displays the file's contents between the tag and the file's ending tag. Assume no nesting of tags, and that all tags have ending tags (denoted with </TAGNAME>).

10. Write a program that takes three command-line arguments (a filename and two strings) and displays to the console all lines in the file that have both strings in the line, either string, only one string, or neither string, based on user input at the beginning of the program (the user will choose which matching mode to use). For all but the "neither string" option, highlight the input string(s) by placing an asterisk (*) at the beginning and end of each string's occurrence when it is displayed.

11. Write a program that takes two command-line arguments (a filename and a string) and counts the number of times the string occurs in the file, even as a substring (but ignoring overlaps). For example, an input string of "ba" would match twice in the word "basketball," but an input string of "ana" would match only once in the word "banana." Display to the console the number of times the string is matched in the file, as

---

well as the average length of the words where the string occurred. (If the string occurs more than once in a word, only count the word once in figuring the average.)

12. Write a program that takes a filename from the command line and profiles the character usage, including punctuation and spaces (all character values of 0x21 [33] through 0x7E [126], as well as the space character). That is, count the number of occurrences of each character in the file, then display the results sorted either sequentially (space, then !, ", #, etc.) or by ascending or descending frequency based on user input at the beginning of the program. For space, display the word "Space" instead of the character ' '. A sample run might look something like this:

```
Format sequentially, ascending, or descending
(S/A/D): D
t:   526
r:   490
etc.
```

13. Using **find( )** and **rfind( )**, write a program that takes two command-line arguments (a filename and a string) and displays the first and last words (and their indexes) not matching the string, as well as the indexes of the first and last instances of the string. Display "Not Found" if any of the searches fail.

14. Using the **find_first_of** "family" of functions (but not exclusively), write a program that will remove all non-alphanumeric characters except spaces and periods from a file, then capitalize the first letter following a period.

15. Again using the **find_first_of** "family" of functions, write a program that accepts a filename as a command-line argument and then formats all numbers in the file to currency. Ignore decimal points after the first until a non-numeric character is found, and round to the nearest hundredth. For example, the string 12.399abc29.00.6a would be formatted (in the USA) to $12.40abc$29.01a.

16. Write a program that accepts two command-line arguments (a filename and a number) and scrambles each word in the file by randomly switching two of its letters the number of times specified in the second argument. (That is, if 0 is passed into your program from the command-line, the words should not be scrambled; if 1 is passed in, one pair of randomly-chosen letters should be swapped, for an input of 2, two random pairs should be swapped, etc.).

---

17. Write a program that accepts a filename from the command line and displays the number of sentences (defined as the number of periods in the file), average number of characters per sentence, and the total number of characters in the file.

18. Prove to yourself that the **at( )** member function really will throw an exception if an attempt is made to go out of bounds, and that the indexing operator (**[ ]**) won't.

4: Iostreams

You can do much more with the general I/O problem than just take standard I/O and turn it into a class.

Wouldn't it be nice if you could make all the usual "receptacles"—standard I/O, files, and even blocks of memory—look the same so that you need to remember only one interface? That's the idea behind iostreams. They're much easier, safer, and sometimes even more efficient than the assorted functions from the Standard C **stdio** library.

The iostreams classes are usually the first part of the C++ library that new C++ programmers learn to use. This chapter discusses how iostreams are an improvement over C's **stdio** facilities and explores the behavior of file and string streams in addition to the standard console streams.

Why iostreams?

You might wonder what's wrong with the good old C library. Why not "wrap" the C library in a class and be done with it? Sometimes this is a fine solution. For example, suppose you want to make sure that the file represented by a **stdio FILE** pointer is always safely opened and properly closed without having to rely on the user to remember to call the **close( )** function. The following program is such an attempt:

```
//: C04:FileClass.h
// stdio files wrapped.
#ifndef FILECLASS_H
#define FILECLASS_H
#include <cstdio>
#include <stdexcept>

class FileClass {
  std::FILE* f;
public:
  struct FileClassError : std::runtime_error {
    FileClassError(const char* msg)
    : std::runtime_error(msg) {}
  };
```

```
    FileClass(const char* fname, const char* mode = "r");
    ~FileClass();
    std::FILE* fp();
};
#endif // FILECLASS_H ///:~
```

When you perform file I/O in C, you work with a naked pointer to a FILE **struct**, but this class wraps around the pointer and guarantees it is properly initialized and cleaned up using the constructor and destructor. The second constructor argument is the file mode, which defaults to "r" for "read."

To fetch the value of the pointer to use in the file I/O functions, you use the **fp( )** access function. Here are the member function definitions:

```
//: C04:FileClass.cpp {O}
// FileClass Implementation.
#include "FileClass.h"
#include <cstdlib>
#include <cstdio>
using namespace std;

FileClass::FileClass(const char* fname, const char* mode) {
  if((f = fopen(fname, mode)) == 0)
    throw FileClassError("Error opening file");
}

FileClass::~FileClass() { fclose(f); }

FILE* FileClass::fp() { return f; } ///:~
```

The constructor calls **fopen( )**, as you would normally do, but it also ensures that the result isn't zero, which indicates a failure upon opening the file. If the file does not open as expected, an exception is thrown.

The destructor closes the file, and the access function **fp( )** returns **f**. Here's a simple example using **FileClass**:

```
//: C04:FileClassTest.cpp
//{L} FileClass
#include <cstdlib>
#include <iostream>
#include "FileClass.h"
using namespace std;
```

```
int main() {
  try {
    FileClass f("FileClassTest.cpp");
    const int BSIZE = 100;
    char buf[BSIZE];
    while(fgets(buf, BSIZE, f.fp()))
      fputs(buf, stdout);
  } catch(FileClass::FileClassError& e) {
    cout << e.what() << endl;
    return EXIT_FAILURE;
  }
  return EXIT_SUCCESS;
} // File automatically closed by destructor
///:~
```

You create the **FileClass** object and use it in normal C file I/O function calls by calling **fp( )**. When you're done with it, just forget about it; the file is closed by the destructor at the end of its scope.

Even though the **FILE** pointer is private, it isn't particularly safe because **fp( )** retrieves it. Since the only effect seems to be guaranteed initialization and cleanup, why not make it public or use a **struct** instead? Notice that while you can get a copy of **f** using **fp( )**, you cannot assign to **f**—that's completely under the control of the class. After capturing the pointer returned by **fp( )**, the client programmer can still assign to the structure elements or even close it, so the safety is in guaranteeing a valid **FILE** pointer rather than proper contents of the structure.

If you want complete safety, you must prevent the user from directly accessing the **FILE** pointer. Some version of all the normal file I/O functions must show up as class members so that everything you can do with the C approach is available in the C++ class:

```
//: C04:Fullwrap.h
// Completely hidden file IO.
#ifndef FULLWRAP_H
#define FULLWRAP_H
#include <cstddef>
#include <cstdio>
#undef getc
#undef putc
#undef ungetc
using std::size_t;
```

```
using std::fpos_t;

class File {
  std::FILE* f;
  std::FILE* F(); // Produces checked pointer to f
public:
  File(); // Create object but don't open file
  File(const char* path, const char* mode = "r");
  ~File();
  int open(const char* path, const char* mode = "r");
  int reopen(const char* path, const char* mode);
  int getc();
  int ungetc(int c);
  int putc(int c);
  int puts(const char* s);
  char* gets(char* s, int n);
  int printf(const char* format, ...);
  size_t read(void* ptr, size_t size, size_t n);
  size_t write(const void* ptr, size_t size, size_t n);
  int eof();
  int close();
  int flush();
  int seek(long offset, int whence);
  int getpos(fpos_t* pos);
  int setpos(const fpos_t* pos);
  long tell();
  void rewind();
  void setbuf(char* buf);
  int setvbuf(char* buf, int type, size_t sz);
  int error();
  void clearErr();
};
#endif // FULLWRAP_H ///:~
```

This class contains almost all the file I/O functions from **<cstdio>**.
(**vfprintf( )** is missing; it implements the **printf( )** member function.)

File has the same constructor as in the previous example, and it also has a
default constructor. The default constructor is important if you want to create
an array of **File** objects or use a **File** object as a member of another class
where the initialization doesn't happen in the constructor, but some time
after the enclosing object is created.

The default constructor sets the private **FILE** pointer **f** to zero. But now, before any reference to **f**, its value must be checked to ensure it isn't zero. This is accomplished with **F( )**, which is **private** because it is intended to be used only by other member functions. (We don't want to give the user direct access to the underlying **FILE** structure in this class.)

This approach is not a terrible solution by any means. It's quite functional, and you could imagine making similar classes for standard (console) I/O and for in-core formatting (reading/writing a piece of memory rather than a file or the console).

The stumbling block is the runtime interpreter used for the variable argument list functions. This is the code that parses your format string at runtime and grabs and interprets arguments from the variable argument list. It's a problem for four reasons.

1.　Even if you use only a fraction of the functionality of the interpreter, the whole thing gets loaded into your executable. So if you say **printf("%c", 'x');**, you'll get the whole package, including the parts that print floating-point numbers and strings. There's no standard option for reducing the amount of space used by the program.

2.　Because the interpretation happens at runtime, you can't get rid of a performance overhead. It's frustrating because all the information is *there* in the format string at compile time, but it's not evaluated until runtime. However, if you could parse the arguments in the format string at compile time, you could make direct function calls that have the potential to be much faster than a runtime interpreter (although the **printf( )** family of functions is usually quite well optimized).

3.　Because the format string is not evaluated until runtime, there can be no compile-time error checking. You're probably familiar with this problem if you've tried to find bugs that came from using the wrong number or type of arguments in a **printf( )** statement. C++ makes a big deal out of compile-time error checking to find errors early and make your life easier. It seems a shame to throw type safety away for an I/O library, especially since I/O is used a lot.

4.　For C++, the most crucial problem is that the **printf( )** family of functions is not particularly extensible. They're really designed to handle only the basic data types in C (**char**, **int**, **float**, **double**,

wchar_t, **char***, **wchar_t***, and **void*)** and their variations. You might think that every time you add a new class, you could add overloaded **printf( )** and **scanf( )** functions (and their variants for files and strings), but remember, overloaded functions must have different types in their argument lists, and the **printf( )** family hides its type information in the format string and in the variable argument list. For a language such as C++, whose goal is to be able to easily add new data types, this is an unacceptable restriction.

Iostreams to the rescue

These issues make it clear that I/O is one of the first priorities for the Standard C++ class libraries. Because "hello, world" is the first program just about everyone writes in a new language, and because I/O is part of virtually every program, the I/O library in C++ must be particularly easy to use. It also has the much greater challenge that it must accommodate any new class. Thus, its constraints require that this foundation class library be a truly inspired design. In addition to gaining a great deal of leverage and clarity in your dealings with I/O and formatting, you'll also see in this chapter how a really powerful C++ library can work.

Inserters and extractors

A *stream* is an object that transports and formats characters of a fixed width. You can have an input stream (via descendants of the **istream** class), an output stream (with **ostream** objects), or a stream that does both simultaneously (with objects derived from **iostream**). The iostreams library provides different types of such classes: **ifstream**, **ofstream**, and **fstream** for files, and **istringstream**, **ostringstream**, and **stringstream** for interfacing with the Standard C++ **string** class. All these stream classes have nearly identical interfaces, so you can use streams in a uniform manner, whether you're working with a file, standard I/O, a region of memory, or a **string** object. The single interface you learn also works for extensions added to support new classes. Some functions implement your formatting commands, and some functions read and write characters without formatting.

The stream classes mentioned earlier are actually template specializations,[1] much like the standard **string** class is a specialization of the **basic_string** template. The basic classes in the iostreams inheritance hierarchy are shown in the following figure:

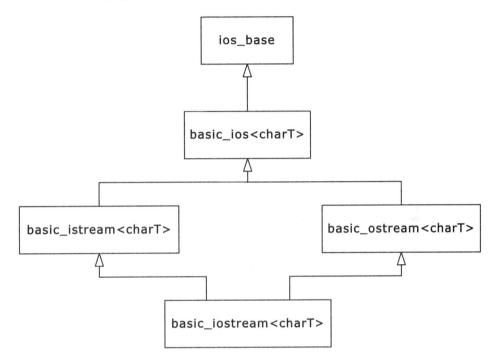

The **ios_base** class declares everything that is common to all streams, independent of the type of character the stream handles. These declarations are mostly constants and functions to manage them, some of which you'll see throughout this chapter. The rest of the classes are templates that have the underlying character type as a parameter. The **istream** class, for example, is defined as follows:

```
typedef basic_istream<char> istream;
```

All the classes mentioned earlier are defined via similar type definitions. There are also type definitions for all stream classes using **wchar_t** (the wide character type discussed in Chapter 3) instead of **char**. We'll look at these at

---

[1] Explained in depth in Chapter 5.

the end of this chapter. The **basic_ios** template defines functions common to both input and output, but that depends on the underlying character type (we won't use these much). The template **basic_istream** defines generic functions for input, and **basic_ostream** does the same for output. The classes for file and string streams introduced later add functionality for their specific stream types.

In the iostreams library, two operators are overloaded to simplify the use of iostreams. The operator << is often referred to as an *inserter* for iostreams, and the operator >> is often referred to as an *extractor*.

Extractors parse the information that's expected by the destination object according to its type. To see an example of this, you can use the **cin** object, which is the iostream equivalent of **stdin** in C, that is, redirectable standard input. This object is predefined whenever you include the **<iostream>** header.

```
int i;
cin >> i;

float f;
cin >> f;

char c;
cin >> c;

char buf[100];
cin >> buf;
```

There's an overloaded **operator >>** for every built-in data type. You can also overload your own, as you'll see later.

To find out what you have in the various variables, you can use the **cout** object (corresponding to standard output; there's also a **cerr** object corresponding to standard error) with the inserter <<:

```
cout << "i = ";
cout << i;
cout << "\n";
cout << "f = ";
cout << f;
cout << "\n";
```

```
cout << "c = ";
cout << c;
cout << "\n";
cout << "buf = ";
cout << buf;
cout << "\n";
```

This is tedious and doesn't seem like much of an improvement over **printf( )**, despite improved type checking. Fortunately, the overloaded inserters and extractors are designed to be chained into a more complex expression that is much easier to write (and read):

```
cout << "i = " << i << endl;
cout << "f = " << f << endl;
cout << "c = " << c << endl;
cout << "buf = " << buf << endl;
```

Defining inserters and extractors for your own classes is just a matter of overloading the associated operators to do the right things, namely:

- Make the first parameter a non-**const** reference to the stream (**istream** for input, **ostream** for output).

- Perform the operation by inserting/extracting data to/from the stream (by processing the components of the object).

- Return a reference to the stream.

The stream should be non-**const** because processing stream data changes the state of the stream. By returning the stream, you allow for chaining stream operations in a single statement, as shown earlier.

As an example, consider how to output the representation of a **Date** object in MM-DD-YYYY format. The following inserter does the job:

```
ostream& operator<<(ostream& os, const Date& d) {
  char fillc = os.fill('0');
  os << setw(2) << d.getMonth() << '-'
     << setw(2) << d.getDay() << '-'
     << setw(4) << setfill(fillc) << d.getYear();
  return os;
}
```

This function cannot be a member of the **Date** class because the left operand of the << operator must be the output stream. The **fill( )** member function of **ostream** changes the padding character used when the width of an output field, determined by the *manipulator* **setw( )**, is greater than needed for the data. We use a '0' character so that months preceding October will display a leading zero, such as "09" for September. The **fill( )** function also returns the previous fill character (which defaults to a single space) so that we can restore it later with the manipulator **setfill( )**. We discuss manipulators in depth later in this chapter.

Extractors require a little more care because things can go wrong with input data. The way to signal a stream error is to set the stream's *fail bit*, as follows:

```
istream& operator>>(istream& is, Date& d) {
  is >> d.month;
  char dash;
  is >> dash;
  if(dash != '-')
    is.setstate(ios::failbit);
  is >> d.day;
  is >> dash;
  if(dash != '-')
    is.setstate(ios::failbit);
  is >> d.year;
  return is;
}
```

When an error bit is set in a stream, all further streams operations are ignored until the stream is restored to a good state (explained shortly). That's why the code above continues extracting even if **ios::failbit** gets set. This implementation is somewhat forgiving in that it allows white space between the numbers and dashes in a date string (because the >> operator skips white space by default when reading built-in types). The following are valid date strings for this extractor:

```
"08-10-2003"
"8-10-2003"
"08 - 10 - 2003"
```

but these are not:

```
"A-10-2003" // No alpha characters allowed
"08%10/2003" // Only dashes allowed as a delimiter
```

We'll discuss stream state in more depth in the section "Handling stream errors" later in this chapter.

Common usage

As the **Date** extractor illustrated, you must be on guard for erroneous input. If the input produces an unexpected value, the process is skewed, and it's difficult to recover. In addition, formatted input defaults to white space delimiters. Consider what happens when we collect the code fragments from earlier in this chapter into a single program:

```
//: C04:Iosexamp.cpp {RunByHand}
// Iostream examples.
#include <iostream>
using namespace std;

int main() {
  int i;
  cin >> i;

  float f;
  cin >> f;

  char c;
  cin >> c;

  char buf[100];
  cin >> buf;

  cout << "i = " << i << endl;
  cout << "f = " << f << endl;
  cout << "c = " << c << endl;
  cout << "buf = " << buf << endl;

  cout << flush;
  cout << hex << "0x" << i << endl;
} ///:~
```

and give it the following input:

```
12 1.4 c this is a test
```

We expect the same output as if we gave it

```
12
1.4
c
this is a test
```

but the output is, somewhat unexpectedly

```
i = 12
f = 1.4
c = c
buf = this
0xc
```

Notice that **buf** got only the first word because the input routine looked for a space to delimit the input, which it saw after "this." In addition, if the continuous input string is longer than the storage allocated for **buf**, we overrun the buffer.

In practice, you'll usually want to get input from interactive programs a line at a time as a sequence of characters, scan them, and then perform conversions once they're safely in a buffer. This way you don't need to worry about the input routine choking on unexpected data.

Another consideration is the whole concept of a command-line interface. This made sense in the past when the console was little more than a glass typewriter, but the world is rapidly changing to one where the graphical user interface (GUI) dominates. What is the meaning of console I/O in such a world? It makes much more sense to ignore **cin** altogether, other than for simple examples or tests, and take the following approaches:

1.   If your program requires input, read that input from a file—you'll soon see that it's remarkably easy to use files with iostreams. Iostreams for files still works fine with a GUI.

2.   Read the input without attempting to convert it, as we just suggested. When the input is some place where it can't foul things up during conversion, you can safely scan it.

3.   Output is different. If you're using a GUI, **cout** doesn't necessarily work, and you must send it to a file (which is identical to sending it to **cout**) or use the GUI facilities for data display. Otherwise it often

makes sense to send it to **cout**. In both cases, the output formatting functions of iostreams are highly useful.

Another common practice saves compile time on large projects. Consider, for example, how you would declare the **Date** stream operators introduced earlier in the chapter in a header file. You only need to include the prototypes for the functions, so it's not really necessary to include the entire **<iostream>** header in **Date.h**. The standard practice is to only declare classes, something like this:

```
class ostream;
```

This is an age-old technique for separating interface from implementation and is often called a *forward declaration* (and **ostream** at this point would be considered an *incomplete type*, since the class definition has not yet been seen by the compiler).

This will not work as is, however, for two reasons:

1. The stream classes are defined in the **std** namespace.

2. They are templates.

The proper declaration would be:

```
namespace std {
  template<class charT, class traits = char_traits<charT> >
    class basic_ostream;
  typedef basic_ostream<char> ostream;
}
```

(As you can see, like the **string** class, the streams classes use the character traits classes mentioned in Chapter 3). Since it would be terribly tedious to type all that for every stream class you want to reference, the standard provides a header that does it for you: **<iosfwd>**. The **Date** header would then look something like this:

```
// Date.h
#include <iosfwd>

class Date {
  friend std::ostream& operator<<(std::ostream&,
                                  const Date&);
  friend std::istream& operator>>(std::istream&, Date&);
```

```
    // Etc.
```

Line-oriented input

To grab input a line at a time, you have three choices:

- The member function **get( )**

- The member function **getline( )**

- The global function **getline( )** defined in the **<string>** header

The first two functions take three arguments:

1. A pointer to a character buffer in which to store the result.
2. The size of that buffer (so it's not overrun).
3. The terminating character, to know when to stop reading input.

The terminating character has a default value of **'\n'**, which is what you'll usually use. Both functions store a zero in the result buffer when they encounter the terminating character in the input.

So what's the difference? Subtle, but important: **get( )** stops when it *sees* the delimiter in the input stream, but it doesn't extract it from the input stream. Thus, if you did another **get( )** using the same delimiter, it would immediately return with no fetched input. (Presumably, you either use a different delimiter in the next **get( )** statement or a different input function.) The **getline( )** function, on the other hand, extracts the delimiter from the input stream, but still doesn't store it in the result buffer.

The **getline( )** function defined in **<string>** is convenient. It is not a member function, but rather a stand-alone function declared in the namespace **std**. It takes only two non-default arguments, the input stream and the **string** object to populate. Like its namesake, it reads characters until it encounters the first occurrence of the delimiter (**'\n'** by default) and consumes and discards the delimiter. The advantage of this function is that it reads into a **string** object, so you don't need to worry about buffer size.

Generally, when you're processing a text file that you read a line at a time, you'll want to use one of the **getline( )** functions.

Overloaded versions of get( )

The **get( )** function also comes in three other overloaded versions: one with no arguments that returns the next character using an **int** return value; one that stuffs a character into its **char** argument using a reference; and one that stores directly into the underlying buffer structure of another iostream object. The latter is explored later in the chapter.

Reading raw bytes

If you know exactly what you're dealing with and want to move the bytes directly into a variable, an array, or a structure in memory, you can use the unformatted I/O function **read( )**. The first argument for this function is a pointer to the destination memory, and the second is the number of bytes to read. This is especially useful if you've previously stored the information to a file, for example, in binary form using the complementary **write( )** member function for an output stream (using the same compiler, of course). You'll see examples of all these functions later.

Handling stream errors

The **Date** extractor shown earlier sets a stream's fail bit under certain conditions. How does the user know when such a failure occurs? You can detect stream errors by either calling certain stream member functions to see if an error state has occurred, or if you don't care what the particular error was, you can just evaluate the stream in a Boolean context. Both techniques derive from the state of a stream's error bits.

Stream state

The **ios_base** class, from which **ios** derives,[2] defines four flags that you can use to test the state of a stream:

Flag	Meaning
badbit	Some fatal (perhaps physical) error occurred. The stream should be considered unusable.

---

[2] For this reason, you can write **ios::failbit** instead of **ios_base::failbit** to save typing.

---

eofbit	End-of-input has occurred (either by encountering the physical end of a file stream or by the user terminating a console stream, such as with Ctrl-Z or Ctrl-D).
failbit	An I/O operation failed, most likely because of invalid data (e.g., letters were found when trying to read a number). The stream is still usable. The failbit flag is also set when end-of-input occurs.
goodbit	All is well; no errors. End-of-input has not yet occurred.

You can test whether any of these conditions have occurred by calling corresponding member functions that return a Boolean value indicating whether any of these have been set. The **good( )** stream member function returns true if none of the other three bits are set. The **eof( )** function returns true if **eofbit** is set, which happens with an attempt to read from a stream that has no more data (usually a file). Because end-of-input happens in C++ when trying to read past the end of the physical medium, **failbit** is also set to indicate that the "expected" data was not successfully read. The **fail( )** function returns true if *either* **failbit** or **badbit** is set, and **bad( )** returns true only if the **badbit** is set.

Once any of the error bits in a stream's state are set, they remain set, which is not always what you want. When reading a file, you might want to reposition to an earlier place in the file before end-of-file occurred. Just moving the file pointer doesn't automatically reset **eofbit** or **failbit**; you must do it yourself with the **clear( )** function, like this:

```
myStream.clear(); // Clears all error bits
```

After calling **clear( )**, **good( )** will return **true** if called immediately. As you saw in the **Date** extractor earlier, the **setstate( )** function sets the bits you pass it. It turns out that **setstate( )** doesn't affect any other bits—if they're already set, they stay set. If you want to set certain bits but at the same time reset all the rest, you can call an overloaded version of **clear( )**, passing it a bitwise expression representing the bits you want to set, as in:

```
myStream.clear(ios::failbit | ios::eofbit);
```

Most of the time you won't be interested in checking the stream state bits individually. Usually you just want to know if everything is okay. This is the case when you read a file from beginning to end; you just want to know when the input data is exhausted. You can use a conversion function defined for **void*** that is automatically called when a stream occurs in a Boolean expression. Reading a stream until end-of-input using this idiom looks like the following:

```
int i;
while(myStream >> i)
   cout << i << endl;
```

Remember that **operator>>( )** returns its stream argument, so the **while** statement above tests the stream as a Boolean expression. This particular example assumes that the input stream **myStream** contains integers separated by white space. The function **ios_base::operator void*( )** simply calls **good( )** on its stream and returns the result.[3] Because most stream operations return their stream, using this idiom is convenient.

Streams and exceptions

Iostreams existed as part of C++ long before there were exceptions, so checking stream state manually was just the way things were done. For backward compatibility, this is still the status quo, but modern iostreams can throw exceptions instead. The **exceptions( )** stream member function takes a parameter representing the state bits for which you want exceptions to be thrown. Whenever the stream encounters such a state, it throws an exception of type **std::ios_base::failure**, which inherits from **std::exception**.

Although you can trigger a failure exception for any of the four stream states, it's not necessarily a good idea to enable exceptions for all of them. As Chapter 1 explains, use exceptions for truly exceptional conditions, but end-of-file is not only *not* exceptional—it's *expected*! For that reason, you might want to enable exceptions only for the errors represented by **badbit**, which you would do like this:

---

[3] It is customary to use **operator void*( )** in preference to **operator bool( )** because the implicit conversions from **bool** to **int** may cause surprises, should you incorrectly place a stream in a context where an integer conversion can be applied. The **operator void*( )** function will only be called implicitly in the body of a Boolean expression.

```
myStream.exceptions(ios::badbit);
```

You enable exceptions on a stream-by-stream basis, since **exceptions( )** is a member function for streams. The **exceptions( )** function returns a bitmask[4] (of type **iostate**, which is some compiler-dependent type convertible to **int**) indicating which stream states will cause exceptions. If those states have already been set, an exception is thrown immediately. Of course, if you use exceptions in connection with streams, you had better be ready to catch them, which means that you need to wrap all stream processing with a **try** block that has an **ios::failure** handler. Many programmers find this tedious and just check states manually where they expect errors to occur (since, for example, they don't expect **bad( )** to return **true** most of the time anyway). This is another reason that having streams throw exceptions is optional and not the default. In any case, you can choose how you want to handle stream errors. For the same reasons that we recommend using exceptions for error handling in other contexts, we do so here.

File iostreams

Manipulating files with iostreams is much easier and safer than using **stdio** in C. All you do to open a file is create an object—the constructor does the work. You don't need to explicitly close a file (although you can, using the **close( )** member function) because the destructor will close it when the object goes out of scope. To create a file that defaults to input, make an **ifstream** object. To create one that defaults to output, make an **ofstream** object. An **fstream** object can do both input and output.

The file stream classes fit into the iostreams classes as shown in the following figure:

---

[4] An integral type used to hold single–bit flags.

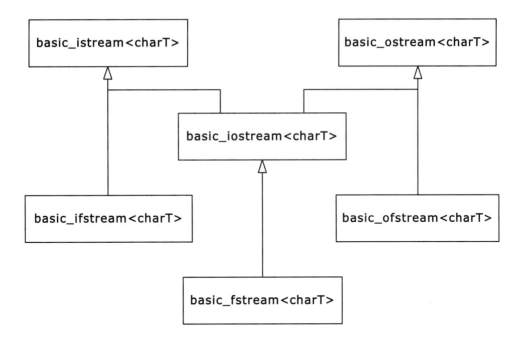

As before, the classes you actually use are template specializations defined by type definitions. For example, **ifstream**, which processes files of **char**, is defined as

```
typedef basic_ifstream<char> ifstream;
```

A File–Processing Example

Here's an example that shows many of the features discussed so far. Notice the inclusion of **<fstream>** to declare the file I/O classes. Although on many platforms this will also include **<iostream>** automatically, compilers are not required to do so. If you want portable code, always include both headers.

```
//: C04:Strfile.cpp
// Stream I/O with files;
// The difference between get() & getline().
#include <fstream>
#include <iostream>
#include "../require.h"
using namespace std;

int main() {
  const int SZ = 100; // Buffer size;
```

```
    char buf[SZ];
    {
      ifstream in("Strfile.cpp"); // Read
      assure(in, "Strfile.cpp"); // Verify open
      ofstream out("Strfile.out"); // Write
      assure(out, "Strfile.out");
      int i = 1; // Line counter

      // A less-convenient approach for line input:
      while(in.get(buf, SZ)) { // Leaves \n in input
        in.get(); // Throw away next character (\n)
        cout << buf << endl; // Must add \n
        // File output just like standard I/O:
        out << i++ << ": " << buf << endl;
      }
    } // Destructors close in & out

    ifstream in("Strfile.out");
    assure(in, "Strfile.out");
    // More convenient line input:
    while(in.getline(buf, SZ)) { // Removes \n
      char* cp = buf;
      while(*cp != ':')
        ++cp;
      cp += 2; // Past ": "
      cout << cp << endl; // Must still add \n
    }
} ///:~
```

The creation of both the **ifstream** and **ofstream** are followed by an
assure( ) to guarantee the file was successfully opened. Here again the
object, used in a situation where the compiler expects a Boolean result,
produces a value that indicates success or failure.

The first **while** loop demonstrates the use of two forms of the **get( )**
function. The first gets characters into a buffer and puts a zero terminator in
the buffer when either **SZ-1** characters have been read or the third argument
(defaulted to '**\n**') is encountered. The **get( )** function leaves the terminator
character in the input stream, so this terminator must be thrown away via
in.get( ) using the form of **get( )** with no argument, which fetches a single
byte and returns it as an **int**. You can also use the **ignore( )** member
function, which has two default arguments. The first argument is the number
of characters to throw away and defaults to one. The second argument is the

character at which the **ignore( )** function quits (after extracting it) and defaults to **EOF**.

Next, you see two output statements that look similar: one to **cout** and one to the file **out**. Notice the convenience here—you don't need to worry about the object type because the formatting statements work the same with all **ostream** objects. The first one echoes the line to standard output, and the second writes the line out to the new file and includes a line number.

To demonstrate **getline( )**, open the file we just created and strip off the line numbers. To ensure the file is properly closed before opening it to read, you have two choices. You can surround the first part of the program with braces to force the **out** object out of scope, thus calling the destructor and closing the file, which is done here. You can also call **close( )** for both files; if you do this, you can even reuse the **in** object by calling the **open( )** member function.

The second **while** loop shows how **getline( )** removes the terminator character (its third argument, which defaults to '**\n**') from the input stream when it's encountered. Although **getline( )**, like **get( )**, puts a zero in the buffer, it still doesn't insert the terminating character.

This example, as well as most of the examples in this chapter, assumes that each call to any overload of **getline( )** will encounter a newline character. If this is not the case, the eofbit state of the stream will be set and the call to **getline( )** will return **false**, causing the program to lose the last line of input.

Open modes

You can control the way a file is opened by overriding the constructor's default arguments. The following table shows the flags that control the mode of the file:

Flag	Function
ios::in	Opens an input file. Use this as an open mode for an **ofstream** to prevent truncating an existing file.

Flag	Function
ios::out	Opens an output file. When used for an **ofstream** without **ios::app**, **ios::ate** or **ios::in**, **ios::trunc** is implied.
ios::app	Opens an output file for appending only.
ios::ate	Opens an existing file (either input or output) and seeks to the end.
ios::trunc	Truncates the old file if it already exists.
ios::binary	Opens a file in *binary mode*. The default is *text mode*.

You can combine these flags using a bitwise *or* operation.

The binary flag, while portable, only has an effect on some non-UNIX systems, such as operating systems derived from MS-DOS, that have special conventions for storing end-of-line delimiters. For example, on MS-DOS systems in text mode (which is the default), every time you output a newline character ('**\n**'), the file system actually outputs two characters, a carriage-return/linefeed pair (CRLF), which is the pair of ASCII characters **0x0D** and **0x0A**. Conversely, when you read such a file back into memory in text mode, each occurrence of this pair of bytes causes a '**\n**' to be sent to the program in its place. If you want to bypass this special processing, you open files in binary mode. Binary mode has nothing whatsoever to do with whether you *can* write raw bytes to a file—you *always* can (by calling **write( )**) . You should, however, open a file in binary mode when you'll be using **read( )** or **write( )**, because these functions take a byte count parameter. Having the extra '**\r**' characters will throw your byte count off in those instances. You should also open a file in binary mode if you're going to use the stream-positioning commands discussed later in this chapter.

You can open a file for both input and output by declaring an **fstream** object. When declaring an **fstream** object, you must use enough of the open mode flags mentioned earlier to let the file system know whether you want to input, output, or both. To switch from output to input, you need to either flush the stream or change the file position. To change from input to output, change the file position. To create a file via an **fstream** object, use the **ios::trunc** open mode flag in the constructor call to do both input and output.

Iostream buffering

Good design practice dictates that, whenever you create a new class, you should endeavor to hide the details of the underlying implementation as much as possible from the user of the class. You show them only what they need to know and make the rest **private** to avoid confusion. When using inserters and extractors, you normally don't know or care where the bytes are being produced or consumed, whether you're dealing with standard I/O, files, memory, or some newly created class or device.

A time comes, however, when it is important to communicate with the part of the iostream that produces and consumes bytes. To provide this part with a common interface and still hide its underlying implementation, the standard library abstracts it into its own class, called **streambuf**. Each iostream object contains a pointer to some kind of **streambuf**. (The type depends on whether it deals with standard I/O, files, memory, and so on.) You can access the **streambuf** directly; for example, you can move raw bytes into and out of the **streambuf** without formatting them through the enclosing iostream. This is accomplished by calling member functions for the **streambuf** object.

Currently, the most important thing for you to know is that every iostream object contains a pointer to a **streambuf** object, and the **streambuf** object has some member functions you can call if necessary. For file and string streams, there are specialized types of stream buffers, as the following figure illustrates:

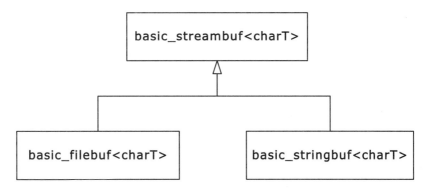

To allow you to access the **streambuf**, every iostream object has a member function called **rdbuf( )** that returns the pointer to the object's **streambuf**. This way you can call any member function for the underlying **streambuf**. However, one of the most interesting things you can do with the **streambuf** pointer is to connect it to another iostream object using the << operator. This drains all the characters from your object into the one on the left side of the <<. If you want to move all the characters from one iostream to another, you don't need to go through the tedium (and potential coding errors) of reading them one character or one line at a time. This is a much more elegant approach.

Here's a simple program that opens a file and sends the contents to standard output (similar to the previous example):

```
//: C04:Stype.cpp
// Type a file to standard output.
#include <fstream>
#include <iostream>
#include "../require.h"
using namespace std;

int main() {
  ifstream in("Stype.cpp");
  assure(in, "Stype.cpp");
  cout << in.rdbuf(); // Outputs entire file
} ///:~
```

An **ifstream** is created using the source code file for this program as an argument. The **assure( )** function reports a failure if the file cannot be opened. All the work really happens in the statement

```
cout << in.rdbuf();
```

which sends the entire contents of the file to **cout**. This is not only more succinct to code, it is often more efficient than moving the bytes one at a time.

A form of **get( )** writes directly into the **streambuf** of another object. The first argument is a reference to the destination **streambuf**, and the second is the terminating character ('\n' by default), which stops the **get( )** function. So there is yet another way to print a file to standard output:

```
//: C04:Sbufget.cpp
```

```
// Copies a file to standard output.
#include <fstream>
#include <iostream>
#include "../require.h"
using namespace std;

int main() {
  ifstream in("Sbufget.cpp");
  assure(in);
  streambuf& sb = *cout.rdbuf();
  while(!in.get(sb).eof()) {
    if(in.fail())              // Found blank line
      in.clear();
    cout << char(in.get()); // Process '\n'
  }
} ///:~
```

The **rdbuf( )** function returns a pointer, so it must be dereferenced to satisfy the function's need to see an object. Stream buffers are not meant to be copied (they have no copy constructor), so we define **sb** as a *reference* to **cout**'s stream buffer. We need the calls to **fail( )** and **clear( )** in case the input file has a blank line (this one does). When this particular overloaded version of **get( )** sees two newlines in a row (evidence of a blank line), it sets the input stream's fail bit, so we must call **clear( )** to reset it so that the stream can continue to be read. The second call to **get( )** extracts and echoes each newline delimiter. (Remember, the **get( )** function doesn't extract its delimiter like **getline( )** does.)

You probably won't need to use a technique like this often, but it's nice to know it exists.[5]

Seeking in iostreams

Each type of iostream has a concept of where its "next" character will come from (if it's an **istream**) or go (if it's an **ostream**). In some situations, you might want to move this stream position. You can do so using two models:

---

[5] A more in-depth treatment of stream buffers and streams in general can be found in Langer & Kreft's, *Standard C++ iostreams and Locales*, Addison-Wesley, 1999.

one uses an absolute location in the stream called the **streampos**; the second works like the Standard C library functions **fseek( )** for a file and moves a given number of bytes from the beginning, end, or current position in the file.

The **streampos** approach requires that you first call a "tell" function: **tellp( )** for an **ostream** or **tellg( )** for an **istream**. (The "p" refers to the "put pointer," and the "g" refers to the "get pointer.") This function returns a **streampos** you can later use in calls to **seekp( )** for an **ostream** or **seekg( )** for an **istream** when you want to return to that position in the stream.

The second approach is a relative seek and uses overloaded versions of **seekp( )** and **seekg( )**. The first argument is the number of characters to move: it can be positive or negative. The second argument is the seek direction:

ios::beg	From beginning of stream
ios::cur	Current position in stream
ios::end	From end of stream

Here's an example that shows the movement through a file, but remember, you're not limited to seeking within files as you are with C's **stdio**. With C++, you can seek in any type of iostream (although the standard stream objects, such as **cin** and **cout**, explicitly disallow it):

```
//: C04:Seeking.cpp
// Seeking in iostreams.
#include <cassert>
#include <cstddef>
#include <cstring>
#include <fstream>
#include "../require.h"
using namespace std;

int main() {
  const int STR_NUM = 5, STR_LEN = 30;
  char origData[STR_NUM][STR_LEN] = {
    "Hickory dickory dus. . .",
```

```
      "Are you tired of C++?",
      "Well, if you have,",
      "That's just too bad,",
      "There's plenty more for us!"
    };
    char readData[STR_NUM][STR_LEN] = {{ 0 }};
    ofstream out("Poem.bin", ios::out | ios::binary);
    assure(out, "Poem.bin");
    for(int i = 0; i < STR_NUM; i++)
      out.write(origData[i], STR_LEN);
    out.close();
    ifstream in("Poem.bin", ios::in | ios::binary);
    assure(in, "Poem.bin");
    in.read(readData[0], STR_LEN);
    assert(strcmp(readData[0], "Hickory dickory dus. . .")
      == 0);
    // Seek -STR_LEN bytes from the end of file
    in.seekg(-STR_LEN, ios::end);
    in.read(readData[1], STR_LEN);
    assert(strcmp(readData[1], "There's plenty more for us!")
      == 0);
    // Absolute seek (like using operator[] with a file)
    in.seekg(3 * STR_LEN);
    in.read(readData[2], STR_LEN);
    assert(strcmp(readData[2], "That's just too bad,") == 0);
    // Seek backwards from current position
    in.seekg(-STR_LEN * 2, ios::cur);
    in.read(readData[3], STR_LEN);
    assert(strcmp(readData[3], "Well, if you have,") == 0);
    // Seek from the begining of the file
    in.seekg(1 * STR_LEN, ios::beg);
    in.read(readData[4], STR_LEN);
    assert(strcmp(readData[4], "Are you tired of C++?")
      == 0);
} ///:~
```

This program writes a poem to a file using a binary output stream. Since we reopen it as an **ifstream**, we use **seekg( )** to position the "get pointer." As you can see, you can seek from the beginning or end of the file or from the current file position. Obviously, you must provide a positive number to move from the beginning of the file and a negative number to move back from the end.

Now that you know about the **streambuf** and how to seek, you can understand an alternative method (besides using an **fstream** object) for creating a stream object that will both read and write a file. The following code first creates an **ifstream** with flags that say it's both an input and an output file. You can't write to an **ifstream**, so you need to create an **ostream** with the underlying stream buffer:

```
ifstream in("filename", ios::in | ios::out);
ostream out(in.rdbuf());
```

You might wonder what happens when you write to one of these objects. Here's an example:

```
//: C04:Iofile.cpp
// Reading & writing one file.
#include <fstream>
#include <iostream>
#include "../require.h"
using namespace std;

int main() {
  ifstream in("Iofile.cpp");
  assure(in, "Iofile.cpp");
  ofstream out("Iofile.out");
  assure(out, "Iofile.out");
  out << in.rdbuf(); // Copy file
  in.close();
  out.close();
  // Open for reading and writing:
  ifstream in2("Iofile.out", ios::in | ios::out);
  assure(in2, "Iofile.out");
  ostream out2(in2.rdbuf());
  cout << in2.rdbuf();  // Print whole file
  out2 << "Where does this end up?";
  out2.seekp(0, ios::beg);
  out2 << "And what about this?";
  in2.seekg(0, ios::beg);
  cout << in2.rdbuf();
} ///:~
```

The first five lines copy the source code for this program into a file called **iofile.out** and then close the files. This gives us a safe text file to play with. Then the aforementioned technique is used to create two objects that read and write to the same file. In **cout << in2.rdbuf( )**, you can see the "get" pointer is initialized to the beginning of the file. The "put" pointer, however, is set to the end of the file because "Where does this end up?" appears appended to the file. However, if the put pointer is moved to the beginning with a **seekp( )**, all the inserted text *overwrites* the existing text. Both writes are seen when the get pointer is moved back to the beginning with a **seekg( )**, and the file is displayed. The file is automatically saved and closed when **out2** goes out of scope and its destructor is called.

String iostreams

A string stream works directly with memory instead of a file or standard output. It uses the same reading and formatting functions that you use with **cin** and **cout** to manipulate bytes in memory. On old computers, the memory was referred to as *core,* so this type of functionality is often called *in-core formatting.*

The class names for string streams echo those for file streams. If you want to create a string stream to extract characters from, you create an **istringstream**. If you want to put characters into a string stream, you create an **ostringstream**. All declarations for string streams are in the standard header **<sstream>**. As usual, there are class templates that fit into the iostreams hierarchy, as shown in the following figure:

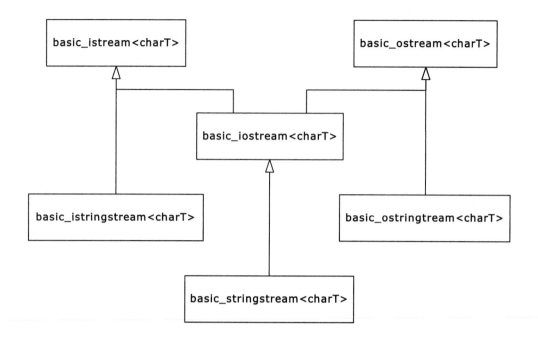

Input string streams

To read from a string using stream operations, you create an **istringstream**
object initialized with the string. The following program shows how to use an
istringstream object:

```
//: C04:Istring.cpp
// Input string streams.
#include <cassert>
#include <cmath>  // For fabs()
#include <iostream>
#include <limits> // For epsilon()
#include <sstream>
#include <string>
using namespace std;

int main() {
  istringstream s("47 1.414 This is a test");
  int i;
  double f;
  s >> i >> f; // Whitespace-delimited input
  assert(i == 47);
  double relerr = (fabs(f) - 1.414) / 1.414;
  assert(relerr <= numeric_limits<double>::epsilon());
```

```
    string buf2;
    s >> buf2;
    assert(buf2 == "This");
    cout << s.rdbuf(); // " is a test"
} ///:~
```

You can see that this is a more flexible and general approach to transforming character strings to typed values than the standard C library functions such as **atof( )** or **atoi( )**, even though the latter may be more efficient for single conversions.

In the expression **s >> i >> f**, the first number is extracted into **i**, and the second into **f**. This isn't "the first whitespace-delimited set of characters" because it depends on the data type it's being extracted into. For example, if the string were instead, "**1.414 47 This is a test**," then **i** would get the value 1 because the input routine would stop at the decimal point. Then **f** would get **0.414**. This could be useful if you want to break a floating-point number into a whole number and a fraction part. Otherwise it would seem to be an error. The second **assert( )** calculates the relative error between what we read and what we expected; it's always better to do this than to compare floating-point numbers for equality. The constant returned by **epsilon( )**, defined in **<limits>**, represents the *machine epsilon* for double-precision numbers, which is the best tolerance you can expect comparisons of **double**s to satisfy.[6]

As you may already have guessed, **buf2** doesn't get the rest of the string, just the next white-space-delimited word. In general, it's best to use the extractor in iostreams when you know the exact sequence of data in the input stream and you're converting to some type other than a character string. However, if you want to extract the rest of the string all at once and send it to another iostream, you can use **rdbuf( )** as shown.

To test the **Date** extractor at the beginning of this chapter, we used an input string stream with the following test program:

---

[6] For more information on machine epsilon and floating-point computation in general, see Chuck's article, "The Standard C Library, Part 3," *C/C++ Users Journal*, March 1995, available at www.freshsources.com/1995006a.htm.

```
//: C04:DateIOTest.cpp
//{L} ../C02/Date
#include <iostream>
#include <sstream>
#include "../C02/Date.h"
using namespace std;

void testDate(const string& s) {
  istringstream os(s);
  Date d;
  os >> d;
  if(os)
    cout << d << endl;
  else
    cout << "input error with \"" << s << "\"" << endl;
}

int main() {
  testDate("08-10-2003");
  testDate("8-10-2003");
  testDate("08 - 10 - 2003");
  testDate("A-10-2003");
  testDate("08%10/2003");
} ///:~
```

Each string literal in **main( )** is passed by reference to **testDate( )**, which in turn wraps it in an **istringstream** so we can test the stream extractor we wrote for **Date** objects. The function **testDate( )** also begins to test the inserter, **operator<<( )**.

Output string streams

To create an output string stream, you just create an **ostringstream** object, which manages a dynamically sized character buffer to hold whatever you insert. To get the formatted result as a **string** object, you call the **str( )** member function. Here's an example:

```
//: C04:Ostring.cpp {RunByHand}
// Illustrates ostringstream.
#include <iostream>
#include <sstream>
#include <string>
using namespace std;
```

```
int main() {
  cout << "type an int, a float and a string: ";
  int i;
  float f;
  cin >> i >> f;
  cin >> ws; // Throw away white space
  string stuff;
  getline(cin, stuff); // Get rest of the line
  ostringstream os;
  os << "integer = " << i << endl;
  os << "float = " << f << endl;
  os << "string = " << stuff << endl;
  string result = os.str();
  cout << result << endl;
} ///:~
```

This is similar to the **lstring.cpp** example earlier that fetched an **int** and a **float**. A sample execution follows (the keyboard input is in bold type).

```
type an int, a float and a string: 10 20.5 the end
integer = 10
float = 20.5
string = the end
```

You can see that, like the other output streams, you can use the ordinary formatting tools, such as the << operator and **endl**, to send bytes to the **ostringstream**. The **str( )** function returns a new **string** object every time you call it so the underlying **stringbuf** object owned by the string stream is left undisturbed.

In the previous chapter, we presented a program, **HTMLStripper.cpp**, that removed all HTML tags and special codes from a text file. As promised, here is a more elegant version using string streams.

```
//: C04:HTMLStripper2.cpp {RunByHand}
//{L} ../C03/ReplaceAll
// Filter to remove html tags and markers.
#include <cstddef>
#include <cstdlib>
#include <fstream>
#include <iostream>
#include <sstream>
#include <stdexcept>
#include <string>
```

```
#include "../C03/ReplaceAll.h"
#include "../require.h"
using namespace std;

string& stripHTMLTags(string& s) throw(runtime_error) {
  size_t leftPos;
  while((leftPos = s.find('<')) != string::npos) {
    size_t rightPos = s.find('>', leftPos+1);
    if(rightPos == string::npos) {
      ostringstream msg;
      msg << "Incomplete HTML tag starting in position "
        << leftPos;
      throw runtime_error(msg.str());
    }
    s.erase(leftPos, rightPos - leftPos + 1);
  }
  // Remove all special HTML characters
  replaceAll(s, "&lt;", "<");
  replaceAll(s, "&gt;", ">");
  replaceAll(s, "&amp;", "&");
  replaceAll(s, " ", " ");
  // Etc...
  return s;
}

int main(int argc, char* argv[]) {
  requireArgs(argc, 1,
    "usage: HTMLStripper2 InputFile");
  ifstream in(argv[1]);
  assure(in, argv[1]);
  // Read entire file into string; then strip
  ostringstream ss;
  ss << in.rdbuf();
  try {
    string s = ss.str();
    cout << stripHTMLTags(s) << endl;
    return EXIT_SUCCESS;
  } catch(runtime_error& x) {
    cout << x.what() << endl;
    return EXIT_FAILURE;
  }
} ///:~
```

In this program we read the entire file into a string by inserting a **rdbuf( )** call to the file stream into an **ostringstream**. Now it's an easy matter to search for HTML delimiter pairs and erase them without having to worry about crossing line boundaries like we had to with the previous version in Chapter 3.

The following example shows how to use a bidirectional (that is, read/write) string stream:

```
//: C04:StringSeeking.cpp {-bor}{-dmc}
// Reads and writes a string stream.
#include <cassert>
#include <sstream>
#include <string>
using namespace std;

int main() {
  string text = "We will hook no fish";
  stringstream ss(text);
  ss.seekp(0, ios::end);
  ss << " before its time.";
  assert(ss.str() ==
    "We will hook no fish before its time.");
  // Change "hook" to "ship"
  ss.seekg(8, ios::beg);
  string word;
  ss >> word;
  assert(word == "hook");
  ss.seekp(8, ios::beg);
  ss << "ship";
  // Change "fish" to "code"
  ss.seekg(16, ios::beg);
  ss >> word;
  assert(word == "fish");
  ss.seekp(16, ios::beg);
  ss << "code";
  assert(ss.str() ==
    "We will ship no code before its time.");
  ss.str("A horse of a different color.");
  assert(ss.str() == "A horse of a different color.");
} ///:~
```

As always, to move the put pointer, you call **seekp( )**, and to reposition the get pointer, you call **seekg( )**. Even though we didn't show it with this example, string streams are a little more forgiving than file streams in that you can switch from reading to writing or vice-versa at any time. You don't need to reposition the get or put pointers or flush the stream. This program also illustrates the overload of **str( )** that replaces the stream's underlying **stringbuf** with a new string.

Output stream formatting

The goal of the iostreams design is to allow you to easily move and/or format characters. It certainly wouldn't be useful if you couldn't do most of the formatting provided by C's **printf( )** family of functions. In this section, you'll learn all the output formatting functions that are available for iostreams, so you can format your bytes the way you want them.

The formatting functions in iostreams can be somewhat confusing at first because there's often more than one way to control the formatting: through both member functions and manipulators. To further confuse things, a generic member function sets state flags to control formatting, such as left or right justification, to use uppercase letters for hex notation, to always use a decimal point for floating-point values, and so on. On the other hand, separate member functions set and read values for the fill character, the field width, and the precision.

In an attempt to clarify all this, we'll first examine the internal formatting data of an iostream, along with the member functions that can modify that data. (Everything can be controlled through the member functions, if desired.) We'll cover the manipulators separately.

Format flags

The class **ios** contains data members to store all the formatting information pertaining to a stream. Some of this data has a range of values and is stored in variables: the floating-point precision, the output field width, and the character used to pad the output (normally a space). The rest of the formatting is determined by flags, which are usually combined to save space and are referred to collectively as the *format flags*. You can find out the value of the format flags with the **ios::flags( )** member function, which takes no arguments and returns an object of type **fmtflags** (usually a synonym for **long**) that contains the current format flags. All the rest of the functions make changes to the format flags and return the previous value of the format flags.

```
fmtflags ios::flags(fmtflags newflags);
fmtflags ios::setf(fmtflags ored_flag);
fmtflags ios::unsetf(fmtflags clear_flag);
fmtflags ios::setf(fmtflags bits, fmtflags field);
```

The first function forces *all* the flags to change, which is sometimes what you want. More often, you change one flag at a time using the remaining three functions.

The use of **setf( )** can seem somewhat confusing. To know which overloaded version to use, you must know what type of flag you're changing. There are two types of flags: those that are simply on or off, and those that work in a group with other flags. The on/off flags are the simplest to understand because you turn them on with **setf(fmtflags)** and off with **unsetf(fmtflags)**. These flags are shown in the following table:

on/off flag	Effect
ios::skipws	Skip white space. (For input; this is the default.)
ios::showbase	Indicate the numeric base (as set, for example, by **dec**, **oct**, or **hex**) when printing an integral value. Input streams also recognize the base prefix when **showbase** is on.
ios::showpoint	Show decimal point and trailing zeros for floating-point values.
ios::uppercase	Display uppercase **A-F** for hexadecimal values and **E** for scientific values.
ios::showpos	Show plus sign (+) for positive values.
ios::unitbuf	"Unit buffering." The stream is flushed after each insertion.

For example, to show the plus sign for **cout**, you say
cout.setf(ios::showpos). To stop showing the plus sign, you say
cout.unsetf(ios::showpos).

The **unitbuf** flag controls *unit buffering*, which means that each insertion is
flushed to its output stream immediately. This is handy for error tracing, so
that in case of a program crash, your data is still written to the log file. The
following program illustrates unit buffering:

```
//: C04:Unitbuf.cpp {RunByHand}
#include <cstdlib>  // For abort()
#include <fstream>
using namespace std;

int main() {
  ofstream out("log.txt");
  out.setf(ios::unitbuf);
  out << "one" << endl;
  out << "two" << endl;
  abort();
} ///:~
```

It is necessary to turn on unit buffering before any insertions are made to the
stream. When we commented out the call to **setf( )**, one particular compiler
had written only the letter 'o' to the file **log.txt**. With unit buffering, no data
was lost.

The standard error output stream **cerr** has unit buffering turned on by
default. There is a cost for unit buffering, so if an output stream is heavily
used, don't enable unit buffering unless efficiency is not a consideration.

Format fields

The second type of formatting flags work in a group. Only one of these flags
can be set at a time, like the buttons on old car radios—you push one in, the
rest pop out. Unfortunately this doesn't happen automatically, and you must
pay attention to what flags you're setting so that you don't accidentally call
the wrong **setf( )** function. For example, there's a flag for each of the number
bases: hexadecimal, decimal, and octal. Collectively, these flags are referred
to as the **ios::basefield**. If the **ios::dec** flag is set and you call
setf(ios::hex), you'll set the **ios::hex** flag, but you *won't* clear the **ios::dec**
bit, resulting in undefined behavior. Instead, call the second form of **setf( )**

like this: **setf(ios::hex, ios::basefield)**. This function first clears all the bits in the **ios::basefield** and *then* sets **ios::hex**. Thus, this form of **setf( )** ensures that the other flags in the group "pop out" whenever you set one. The **ios::hex** manipulator does all this for you, automatically, so you don't need to concern yourself with the internal details of the implementation of this class or to even *care* that it's a set of binary flags. Later you'll see that there are manipulators to provide equivalent functionality in all the places you would use **setf( )**.

Here are the flag groups and their effects:

ios::basefield	Effect
ios::dec	Format integral values in base 10 (decimal) (the default radix—no prefix is visible).
ios::hex	Format integral values in base 16 (hexadecimal).
ios::oct	Format integral values in base 8 (octal).

ios::floatfield	Effect
ios::scientific	Display floating-point numbers in scientific format. Precision field indicates number of digits after the decimal point.
ios::fixed	Display floating-point numbers in fixed format. Precision field indicates number of digits after the decimal point.
"automatic" (Neither bit is set.)	Precision field indicates the total number of significant digits.

ios::adjustfield	Effect
ios::left	Left-align values; pad on the right with the fill character.
ios::right	Right-align values. Pad on the left with the fill character. This is the default alignment.
ios::internal	Add fill characters after any leading sign or base indicator, but before the value. (In other words, the sign, if printed, is left-justified while the number is right-justified.)

Width, fill, and precision

The internal variables that control the width of the output field, the fill character used to pad an output field, and the precision for printing floating-point numbers are read and written by member functions of the same name.

Function	Effect
int ios::width( )	Returns the current width. Default is 0. Used for both insertion and extraction.
int ios::width(int n)	Sets the width, returns the previous width.
int ios::fill( )	Returns the current fill character. Default is space.
int ios::fill(int n)	Sets the fill character, returns the previous fill character.
int ios::precision( )	Returns current floating-point precision. Default is 6.

Function	Effect
int ios::precision(int n)	Sets floating-point precision, returns previous precision. See **ios::floatfield** table for the meaning of "precision."

The **fill** and **precision** values are fairly straightforward, but **width** requires some explanation. When the width is zero, inserting a value produces the minimum number of characters necessary to represent that value. A positive width means that inserting a value will produce at least as many characters as the width; if the value has fewer than width characters, the fill character pad the field. However, the value will never be truncated, so if you try to print 123 with a width of two, you'll still get 123. The field width specifies a *minimum* number of characters; there's no way to specify a maximum number.

The width is also distinctly different because it's reset to zero by each inserter or extractor that could be influenced by its value. It's really not a state variable, but rather an implicit argument to the inserters and extractors. If you want a constant width, call **width( )** after each insertion or extraction.

An exhaustive example

To make sure you know how to call all the functions previously discussed, here's an example that calls them all:

```
//: C04:Format.cpp
// Formatting Functions.
#include <fstream>
#include <iostream>
#include "../require.h"
using namespace std;
#define D(A) T << #A << endl; A

int main() {
  ofstream T("format.out");
  assure(T);
  D(int i = 47;)
  D(float f = 2300114.414159;)
  const char* s = "Is there any more?";
```

```
D(T.setf(ios::unitbuf);)
D(T.setf(ios::showbase);)
D(T.setf(ios::uppercase | ios::showpos);)
D(T << i << endl;) // Default is dec
D(T.setf(ios::hex, ios::basefield);)
D(T << i << endl;)
D(T.setf(ios::oct, ios::basefield);)
D(T << i << endl;)
D(T.unsetf(ios::showbase);)
D(T.setf(ios::dec, ios::basefield);)
D(T.setf(ios::left, ios::adjustfield);)
D(T.fill('0');)
D(T << "fill char: " << T.fill() << endl;)
D(T.width(10);)
T << i << endl;
D(T.setf(ios::right, ios::adjustfield);)
D(T.width(10);)
T << i << endl;
D(T.setf(ios::internal, ios::adjustfield);)
D(T.width(10);)
T << i << endl;
D(T << i << endl;) // Without width(10)

D(T.unsetf(ios::showpos);)
D(T.setf(ios::showpoint);)
D(T << "prec = " << T.precision() << endl;)
D(T.setf(ios::scientific, ios::floatfield);)
D(T << endl << f << endl;)
D(T.unsetf(ios::uppercase);)
D(T << endl << f << endl;)
D(T.setf(ios::fixed, ios::floatfield);)
D(T << f << endl;)
D(T.precision(20);)
D(T << "prec = " << T.precision() << endl;)
D(T << endl << f << endl;)
D(T.setf(ios::scientific, ios::floatfield);)
D(T << endl << f << endl;)
D(T.setf(ios::fixed, ios::floatfield);)
D(T << f << endl;)

D(T.width(10);)
T << s << endl;
D(T.width(40);)
T << s << endl;
D(T.setf(ios::left, ios::adjustfield);)
```

```
  D(T.width(40);)
  T << s << endl;
} ///:~
```

This example uses a trick to create a trace file so that you can monitor what's happening. The macro **D(a)** uses the preprocessor "stringizing" to turn **a** into a string to display. Then it reiterates **a** so the statement is executed. The macro sends all the information to a file called **T**, which is the trace file. The output is

```
int i = 47;
float f = 2300114.414159;
T.setf(ios::unitbuf);
T.setf(ios::showbase);
T.setf(ios::uppercase | ios::showpos);
T << i << endl;
+47
T.setf(ios::hex, ios::basefield);
T << i << endl;
0X2F
T.setf(ios::oct, ios::basefield);
T << i << endl;
057
T.unsetf(ios::showbase);
T.setf(ios::dec, ios::basefield);
T.setf(ios::left, ios::adjustfield);
T.fill('0');
T << "fill char: " << T.fill() << endl;
fill char: 0
T.width(10);
+470000000
T.setf(ios::right, ios::adjustfield);
T.width(10);
0000000+47
T.setf(ios::internal, ios::adjustfield);
T.width(10);
+000000047
T << i << endl;
+47
T.unsetf(ios::showpos);
T.setf(ios::showpoint);
T << "prec = " << T.precision() << endl;
prec = 6
T.setf(ios::scientific, ios::floatfield);
```

```
T << endl << f << endl;

2.300114E+06
T.unsetf(ios::uppercase);
T << endl << f << endl;

2.300114e+06
T.setf(ios::fixed, ios::floatfield);
T << f << endl;
2300114.500000
T.precision(20);
T << "prec = " << T.precision() << endl;
prec = 20
T << endl << f << endl;

2300114.50000000000000000000
T.setf(ios::scientific, ios::floatfield);
T << endl << f << endl;

2.3001145000000000000000e+06
T.setf(ios::fixed, ios::floatfield);
T << f << endl;
2300114.50000000000000000000
T.width(10);
Is there any more?
T.width(40);
00000000000000000000000Is there any more?
T.setf(ios::left, ios::adjustfield);
T.width(40);
Is there any more?00000000000000000000000
```

Studying this output should clarify your understanding of the iostream formatting member functions.

Manipulators

As you can see from the previous program, calling the member functions for stream formatting operations can get a bit tedious. To make things easier to read and write, a set of *manipulators* is supplied to duplicate the actions provided by the member functions. Manipulators are a convenience because you can insert them for their effect within a containing expression; you don't need to create a separate function-call statement.

Manipulators change the state of the stream instead of (or in addition to) processing data. When you insert **endl** in an output expression, for example, it not only inserts a newline character, but it also *flushes* the stream (that is, puts out all pending characters that have been stored in the internal stream buffer but not yet output). You can also just flush a stream like this:

```
cout << flush;
```

which causes a call to the **flush( )** member function, as in:

```
cout.flush();
```

as a side effect (nothing is inserted into the stream). Additional basic manipulators will change the number base to **oct** (octal), **dec** (decimal) or **hex** (hexadecimal):

```
cout << hex << "0x" << i << endl;
```

In this case, numeric output will continue in hexadecimal mode until you change it by inserting either **dec** or **oct** in the output stream.

There's also a manipulator for extraction that "eats" white space:

```
cin >> ws;
```

Manipulators with no arguments are provided in **<iostream>**. These include **dec**, **oct**, and **hex**, which perform the same action as, respectively, **setf(ios::dec, ios::basefield)**, **setf(ios::oct, ios::basefield)**, and **setf(ios::hex, ios::basefield)**, albeit more succinctly. The **<iostream>** header also includes **ws**, **endl**, and **flush** and the additional set shown here:

Manipulator	Effect
showbase **noshowbase**	Indicate the numeric base (**dec**, **oct**, or **hex**) when printing an integral value.
showpos **noshowpos**	Show plus sign (+) for positive values.
uppercase **nouppercase**	Display uppercase A-F for hexadecimal values, and display E for scientific values.

Manipulator	Effect
showpoint **noshowpoint**	Show decimal point and trailing zeros for floating-point values.
skipws **noskipws**	Skip white space on input.
left **right** **internal**	Left-align, pad on right. Right-align, pad on left. Fill between leading sign or base indicator and value.
scientific **fixed**	Indicates the display preference for floating-point output (scientific notation vs. fixed-point decimal).

Manipulators with arguments

There are six standard manipulators, such as **setw( )**, that take arguments. These are defined in the header file **<iomanip>**, and are summarized in the following table:

Manipulator	effect
setiosflags(fmtflags n)	Equivalent to a call to **setf(n)**. The setting remains in effect until the next change, such as **ios::setf( )**.
resetiosflags(fmtflags n)	Clears only the format flags specified by **n**. The setting remains in effect until the next change, such as **ios::unsetf( )**.

Manipulator	effect
setbase(base n)	Changes base to **n**, where **n** is 10, 8, or 16. (Anything else results in 0.) If **n** is zero, output is base 10, but input uses the C conventions: 10 is 10, 010 is 8, and 0xf is 15. You might as well use **dec**, **oct**, and **hex** for output.
setfill(char n)	Changes the fill character to **n**, such as **ios::fill( )**.
setprecision(int n)	Changes the precision to **n**, such as **ios::precision( )**.
setw(int n)	Changes the field width to **n**, such as **ios::width( )**.

If you're doing a lot of formatting, you can see how using manipulators instead of calling stream member functions can clean up your code. As an example, here's the program from the previous section rewritten to use the manipulators. (The **D( )** macro is removed to make it easier to read.)

```
//: C04:Manips.cpp
// Format.cpp using manipulators.
#include <fstream>
#include <iomanip>
#include <iostream>
using namespace std;

int main() {
  ofstream trc("trace.out");
  int i = 47;
  float f = 2300114.414159;
  char* s = "Is there any more?";

  trc << setiosflags(ios::unitbuf
          | ios::showbase | ios::uppercase
          | ios::showpos);
  trc << i << endl;
  trc << hex << i << endl
```

```
        << oct << i << endl;
  trc.setf(ios::left, ios::adjustfield);
  trc << resetiosflags(ios::showbase)
        << dec << setfill('0');
  trc << "fill char: " << trc.fill() << endl;
  trc << setw(10) << i << endl;
  trc.setf(ios::right, ios::adjustfield);
  trc << setw(10) << i << endl;
  trc.setf(ios::internal, ios::adjustfield);
  trc << setw(10) << i << endl;
  trc << i << endl; // Without setw(10)

  trc << resetiosflags(ios::showpos)
        << setiosflags(ios::showpoint)
        << "prec = " << trc.precision() << endl;
  trc.setf(ios::scientific, ios::floatfield);
  trc << f << resetiosflags(ios::uppercase) << endl;
  trc.setf(ios::fixed, ios::floatfield);
  trc << f << endl;
  trc << f << endl;
  trc << setprecision(20);
  trc << "prec = " << trc.precision() << endl;
  trc << f << endl;
  trc.setf(ios::scientific, ios::floatfield);
  trc << f << endl;
  trc.setf(ios::fixed, ios::floatfield);
  trc << f << endl;
  trc << f << endl;

  trc << setw(10) << s << endl;
  trc << setw(40) << s << endl;
  trc.setf(ios::left, ios::adjustfield);
  trc << setw(40) << s << endl;
} ///:~
```

You can see that a lot of the multiple statements have been condensed into a single chained insertion. Notice the call to **setiosflags( )** in which the bitwise-OR of the flags is passed. This could also have been done with **setf( )** and **unsetf( )** as in the previous example.

When using **setw( )** with an output stream, the output expression is formatted into a temporary string that is padded with the current fill character if needed, as determined by comparing the length of the formatted result to the argument of **setw( )**. In other words, **setw( )** affects the *result* *string* of a formatted output operation. Likewise, using **setw( )** with input streams only is meaningful when reading *strings*, as the following example makes clear:

```
//: C04:InputWidth.cpp
// Shows limitations of setw with input.
#include <cassert>
#include <cmath>
#include <iomanip>
#include <limits>
#include <sstream>
#include <string>
using namespace std;

int main() {
  istringstream is("one 2.34 five");
  string temp;
  is >> setw(2) >> temp;
  assert(temp == "on");
  is >> setw(2) >> temp;
  assert(temp == "e");
  double x;
  is >> setw(2) >> x;
  double relerr = fabs(x - 2.34) / x;
  assert(relerr <= numeric_limits<double>::epsilon());
} ///:~
```

If you attempt to read a string, **setw( )** will control the number of characters extracted quite nicely... up to a point. The first extraction gets two characters, but the second only gets one, even though we asked for two. That is because **operator>>( )** uses white space as a delimiter (unless you turn off the **skipws** flag). When trying to read a number, however, such as **x**, you cannot use **setw( )** to limit the characters read. With input streams, use only **setw( )** for extracting strings.

Creating manipulators

Sometimes you'd like to create your own manipulators, and it turns out to be remarkably simple. A zero-argument manipulator such as **endl** is simply a function that takes as its argument an **ostream** reference and returns an **ostream** reference. The declaration for **endl** is

```
ostream& endl(ostream&);
```

Now, when you say:

```
cout << "howdy" << endl;
```

the **endl** produces the *address* of that function. So the compiler asks, "Is there a function that can be applied here that takes the address of a function as its argument?" Predefined functions in **<iostream>** do this; they're called *applicators* (because they *apply* a function to a stream). The applicator calls its function argument, passing it the **ostream** object as its argument. You don't need to know how applicators work to create your own manipulator; you only need to know that they exist. Here's the (simplified) code for an **ostream** applicator:

```
ostream& ostream::operator<<(ostream& (*pf)(ostream&)) {
   return pf(*this);
}
```

The actual definition is a little more complicated since it involves templates, but this code illustrates the technique. When a function such as ***pf** (that takes a stream parameter and returns a stream reference) is inserted into a stream, this applicator function is called, which in turn executes the function to which **pf** points. Applicators for **ios_base**, **basic_ios**, **basic_ostream**, and **basic_istream** are predefined in the Standard C++ library.

To illustrate the process, here's a trivial example that creates a manipulator called **nl** that is equivalent to just inserting a newline into a stream (i.e., no flushing of the stream occurs, as with **endl**):

```
//: C04:nl.cpp
// Creating a manipulator.
#include <iostream>
using namespace std;

ostream& nl(ostream& os) {
   return os << '\n';
}

int main() {
   cout << "newlines" << nl << "between" << nl
        << "each" << nl << "word" << nl;
} ///:~
```

When you insert **nl** into an output stream, such as **cout**, the following sequence of calls ensues:

```
cout.operator<<(nl) ➜ nl(cout)
```

The expression

```
os << '\n';
```

inside **nl( )** calls **ostream::operator(char)**, which returns the stream, which is what is ultimately returned from **nl( )**.[7]

Effectors

As you've seen, zero-argument manipulators are easy to create. But what if you want to create a manipulator that takes arguments? If you inspect the **<iomanip>** header, you'll see a type called **smanip**, which is what the manipulators with arguments return. You might be tempted to somehow use that type to define your own manipulators, but don't do it. The **smanip** type is implementation-dependent and thus not portable. Fortunately, you can define such manipulators in a straightforward way without any special machinery, based on a technique introduced by Jerry Schwarz, called an *effector*.[8] An effector is a simple class whose constructor formats a string representing the desired operation, along with an overloaded **operator<<** to insert that string into a stream. Here's an example with two effectors. The first outputs a truncated character string, and the second prints a number in binary.

```
//: C04:Effector.cpp
// Jerry Schwarz's "effectors."
#include <cassert>
#include <limits>   // For max()
#include <sstream>
#include <string>
using namespace std;

// Put out a prefix of a string:
class Fixw {
```

---

[7] Before putting **nl** into a header file, make it an **inline** function.
[8] Jerry Schwarz is the designer of iostreams.

```
    string str;
public:
  Fixw(const string& s, int width) : str(s, 0, width) {}
  friend ostream& operator<<(ostream& os, const Fixw& fw) {
    return os << fw.str;
  }
};

// Print a number in binary:
typedef unsigned long ulong;

class Bin {
  ulong n;
public:
  Bin(ulong nn) { n = nn; }
  friend ostream& operator<<(ostream& os, const Bin& b) {
    const ulong ULMAX = numeric_limits<ulong>::max();
    ulong bit = ~(ULMAX >> 1); // Top bit set
    while(bit) {
      os << (b.n & bit ? '1' : '0');
      bit >>= 1;
    }
    return os;
  }
};

int main() {
  string words = "Things that make us happy, make us wise";
  for(int i = words.size(); --i >= 0;) {
    ostringstream s;
    s << Fixw(words, i);
    assert(s.str() == words.substr(0, i));
  }
  ostringstream xs, ys;
  xs << Bin(0xCAFEBABEUL);
  assert(xs.str() ==
    "1100""1010""1111""1110""1011""1010""1011""1110");
  ys << Bin(0x76543210UL);
  assert(ys.str() ==
    "0111""0110""0101""0100""0011""0010""0001""0000");
} ///:~
```

The constructor for **Fixw** creates a shortened copy of its **char*** argument, and the destructor releases the memory created for this copy. The overloaded

operator<< takes the contents of its second argument, the **Fixw** object, inserts it into the first argument, the **ostream**, and then returns the **ostream** so that it can be used in a chained expression. When you use **Fixw** in an expression like this:

```
cout << Fixw(string, i) << endl;
```

a *temporary object* is created by the call to the **Fixw** constructor, and that temporary object is passed to **operator<<**. The effect is that of a manipulator with arguments. The temporary **Fixw** object persists until the end of the statement.

The **Bin** effector relies on the fact that shifting an unsigned number to the right shifts zeros into the high bits. We use **numeric_limits<unsigned long>::max( )** (the largest **unsigned long** value, from the standard header **<limits>**) to produce a value with the high bit set, and this value is moved across the number in question (by shifting it to the right), masking each bit in turn. We've juxtaposed string literals in the code for readability; the separate strings are concatenated into a single string by the compiler.

Historically, the problem with this technique was that once you created a class called **Fixw** for **char*** or **Bin** for **unsigned long**, no one else could create a different **Fixw** or **Bin** class for their type. However, with namespaces, this problem is eliminated. Effectors and manipulators aren't equivalent, although they can often be used to solve the same problem. If you find that an effector isn't enough, you will need to conquer the complexity of manipulators.

Iostream examples

In this section you'll see examples that use what you've learned in this chapter. Although many tools exist to manipulate bytes (stream editors such as **sed** and **awk** from UNIX are perhaps the most well known, but a text editor also fits this category), they generally have some limitations. Both **sed** and **awk** can be slow and can only handle lines in a forward sequence, and text editors usually require human interaction, or at least learning a proprietary macro language. The programs you write with iostreams have none of these limitations: they're fast, portable, and flexible.

Maintaining class library source code

Generally, when you create a class, you think in library terms: you make a header file **Name.h** for the class declaration, and then create a file called **Name.cpp** where the member functions are implemented. These files have certain requirements: a particular coding standard (the program shown here uses the coding format for this book), and preprocessor statements surrounding the code in the header file to prevent multiple declarations of classes. (Multiple declarations confuse the compiler—it doesn't know which one you want to use. They could be different, so it throws up its hands and gives an error message.)

This example creates a new header/implementation pair of files or modifies an existing pair. If the files already exist, it checks and potentially modifies the files, but if they don't exist, it creates them using the proper format.

```
//: C04:Cppcheck.cpp
// Configures .h & .cpp files to conform to style
// standard. Tests existing files for conformance.
#include <fstream>
#include <sstream>
#include <string>
#include <cstddef>
#include "../require.h"
using namespace std;

bool startsWith(const string& base, const string& key) {
  return base.compare(0, key.size(), key) == 0;
}

void cppCheck(string fileName) {
  enum bufs { BASE, HEADER, IMPLEMENT, HLINE1, GUARD1,
    GUARD2, GUARD3, CPPLINE1, INCLUDE, BUFNUM };
  string part[BUFNUM];
  part[BASE] = fileName;
  // Find any '.' in the string:
  size_t loc = part[BASE].find('.');
  if(loc != string::npos)
    part[BASE].erase(loc); // Strip extension
  // Force to upper case:
  for(size_t i = 0; i < part[BASE].size(); i++)
    part[BASE][i] = toupper(part[BASE][i]);
  // Create file names and internal lines:
```

```cpp
  part[HEADER] = part[BASE] + ".h";
  part[IMPLEMENT] = part[BASE] + ".cpp";
  part[HLINE1] = "//" ": " + part[HEADER];
  part[GUARD1] = "#ifndef " + part[BASE] + "_H";
  part[GUARD2] = "#define " + part[BASE] + "_H";
  part[GUARD3] = "#endif // " + part[BASE] +"_H";
  part[CPPLINE1] = string("//") + ": " + part[IMPLEMENT];
  part[INCLUDE] = "#include \"" + part[HEADER] + "\"";
  // First, try to open existing files:
  ifstream existh(part[HEADER].c_str()),
           existcpp(part[IMPLEMENT].c_str());
  if(!existh) { // Doesn't exist; create it
    ofstream newheader(part[HEADER].c_str());
    assure(newheader, part[HEADER].c_str());
    newheader << part[HLINE1] << endl
              << part[GUARD1] << endl
              << part[GUARD2] << endl << endl
              << part[GUARD3] << endl;
  } else { // Already exists; verify it
    stringstream hfile; // Write & read
    ostringstream newheader; // Write
    hfile << existh.rdbuf();
    // Check that first three lines conform:
    bool changed = false;
    string s;
    hfile.seekg(0);
    getline(hfile, s);
    bool lineUsed = false;
    // The call to good() is for Microsoft (later too):
    for(int line = HLINE1; hfile.good() && line <= GUARD2;
        ++line) {
      if(startsWith(s, part[line])) {
        newheader << s << endl;
        lineUsed = true;
        if(getline(hfile, s))
          lineUsed = false;
      } else {
        newheader << part[line] << endl;
        changed = true;
        lineUsed = false;
      }
    }
    // Copy rest of file
    if(!lineUsed)
      newheader << s << endl;
```

```cpp
    newheader << hfile.rdbuf();
    // Check for GUARD3
    string head = hfile.str();
    if(head.find(part[GUARD3]) == string::npos) {
      newheader << part[GUARD3] << endl;
      changed = true;
    }
    // If there were changes, overwrite file:
    if(changed) {
      existh.close();
      ofstream newH(part[HEADER].c_str());
      assure(newH, part[HEADER].c_str());
      newH << "//@//\n"  // Change marker
           << newheader.str();
    }
  }
  if(!existcpp) { // Create cpp file
    ofstream newcpp(part[IMPLEMENT].c_str());
    assure(newcpp, part[IMPLEMENT].c_str());
    newcpp << part[CPPLINE1] << endl
           << part[INCLUDE] << endl;
  } else { // Already exists; verify it
    stringstream cppfile;
    ostringstream newcpp;
    cppfile << existcpp.rdbuf();
    // Check that first two lines conform:
    bool changed = false;
    string s;
    cppfile.seekg(0);
    getline(cppfile, s);
    bool lineUsed = false;
    for(int line = CPPLINE1;
        cppfile.good() && line <= INCLUDE; ++line) {
      if(startsWith(s, part[line])) {
        newcpp << s << endl;
        lineUsed = true;
        if(getline(cppfile, s))
          lineUsed = false;
      } else {
        newcpp << part[line] << endl;
        changed = true;
        lineUsed = false;
      }
    }
    // Copy rest of file
```

```
    if(!lineUsed)
      newcpp << s << endl;
    newcpp << cppfile.rdbuf();
    // If there were changes, overwrite file:
    if(changed) {
      existcpp.close();
      ofstream newCPP(part[IMPLEMENT].c_str());
      assure(newCPP, part[IMPLEMENT].c_str());
      newCPP << "//@//\n"  // Change marker
             << newcpp.str();
    }
  }
}

int main(int argc, char* argv[]) {
  if(argc > 1)
    cppCheck(argv[1]);
  else
    cppCheck("cppCheckTest.h");
} ///:~
```

First notice the useful function **startsWith( )**, which does just what its name says—it returns **true** if the first string argument starts with the second argument. This is used when looking for the expected comments and include-related statements. Having the array of strings, **part**, allows for easy looping through the series of expected statements in source code. If the source file doesn't exist, we merely write the statements to a new file of the given name. If the file does exist, we search a line at a time, verifying that the expected lines occur. If they are not present, they are inserted. Special care must be taken to make sure we don't drop existing lines (see where we use the Boolean variable **lineUsed**). Notice that we use a **stringstream** for an existing file, so we can first write the contents of the file to it and then read from and search it.

The names in the enumeration are **BASE**, the capitalized base file name without extension; **HEADER**, the header file name; **IMPLEMENT**, the implementation file (**cpp**) name; **HLINE1**, the skeleton first line of the header file; **GUARD1**, **GUARD2**, and **GUARD3**, the "guard" lines in the header file (to prevent multiple inclusion); **CPPLINE1**, the skeleton first line of the **cpp** file; and **INCLUDE**, the line in the **cpp** file that includes the header file.

If you run this program without any arguments, the following two files are created:

```
// CPPCHECKTEST.h
#ifndef CPPCHECKTEST_H
#define CPPCHECKTEST_H

#endif // CPPCHECKTEST_H
// CPPCHECKTEST.cpp
#include "CPPCHECKTEST.h"
```

(We removed the colon after the double-slash in the first comment lines so as not to confuse the book's code extractor. It will appear in the actual output produced by **cppCheck**.)

You can experiment by removing selected lines from these files and re-running the program. Each time you will see that the correct lines are added back in. When a file is modified, the string "//@//" is placed as the first line of the file to bring the change to your attention. You will need to remove this line before you process the file again (otherwise **cppcheck** will assume the initial comment line is missing).

Detecting compiler errors

All the code in this book is designed to compile as shown without errors. Lines of code that should generate a compile-time error may be commented out with the special comment sequence "//!". The following program will remove these special comments and append a numbered comment to the line. When you run your compiler, it should generate error messages, and you will see all the numbers appear when you compile all the files. This program also appends the modified line to a special file so that you can easily locate any lines that don't generate errors.

```
//: C04:Showerr.cpp {RunByHand}
// Un-comment error generators.
#include <cstddef>
#include <cstdlib>
#include <cstdio>
#include <fstream>
#include <iostream>
#include <sstream>
#include <string>
```

```cpp
#include "../require.h"
using namespace std;

const string USAGE =
  "usage: showerr filename chapnum\n"
  "where filename is a C++ source file\n"
  "and chapnum is the chapter name it's in.\n"
  "Finds lines commented with //! and removes\n"
  "the comment, appending //(#) where # is unique\n"
  "across all files, so you can determine\n"
  "if your compiler finds the error.\n"
  "showerr /r\n"
  "resets the unique counter.";

class Showerr {
  const int CHAP;
  const string MARKER, FNAME;
  // File containing error number counter:
  const string ERRNUM;
  // File containing error lines:
  const string ERRFILE;
  stringstream edited; // Edited file
  int counter;
public:
  Showerr(const string& f, const string& en,
    const string& ef, int c)
  : CHAP(c), MARKER("//!"), FNAME(f), ERRNUM(en),
    ERRFILE(ef), counter(0) {}
  void replaceErrors() {
    ifstream infile(FNAME.c_str());
    assure(infile, FNAME.c_str());
    ifstream count(ERRNUM.c_str());
    if(count) count >> counter;
    int linecount = 1;
    string buf;
    ofstream errlines(ERRFILE.c_str(), ios::app);
    assure(errlines, ERRFILE.c_str());
    while(getline(infile, buf)) {
      // Find marker at start of line:
      size_t pos = buf.find(MARKER);
      if(pos != string::npos) {
        // Erase marker:
        buf.erase(pos, MARKER.size() + 1);
        // Append counter & error info:
        ostringstream out;
```

```
          out << buf << " // (" << ++counter << ") "
              << "Chapter " << CHAP
              << " File: " << FNAME
              << " Line " << linecount << endl;
          edited << out.str();
          errlines << out.str(); // Append error file
        }
        else
          edited << buf << "\n"; // Just copy
        ++linecount;
      }
    }
  void saveFiles() {
    ofstream outfile(FNAME.c_str()); // Overwrites
    assure(outfile, FNAME.c_str());
    outfile << edited.rdbuf();
    ofstream count(ERRNUM.c_str()); // Overwrites
    assure(count, ERRNUM.c_str());
    count << counter; // Save new counter
  }
};

int main(int argc, char* argv[]) {
  const string ERRCOUNT("../errnum.txt"),
    ERRFILE("../errlines.txt");
  requireMinArgs(argc, 1, USAGE.c_str());
  if(argv[1][0] == '/' || argv[1][0] == '-') {
    // Allow for other switches:
    switch(argv[1][1]) {
      case 'r': case 'R':
        cout << "reset counter" << endl;
        remove(ERRCOUNT.c_str()); // Delete files
        remove(ERRFILE.c_str());
        return EXIT_SUCCESS;
      default:
        cerr << USAGE << endl;
        return EXIT_FAILURE;
    }
  }
  if(argc == 3) {
    Showerr s(argv[1], ERRCOUNT, ERRFILE, atoi(argv[2]));
    s.replaceErrors();
    s.saveFiles();
  }
} ///:~
```

You can replace the marker with one of your choice.

Each file is read a line at a time, and each line is searched for the marker appearing at the head of the line; the line is modified and put into the error line list and into the string stream, **edited**. When the whole file is processed, it is closed (by reaching the end of a scope), it is reopened as an output file, and **edited** is poured into the file. Also notice the counter is saved in an external file. The next time this program is invoked, it continues to increment the counter.

A simple data logger

This example shows an approach you might take to log data to disk and later retrieve it for processing. It is meant to produce a temperature-depth profile of the ocean at various points. The **DataPoint** class holds the data:

```
//: C04:DataLogger.h
// Datalogger record layout.
#ifndef DATALOG_H
#define DATALOG_H
#include <ctime>
#include <iosfwd>
#include <string>
using std::ostream;

struct Coord {
  int deg, min, sec;
  Coord(int d = 0, int m = 0, int s = 0)
  : deg(d), min(m), sec(s) {}
  std::string toString() const;
};

ostream& operator<<(ostream&, const Coord&);

class DataPoint {
  std::time_t timestamp; // Time & day
  Coord latitude, longitude;
  double depth, temperature;
public:
  DataPoint(std::time_t ts, const Coord& lat,
            const Coord& lon, double dep, double temp)
  : timestamp(ts), latitude(lat), longitude(lon),
      depth(dep), temperature(temp) {}
```

```
    DataPoint() : timestamp(0), depth(0), temperature(0) {}
    friend ostream& operator<<(ostream&, const DataPoint&);
};
#endif // DATALOG_H ///:~
```

A **DataPoint** consists of a time stamp, which is stored as a **time_t** value as defined in **<ctime>**, longitude and latitude coordinates, and values for depth and temperature. We use inserters for easy formatting. Here's the implementation file:

```
//: C04:DataLogger.cpp {O}
// Datapoint implementations.
#include "DataLogger.h"
#include <iomanip>
#include <iostream>
#include <sstream>
#include <string>
using namespace std;

ostream& operator<<(ostream& os, const Coord& c) {
  return os << c.deg << '*' << c.min << '\''
            << c.sec << '"';
}

string Coord::toString() const {
  ostringstream os;
  os << *this;
  return os.str();
}

ostream& operator<<(ostream& os, const DataPoint& d) {
  os.setf(ios::fixed, ios::floatfield);
  char fillc = os.fill('0'); // Pad on left with '0'
  tm* tdata = localtime(&d.timestamp);
  os << setw(2) << tdata->tm_mon + 1 << '\\'
     << setw(2) << tdata->tm_mday << '\\'
     << setw(2) << tdata->tm_year+1900 << ' '
     << setw(2) << tdata->tm_hour << ':'
     << setw(2) << tdata->tm_min << ':'
     << setw(2) << tdata->tm_sec;
  os.fill(' '); // Pad on left with ' '
  streamsize prec = os.precision(4);
  os << " Lat:"   << setw(9) << d.latitude.toString()
     << ", Long:" << setw(9) << d.longitude.toString()
```

```
       << ", depth:" << setw(9) << d.depth
       << ", temp:"  << setw(9) << d.temperature;
  os.fill(fillc);
  os.precision(prec);
  return os;
} ///:~
```

The **Coord::toString( )** function is necessary because the **DataPoint**
inserter calls **setw( )** before it prints the latitude and longitude. If we used
the stream inserter for **Coord** instead, the width would only apply to the first
insertion (that is, to **Coord::deg**), since width changes are always reset
immediately. The call to **setf( )** causes the floating-point output to be fixed-
precision, and **precision( )** sets the number of decimal places to four. Notice
how we restore the fill character and precision to whatever they were before
the inserter was called.

To get the values from the time encoding stored in **DataPoint::timestamp**,
we call the function **std::localtime( )**, which returns a static pointer to a **tm**
object. The **tm struct** has the following layout:

```
struct tm {
  int tm_sec; // 0-59 seconds
  int tm_min; // 0-59 minutes
  int tm_hour; // 0-23 hours
  int tm_mday; // Day of month
  int tm_mon; // 0-11 months
  int tm_year; // Years since 1900
  int tm_wday; // Sunday == 0, etc.
  int tm_yday; // 0-365 day of year
  int tm_isdst; // Daylight savings?
};
```

Generating test data

Here's a program that creates a file of test data in binary form (using
write( )) and a second file in ASCII form using the **DataPoint** inserter. You
can also print it out to the screen, but it's easier to inspect in file form.

```
//: C04:Datagen.cpp
// Test data generator.
//{L} DataLogger
#include <cstdlib>
#include <ctime>
#include <cstring>
```

```
#include <fstream>
#include "DataLogger.h"
#include "../require.h"
using namespace std;

int main() {
  time_t timer;
  srand(time(&timer)); // Seed the random number generator
  ofstream data("data.txt");
  assure(data, "data.txt");
  ofstream bindata("data.bin", ios::binary);
  assure(bindata, "data.bin");
  for(int i = 0; i < 100; i++, timer += 55) {
    // Zero to 199 meters:
    double newdepth  = rand() % 200;
    double fraction = rand() % 100 + 1;
    newdepth += 1.0 / fraction;
    double newtemp = 150 + rand() % 200; // Kelvin
    fraction = rand() % 100 + 1;
    newtemp += 1.0 / fraction;
    const DataPoint d(timer, Coord(45,20,31),
                      Coord(22,34,18), newdepth,
                      newtemp);
    data << d << endl;
    bindata.write(reinterpret_cast<const char*>(&d),
                  sizeof(d));
  }
} ///:~
```

The file **data.txt** is created in the ordinary way as an ASCII file, but **data.bin** has the flag **ios::binary** to tell the constructor to set it up as a binary file. To illustrate the formatting used for the text file, here is the first line of **data.txt** (the line wraps because it's longer than this page will allow):

```
07\28\2003 12:54:40 Lat:45*20'31", Long:22*34'18", depth:
16.0164, temp: 242.0122
```

The Standard C library function **time( )** updates the **time_t** value its argument points to with an encoding of the current time, which on most platforms is the number of seconds elapsed since 00: 00: 00 GMT, January 1 1970 (the dawning of the age of Aquarius?). The current time is also a convenient way to seed the random number generator with the Standard C library function **srand( )**, as is done here.

After this, the **timer** is incremented by 55 seconds to give an interesting interval between readings in this simulation.

The latitude and longitude used are fixed values to indicate a set of readings at a single location. Both the depth and the temperature are generated with the Standard C library **rand( )** function, which returns a pseudorandom number between zero and a platform-dependent constant, **RAND_MAX**, defined in **<cstdlib>** (usually the value of the platform's largest unsigned integer). To put this in a desired range, use the remainder operator **%** and the upper end of the range. These numbers are integral; to add a fractional part, a second call to **rand( )** is made, and the value is inverted after adding one (to prevent divide-by-zero errors).

In effect, the **data.bin** file is being used as a container for the data in the program, even though the container exists on disk and not in RAM. **write( )** sends the data out to the disk in binary form. The first argument is the starting address of the source block—notice it must be cast to a **char*** because that's what **write( )** expects for narrow streams. The second argument is the number of characters to write, which in this case is the size of the **DataPoint** object (again, because we're using *narrow streams*). Because no pointers are contained in **DataPoint**, there is no problem in writing the object to disk. If the object is more sophisticated, you must implement a scheme for *serialization*, which writes the data referred to by pointers and defines new pointers when read back in later. (We don't talk about serialization in this volume—most vendor class libraries have some sort of serialization structure built into them.)

Verifying and viewing the data

To check the validity of the data stored in binary format, you can read it into memory with the **read( )** member function for input streams, and compare it to the text file created earlier by **Datagen.cpp**. The following example just writes the formatted results to **cout**, but you can redirect this to a file and then use a file comparison utility to verify that it is identical to the original:

```
//: C04:Datascan.cpp
//{L} DataLogger
#include <fstream>
#include <iostream>
#include "DataLogger.h"
#include "../require.h"
using namespace std;
```

Exercises

Solutions to selected exercises can be found in the electronic document *The Thinking in C++ Volume 2 Annotated Solution Guide*, available for a small fee from *www.MindView.net*.

1. Open a file by creating an **ifstream** object. Make an **ostringstream** object and read the entire contents into the **ostringstream** using the **rdbuf( )** member function. Extract a **string** copy of the underlying buffer and capitalize every character in the file using the Standard C **toupper( )** macro defined in **<cctype>**. Write the result out to a new file.

2. Create a program that opens a file (the first argument on the command line) and searches it for any one of a set of words (the remaining arguments on the command line). Read the input a line at a time, and write out the lines (with line numbers) that match to the new file.

3. Write a program that adds a copyright notice to the beginning of all source-code files indicated by the program's command-line arguments.

4. Use your favorite text-searching program (**grep**, for example) to output the names (only) of all the files that contain a particular pattern. Redirect the output into a file. Write a program that uses the contents of that file to generate a batch file that invokes your editor on each of the files found by the search program.

5. We know that **setw( )** allows for a minimum of characters read in, but what if you wanted to read a maximum? Write an effector that allows the user to specify a maximum number of characters to extract. Have your effector also work for output, in such a way that output fields are truncated, if necessary, to stay within width limits.

6. Demonstrate to yourself that if the fail or bad bit is set, and you subsequently turn on stream exceptions, that the stream will immediately throw an exception.

7. String streams accommodate easy conversions, but they come with a price. Write a program that races **atoi( )** against the **stringstream** conversion system to see the effect of the overhead involved with **stringstream**.

8. Make a **Person** struct with fields such as name, age, address, etc. Make the string fields fixed-size arrays. The social security number

will be the key for each record. Implement the following **Database** class:

```
class DataBase {
public:
  // Find where a record is on disk
  size_t query(size_t ssn);
  // Return the person at rn (record number)
  Person retrieve(size_t rn);
  // Record a record on disk
  void add(const Person& p);
};
```

Write some **Person** records to disk (do not keep them all in memory). When the user requests a record, read it off the disk and return it. The I/O operations in the **DataBase** class use **read( )** and **write( )** to process all **Person** records.

9. Write an **operator<<** inserter for the **Person** struct that can be used to display records in a format for easy reading. Demonstrate it by writing data out to a file.

10. Suppose the database for your **Person** structs was lost but that you have the file you wrote from the previous exercise. Recreate your database using this file. Be sure to use error checking.

11. Write **size_t(-1)** (the largest **unsigned int** on your platform) to a text file 1,000,000 times. Repeat, but write to a binary file. Compare the size of the two files, and see how much room is saved using the binary format. (You may first want to calculate how much will be saved on your platform.)

12. Discover the maximum number of digits of precision your implementation of iostreams will print by repeatedly increasing the value of the argument to **precision( )** when printing a transcendental number such as **sqrt(2.0)**.

13. Write a program that reads real numbers from a file and prints their sum, average, minimum, and maximum.

14. Determine the output of the following program before it is executed:

```
//: C04:Exercise14.cpp
#include <fstream>
#include <iostream>
#include <sstream>
#include "../require.h"
```

4: Iostreams   223

independent of the type of objects being held. For this reason you can use a type parameter to represent the contained type:

```
template<class T> class Stack {
  T* data;
  size_t count;
public:
  void push(const T& t);
  // Etc.
};
```

The actual type to be used for a particular **Stack** instance is determined by the argument for the parameter **T**:

```
Stack<int> myStack;  // A Stack of ints
```

The compiler then provides an **int**-version of **Stack** by substituting **int** for **T** and generating the corresponding code. The name of the class instance generated from the template in this case is **Stack<int>**.

Non–type template parameters

A non-type template parameter must be an integral value that is known at compile time. You can make a fixed-size **Stack**, for instance, by specifying a non-type parameter to be used as the dimension for the underlying array, as follows.

```
template<class T, size_t N> class Stack {
  T data[N];  // Fixed capacity is N
  size_t count;
public:
  void push(const T& t);
  // Etc.
};
```

You must provide a compile-time constant value for the parameter **N** when you request an instance of this template, such as

```
Stack<int, 100> myFixedStack;
```

Because the value of **N** is known at compile time, the underlying array (**data**) can be placed on the runtime stack instead of on the free store. This can improve runtime performance by avoiding the overhead associated with dynamic memory allocation. Following the pattern mentioned earlier, the name of the class above is **Stack<int, 100>**. This means that each distinct value of **N** results in a unique class type. For example, **Stack<int, 99>** is a distinct class from **Stack<int, 100>**.

The **bitset** class template, discussed in detail in Chapter 7, is the only class in the Standard C++ library that uses a non-type template parameter (which specifies the number of bits the **bitset** object can hold). The following random number generator example uses a **bitset** to track numbers so all the numbers in its range are returned in random order without repetition before starting over. This example also overloads **operator( )** to produce a familiar function-call syntax.

```
//: C05:Urand.h {-bor}
// Unique randomizer.
#ifndef URAND_H
#define URAND_H
#include <bitset>
#include <cstddef>
#include <cstdlib>
#include <ctime>
using std::size_t;
using std::bitset;

template<size_t UpperBound> class Urand {
  bitset<UpperBound> used;
public:
  Urand() { srand(time(0)); } // Randomize
  size_t operator()(); // The "generator" function
};

template<size_t UpperBound>
inline size_t Urand<UpperBound>::operator()() {
  if(used.count() == UpperBound)
    used.reset();  // Start over (clear bitset)
  size_t newval;
  while(used[newval = rand() % UpperBound])
    ; // Until unique value is found
  used[newval] = true;
  return newval;
}
#endif // URAND_H ///:~
```

The numbers generated by **Urand** are unique because the **bitset used** tracks all the possible numbers in the random space (the upper bound is set with the template argument) and records each used number by setting the corresponding position bit. When the numbers are all used up, the **bitset** is cleared to start over. Here's a simple driver that illustrates how to use a **Urand** object:

```
//: C05:UrandTest.cpp {-bor}
#include <iostream>
#include "Urand.h"
using namespace std;

int main() {
  Urand<10> u;
  for(int i = 0; i < 20; ++i)
    cout << u() << ' ';
} ///:~
```

As we explain later in this chapter, non-type template arguments are also important in the optimization of numeric computations.

Default template arguments

You can provide default arguments for template parameters in class templates, but not function templates. As with default function arguments, they should only be defined once, the first time a template declaration or definition is seen by the compiler. Once you introduce a default argument, all the subsequent template parameters must also have defaults. To make the fixed-size **Stack** template shown earlier a little friendlier, for example, you can add a default argument like this:

```
template<class T, size_t N = 100> class Stack {
  T data[N];  // Fixed capacity is N
  size_t count;
public:
  void push(const T& t);
  // Etc.
};
```

Now, if you omit the second template argument when declaring a **Stack** object, the value for **N** will default to 100.

You can choose to provide defaults for all arguments, but you must use an empty set of brackets when declaring an instance so that the compiler knows that a class template is involved:

```
template<class T = int, size_t N = 100>  // Both defaulted
class Stack {
  T data[N];  // Fixed capacity is N
  size_t count;
public:
  void push(const T& t);
  // Etc.
};

Stack<> myStack;  // Same as Stack<int, 100>
```

Default arguments are used heavily in the Standard C++ library. The **vector** class template, for instance, is declared as follows:

```
template<class T, class Allocator = allocator<T> >
class vector;
```

Note the space between the last two right angle bracket characters. This prevents the compiler from interpreting those two characters (>>) as the right-shift operator.

This declaration reveals that **vector** takes two arguments: the type of the contained objects it holds, and a type that represents the allocator used by the **vector**. Whenever you omit the second argument, the standard **allocator** template is used, parameterized by the first template parameter. This declaration also shows that you can use template parameters in subsequent template parameters, as **T** is used here.

Although you cannot use default template arguments in function templates, you can use template parameters as default arguments to normal functions. The following function template adds the elements in a sequence:

```
//: C05:FuncDef.cpp
#include <iostream>
using namespace std;

template<class T> T sum(T* b, T* e, T init = T()) {
  while(b != e)
    init += *b++;
```

```
    return init;
}

int main() {
  int a[] = { 1, 2, 3 };
  cout << sum(a, a + sizeof a / sizeof a[0]) << endl; // 6
} ///:~
```

The third argument to **sum( )** is the initial value for the accumulation of the elements. Since we omitted it, this argument defaults to **T( )**, which in the case of **int** and other built-in types invokes a pseudo-constructor that performs zero-initialization.

Template template parameters

The third type of parameter a template can accept is another class template. If you are going to use a template type parameter itself as a template in your code, the compiler needs to know that the parameter is a template in the first place. The following example illustrates a template template parameter:

```
//: C05:TempTemp.cpp
// Illustrates a template template parameter.
#include <cstddef>
#include <iostream>
using namespace std;

template<class T>
class Array { // A simple, expandable sequence
  enum { INIT = 10 };
  T* data;
  size_t capacity;
  size_t count;
public:
  Array() {
    count = 0;
    data = new T[capacity = INIT];
  }
  ~Array() { delete [] data; }
  void push_back(const T& t) {
    if(count == capacity) {
      // Grow underlying array
      size_t newCap = 2 * capacity;
      T* newData = new T[newCap];
      for(size_t i = 0; i < count; ++i)
```

```
        newData[i] = data[i];
      delete [] data;
      data = newData;
      capacity = newCap;
    }
    data[count++] = t;
  }
  void pop_back() {
    if(count > 0)
      --count;
  }
  T* begin() { return data; }
  T* end() { return data + count; }
};

template<class T, template<class> class Seq>
class Container {
  Seq<T> seq;
public:
  void append(const T& t) { seq.push_back(t); }
  T* begin() { return seq.begin(); }
  T* end() { return seq.end(); }
};

int main() {
  Container<int, Array> container;
  container.append(1);
  container.append(2);
  int* p = container.begin();
  while(p != container.end())
    cout << *p++ << endl;
} ///:~
```

The **Array** class template is a trivial sequence container. The **Container** template takes two parameters: the type that it holds, and a sequence data structure to do the holding. The following line in the implementation of the **Container** class requires that we inform the compiler that **Seq** is a template:

```
  Seq<T> seq;
```

If we hadn't declared **Seq** to be a template template parameter, the compiler would complain here that **Seq** is not a template, since we're using it as such. In **main( )** a **Container** is instantiated to use an **Array** to hold integers, so **Seq** stands for **Array** in this example.

Note that it is not necessary in this case to name the parameter for **Seq** inside **Container**'s declaration. The line in question is:

```
template<class T, template<class> class Seq>
```

Although we could have written

```
template<class T, template<class U> class Seq>
```

the parameter **U** is not needed anywhere. All that matters is that **Seq** is a class template that takes a single type parameter. This is analogous to omitting the names of function parameters when they're not needed, such as when you overload the post-increment operator:

```
T operator++(int);
```

The **int** here is merely a placeholder and so needs no name.

The following program uses a fixed-size array, which has an extra template parameter representing the array length:

```
//: C05:TempTemp2.cpp
// A multi-variate template template parameter.
#include <cstddef>
#include <iostream>
using namespace std;

template<class T, size_t N> class Array {
  T data[N];
  size_t count;
public:
  Array() { count = 0; }
  void push_back(const T& t) {
    if(count < N)
      data[count++] = t;
  }
  void pop_back() {
    if(count > 0)
      --count;
  }
  T* begin() { return data; }
  T* end() { return data + count; }
};
```

```
template<class T,size_t N,template<class,size_t> class Seq>
class Container {
  Seq<T,N> seq;
public:
  void append(const T& t) { seq.push_back(t); }
  T* begin() { return seq.begin(); }
  T* end() { return seq.end(); }
};

int main() {
  const size_t N = 10;
  Container<int, N, Array> container;
  container.append(1);
  container.append(2);
  int* p = container.begin();
  while(p != container.end())
    cout << *p++ << endl;
} ///:~
```

Once again, parameter names are not needed in the declaration of **Seq** inside **Container**'s declaration, but we need two parameters to declare the data member **seq**, hence the appearance of the non-type parameter **N** at the top level.

Combining default arguments with template template parameters is slightly more problematic. When the compiler looks at the inner parameters of a template template parameter, default arguments are not considered, so you have to repeat the defaults in order to get an exact match. The following example uses a default argument for the fixed-size **Array** template and shows how to accommodate this quirk in the language:

```
//: C05:TempTemp3.cpp {-bor}{-msc}
// Template template parameters and default arguments.
#include <cstddef>
#include <iostream>
using namespace std;

template<class T, size_t N = 10>  // A default argument
class Array {
  T data[N];
  size_t count;
public:
  Array() { count = 0; }
  void push_back(const T& t) {
```

```
    if(count < N)
      data[count++] = t;
  }
  void pop_back() {
    if(count > 0)
      --count;
  }
  T* begin() { return data; }
  T* end() { return data + count; }
};

template<class T, template<class, size_t = 10> class Seq>
class Container {
  Seq<T> seq;  // Default used
public:
  void append(const T& t) { seq.push_back(t); }
  T* begin() { return seq.begin(); }
  T* end() { return seq.end(); }
};

int main() {
  Container<int, Array> container;
  container.append(1);
  container.append(2);
  int* p = container.begin();
  while(p != container.end())
    cout << *p++ << endl;
} ///:~
```

The default dimension of 10 is required in the line:

```
template<class T, template<class, size_t = 10> class Seq>
```

Both the definition of **seq** in **Container** and **container** in **main( )** use the default. The only way to use something other than the default value was shown in **TempTemp2.cpp**. This is the only exception to the rule stated earlier that default arguments should appear only once in a compilation unit.

Since the standard sequence containers (**vector, list**, and **deque**, discussed in depth in Chapter 7) have a default allocator argument, the technique shown above is helpful should you ever want to pass one of these sequences as a template parameter. The following program passes a **vector** and then a **list** to two instances of **Container**:

```
//: C05:TempTemp4.cpp {-bor}{-msc}
// Passes standard sequences as template arguments.
#include <iostream>
#include <list>
#include <memory>  // Declares allocator<T>
#include <vector>
using namespace std;

template<class T, template<class U, class = allocator<U> >
         class Seq>
class Container {
  Seq<T> seq; // Default of allocator<T> applied implicitly
public:
  void push_back(const T& t) { seq.push_back(t); }
  typename Seq<T>::iterator begin() { return seq.begin(); }
  typename Seq<T>::iterator end() { return seq.end(); }
};

int main() {
  // Use a vector
  Container<int, vector> vContainer;
  vContainer.push_back(1);
  vContainer.push_back(2);
  for(vector<int>::iterator p = vContainer.begin();
      p != vContainer.end(); ++p) {
    cout << *p << endl;
  }
  // Use a list
  Container<int, list> lContainer;
  lContainer.push_back(3);
  lContainer.push_back(4);
  for(list<int>::iterator p2 = lContainer.begin();
      p2 != lContainer.end(); ++p2) {
    cout << *p2 << endl;
  }
} ///:~
```

Here we name the first parameter of the inner template **Seq** (with the name
U) because the allocators in the standard sequences must themselves be
parameterized with the same type as the contained objects in the sequence.
Also, since the default **allocator** parameter is known, we can omit it in the
subsequent references to **Seq<T>**, as we did in the previous program. To
fully explain this example, however, we have to discuss the semantics of the
typename keyword.

The typename keyword

Consider the following:

```
//: C05:TypenamedID.cpp {-bor}
// Uses 'typename' as a prefix for nested types.

template<class T> class X {
  // Without typename, you should get an error:
  typename T::id i;
public:
  void f() { i.g(); }
};

class Y {
public:
  class id {
  public:
    void g() {}
  };
};

int main() {
  X<Y> xy;
  xy.f();
} ///:~
```

The template definition assumes that the class **T** that you hand it must have a nested identifier of some kind called **id**. Yet **id** could also be a static data member of **T**, in which case you can perform operations on **id** directly, but you can't "create an object" of "the type **id**." In this example, the identifier **id** is being treated as if it were a nested type inside **T**. In the case of class **Y**, **id** is in fact a nested type, but (without the **typename** keyword) the compiler can't know that when it's compiling **X**.

If the compiler has the option of treating an identifier as a type or as something other than a type when it sees an identifier in a template, it will assume that the identifier refers to something other than a type. That is, it will assume that the identifier refers to an object (including variables of primitive types), an enumeration, or something similar. However, it will not—cannot—just assume that it is a type.

Because the default behavior of the compiler is to assume that a name that fits the above two points is not a type, you must use **typename** for nested names (except in constructor initializer lists, where it is neither needed nor allowed). In the above example, when the compiler sees **typename T::id**, it knows (because of the **typename** keyword) that **id** refers to a nested type and thus it can create an object of that type.

The short version of the rule is: if a type referred to inside template code is qualified by a template type parameter, you must use the **typename** keyword as a prefix, unless it appears in a base class specification or initializer list in the same scope (in which case you must not).

The above explains the use of the **typename** keyword in the program **TempTemp4.cpp**. Without it, the compiler would assume that the expression **Seq<T>::iterator** is not a type, but we were using it to define the return type of the **begin( )** and **end( )** member functions.

The following example, which defines a function template that can print any Standard C++ sequence, shows a similar use of **typename**:

```
//: C05:PrintSeq.cpp {-msc}{-mwcc}
// A print function for Standard C++ sequences.
#include <iostream>
#include <list>
#include <memory>
#include <vector>
using namespace std;

template<class T, template<class U, class = allocator<U> >
        class Seq>
void printSeq(Seq<T>& seq) {
  for(typename Seq<T>::iterator b = seq.begin();
      b != seq.end();)
    cout << *b++ << endl;
}

int main() {
  // Process a vector
  vector<int> v;
  v.push_back(1);
  v.push_back(2);
  printSeq(v);
  // Process a list
```

```
    list<int> lst;
    lst.push_back(3);
    lst.push_back(4);
    printSeq(lst);
} ///:~
```

Once again, without the **typename** keyword the compiler will interpret
iterator as a static data member of **Seq<T>**, which is a syntax error, since a
type is required.

Typedefing a typename

It's important not to assume that the **typename** keyword creates a new type
name. It doesn't. Its purpose is to inform the compiler that the qualified
identifier is to be interpreted as a type. A line that reads:

```
typename Seq<T>::iterator It;
```

causes a variable named **It** to be declared of type **Seq<T>::iterator**. If you
mean to create a new type name, you should use **typedef**, as usual, as in:

```
typedef typename Seq<It>::iterator It;
```

Using typename instead of class

Another role of the **typename** keyword is to provide you the option of using
typename instead of **class** in the template argument list of a template
definition:

```
//: C05:UsingTypename.cpp
// Using 'typename' in the template argument list.

template<typename T> class X {};

int main() {
  X<int> x;
} ///:~
```

To some, this produces clearer code.

Using the template keyword as a hint

Just as the **typename** keyword helps the compiler when a type identifier is
not expected, there is also a potential difficulty with tokens that are not
identifiers, such as the < and > characters. Sometimes these represent the

less-than or greater-than symbols, and sometimes they delimit template parameter lists. As an example, we'll once more use the **bitset** class:

```
//: C05:DotTemplate.cpp
// Illustrate the .template construct.
#include <bitset>
#include <cstddef>
#include <iostream>
#include <string>
using namespace std;

template<class charT, size_t N>
basic_string<charT> bitsetToString(const bitset<N>& bs) {
  return bs. template to_string<charT, char_traits<charT>,
                              allocator<charT> >();
}

int main() {
  bitset<10> bs;
  bs.set(1);
  bs.set(5);
  cout << bs << endl; // 0000100010
  string s = bitsetToString<char>(bs);
  cout << s << endl;  // 0000100010
} ///:~
```

The **bitset** class supports conversion to string object via its **to_string** member function. To support multiple string classes, **to_string** is itself a template, following the pattern established by the **basic_string** template discussed in Chapter 3. The declaration of **to_string** inside of **bitset** looks like this:

```
template<class charT, class traits, class Allocator>
basic_string<charT, traits, Allocator> to_string() const;
```

Our **bitsetToString( )** function template above requests different types of string representations of a **bitset**. To get a wide string, for instance, you change the call to the following:

```
  wstring s = bitsetToString<wchar_t>(bs);
```

Note that **basic_string** uses default template arguments, so we don't need to repeat the **char_traits** and **allocator** arguments in the return value. Unfortunately, **bitset::to_string** does not use default arguments. Using

---

bitsetToString<char>(bs) is more convenient than typing a fully-qualified call to **bs.template to_string<char, char_traits, allocator<char> >( )** every time.

The return statement in **bitsetToString( )** contains the **template** keyword in an odd place—right after the dot operator applied to the **bitset** object **bs**. This is because when the template is parsed, the < character after the **to_string** token would be interpreted as a less-than operation instead of the beginning of a template argument list. The **template** keyword used in this context tells the compiler that what follows is the name of a template, causing the < character to be interpreted correctly. The same reasoning applies to the -> and ::operators when applied to templates. As with the **typename** keyword, this template disambiguation technique can only be used within template code.[2]

Member Templates

The **bitset::to_string( )** function template is an example of a *member template*: a template declared within another class or class template. This allows many combinations of independent template arguments to be combined. A useful example is found in the **complex** class template in the Standard C++ library. The **complex** template has a type parameter meant to represent an underlying floating-point type to hold the real and imaginary parts of a complex number. The following code snippet from the standard library shows a member-template constructor in the **complex** class template:

```
template<typename T> class complex {
public:
    template<class X> complex(const complex<X>&);
```

The standard **complex** template comes ready-made with specializations that use **float**, **double**, and **long double** for the parameter **T**. The member-template constructor above creates a new complex number that uses a different floating-point type as its base type, as seen in the code below:

---

[2] The C++ Standards Committee is considering relaxing the only–within–a–template rule for these disambiguation hints, and some compilers allow them in non–template code already.

```
complex<float> z(1, 2);
complex<double> w(z);
```

In the declaration of **w**, the **complex** template parameter **T** is **double** and **X** is **float**. Member templates make this kind of flexible conversion easy.

Defining a template within a template is a nesting operation, so the prefixes that introduce the templates must reflect this nesting if you define the member template outside the outer class definition. For example, if you implement the **complex** class template, and if you define the member-template constructor outside the **complex** template class definition, you do it like this:

```
template<typename T>
template<typename X>
complex<T>::complex(const complex<X>& c) {/* Body here… */}
```

Another use of member function templates in the standard library is in the initialization of containers. Suppose we have a **vector** of **int**s and we want to initialize a new **vector** of **doubles** with it, like this:

```
int data[5] = { 1, 2, 3, 4, 5 };
vector<int> v1(data, data+5);
vector<double> v2(v1.begin(), v1.end());
```

As long as the elements in **v1** are assignment-compatible with the elements in **v2** (as **double** and **int** are here), all is well. The **vector** class template has the following member template constructor:

```
template<class InputIterator>
vector(InputIterator first, InputIterator last,
       const Allocator& = Allocator());
```

This constructor is used twice in the **vector** declarations above. When **v1** is initialized from the array of **int**s, the type **InputIterator** is **int***. When **v2** is initialized from **v1**, an instance of the member template constructor is used with **InputIterator** representing **vector<int>::iterator**.

Member templates can also be classes. (They don't need to be functions.) The following example shows a member class template inside an outer class template:

```
//: C05:MemberClass.cpp
```

```
// A member class template.
#include <iostream>
#include <typeinfo>
using namespace std;

template<class T> class Outer {
public:
  template<class R> class Inner {
  public:
    void f();
  };
};

template<class T> template<class R>
void Outer<T>::Inner<R>::f() {
  cout << "Outer == " << typeid(T).name() << endl;
  cout << "Inner == " << typeid(R).name() << endl;
  cout << "Full Inner == " << typeid(*this).name() << endl;
}

int main() {
  Outer<int>::Inner<bool> inner;
  inner.f();
} ///:~
```

The **typeid** operator, covered in Chapter 8, takes a single argument and
returns a **type_info** object whose **name( )** function yields a string
representing the argument type. For example, **typeid(int).name( )** might
return the string "**int**." (The actual string is platform-dependent.) The **typeid**
operator can also take an expression and return a **type_info** object
representing the type of that expression. For example, with **int i**,
typeid(i).name( ) returns something like "**int**," and **typeid(&i).name( )**
returns something like "**int ***."

The output of the program above should be something like this:

```
Outer == int
Inner == bool
Full Inner == Outer<int>::Inner<bool>
```

The declaration of the variable **inner** in the main program instantiates both
Inner<bool> and **Outer<int>**.

Member template functions cannot be declared **virtual**. Current compiler technology expects to be able to determine the size of a class's virtual function table when the class is parsed. Allowing virtual member template functions would require knowing all calls to such member functions everywhere in the program ahead of time. This is not feasible, especially for multi-file projects.

Function template issues

Just as a class template describes a family of classes, a function template describes a family of functions. The syntax for creating either type of template is virtually identical, but they differ somewhat in how they are used. You must always use angle brackets when instantiating class templates and you must supply all non-default template arguments. However, with function templates you can often omit the template arguments, and default template arguments are not even allowed. Consider a typical implementation of the **min( )** function template declared in the **<algorithm>** header, which looks something like this:

```
template<typename T> const T& min(const T& a, const T& b) {
  return (a < b) ? a : b;
}
```

You could invoke this template by providing the type of the arguments in angle brackets, just like you do with class templates, as in:

```
int z = min<int>(i, j);
```

This syntax tells the compiler that a specialization of the **min( )** template is needed with **int** used in place of the parameter **T**, whereupon the compiler generates the corresponding code. Following the pattern of naming the classes generated from class templates, you can think of the name of the instantiated function as **min<int>( )**.

Type deduction of function template arguments

You can always use such explicit function template specification as in the example above, but it is often convenient to leave off the template arguments and let the compiler deduce them from the function arguments, like this:

```
int z = min(i, j);
```

If both **i** and **j** are **int**s, the compiler knows that you need **min<int>( )**, which it then instantiates automatically. The types must be identical because the template was originally specified with only one template type argument used for both function parameters. No standard conversions are applied for function arguments whose type is specified by a template parameter. For example, if you wanted to find the minimum of an **int** and a **double**, the following attempt at a call to **min( )** would fail:

```
int z = min(x, j); // x is a double
```

Since **x** and **j** are distinct types, no single parameter matches the template parameter **T** in the definition of **min( )**, so the call does not match the template declaration. You can work around this difficulty by casting one argument to the other's type or by reverting to the fully-specified call syntax, as in:

```
int z = min<double>(x, j);
```

This tells the compiler to generate the **double** version of **min( )**, after which **j** can be promoted to a **double** by normal standard conversion rules (because the function **min<double>(const double&, const double&)** would then exist).

You might be tempted to require two parameters for **min( )**, allowing the types of the arguments to be independent, like this:

```
template<typename T, typename U>
const T& min(const T& a, const U& b) {
  return (a < b) ? a : b;
}
```

This is often a good strategy, but here it is problematic because **min( )** must return a value, and there is no satisfactory way to determine which type it should be (**T** or **U**?).

If the return type of a function template is an independent template parameter, you must always specify its type explicitly when you call it, since there is no argument from which to deduce it. Such is the case with the **fromString** template below.

```
//: C05:StringConv.h
// Function templates to convert to and from strings.
```

```
#ifndef STRINGCONV_H
#define STRINGCONV_H
#include <string>
#include <sstream>

template<typename T> T fromString(const std::string& s) {
  std::istringstream is(s);
  T t;
  is >> t;
  return t;
}

template<typename T> std::string toString(const T& t) {
  std::ostringstream s;
  s << t;
  return s.str();
}
#endif // STRINGCONV_H ///:~
```

These function templates provide conversions to and from **std::string** for any types that provide a stream inserter or extractor, respectively. Here's a test program that includes the use of the standard library **complex** number type:

```
//: C05:StringConvTest.cpp
#include <complex>
#include <iostream>
#include "StringConv.h"
using namespace std;

int main() {
  int i = 1234;
  cout << "i == \"" << toString(i) << "\"" << endl;
  float x = 567.89;
  cout << "x == \"" << toString(x) << "\"" << endl;
  complex<float> c(1.0, 2.0);
  cout << "c == \"" << toString(c) << "\"" << endl;
  cout << endl;

  i = fromString<int>(string("1234"));
  cout << "i == " << i << endl;
  x = fromString<float>(string("567.89"));
  cout << "x == " << x << endl;
  c = fromString<complex<float> >(string("(1.0,2.0)"));
```

```
    cout << "c == " << c << endl;
} ///:~
```

The output is what you'd expect:

```
i == "1234"
x == "567.89"
c == "(1,2)"

i == 1234
x == 567.89
c == (1,2)
```

Notice that in each of the instantiations of **fromString( )**, the template parameter is specified in the call. If you have a function template with template parameters for the parameter types as well as the return types, it is important to declare the return type parameter first, otherwise you won't be able to omit the type parameters for the function parameters. As an illustration, consider the following well-known function template:[3]

```
//: C05:ImplicitCast.cpp

template<typename R, typename P>
R implicit_cast(const P& p) {
  return p;
}

int main() {
  int i = 1;
  float x = implicit_cast<float>(i);
  int j = implicit_cast<int>(x);
  //! char* p = implicit_cast<char*>(i);
} ///:~
```

If you interchange **R** and **P** in the template parameter list near the top of the file, it will be impossible to compile this program because the return type will remain unspecified (the first template parameter would be the function's parameter type). The last line (which is commented out) is illegal because

---

[3] See Stroustrup, *The C++ Programming Language*, 3rd Edition, Addison Wesley, pp. 335–336.

there is no standard conversion from **int** to **char***. **implicit_cast** is for revealing conversions in your code that are allowed naturally.

With a little care you can even deduce array dimensions. This example has an array-initialization function template (**init2**) that performs such a deduction:

```
//: C05:ArraySize.cpp
#include <cstddef>
using std::size_t;

template<size_t R, size_t C, typename T>
void init1(T a[R][C]) {
  for(size_t i = 0; i < R; ++i)
    for(size_t j = 0; j < C; ++j)
      a[i][j] = T();
}

template<size_t R, size_t C, class T>
void init2(T (&a)[R][C]) {  // Reference parameter
  for(size_t i = 0; i < R; ++i)
    for(size_t j = 0; j < C; ++j)
      a[i][j] = T();
}

int main() {
  int a[10][20];
  init1<10,20>(a);  // Must specify
  init2(a);         // Sizes deduced
} ///:~
```

Array dimensions are not passed as part of a function parameter's type unless that parameter is passed by pointer or reference. The function template **init2** declares **a** to be a reference to a two-dimensional array, so its dimensions **R** and **C** are deduced by the template facility, making **init2** a handy way to initialize a two-dimensional array of any size. The template **init1** does not pass the array by reference, so the sizes must be explicitly specified, although the type parameter can still be deduced.

Function template overloading

As with ordinary functions, you can overload function templates that have the same name. When the compiler processes a function call in a program, it has to decide which template or ordinary function is the "best" fit for the call.

Along with the **min( )** function template introduced earlier, let's add some ordinary functions to the mix:

```
//: C05:MinTest.cpp
#include <cstring>
#include <iostream>
using std::strcmp;
using std::cout;
using std::endl;

template<typename T> const T& min(const T& a, const T& b) {
  return (a < b) ? a : b;
}

const char* min(const char* a, const char* b) {
  return (strcmp(a, b) < 0) ? a : b;
}

double min(double x, double y) {
  return (x < y) ? x : y;
}

int main() {
  const char *s2 = "say \"Ni-!\"", *s1 = "knights who";
  cout << min(1, 2) << endl;       // 1: 1 (template)
  cout << min(1.0, 2.0) << endl;   // 2: 1 (double)
  cout << min(1, 2.0) << endl;     // 3: 1 (double)
  cout << min(s1, s2) << endl;     // 4: knights who (const
                                   //                   char*)
  cout << min<>(s1, s2) << endl;   // 5: say "Ni-!"
                                   //    (template)
} ///:~
```

In addition to the function template, this program defines two non-template functions: a C-style string version of **min( )** and a **double** version. If the template doesn't exist, the call in line 1 above invokes the **double** version of **min( )** because of the standard conversion from **int** to **double**. The template can generate an **int** version which is considered a better match, so that's what happens. The call in line 2 is an exact match for the **double** version, and the call in line 3 also invokes the same function, implicitly converting 1 to 1.0. In line 4 the **const char*** version of **min( )** is called directly. In line 5 we force the compiler to use the template facility by appending empty angle brackets to the function name, whereupon it generates a **const char*** version from the template and uses it (which is verified by the wrong answer—it's just comparing addresses![4]). If you're wondering why we have **using** declarations in lieu of the **using namespace std** directive, it's because some compilers include headers behind the scenes that bring in **std::min( )**, which would conflict with our declarations of the name **min( )**.

As stated above, you can overload templates of the same name, as long as they can be distinguished by the compiler. You could, for example, declare a **min( )** function template that processes three arguments:

```
template<typename T>
const T& min(const T& a, const T& b, const T& c);
```

Versions of this template will be generated only for calls to **min( )** that have three arguments of the same type.

Taking the address of a generated function template

In some situations you need to take the address of a function. For example, you may have a function that takes an argument of a pointer to another function. It's possible that this other function might be generated from a template function, so you need some way to take that kind of address:[5]

```
//: C05:TemplateFunctionAddress.cpp {-mwcc}
// Taking the address of a function generated
// from a template.

template<typename T> void f(T*) {}

void h(void (*pf)(int*)) {}

template<typename T> void g(void (*pf)(T*)) {}

int main() {
  h(&f<int>); // Full type specification
```

---

[4] Technically, comparing two pointers that are not inside the same array is undefined behavior, but today's compilers don't complain about this. All the more reason to do it right.
[5] We are indebted to Nathan Myers for this example.

```
    h(&f); // Type deduction
    g<int>(&f<int>); // Full type specification
    g(&f<int>); // Type deduction
    g<int>(&f); // Partial (but sufficient) specification
} ///:~
```

This example demonstrates a number of issues. First, even though you're using templates, the signatures must match. The function **h( )** takes a pointer to a function that takes an **int*** and returns **void**, and that's what the template **f( )** produces. Second, the function that wants the function pointer as an argument can itself be a template, as in the case of the template **g( )**.

In **main( )** you can see that type deduction works here, too. The first call to **h( )** explicitly gives the template argument for **f( )**, but since **h( )** says that it will only take the address of a function that takes an **int***, that part can be deduced by the compiler. With **g( )** the situation is even more interesting because two templates are involved. The compiler cannot deduce the type with nothing to go on, but if either **f( )** or **g( )** is given **int**, the rest can be deduced.

An obscure issue arises when trying to pass the functions **tolower** or **toupper**, declared in **<cctype>**, as parameters. It is possible to use these, for example, with the **transform** algorithm (which is covered in detail in the next chapter) to convert a string to lower or upper case. You must be careful because there are multiple declarations for these functions. A naive approach would be something like this:

```
// The variable s is a std::string
transform(s.begin(), s.end(), s.begin(), tolower);
```

The **transform** algorithm applies its fourth parameter (**tolower( )** in this case) to each character in the string **s** and places the result in **s** itself, thus overwriting each character in **s** with its lower-case equivalent. As it is written, this statement may or may not work! It fails in the following context:

```
//: C05:FailedTransform.cpp {-xo}
#include <algorithm>
#include <cctype>
#include <iostream>
#include <string>
using namespace std;
```

```
int main() {
  string s("LOWER");
  transform(s.begin(), s.end(), s.begin(), tolower);
  cout << s << endl;
} ///:~
```

Even if your compiler lets you get away with this, it is illegal. The reason is that the **<iostream>** header also makes available a two-argument version of **tolower( )** and **toupper( )**:

```
template<class charT> charT toupper(charT c,
                              const locale& loc);
template<class charT> charT tolower(charT c,
                              const locale& loc);
```

These function templates take a second argument of type **locale**. The compiler has no way of knowing whether it should use the one-argument version of **tolower( )** defined in **<cctype>** or the one mentioned above. You can solve this problem (almost!) with a cast in the call to **transform**, as follows:

```
transform(s.begin(),s.end(),s.begin()
          static_cast<int (*)(int)>(tolower));
```

(Recall that **tolower( )** and **toupper( )** work with **int** instead of **char**.) The cast above makes clear that the single-argument version of **tolower( )** is desired. This works with some compilers, but it is not required to. The reason, albeit obscure, is that a library implementation is allowed to give "C linkage" (meaning that the function name does not contain all the auxiliary information[6] that normal C++ functions do) to functions inherited from the C language. If this is the case, the cast fails because **transform** is a C++ function template and expects its fourth argument to have C++ linkage—and a cast is not allowed to change the linkage. What a predicament!

The solution is to place **tolower( )** calls in an unambiguous context. For example, you could write a function named **strTolower( )** and place it in its own file without including **<iostream>**, like this:

```
//: C05:StrTolower.cpp {O} {-mwcc}
```

---

[6] Such as type information encoded in a decorated name.

```
#include <algorithm>
#include <cctype>
#include <string>
using namespace std;

string strTolower(string s) {
  transform(s.begin(), s.end(), s.begin(), tolower);
  return s;
} ///:~
```

The header **<iostream>** is not involved here, and the compilers we use do not introduce the two-argument version of **tolower( )** in this context,[7] so there's no problem. You can then use this function normally:

```
//: C05:Tolower.cpp {-mwcc}
//{L} StrTolower
#include <algorithm>
#include <cctype>
#include <iostream>
#include <string>
using namespace std;
string strTolower(string);

int main() {
  string s("LOWER");
  cout << strTolower(s) << endl;
} ///:~
```

Another solution is to write a wrapper function template that calls the correct version of **tolower( )** explicitly:

```
//: C05:ToLower2.cpp {-mwcc}
#include <algorithm>
#include <cctype>
#include <iostream>
#include <string>
using namespace std;

template<class charT> charT strTolower(charT c) {
  return tolower(c);  // One-arg version called
```

---

[7] C++ compilers can introduce names anywhere they want, however. Fortunately, most don't declare names they don't need.

```
  }

int main() {
  string s("LOWER");
  transform(s.begin(),s.end(),s.begin(),&strTolower<char>);
  cout << s << endl;
} ///:~
```

This version has the advantage that it can process both wide and narrow strings since the underlying character type is a template parameter. The C++ Standards Committee is working on modifying the language so that the first example (without the cast) will work, and some day these workarounds can be ignored.[8]

Applying a function to an STL sequence

Suppose you want to take an STL sequence container (which you'll learn more about in subsequent chapters; for now we can just use the familiar **vector**) and apply a member function to all the objects it contains. Because a **vector** can contain any type of object, you need a function that works with any type of **vector**:

```
//: C05:ApplySequence.h
// Apply a function to an STL sequence container.

// const, 0 arguments, any type of return value:
template<class Seq, class T, class R>
void apply(Seq& sq, R (T::*f)() const) {
  typename Seq::iterator it = sq.begin();
  while(it != sq.end())
    ((*it++)->*f)();
}

// const, 1 argument, any type of return value:
template<class Seq, class T, class R, class A>
void apply(Seq& sq, R(T::*f)(A) const, A a) {
  typename Seq::iterator it = sq.begin();
  while(it != sq.end())
    ((*it++)->*f)(a);
}
```

---

[8] If you're interested in seeing the proposal, it's Core Issue 352.

```
// const, 2 arguments, any type of return value:
template<class Seq, class T, class R,
         class A1, class A2>
void apply(Seq& sq, R(T::*f)(A1, A2) const,
    A1 a1, A2 a2) {
  typename Seq::iterator it = sq.begin();
  while(it != sq.end())
    ((*it++)->*f)(a1, a2);
}

// Non-const, 0 arguments, any type of return value:
template<class Seq, class T, class R>
void apply(Seq& sq, R (T::*f)()) {
  typename Seq::iterator it = sq.begin();
  while(it != sq.end())
    ((*it++)->*f)();
}

// Non-const, 1 argument, any type of return value:
template<class Seq, class T, class R, class A>
void apply(Seq& sq, R(T::*f)(A), A a) {
  typename Seq::iterator it = sq.begin();
  while(it != sq.end())
    ((*it++)->*f)(a);
}

// Non-const, 2 arguments, any type of return value:
template<class Seq, class T, class R,
         class A1, class A2>
void apply(Seq& sq, R(T::*f)(A1, A2),
    A1 a1, A2 a2) {
  typename Seq::iterator it = sq.begin();
  while(it != sq.end())
    ((*it++)->*f)(a1, a2);
}
// Etc., to handle maximum likely arguments ///:~
```

The **apply( )** function template above takes a reference to the container class and a pointer-to-member for a member function of the objects contained in the class. It uses an iterator to move through the sequence and apply the function to every object. We have overloaded on the **const**-ness of the function so you can use it with both **const** and non-**const** functions.

Notice that there are no STL header files (or any header files, for that matter) included in **applySequence.h**, so it is not limited to use with an STL container. However, it does make assumptions (primarily, the name and behavior of the **iterator**) that apply to STL sequences, and it also assumes that the elements of the container be of pointer type.

You can see there is more than one version of **apply( )**, further illustrating overloading of function templates. Although these templates allow any type of return value (which is ignored, but the type information is required to match the pointer-to-member), each version takes a different number of arguments, and because it's a template, those arguments can be of any type. The only limitation here is that there's no "super template" to create templates for you; you must decide how many arguments will ever be required and make the appropriate definitions.

To test the various overloaded versions of **apply( )**, the class **Gromit**[9] is created containing functions with different numbers of arguments, and both **const** and non-**const** member functions:

```
//: C05:Gromit.h
// The techno-dog. Has member functions
// with various numbers of arguments.
#include <iostream>

class Gromit {
  int arf;
  int totalBarks;
public:
  Gromit(int arf = 1) : arf(arf + 1), totalBarks(0) {}
  void speak(int) {
    for(int i = 0; i < arf; i++) {
      std::cout << "arf! ";
      ++totalBarks;
    }
    std::cout << std::endl;
  }
  char eat(float) const {
    std::cout << "chomp!" << std::endl;
```

---

[9] A reference to the British animated short films by Nick Park featuring Wallace and Gromit.

```
      return 'z';
  }
  int sleep(char, double) const {
    std::cout << "zzz..." << std::endl;
    return 0;
  }
  void sit() const {
    std::cout << "Sitting..." << std::endl;
  }
}; ///:~
```

Now you can use the **apply( )** template functions to apply the **Gromit** member functions to a **vector<Gromit*>**, like this:

```
//: C05:ApplyGromit.cpp
// Test ApplySequence.h.
#include <cstddef>
#include <iostream>
#include <vector>
#include "ApplySequence.h"
#include "Gromit.h"
#include "../purge.h"
using namespace std;

int main() {
  vector<Gromit*> dogs;
  for(size_t i = 0; i < 5; i++)
    dogs.push_back(new Gromit(i));
  apply(dogs, &Gromit::speak, 1);
  apply(dogs, &Gromit::eat, 2.0f);
  apply(dogs, &Gromit::sleep, 'z', 3.0);
  apply(dogs, &Gromit::sit);
  purge(dogs);
} ///:~
```

The **purge( )** function is a small utility that calls **delete** on every element of sequence. You'll find it defined in Chapter 7, and used various places in this book.

Although the definition of **apply( )** is somewhat complex and not something you'd ever expect a novice to understand, its use is remarkably clean and simple, and a novice could use it knowing only *what* it is intended to accomplish, not *how*. This is the type of division you should strive for in all your program components. The tough details are all isolated on the designer's side of the wall. Users are concerned only with accomplishing their goals and don't see, know about, or depend on details of the underlying implementation. We'll explore even more flexible ways to apply functions to sequences in the next chapter.

Partial ordering of function templates

We mentioned earlier that an ordinary function overload of **min( )** is preferable to using the template. If a function already exists to match a function call, why generate another? In the absence of ordinary functions, however, it is possible that overloaded function templates can lead to ambiguities. To minimize the chances of this, an ordering is defined for function templates, which chooses the *most specialized* template, if such exists. A function template is considered more specialized than another if every possible list of arguments that matches it also matches the other, but not the other way around. Consider the following function template declarations, taken from an example in the C++ Standard document:

```
template<class T> void f(T);
template<class T> void f(T*);
template<class T> void f(const T*);
```

The first template can be matched with any type. The second template is more specialized than the first because only pointer types match it. In other words, you can look upon the set of possible calls that match the second template as a subset of the first. A similar relationship exists between the second and third template declarations above: the third can only be called for pointers to **const**, but the second accommodates any pointer type. The following program illustrates these rules:

```
//: C05:PartialOrder.cpp
// Reveals ordering of function templates.
#include <iostream>
using namespace std;

template<class T> void f(T) {
  cout << "T" << endl;
}

template<class T> void f(T*) {
  cout << "T*" << endl;
}
```

```
template<class T> void f(const T*) {
  cout << "const T*" << endl;
}

int main() {
  f(0);                // T
  int i = 0;
  f(&i);               // T*
  const int j = 0;
  f(&j);               // const T*
} ///:~
```

The call **f(&i)** certainly matches the first template, but since the second is more specialized, it is called. The third can't be called here since the pointer is not a pointer to **const**. The call **f(&j)** matches all three templates (for example, **T** would be **const int** in the second template), but again, the third template is more specialized, so it is used instead.

If there is no "most specialized" template among a set of overloaded function templates, an ambiguity remains, and the compiler will report an error. That is why this feature is called a "partial ordering"—it may not be able to resolve all possibilities. Similar rules exist for class templates (see the section "Partial specialization" below).

Template specialization

The term *specialization* has a specific, template-related meaning in C++. A template definition is, by its very nature, a *generalization*, because it describes a family of functions or classes in general terms. When template arguments are supplied, the result is a specialization of the template because it determines a unique instance out of the many possible instances of the family of functions or classes. The **min( )** function template seen at the beginning of this chapter is a generalization of a minimum-finding function because the type of its parameters is not specified. When you supply the type for the template parameter, whether explicitly or implicitly via argument deduction, the resultant code generated by the compiler (for example, **min<int>( )**) is a specialization of the template. The code generated is also considered an *instantiation* of the template, as are all code bodies generated by the template facility.

Explicit specialization

You can also provide the code yourself for a given template specialization, should the need arise. Providing your own template specializations is often needed with class templates, but we will begin with the **min( )** function template to introduce the syntax.

Recall that in **MinTest.cpp** earlier in this chapter we introduced the following ordinary function:

```
const char* min(const char* a, const char* b) {
  return (strcmp(a, b) < 0) ? a : b;
}
```

This was so that a call to **min( )** would compare strings and not addresses. Although it would provide no advantage here, we could instead define a **const char*** specialization for **min( )**, as in the following program:

```
//: C05:MinTest2.cpp
#include <cstring>
#include <iostream>
using std::strcmp;
using std::cout;
using std::endl;

template<class T> const T& min(const T& a, const T& b) {
  return (a < b) ? a : b;
}

// An explicit specialization of the min template
template<>
const char* const& min<const char*>(const char* const& a,
                                    const char* const& b) {
  return (strcmp(a, b) < 0) ? a : b;
}

int main() {
  const char *s2 = "say \"Ni-!\"", *s1 = "knights who";
  cout << min(s1, s2) << endl;
  cout << min<>(s1, s2) << endl;
} ///:~
```

The "**template<>**" prefix tells the compiler that what follows is a specialization of a template. The type for the specialization must appear in angle brackets immediately following the function name, as it normally would in an explicitly specified call. Note that we *carefully* substitute **const char*** for **T** in the explicit specialization. Whenever the original template specifies **const T**, that **const** modifies the *whole* type **T**. It is the pointer to a **const char*** that is **const**. So we must write **const char* const** in place of **const T** in the specialization. When the compiler sees a call to **min( )** with **const char*** arguments in the program, it will instantiate our **const char*** version of **min( )** so it can be called. The two calls to **min( )** in this program call the same specialization of **min( )**.

Explicit specializations tend to be more useful for class templates than for function templates. When you provide a full specialization for a class template, though, you may need to implement all the member functions. This is because you are providing a separate class, and client code may expect the complete interface to be implemented.

The standard library has an explicit specialization for **vector** when it holds objects of type **bool**. The purpose for **vector<bool>** is to allow library implementations to save space by packing bits into integers.[10]

As you saw earlier in this chapter, the declaration for the primary **vector** class template is:

```
template<class T, class Allocator = allocator<T> >
class vector {...};
```

To specialize for objects of type **bool**, you could declare an explicit specialization as follows:

```
template<> class vector<bool, allocator<bool> > {...};
```

Again, this is quickly recognized as a full, explicit specialization because of the **template<>** prefix and because all the primary template's parameters are satisfied by the argument list appended to the class name.

It turns out that **vector<bool>** is a little more flexible than we have described, as seen in the next section.

---

[10] We discuss **vector<bool>** in depth in Chapter 7.

Partial Specialization

Class templates can also be partially specialized, meaning that at least one of the template parameters is left "open" in some way in the specialization. **vector<bool>** specifies the object type (**bool**), but leaves the allocator type unspecified. Here is the actual declaration of **vector<bool>**:

```
template<class Allocator> class vector<bool, Allocator>;
```

You can recognize a partial specialization because non-empty parameter lists appear in angle brackets both after the template keyword (the unspecified parameters) and after the class (the specified arguments). Because of the way **vector<bool>** is defined, a user can provide a custom allocator type, even though the contained type of **bool** is fixed. In other words, specialization, and partial specialization in particular, constitute a sort of "overloading" for class templates.

Partial ordering of class templates

The rules that determine which template is selected for instantiation are similar to the partial ordering for function templates—the "most specialized" template is selected. The string in each **f( )** member function in the illustration below explains the role of each template definition:

```cpp
//: C05:PartialOrder2.cpp
// Reveals partial ordering of class templates.
#include <iostream>
using namespace std;

template<class T, class U> class C {
public:
  void f() { cout << "Primary Template\n"; }
};

template<class U> class C<int, U> {
public:
  void f() { cout << "T == int\n"; }
};

template<class T> class C<T, double> {
public:
  void f() { cout << "U == double\n"; }
};
```

```
template<class T, class U> class C<T*, U> {
public:
  void f() { cout << "T* used\n"; }
};

template<class T, class U> class C<T, U*> {
public:
  void f() { cout << "U* used\n"; }
};

template<class T, class U> class C<T*, U*> {
public:
  void f() { cout << "T* and U* used\n"; }
};

template<class T> class C<T, T> {
public:
  void f() { cout << "T == U\n"; }
};

int main() {
  C<float, int>().f();    // 1: Primary template
  C<int, float>().f();    // 2: T == int
  C<float, double>().f(); // 3: U == double
  C<float, float>().f();  // 4: T == U
  C<float*, float>().f(); // 5: T* used [T is float]
  C<float, float*>().f(); // 6: U* used [U is float]
  C<float*, int*>().f();  // 7: T* and U* used [float,int]
  // The following are ambiguous:
//    8: C<int, int>().f();
//    9: C<double, double>().f();
//   10: C<float*, float*>().f();
//   11: C<int, int*>().f();
//   12: C<int*, int*>().f();
} ///:~
```

As you can see, you can partially specify template parameters according to whether they are pointer types, or whether they are equal. When the **T***
specialization is used, such as is the case in line 5, **T** itself is not the top-level pointer type that was passed—it is the type that the pointer refers to (**float**, in this case). The **T*** specification is a pattern to allow matching against pointer types. If you use **int*** as the first template argument, **T** becomes **int***. Line 8 is ambiguous because having the first parameter as an **int** versus having the

two parameters equal are independent issues—one is not more specialized than the other. Similar logic applies to lines 9 through 12.

A practical example

You can easily derive from a class template, and you can create a new template that instantiates and inherits from an existing template. If the **vector** template does most everything you want, for example, but in a certain application you'd also like a version that can sort itself, you can easily reuse the **vector** code. The following example derives from **vector<T>** and adds sorting. Note that deriving from **vector**, which doesn't have a virtual destructor, would be dangerous if we needed to perform cleanup in our destructor.

```
//: C05:Sortable.h
// Template specialization.
#ifndef SORTABLE_H
#define SORTABLE_H
#include <cstring>
#include <cstddef>
#include <string>
#include <vector>
using std::size_t;

template<class T>
class Sortable : public std::vector<T> {
public:
  void sort();
};

template<class T>
void Sortable<T>::sort() { // A simple sort
  for(size_t i = this->size(); i > 0; --i)
    for(size_t j = 1; j < i; ++j)
      if(this->at(j-1) > this->at(j)) {
        T t = this->at(j-1);
        this->at(j-1) = this->at(j);
        this->at(j) = t;
      }
}
```

```
// Partial specialization for pointers:
template<class T>
class Sortable<T*> : public std::vector<T*> {
public:
  void sort();
};

template<class T>
void Sortable<T*>::sort() {
  for(size_t i = this->size(); i > 0; --i)
    for(size_t j = 1; j < i; ++j)
      if(*this->at(j-1) > *this->at(j)) {
        T* t = this->at(j-1);
        this->at(j-1) = this->at(j);
        this->at(j) = t;
      }
}

// Full specialization for char*
// (Made inline here for convenience -- normally you would
// place the function body in a separate file and only
// leave the declaration here).
template<> inline void Sortable<char*>::sort() {
  for(size_t i = this->size(); i > 0; --i)
    for(size_t j = 1; j < i; ++j)
      if(std::strcmp(this->at(j-1), this->at(j)) > 0) {
        char* t = this->at(j-1);
        this->at(j-1) = this->at(j);
        this->at(j) = t;
      }
}
#endif // SORTABLE_H ///:~
```

The **Sortable** template imposes a restriction on all but one of the classes for which it is instantiated: they must contain a > operator. It works correctly only with non-pointer objects (including objects of built-in types). The full specialization compares the elements using **strcmp( )** to sort **vector**s of **char*** according to the null-terminated strings to which they refer. The use of "**this->**" above is mandatory[11] and is explained in the section entitled "Name lookup issues" later in this chapter.[12]

Here's a driver for **Sortable.h** that uses the randomizer introduced earlier in the chapter:

```
//: C05:Sortable.cpp
//{-bor} (Because of bitset in Urand.h)
// Testing template specialization.
#include <cstddef>
#include <iostream>
#include "Sortable.h"
#include "Urand.h"
using namespace std;

#define asz(a) (sizeof a / sizeof a[0])

char* words[] = { "is", "running", "big", "dog", "a", };
char* words2[] = { "this", "that", "theother", };

int main() {
  Sortable<int> is;
  Urand<47> rnd;
  for(size_t i = 0; i < 15; ++i)
    is.push_back(rnd());
  for(size_t i = 0; i < is.size(); ++i)
    cout << is[i] << ' ';
  cout << endl;
  is.sort();
  for(size_t i = 0; i < is.size(); ++i)
    cout << is[i] << ' ';
  cout << endl;

  // Uses the template partial specialization:
  Sortable<string*> ss;
  for(size_t i = 0; i < asz(words); ++i)
    ss.push_back(new string(words[i]));
  for(size_t i = 0; i < ss.size(); ++i)
```

---

[11] Instead of **this->** you could use any valid qualification, such as **Sortable::at( )** or **vector<T>::at( )**. The point is that it must be qualified.
[12] See also the explanation accompanying **PriorityQueue6.cpp** in Chapter 7.

5: Templates in Depth

```
      cout << *ss[i] << ' ';
  cout << endl;
  ss.sort();
  for(size_t i = 0; i < ss.size(); ++i) {
    cout << *ss[i] << ' ';
    delete ss[i];
  }
  cout << endl;

  // Uses the full char* specialization:
  Sortable<char*> scp;
  for(size_t i = 0; i < asz(words2); ++i)
    scp.push_back(words2[i]);
  for(size_t i = 0; i < scp.size(); ++i)
    cout << scp[i] << ' ';
  cout << endl;
  scp.sort();
  for(size_t i = 0; i < scp.size(); ++i)
    cout << scp[i] << ' ';
  cout << endl;
} ///:~
```

Each of the template instantiations above uses a different version of the template. **Sortable<int>** uses the primary template. **Sortable<string*>** uses the partial specialization for pointers. Last, **Sortable<char*>** uses the full specialization for **char***. Without this full specialization, you could be fooled into thinking that things were working correctly because the **words** array would still sort out to "a big dog is running" since the partial specialization would end up comparing the first character of each array. However, **words2** would not sort correctly.

Preventing template code bloat

Whenever a class template is instantiated, the code from the class definition for the particular specialization is generated, along with all the member functions that are called in the program. Only the member functions that are called are generated. This is good, as you can see in the following program:

```
//: C05:DelayedInstantiation.cpp
// Member functions of class templates are not
// instantiated until they're needed.

class X {
```

```
public:
  void f() {}
};

class Y {
public:
  void g() {}
};

template<typename T> class Z {
  T t;
public:
  void a() { t.f(); }
  void b() { t.g(); }
};

int main() {
  Z<X> zx;
  zx.a(); // Doesn't create Z<X>::b()
  Z<Y> zy;
  zy.b(); // Doesn't create Z<Y>::a()
} ///:~
```

Here, even though the template **Z** purports to use both **f( )** and **g( )** member functions of **T**, the fact that the program compiles shows you that it only generates **Z<X>::a( )** when it is explicitly called for **zx**. (If **Z<X>::b( )** were also generated at the same time, a compile-time error message would be generated because it would attempt to call **X::g( )**, which doesn't exist.) Similarly, the call to **zy.b( )** doesn't generate **Z<Y>::a( )**. As a result, the **Z** template can be used with **X** and **Y**, whereas if all the member functions were generated when the class was first instantiated the use of many templates would become significantly limited.

Suppose you have a templatized **Stack** container and you use specializations for **int**, **int***, and **char***. Three versions of **Stack** code will be generated and linked as part of your program. One of the reasons for using a template in the first place is so you don't need to replicate code by hand; but code still gets replicated—it's just the compiler that does it instead of you. You can factor the bulk of the implementation for storing pointer types into a single class by using a combination of full and partial specialization. The key is to fully specialize for **void*** and then derive all other pointer types from the **void***

implementation so the common code can be shared. The program below illustrates this technique:

```
//: C05:Nobloat.h
// Shares code for storing pointers in a Stack.
#ifndef NOBLOAT_H
#define NOBLOAT_H
#include <cassert>
#include <cstddef>
#include <cstring>

// The primary template
template<class T> class Stack {
  T* data;
  std::size_t count;
  std::size_t capacity;
  enum { INIT = 5 };
public:
  Stack() {
    count = 0;
    capacity = INIT;
    data = new T[INIT];
  }
  void push(const T& t) {
    if(count == capacity) {
      // Grow array store
      std::size_t newCapacity = 2 * capacity;
      T* newData = new T[newCapacity];
      for(size_t i = 0; i < count; ++i)
        newData[i] = data[i];
      delete [] data;
      data = newData;
      capacity = newCapacity;
    }
    assert(count < capacity);
    data[count++] = t;
  }
  void pop() {
    assert(count > 0);
    --count;
  }
  T top() const {
    assert(count > 0);
    return data[count-1];
```

```
  }
  std::size_t size() const { return count; }
};

// Full specialization for void*
template<> class Stack<void *> {
  void** data;
  std::size_t count;
  std::size_t capacity;
  enum { INIT = 5 };
public:
  Stack() {
    count = 0;
    capacity = INIT;
    data = new void*[INIT];
  }
  void push(void* const & t) {
    if(count == capacity) {
      std::size_t newCapacity = 2*capacity;
      void** newData = new void*[newCapacity];
      std::memcpy(newData, data, count*sizeof(void*));
      delete [] data;
      data = newData;
      capacity = newCapacity;
    }
    assert(count < capacity);
    data[count++] = t;
  }
  void pop() {
    assert(count > 0);
    --count;
  }
  void* top() const {
    assert(count > 0);
    return data[count-1];
  }
  std::size_t size() const { return count; }
};

// Partial specialization for other pointer types
template<class T> class Stack<T*> : private Stack<void *> {
  typedef Stack<void *> Base;
public:
  void push(T* const & t) { Base::push(t); }
  void pop() {Base::pop();}
```

```
  T* top() const { return static_cast<T*>(Base::top()); }
  std::size_t size() { return Base::size(); }
};
#endif // NOBLOAT_H ///:~
```

This simple stack expands as it fills its capacity. The **void*** specialization stands out as a full specialization by virtue of the **template<>** prefix (that is, the template parameter list is empty). As mentioned earlier, it is necessary to implement all member functions in a class template specialization. The savings occurs with all other pointer types. The partial specialization for other pointer types derives from **Stack<void*>** privately, since we are merely using **Stack<void*>** for implementation purposes, and do not wish to expose any of its interface directly to the user. The member functions for each pointer instantiation are small forwarding functions to the corresponding functions in **Stack<void*>**. Hence, whenever a pointer type other than **void*** is instantiated, it is a fraction of the size it would have been had the primary template alone been used.[13] Here is a driver program:

```
//: C05:NobloatTest.cpp
#include <iostream>
#include <string>
#include "Nobloat.h"
using namespace std;

template<class StackType>
void emptyTheStack(StackType& stk) {
  while(stk.size() > 0) {
    cout << stk.top() << endl;
    stk.pop();
  }
}

// An overload for emptyTheStack (not a specialization!)
template<class T>
void emptyTheStack(Stack<T*>& stk) {
  while(stk.size() > 0) {
    cout << *stk.top() << endl;
    stk.pop();
  }
```

---

[13] Since the forwarding functions are inline, no code for Stack<void*> is generated at all!

```
}

int main() {
  Stack<int> s1;
  s1.push(1);
  s1.push(2);
  emptyTheStack(s1);
  Stack<int *> s2;
  int i = 3;
  int j = 4;
  s2.push(&i);
  s2.push(&j);
  emptyTheStack(s2);
} ///:~
```

For convenience we include two **emptyStack** function templates. Since function templates don't support partial specialization, we provide overloaded templates. The second version of **emptyStack** is more specialized than the first, so it is chosen whenever pointer types are used. Three class templates are instantiated in this program: **Stack<int>**, **Stack<void*>**, and **Stack<int*>**. **Stack<void*>** is implicitly instantiated because **Stack<int*>** derives from it. A program using instantiations for many pointer types can produce substantial savings in code size over just using a single **Stack** template.

Name lookup issues

When the compiler encounters an identifier it must determine the type and scope (and in the case of variables, the lifetime) of the entity the identifier represents. Templates add complexity to the situation. Because the compiler doesn't know everything about a template when it first sees the definition, it can't tell whether the template is being used properly until it sees the template instantiation. This predicament leads to a two-phase process for template compilation.

Names in templates

In the first phase, the compiler parses the template definition looking for obvious syntax errors and resolving all the names it can. It can resolve names that do not depend on template parameters using normal name lookup, and if necessary through argument-dependent lookup (discussed below). The names it can't resolve are the so-called *dependent names*, which depend on template parameters in some way. These can't be resolved until the template is instantiated with its actual arguments. So instantiation is the second phase of template compilation. Here, the compiler determines whether to use an explicit specialization of the template instead of the primary template.

Before you see an example, you must understand two more terms. A *qualified name* is a name with a class-name prefix, a name with an object name and a dot operator, or a name with a pointer to an object and an arrow operator. Examples of qualified names are:

```
MyClass::f();
x.f();
p->f();
```

We use qualified names many times in this book, and most recently in connection with the **typename** keyword. These are called qualified names because the target names (like **f** above) are explicitly associated with a class or namespace, which tells the compiler where to look for the declarations of those names.

The other term is *argument-dependent lookup*[14] (ADL), a mechanism originally designed to simplify non-member function calls (including operators) declared in namespaces. Consider the following:

```
#include <iostream>
#include <string>
// ...
  std::string s("hello");
  std::cout << s << std::endl;
```

Note that, following the typical practice in header files, there is no **using namespace std** directive. Without such a directive, you must use the "**std::**" qualifier on the items that are in the **std** namespace. We have, however, not qualified everything from **std** that we are using. Can you see what is unqualified?

---

[14] Also called *Koenig lookup*, after Andrew Koenig, who first proposed the technique to the C++ Standards Committee. ADL applies universally, whether templates are involved or not.

We have not specified which operator functions to use. We want the following to happen, but we don't want to have to type it!

```
std::operator<<(std::operator<<(std::cout,s),std::endl);
```

To make the original output statement work as desired, ADL specifies that when an unqualified function call appears and its declaration is not in (normal) scope, the namespaces of each of its arguments are searched for a matching function declaration. In the original statement, the first function call is:

```
operator<<(std::cout, s);
```

Since there is no such function in scope in our original excerpt, the compiler notes that this function's first argument (**std::cout**) is in the namespace **std;** so it adds that namespace to the list of scopes to search for a unique function that best matches the signature **operator<<(std::ostream&, std::string)**. It finds this function declared in the **std** namespace via the **<string>** header.

Namespaces would be very inconvenient without ADL. Note that ADL generally brings in *all* declarations of the name in question from all eligible namespaces—if there is no single best match, an ambiguity will result.

To turn off ADL, you can enclose the function name in parentheses:

```
(f)(x, y);  // ADL suppressed
```

Now consider the following program:[15]

```
//: C05:Lookup.cpp
// Only produces correct behavior with EDG,
// and Metrowerks using a special option.
#include <iostream>
using std::cout;
using std::endl;

void f(double) { cout << "f(double)" << endl; }

template<class T> class X {
```

---

[15] From a presentation by Herb Sutter.

```
public:
  void g() { f(1); }
};

void f(int) { cout << "f(int)" << endl; }

int main() {
  X<int>().g();
} ///:~
```

The only compiler we have that produces correct behavior without modification is the Edison Design Group front end,[16] although some compilers, such as Metrowerks, have an option to enable the correct lookup behavior. The output should be:

```
f(double)
```

because **f** is a non-dependent name that can be resolved early by looking in the context where the template is defined, when only **f(double)** is in scope. Unfortunately, there is a lot of existing code in the industry that depends on the non-standard behavior of binding the call to **f(1)** inside **g( )** to the latter **f(int)**, so compiler writers have been reluctant to make the change.

Here is a more detailed example:[17]

```
//: C05:Lookup2.cpp {-bor}{-g++}{-dmc}
// Microsoft: use option -Za (ANSI mode)
#include <algorithm>
#include <iostream>
#include <typeinfo>
using std::cout;
using std::endl;

void g() { cout << "global g()" << endl; }

template<class T> class Y {
public:
  void g() {
    cout << "Y<" << typeid(T).name() << ">::g()" << endl;
```

---

[16] A number of compilers use this front end, including Comeau C++.
[17] Also based on an example by Herb Sutter.

```
    }
  void h() {
    cout << "Y<" << typeid(T).name() << ">::h()" << endl;
  }
  typedef int E;
};

typedef double E;

template<class T> void swap(T& t1, T& t2) {
  cout << "global swap" << endl;
  T temp = t1;
  t1 = t2;
  t2 = temp;
}

template<class T> class X : public Y<T> {
public:
  E f() {
    g();
    this->h();
    T t1 = T(), t2 = T(1);
    cout << t1 << endl;
    swap(t1, t2);
    std::swap(t1, t2);
    cout << typeid(E).name() << endl;
    return E(t2);
  }
};

int main() {
  X<int> x;
  cout << x.f() << endl;
} ///:~
```

The output from this program should be:

```
global g()
Y<int>::h()
0
global swap
double
1
```

Looking at the declarations inside of **X::f( )**:

- **E**, the return type of **X::f( )**, is not a dependent name, so it is looked up when the template is parsed, and the **typedef** naming **E** as a **double** is found. This may seem strange, since with non-template classes the declaration of **E** in the base class would be found first, but those are the rules. (The base class, **Y**, is a *dependent base class*, so it can't be searched at template definition time).

- The call to **g( )** is also non-dependent, since there is no mention of **T**. If **g** had parameters that were of class type of defined in another namespace, ADL would take over, since there is no **g** with parameters in scope. As it is, this call matches the global declaration of **g( )**.

- The call **this->h( )** is a qualified name, and the object that qualifies it (**this**) refers to the current object, which is of type **X**, which in turn depends on the name **Y<T>** by inheritance. There is no function **h( )** inside of **X**, so the lookup will search the scope of **X**'s base class, **Y<T>**. Since this is a dependent name, it is looked up at instantiation time, when **Y<T>** are reliably known (including any potential specializations that might have been written after the definition of **X**), so it calls **Y<int>::h( )**.

- The declarations of **t1** and **t2** are dependent.

- The call to **operator<<(cout, t1)** is dependent, since **t1** is of type **T**. This is looked up later when **T** is **int**, and the inserter for **int** is found in **std**.

- The unqualified call to **swap( )** is dependent because its arguments are of type **T**. This ultimately causes a global **swap(int&, int&)** to be instantiated.

- The qualified call to **std::swap( )** is *not* dependent, because **std** is a fixed namespace. The compiler knows to look in **std** for the proper declaration. (The qualifier on the left of the "**::**" must mention a template parameter for a qualified name to be considered dependent.) The **std::swap( )** function template later generates **std::swap(int&, int&)**, at instantiation time. No more dependent names remain in **X<T>::f( )**.

To clarify and summarize: name lookup is done at the point of instantiation if the name is dependent, except that for unqualified dependent names the normal name lookup is also attempted early, at the point of definition. All non-dependent names in templates are looked up early, at the time the template definition is parsed. (If necessary, another lookup occurs at instantiation time, when the type of the actual argument is known.)

If you have studied this example to the point that you understand it, prepare yourself for yet another surprise in the following section on **friend** declarations.

Templates and friends

A friend function declaration inside a class allows a non-member function to access non-public members of that class. If the friend function name is qualified, it will be found in the namespace or class that qualifies it. If it is unqualified, however, the compiler must make an assumption about where the definition of the friend function will be, since all identifiers must have a unique scope. The expectation is that the function will be defined in the nearest enclosing namespace (non-class) scope that contains the class granting friendship. Often this is just the global scope. The following non-template example clarifies this issue:

```
//: C05:FriendScope.cpp
#include <iostream>
using namespace std;

class Friendly {
  int i;
public:
  Friendly(int theInt) { i = theInt; }
  friend void f(const Friendly&); // Needs global def.
  void g() { f(*this); }
};

void h() {
  f(Friendly(1));  // Uses ADL
}

void f(const Friendly& fo) {  // Definition of friend
  cout << fo.i << endl;
}
```

```
int main() {
  h(); // Prints 1
  Friendly(2).g(); // Prints 2
} ///:~
```

The declaration of **f( )** inside the **Friendly** class is unqualified, so the compiler will expect to be able to eventually link that declaration to a definition at file scope (the namespace scope that contains **Friendly** in this case). That definition appears after the definition of the function **h( )**. The linking of the call to **f( )** inside **h( )** to the same function is a separate matter, however. This is resolved by ADL. Since the argument of **f( )** inside **h( )** is a **Friendly** object, the **Friendly** class is searched for a declaration of **f( )**, which succeeds. If the call were **f(1)** instead (which makes some sense since 1 can be implicitly converted to **Friendly(1)**), the call should fail, since there is no hint of where the compiler should look for the declaration of **f( )**. The EDG compiler correctly complains that **f** is undefined in that case.

Now suppose that **Friendly** and **f** are both templates, as in the following program:

```
//: C05:FriendScope2.cpp
#include <iostream>
using namespace std;

// Necessary forward declarations:
template<class T> class Friendly;
template<class T> void f(const Friendly<T>&);

template<class T> class Friendly {
  T t;
public:
  Friendly(const T& theT) : t(theT) {}
  friend void f<>(const Friendly<T>&);
  void g() { f(*this); }
};

void h() {
  f(Friendly<int>(1));
}

template<class T> void f(const Friendly<T>& fo) {
  cout << fo.t << endl;
```

```
}

int main() {
  h();
  Friendly<int>(2).g();
} ///:~
```

First notice that angle brackets in the declaration of **f** inside **Friendly**. This is necessary to tell the compiler that **f** is a template. Otherwise, the compiler will look for an ordinary function named **f** and not find it. We could have inserted the template parameter (**<T>**) in the brackets, but it is easily deduced from the declaration.

The forward declaration of the function template **f** before the class definition is necessary, even though it wasn't in the previous example when **f** was a not a template; the language specifies that friend function templates must be previously declared. To properly declare **f**, **Friendly** must also have been declared, since **f** takes a **Friendly** argument, hence the forward declaration of **Friendly** in the beginning. We could have placed the full definition of **f** right after the initial declaration of **Friendly** instead of separating its definition and declaration, but we chose instead to leave it in a form that more closely resembles the previous example.

One last option remains for using friends inside templates: fully define them inside the host class template definition itself. Here is how the previous example would appear with that change:

```
//: C05:FriendScope3.cpp {-bor}
// Microsoft: use the -Za (ANSI-compliant) option
#include <iostream>
using namespace std;

template<class T> class Friendly {
  T t;
public:
  Friendly(const T& theT) : t(theT) {}
  friend void f(const Friendly<T>& fo) {
    cout << fo.t << endl;
  }
  void g() { f(*this); }
};

void h() {
```

```
    f(Friendly<int>(1));
}

int main() {
  h();
  Friendly<int>(2).g();
} ///:~
```

There is an important difference between this and the previous example: **f** is not a template here, but is an ordinary function. (Remember that angle brackets were necessary before to imply that **f( )** was a template.) Every time the **Friendly** class template is instantiated, a new, ordinary function overload is created that takes an argument of the current **Friendly** specialization. This is what Dan Saks has called "making new friends."[18] This is the most convenient way to define friend functions for templates.

To clarify, suppose you want to add non-member friend operators to a class template. Here is a class template that simply holds a generic value:

```
template<class T> class Box {
  T t;
public:
  Box(const T& theT) : t(theT) {}
};
```

Without understanding the previous examples in this section, novices find themselves frustrated because they can't get a simple stream output inserter to work. If you don't define your operators inside the definition of **Box**, you must provide the forward declarations we showed earlier:

```
//: C05:Box1.cpp
// Defines template operators.
#include <iostream>
using namespace std;

// Forward declarations
template<class T> class Box;

template<class T>
Box<T> operator+(const Box<T>&, const Box<T>&);
```

---

[18] In a talk given at *The C++ Seminar*, Portland, OR, September, 2001.

```
template<class T>
ostream& operator<<(ostream&, const Box<T>&);

template<class T> class Box {
  T t;
public:
  Box(const T& theT) : t(theT) {}
  friend Box operator+<>(const Box<T>&, const Box<T>&);
  friend ostream& operator<< <>(ostream&, const Box<T>&);
};

template<class T>
Box<T> operator+(const Box<T>& b1, const Box<T>& b2) {
  return Box<T>(b1.t + b2.t);
}

template<class T>
ostream& operator<<(ostream& os, const Box<T>& b) {
  return os << '[' << b.t << ']';
}

int main() {
  Box<int> b1(1), b2(2);
  cout << b1 + b2 << endl;  // [3]
// cout << b1 + 2 << endl; // No implicit conversions!
} ///:~
```

Here we are defining both an addition operator and an output stream operator. The main program reveals a disadvantage of this approach: you can't depend on implicit conversions (the expression **b1 + 2**) because templates do not provide them. Using the in-class, non-template approach is shorter and more robust:

```
//: C05:Box2.cpp
// Defines non-template operators.
#include <iostream>
using namespace std;

template<class T> class Box {
  T t;
public:
  Box(const T& theT) : t(theT) {}
  friend Box<T> operator+(const Box<T>& b1,
```

```
                    const Box<T>& b2) {
    return Box<T>(b1.t + b2.t);
  }
  friend ostream&
  operator<<(ostream& os, const Box<T>& b) {
    return os << '[' << b.t << ']';
  }
};

int main() {
  Box<int> b1(1), b2(2);
  cout << b1 + b2 << endl; // [3]
  cout << b1 + 2 << endl; // [3]
} ///:~
```

Because the operators are normal functions (overloaded for each specialization of **Box**—just **int** in this case), implicit conversions are applied as normal; so the expression **b1 + 2** is valid.

Note that there's one type in particular that cannot be made a friend of **Box**, or any other class template for that matter, and that type is **T**—or rather, the type that the class template is parameterized upon. To the best of our knowledge, there are really no good reasons why this shouldn't be allowed, but as is, the declaration **friend class T** is illegal, and should not compile.

Friend templates

You can be precise as to which specializations of a template are friends of a class. In the examples in the previous section, only the specialization of the function template **f** with the same type that specialized **Friendly** was a friend. For example, only the specialization **f<int>(const Friendly<int>&)** is a friend of the class **Friendly<int>**. This was accomplished by using the template parameter for **Friendly** to specialize **f** in its friend declaration. If we had wanted to, we could have made a particular, fixed specialization of **f** a friend to all instances of **Friendly**, like this:

```
  // Inside Friendly:
  friend void f<>(const Friendly<double>&);
```

By using **double** instead of **T**, the **double** specialization of **f** has access to the non-public members of any **Friendly** specialization. The specialization **f<double>( )** still isn't instantiated unless it is explicitly called.

Likewise, if you declare a non-template function with no parameters dependent on **T**, that single function is a friend to all instances of **Friendly**:

```
// Inside Friendly:
friend void g(int);   // g(int) befriends all Friendlys
```

As always, since **g(int)** is unqualified, it must be defined at file scope (the namespace scope containing **Friendly**).

It is also possible to arrange for all specializations of **f** to be friends for all specializations of **Friendly**, with a so-called *friend template*, as follows:

```
template<class T> class Friendly {
  template<class U> friend void f<>(const Friendly<U>&);
```

Since the template argument for the friend declaration is independent of **T**, any combination of **T** and **U** is allowed, achieving the friendship objective. Like member templates, friend templates can appear within non-template classes as well.

Template programming idioms

Since language is a tool of thought, new language features tend to spawn new programming techniques. In this section we cover some commonly used template programming idioms that have emerged in the years since templates were added to the C++ language.[19]

Traits

The traits template technique, pioneered by Nathan Myers, is a means of bundling type-dependent declarations together. In essence, using traits you can "mix and match" certain types and values with contexts that use them in a flexible manner, while keeping your code readable and maintainable.

The simplest example of a traits template is the **numeric_limits** class template defined in **<limits>**. The primary template is defined as follows:

```
template<class T> class numeric_limits {
```

---

[19] Another template idiom, mixin inheritance, is covered in Chapter 9.

```
public:
  static const bool is_specialized = false;
  static T min() throw();
  static T max() throw();
  static const int digits = 0;
  static const int digits10 = 0;
  static const bool is_signed = false;
  static const bool is_integer = false;
  static const bool is_exact = false;
  static const int radix = 0;
  static T epsilon() throw();
  static T round_error() throw();
  static const int min_exponent = 0;
  static const int min_exponent10 = 0;
  static const int max_exponent = 0;
  static const int max_exponent10 = 0;
  static const bool has_infinity = false;
  static const bool has_quiet_NaN = false;
  static const bool has_signaling_NaN = false;
  static const float_denorm_style has_denorm =
                                  denorm_absent;
  static const bool has_denorm_loss = false;
  static T infinity() throw();
  static T quiet_NaN() throw();
  static T signaling_NaN() throw();
  static T denorm_min() throw();
  static const bool is_iec559 = false;
  static const bool is_bounded = false;
  static const bool is_modulo = false;
  static const bool traps = false;
  static const bool tinyness_before = false;
  static const float_round_style round_style =
                                  round_toward_zero;
};
```

The **<limits>** header defines specializations for all fundamental, numeric types (when the member **is_specialized** is set to **true**). To obtain the base for the **double** version of your floating-point number system, for example, you can use the expression **numeric_limits<double>::radix**. To find the smallest integer value available, you can use **numeric_limits<int>::min( )**. Not all members of **numeric_limits** apply to all fundamental types. (For example, **epsilon( )** is only meaningful for floating-point types.)

The values that will always be integral are static data members of **numeric_limits**. Those that may not be integral, such as the minimum value for **float**, are implemented as static inline member functions. This is because C++ allows only *integral* static data member constants to be initialized inside a class definition.

In Chapter 3 you saw how traits are used to control the character-processing functionality used by the string classes. The classes **std::string** and **std::wstring** are specializations of the **std::basic_string** template, which is defined as follows:

```
template<class charT,
  class traits = char_traits<charT>,
  class allocator = allocator<charT> >
  class basic_string;
```

The template parameter **charT** represents the underlying character type, which is usually either **char** or **wchar_t**. The primary **char_traits** template is typically empty, and specializations for **char** and **wchar_t** are provided by the standard library. Here is the specification of the specialization **char_traits<char>** according to the C++ Standard:

```
template<> struct char_traits<char> {
  typedef char char_type;
  typedef int int_type;
  typedef streamoff off_type;
  typedef streampos pos_type;
  typedef mbstate_t state_type;
  static void assign(char_type& c1, const char_type& c2);
  static bool eq(const char_type& c1, const char_type& c2);
  static bool lt(const char_type& c1, const char_type& c2);
  static int compare(const char_type* s1,
                const char_type* s2, size_t n);
  static size_t length(const char_type* s);
  static const char_type* find(const char_type* s,
                        size_t n,
                        const char_type& a);
  static char_type* move(char_type* s1,
                const char_type* s2, size_t n);
  static char_type* copy(char_type* s1,
                const char_type* s2, size_t n);
  static char_type* assign(char_type* s, size_t n,
                    char_type a);
```

```
    static int_type not_eof(const int_type& c);
    static char_type to_char_type(const int_type& c);
    static int_type to_int_type(const char_type& c);
    static bool eq_int_type(const int_type& c1,
                            const int_type& c2);
    static int_type eof();
};
```

These functions are used by the **basic_string** class template for character-based operations common to string processing. When you declare a **string** variable, such as:

```
std::string s;
```

you are actually declaring **s** as follows (because of the default template arguments in the specification of **basic_string**):

```
std::basic_string<char, std::char_traits<char>,
                  std::allocator<char> > s;
```

Because the character traits have been separated from the **basic_string** class template, you can supply a custom traits class to replace **std::char_traits**. The following example illustrates this flexibility:

```
//: C05:BearCorner.h
#ifndef BEARCORNER_H
#define BEARCORNER_H
#include <iostream>
using std::ostream;

// Item classes (traits of guests):
class Milk {
public:
  friend ostream& operator<<(ostream& os, const Milk&) {
    return os << "Milk";
  }
};

class CondensedMilk {
public:
  friend ostream&
  operator<<(ostream& os, const CondensedMilk &) {
    return os << "Condensed Milk";
  }
};
```

```cpp
class Honey {
public:
  friend ostream& operator<<(ostream& os, const Honey&) {
    return os << "Honey";
  }
};

class Cookies {
public:
  friend ostream& operator<<(ostream& os, const Cookies&) {
    return os << "Cookies";
  }
};

// Guest classes:
class Bear {
public:
  friend ostream& operator<<(ostream& os, const Bear&) {
    return os << "Theodore";
  }
};

class Boy {
public:
  friend ostream& operator<<(ostream& os, const Boy&) {
    return os << "Patrick";
  }
};

// Primary traits template (empty-could hold common types)
template<class Guest> class GuestTraits;

// Traits specializations for Guest types
template<> class GuestTraits<Bear> {
public:
  typedef CondensedMilk beverage_type;
  typedef Honey snack_type;
};

template<> class GuestTraits<Boy> {
public:
  typedef Milk beverage_type;
  typedef Cookies snack_type;
};
```

```
#endif // BEARCORNER_H ///:~

//: C05:BearCorner.cpp
// Illustrates traits classes.
#include <iostream>
#include "BearCorner.h"
using namespace std;

// A custom traits class
class MixedUpTraits {
public:
  typedef Milk beverage_type;
  typedef Honey snack_type;
};

// The Guest template (uses a traits class)
template<class Guest, class traits = GuestTraits<Guest> >
class BearCorner {
  Guest theGuest;
  typedef typename traits::beverage_type beverage_type;
  typedef typename traits::snack_type snack_type;
  beverage_type bev;
  snack_type snack;
public:
  BearCorner(const Guest& g) : theGuest(g) {}
  void entertain() {
    cout << "Entertaining " << theGuest
         << " serving " << bev
         << " and " << snack << endl;
  }
};

int main() {
  Boy cr;
  BearCorner<Boy> pc1(cr);
  pc1.entertain();
  Bear pb;
  BearCorner<Bear> pc2(pb);
  pc2.entertain();
  BearCorner<Bear, MixedUpTraits> pc3(pb);
  pc3.entertain();
} ///:~
```

In this program, instances of the guest classes **Boy** and **Bear** are served
items appropriate to their tastes. **Boy**s like milk and cookies, and **Bear**s like

condensed milk and honey. This association of guests to items is done via specializations of a primary (empty) traits class template. The default arguments to **BearCorner** ensure that guests get their proper items, but you can override this by simply providing a class that meets the requirements of the traits class, as we do with the **MixedUpTraits** class above. The output of this program is:

```
Entertaining Patrick serving Milk and Cookies
Entertaining Theodore serving Condensed Milk and Honey
Entertaining Theodore serving Milk and Honey
```

Using traits provides two key advantages: (1) it allows flexibility and extensibility in pairing objects with associated attributes or functionality, and (2) it keeps template parameter lists small and readable. If 30 types were associated with a guest, it would be inconvenient to have to specify all 30 arguments directly in each **BearCorner** declaration. Factoring the types into a separate traits class simplifies things considerably.

The traits technique is also used in implementing streams and locales, as we showed in Chapter 4. An example of iterator traits is found in the header file **PrintSequence.h** in Chapter 6.

Policies

If you inspect the **char_traits** specialization for **wchar_t**, you'll see that it is practically identical to its **char** counterpart:

```
template<> struct char_traits<wchar_t> {
  typedef wchar_t char_type;
  typedef wint_t int_type;
  typedef streamoff off_type;
  typedef wstreampos pos_type;
  typedef mbstate_t state_type;
  static void assign(char_type& c1, const char_type& c2);
  static bool eq(const char_type& c1, const char_type& c2);
  static bool lt(const char_type& c1, const char_type& c2);
  static int compare(const char_type* s1,
                     const char_type* s2, size_t n);
  static size_t length(const char_type* s);
  static const char_type* find(const char_type* s,
                               size_t n,
                               const char_type& a);
  static char_type* move(char_type* s1,
```

```
                        const char_type* s2, size_t n);
  static char_type* copy(char_type* s1,
                        const char_type* s2, size_t n);
  static char_type* assign(char_type* s, size_t n,
                          char_type a);
  static int_type not_eof(const int_type& c);
  static char_type to_char_type(const int_type& c);
  static int_type to_int_type(const char_type& c);
  static bool eq_int_type(const int_type& c1,
                         const int_type& c2);
  static int_type eof();
};
```

The only real difference between the two versions is the set of types involved (**char** and **int** vs. **wchar_t** and **wint_t**). The functionality provided is the same.[20] This highlights the fact that traits classes are indeed for *traits*, and the things that change between related traits classes are usually types and constant values, or fixed algorithms that use type-related template parameters. Traits classes tend to be templates themselves, since the types and constants they contain are seen as characteristics of the primary template parameter(s) (for example, **char** and **wchar_t**).

It is also useful to be able to associate *functionality* with template arguments, so that client programmers can easily customize behavior when they code. The following version of the **BearCorner** program, for instance, supports different types of entertainment:

```
//: C05:BearCorner2.cpp
// Illustrates policy classes.
#include <iostream>
#include "BearCorner.h"
using namespace std;

// Policy classes (require a static doAction() function):
class Feed {
public:
  static const char* doAction() { return "Feeding"; }
};
```

---

[20] The fact that **char_traits<>::compare( )** may call **strcmp( )** in one instance vs. **wcscmp( )** in another, for example, is immaterial to the point we make here: the "function" performed by **compare( )** is the same.

```
class Stuff {
public:
  static const char* doAction() { return "Stuffing"; }
};

// The Guest template (uses a policy and a traits class)
template<class Guest, class Action,
         class traits = GuestTraits<Guest> >
class BearCorner {
  Guest theGuest;
  typedef typename traits::beverage_type beverage_type;
  typedef typename traits::snack_type snack_type;
  beverage_type bev;
  snack_type snack;
public:
  BearCorner(const Guest& g) : theGuest(g) {}
  void entertain() {
    cout << Action::doAction() << " " << theGuest
         << " with " << bev
         << " and " << snack << endl;
  }
};

int main() {
  Boy cr;
  BearCorner<Boy, Feed> pc1(cr);
  pc1.entertain();
  Bear pb;
  BearCorner<Bear, Stuff> pc2(pb);
  pc2.entertain();
} ///:~
```

The **Action** template parameter in the **BearCorner** class expects to have a static member function named **doAction( )**, which is used in **BearCorner<>::entertain( )**. Users can choose **Feed** or **Stuff** at will, both of which provide the required function. Classes that encapsulate functionality in this way are referred to as *policy classes*. The entertainment "policies" are provided above through **Feed::doAction( )** and **Stuff::doAction( )**. These policy classes happen to be ordinary classes, but they can be templates, and can be combined with inheritance to great advantage. For more in-depth information on policy-based design, see Andrei Alexandrescu's book,[21] the definitive source on the subject.

The curiously recurring template pattern

Any novice C++ programmer can figure out how to modify a class to keep track of the number of objects of that class that currently exist. All you have to do is to add static members, and modify constructor and destructor logic, as follows:

```
//: C05:CountedClass.cpp
// Object counting via static members.
#include <iostream>
using namespace std;

class CountedClass {
  static int count;
public:
  CountedClass() { ++count; }
  CountedClass(const CountedClass&) { ++count; }
  ~CountedClass() { --count; }
  static int getCount() { return count; }
};

int CountedClass::count = 0;

int main() {
  CountedClass a;
  cout << CountedClass::getCount() << endl;    // 1
  CountedClass b;
  cout << CountedClass::getCount() << endl;    // 2
  { // An arbitrary scope:
    CountedClass c(b);
    cout << CountedClass::getCount() << endl; // 3
    a = c;
    cout << CountedClass::getCount() << endl; // 3
  }
  cout << CountedClass::getCount() << endl;    // 2
} ///:~
```

---

[21] *Modern C++ Design: Generic Programming and Design Patterns Applied*, Addison Wesley, 2001.

All constructors of **CountedClass** increment the static data member **count**, and the destructor decrements it. The static member function **getCount( )** yields the current number of objects.

It would be tedious to manually add these members every time you wanted to add object counting to a class. The usual object-oriented device used to repeat or share code is inheritance, which is only half a solution in this case. Observe what happens when we collect the counting logic into a base class.

```
//: C05:CountedClass2.cpp
// Erroneous attempt to count objects.
#include <iostream>
using namespace std;

class Counted {
  static int count;
public:
  Counted() { ++count; }
  Counted(const Counted&) { ++count; }
  ~Counted() { --count; }
  static int getCount() { return count; }
};

int Counted::count = 0;

class CountedClass : public Counted {};
class CountedClass2 : public Counted {};

int main() {
  CountedClass a;
  cout << CountedClass::getCount() << endl;     // 1
  CountedClass b;
  cout << CountedClass::getCount() << endl;     // 2
  CountedClass2 c;
  cout << CountedClass2::getCount() << endl;    // 3 (Error)
} ///:~
```

All classes that derive from **Counted** share the same, single static data member, so the number of objects is tracked collectively across all classes in the **Counted** hierarchy. What is needed is a way to automatically generate a *different* base class for each derived class. This is accomplished by the curious template construct illustrated below:

```
//: C05:CountedClass3.cpp
#include <iostream>
using namespace std;

template<class T> class Counted {
  static int count;
public:
  Counted() { ++count; }
  Counted(const Counted<T>&) { ++count; }
  ~Counted() { --count; }
  static int getCount() { return count; }
};

template<class T> int Counted<T>::count = 0;

// Curious class definitions
class CountedClass : public Counted<CountedClass> {};
class CountedClass2 : public Counted<CountedClass2> {};

int main() {
  CountedClass a;
  cout << CountedClass::getCount() << endl;     // 1
  CountedClass b;
  cout << CountedClass::getCount() << endl;     // 2
  CountedClass2 c;
  cout << CountedClass2::getCount() << endl;    // 1 (!)
} ///:~
```

Each derived class derives from a unique base class that is determined by using itself (the derived class) as a template parameter! This may seem like a circular definition, and it would be, had any base class members used the template argument in a computation. Since no data members of **Counted** are dependent on **T**, the size of **Counted** (which is zero!) is known when the template is parsed. So it doesn't matter which argument is used to instantiate **Counted** because the size is always the same. Any derivation from an instance of **Counted** can be completed when it is parsed, and there is no recursion. Since each base class is unique, it has its own static data, thus constituting a handy technique for adding counting to any class whatsoever. Jim Coplien was the first to mention this interesting derivation idiom in print, which he cited in an article, entitled "Curiously Recurring Template Patterns." [22]

Template metaprogramming

In 1993 compilers were beginning to support simple template constructs so that users could define generic containers and functions. About the same time that the STL was being considered for adoption into Standard C++, clever and surprising examples such as the following were passed around among members of the C++ Standards Committee:[23]

```
//: C05:Factorial.cpp
// Compile-time computation using templates.
#include <iostream>
using namespace std;

template<int n> struct Factorial {
  enum { val = Factorial<n-1>::val * n };
};

template<> struct Factorial<0> {
  enum { val = 1 };
};

int main() {
  cout << Factorial<12>::val << endl; // 479001600
} ///:~
```

That this program prints the correct value of **12!** is not alarming. What is alarming is that the computation is complete before the program even runs!

When the compiler attempts to instantiate **Factorial<12>**, it finds it must also instantiate **Factorial<11>**, which requires **Factorial<10>**, and so on. Eventually the recursion ends with the specialization **Factorial<1>**, and the computation unwinds. Eventually, **Factorial<12>::val** is replaced by the integral constant 479001600, and compilation ends. Since all the

---

[22] *C++ Gems*, edited by Stan Lippman, SIGS, 1996.

[23] These are technically compile–time constants, so you could argue that the identifiers should be all uppercase letters to follow the usual form. We left them lowercased because they are simulations of variables.

computation is done by the compiler, the values involved must be compile-time constants, hence the use of **enum**. When the program runs, the only work left to do is print that constant followed by a newline. To convince yourself that a specialization of **Factorial** results in the correct compile-time value, you could use it as an array dimension, such as:

```
double nums[Factorial<5>::val];
assert(sizeof nums == sizeof(double)*120);
```

Compile–time programming

So what was meant to be a convenient way to perform type parameter substitution turned out to be a mechanism to support compile-time programming. Such a program is called a **template metaprogram** (since you're in effect "programming a program"), and it turns out that you can do quite a lot with it. In fact, template metaprogramming is *Turing complete* because it supports selection (if-else) and looping (through recursion). Theoretically, then, you can perform any computation with it.[24] The factorial example above shows how to implement repetition: write a recursive template and provide a stopping criterion via a specialization. The following example shows how to compute Fibonacci numbers at compile time by the same technique:

```
//: C05:Fibonacci.cpp
#include <iostream>
using namespace std;

template<int n> struct Fib {
  enum { val = Fib<n-1>::val + Fib<n-2>::val };
};

template<> struct Fib<1> { enum { val = 1 }; };

template<> struct Fib<0> { enum { val = 0 }; };

int main() {
```

---

[24] In 1966 Böhm and Jacopini proved that any language supporting selection and repetition, along with the ability to use an arbitrary number of variables, is equivalent to a Turing machine, which is believed capable of expressing any algorithm.

```
  cout << Fib<5>::val << endl;    // 6
  cout << Fib<20>::val << endl;   // 6765
} ///:~
```

Fibonacci numbers are defined mathematically as:

$$f_n = \begin{cases} 0, n = 0 \\ 1, n = 1 \\ f_{n-2} + f_{n-1}, n > 1 \end{cases}$$

The first two cases lead to the template specializations above, and the rule in the third line becomes the primary template.

Compile-time looping

To compute any loop in a template metaprogram, it must first be reformulated recursively. For example, to raise the integer **n** to the power **p**, instead of using a loop such as in the following lines:

```
int val = 1;
while(p--)
  val *= n;
```

you cast it as a recursive procedure:

```
int power(int n, int p) {
  return (p == 0) ? 1 : n*power(n, p - 1);
}
```

This can now be easily rendered as a template metaprogram:

```
//: C05:Power.cpp
#include <iostream>
using namespace std;

template<int N, int P> struct Power {
  enum { val = N * Power<N, P-1>::val };
};

template<int N> struct Power<N, 0> {
  enum { val = 1 };
};

int main() {
```

```
  cout << Power<2, 5>::val << endl;    // 32
} ///:~
```

We need to use a partial specialization for the stopping condition, since the value **N** is still a free template parameter. Note that this program only works for non-negative powers.

The following metaprogram adapted from Czarnecki and Eisenecker[25] is interesting in that it uses a template template parameter, and simulates passing a function as a parameter to another function, which "loops through" the numbers **0..n**:

```
//: C05:Accumulate.cpp
// Passes a "function" as a parameter at compile time.
#include <iostream>
using namespace std;

// Accumulates the results of F(0)..F(n)
template<int n, template<int> class F> struct Accumulate {
  enum { val = Accumulate<n-1, F>::val + F<n>::val };
};

// The stopping criterion (returns the value F(0))
template<template<int> class F> struct Accumulate<0, F> {
  enum { val = F<0>::val };
};

// Various "functions":
template<int n> struct Identity {
  enum { val = n };
};

template<int n> struct Square {
  enum { val = n*n };
};

template<int n> struct Cube {
  enum { val = n*n*n };
};
```

---

[25] Czarnecki and Eisenecker, *Generative Programming: Methods, Tools, and Applications*, Addison Wesley, 2000, p. 417.

```
int main() {
  cout << Accumulate<4, Identity>::val << endl; // 10
  cout << Accumulate<4, Square>::val << endl;   // 30
  cout << Accumulate<4, Cube>::val << endl;     // 100
} ///:~
```

The primary **Accumulate** template attempts to compute the sum
F(n)+F(n-1)...F(0). The stopping criterion is obtained by a partial
specialization, which "returns" **F(0)**. The parameter **F** is itself a template,
and acts like a function as in the previous examples in this section. The
templates **Identity, Square,** and **Cube** compute the corresponding
functions of their template parameter that their names suggest. The first
instantiation of **Accumulate** in **main( )** computes the sum 4+3+2+1+0,
because the **Identity** function simply "returns" its template parameter. The
second line in **main( )** adds the squares of those numbers (16+9+4+1+0),
and the last computes the sum of the cubes (64+27+8+1+0).

Loop unrolling

Algorithm designers have always endeavored to optimize their programs. One
time-honored optimization, especially for numeric programming, is loop
unrolling, a technique that minimizes loop overhead. The quintessential loop-
unrolling example is matrix multiplication. The following function multiplies
a matrix and a vector. (Assume that the constants **ROWS** and **COLS** have
been previously defined.):

```
void mult(int a[ROWS][COLS], int x[COLS], int y[COLS]) {
  for(int i = 0; i < ROWS; ++i) {
      y[i] = 0;
      for(int j = 0; j < COLS; ++j)
        y[i] += a[i][j]*x[j];
  }
}
```

If **COLS** is an even number, the overhead of incrementing and comparing the
loop control variable **j** can be cut in half by "unrolling" the computation into
pairs in the inner loop:

```
void mult(int a[ROWS][COLS], int x[COLS], int y[COLS]) {
  for(int i = 0; i < ROWS; ++i) {
      y[i] = 0;
      for(int j = 0; j < COLS; j += 2)
        y[i] += a[i][j]*x[j] + a[i][j+1]*x[j+1];
  }
```

```
}
```

In general, if **COLS** is a factor of **k**, **k** operations can be performed each time the inner loop iterates, greatly reducing the overhead. The savings is only noticeable on large arrays, but that is precisely the case with industrial-strength mathematical computations.

Function inlining also constitutes a form of loop unrolling. Consider the following approach to computing powers of integers:

```
//: C05:Unroll.cpp
// Unrolls an implicit loop via inlining.
#include <iostream>
using namespace std;

template<int n> inline int power(int m) {
  return power<n-1>(m) * m;
}

template<> inline int power<1>(int m) {
  return m;
}

template<> inline int power<0>(int m) {
  return 1;
}

int main() {
  int m = 4;
  cout << power<3>(m) << endl;
} ///:~
```

Conceptually, the compiler must generate three specializations of **power<>**, one each for the template parameters 3, 2, and 1. Because the code for each of these functions can be inlined, the actual code that is inserted into **main( )** is the single expression **m*m*m**. Thus, a simple template specialization coupled with inlining provides a way to totally avoid loop control overhead.[26] This approach to loop unrolling is limited by your compiler's inlining depth.

---

[26] There is a much better way to compute powers of integers: the Russian Peasant Algorithm.

Compile–time selection

To simulate conditionals at compile time, you can use the conditional ternary operator in an **enum** declaration. The following program uses this technique to calculate the maximum of two integers at compile time:

```
//: C05:Max.cpp
#include <iostream>
using namespace std;

template<int n1, int n2> struct Max {
  enum { val = n1 > n2 ? n1 : n2 };
};

int main() {
  cout << Max<10, 20>::val << endl;   // 20
} ///:~
```

If you want to use compile-time conditions to govern custom code generation, you can use specializations of the values **true** and **false**:

```
//: C05:Conditionals.cpp
// Uses compile-time conditions to choose code.
#include <iostream>
using namespace std;

template<bool cond> struct Select {};

template<> class Select<true> {
  static void statement1() {
    cout << "This is statement1 executing\n";
  }
public:
  static void f() { statement1(); }
};

template<> class Select<false> {
  static void statement2() {
    cout << "This is statement2 executing\n";
  }
public:
  static void f() { statement2(); }
};

template<bool cond> void execute() {
```

```
    Select<cond>::f();
}

int main() {
  execute<sizeof(int) == 4>();
} ///:~
```

This program is equivalent to the expression:

```
if(cond)
  statement1();
else
  statement2();
```

except that the condition **cond** is evaluated at compile time, and the appropriate versions of **execute<>( )** and **Select<>** are instantiated by the compiler. The function **Select<>::f( )** executes at runtime. A **switch** statement can be emulated in similar fashion, but specializing on each case value instead of the values **true** and **false**.

Compile-time assertions

In Chapter 2 we touted the virtues of using assertions as part of an overall defensive programming strategy. An assertion is basically an evaluation of a Boolean expression followed by a suitable action: do nothing if the condition is true, or halt with a diagnostic message otherwise. It's best to discover assertion failures as soon as possible. If you can evaluate an expression at compile time, use a compile-time assertion. The following example uses a technique that maps a Boolean expression to an array declaration:

```
//: C05:StaticAssert1.cpp {-xo}
// A simple, compile-time assertion facility

#define STATIC_ASSERT(x) \
  do { typedef int a[(x) ? 1 : -1]; } while(0)

int main() {
  STATIC_ASSERT(sizeof(int) <= sizeof(long)); // Passes
  STATIC_ASSERT(sizeof(double) <= sizeof(int)); // Fails
} ///:~
```

The **do** loop creates a temporary scope for the definition of an array, **a**, whose size is determined by the condition in question. It is illegal to define an array of size -1, so when the condition is false the statement should fail.

The previous section showed how to evaluate compile-time Boolean expressions. The remaining challenge in emulating assertions at compile time is to print a meaningful error message and halt. All that is required to halt the compiler is a compile error; the trick is to insert helpful text in the error message. The following example from Alexandrescu[27] uses template specialization, a local class, and a little macro magic to do the job:

```
//: C05:StaticAssert2.cpp {-g++}
#include <iostream>
using namespace std;

// A template and a specialization
template<bool> struct StaticCheck {
  StaticCheck(...);
};

template<> struct StaticCheck<false> {};

// The macro (generates a local class)
#define STATIC_CHECK(expr, msg) {                 \
  class Error_##msg {};                           \
  sizeof((StaticCheck<expr>(Error_##msg()))); \
}

// Detects narrowing conversions
template<class To, class From> To safe_cast(From from) {
  STATIC_CHECK(sizeof(From) <= sizeof(To),
               NarrowingConversion);
  return reinterpret_cast<To>(from);
}

int main() {
  void* p = 0;
  int i = safe_cast<int>(p);
  cout << "int cast okay" << endl;
  //! char c = safe_cast<char>(p);
} ///:~
```

This example defines a function template, **safe_cast<>( )**, that checks to see if the object it is casting from is no larger than the type of object it casts to. If the size of the target object type is smaller, then the user will be notified at

---

[27] *Modern C++ Design*, pp. 23–26.

compile time that a narrowing conversion was attempted. Notice that the **StaticCheck** class template has the curious feature that *anything* can be converted to an instance of **StaticCheck<true>** (because of the ellipsis in its constructor[28]), and *nothing* can be converted to a **StaticCheck<false>** because no conversions are supplied for that specialization. The idea is to attempt to create an instance of a new class and attempt to convert it to **StaticCheck<true>** *at compile time* whenever the condition of interest is true, or to a **StaticCheck<false>** object when the condition being tested is false. Since the **sizeof** operator does its work at compile time, it is used to attempt the conversion. If the condition is false, the compiler will complain that it doesn't know how to convert from the new class type to **StaticCheck<false>**. (The extra parentheses inside the **sizeof** invocation in **STATIC_CHECK( )** are to prevent the compiler from thinking that we're trying to invoke **sizeof** on a function, which is illegal.) To get some meaningful information inserted into the error message, the new class name carries key text in its name.

The best way to understand this technique is to walk through a specific case. Consider the line in **main( )** above which reads:

```
int i = safe_cast<int>(p);
```

The call to **safe_cast<int>(p)** contains the following macro expansion replacing its first line of code:

```
{                                                      \
   class Error_NarrowingConversion {};                 \
   sizeof(StaticCheck<sizeof(void*) <= sizeof(int)> \
         (Error_NarrowingConversion()));               \
}
```

(Recall that the token-pasting preprocessing operator, **##**, concatenates its operand into a single token, so **Error_##NarrowingConversion** becomes the token **Error_NarrowingConversion** after preprocessing). The class **Error_NarrowingConversion** is a *local class* (meaning that it is declared inside a non-namespace scope) because it is not needed elsewhere in

---

[28] You are not allowed to pass object types (other than built-ins) to an ellipsis parameter specification, but since we are only asking for its size (a compile-time operation), the expression is never actually evaluated at runtime.

the program. The application of the **sizeof** operator here attempts to determine the size of an instance of **StaticCheck<true>** (because **sizeof(void*) <= sizeof(int)** is true on our platforms), created implicitly from the temporary object returned by the call **Error_NarrowingConversion( )**. The compiler knows the size of the new class **Error_NarrowingConversion** (it's empty), and so the compile-time use of **sizeof** at the outer level in **STATIC_CHECK( )** is valid. Since the conversion from the **Error_NarrowingConversion** temporary to **StaticCheck<true>** succeeds, so does this outer application of **sizeof**, and execution continues.

Now consider what would happen if the comment were removed from the last line of **main( )**:

```
char c = safe_cast<char>(p);
```

Here the **STATIC_CHECK( )** macro inside **safe_cast<char>(p)** expands to:

```
{                                                              \
   class Error_NarrowingConversion {};                         \
   sizeof(StaticCheck<sizeof(void*) <= sizeof(char)> \
         (Error_NarrowingConversion()));                       \
}
```

Since the expression **sizeof(void*) <= sizeof(char)** is false, a conversion from an **Error_NarrowingConversion** temporary to **StaticCheck<false>** is attempted, as follows:

```
sizeof(StaticCheck<false>(Error_NarrowingConversion()));
```

which fails, so the compiler halts with a message something like the following:

```
Cannot cast from 'Error_NarrowingConversion' to
'StaticCheck<0>' in function
char safe_cast<char,void *>(void *)
```

The class name **Error_NarrowingConversion** is the meaningful message judiciously arranged by the coder. In general, to perform a static assertion with this technique, you just invoke the **STATIC_CHECK** macro with the compile-time condition to check and with a meaningful name to describe the error.

Expression templates

Perhaps the most powerful application of templates is a technique discovered independently in 1994 by Todd Veldhuizen[29] and Daveed Vandevoorde:[30] *expression templates*. Expression templates enable extensive compile-time optimization of certain computations that result in code that is at least as fast as hand-optimized Fortran, and yet preserves the natural notation of mathematics via operator overloading. Although you wouldn't be likely to use this technique in everyday programming, it is the basis for a number of sophisticated, high-performance mathematical libraries written in C++.[31]

To motivate the need for expression templates, consider typical numerical linear algebra operations, such as adding together two matrices or vectors,[32] such as in the following:

```
D = A + B + C;
```

In naive implementations, this expression would result in a number of temporaries—one for **A+B**, and one for **(A+B)+C**. When these variables represent immense matrices or vectors, the coincident drain on resources is unacceptable. Expression templates allow you to use the same expression without temporaries.

The following program defines a **MyVector** class to simulate mathematical vectors of any size. We use a non-type template argument for the length of

---

[29] A reprint of Todd's original article can be found in Lippman, *C++ Gems*, SIGS, 1996. It should also be noted that besides retaining mathematical notation and optimized code, expression templates also allow for C++ libraries to incorporate paradigms and mechanisms found in other programming languages, such as lambda expressions. Another example is the fantastic class library Spirit, which is a parser that makes heavy use of expression templates, allowing for (an approximate) EBNF notation directly in C++, resulting in extremely efficient parsers. Visit http://spirit.sourceforge.net/.

[30] See his and Nico's book, *C++ Templates*, book cited earlier.

[31] Namely, Blitz++ (http://www.oonumerics.org/blitz/), the Matrix Template Library (http://www.osl.iu.edu/research/mtl/), and POOMA (http://www.acl.lanl.gov/pooma/).

[32] We mean "vector" in the mathematical sense, as a fixed–length, one–dimensional, numerical array.

---

the vector. We also define a **MyVectorSum** class to act as a proxy class for a sum of **MyVector** objects. This allows us to use lazy evaluation, so the addition of vector components is performed on demand without the need for temporaries.

```cpp
//: C05:MyVector.cpp
// Optimizes away temporaries via templates.
#include <cstddef>
#include <cstdlib>
#include <ctime>
#include <iostream>
using namespace std;

// A proxy class for sums of vectors
template<class, size_t> class MyVectorSum;

template<class T, size_t N> class MyVector {
  T data[N];
public:
  MyVector<T,N>& operator=(const MyVector<T,N>& right) {
    for(size_t i = 0; i < N; ++i)
      data[i] = right.data[i];
    return *this;
  }
  MyVector<T,N>& operator=(const MyVectorSum<T,N>& right);
  const T& operator[](size_t i) const { return data[i]; }
  T& operator[](size_t i) { return data[i]; }
};

// Proxy class hold references; uses lazy addition
template<class T, size_t N> class MyVectorSum {
  const MyVector<T,N>& left;
  const MyVector<T,N>& right;
public:
  MyVectorSum(const MyVector<T,N>& lhs,
              const MyVector<T,N>& rhs)
  : left(lhs), right(rhs) {}
  T operator[](size_t i) const {
    return left[i] + right[i];
  }
};

// Operator to support v3 = v1 + v2
template<class T, size_t N> MyVector<T,N>&
```

```
MyVector<T,N>::operator=(const MyVectorSum<T,N>& right) {
  for(size_t i = 0; i < N; ++i)
    data[i] = right[i];
  return *this;
}

// operator+ just stores references
template<class T, size_t N> inline MyVectorSum<T,N>
operator+(const MyVector<T,N>& left,
          const MyVector<T,N>& right) {
  return MyVectorSum<T,N>(left, right);
}

// Convenience functions for the test program below
template<class T, size_t N> void init(MyVector<T,N>& v) {
  for(size_t i = 0; i < N; ++i)
    v[i] = rand() % 100;
}

template<class T, size_t N> void print(MyVector<T,N>& v) {
  for(size_t i = 0; i < N; ++i)
    cout << v[i] << ' ';
  cout << endl;
}

int main() {
  srand(time(0));
  MyVector<int, 5> v1;
  init(v1);
  print(v1);
  MyVector<int, 5> v2;
  init(v2);
  print(v2);
  MyVector<int, 5> v3;
  v3 = v1 + v2;
  print(v3);
  MyVector<int, 5> v4;
  // Not yet supported:
//!   v4 = v1 + v2 + v3;
} ///:~
```

The **MyVectorSum** class does no computation when it is created; it merely holds references to the two vectors to be added. Calculations happen only when you access a component of a vector sum (see its **operator[ ]( )**). The

overload of the assignment operator for **MyVector** that takes a
MyVectorSum argument is for an expression such as:

```
v1 = v2 + v3;   // Add two vectors
```

When the expression **v1+v2** is evaluated, a **MyVectorSum** object is
returned (or actually, inserted inline, since that **operator+( )** is declared
inline). This is a small, fixed-size object (it holds only two references). Then
the assignment operator mentioned above is invoked:

```
v3.operator=<int,5>(MyVectorSum<int,5>(v2, v3));
```

This assigns to each element of **v3** the sum of the corresponding elements of
v1 and **v2**, computed in real time. No temporary **MyVector** objects are
created.

This program does not support an expression that has more than two
operands, however, such as

```
v4 = v1 + v2 + v3;
```

The reason is that, after the first addition, a second addition is attempted:

```
(v1 + v2) + v3;
```

which would require an **operator+( )** with a first argument of
MyVectorSum and a second argument of type **MyVector**. We could
attempt to provide a number of overloads to meet all situations, but it is
better to let templates do the work, as in the following version of the
program:

```
//: C05:MyVector2.cpp
// Handles sums of any length with expression templates.
#include <cstddef>
#include <cstdlib>
#include <ctime>
#include <iostream>
using namespace std;

// A proxy class for sums of vectors
template<class, size_t, class, class> class MyVectorSum;

template<class T, size_t N> class MyVector {
  T data[N];
```

```
public:
  MyVector<T,N>& operator=(const MyVector<T,N>& right) {
    for(size_t i = 0; i < N; ++i)
      data[i] = right.data[i];
    return *this;
  }
  template<class Left, class Right> MyVector<T,N>&
  operator=(const MyVectorSum<T,N,Left,Right>& right);
  const T& operator[](size_t i) const {
    return data[i];
  }
  T& operator[](size_t i) {
    return data[i];
  }
};

// Allows mixing MyVector and MyVectorSum
template<class T, size_t N, class Left, class Right>
class MyVectorSum {
  const Left& left;
  const Right& right;
public:
  MyVectorSum(const Left& lhs, const Right& rhs)
  : left(lhs), right(rhs) {}
  T operator[](size_t i) const {
    return left[i] + right[i];
  }
};

template<class T, size_t N>
template<class Left, class Right>
MyVector<T,N>&
MyVector<T,N>::
operator=(const MyVectorSum<T,N,Left,Right>& right) {
  for(size_t i = 0; i < N; ++i)
    data[i] = right[i];
  return *this;
}
// operator+ just stores references
template<class T, size_t N>
inline MyVectorSum<T,N,MyVector<T,N>,MyVector<T,N> >
operator+(const MyVector<T,N>& left,
          const MyVector<T,N>& right) {
  return MyVectorSum<T,N,MyVector<T,N>,MyVector<T,N> >
      (left,right);
```

```
}

template<class T, size_t N, class Left, class Right>
inline MyVectorSum<T, N, MyVectorSum<T,N,Left,Right>,
          MyVector<T,N> >
operator+(const MyVectorSum<T,N,Left,Right>& left,
          const MyVector<T,N>& right) {
  return MyVectorSum<T,N,MyVectorSum<T,N,Left,Right>,
                      MyVector<T,N> >
    (left, right);
}
// Convenience functions for the test program below
template<class T, size_t N> void init(MyVector<T,N>& v) {
  for(size_t i = 0; i < N; ++i)
    v[i] = rand() % 100;
}

template<class T, size_t N> void print(MyVector<T,N>& v) {
  for(size_t i = 0; i < N; ++i)
    cout << v[i] << ' ';
  cout << endl;
}

int main() {
  srand(time(0));
  MyVector<int, 5> v1;
  init(v1);
  print(v1);
  MyVector<int, 5> v2;
  init(v2);
  print(v2);
  MyVector<int, 5> v3;
  v3 = v1 + v2;
  print(v3);
  // Now supported:
  MyVector<int, 5> v4;
  v4 = v1 + v2 + v3;
  print(v4);
  MyVector<int, 5> v5;
  v5 = v1 + v2 + v3 + v4;
  print(v5);
} ///:~
```

The template facility deduces the argument types of a sum using the template
arguments, **Left** and **Right**, instead of committing to those types ahead of

time. The **MyVectorSum** template takes these extra two parameters so it can represent a sum of any combination of pairs of **MyVector** and **MyVectorSum**.

The assignment operator is now a member function template. This allows any <**T, N**> pair to be coupled with any <**Left, Right**> pair, so a **MyVector** object can be assigned from a **MyVectorSum** holding references to any possible pair of the types **MyVector** and **MyVectorSum**.

As we did before, let's trace through a sample assignment to understand exactly what takes place, beginning with the expression

```
v4 = v1 + v2 + v3;
```

Since the resulting expressions become quite unwieldy, in the explanation that follows, we will use **MVS** as shorthand for **MyVectorSum**, and will omit the template arguments.

The first operation is **v1+v2**, which invokes the inline **operator+( )**, which in turn inserts **MVS(v1, v2)** into the compilation stream. This is then added to **v3**, which results in a temporary object according to the expression **MVS(MVS(v1, v2), v3)**. The final representation of the entire statement is

```
v4.operator+(MVS(MVS(v1, v2), v3));
```

This transformation is all arranged by the compiler and explains why this technique carries the moniker "expression templates." The template **MyVectorSum** represents an expression (an addition, in this case), and the nested calls above are reminiscent of the parse tree of the left-associative expression **v1+v2+v3**.

An excellent article by Angelika Langer and Klaus Kreft explains how this technique can be extended to more complex computations.[33]

---

[33] Langer and Kreft, "C++ Expression Templates," *C/C++ Users Journal*, March 2003. See also the article on expression templates by Thomas Becker in the June 2003 issue of the same journal (that article was the inspiration for the material in this section).

Template compilation models

You may have noticed that all our template examples place fully-defined templates within each compilation unit. (For example, we place them completely within single-file programs, or in header files for multi-file programs.) This runs counter to the conventional practice of separating ordinary function definitions from their declarations by placing the latter in header files and the function implementations in separate (that is, **.cpp**) files.

The reasons for this traditional separation are:

- Non-inline function bodies in header files lead to multiple function definitions, resulting in linker errors.

- Hiding the implementation from clients helps reduce compile-time coupling.

- Vendors can distribute pre-compiled code (for a particular compiler) along with headers so that users cannot see the function implementations.

- Compile times are shorter since header files are smaller.

The inclusion model

Templates, on the other hand, are not code per se, but instructions for code generation. Only template instantiations are real code. When a compiler has seen a complete template definition during a compilation and then encounters a point of instantiation for that template in the same translation unit, it must deal with the fact that an equivalent point of instantiation may be present in another translation unit. The most common approach consists of generating the code for the instantiation in every translation unit and letting the linker weed out duplicates. That particular approach also works well with inline functions that cannot be inlined and with virtual function tables, which is one of the reasons for its popularity. Nonetheless, several compilers prefer instead to rely on more complex schemes to avoid generating a particular instantiation more than once. Either way, it is the responsibility of the C++ translation system to avoid errors due to multiple equivalent points of instantiation.

A drawback of this approach is that all template source code is visible to the client, so there is little opportunity for library vendors to hide their implementation strategies. Another disadvantage of the inclusion model is that header files are much larger than they would be if function bodies were compiled separately. This can increase compile times dramatically over traditional compilation models.

To help reduce the large headers required by the inclusion model, C++ offers two (non-exclusive) alternative code organization mechanisms: you can manually instantiate each specialization using *explicit instantiation* or you can use *exported templates*, which support a large degree of separate compilation.

Explicit instantiation

You can manually direct the compiler to instantiate any template specializations of your choice. When you use this technique, there must be one and only one such directive for each such specialization; otherwise you might get multiple definition errors, just as you would with ordinary, non-inline functions with identical signatures. To illustrate, we first (erroneously) separate the declaration of the **min( )** template from earlier in this chapter from its definition, following the normal pattern for ordinary, non-inline functions. The following example consists of five files:

- **OurMin.h**: contains the declaration of the **min( )** function template.

- **OurMin.cpp**: contains the definition of the **min( )** function template.

- **UseMin1.cpp**: attempts to use an **int**-instantiation of **min( )**.

- **UseMin2.cpp**: attempts to use a **double**-instantiation of **min( )**.

- **MinMain.cpp**: calls **usemin1( )** and **usemin2( )**.

```
//: C05:OurMin.h
#ifndef OURMIN_H
#define OURMIN_H
// The declaration of min()
template<typename T> const T& min(const T&, const T&);
#endif // OURMIN_H ///:~

// OurMin.cpp
#include "OurMin.h"
```

```
// The definition of min()
template<typename T> const T& min(const T& a, const T& b) {
  return (a < b) ? a : b;
}
```

```
//: C05:UseMin1.cpp {O}
#include <iostream>
#include "OurMin.h"
void usemin1() {
  std::cout << min(1,2) << std::endl;
} ///:~
```

```
//: C05:UseMin2.cpp {O}
#include <iostream>
#include "OurMin.h"
void usemin2() {
  std::cout << min(3.1,4.2) << std::endl;
} ///:~
```

```
//: C05:MinMain.cpp
//{L} UseMin1 UseMin2 MinInstances
void usemin1();
void usemin2();

int main() {
  usemin1();
  usemin2();
} ///:~
```

When we attempt to build this program, the linker reports unresolved
external references for **min<int>( )** and **min<double>( )**. The reason is
that when the compiler encounters the calls to specializations of **min( )** in
UseMin1 and **UseMin2**, only the declaration of **min( )** is visible. Since the
definition is not available, the compiler assumes it will come from some other
translation unit, and the needed specializations are thus not instantiated at
that point, leaving the linker to eventually complain that it cannot find them.

To solve this problem, we will introduce a new file, **MinInstances.cpp**, that
explicitly instantiates the needed specializations of **min( )**:

```
//: C05:MinInstances.cpp {O}
#include "OurMin.cpp"

// Explicit Instantiations for int and double
template const int& min<int>(const int&, const int&);
```

```
template const double& min<double>(const double&,
                                    const double&);
///:~
```

To manually instantiate a particular template specialization, you precede the specialization's declaration with the **template** keyword. Note that we must include **OurMin.cpp**, not **OurMin.h**, here, because the compiler needs the template definition to perform the instantiation. This is the only place where we have to do this in this program,[34] however, since it gives us the unique instantiations of **min( )** that we need—the declarations alone suffice for the other files. Since we are including **OurMin.cpp** with the macro preprocessor, we add include guards:

```
//: C05:OurMin.cpp {0}
#ifndef OURMIN_CPP
#define OURMIN_CPP
#include "OurMin.h"

template<typename T> const T& min(const T& a, const T& b) {
  return (a < b) ? a : b;
}
#endif // OURMIN_CPP ///:~
```

Now when we compile all the files together into a complete program, the unique instances of **min( )** are found, and the program executes correctly, giving the output:

```
1
3.1
```

You can also manually instantiate classes and static data members. When explicitly instantiating a class, all member functions for the requested specialization are instantiated, except any that may have been explicitly instantiated previously. This is important, as it will render many templates useless when using this mechanism—specifically, templates that implement different functionality depending on their parameterization type. Implicit instantiation has the advantage here: only member functions that get called are instantiated.

---

[34] As explained earlier, you must explicitly instantiate a template only once per program.

Explicit instantiation is intended for large projects where a hefty chunk of compilation time can be avoided. Whether you use implicit or explicit instantiation is independent of which template compilation you use. You can use manual instantiation with either the inclusion model or the separation model (discussed in the next section).

The separation model

The separation model of template compilation separates function template definitions or static data member definitions from their declarations across translation units, just like you do with ordinary functions and data, by *exporting* templates. After reading the preceding two sections, this must sound strange. Why bother to have the inclusion model in the first place if you can just adhere to the status quo? The reasons are both historical and technical.

Historically, the inclusion model was the first to experience widespread commercial use—all C++ compilers support the inclusion model. Part of the reason for that was that the separation model was not well specified until late in the standardization process, but also that the inclusion model is easier to implement. A lot of working code was in existence long before the semantics of the separation model were finalized.

The separation model is so difficult to implement that, as of Summer 2003, only one compiler front end (EDG) supports the separation model, and at the moment it still requires that template source code be available at compile time to perform instantiation on demand. Plans are in place to use some form of intermediate code instead of requiring that the original source be at hand, at which point you will be able to ship "pre-compiled" templates without shipping source code. Because of the lookup complexities explained earlier in this chapter (about dependent names being looked up in the template definition context), a full template definition still has to be available in some form when you compile a program that instantiates it.

The syntax to separate the source code of a template definition from its declaration is easy enough. You use the **export** keyword:

```
// C05:OurMin2.h
// Declares min as an exported template
// (Only works with EDG-based compilers)
#ifndef OURMIN2_H
```

```
#define OURMIN2_H
export template<typename T> const T& min(const T&,
                                         const T&);
#endif // OURMIN2_H ///:~
```

Similar to **inline** or **virtual**, the **export** keyword need only be mentioned once in a compilation stream, where an exported template is introduced. For this reason, we need not repeat it in the implementation file, but it is considered good practice to do so:

```
// C05:OurMin2.cpp
// The definition of the exported min template
// (Only works with EDG-based compilers)
#include "OurMin2.h"
export
template<typename T> const T& min(const T& a, const T& b) {
  return (a < b) ? a : b;
} ///:~
```

The **UseMin** files used previously only need to include the correct header file (**OurMin2.h**), and the main program doesn't change. Although this appears to give true separation, the file with the template definition (**OurMin2.cpp**) must still be shipped to users (because it must be processed for each instantiation of **min( )**) until such time as some form of intermediate code representation of template definitions is supported. So while the standard does provide for a true separation model, not all of its benefits can be reaped today. Only one family of compilers currently supports **export** (those based on the EDG front end), and these compilers currently do not exploit the potential ability to distribute template definitions in compiled form.

Summary

Templates go far beyond simple type parameterization. When you combine argument type deduction, custom specialization, and template metaprogramming, C++ templates emerge as a powerful code generation mechanism.

One of the weaknesses of C++ templates that we did not mention is the difficulty in interpreting compile-time error messages. The quantity of inscrutable text spewed out by the compiler can be quite overwhelming. C++ compilers have improved their template error messages, and Leor Zolman has written a tool called **STLFilt** that renders these error messages much more readable by extracting the useful information and throwing away the rest.[35]

Another important idea to take away from this chapter is that *a template implies an interface*. That is, even though the **template** keyword says "I'll take any type," the code in a template definition requires that certain operators and member functions be supported—that's the interface. So in reality, a template definition is saying, "I'll take any type that supports this interface." Things would be much nicer if the compiler could simply say, "Hey, this type that you're trying to instantiate the template with doesn't support that interface—can't do it." Using templates constitutes a sort of "latent type checking" that is more flexible than the pure object-oriented practice of requiring all types to derive from certain base classes.

In Chapters 6 and 7 we explore in depth the most famous application of templates, the subset of the Standard C++ library commonly known as the Standard Template Library (STL). Chapters 9 and 10 also use template techniques not found in this chapter.

Exercises

Solutions to selected exercises can be found in the electronic document *The Thinking in C++ Volume 2 Annotated Solution Guide*, available for a small fee from *www.MindView.net*.

1. Write a unary function template that takes a single type template parameter. Create a full specialization for the type **int**. Also create a non-template overload for this function that takes a single **int** parameter. Have your main program invoke three function variations.

2. Write a class template that uses a **vector** to implement a stack data structure.

3. Modify your solution to the previous exercise so that the type of the container used to implement the stack is a template template parameter.

---

[35] Visit http://www.bdsoft.com/tools/stlfilt.html.

4. In the following code, the class **NonComparable** does not have an **operator=( )**. Why would the presence of the class **HardLogic** cause a compile error, but **SoftLogic** would not?

```
//: C05:Exercise4.cpp {-xo}
class Noncomparable {};

struct HardLogic {
  Noncomparable nc1, nc2;
  void compare() {
    return nc1 == nc2; // Compiler error
  }
};

template<class T> struct SoftLogic {
  Noncomparable nc1, nc2;
  void noOp() {}
  void compare() {
    nc1 == nc2;
  }
};

int main() {
  SoftLogic<Noncomparable> l;
  l.noOp();
} ///:~
```

5. Write a function template that takes a single type parameter (**T**) and accepts four function arguments: an array of **T**, a start index, a stop index (inclusive), and an optional initial value. The function returns the sum of all the array elements in the specified range and the initial value. Use the default constructor of **T** for the default initial value.

6. Repeat the previous exercise but use explicit instantiation to manually create specializations for **int** and **double**, following the technique explained in this chapter.

7. Why does the following code not compile? (Hint: what do class member functions have access to?)

```
//: C05:Exercise7.cpp {-xo}
class Buddy {};

template<class T> class My {
  int i;
```

```
public:
  void play(My<Buddy>& s) {
    s.i = 3;
  }
};

int main() {
  My<int> h;
  My<Buddy> me, bud;
  h.play(bud);
  me.play(bud);
} ///:~
```

8.   Why does the following code not compile?

```
//: C05:Exercise8.cpp {-xo}
template<class T> double pythag(T a, T b, T c) {
  return (-b + sqrt(double(b*b - 4*a*c))) / 2*a;
}

int main() {
  pythag(1, 2, 3);
  pythag(1.0, 2.0, 3.0);
  pythag(1, 2.0, 3.0);
  pythag<double>(1, 2.0, 3.0);
} ///:~
```

9.   Write templates that take non-type parameters of the following
     variety: an **int**, a pointer to an **int**, a pointer to a static class
     member of type **int**, and a pointer to a static member function.

10. Write a class template that takes two type parameters. Define a
     partial specialization for the first parameter, and another partial
     specialization that specifies the second parameter. In each
     specialization, introduce members that are not in the primary
     template.

11. Define a class template named **Bob** that takes a single type
     parameter. Make **Bob** a friend of all instances of a template class
     named **Friendly**, and a friend of a class template named **Picky**
     only when the type parameter of **Bob** and **Picky** are identical.
     Give **Bob** member functions that demonstrate its friendship.

6: Generic Algorithms

Algorithms are at the core of computing. To be able to write an algorithm that works with any type of sequence makes your programs both simpler and safer. The ability to customize algorithms at runtime has revolutionized software development.

The subset of the Standard C++ library known as the Standard Template Library (STL) was originally designed around *generic algorithms*—code that processes sequences of any type of values in a type-safe manner. The goal was to use predefined algorithms for almost every task, instead of hand-coding loops every time you need to process a collection of data. This power comes with a bit of a learning curve, however. By the time you get to the end of this chapter, you should be able to decide for yourself whether you find the algorithms addictive or too confusing to remember. If you're like most people, you'll resist them at first but then tend to use them more and more as time goes on.

A first look

Among other things, the generic algorithms in the standard library provide a vocabulary with which to describe solutions. Once you become familiar with the algorithms, you'll have a new set of words with which to discuss what you're doing, and these words are at a higher level than what you had before. You don't need to say, "This loop moves through and assigns from here to there ... oh, I see, it's copying!" Instead, you just say **copy( )**. This is what we've been doing in computer programming from the beginning—creating high-level abstractions to express *what* you're doing and spending less time saying *how* you're doing it. The *how* has been solved once and for all and is hidden in the algorithm's code, ready to be reused on demand.

Here's an example of how to use the **copy** algorithm:

```
//: C06:CopyInts.cpp
// Copies ints without an explicit loop.
#include <algorithm>
```

```
#include <cassert>
#include <cstddef>  // For size_t
using namespace std;

int main() {
  int a[] = { 10, 20, 30 };
  const size_t SIZE = sizeof a / sizeof a[0];
  int b[SIZE];
  copy(a, a + SIZE, b);
  for(size_t i = 0; i < SIZE; ++i)
    assert(a[i] == b[i]);
} ///:~
```

The **copy( )** algorithm's first two parameters represent the *range* of the input sequence—in this case the array **a**. Ranges are denoted by a pair of pointers. The first points to the first element of the sequence, and the second points one position *past the end* of the array (right after the last element). This may seem strange at first, but it is an old C idiom that comes in quite handy. For example, the difference of these two pointers yields the number of elements in the sequence. More important, in implementing **copy**, the second pointer can act as a sentinel to stop the iteration through the sequence. The third argument refers to the beginning of the output sequence, which is the array **b** in this example. It is assumed that the array that **b** represents has enough space to receive the copied elements.

The **copy( )** algorithm wouldn't be very exciting if it could only process integers. It can copy any kind of sequence. The following example copies **string** objects:

```
//: C06:CopyStrings.cpp
// Copies strings.
#include <algorithm>
#include <cassert>
#include <cstddef>
#include <string>
using namespace std;

int main() {
  string a[] = {"read", "my", "lips"};
  const size_t SIZE = sizeof a / sizeof a[0];
  string b[SIZE];
  copy(a, a + SIZE, b);
  assert(equal(a, a + SIZE, b));
```

```
} ///:~
```

This example introduces another algorithm, **equal( )**, which returns **true** only if each element in the first sequence is equal (using its **operator==( )**) to the corresponding element in the second sequence. This example traverses each sequence twice, once for the copy, and once for the comparison, without a single explicit loop!

Generic algorithms achieve this flexibility because they are function templates. If you think that the implementation of **copy( )** looks like the following, you're almost right:

```
template<typename T> void copy(T* begin, T* end, T* dest) {
  while(begin != end)
    *dest++ = *begin++;
}
```

We say "almost" because **copy( )** can process sequences delimited by anything that acts like a pointer, such as an iterator. In this way, **copy( )** can be used to duplicate a **vector**:

```
//: C06:CopyVector.cpp
// Copies the contents of a vector.
#include <algorithm>
#include <cassert>
#include <cstddef>
#include <vector>
using namespace std;

int main() {
  int a[] = { 10, 20, 30 };
  const size_t SIZE = sizeof a / sizeof a[0];
  vector<int> v1(a, a + SIZE);
  vector<int> v2(SIZE);
  copy(v1.begin(), v1.end(), v2.begin());
  assert(equal(v1.begin(), v1.end(), v2.begin()));
} ///:~
```

The first **vector, v1,** is initialized from the sequence of integers in the array **a.** The definition of the **vector v2** uses a different **vector** constructor that makes room for **SIZE** elements, initialized to zero (the default value for integers).

As with the array example earlier, it's important that **v2** have enough space to receive a copy of the contents of **v1**. For convenience, a special library function, **back_inserter( )**, returns a special type of iterator that *inserts* elements instead of *overwriting* them, so memory is expanded automatically by the container as needed. The following example uses **back_inserter( )**, so it doesn't have to establish the size of the output **vector, v2**, ahead of time:

```
//: C06:InsertVector.cpp
// Appends the contents of a vector to another.
#include <algorithm>
#include <cassert>
#include <cstddef>
#include <iterator>
#include <vector>
using namespace std;

int main() {
  int a[] = { 10, 20, 30 };
  const size_t SIZE = sizeof a / sizeof a[0];
  vector<int> v1(a, a + SIZE);
  vector<int> v2; // v2 is empty here
  copy(v1.begin(), v1.end(), back_inserter(v2));
  assert(equal(v1.begin(), v1.end(), v2.begin()));
} ///:~
```

The **back_inserter( )** function is defined in the **<iterator>** header. We'll explain how insert iterators work in depth in the next chapter.

Since iterators are identical to pointers in all essential ways, you can write the algorithms in the standard library in such a way as to allow both pointer and iterator arguments. For this reason, the implementation of **copy( )** looks more like the following code:

```
template<typename Iterator>
void copy(Iterator begin, Iterator end, Iterator dest) {
  while(begin != end)
    *begin++ = *dest++;
}
```

Whichever argument type you use in the call, **copy( )** assumes it properly implements the indirection and increment operators. If it doesn't, you'll get a compile-time error.

Predicates

At times, you might want to copy only a well-defined subset of one sequence to another, such as only those elements that satisfy a particular condition. To achieve this flexibility, many algorithms have alternate calling sequences that allow you to supply a *predicate*, which is simply a function that returns a Boolean value based on some criterion. Suppose, for example, that you only want to extract from a sequence of integers those numbers that are less than or equal to 15. A version of **copy( )** called **remove_copy_if( )** can do the job, like this:

```
//: C06:CopyInts2.cpp
// Ignores ints that satisfy a predicate.
#include <algorithm>
#include <cstddef>
#include <iostream>
using namespace std;

// You supply this predicate
bool gt15(int x) { return 15 < x; }

int main() {
  int a[] = { 10, 20, 30 };
  const size_t SIZE = sizeof a / sizeof a[0];
  int b[SIZE];
  int* endb = remove_copy_if(a, a+SIZE, b, gt15);
  int* beginb = b;
  while(beginb != endb)
    cout << *beginb++ << endl; // Prints 10 only
} ///:~
```

The **remove_copy_if( )** function template takes the usual range-delimiting pointers, followed by a predicate of your choosing. The predicate must be a pointer to a function[1] that takes a single argument of the same type as the elements in the sequence, and it must return a **bool**. Here, the function **gt15** returns **true** if its argument is greater than 15. The **remove_copy_if( )** algorithm applies **gt15( )** to each element in the input sequence and ignores those elements where the predicate yields true when writing to the output sequence.

---

[1] Or something that is callable as a function, as you'll see shortly.

The following program illustrates yet another variation of the **copy** algorithm:

```
//: C06:CopyStrings2.cpp
// Replaces strings that satisfy a predicate.
#include <algorithm>
#include <cstddef>
#include <iostream>
#include <string>
using namespace std;

// The predicate
bool contains_e(const string& s) {
  return s.find('e') != string::npos;
}

int main() {
  string a[] = {"read", "my", "lips"};
  const size_t SIZE = sizeof a / sizeof a[0];
  string b[SIZE];
  string* endb = replace_copy_if(a, a + SIZE, b,
    contains_e, string("kiss"));
  string* beginb = b;
  while(beginb != endb)
    cout << *beginb++ << endl;
} ///:~
```

Instead of just ignoring elements that don't satisfy the predicate, **replace_copy_if( )** substitutes a fixed value for such elements when populating the output sequence. The output is:

```
kiss
my
lips
```

because the original occurrence of "read," the only input string containing the letter *e*, is replaced by the word "kiss," as specified in the last argument in the call to **replace_copy_if( )**.

The **replace_if( )** algorithm changes the original sequence in place, instead of writing to a separate output sequence, as the following program shows:

```
//: C06:ReplaceStrings.cpp
// Replaces strings in-place.
```

```
#include <algorithm>
#include <cstddef>
#include <iostream>
#include <string>
using namespace std;

bool contains_e(const string& s) {
  return s.find('e') != string::npos;
}

int main() {
  string a[] = {"read", "my", "lips"};
  const size_t SIZE = sizeof a / sizeof a[0];
  replace_if(a, a + SIZE, contains_e, string("kiss"));
  string* p = a;
  while(p != a + SIZE)
    cout << *p++ << endl;
} ///:~
```

Stream iterators

Like any good software library, the Standard C++ Library attempts to provide
convenient ways to automate common tasks. We mentioned in the beginning
of this chapter that you can use generic algorithms in place of looping
constructs. So far, however, our examples have still used an explicit loop to
print their output. Since printing output is one of the most common tasks,
you would hope for a way to automate that too.

That's where *stream iterators* come in. A stream iterator uses a stream as
either an input or an output sequence. To eliminate the output loop in the
CopyInts2.cpp program, for instance, you can do something like the
following:

```
//: C06:CopyInts3.cpp
// Uses an output stream iterator.
#include <algorithm>
#include <cstddef>
#include <iostream>
#include <iterator>
using namespace std;

bool gt15(int x) { return 15 < x; }
```

```
int main() {
  int a[] = { 10, 20, 30 };
  const size_t SIZE = sizeof a / sizeof a[0];
  remove_copy_if(a, a + SIZE,
              ostream_iterator<int>(cout, "\n"), gt15);
} ///:~
```

In this example we've replaced the output sequence **b** in the third argument of **remove_copy_if( )** with an *output* stream iterator, which is an instance of the **ostream_iterator** class template declared in the **<iterator>** header. Output stream iterators overload their copy-assignment operators to write to their stream. This particular instance of **ostream_iterator** is attached to the output stream **cout**. Every time **remove_copy_if( )** assigns an integer from the sequence **a** to **cout** through this iterator, the iterator writes the integer to **cout** and also automatically writes an instance of the separator string found in its second argument, which in this case contains the newline character.

It is just as easy to write to a file by providing an output file stream, instead of **cout**:

```
//: C06:CopyIntsToFile.cpp
// Uses an output file stream iterator.
#include <algorithm>
#include <cstddef>
#include <fstream>
#include <iterator>
using namespace std;

bool gt15(int x) { return 15 < x; }

int main() {
  int a[] = { 10, 20, 30 };
  const size_t SIZE = sizeof a / sizeof a[0];
  ofstream outf("ints.out");
  remove_copy_if(a, a + SIZE,
              ostream_iterator<int>(outf, "\n"), gt15);
} ///:~
```

An *input* stream iterator allows an algorithm to get its input sequence from an input stream. This is accomplished by having both the constructor and **operator++( )** read the next element from the underlying stream and by overloading **operator*( )** to yield the value previously read. Since algorithms require two pointers to delimit an input sequence, you can construct an **istream_iterator** in two ways, as you can see in the program that follows.

```
//: C06:CopyIntsFromFile.cpp
// Uses an input stream iterator.
#include <algorithm>
#include <fstream>
#include <iostream>
#include <iterator>
#include "../require.h"
using namespace std;

bool gt15(int x) { return 15 < x; }

int main() {
  ofstream ints("someInts.dat");
  ints << "1 3 47 5 84 9";
  ints.close();
  ifstream inf("someInts.dat");
  assure(inf, "someInts.dat");
  remove_copy_if(istream_iterator<int>(inf),
                 istream_iterator<int>(),
                 ostream_iterator<int>(cout, "\n"), gt15);
} ///:~
```

The first argument to **replace_copy_if( )** in this program attaches an **istream_iterator** object to the input file stream containing **int**s. The second argument uses the default constructor of the **istream_iterator** class. This call constructs a special value of **istream_iterator** that indicates end-of-file, so that when the first iterator finally encounters the end of the physical file, it compares equal to the value **istream_iterator<int>( )**, allowing the algorithm to terminate correctly. Note that this example avoids using an explicit array altogether.

Algorithm complexity

Using a software library is a matter of trust. You trust the implementers to not only provide correct functionality, but you also hope that the functions execute as efficiently as possible. It's better to write your own loops than to use algorithms that degrade performance.

To guarantee quality library implementations, the C++ Standard not only specifies what an algorithm should do, but how fast it should do it and sometimes how much space it should use. Any algorithm that does not meet the performance requirements does not conform to the standard. The measure of an algorithm's operational efficiency is called its *complexity*.

When possible, the standard specifies the exact number of operation counts an algorithm should use. The **count_if( )** algorithm, for example, returns the number of elements in a sequence satisfying a given predicate. The following call to **count_if( )**, if applied to a sequence of integers similar to the examples earlier in this chapter, yields the number of integer elements that are greater than 15:

```
size_t n = count_if(a, a + SIZE, gt15);
```

Since **count_if( )** must look at every element exactly once, it is specified to make a number of comparisons exactly equal to the number of elements in the sequence. The **copy( )** algorithm has the same specification.

Other algorithms can be specified to take *at most* a certain number of operations. The **find( )** algorithm searches through a sequence in order until it encounters an element equal to its third argument:

```
int* p = find(a, a + SIZE, 20);
```

It stops as soon as the element is found and returns a pointer to that first occurrence. If it doesn't find one, it returns a pointer one position past the end of the sequence (**a+SIZE** in this example). So **find()** makes at most a number of comparisons equal to the number of elements in the sequence.

Sometimes the number of operations an algorithm takes cannot be measured with such precision. In such cases, the standard specifies the algorithm's *asymptotic complexity*, which is a measure of how the algorithm behaves with large sequences compared to well-known formulas. A good example is the **sort( )** algorithm, which the standard says takes "approximately **n log n** comparisons on average" (**n** is the number of elements in the sequence).[2]

---

[2] This is simply an English rendition of **O(n log n)**, which is the mathematical way of saying that for large **n**, the number of comparisons grows in direct proportion to the function **f(n) = n log n**.

Such complexity measures give a "feel" for the cost of an algorithm and at least give a meaningful basis for comparing algorithms. As you'll see in the next chapter, the **find( )** member function for the **set** container has logarithmic complexity, which means that the cost of searching for an element in a **set** will, for large sets, be proportional to the logarithm of the number of elements. This is much smaller than the number of elements for large **n**, so it is always better to search a **set** by using its **find( )** member function rather than by using the generic **find( )** algorithm.

Function objects

As you study some of the examples earlier in this chapter, you will probably notice the limited utility of the function **gt15( )**. What if you want to use a number other than 15 as a comparison threshold? You may need a **gt20( )** or **gt25( )** or others as well. Having to write a separate function is time consuming, but also unreasonable because you must know all required values when you write your application code.

The latter limitation means that you can't use runtime values[3] to govern your searches, which is unacceptable. Overcoming this difficulty requires a way to pass information to predicates at runtime. For example, you would need a greater-than function that you can initialize with an arbitrary comparison value. Unfortunately, you can't pass that value as a function parameter because unary predicates, such as our **gt15( )**, are applied to each value in a sequence individually and must therefore take only one parameter.

The way out of this dilemma is, as always, to create an abstraction. Here, we need an abstraction that can act like a function as well as store state, without disturbing the number of function parameters it accepts when used. This abstraction is called a *function object*.[4]

A function object is an instance of a class that overloads **operator( )**, the function call operator. This operator allows an object to be used with function

---

[3] Unless you do something ungainly using global variables.
[4] Function objects are also called *functors*, after a mathematical concept with similar behavior.

call syntax. As with any other object, you can initialize it via its constructors. Here is a function object that can be used in place of **gt15( )**:

```
//: C06:GreaterThanN.cpp
#include <iostream>
using namespace std;

class gt_n {
  int value;
public:
  gt_n(int val) : value(val) {}
  bool operator()(int n) { return n > value; }
};

int main() {
  gt_n f(4);
  cout << f(3) << endl;  // Prints 0 (for false)
  cout << f(5) << endl;  // Prints 1 (for true)
} ///:~
```

The fixed value to compare against (4) is passed when the function object **f** is created. The expression **f(3)** is then evaluated by the compiler as the following function call:

```
f.operator()(3);
```

which returns the value of the expression **3 > value**, which is false when **value** is 4, as it is in this example.

Since such comparisons apply to types other than **int**, it would make sense to define **gt_n( )** as a class template. It turns out you don't need to do it yourself, though—the standard library has already done it for you. The following descriptions of function objects should not only make that topic clear, but also give you a better understanding of how the generic algorithms work.

Classification of function objects

The Standard C++ library classifies a function object based on the number of arguments its **operator( )** takes and the kind of value it returns. This classification is based on whether a function object's **operator( )** takes zero, one, or two arguments:

Generator: A type of function object that takes no arguments and returns a value of an arbitrary type. A random number generator is an example of a generator. The standard library provides one generator, the function **rand( )** declared in **<cstdlib>**, and has some algorithms, such as **generate_n( )**, which apply generators to a sequence.

Unary Function: A type of function object that takes a single argument of any type and returns a value that may be of a different type (which may be **void**).

Binary Function: A type of function object that takes two arguments of any two (possibly distinct) types and returns a value of any type (including **void**).

Unary Predicate: A Unary Function that returns a **bool**.

Binary Predicate: A Binary Function that returns a **bool**.

Strict Weak Ordering: A binary predicate that allows for a more general interpretation of "equality." Some of the standard containers consider two elements equivalent if neither is less than the other (using **operator<( )**). This is important when comparing floating-point values, and objects of other types where **operator==( )** is unreliable or unavailable. This notion also applies if you want to sort a sequence of data records (**struct**s) on a subset of the **struct**'s fields. That comparison scheme is considered a strict weak ordering because two records with equal keys are not really "equal" as total objects, but they are equal as far as the comparison you're using is concerned. The importance of this concept will become clearer in the next chapter.

In addition, certain algorithms make assumptions about the operations available for the types of objects they process. We will use the following terms to indicate these assumptions:

LessThanComparable: A class that has a less-than **operator<**.

Assignable: A class that has a copy-assignment **operator=** for its own type.

EqualityComparable: A class that has an equivalence **operator==** for its own type.

We will use these terms later in this chapter to describe the generic algorithms in the standard library.

Automatic creation of function objects

The **<functional>** header defines a number of useful generic function objects. They are admittedly simple, but you can use them to compose more complicated function objects. Consequently, in many instances, you can construct complicated predicates without writing a single function. You do so by using *function object adaptors*[5] to take the simple function objects and adapt them for use with other function objects in a chain of operations.

To illustrate, let's use only standard function objects to accomplish what **gt15( )** did earlier. The standard function object, **greater**, is a *binary* function object that returns **true** if its first argument is greater than its second argument. We cannot apply this directly to a sequence of integers through an algorithm such as **remove_copy_if( )** because **remove_copy_if( )** expects a *unary* predicate. We can construct a unary predicate on the fly that uses **greater** to compare its first argument to a *fixed value*. We fix the value of the second parameter at 15 using the function object adaptor **bind2nd**, like this:

```
//: C06:CopyInts4.cpp
// Uses a standard function object and adaptor.
#include <algorithm>
#include <cstddef>
#include <functional>
#include <iostream>
#include <iterator>
using namespace std;

int main() {
  int a[] = { 10, 20, 30 };
  const size_t SIZE = sizeof a / sizeof a[0];
  remove_copy_if(a, a + SIZE,
                 ostream_iterator<int>(cout, "\n"),
                 bind2nd(greater<int>(), 15));
} ///:~
```

---

[5] The spelling here is *adaptor*, following the use in the C++ Standard. Elsewhere you will see it spelled *adapter* when used in the context of design patterns, following the common spelling there. Both spellings are considered acceptable by dictionaries.

This program produces the same result as **CopyInts3.cpp**, but without writing our own predicate function **gt15( )**. The function object adaptor **bind2nd( )** is a template function that creates a function object of type **binder2nd**, which simply stores the two arguments passed to **bind2nd( )**, the first of which must be a binary function or function object (that is, anything that can be called with two arguments). The **operator( )** function in **binder2nd**, which is itself a unary function, calls the binary function it stored, passing it its incoming parameter and the fixed value it stored.

To make the explanation concrete for this example, let's call the instance of **binder2nd** created by **bind2nd( )** by the name **b**. When **b** is created, it receives two parameters (**greater<int>( )** and 15) and stores them. Let's call the instance of **greater<int>** by the name **g**, and call the instance of the output stream iterator by the name **o**. Then the call to **remove_copy_if( )** earlier conceptually becomes the following:

```
remove_copy_if(a, a + SIZE, o, b(g, 15).operator());
```

As **remove_copy_if( )** iterates through the sequence, it calls **b** on each element, to determine whether to ignore the element when copying to the destination. If we denote the current element by the name **e**, that call inside **remove_copy_if( )** is equivalent to

```
if(b(e))
```

but **binder2nd**'s function call operator just turns around and calls **g(e,15)**, so the earlier call is the same as

```
if(greater<int>(e, 15))
```

which is the comparison we were seeking. There is also a **bind1st( )** adaptor that creates a **binder1st** object, which fixes the *first* argument of the associated input binary function.

As another example, let's count the number of elements in the sequence not equal to 20. This time we'll use the algorithm **count_if( )**, introduced earlier. There is a standard binary function object, **equal_to**, and also a function object adaptor, **not1( )**, that takes a unary function object as a parameter and invert its truth value. The following program will do the job:

```
//: C06:CountNotEqual.cpp
// Count elements not equal to 20.
```

```
#include <algorithm>
#include <cstddef>
#include <functional>
#include <iostream>
using namespace std;

int main() {
  int a[] = { 10, 20, 30 };
  const size_t SIZE = sizeof a / sizeof a[0];
  cout << count_if(a, a + SIZE,
                   not1(bind1st(equal_to<int>(), 20)));// 2
} ///:~
```

As **remove_copy_if( )** did in the previous example, **count_if( )** calls the predicate in its third argument (let's call it **n**) for each element of its sequence and increments its internal counter each time **true** is returned. If, as before, we call the current element of the sequence by the name **e**, the statement

```
if(n(e))
```

in the implementation of **count_if** is interpreted as

```
if(!bind1st(equal_to<int>, 20)(e))
```

which ends up as

```
if(!equal_to<int>(20, e))
```

because **not1( )** returns the logical negation of the result of calling its unary function argument. The first argument to **equal_to** is 20 because we used **bind1st( )** instead of **bind2nd( )**. Since testing for equality is symmetric in its arguments, we could have used either **bind1st( )** or **bind2nd( )** in this example.

The following table shows the templates that generate the standard function objects, along with the kinds of expressions to which they apply:

Name	Type	Result produced
plus	BinaryFunction	arg1 + arg2
minus	BinaryFunction	arg1 - arg2

Name	Type	Result produced
multiplies	BinaryFunction	arg1 * arg2
divides	BinaryFunction	arg1 / arg2
modulus	BinaryFunction	arg1 % arg2
negate	UnaryFunction	- arg1
equal_to	BinaryPredicate	arg1 == arg2
not_equal_to	BinaryPredicate	arg1 != arg2
greater	BinaryPredicate	arg1 > arg2
less	BinaryPredicate	arg1 < arg2
greater_equal	BinaryPredicate	arg1 >= arg2
less_equal	BinaryPredicate	arg1 <= arg2
logical_and	BinaryPredicate	arg1 && arg2
Logical_or	BinaryPredicate	arg1 || arg2
logical_not	UnaryPredicate	!arg1
unary_negate	Unary Logical	!(UnaryPredicate(arg1))
binary_negate	Binary Logical	!(BinaryPredicate(arg1, arg2))

Adaptable function objects

Standard function adaptors such as **bind1st( )** and **bind2nd( )** make some assumptions about the function objects they process. Consider the following expression from the last line of the earlier **CountNotEqual.cpp** program:

```
not1(bind1st(equal_to<int>(), 20))
```

The **bind1st( )** adaptor creates a unary function object of type **binder1st**, which simply stores an instance of **equal_to<int>** and the value 20. The **binder1st::operator( )** function needs to know its argument type and its return type; otherwise, it will not have a valid declaration. The convention to solve this problem is to expect all function objects to provide nested type definitions for these types. For unary functions, the type names are **argument_type** and **result_type**; for binary function objects they are **first_argument_type**, **second_argument_type**, and **result_type**. Looking at the implementation of **bind1st( )** and **binder1st** in the **<functional>** header reveals these expectations. First inspect **bind1st( )**, as it might appear in a typical library implementation:

```
template<class Op, class T>
binder1st<Op> bind1st(const Op& f, const T& val) {
  typedef typename Op::first_argument_type Arg1_t;
  return binder1st<Op>(f, Arg1_t(val));
}
```

Note that the template parameter, **Op**, which represents the type of the binary function being adapted by **bind1st( )**, must have a nested type named **first_argument_type**. (Note also the use of **typename** to inform the compiler that it is a member *type* name, as explained in Chapter 5.) Now see how **binder1st** uses the type names in **Op** in its declaration of its function call operator:

```
// Inside the implementation for binder1st<Op>
typename Op::result_type
operator()(const typename Op::second_argument_type& x)
  const;
```

Function objects whose classes provide these type names are called *adaptable function objects*.

Since these names are expected of all standard function objects as well as of any function objects you create to use with function object adaptors, the **<functional>** header provides two templates that define these types for you: **unary_function** and **binary_function**. You simply derive from these classes while filling in the argument types as template parameters. Suppose, for example, that we want to make the function object **gt_n**, defined earlier in this chapter, adaptable. All we need to do is the following:

```
class gt_n : public unary_function<int, bool> {
```

```
    int value;
public:
  gt_n(int val) : value(val) {}
  bool operator()(int n) {
    return n > value;
  }
};
```

All **unary_function** does is to provide the appropriate type definitions, which it infers from its template parameters as you can see in its definition:

```
template<class Arg, class Result> struct unary_function {
  typedef Arg argument_type;
  typedef Result result_type;
};
```

These types become accessible through **gt_n** because it derives publicly from **unary_function**. The **binary_function** template behaves in a similar manner.

More function object examples

The following **FunctionObjects.cpp** example provides simple tests for most of the built-in basic function object templates. This way, you can see how to use each template, along with the resulting behavior. This example uses one of the following generators for convenience:

```
//: C06:Generators.h
// Different ways to fill sequences.
#ifndef GENERATORS_H
#define GENERATORS_H
#include <cstring>
#include <set>
#include <cstdlib>

// A generator that can skip over numbers:
class SkipGen {
  int i;
  int skp;
public:
  SkipGen(int start = 0, int skip = 1)
  : i(start), skp(skip) {}
  int operator()() {
    int r = i;
```

```
      i += skp;
      return r;
    }
};

// Generate unique random numbers from 0 to mod:
class URandGen {
  std::set<int> used;
  int limit;
public:
  URandGen(int lim) : limit(lim) {}
  int operator()() {
    while(true) {
      int i = int(std::rand()) % limit;
      if(used.find(i) == used.end()) {
        used.insert(i);
        return i;
      }
    }
  }
};

// Produces random characters:
class CharGen {
  static const char* source;
  static const int len;
public:
  char operator()() {
    return source[std::rand() % len];
  }
};
#endif // GENERATORS_H ///:~

//: C06:Generators.cpp {O}
#include "Generators.h"
const char* CharGen::source = "ABCDEFGHIJK"
  "LMNOPQRSTUVWXYZabcdefghijklmnopqrstuvwxyz";
const int CharGen::len = std::strlen(source);
///:~
```

We'll be using these generating functions in various examples throughout this chapter. The **SkipGen** function object returns the next number of an arithmetic sequence whose common difference is held in its **skp** data member. A **URandGen** object generates a unique random number in a specified range. (It uses a **set** container, which we'll discuss in the next chapter.) A **CharGen** object returns a random alphabetic character. Here is a sample program using **UrandGen**:

```
//: C06:FunctionObjects.cpp {-bor}
// Illustrates selected predefined function object
// templates from the Standard C++ library.
//{L} Generators
#include <algorithm>
#include <cstdlib>
#include <ctime>
#include <functional>
#include <iostream>
#include <iterator>
#include <vector>
#include "Generators.h"
#include "PrintSequence.h"
using namespace std;

template<typename Contain, typename UnaryFunc>
void testUnary(Contain& source, Contain& dest,
  UnaryFunc f) {
    transform(source.begin(), source.end(), dest.begin(), f);
}

template<typename Contain1, typename Contain2,
  typename BinaryFunc>
void testBinary(Contain1& src1, Contain1& src2,
  Contain2& dest, BinaryFunc f) {
    transform(src1.begin(), src1.end(),
      src2.begin(), dest.begin(), f);
}

// Executes the expression, then stringizes the
// expression into the print statement:
#define T(EXPR) EXPR; print(r.begin(), r.end(), \
  "After " #EXPR);
// For Boolean tests:
#define B(EXPR) EXPR; print(br.begin(), br.end(), \
  "After " #EXPR);

// Boolean random generator:
struct BRand {
  bool operator()() { return rand() % 2 == 0; }
};
```

```
int main() {
  const int SZ = 10;
  const int MAX = 50;
  vector<int> x(SZ), y(SZ), r(SZ);
  // An integer random number generator:
  URandGen urg(MAX);
  srand(time(0));  // Randomize
  generate_n(x.begin(), SZ, urg);
  generate_n(y.begin(), SZ, urg);
  // Add one to each to guarantee nonzero divide:
  transform(y.begin(), y.end(), y.begin(),
    bind2nd(plus<int>(), 1));
  // Guarantee one pair of elements is ==:
  x[0] = y[0];
  print(x.begin(), x.end(), "x");
  print(y.begin(), y.end(), "y");
  // Operate on each element pair of x & y,
  // putting the result into r:
  T(testBinary(x, y, r, plus<int>()));
  T(testBinary(x, y, r, minus<int>()));
  T(testBinary(x, y, r, multiplies<int>()));
  T(testBinary(x, y, r, divides<int>()));
  T(testBinary(x, y, r, modulus<int>()));
  T(testUnary(x, r, negate<int>()));
  vector<bool> br(SZ); // For Boolean results
  B(testBinary(x, y, br, equal_to<int>()));
  B(testBinary(x, y, br, not_equal_to<int>()));
  B(testBinary(x, y, br, greater<int>()));
  B(testBinary(x, y, br, less<int>()));
  B(testBinary(x, y, br, greater_equal<int>()));
  B(testBinary(x, y, br, less_equal<int>()));
  B(testBinary(x, y, br, not2(greater_equal<int>())));
  B(testBinary(x,y,br,not2(less_equal<int>())));
  vector<bool> b1(SZ), b2(SZ);
  generate_n(b1.begin(), SZ, BRand());
  generate_n(b2.begin(), SZ, BRand());
  print(b1.begin(), b1.end(), "b1");
  print(b2.begin(), b2.end(), "b2");
  B(testBinary(b1, b2, br, logical_and<int>()));
  B(testBinary(b1, b2, br, logical_or<int>()));
  B(testUnary(b1, br, logical_not<int>()));
  B(testUnary(b1, br, not1(logical_not<int>())));
} ///:~
```

This example uses a handy function template, **print( )**, which is capable of printing a sequence of any type along with an optional message. This template appears in the header file **PrintSequence.h**, and is explained later in this chapter.

The two template functions automate the process of testing the various function object templates. There are two because the function objects are either unary or binary. The **testUnary( )** function takes a source **vector**, a destination **vector**, and a unary function object to apply to the source **vector** to produce the destination **vector**. In **testBinary( )**, two source **vector**s are fed to a binary function to produce the destination **vector**. In both cases, the template functions simply turn around and call the **transform( )** algorithm, which applies the unary function or function object found in its fourth parameter to each sequence element, writing the result to the sequence indicated by its third parameter, which in this case is the same as the input sequence.

For each test, you want to see a string describing the test, followed by the results of the test. To automate this, the preprocessor comes in handy; the **T( )** and **B( )** macros each take the expression you want to execute. After evaluating the expression, they pass the appropriate range to **print( )**. To produce the message the expression is "stringized" using the preprocessor. That way you see the code of the expression that is executed followed by the result **vector**.

The last little tool, **BRand**, is a generator object that creates random **bool** values. To do this, it gets a random number from **rand( )** and tests to see if it's greater than **(RAND_MAX+1)/2**. If the random numbers are evenly distributed, this should happen half the time.

In **main( )**, three **vector**s of **int** are created: **x** and **y** for source values, and **r** for results. To initialize **x** and **y** with random values no greater than 50, a generator of type **URandGen** from **Generators.h** is used. The standard **generate_n( )** algorithm populates the sequence specified in its first argument by invoking its third argument (which must be a generator) a given number of times (specified in its second argument). Since there is one operation where elements of **x** are divided by elements of **y**, we must ensure that there are no zero values of **y**. This is accomplished by once again using the **transform( )** algorithm, taking the source values from **y** and putting the results back into **y**. The function object for this is created with the expression:

```
bind2nd(plus<int>(), 1)
```

This expression uses the **plus** function object to add 1 to its first argument. As we did earlier in this chapter, we use a binder adaptor to make this a unary function so it can applied to the sequence by a single call to **transform( )**.

Another test in the program compares the elements in the two **vector**s for equality, so it is interesting to guarantee that at least one pair of elements is equivalent; here element zero is chosen.

Once the two **vector**s are printed, **T( )** tests each of the function objects that produces a numeric value, and then **B( )** tests each function object that produces a Boolean result. The result is placed into a **vector<bool>**, and when this **vector** is printed, it produces a '**1**' for a true value and a '**0**' for a false value. Here is the output from an execution of **FunctionObjects.cpp**:

```
x:
4 8 18 36 22 6 29 19 25 47
y:
4 14 23 9 11 32 13 15 44 30
After testBinary(x, y, r, plus<int>()):
8 22 41 45 33 38 42 34 69 77
After testBinary(x, y, r, minus<int>()):
0 -6 -5 27 11 -26 16 4 -19 17
After testBinary(x, y, r, multiplies<int>()):
16 112 414 324 242 192 377 285 1100 1410
After testBinary(x, y, r, divides<int>()):
1 0 0 4 2 0 2 1 0 1
After testBinary(x, y, r, limit<int>()):
0 8 18 0 0 6 3 4 25 17
After testUnary(x, r, negate<int>()):
-4 -8 -18 -36 -22 -6 -29 -19 -25 -47
After testBinary(x, y, br, equal_to<int>()):
1 0 0 0 0 0 0 0 0 0
After testBinary(x, y, br, not_equal_to<int>()):
0 1 1 1 1 1 1 1 1 1
After testBinary(x, y, br, greater<int>()):
0 0 0 1 1 0 1 1 0 1
After testBinary(x, y, br, less<int>()):
0 1 1 0 0 1 0 0 1 0
After testBinary(x, y, br, greater_equal<int>()):
1 0 0 1 1 0 1 1 0 1
After testBinary(x, y, br, less_equal<int>()):
```

```
1 1 1 0 0 1 0 0 1 0
After testBinary(x, y, br, not2(greater_equal<int>())):
0 1 1 0 0 1 0 0 1 0
After testBinary(x,y,br,not2(less_equal<int>())):
0 0 0 1 1 0 1 1 0 1
b1:
0 1 1 0 0 0 1 0 1 1
b2:
0 1 1 0 0 0 1 0 1 1
After testBinary(b1, b2, br, logical_and<int>()):
0 1 1 0 0 0 1 0 1 1
After testBinary(b1, b2, br, logical_or<int>()):
0 1 1 0 0 0 1 0 1 1
After testUnary(b1, br, logical_not<int>()):
1 0 0 1 1 1 0 1 0 0
After testUnary(b1, br, not1(logical_not<int>())):
0 1 1 0 0 0 1 0 1 1
```

If you want the Boolean values to display as "true" and "false" instead of 1 and 0, call **cout.setf(ios::boolalpha)**.

A binder doesn't have to produce a unary *predicate*; it can also create any unary *function* (that is, a function that returns something other than **bool**). For example, you can to multiply every element in a **vector** by 10 using a binder with the **transform( )** algorithm:

```
//: C06:FBinder.cpp
// Binders aren't limited to producing predicates.
//{L} Generators
#include <algorithm>
#include <cstdlib>
#include <ctime>
#include <functional>
#include <iostream>
#include <iterator>
#include <vector>
#include "Generators.h"
using namespace std;

int main() {
  ostream_iterator<int> out(cout," ");
  vector<int> v(15);
  srand(time(0));   // Randomize
  generate(v.begin(), v.end(), URandGen(20));
```

```
    copy(v.begin(), v.end(), out);
    transform(v.begin(), v.end(), v.begin(),
              bind2nd(multiplies<int>(), 10));
    copy(v.begin(), v.end(), out);
} ///:~
```

Since the third argument to **transform( )** is the same as the first, the
resulting elements are copied back into the source **vector**. The function
object created by **bind2nd( )** in this case produces an **int** result.

The "bound" argument to a binder cannot be a function object, but it does not
have to be a compile-time constant. For example:

```
//: C06:BinderValue.cpp
// The bound argument can vary.
#include <algorithm>
#include <functional>
#include <iostream>
#include <iterator>
#include <cstdlib>
using namespace std;

int boundedRand() { return rand() % 100; }

int main() {
  const int SZ = 20;
  int a[SZ], b[SZ] = {0};
  generate(a, a + SZ, boundedRand);
  int val = boundedRand();
  int* end = remove_copy_if(a, a + SZ, b,
                            bind2nd(greater<int>(), val));
  // Sort for easier viewing:
  sort(a, a + SZ);
  sort(b, end);
  ostream_iterator<int> out(cout, " ");
  cout << "Original Sequence:" << endl;
  copy(a, a + SZ, out); cout << endl;
  cout << "Values <= " << val << endl;
  copy(b, end, out); cout << endl;
} ///:~
```

Here, an array is filled with 20 random numbers between 0 and 100, and the
user provides a value on the command line. In the **remove_copy_if( )** call,

you can see that the bound argument to **bind2nd( )** is random number in the same range as the sequence. Here is the output from one run:

```
Original Sequence:
4 12 15 17 19 21 26 30 47 48 56 58 60 63 71 79 82 90 92 95
Values <= 41
4 12 15 17 19 21 26 30
```

Function pointer adaptors

Wherever a function-like entity is expected by an algorithm, you can supply either a pointer to an ordinary function or a function object. When the algorithm issues a call, if it is through a function pointer, than the native function-call mechanism is used. If it is through a function object, then that object's **operator( )** member executes. In **CopyInts2.cpp**, we passed the raw function **gt15( )** as a predicate to **remove_copy_if( )**. We also passed pointers to functions returning random numbers to **generate( )** and **generate_n( )**.

You cannot use raw functions with function object adaptors such as **bind2nd( )** because they assume the existence of type definitions for the argument and result types. Instead of manually converting your native functions into function objects yourself, the standard library provides a family of adaptors to do the work for you. The **ptr_fun( )** adaptors take a pointer to a function and turn it into a function object. They are not designed for a function that takes no arguments—they must only be used with unary functions or binary functions.

The following program uses **ptr_fun( )** to wrap a unary function:

```
//: C06:PtrFun1.cpp
// Using ptr_fun() with a unary function.
#include <algorithm>
#include <cmath>
#include <functional>
#include <iostream>
#include <iterator>
#include <vector>
using namespace std;

int d[] = { 123, 94, 10, 314, 315 };
const int DSZ = sizeof d / sizeof *d;
```

```
bool isEven(int x) { return x % 2 == 0; }

int main() {
  vector<bool> vb;
  transform(d, d + DSZ, back_inserter(vb),
    not1(ptr_fun(isEven)));
  copy(vb.begin(), vb.end(),
    ostream_iterator<bool>(cout, " "));
  cout << endl;
  // Output: 1 0 0 0 1
} ///:~
```

We can't simply pass **isEven** to **not1**, because **not1** needs to know the actual argument type and return type its argument uses. The **ptr_fun( )** adaptor deduces those types through template argument deduction. The definition of the unary version of **ptr_fun( )** looks something like this:

```
template<class Arg, class Result>
pointer_to_unary_function<Arg, Result>
ptr_fun(Result (*fptr)(Arg)) {
  return pointer_to_unary_function<Arg, Result>(fptr);
}
```

As you can see, this version of **ptr_fun( )** deduces the argument and result types from **fptr** and uses them to initialize a **pointer_to_unary_function** object that stores **fptr**. The function call operator for **pointer_to_unary_function** just calls **fptr**, as you can see by the last line of its code:

```
template<class Arg, class Result>
class pointer_to_unary_function
: public unary_function<Arg, Result> {
  Result (*fptr)(Arg); // Stores the f-ptr
public:
  pointer_to_unary_function(Result (*x)(Arg)) : fptr(x) {}
  Result operator()(Arg x) const { return fptr(x); }
};
```

Since **pointer_to_unary_function** derives from **unary_function**, the appropriate type definitions come along for the ride and are available to **not1**.

There is also a binary version of **ptr_fun( )**, which returns a **pointer_to_binary_function** object (which derives from **binary_function**) that behaves analogously to the unary case. The following program uses the binary version of **ptr_fun( )** to raise numbers in a sequence to a power. It also reveals a pitfall when passing overloaded functions to **ptr_fun( )**.

```cpp
//: C06:PtrFun2.cpp {-edg}
// Using ptr_fun() for a binary function.
#include <algorithm>
#include <cmath>
#include <functional>
#include <iostream>
#include <iterator>
#include <vector>
using namespace std;

double d[] = { 01.23, 91.370, 56.661,
  023.230, 19.959, 1.0, 3.14159 };
const int DSZ = sizeof d / sizeof *d;

int main() {
  vector<double> vd;
  transform(d, d + DSZ, back_inserter(vd),
    bind2nd(ptr_fun<double, double, double>(pow), 2.0));
  copy(vd.begin(), vd.end(),
    ostream_iterator<double>(cout, " "));
  cout << endl;
} ///:~
```

The **pow( )** function is overloaded in the Standard C++ header **<cmath>** for each of the floating-point data types, as follows:

```cpp
float pow(float, int);  // Efficient int power versions ...
double pow(double, int);
long double pow(long double, int);
float pow(float, float);
double pow(double, double);
long double pow(long double, long double);
```

Since there are multiple versions of **pow( )**, the compiler has no way of knowing which to choose. Here, we have to help the compiler by using explicit function template specialization, as explained in the previous chapter.[6]

It's even trickier to convert a member function into a function object suitable for using with the generic algorithms. As a simple example, suppose we have the classical "shape" problem and want to apply the **draw( )** member function to each pointer in a container of **Shape**:

```
//: C06:MemFun1.cpp
// Applying pointers to member functions.
#include <algorithm>
#include <functional>
#include <iostream>
#include <vector>
#include "../purge.h"
using namespace std;

class Shape {
public:
  virtual void draw() = 0;
  virtual ~Shape() {}
};

class Circle : public Shape {
public:
  virtual void draw() { cout << "Circle::Draw()" << endl; }
  ~Circle() { cout << "Circle::~Circle()" << endl; }
};

class Square : public Shape {
public:
  virtual void draw() { cout << "Square::Draw()" << endl; }
  ~Square() { cout << "Square::~Square()" << endl; }
};

int main() {
  vector<Shape*> vs;
```

___

[6] There's a complication with different library implementations. If **pow( )** has C linkage, meaning its name is not "mangled" like C++ functions, then this example won't compile. **ptr_fun** requires a pointer to a normal, overloadable C++ function.

```
    vs.push_back(new Circle);
    vs.push_back(new Square);
    for_each(vs.begin(), vs.end(), mem_fun(&Shape::draw));
    purge(vs);
} ///:~
```

The **for_each( )** algorithm passes each element in a sequence to the function object denoted by its third argument. Here, we want the function object to wrap one of the member functions of the class itself, and so the function object's "argument" becomes the pointer to the object for the member function call. To produce such a function object, the **mem_fun( )** template takes a pointer to a member as its argument.

The **mem_fun( )** functions are for producing function objects that are called using a pointer to the object that the member function is called for, while **mem_fun_ref( )** calls the member function directly for an object. One set of overloads of both **mem_fun( )** and **mem_fun_ref( )** is for member functions that take zero arguments and one argument, and this is multiplied by two to handle **const** vs. non-**const** member functions. However, templates and overloading take care of sorting all that out—all you need to remember is when to use **mem_fun( )** vs. **mem_fun_ref( )**.

Suppose you have a container of objects (not pointers), and you want to call a member function that takes an argument. The argument you pass should come from a second container of objects. To accomplish this, use the second overloaded form of the **transform( )** algorithm:

```
//: C06:MemFun2.cpp
// Calling member functions through an object reference.
#include <algorithm>
#include <functional>
#include <iostream>
#include <iterator>
#include <vector>
using namespace std;

class Angle {
  int degrees;
public:
  Angle(int deg) : degrees(deg) {}
  int mul(int times) { return degrees *= times; }
};
```

```
int main() {
  vector<Angle> va;
  for(int i = 0; i < 50; i += 10)
    va.push_back(Angle(i));
  int x[] = { 1, 2, 3, 4, 5 };
  transform(va.begin(), va.end(), x,
    ostream_iterator<int>(cout, " "),
    mem_fun_ref(&Angle::mul));
  cout << endl;
  // Output: 0 20 60 120 200
} ///:~
```

Because the container is holding objects, **mem_fun_ref( )** must be used with the pointer-to-member function. This version of **transform( )** takes the start and end point of the first range (where the objects live); the starting point of the second range, which holds the arguments to the member function; the destination iterator, which in this case is standard output; and the function object to call for each object. This function object is created with **mem_fun_ref( )** and the desired pointer to member. Notice that the **transform( )** and **for_each( )** template functions are incomplete; **transform( )** requires that the function it calls return a value, and there is no **for_each( )** that passes two arguments to the function it calls. Thus, you cannot call a member function that returns **void** and takes an argument using **transform( )** or **for_each( )**.

Most any member function works with **mem_fun_ref( )**. You can also use standard library member functions, if your compiler doesn't add any default arguments beyond the normal arguments specified in the standard.[7] For example, suppose you'd like to read a file and search for blank lines. Your compiler may allow you to use the **string::empty( )** member function like this:

```
//: C06:FindBlanks.cpp
// Demonstrates mem_fun_ref() with string::empty().
```

---

[7] If a compiler were to define **string::empty** with default arguments (which is allowed), then the expression **&string::empty** would define a pointer to a member function taking the total number of arguments. Since there is no way for the compiler to provide the extra defaults, there would be a "missing argument" error when an algorithm applied **string::empty** via **mem_fun_ref**.

```cpp
#include <algorithm>
#include <cassert>
#include <cstddef>
#include <fstream>
#include <functional>
#include <string>
#include <vector>
#include "../require.h"
using namespace std;

typedef vector<string>::iterator LSI;

int main(int argc, char* argv[]) {
  char* fname = "FindBlanks.cpp";
  if(argc > 1) fname = argv[1];
  ifstream in(fname);
  assure(in, fname);
  vector<string> vs;
  string s;
  while(getline(in, s))
    vs.push_back(s);
  vector<string> cpy = vs; // For testing
  LSI lsi = find_if(vs.begin(), vs.end(),
    mem_fun_ref(&string::empty));
  while(lsi != vs.end()) {
    *lsi = "A BLANK LINE";
    lsi = find_if(vs.begin(), vs.end(),
      mem_fun_ref(&string::empty));
  }
  for(size_t i = 0; i < cpy.size(); i++)
    if(cpy[i].size() == 0)
      assert(vs[i] == "A BLANK LINE");
    else
      assert(vs[i] != "A BLANK LINE");
} ///:~
```

This example uses **find_if( )** to locate the first blank line in the given range
using **mem_fun_ref( )** with **string::empty( )**. After the file is opened and
read into the **vector**, the process is repeated to find every blank line in the
file. Each time a blank line is found, it is replaced with the characters "A
BLANK LINE." All you have to do to accomplish this is dereference the
iterator to select the current string.

Writing your own function object adaptors

Consider how to write a program that converts strings representing floating-point numbers to their actual numeric values. To get things started, here's a generator that creates the strings:

```
//: C06:NumStringGen.h
// A random number generator that produces
// strings representing floating-point numbers.
#ifndef NUMSTRINGGEN_H
#define NUMSTRINGGEN_H
#include <cstdlib>
#include <string>

class NumStringGen {
  const int sz; // Number of digits to make
public:
  NumStringGen(int ssz = 5) : sz(ssz) {}
  std::string operator()() {
    std::string digits("0123456789");
    const int ndigits = digits.size();
    std::string r(sz, ' ');
    // Don't want a zero as the first digit
    r[0] = digits[std::rand() % (ndigits - 1)] + 1;
    // Now assign the rest
    for(int i = 1; i < sz; ++i)
      if(sz >= 3 && i == sz/2)
        r[i] = '.'; // Insert a decimal point
      else
        r[i] = digits[std::rand() % ndigits];
    return r;
  }
};
#endif // NUMSTRINGGEN_H ///:~
```

You tell it how big the strings should be when you create the **NumStringGen** object. The random number generator selects digits, and a decimal point is placed in the middle.

The following program uses **NumStringGen** to fill a **vector<string>**. However, to use the standard C library function **atof( )** to convert the strings to floating-point numbers, the **string** objects must first be turned into **char** pointers, since there is no automatic type conversion from **string** to **char***. The **transform( )** algorithm can be used with **mem_fun_ref( )** and

string::c_str( ) to convert all the **string**s to **char***, and then these can be transformed using **atof**.

```
//: C06:MemFun3.cpp
// Using mem_fun().
#include <algorithm>
#include <cstdlib>
#include <ctime>
#include <functional>
#include <iostream>
#include <iterator>
#include <string>
#include <vector>
#include "NumStringGen.h"
using namespace std;

int main() {
  const int SZ = 9;
  vector<string> vs(SZ);
  // Fill it with random number strings:
  srand(time(0)); // Randomize
  generate(vs.begin(), vs.end(), NumStringGen());
  copy(vs.begin(), vs.end(),
    ostream_iterator<string>(cout, "\t"));
  cout << endl;
  const char* vcp[SZ];
  transform(vs.begin(), vs.end(), vcp,
    mem_fun_ref(&string::c_str));
  vector<double> vd;
  transform(vcp, vcp + SZ, back_inserter(vd),
    std::atof);
  cout.precision(4);
  cout.setf(ios::showpoint);
  copy(vd.begin(), vd.end(),
    ostream_iterator<double>(cout, "\t"));
  cout << endl;
} ///:~
```

This program does two transformations: one to convert strings to C-style strings (arrays of characters), and one to convert the C-style strings to numbers via **atof( )**. It would be nice to combine these two operations into one. After all, we can compose functions in mathematics, so why not C++?

The obvious approach takes the two functions as arguments and applies them in the proper order:

```
//: C06:ComposeTry.cpp
// A first attempt at implementing function composition.
#include <cassert>
#include <cstdlib>
#include <functional>
#include <iostream>
#include <string>
using namespace std;

template<typename R, typename E, typename F1, typename F2>
class unary_composer {
  F1 f1;
  F2 f2;
public:
  unary_composer(F1 fone, F2 ftwo) : f1(fone), f2(ftwo) {}
  R operator()(E x) { return f1(f2(x)); }
};

template<typename R, typename E, typename F1, typename F2>
unary_composer<R, E, F1, F2> compose(F1 f1, F2 f2) {
  return unary_composer<R, E, F1, F2>(f1, f2);
}

int main() {
  double x = compose<double, const string&>(
    atof, mem_fun_ref(&string::c_str))("12.34");
  assert(x == 12.34);
} ///:~
```

The **unary_composer** object in this example stores the function pointers **atof** and **string::c_str** such that the latter function is applied first when its **operator( )** is called. The **compose( )** function adaptor is a convenience, so we don't need to supply all four template arguments explicitly—**F1** and **F2** are deduced from the call.

It would be much better if we didn't need to supply any template arguments. This is achieved by adhering to the convention for type definitions for adaptable function objects. In other words, we will assume that the functions to be composed are adaptable. This requires that we use **ptr_fun( )** for **atof( )**. For maximum flexibility, we also make **unary_composer** adaptable in case it gets passed to a function adaptor. The following program does so and easily solves the original problem:

```cpp
//: C06:ComposeFinal.cpp {-edg}
// An adaptable composer.
#include <algorithm>
#include <cassert>
#include <cstdlib>
#include <functional>
#include <iostream>
#include <iterator>
#include <string>
#include <vector>
#include "NumStringGen.h"
using namespace std;

template<typename F1, typename F2> class unary_composer
: public unary_function<typename F2::argument_type,
                        typename F1::result_type> {
  F1 f1;
  F2 f2;
public:
  unary_composer(F1 f1, F2 f2) : f1(f1), f2(f2) {}
  typename F1::result_type
  operator()(typename F2::argument_type x) {
    return f1(f2(x));
  }
};

template<typename F1, typename F2>
unary_composer<F1, F2> compose(F1 f1, F2 f2) {
  return unary_composer<F1, F2>(f1, f2);
}

int main() {
  const int SZ = 9;
  vector<string> vs(SZ);
  // Fill it with random number strings:
  generate(vs.begin(), vs.end(), NumStringGen());
  copy(vs.begin(), vs.end(),
    ostream_iterator<string>(cout, "\t"));
  cout << endl;
  vector<double> vd;
  transform(vs.begin(), vs.end(), back_inserter(vd),
```

```
      compose(ptr_fun(atof), mem_fun_ref(&string::c_str)));
  copy(vd.begin(), vd.end(),
    ostream_iterator<double>(cout, "\t"));
  cout << endl;
} ///:~
```

Once again we must use **typename** to let the compiler know that the
member we are referring to is a nested type.

Some implementations[8] support composition of function objects as an
extension, and the C++ Standards Committee is likely to add these
capabilities to the next version of Standard C++.

A catalog of STL algorithms

This section provides a quick reference when you're searching for the
appropriate algorithm. We leave the full exploration of all the STL algorithms
to other references (see the end of this chapter, and Appendix A), along with
the more intimate details of issues like performance. Our goal here is for you
to rapidly become comfortable with the algorithms, and we'll assume you will
look into the more specialized references if you need more detail.

Although you will often see the algorithms described using their full template
declaration syntax, we're not doing that here because you already know they
are templates, and it's quite easy to see what the template arguments are
from the function declarations. The type names for the arguments provide
descriptions for the types of iterators required. We think you'll find this form
is easier to read, and you can quickly find the full declaration in the template
header file if you need it.

The reason for all the fuss about iterators is to accommodate any type of
container that meets the requirements in the standard library. So far we have
illustrated the generic algorithms with only arrays and **vector**s as sequences,
but in the next chapter you'll see a broad range of data structures that support
less robust iteration. For this reason, the algorithms are categorized in part by
the types of iteration facilities they require.

---

[8] STLPort, for instance, which comes with version 6 of Borland C++
Builder and the Digital Mars compiler, and is based on SGI STL.

The names of the iterator classes describe the iterator type to which they must conform. There are no interface base classes to enforce these iteration operations—they are just expected to be there. If they are not, your compiler will complain. The various flavors of iterators are described briefly as follows.

InputIterator. An input iterator only allows *reading* elements of its sequence in a single, forward pass using **operator++** and **operator***. Input iterators can also be tested with **operator==** and **operator!=**. That's the extent of the constraints.

OutputIterator. An output iterator only allows *writing* elements to a sequence in a single, forward pass using **operator++** and **operator***. **OutputIterator**s cannot be tested with **operator==** and **operator!=**, however, because you assume that you can just keep sending elements to the destination and that you don't need to see if the destination's end marker was reached. That is, the container that an **OutputIterator** references can take an infinite number of objects, so no end-checking is necessary. This requirement is important so that an **OutputIterator** can be used with **ostream**s (via **ostream_iterator**), but you'll also commonly use the "insert" iterators such as are the type of iterator returned by **back_inserter( )**.

There is no way to determine whether multiple **InputIterators** or **OutputIterators** point within the same range, so there is no way to use such iterators together. Just think in terms of iterators to support **istream**s and **ostream**s, and **InputIterator** and **OutputIterator** will make perfect sense. Also note that algorithms that use **InputIterators** or **OutputIterators** put the weakest restrictions on the types of iterators they will accept, which means that you can use any "more sophisticated" type of iterator when you see **InputIterator** or **OutputIterator** used as STL algorithm template arguments.

ForwardIterator. Because you can only read from an **InputIterator** and write to an **OutputIterator**, you can't use either of them to simultaneously read and modify a range, and you can't dereference such an iterator more than once. With a **ForwardIterator** these restrictions are relaxed; you can still only move forward using **operator++**, but you can both write and read, and you can compare such iterators in the same range for equality. Since forward iterators can both read and write, they can be used in place of an **InputIterator** or **OutputIterator**.

BidirectionalIterator. Effectively, this is a **ForwardIterator** that can also go backward. That is, a **BidirectionalIterator** supports all the operations that a **ForwardIterator** does, but in addition it has an **operator--**.

RandomAccessIterator. This type of iterator supports all the operations that a regular pointer does: you can add and subtract integral values to move it forward and backward by jumps (rather than just one element at a time), you can subscript it with **operator[ ]**, you can subtract one iterator from another, and you can compare iterators to see which is greater using **operator<, operator>**, and so on. If you're implementing a sorting routine or something similar, random access iterators are necessary to be able to create an efficient algorithm.

The names used for the template parameter types in the algorithm descriptions later in this chapter consist of the listed iterator types (sometimes with a '1' or '2' appended to distinguish different template arguments) and can also include other arguments, often function objects.

When describing the group of elements passed to an operation, mathematical "range" notation is often used. In this, the square bracket means "includes the end point," and the parenthesis means "does not include the end point." When using iterators, a range is determined by the iterator pointing to the initial element and by the "past-the-end" iterator, pointing past the last element. Since the past-the-end element is never used, the range determined by a pair of iterators can be expressed as **[first, last)**, where **first** is the iterator pointing to the initial element, and **last** is the past-the-end iterator.

Most books and discussions of the STL algorithms arrange them according to side-effects: *non-mutating* algorithms don't change the elements in the range, *mutating* algorithms do change the elements, and so on. These descriptions are based primarily on the underlying behavior or implementation of the algorithm—that is, on the designer's perspective. In practice, we don't find this a useful categorization, so instead we'll organize them according to the problem you want to solve: Are you searching for an element or set of elements, performing an operation on each element, counting elements, replacing elements, and so on? This should help you find the algorithm you want more easily.

If you do not see a different header such as **<utility>** or **<numeric>** above the function declarations, it appears in **<algorithm>**. Also, all the algorithms are in the namespace **std**.

Support tools for example creation

It's useful to create some basic tools to test the algorithms. In the examples that follow we'll use the generators mentioned earlier in **Generators.h**, as well as what appears below.

Displaying a range is a frequent task, so here is a function template to print any sequence, regardless of the type contained in that sequence:

```
//: C06:PrintSequence.h
// Prints the contents of any sequence.
#ifndef PRINTSEQUENCE_H
#define PRINTSEQUENCE_H
#include <algorithm>
#include <iostream>
#include <iterator>

template<typename Iter>
void print(Iter first, Iter last, const char* nm = "",
           const char* sep = "\n",
           std::ostream& os = std::cout) {
  if(nm != 0 && *nm != '\0')
    os << nm << ": " << sep;
  typedef typename
    std::iterator_traits<Iter>::value_type T;
  std::copy(first, last,
            std::ostream_iterator<T>(std::cout, sep));
  os << std::endl;
}
#endif // PRINTSEQUENCE_H ///:~
```

By default this function template prints to **cout** with newlines as separators, but you can change that by modifying the default argument. You can also provide a message to print at the head of the output. Since **print( )** uses the **copy( )** algorithm to send objects to **cout** via an **ostream_iterator**, the **ostream_iterator** must know the type of object it is printing, which we infer from the **value_type** member of the iterator passed.

The **std::iterator_traits** template enables the **print( )** function template to process sequences delimited by any type of iterator. The iterator types returned by the standard containers such as **vector** define a nested type, **value_type**, which represents the element type, but when using arrays, the iterators are just pointers, which can have no nested types. To supply the conventional types associated with iterators in the standard library, **std::iterator_traits** provides the following partial specialization for pointer types:

```
template<class T>
  struct iterator_traits<T*> {
    typedef random_access_iterator_tag iterator_category;
    typedef T value_type;
    typedef ptrdiff_t difference_type;
    typedef T* pointer;
    typedef T& reference;
  };
```

This makes the type of the elements pointed at (namely, **T**) available via the type name **value_type**.

Stable vs. unstable reordering

A number of the STL algorithms that move elements of a sequence around distinguish between *stable* and *unstable* reordering of a sequence. A stable sort preserves the original relative order of the elements that are equivalent as far as the comparison function is concerned. For example, consider a sequence **{ c(1), b(1), c(2), a(1), b(2), a(2) }**. These elements are tested for equivalence based on their letters, but their numbers indicate how they first appeared in the sequence. If you sort (for example) this sequence using an unstable sort, there's no guarantee of any particular order among equivalent letters, so you could end up with **{ a(2), a(1), b(1), b(2), c(2), c(1) }**. However, if you use a stable sort, you will get **{ a(1), a(2), b(1), b(2), c(1), c(2) }**. The STL **sort( )** algorithm uses a variation of *quicksort* and is thus unstable, but a **stable_sort( )** is also provided.[9]

To demonstrate the stability versus instability of algorithms that reorder a sequence, we need some way to keep track of how the elements originally

---

[9] The **stable_sort( )** algorithm uses *mergesort*, which is indeed stable, but tends to run slower than *quicksort* on average.

appeared. The following is a kind of **string** object that keeps track of the order in which that particular object originally appeared, using a **static map** that maps **NString**s to **Counter**s. Each **NString** then contains an **occurrence** field that indicates the order in which this **NString** was discovered.

```
//: C06:NString.h
// A "numbered string" that keeps track of the
// number of occurrences of the word it contains.
#ifndef NSTRING_H
#define NSTRING_H
#include <algorithm>
#include <iostream>
#include <string>
#include <utility>
#include <vector>

typedef std::pair<std::string, int> psi;

// Only compare on the first element
bool operator==(const psi& l, const psi& r) {
  return l.first == r.first;
}

class NString {
  std::string s;
  int thisOccurrence;
  // Keep track of the number of occurrences:
  typedef std::vector<psi> vp;
  typedef vp::iterator vpit;
  static vp words;
  void addString(const std::string& x) {
    psi p(x, 0);
    vpit it = std::find(words.begin(), words.end(), p);
    if(it != words.end())
      thisOccurrence = ++it->second;
    else {
      thisOccurrence = 0;
      words.push_back(p);
    }
  }
public:
  NString() : thisOccurrence(0) {}
  NString(const std::string& x) : s(x) { addString(x); }
```

```
NString(const char* x) : s(x) { addString(x); }
// Implicit operator= and copy-constructor are OK here.
friend std::ostream& operator<<(
  std::ostream& os, const NString& ns) {
  return os << ns.s << " [" << ns.thisOccurrence << "]";
}
// Need this for sorting. Notice it only
// compares strings, not occurrences:
friend bool
operator<(const NString& l, const NString& r) {
  return l.s < r.s;
}
friend
bool operator==(const NString& l, const NString& r) {
  return l.s == r.s;
}
// For sorting with greater<NString>:
friend bool
operator>(const NString& l, const NString& r) {
  return l.s > r.s;
}
// To get at the string directly:
operator const std::string&() const { return s; }
};

// Because NString::vp is a template and we are using the
// inclusion model, it must be defined in this header file:
NString::vp NString::words;
#endif // NSTRING_H ///:~
```

We would normally use a **map** container to associate a string with its number of occurrences, but maps don't appear until the next chapter, so we use a **vector** of pairs instead. You'll see plenty of similar examples in Chapter 7.

The only operator necessary to perform an ordinary ascending sort is **NString::operator<( )**. To sort in reverse order, the **operator>( )** is also provided so that the **greater** template can call it.

Filling and generating

These algorithms let you automatically fill a range with a particular value or generate a set of values for a particular range. The "fill" functions insert a single value multiple times into the container. The "generate" functions use

---

generators such as those described earlier to produce values to insert into the container.

```
void fill(ForwardIterator first, ForwardIterator last,
  const T& value);
void fill_n(OutputIterator first, Size n, const T& value);
```

fill( ) assigns **value** to every element in the range **[first, last)**. **fill_n( )** assigns **value** to **n** elements starting at **first**.

```
void generate(ForwardIterator first, ForwardIterator last,
  Generator gen);
void generate_n(OutputIterator first, Size n, Generator
  gen);
```

generate( ) makes a call to **gen( )** for each element in the range **[first, last)**, presumably to produce a different value for each element. **generate_n( )** calls **gen( )** **n** times and assigns each result to **n** elements starting at **first**.

Example
The following example fills and generates into **vector**s. It also shows the use of **print( )**:

```
//: C06:FillGenerateTest.cpp
// Demonstrates "fill" and "generate."
//{L} Generators
#include <vector>
#include <algorithm>
#include <string>
#include "Generators.h"
#include "PrintSequence.h"
using namespace std;

int main() {
  vector<string> v1(5);
  fill(v1.begin(), v1.end(), "howdy");
  print(v1.begin(), v1.end(), "v1", " ");
  vector<string> v2;
  fill_n(back_inserter(v2), 7, "bye");
  print(v2.begin(), v2.end(), "v2");
  vector<int> v3(10);
```

```
    generate(v3.begin(), v3.end(), SkipGen(4,5));
    print(v3.begin(), v3.end(), "v3", " ");
    vector<int> v4;
    generate_n(back_inserter(v4),15, URandGen(30));
    print(v4.begin(), v4.end(), "v4", " ");
} ///:~
```

A **vector<string>** is created with a predefined size. Since storage has already been created for all the **string** objects in the **vector, fill( )** can use its assignment operator to assign a copy of "howdy" to each space in the **vector**. Also, the default newline separator is replaced with a space.

The second **vector<string> v2** is not given an initial size, so **back_inserter( )** must be used to force new elements in instead of trying to assign to existing locations.

The **generate( )** and **generate_n( )** functions have the same form as the "fill" functions except that they use a generator instead of a constant value. Here, both generators are demonstrated.

Counting

All containers have a member function **size( )** that tells you how many elements they hold. The return type of **size( )** is the iterator's **difference_type**[10] (usually **ptrdiff_t**), which we denote by **IntegralValue** in the following. The following two algorithms count objects that satisfy certain criteria.

```
IntegralValue count(InputIterator first, InputIterator
    last, const EqualityComparable& value);
```

Produces the number of elements in **[first, last)** that are equivalent to **value** (when tested using **operator==**).

```
IntegralValue count_if(InputIterator first, InputIterator
    last, Predicate pred);
```

---

[10] Iterators are discussed in more depth in the next chapter.

Produces the number of elements in **[first, last)** that each cause **pred** to return **true**.

Example
Here, a **vector\<char\> v** is filled with random characters (including some duplicates). A **set\<char\>** is initialized from **v**, so it holds only one of each letter represented in **v**. This **set** counts all the instances of all the characters, which are then displayed:

```
//: C06:Counting.cpp
// The counting algorithms.
//{L} Generators
#include <algorithm>
#include <functional>
#include <iterator>
#include <set>
#include <vector>
#include "Generators.h"
#include "PrintSequence.h"
using namespace std;

int main() {
  vector<char> v;
  generate_n(back_inserter(v), 50, CharGen());
  print(v.begin(), v.end(), "v", "");
  // Create a set of the characters in v:
  set<char> cs(v.begin(), v.end());
  typedef set<char>::iterator sci;
  for(sci it = cs.begin(); it != cs.end(); it++) {
    int n = count(v.begin(), v.end(), *it);
    cout << *it << ": " << n << ", ";
  }
  int lc = count_if(v.begin(), v.end(),
    bind2nd(greater<char>(), 'a'));
  cout << "\nLowercase letters: " << lc << endl;
  sort(v.begin(), v.end());
  print(v.begin(), v.end(), "sorted", "");
} ///:~
```

The **count_if( )** algorithm is demonstrated by counting all the lowercase letters; the predicate is created using the **bind2nd( )** and **greater** function object templates.

Manipulating sequences

These algorithms let you move sequences around.

```
OutputIterator copy(InputIterator first, InputIterator
   last, OutputIterator destination);
```

Using assignment, copies from **[first, last)** to **destination**, incrementing **destination** after each assignment. This is essentially a "shuffle-left" operation, and so the source sequence must not contain the destination. Because assignment is used, you cannot directly insert elements into an empty container or at the end of a container, but instead you must wrap the **destination** iterator in an **insert_iterator** (typically by using **back_inserter( )** or by using **inserter( )** in the case of an associative container).

```
BidirectionalIterator2 copy_backward(BidirectionalIterator1
   first, BidirectionalIterator1 last,
   BidirectionalIterator2 destinationEnd);
```

Like **copy( )**, but copies the elements in reverse order. This is essentially a "shuffle-right" operation, and, like **copy( )**, the source sequence must not contain the destination. The source range **[first, last)** is copied to the destination, but the first destination element is **destinationEnd - 1**. This iterator is then decremented after each assignment. The space in the destination range must already exist (to allow assignment), and the destination range cannot be within the source range.

```
void reverse(BidirectionalIterator first,
   BidirectionalIterator last);
OutputIterator reverse_copy(BidirectionalIterator first,
   BidirectionalIterator last, OutputIterator destination);
```

Both forms of this function reverse the range **[first, last). reverse( )** reverses the range in place, and **reverse_copy( )** leaves the original range alone and copies the reversed elements into **destination**, returning the past-the-end iterator of the resulting range.

```
ForwardIterator2 swap_ranges(ForwardIterator1 first1,
   ForwardIterator1 last1, ForwardIterator2 first2);
```

Exchanges the contents of two ranges of equal size by swapping corresponding elements.

```
void rotate(ForwardIterator first, ForwardIterator middle,
  ForwardIterator last);
OutputIterator rotate_copy(ForwardIterator first,
  ForwardIterator middle, ForwardIterator last,
  OutputIterator destination);
```

Moves the contents of **[first, middle)** to the end of the sequence, and the contents of **[middle, last)** to the beginning. With **rotate( )**, the swap is performed in place; and with **rotate_copy( )** the original range is untouched, and the rotated version is copied into **destination**, returning the past-the-end iterator of the resulting range. Note that while **swap_ranges( )** requires that the two ranges be exactly the same size, the "rotate" functions do not.

```
bool next_permutation(BidirectionalIterator first,
  BidirectionalIterator last);
bool next_permutation(BidirectionalIterator first,
  BidirectionalIterator last, StrictWeakOrdering
  binary_pred);
bool prev_permutation(BidirectionalIterator first,
  BidirectionalIterator last);
bool prev_permutation(BidirectionalIterator first,
  BidirectionalIterator last, StrictWeakOrdering
  binary_pred);
```

A *permutation* is one unique ordering of a set of elements. If you have **n** unique elements, there are **n!** (**n** factorial) distinct possible combinations of those elements. All these combinations can be conceptually sorted into a sequence using a lexicographical (dictionary-like) ordering and thus produce a concept of a "next" and "previous" permutation. So whatever the current ordering of elements in the range, there is a distinct "next" and "previous" permutation in the sequence of permutations.

The **next_permutation( )** and **prev_permutation( )** functions rearrange the elements into their next or previous permutation and, if successful, return **true**. If there are no more "next" permutations, the elements are in sorted order so **next_permutation( )** returns **false**. If there are no more "previous" permutations, the elements are in descending sorted order so **previous_permutation( )** returns **false**.

The versions of the functions that have a **StrictWeakOrdering** argument perform the comparisons using **binary_pred** instead of **operator<**.

```
void random_shuffle(RandomAccessIterator first,
  RandomAccessIterator last);
void random_shuffle(RandomAccessIterator first,
  RandomAccessIterator last RandomNumberGenerator& rand);
```

This function randomly rearranges the elements in the range. It yields uniformly distributed results if the random-number generator does. The first form uses an internal random number generator, and the second uses a user-supplied random-number generator. The generator must return a value in the range **[0, n)** for some positive **n**.

```
BidirectionalIterator partition(BidirectionalIterator
  first, BidirectionalIterator last, Predicate pred);
BidirectionalIterator
stable_partition(BidirectionalIterator first,
  BidirectionalIterator last, Predicate pred);
```

The "partition" functions move elements that satisfy **pred** to the beginning of the sequence. An iterator pointing one past the last of those elements is returned (which is, in effect, an "end" iterator" for the initial subsequence of elements that satisfy **pred**). This location is often called the "partition point."

With **partition( )**, the order of the elements in each resulting subsequence after the function call is not specified, but with **stable_partition( )**, the relative order of the elements before and after the partition point will be the same as before the partitioning process.

Example
This gives a basic demonstration of sequence manipulation:

```
//: C06:Manipulations.cpp
// Shows basic manipulations.
//{L} Generators
// NString
#include <vector>
```

```cpp
#include <string>
#include <algorithm>
#include "PrintSequence.h"
#include "NString.h"
#include "Generators.h"
using namespace std;

int main() {
  vector<int> v1(10);
  // Simple counting:
  generate(v1.begin(), v1.end(), SkipGen());
  print(v1.begin(), v1.end(), "v1", " ");
  vector<int> v2(v1.size());
  copy_backward(v1.begin(), v1.end(), v2.end());
  print(v2.begin(), v2.end(), "copy_backward", " ");
  reverse_copy(v1.begin(), v1.end(), v2.begin());
  print(v2.begin(), v2.end(), "reverse_copy", " ");
  reverse(v1.begin(), v1.end());
  print(v1.begin(), v1.end(), "reverse", " ");
  int half = v1.size() / 2;
  // Ranges must be exactly the same size:
  swap_ranges(v1.begin(), v1.begin() + half,
    v1.begin() + half);
  print(v1.begin(), v1.end(), "swap_ranges", " ");
  // Start with a fresh sequence:
  generate(v1.begin(), v1.end(), SkipGen());
  print(v1.begin(), v1.end(), "v1", " ");
  int third = v1.size() / 3;
  for(int i = 0; i < 10; i++) {
    rotate(v1.begin(), v1.begin() + third, v1.end());
    print(v1.begin(), v1.end(), "rotate", " ");
  }
  cout << "Second rotate example:" << endl;
  char c[] = "aabbccddeeffgghhiijj";
  const char CSZ = strlen(c);
  for(int i = 0; i < 10; i++) {
    rotate(c, c + 2, c + CSZ);
    print(c, c + CSZ, "", "");
  }
  cout << "All n! permutations of abcd:" << endl;
  int nf = 4 * 3 * 2 * 1;
  char p[] = "abcd";
  for(int i = 0; i < nf; i++) {
    next_permutation(p, p + 4);
    print(p, p + 4, "", "");
```

```
  }
  cout << "Using prev_permutation:" << endl;
  for(int i = 0; i < nf; i++) {
    prev_permutation(p, p + 4);
    print(p, p + 4, "", "");
  }
  cout << "random_shuffling a word:" << endl;
  string s("hello");
  cout << s << endl;
  for(int i = 0; i < 5; i++) {
    random_shuffle(s.begin(), s.end());
    cout << s << endl;
  }
  NString sa[] = { "a", "b", "c", "d", "a", "b",
    "c", "d", "a", "b", "c", "d", "a", "b", "c"};
  const int SASZ = sizeof sa / sizeof *sa;
  vector<NString> ns(sa, sa + SASZ);
  print(ns.begin(), ns.end(), "ns", " ");
  vector<NString>::iterator it =
    partition(ns.begin(), ns.end(),
      bind2nd(greater<NString>(), "b"));
  cout << "Partition point: " << *it << endl;
  print(ns.begin(), ns.end(), "", " ");
  // Reload vector:
  copy(sa, sa + SASZ, ns.begin());
  it = stable_partition(ns.begin(), ns.end(),
    bind2nd(greater<NString>(), "b"));
  cout << "Stable partition" << endl;
  cout << "Partition point: " << *it << endl;
  print(ns.begin(), ns.end(), "", " ");
} ///:~
```

The best way to see the results of this program is to run it. (You'll probably want to redirect the output to a file.)

The **vector<int> v1** is initially loaded with a simple ascending sequence and printed. You'll see that the effect of **copy_backward( )** (which copies into **v2**, which is the same size as **v1**) is the same as an ordinary copy. Again, **copy_backward( )** does the same thing as **copy( )**—it just performs the operations in reverse order.

reverse_copy( ) actually does create a reversed copy, and **reverse( )** performs the reversal in place. Next, **swap_ranges( )** swaps the upper half of the reversed sequence with the lower half. The ranges could be smaller subsets of the entire **vector**, as long as they are of equivalent size.

After re-creating the ascending sequence, **rotate( )** is demonstrated by rotating one third of **v1** multiple times. A second **rotate( )** example uses characters and just rotates two characters at a time. This also demonstrates the flexibility of both the STL algorithms and the **print( )** template, since they can both be used with arrays of **char** as easily as with anything else.

To demonstrate **next_permutation( )** and **prev_permutation( )**, a set of four characters "abcd" is permuted through all **n!** (**n** factorial) possible combinations. You'll see from the output that the permutations move through a strictly defined order (that is, permuting is a deterministic process).

A quick-and-dirty demonstration of **random_shuffle( )** is to apply it to a **string** and see what words result. Because a **string** object has **begin( )** and **end( )** member functions that return the appropriate iterators, it too can be easily used with many of the STL algorithms. An array of **char** could also have been used.

Finally, the **partition( )** and **stable_partition( )** are demonstrated, using an array of **NString**. You'll note that the aggregate initialization expression uses **char** arrays, but **NString** has a **char*** constructor that is automatically used.

You'll see from the output that with the unstable partition, the objects are correctly above and below the partition point, but in no particular order; whereas with the stable partition, their original order is maintained.

Searching and replacing

All these algorithms are used for searching for one or more objects within a range defined by the first two iterator arguments.

```
InputIterator find(InputIterator first, InputIterator last,
    const EqualityComparable& value);
```

Searches for **value** within a range of elements. Returns an iterator in the range **[first, last)** that points to the first occurrence of **value**. If **value** isn't in the range, **find( )** returns **last**. This is a *linear search*; that is, it starts at the beginning and looks at each sequential element without making any assumptions about the way the elements are ordered. In contrast, a **binary_search( )** (defined later) works on a sorted sequence and can thus be much faster.

```
InputIterator find_if(InputIterator first, InputIterator
  last, Predicate pred);
```

Just like **find( )**, **find_if( )** performs a linear search through the range. However, instead of searching for **value**, **find_if( )** looks for an element such that the **Predicate pred** returns **true** when applied to that element. Returns **last** if no such element can be found.

```
ForwardIterator adjacent_find(ForwardIterator first,
  ForwardIterator last);
ForwardIterator adjacent_find(ForwardIterator first,
  ForwardIterator last, BinaryPredicate binary_pred);
```

Like **find( )**, performs a linear search through the range, but instead of looking for only one element, it searches for two adjacent elements that are equivalent. The first form of the function looks for two elements that are equivalent (via **operator==**). The second form looks for two adjacent elements that, when passed together to **binary_pred**, produce a **true** result. An iterator to the first of the two elements is returned if a pair is found; otherwise, **last** is returned.

```
ForwardIterator1 find_first_of(ForwardIterator1 first1,
  ForwardIterator1 last1, ForwardIterator2 first2,
  ForwardIterator2 last2);
ForwardIterator1 find_first_of(ForwardIterator1 first1,
  ForwardIterator1 last1, ForwardIterator2 first2,
  ForwardIterator2 last2, BinaryPredicate binary_pred);
```

Like **find( )**, performs a linear search through the range. Both forms search for an element in the second range that's equivalent to one in the first, the first form using **operator==**, and the second using the supplied predicate. In the second form, the current element from the first range becomes the first argument to **binary_pred**, and the element from the second range becomes the second argument.

```
ForwardIterator1 search(ForwardIterator1 first1,
   ForwardIterator1 last1, ForwardIterator2 first2,
   ForwardIterator2 last2);
ForwardIterator1 search(ForwardIterator1 first1,
   ForwardIterator1 last1, ForwardIterator2 first2,
   ForwardIterator2 last2 BinaryPredicate binary_pred);
```

Checks to see if the second range occurs (in the exact order of the second range) within the first range, and if so returns an iterator pointing to the place in the first range where the second range begins. Returns **last1** if no subset can be found. The first form performs its test using **operator==**, and the second checks to see if each pair of objects being compared causes **binary_pred** to return **true**.

```
ForwardIterator1 find_end(ForwardIterator1 first1,
   ForwardIterator1 last1, ForwardIterator2 first2,
   ForwardIterator2 last2);
ForwardIterator1 find_end(ForwardIterator1 first1,
   ForwardIterator1 last1, ForwardIterator2 first2,
   ForwardIterator2 last2, BinaryPredicate binary_pred);
```

The forms and arguments are just like **search( )** in that they look for the second range appearing as a subset of the first range, but while **search( )** looks for the first occurrence of the subset, **find_end( )** looks for the *last* occurrence and returns an iterator to its first element.

```
ForwardIterator search_n(ForwardIterator first,
   ForwardIterator last, Size count, const T& value);
ForwardIterator search_n(ForwardIterator first,
   ForwardIterator last, Size count, const T& value,
   BinaryPredicate binary_pred);
```

Looks for a group of **count** consecutive values in **[first, last)** that are all equal to **value** (in the first form) or that all cause a return value of **true** when passed into **binary_pred** along with **value** (in the second form). Returns **last** if such a group cannot be found.

```
ForwardIterator min_element(ForwardIterator first,
   ForwardIterator last);
```

```
ForwardIterator min_element(ForwardIterator first,
    ForwardIterator last, BinaryPredicate binary_pred);
```

Returns an iterator pointing to the first occurrence of the "smallest" value in the range (as explained below—there may be multiple occurrences of this value.) Returns **last** if the range is empty. The first version performs comparisons with **operator<**, and the value **r** returned is such that *****e < *****r is false for every element **e** in the range **[first, r)**. The second version compares using **binary_pred**, and the value **r** returned is such that **binary_pred(*e, *r)** is false for every element **e** in the range **[first, r)**.

```
ForwardIterator max_element(ForwardIterator first,
    ForwardIterator last);
ForwardIterator max_element(ForwardIterator first,
    ForwardIterator last, BinaryPredicate binary_pred);
```

Returns an iterator pointing to the first occurrence of the largest value in the range. (There may be multiple occurrences of the largest value.) Returns **last** if the range is empty. The first version performs comparisons with **operator<**, and the value **r** returned is such that *****r < *****e is false for every element **e** in the range **[first, r)**. The second version compares using **binary_pred**, and the value **r** returned is such that **binary_pred(*r, *e)** is false for every element **e** in the range **[first, r)**.

```
void replace(ForwardIterator first, ForwardIterator last,
    const T& old_value, const T& new_value);
void replace_if(ForwardIterator first, ForwardIterator
    last, Predicate pred, const T& new_value);
OutputIterator replace_copy(InputIterator first,
    InputIterator last, OutputIterator result, const T&
    old_value, const T& new_value);
OutputIterator replace_copy_if(InputIterator first,
    InputIterator last, OutputIterator result, Predicate
    pred, const T& new_value);
```

Each of the "replace" forms moves through the range **[first, last)**, finding values that match a criterion and replacing them with **new_value**. Both **replace( )** and **replace_copy( )** simply look for **old_value** to replace; **replace_if( )** and **replace_copy_if( )** look for values that satisfy the predicate **pred**. The "copy" versions of the functions do not modify the original range but instead make a copy with the replacements into **result** (incrementing **result** after each assignment).

Example
To provide easy viewing of the results, this example manipulates **vector**s of **int**. Again, not every possible version of each algorithm is shown. (Some that should be obvious have been omitted.)

```
//: C06:SearchReplace.cpp
// The STL search and replace algorithms.
#include <algorithm>
#include <functional>
#include <vector>
#include "PrintSequence.h"
using namespace std;

struct PlusOne {
  bool operator()(int i, int j) { return j == i + 1; }
};

class MulMoreThan {
  int value;
public:
  MulMoreThan(int val) : value(val) {}
  bool operator()(int v, int m) { return v * m > value; }
};

int main() {
  int a[] = { 1, 2, 3, 4, 5, 6, 6, 7, 7, 7,
    8, 8, 8, 8, 11, 11, 11, 11, 11 };
  const int ASZ = sizeof a / sizeof *a;
  vector<int> v(a, a + ASZ);
  print(v.begin(), v.end(), "v", " ");
  vector<int>::iterator it = find(v.begin(), v.end(), 4);
  cout << "find: " << *it << endl;
  it = find_if(v.begin(), v.end(),
    bind2nd(greater<int>(), 8));
  cout << "find_if: " << *it << endl;
  it = adjacent_find(v.begin(), v.end());
  while(it != v.end()) {
    cout << "adjacent_find: " << *it
         << ", " << *(it + 1) << endl;
    it = adjacent_find(it + 1, v.end());
  }
}
```

```
it = adjacent_find(v.begin(), v.end(), PlusOne());
while(it != v.end()) {
  cout << "adjacent_find PlusOne: " << *it
       << ", " << *(it + 1) << endl;
  it = adjacent_find(it + 1, v.end(), PlusOne());
}
int b[] = { 8, 11 };
const int BSZ = sizeof b / sizeof *b;
print(b, b + BSZ, "b", " ");
it = find_first_of(v.begin(), v.end(), b, b + BSZ);
print(it, it + BSZ, "find_first_of", " ");
it = find_first_of(v.begin(), v.end(),
  b, b + BSZ, PlusOne());
print(it,it + BSZ,"find_first_of PlusOne"," ");
it = search(v.begin(), v.end(), b, b + BSZ);
print(it, it + BSZ, "search", " ");
int c[] = { 5, 6, 7 };
const int CSZ = sizeof c / sizeof *c;
print(c, c + CSZ, "c", " ");
it = search(v.begin(), v.end(), c, c + CSZ, PlusOne());
print(it, it + CSZ,"search PlusOne", " ");
int d[] = { 11, 11, 11 };
const int DSZ = sizeof d / sizeof *d;
print(d, d + DSZ, "d", " ");
it = find_end(v.begin(), v.end(), d, d + DSZ);
print(it, v.end(),"find_end", " ");
int e[] = { 9, 9 };
print(e, e + 2, "e", " ");
it = find_end(v.begin(), v.end(), e, e + 2, PlusOne());
print(it, v.end(),"find_end PlusOne"," ");
it = search_n(v.begin(), v.end(), 3, 7);
print(it, it + 3, "search_n 3, 7", " ");
it = search_n(v.begin(), v.end(),
  6, 15, MulMoreThan(100));
print(it, it + 6,
  "search_n 6, 15, MulMoreThan(100)", " ");
cout << "min_element: "
     << *min_element(v.begin(), v.end()) << endl;
cout << "max_element: "
     << *max_element(v.begin(), v.end()) << endl;
vector<int> v2;
replace_copy(v.begin(), v.end(),
  back_inserter(v2), 8, 47);
print(v2.begin(), v2.end(), "replace_copy 8 -> 47", " ");
replace_if(v.begin(), v.end(),
```

```
      bind2nd(greater_equal<int>(), 7), -1);
   print(v.begin(), v.end(), "replace_if >= 7 -> -1", " ");
} ///:~
```

The example begins with two predicates: **PlusOne**, which is a binary predicate that returns **true** if the second argument is equivalent to one plus the first argument; and **MulMoreThan**, which returns **true** if the first argument times the second argument is greater than a value stored in the object. These binary predicates are used as tests in the example.

In **main( )**, an array **a** is created and fed to the constructor for **vector<int> v**. This **vector** is the target for the search and replace activities, and you'll note that there are duplicate elements—these are discovered by some of the search/replace routines.

The first test demonstrates **find( )**, discovering the value 4 in **v**. The return value is the iterator pointing to the first instance of 4, or the end of the input range (**v.end( )**) if the search value is not found.

The **find_if( )** algorithm uses a predicate to determine if it has discovered the correct element. In this example, this predicate is created on the fly using **greater<int>** (that is, "see if the first **int** argument is greater than the second") and **bind2nd( )** to fix the second argument to 8. Thus, it returns true if the value in **v** is greater than 8.

Since two identical objects appear next to each other in a number of cases in **v**, the test of **adjacent_find( )** is designed to find them all. It starts looking from the beginning and then drops into a **while** loop, making sure that the iterator **it** has not reached the end of the input sequence (which would mean that no more matches can be found). For each match it finds, the loop prints the matches and then performs the next **adjacent_find( )**, this time using **it + 1** as the first argument (this way, it will still find two pairs in a triple).

You might look at the **while** loop and think that you can do it a bit more cleverly, like this:

```
while(it != v.end()) {
   cout << "adjacent_find: " << *it++
        << ", " << *it++ << endl;
   it = adjacent_find(it, v.end());
}
```

This is exactly what we tried first. However, we did not get the output we expected, on any compiler. This is because there is no guarantee about when the increments occur in this expression.

The next test uses **adjacent_find( )** with the **PlusOne** predicate, which discovers all the places where the next number in the sequence **v** changes from the previous by one. The same **while** approach finds all the cases.

The **find_first_of( )** algorithm requires a second range of objects for which to hunt; this is provided in the array **b**. Because the first range and the second range in **find_first_of( )** are controlled by separate template arguments, those ranges can refer to two different types of containers, as seen here. The second form of **find_first_of( )** is also tested, using **PlusOne**.

The **search( )** algorithm finds exactly the second range inside the first one, with the elements in the same order. The second form of **search( )** uses a predicate, which is typically just something that defines equivalence, but it also presents some interesting possibilities—here, the **PlusOne** predicate causes the range **{ 4, 5, 6 }** to be found.

The **find_end( )** test discovers the *last* occurrence of the entire sequence **{ 11, 11, 11 }**. To show that it has in fact found the last occurrence, the rest of **v** starting from **it** is printed.

The first **search_n( )** test looks for 3 copies of the value 7, which it finds and prints. When using the second version of **search_n( )**, the predicate is ordinarily meant to be used to determine equivalence between two elements, but we've taken some liberties and used a function object that multiplies the value in the sequence by (in this case) 15 and checks to see if it's greater than 100. That is, the **search_n( )** test says "find me 6 consecutive values that, when multiplied by 15, each produce a number greater than 100." Not exactly what you normally expect to do, but it might give you some ideas the next time you have an odd searching problem.

The **min_element( )** and **max_element( )** algorithms are straightforward, but they look odd, as if the function is being dereferenced with a '*'. Actually, the returned iterator is being dereferenced to produce the value for printing.

To test replacements, **replace_copy( )** is used first (so it doesn't modify the original **vector**) to replace all values of 8 with the value 47. Notice the use of **back_inserter( )** with the empty **vector v2**. To demonstrate **replace_if( )**, a function object is created using the standard template **greater_equal** along with **bind2nd** to replace all the values that are greater than or equal to 7 with the value -1.

Comparing ranges

These algorithms provide ways to compare two ranges. At first glance, the operations they perform seem similar to the **search( )** function. However, **search( )** tells you where the second sequence appears within the first, and **equal( )** and **lexicographical_compare( )** simply tell you how two sequences compare. On the other hand, **mismatch( )** does tell you where the two sequences go out of sync, but those sequences must be exactly the same length.

```
bool equal(InputIterator first1, InputIterator last1,
  InputIterator first2);
bool equal(InputIterator first1, InputIterator last1,
  InputIterator first2 BinaryPredicate binary_pred);
```

In both these functions, the first range is the typical one, **[first1, last1)**. The second range starts at **first2**, but there is no "last2" because its length is determined by the length of the first range. The **equal( )** function returns true if both ranges are exactly the same (the same elements in the same order). In the first case, the **operator==** performs the comparison, and in the second case **binary_pred** decides if two elements are the same.

```
bool lexicographical_compare(InputIterator1 first1,
  InputIterator1 last1, InputIterator2 first2,
  InputIterator2 last2);
bool lexicographical_compare(InputIterator1 first1,
  InputIterator1 last1, InputIterator2 first2,
  InputIterator2 last2, BinaryPredicate binary_pred);
```

These two functions determine if the first range is "lexicographically less" than the second. (They return **true** if range 1 is less than range 2, and false otherwise.) *Lexicographical comparison*, or "dictionary" comparison, means that the comparison is done in the same way that we establish the order of strings in a dictionary: one element at a time. The first elements determine the result if these elements are different, but if they're equal, the algorithm moves on to the next elements and looks at those, and so on until it finds a mismatch. At that point, it looks at the elements, and if the element from range 1 is less than the element from range two, **lexicographical_compare( )** returns **true**; otherwise, it returns **false**. If it gets all the way through one range or the other (the ranges may be different lengths for this algorithm) without finding an inequality, range 1 is *not* less than range 2, so the function returns **false**.

If the two ranges are different lengths, a missing element in one range acts as one that "precedes" an element that exists in the other range, so "abc" precedes "abcd." If the algorithm reaches the end of one of the ranges without a mismatch, then the shorter range comes first. In that case, if the shorter range is the first range, the result is **true**, otherwise it is **false**.

In the first version of the function, **operator<** performs the comparisons, and in the second version, **binary_pred** is used.

```
pair<InputIterator1, InputIterator2>
mismatch(InputIterator1 first1, InputIterator1 last1,
   InputIterator2 first2);
pair<InputIterator1, InputIterator2>
mismatch(InputIterator1 first1, InputIterator1 last1,
   InputIterator2 first2, BinaryPredicate binary_pred);
```

As in **equal( )**, the length of both ranges is exactly the same, so only the first iterator in the second range is necessary, and the length of the first range is used as the length of the second range. Whereas **equal( )** just tells you whether the two ranges are the same, **mismatch( )** tells you where they begin to differ. To accomplish this, you must be told (1) the element in the first range where the mismatch occurred and (2) the element in the second range where the mismatch occurred. These two iterators are packaged together into a **pair** object and returned. If no mismatch occurs, the return value is **last1** combined with the past-the-end iterator of the second range. The **pair** template class is a **struct** with two elements denoted by the member names **first** and **second** and is defined in the **<utility>** header.

As in **equal( )**, the first function tests for equality using **operator==** while the second one uses **binary_pred**.

Example

Because the Standard C++ **string** class is built like a container (it has **begin( )** and **end( )** member functions that produce objects of type **string::iterator**), it can be used to conveniently create ranges of characters to test with the STL comparison algorithms. However, note that **string** has a fairly complete set of native operations, so look at the **string** class before using the STL algorithms to perform operations.

```
//: C06:Comparison.cpp
// The STL range comparison algorithms.
#include <algorithm>
#include <functional>
#include <string>
#include <vector>
#include "PrintSequence.h"
using namespace std;

int main() {
  // Strings provide a convenient way to create
  // ranges of characters, but you should
  // normally look for native string operations:
  string s1("This is a test");
  string s2("This is a Test");
  cout << "s1: " << s1 << endl << "s2: " << s2 << endl;
  cout << "compare s1 & s1: "
       << equal(s1.begin(), s1.end(), s1.begin()) << endl;
  cout << "compare s1 & s2: "
       << equal(s1.begin(), s1.end(), s2.begin()) << endl;
  cout << "lexicographical_compare s1 & s1: "
       << lexicographical_compare(s1.begin(), s1.end(),
          s1.begin(), s1.end()) <<  endl;
  cout << "lexicographical_compare s1 & s2: "
       << lexicographical_compare(s1.begin(), s1.end(),
          s2.begin(), s2.end()) << endl;
  cout << "lexicographical_compare s2 & s1: "
       << lexicographical_compare(s2.begin(), s2.end(),
          s1.begin(), s1.end()) << endl;
  cout << "lexicographical_compare shortened "
          "s1 & full-length s2: " << endl;
  string s3(s1);
  while(s3.length() != 0) {
    bool result = lexicographical_compare(
      s3.begin(), s3.end(), s2.begin(),s2.end());
    cout << s3 << endl << s2 << ", result = "
```

```
        << result << endl;
    if(result == true) break;
    s3 = s3.substr(0, s3.length() - 1);
  }
  pair<string::iterator, string::iterator> p =
    mismatch(s1.begin(), s1.end(), s2.begin());
  print(p.first, s1.end(), "p.first", "");
  print(p.second, s2.end(), "p.second","");
} ///:~
```

Note that the only difference between **s1** and **s2** is the capital 'T' in **s2**'s "Test." Comparing **s1** and **s1** for equality yields **true**, as expected, while **s1** and **s2** are not equal because of the capital 'T'.

To understand the output of the **lexicographical_compare( )** tests, remember two things: first, the comparison is performed character-by-character, and second, on our platform capital letters "precede" lowercase letters. In the first test, **s1** is compared to **s1**. These are exactly equivalent. One is *not* lexicographically less than the other (which is what the comparison is looking for), and thus the result is **false**. The second test is asking "does **s1** precede **s2**?" When the comparison gets to the 't' in "test", it discovers that the lowercase 't' in **s1** is "greater" than the uppercase 'T' in **s2**, so the answer is again **false**. However, if we test to see whether **s2** precedes **s1**, the answer is **true**.

To further examine lexicographical comparison, the next test in this example compares **s1** with **s2** again (which returned **false** before). But this time it repeats the comparison, trimming one character off the end of **s1** (which is first copied into **s3**) each time through the loop until the test evaluates to **true**. What you'll see is that, as soon as the uppercase 'T' is trimmed off **s3** (the copy of **s1**), the characters, which are exactly equal up to that point, no longer count. Because **s3** is shorter than **s2**, it lexicographically precedes **s2**.

The final test uses **mismatch( )**. To capture the return value, create the appropriate **pair p**, constructing the template using the iterator type from the first range and the iterator type from the second range (in this case, both **string::iterator**s). To print the results, the iterator for the mismatch in the first range is **p.first**, and for the second range is **p.second**. In both cases, the range is printed from the mismatch iterator to the end of the range so you can see exactly where the iterator points.

Removing elements

Because of the genericity of the STL, the concept of removal is a bit constrained. Since elements can only be "removed" via iterators, and iterators can point to arrays, **vector**s, **list**s, and so on, it is not safe or reasonable to try to destroy the elements that are being removed and to change the size of the input range **[first, last)**. (An array, for example, cannot have its size changed.) So instead, what the STL "remove" functions do is rearrange the sequence so that the "removed" elements are at the end of the sequence, and the "un-removed" elements are at the beginning of the sequence (in the same order that they were before, minus the removed elements—that is, this is a *stable* operation). Then the function will return an iterator to the "new last" element of the sequence, which is the end of the sequence without the removed elements and the beginning of the sequence of the removed elements. In other words, if **new_last** is the iterator that is returned from the "remove" function, **[first, new_last)** is the sequence without any of the removed elements, and **[new_last, last)** is the sequence of removed elements.

If you are simply using your sequence, including the removed elements, with more STL algorithms, you can just use **new_last** as the new past-the-end iterator. However, if you're using a resizable container **c** (not an array) and you want to eliminate the removed elements from the container, you can use **erase( )** to do so, for example:

```
c.erase(remove(c.begin(), c.end(), value), c.end());
```

You can also use the **resize( )** member function that belongs to all standard sequences (more on this in the next chapter).

The return value of **remove( )** is the **new_last** iterator, so **erase( )** deletes all the removed elements from **c**.

The iterators in **[new_last, last)** are dereferenceable, but the element values are unspecified and should not be used.

```
ForwardIterator remove(ForwardIterator first,
  ForwardIterator last, const T& value);
ForwardIterator remove_if(ForwardIterator first,
  ForwardIterator last, Predicate pred);
OutputIterator remove_copy(InputIterator first,
```

```
    InputIterator last, OutputIterator result, const T&
    value);
OutputIterator remove_copy_if(InputIterator first,
    InputIterator last, OutputIterator result, Predicate
    pred);
```

Each of the "remove" forms moves through the range **[first, last)**, finding values that match a removal criterion and copying the unremoved elements over the removed elements (thus effectively removing them). The original order of the unremoved elements is maintained. The return value is an iterator pointing past the end of the range that contains none of the removed elements. The values that this iterator points to are unspecified.

The "if" versions pass each element to **pred( )** to determine whether it should be removed. (If **pred( )** returns **true**, the element is removed.) The "copy" versions do not modify the original sequence, but instead copy the unremoved values into a range beginning at **result** and return an iterator indicating the past-the-end value of this new range.

```
ForwardIterator unique(ForwardIterator first,
    ForwardIterator last);
ForwardIterator unique(ForwardIterator first,
    ForwardIterator last, BinaryPredicate binary_pred);
OutputIterator unique_copy(InputIterator first,
    InputIterator last, OutputIterator result);
OutputIterator unique_copy(InputIterator first,
    InputIterator last, OutputIterator result,
    BinaryPredicate binary_pred);
```

Each of the "unique" functions moves through the range **[first, last)**, finding adjacent values that are equivalent (that is, duplicates) and "removing" the duplicate elements by copying over them. The original order of the unremoved elements is maintained. The return value is an iterator pointing past the end of the range that has the adjacent duplicates removed.

Because only duplicates that are adjacent are removed, it's likely that you'll want to call **sort( )** before calling a "unique" algorithm, since that will guarantee that *all* the duplicates are removed.

For each iterator value **i** in the input range, the versions containing **binary_pred** call:

```
binary_pred(*i, *(i-1));
```

and if the result is **true**, ***i** is considered a duplicate.

The "copy" versions do not modify the original sequence, but instead copy the unremoved values into a range beginning at **result** and return an iterator indicating the past-the-end value of this new range.

Example
This example gives a visual demonstration of the way the "remove" and "unique" functions work.

```cpp
//: C06:Removing.cpp
// The removing algorithms.
//{L} Generators
#include <algorithm>
#include <cctype>
#include <string>
#include "Generators.h"
#include "PrintSequence.h"
using namespace std;

struct IsUpper {
  bool operator()(char c) { return isupper(c); }
};

int main() {
  string v;
  v.resize(25);
  generate(v.begin(), v.end(), CharGen());
  print(v.begin(), v.end(), "v original", "");
  // Create a set of the characters in v:
  string us(v.begin(), v.end());
  sort(us.begin(), us.end());
  string::iterator it = us.begin(), cit = v.end(),
    uend = unique(us.begin(), us.end());
  // Step through and remove everything:
  while(it != uend) {
    cit = remove(v.begin(), cit, *it);
    print(v.begin(), v.end(), "Complete v", "");
    print(v.begin(), cit, "Pseudo v ", " ");
```

```
    cout << "Removed element:\t" << *it
         << "\nPsuedo Last Element:\t"
         << *cit << endl << endl;
    ++it;
  }
  generate(v.begin(), v.end(), CharGen());
  print(v.begin(), v.end(), "v", "");
  cit = remove_if(v.begin(), v.end(), IsUpper());
  print(v.begin(), cit, "v after remove_if IsUpper", " ");
  // Copying versions are not shown for remove()
  // and remove_if().
  sort(v.begin(), cit);
  print(v.begin(), cit, "sorted", " ");
  string v2;
  v2.resize(cit - v.begin());
  unique_copy(v.begin(), cit, v2.begin());
  print(v2.begin(), v2.end(), "unique_copy", " ");
  // Same behavior:
  cit = unique(v.begin(), cit, equal_to<char>());
  print(v.begin(), cit, "unique equal_to<char>", " ");
} ///:~
```

The string **v** is a container of characters filled with randomly generated characters. Each character is used in a **remove** statement, but the entire string **v** is displayed each time so you can see what happens to the rest of the range, after the resulting endpoint (which is stored in **cit**).

To demonstrate **remove_if( )**, the standard C library function **isupper( )** (in **<cctype>**) is called inside the function object class **IsUpper**, an object of which is passed as the predicate for **remove_if( )**. This returns **true** only if a character is uppercase, so only lowercase characters will remain. Here, the end of the range is used in the call to **print( )** so only the remaining elements will appear. The copying versions of **remove( )** and **remove_if( )** are not shown because they are a simple variation on the noncopying versions, which you should be able to use without an example.

The range of lowercase letters is sorted in preparation for testing the "unique" functions. (The "unique" functions are not undefined if the range isn't sorted, but it's probably not what you want.) First, **unique_copy( )** puts the unique elements into a new **vector** using the default element comparison, and then uses the form of **unique( )** that takes a predicate. The predicate is the built-in function object **equal_to( )**, which produces the same results as the default element comparison.

Sorting and operations on sorted ranges

A significant category of STL algorithms must operate on a sorted range. STL provides a number of separate sorting algorithms, depending on whether the sort should be stable, partial, or just regular (non-stable). Oddly enough, only the partial sort has a copying version. If you're using another sort and you need to work on a copy, you'll have to make your own copy before sorting.

Once your sequence is sorted, you can perform many operations on that sequence, from simply locating an element or group of elements to merging with another sorted sequence or manipulating sequences as mathematical sets.

Each algorithm involved with sorting or operations on sorted sequences has two versions. The first uses the object's own **operator<** to perform the comparison, and the second uses **operator( )(a, b)** to determine the relative order of **a** and **b**. Other than this, there are no differences, so this distinction will not be pointed out in the description of each algorithm.

Sorting

The sort algorithms require ranges delimited by random-access iterators, such as a **vector** or **deque**. The **list** container has its own built-in **sort( )** function, since it only supports bi-directional iteration.

```
void sort(RandomAccessIterator first, RandomAccessIterator
    last);
void sort(RandomAccessIterator first, RandomAccessIterator
    last, StrictWeakOrdering binary_pred);
```

Sorts **[first, last)** into ascending order. The first form uses **operator<** and the second form uses the supplied comparator object to determine the order.

```
void stable_sort(RandomAccessIterator first,
    RandomAccessIterator last);
void stable_sort(RandomAccessIterator first,
    RandomAccessIterator last, StrictWeakOrdering
    binary_pred);
```

Sorts **[first, last)** into ascending order, preserving the original ordering of equivalent elements. (This is important if elements can be equivalent but not identical.)

```
void partial_sort(RandomAccessIterator first,
  RandomAccessIterator middle, RandomAccessIterator last);
void partial_sort(RandomAccessIterator first,
  RandomAccessIterator middle, RandomAccessIterator last,
  StrictWeakOrdering binary_pred);
```

Sorts the number of elements from **[first, last)** that can be placed in the range **[first, middle)**. The rest of the elements end up in **[middle, last)** and have no guaranteed order.

```
RandomAccessIterator partial_sort_copy(InputIterator first,
  InputIterator last, RandomAccessIterator result_first,
  RandomAccessIterator result_last);
RandomAccessIterator partial_sort_copy(InputIterator first,
  InputIterator last, RandomAccessIterator result_first,
  RandomAccessIterator result_last, StrictWeakOrdering
  binary_pred);
```

Sorts the number of elements from **[first, last)** that can be placed in the range **[result_first, result_last)** and copies those elements into **[result_first, result_last)**. If the range **[first, last)** is smaller than **[result_first, result_last)**, the smaller number of elements is used.

```
void nth_element(RandomAccessIterator first,
  RandomAccessIterator nth, RandomAccessIterator last);
void nth_element(RandomAccessIterator first,
  RandomAccessIterator nth, RandomAccessIterator last,
  StrictWeakOrdering binary_pred);
```

Just like **partial_sort( )**, **nth_element( )** partially orders a range of elements. However, it's much "less ordered" than **partial_sort( )**. The only guarantee from **nth_element( )** is that whatever *location* you choose will become a dividing point. All the elements in the range **[first, nth)** will pairwise satisfy the binary predicate (**operator<** by default, as usual), and all the elements in the range **(nth, last]** will not. However, neither subrange is in any particular order, unlike **partial_sort( )** which has the first range in sorted order.

If all you need is this very weak ordering (if, for example, you're determining medians, percentiles, and so on), this algorithm is faster than **partial_sort( )**.

Locating elements in sorted ranges

Once a range is sorted, you can use a group of operations to find elements within those ranges. In the following functions, there are always two forms. One assumes that the intrinsic **operator<** performs the sort, and the second operator must be used if some other comparison function object performs the sort. You must use the same comparison for locating elements as you do to perform the sort; otherwise, the results are undefined. In addition, if you try to use these functions on unsorted ranges, the results will be undefined.

```
bool binary_search(ForwardIterator first, ForwardIterator
  last, const T& value);
bool binary_search(ForwardIterator first, ForwardIterator
  last, const T& value, StrictWeakOrdering binary_pred);
```

Tells you whether **value** appears in the sorted range **[first, last)**.

```
ForwardIterator lower_bound(ForwardIterator first,
  ForwardIterator last, const T& value);
ForwardIterator lower_bound(ForwardIterator first,
  ForwardIterator last, const T& value, StrictWeakOrdering
  binary_pred);
```

Returns an iterator indicating the first occurrence of **value** in the sorted range **[first, last)**. If **value** is not present, an iterator to where it would fit in the sequence is returned.

```
ForwardIterator upper_bound(ForwardIterator first,
  ForwardIterator last, const T& value);
ForwardIterator upper_bound(ForwardIterator first,
  ForwardIterator last, const T& value, StrictWeakOrdering
  binary_pred);
```

Returns an iterator indicating one past the last occurrence of **value** in the sorted range **[first, last)**. If **value** is not present, an iterator to where it would fit in the sequence is returned.

```
pair<ForwardIterator, ForwardIterator>
equal_range(ForwardIterator first, ForwardIterator last,
  const T& value);
pair<ForwardIterator, ForwardIterator>
equal_range(ForwardIterator first, ForwardIterator last,
  const T& value, StrictWeakOrdering binary_pred);
```

Essentially combines **lower_bound( )** and **upper_bound( )** to return a **pair** indicating the first and one-past-the-last occurrences of **value** in the sorted range **[first, last)**. Both iterators indicate the location where **value** would fit if it is not found.

You may find it surprising that the binary search algorithms take a forward iterator instead of a random access iterator. (Most explanations of binary search use indexing.) Remember that a random access iterator "is-a" forward iterator, and can be used wherever the latter is specified. If the iterator passed to one of these algorithms in fact supports random access, then the efficient logarithmic-time procedure is used, otherwise a linear search is performed.[11]

Example
The following example turns each input word into an **NString** and adds it to a **vector<NString>**. The **vector** is then used to demonstrate the various sorting and searching algorithms.

```
//: C06:SortedSearchTest.cpp
// Test searching in sorted ranges.
// NString
#include <algorithm>
#include <cassert>
#include <ctime>
#include <cstdlib>
#include <cstddef>
#include <fstream>
```

---

[11] Algorithms can determine the type of an iterator by reading its **tag**, discussed in the next chapter.

```cpp
#include <iostream>
#include <iterator>
#include <vector>
#include "NString.h"
#include "PrintSequence.h"
#include "../require.h"
using namespace std;

int main(int argc, char* argv[]) {
  typedef vector<NString>::iterator sit;
  char* fname = "Test.txt";
  if(argc > 1) fname = argv[1];
  ifstream in(fname);
  assure(in, fname);
  srand(time(0));
  cout.setf(ios::boolalpha);
  vector<NString> original;
  copy(istream_iterator<string>(in),
    istream_iterator<string>(), back_inserter(original));
  require(original.size() >= 4, "Must have four elements");
  vector<NString> v(original.begin(), original.end()),
    w(original.size() / 2);
  sort(v.begin(), v.end());
  print(v.begin(), v.end(), "sort");
  v = original;
  stable_sort(v.begin(), v.end());
  print(v.begin(), v.end(), "stable_sort");
  v = original;
  sit it = v.begin(), it2;
  // Move iterator to middle
  for(size_t i = 0; i < v.size() / 2; i++)
    ++it;
  partial_sort(v.begin(), it, v.end());
  cout << "middle = " << *it << endl;
  print(v.begin(), v.end(), "partial_sort");
  v = original;
  // Move iterator to a quarter position
  it = v.begin();
  for(size_t i = 0; i < v.size() / 4; i++)
    ++it;
  // Less elements to copy from than to the destination
  partial_sort_copy(v.begin(), it, w.begin(), w.end());
  print(w.begin(), w.end(), "partial_sort_copy");
  // Not enough room in destination
  partial_sort_copy(v.begin(), v.end(), w.begin(),w.end());
```

```
    print(w.begin(), w.end(), "w partial_sort_copy");
    // v remains the same through all this process
    assert(v == original);
    nth_element(v.begin(), it, v.end());
    cout << "The nth_element = " << *it << endl;
    print(v.begin(), v.end(), "nth_element");
    string f = original[rand() % original.size()];
    cout << "binary search: "
         << binary_search(v.begin(), v.end(), f) << endl;
    sort(v.begin(), v.end());
    it = lower_bound(v.begin(), v.end(), f);
    it2 = upper_bound(v.begin(), v.end(), f);
    print(it, it2, "found range");
    pair<sit, sit> ip = equal_range(v.begin(), v.end(), f);
    print(ip.first, ip.second, "equal_range");
} ///:~
```

This example uses the **NString** class seen earlier, which stores an occurrence
number with copies of a string. The call to **stable_sort( )** shows how the
original order for objects with equal strings is preserved. You can also see
what happens during a partial sort (the remaining unsorted elements are in
no particular order). There is no "partial stable sort."

Notice in the call to **nth_element( )** that, whatever the nth element turns
out to be (which will vary from one run to another because of **URandGen**),
the elements before that are less, and after that are greater, but the elements
have no particular order other than that. Because of **URandGen**, there are
no duplicates, but if you use a generator that allows duplicates, you'll see that
the elements before the nth element will be less than or equal to the nth
element.

This example also illustrates all three binary search algorithms. As
advertised, **lower_bound( )** refers to the first element in the sequence
equal to a given key, **upper_bound( )** points one past the last, and
equal_range( ) returns both results as a pair.

Merging sorted ranges
As before, the first form of each function assumes that the intrinsic
operator< performs the sort. The second form must be used if some other
comparison function object performs the sort. You must use the same
comparison for locating elements as you do to perform the sort; otherwise,

the results are undefined. In addition, if you try to use these functions on unsorted ranges, the results will be undefined.

```
OutputIterator merge(InputIterator1 first1, InputIterator1
   last1, InputIterator2 first2, InputIterator2 last2,
   OutputIterator result);
OutputIterator merge(InputIterator1 first1, InputIterator1
   last1, InputIterator2 first2, InputIterator2 last2,
   OutputIterator result, StrictWeakOrdering binary_pred);
```

Copies elements from **[first1, last1)** and **[first2, last2)** into **result**, such that the resulting range is sorted in ascending order. This is a stable operation.

```
void inplace_merge(BidirectionalIterator first,
   BidirectionalIterator middle, BidirectionalIterator
   last);
void inplace_merge(BidirectionalIterator first,
   BidirectionalIterator middle, BidirectionalIterator last,
   StrictWeakOrdering binary_pred);
```

This assumes that **[first, middle)** and **[middle, last)** are each sorted ranges in the same sequence. The two ranges are merged so that the resulting range **[first, last)** contains the combined ranges in sorted order.

Example

It's easier to see what goes on with merging if **int**s are used. The following example also emphasizes how the algorithms (and our own **print** template) work with arrays as well as containers:

```
//: C06:MergeTest.cpp
// Test merging in sorted ranges.
//{L} Generators
#include <algorithm>
#include "PrintSequence.h"
#include "Generators.h"
using namespace std;

int main() {
  const int SZ = 15;
  int a[SZ*2] = {0};
```

```
    // Both ranges go in the same array:
    generate(a, a + SZ, SkipGen(0, 2));
    a[3] = 4;
    a[4] = 4;
    generate(a + SZ, a + SZ*2, SkipGen(1, 3));
    print(a, a + SZ, "range1", " ");
    print(a + SZ, a + SZ*2, "range2", " ");
    int b[SZ*2] = {0}; // Initialize all to zero
    merge(a, a + SZ, a + SZ, a + SZ*2, b);
    print(b, b + SZ*2, "merge", " ");
    // Reset b
    for(int i = 0; i < SZ*2; i++)
        b[i] = 0;
    inplace_merge(a, a + SZ, a + SZ*2);
    print(a, a + SZ*2, "inplace_merge", " ");
    int* end = set_union(a, a + SZ, a + SZ, a + SZ*2, b);
    print(b, end, "set_union", " ");
} ///:~
```

In **main( )**, instead of creating two separate arrays, both ranges are created end to end in the array **a**. (This will come in handy for the **inplace_merge**.) The first call to **merge( )** places the result in a different array, **b**. For comparison, **set_union( )** is also called, which has the same signature and similar behavior, except that it removes duplicates from the second set. Finally, **inplace_merge( )** combines both parts of **a**.

Set operations on sorted ranges
Once ranges have been sorted, you can perform mathematical set operations on them.

```
bool includes(InputIterator1 first1, InputIterator1 last1,
    InputIterator2 first2, InputIterator2 last2);
bool includes(InputIterator1 first1, InputIterator1 last1,
    InputIterator2 first2, InputIterator2 last2,
    StrictWeakOrdering binary_pred);
```

Returns **true** if [**first2, last2**) is a subset of [**first1, last1**). Neither range is required to hold only unique elements, but if [**first2, last2**) holds **n** elements of a particular value, [**first1, last1**) must also hold at least **n** elements if the result is to be **true**.

```
OutputIterator set_union(InputIterator1 first1,
    InputIterator1 last1, InputIterator2 first2,
    InputIterator2 last2, OutputIterator result);
OutputIterator set_union(InputIterator1 first1,
    InputIterator1 last1, InputIterator2 first2,
    InputIterator2 last2, OutputIterator result,
    StrictWeakOrdering binary_pred);
```

Creates the mathematical union of two sorted ranges in the **result** range,
returning the end of the output range. Neither input range is required to hold
only unique elements, but if a particular value appears multiple times in both
input sets, the resulting set will contain the larger number of identical values.

```
OutputIterator set_intersection(InputIterator1 first1,
    InputIterator1 last1, InputIterator2 first2,
    InputIterator2 last2, OutputIterator result);
OutputIterator set_intersection(InputIterator1 first1,
    InputIterator1 last1, InputIterator2 first2,
    InputIterator2 last2, OutputIterator result,
    StrictWeakOrdering binary_pred);
```

Produces, in **result**, the intersection of the two input sets, returning the end
of the output range—that is, the set of values that appear in both input sets.
Neither input range is required to hold only unique elements, but if a
particular value appears multiple times in both input sets, the resulting set
will contain the smaller number of identical values.

```
OutputIterator set_difference(InputIterator1 first1,
    InputIterator1 last1, InputIterator2 first2,
    InputIterator2 last2, OutputIterator result);
OutputIterator set_difference(InputIterator1 first1,
    InputIterator1 last1, InputIterator2 first2,
    InputIterator2 last2, OutputIterator result,
    StrictWeakOrdering binary_pred);
```

Produces, in **result**, the mathematical set difference, returning the end of the
output range. All the elements that are in **[first1, last1)** but not in **[first2,
last2)** are placed in the result set. Neither input range is required to hold
only unique elements, but if a particular value appears multiple times in both

input sets (**n** times in set 1 and **m** times in set 2), the resulting set will contain **max(n-m, 0)** copies of that value.

```
OutputIterator set_symmetric_difference(InputIterator1
    first1, InputIterator1 last1, InputIterator2 first2,
    InputIterator2 last2, OutputIterator result);
OutputIterator set_symmetric_difference(InputIterator1
    first1, InputIterator1 last1, InputIterator2 first2,
    InputIterator2 last2, OutputIterator result,
    StrictWeakOrdering binary_pred);
```

Constructs, in **result**, the set containing:

1. All the elements in set 1 that are not in set 2.

2. All the elements in set 2 that are not in set 1.

Neither input range is required to hold only unique elements, but if a particular value appears multiple times in both input sets (**n** times in set 1 and **m** times in set 2), the resulting set will contain **abs(n-m)** copies of that value, where **abs( )** is the absolute value. The return value is the end of the output range.

Example
It's easiest to see the set operations demonstrated using simple **vector**s of characters. These characters are randomly generated and then sorted, but the duplicates are retained so that you can see what the set operations do when there are duplicates.

```
//: C06:SetOperations.cpp
// Set operations on sorted ranges.
//{L} Generators
#include <algorithm>
#include <vector>
#include "Generators.h"
#include "PrintSequence.h"
using namespace std;

int main() {
  const int SZ = 30;
  char v[SZ + 1], v2[SZ + 1];
  CharGen g;
```

```
    generate(v, v + SZ, g);
    generate(v2, v2 + SZ, g);
    sort(v, v + SZ);
    sort(v2, v2 + SZ);
    print(v, v + SZ, "v", "");
    print(v2, v2 + SZ, "v2", "");
    bool b = includes(v, v + SZ, v + SZ/2, v + SZ);
    cout.setf(ios::boolalpha);
    cout << "includes: " << b << endl;
    char v3[SZ*2 + 1], *end;
    end = set_union(v, v + SZ, v2, v2 + SZ, v3);
    print(v3, end, "set_union", "");
    end = set_intersection(v, v + SZ, v2, v2 + SZ, v3);
    print(v3, end, "set_intersection", "");
    end = set_difference(v, v + SZ, v2, v2 + SZ, v3);
    print(v3, end, "set_difference", "");
    end = set_symmetric_difference(v, v + SZ,
      v2, v2 + SZ, v3);
    print(v3, end, "set_symmetric_difference","");
} ///:~
```

After **v** and **v2** are generated, sorted, and printed, the **includes( )** algorithm is tested by seeing if the entire range of **v** contains the last half of **v**. It does, so the result should always be true. The array **v3** holds the output of **set_union( )**, **set_intersection( )**, **set_difference( )**, and **set_symmetric_difference( )**, and the results of each are displayed so you can ponder them and convince yourself that the algorithms work as promised.

Heap operations

A heap is an array-like data structure used to implement a "priority queue," which is just a range that is organized in a way that accommodates retrieving elements by priority according to some comparison function. The heap operations in the standard library allow a sequence to be treated as a "heap" data structure, which always efficiently returns the element of highest priority, without fully ordering the entire sequence.

As with the "sort" operations, there are two versions of each function. The first uses the object's own **operator<** to perform the comparison; the second uses an additional **StrictWeakOrdering** object's **operator( )(a, b)** to compare two objects for **a < b**.

```
void make_heap(RandomAccessIterator first,
  RandomAccessIterator last);
void make_heap(RandomAccessIterator first,
  RandomAccessIterator last,
  StrictWeakOrdering binary_pred);
```

Turns an arbitrary range into a heap.

```
void push_heap(RandomAccessIterator first,
  RandomAccessIterator last);
void push_heap(RandomAccessIterator first,
  RandomAccessIterator last,
  StrictWeakOrdering binary_pred);
```

Adds the element *(last-1) to the heap determined by the range [first, last-1). In other words, it places the last element in its proper location in the heap.

```
void pop_heap(RandomAccessIterator first,
  RandomAccessIterator last);
void pop_heap(RandomAccessIterator first,
  RandomAccessIterator last,
  StrictWeakOrdering binary_pred);
```

Places the largest element (which is actually in *first, before the operation, because of the way heaps are defined) into the position *(last-1) and reorganizes the remaining range so that it's still in heap order. If you simply grabbed *first, the next element would not be the next-largest element; so you must use pop_heap( ) if you want to maintain the heap in its proper priority-queue order.

```
void sort_heap(RandomAccessIterator first,
  RandomAccessIterator last);
void sort_heap(RandomAccessIterator first,
  RandomAccessIterator last,
  StrictWeakOrdering binary_pred);
```

This could be thought of as the complement to make_heap( ). It takes a range that is in heap order and turns it into ordinary sorted order, so it is no longer a heap. That means that if you call sort_heap( ), you can no longer use **push_heap( )** or **pop_heap( )** on that range. (Rather, you can use those functions, but they won't do anything sensible.) This is not a stable sort.

Applying an operation to each element in a range

These algorithms move through the entire range and perform an operation on each element. They differ in what they do with the results of that operation: **for_each( )** discards the return value of the operation, and **transform( )** places the results of each operation into a destination sequence (which can be the original sequence).

```
UnaryFunction for_each(InputIterator first, InputIterator
    last, UnaryFunction f);
```

Applies the function object **f** to each element in **[first, last)**, discarding the return value from each individual application of **f**. If **f** is just a function pointer, you are typically not interested in the return value; but if **f** is an object that maintains some internal state, it can capture the combined return value of being applied to the range. The final return value of **for_each( )** is **f**.

```
OutputIterator transform(InputIterator first, InputIterator
    last, OutputIterator result, UnaryFunction f);
OutputIterator transform(InputIterator1 first,
    InputIterator1 last, InputIterator2 first2,
    OutputIterator result, BinaryFunction f);
```

Like **for_each( )**, **transform( )** applies a function object **f** to each element in the range **[first, last)**. However, instead of discarding the result of each function call, **transform( )** copies the result (using **operator=**) into ***result**, incrementing **result** after each copy. (The sequence pointed to by **result** must have enough storage; otherwise, use an inserter to force insertions instead of assignments.)

The first form of **transform( )** simply calls **f(*first)**, where first ranges through the input sequence. Similarly, the second form calls **f(*first1, *first2)**. (Note that the length of the second input range is determined by the length of the first.) The return value in both cases is the past-the-end iterator for the resulting output range.

Examples

Since much of what you do with objects in a container is to apply an operation to all those objects, these are fairly important algorithms and merit several illustrations.

First, consider **for_each( )**. This sweeps through the range, pulling out each element and passing it as an argument as it calls whatever function object it's been given. Thus, **for_each( )** performs operations that you might normally write out by hand. If you look in your compiler's header file at the template defining **for_each( )**, you'll see something like this:

```
template<class InputIterator, class Function>
Function for_each(InputIterator first, InputIterator last,
                  Function f) {
    while(first != last)
      f(*first++);
    return f;
}
```

The following example shows several ways this template can be expanded. First, we need a class that keeps track of its objects so we can know that it's being properly destroyed:

```
//: C06:Counted.h
// An object that keeps track of itself.
#ifndef COUNTED_H
#define COUNTED_H
#include <vector>
#include <iostream>

class Counted {
  static int count;
  char* ident;
public:
  Counted(char* id) : ident(id) { ++count; }
  ~Counted() {
    std::cout << ident << " count = "
              << --count << std::endl;
  }
};

class CountedVector : public std::vector<Counted*> {
public:
  CountedVector(char* id) {
```

```
    for(int i = 0; i < 5; i++)
      push_back(new Counted(id));
  }
};
#endif // COUNTED_H ///:~

//: C06:Counted.cpp {O}
#include "Counted.h"
int Counted::count = 0;
///:~
```

The **class Counted** keeps a static count of the number of **Counted** objects that have been created, and notifies you as they are destroyed.[12] In addition, each **Counted** keeps a **char*** identifier to make tracking the output easier.

The **CountedVector** is derived from **vector<Counted*>**, and in the constructor it creates some **Counted** objects, handing each one your desired **char***. The **CountedVector** makes testing quite simple, as you can see here:

```
//: C06:ForEach.cpp {-mwcc}
// Use of STL for_each() algorithm.
//{L} Counted
#include <algorithm>
#include <iostream>
#include "Counted.h"
using namespace std;

// Function object:
template<class T> class DeleteT {
public:
  void operator()(T* x) { delete x; }
};

// Template function:
template<class T> void wipe(T* x) { delete x; }

int main() {
  CountedVector B("two");
  for_each(B.begin(), B.end(), DeleteT<Counted>());
  CountedVector C("three");
```

---

[12] We're ignoring the copy constructor and assignment operator in this example, since they don't apply.

```
  for_each(C.begin(), C.end(), wipe<Counted>);
} ///:~
```

Since this is obviously something you might want to do a lot, why not create an algorithm to **delete** all the pointers in a container? You could use **transform( )**. The value of **transform( )** over **for_each( )** is that **transform( )** assigns the result of calling the function object into a resulting range, which can actually be the input range. That case means a literal transformation for the input range, since each element would be a modification of its previous value. In this example, this approach would be especially useful since it's more appropriate to assign to each pointer the safe value of zero after calling **delete** for that pointer. **Transform( )** can easily do this:

```
//: C06:Transform.cpp {-mwcc}
// Use of STL transform() algorithm.
//{L} Counted
#include <iostream>
#include <vector>
#include <algorithm>
#include "Counted.h"
using namespace std;

template<class T> T* deleteP(T* x) { delete x; return 0; }

template<class T> struct Deleter {
  T* operator()(T* x) { delete x; return 0; }
};

int main() {
  CountedVector cv("one");
  transform(cv.begin(), cv.end(), cv.begin(),
    deleteP<Counted>);
  CountedVector cv2("two");
  transform(cv2.begin(), cv2.end(), cv2.begin(),
    Deleter<Counted>());
} ///:~
```

This shows both approaches: using a template function or a templatized function object. After the call to **transform( )**, the **vector** contains five null pointers, which is safer since any duplicate **delete**s will have no effect.

One thing you cannot do is **delete** every pointer in a collection without wrapping the call to **delete** inside a function or an object. That is, you do the following:

```
for_each(a.begin(), a.end(), ptr_fun(operator delete));
```

This has the same problem as the call to **destroy( )** did earlier: **operator delete( )** takes a **void***, but iterators aren't pointers. Even if you could make it compile, what you'd get is a sequence of calls to the function that releases the storage. You will not get the effect of calling **delete** for each pointer in **a**, however—the destructor will not be called. This is typically not what you want, so you will need to wrap your calls to **delete**.

In the previous example of **for_each( )**, the return value of the algorithm was ignored. This return value is the function that is passed into **for_each( )**. If the function is just a pointer to a function, the return value is not very useful, but if it is a function object, that function object may have internal member data that it uses to accumulate information about all the objects that it sees during **for_each( )**.

For example, consider a simple model of inventory. Each **Inventory** object has the type of product it represents (here, single characters will be used for product names), the quantity of that product, and the price of each item:

```
//: C06:Inventory.h
#ifndef INVENTORY_H
#define INVENTORY_H
#include <iostream>
#include <cstdlib>
using std::rand;

class Inventory {
  char item;
  int quantity;
  int value;
public:
  Inventory(char it, int quant, int val)
  : item(it), quantity(quant), value(val) {}
  // Synthesized operator= & copy-constructor OK
  char getItem() const { return item; }
  int getQuantity() const { return quantity; }
  void setQuantity(int q) { quantity = q; }
  int getValue() const { return value; }
```

```
    void setValue(int val) { value = val; }
    friend std::ostream& operator<<(
      std::ostream& os, const Inventory& inv) {
      return os << inv.item << ": "
        << "quantity " << inv.quantity
        << ", value " << inv.value;
    }
};

// A generator:
struct InvenGen {
  Inventory operator()() {
    static char c = 'a';
    int q = rand() % 100;
    int v = rand() % 500;
    return Inventory(c++, q, v);
  }
};
#endif // INVENTORY_H ///:~
```

Member functions get the item name and get and set quantity and value. An **operator<<** prints the **Inventory** object to an **ostream**. A generator creates objects that have sequentially labeled items and random quantities and values.

To find out the total number of items and total value, you can create a function object to use with **for_each( )** that has data members to hold the totals:

```
//: C06:CalcInventory.cpp
// More use of for_each().
#include <algorithm>
#include <ctime>
#include <vector>
#include "Inventory.h"
#include "PrintSequence.h"
using namespace std;

// To calculate inventory totals:
class InvAccum {
  int quantity;
  int value;
public:
  InvAccum() : quantity(0), value(0) {}
```

```
    void operator()(const Inventory& inv) {
      quantity += inv.getQuantity();
      value += inv.getQuantity() * inv.getValue();
    }
    friend ostream&
    operator<<(ostream& os, const InvAccum& ia) {
      return os << "total quantity: " << ia.quantity
                << ", total value: " << ia.value;
    }
};

int main() {
  vector<Inventory> vi;
  srand(time(0));   // Randomize
  generate_n(back_inserter(vi), 15, InvenGen());
  print(vi.begin(), vi.end(), "vi");
  InvAccum ia = for_each(vi.begin(),vi.end(), InvAccum());
  cout << ia << endl;
} ///:~
```

InvAccum's **operator( )** takes a single argument, as required by
for_each( ). As **for_each( )** moves through its range, it takes each object
in that range and passes it to **InvAccum::operator( )**, which performs
calculations and saves the result. At the end of this process, **for_each( )**
returns the **InvAccum** object, which is printed.

You can do most things to the **Inventory** objects using **for_each( )**. For
example, **for_each( )** can handily increase all the prices by 10%. But you'll
notice that the **Inventory** objects have no way to change the **item** value. The
programmers who designed **Inventory** thought this was a good idea. After
all, why would you want to change the name of an item? But marketing has
decided that they want a "new, improved" look by changing all the item
names to uppercase. They've done studies and determined that the new
names will boost sales (well, marketing needs to have *something* to do...). So
for_each( ) will not work here, but **transform( )** will:

```
//: C06:TransformNames.cpp
// More use of transform().
#include <algorithm>
#include <cctype>
#include <ctime>
#include <vector>
#include "Inventory.h"
```

```
#include "PrintSequence.h"
using namespace std;

struct NewImproved {
  Inventory operator()(const Inventory& inv) {
    return Inventory(toupper(inv.getItem()),
      inv.getQuantity(), inv.getValue());
  }
};

int main() {
  vector<Inventory> vi;
  srand(time(0));  // Randomize
  generate_n(back_inserter(vi), 15, InvenGen());
  print(vi.begin(), vi.end(), "vi");
  transform(vi.begin(),vi.end(),vi.begin(),NewImproved());
  print(vi.begin(), vi.end(), "vi");
} ///:~
```

Notice that the resulting range is the same as the input range; that is, the transformation is performed in place.

Now suppose that the sales department needs to generate special price lists with different discounts for each item. The original list must stay the same, and any number of special lists need to be generated. Sales will give you a separate list of discounts for each new list. To solve this problem, we can use the second version of **transform( )**:

```
//: C06:SpecialList.cpp
// Using the second version of transform().
#include <algorithm>
#include <ctime>
#include <vector>
#include "Inventory.h"
#include "PrintSequence.h"
using namespace std;

struct Discounter {
  Inventory operator()(const Inventory& inv,
    float discount) {
    return Inventory(inv.getItem(), inv.getQuantity(),
      int(inv.getValue() * (1 - discount)));
  }
};
```

```
struct DiscGen {
  float operator()() {
    float r = float(rand() % 10);
    return r / 100.0;
  }
};

int main() {
  vector<Inventory> vi;
  srand(time(0));  // Randomize
  generate_n(back_inserter(vi), 15, InvenGen());
  print(vi.begin(), vi.end(), "vi");
  vector<float> disc;
  generate_n(back_inserter(disc), 15, DiscGen());
  print(disc.begin(), disc.end(), "Discounts:");
  vector<Inventory> discounted;
  transform(vi.begin(),vi.end(), disc.begin(),
    back_inserter(discounted), Discounter());
  print(discounted.begin(), discounted.end(),"discounted");
} ///:~
```

Given an **Inventory** object and a discount percentage, the **Discounter** function object produces a new **Inventory** with the discounted price. The **DiscGen** function object just generates random discount values between 1% and 10% to use for testing. In **main( )**, two **vector**s are created, one for **Inventory** and one for discounts. These are passed to **transform( )** along with a **Discounter** object, and **transform( )** fills a new **vector<Inventory>** called **discounted**.

Numeric algorithms

These algorithms are all tucked into the header **<numeric>**, since they are primarily useful for performing numeric calculations.

```
T accumulate(InputIterator first, InputIterator last, T
  result);
T accumulate(InputIterator first, InputIterator last, T
  result, BinaryFunction f);
```

The first form is a generalized summation; for each element pointed to by an iterator **i** in **[first, last)**, it performs the operation **result = result + *i**, where **result** is of type **T**. However, the second form is more general; it applies the function **f(result, *i)** on each element ***i** in the range from beginning to end.

Note the similarity between the second form of **transform( )** and the second form of **accumulate( )**.

```
T inner_product(InputIterator1 first1, InputIterator1
    last1, InputIterator2 first2, T init);
T inner_product(InputIterator1 first1, InputIterator1
    last1, InputIterator2 first2, T init, BinaryFunction1
    op1, BinaryFunction2 op2);
```

Calculates a generalized inner product of the two ranges **[first1, last1)** and **[first2, first2 + (last1 - first1))**. The return value is produced by multiplying the element from the first sequence by the "parallel" element in the second sequence and then adding it to the sum. Thus, if you have two sequences **{1, 1, 2, 2}** and **{1, 2, 3, 4}**, the inner product becomes

```
(1*1) + (1*2) + (2*3) + (2*4)
```

which is 17. The **init** argument is the initial value for the inner product—this is probably zero but may be anything and is especially important for an empty first sequence, because then it becomes the default return value. The second sequence must have at least as many elements as the first.

The second form simply applies a pair of functions to its sequence. The **op1** function is used in place of addition and **op2** is used instead of multiplication. Thus, if you applied the second version of **inner_product( )** to the sequence, the result would be the following operations:

```
init = op1(init, op2(1,1));
init = op1(init, op2(1,2));
init = op1(init, op2(2,3));
init = op1(init, op2(2,4));
```

Thus, it's similar to **transform( )**, but two operations are performed instead of one.

```
OutputIterator partial_sum(InputIterator first,
    InputIterator last, OutputIterator result);
OutputIterator partial_sum(InputIterator first,
```

```
InputIterator last, OutputIterator result,
BinaryFunction op);
```

Calculates a generalized partial sum. A new sequence is created, beginning at **result**. Each element is the sum of all the elements up to the currently selected element in **[first, last)**. For example, if the original sequence is **{1, 1, 2, 2, 3}**, the generated sequence is **{1, 1 + 1, 1 + 1 + 2, 1 + 1 + 2 + 2, 1 + 1 + 2 + 2 + 3}**, that is, **{1, 2, 4, 6, 9}**.

In the second version, the binary function **op** is used instead of the + operator to take all the "summation" up to that point and combine it with the new value. For example, if you use **multiplies<int>( )** as the object for the sequence, the output is **{1, 1, 2, 4, 12}**. Note that the first output value is always the same as the first input value.

The return value is the end of the output range **[result, result + (last - first))**.

```
OutputIterator adjacent_difference(InputIterator first,
    InputIterator last, OutputIterator result);
OutputIterator adjacent_difference(InputIterator first,
    InputIterator last, OutputIterator result, BinaryFunction
    op);
```

Calculates the differences of adjacent elements throughout the range **[first, last)**. This means that in the new sequence, the value is the value of the difference of the current element and the previous element in the original sequence (the first value is unchanged). For example, if the original sequence is **{1, 1, 2, 2, 3}**, the resulting sequence is **{1, 1 − 1, 2 − 1, 2 − 2, 3 − 2}**, that is: **{1, 0, 1, 0, 1}**.

The second form uses the binary function **op** instead of the '−' operator to perform the "differencing." For example, if you use **multiplies<int>( )** as the function object for the sequence, the output is **{1, 1, 2, 4, 6}**.

The return value is the end of the output range **[result, result + (last - first))**.

Example

This program tests all the algorithms in **\<numeric\>** in both forms, on integer arrays. You'll notice that in the test of the form where you supply the function or functions, the function objects used are the ones that produce the same result as form one, so the results will be exactly the same. This should also demonstrate a bit more clearly the operations that are going on and how to substitute your own operations.

```
//: C06:NumericTest.cpp
#include <algorithm>
#include <iostream>
#include <iterator>
#include <functional>
#include <numeric>
#include "PrintSequence.h"
using namespace std;

int main() {
  int a[] = { 1, 1, 2, 2, 3, 5, 7, 9, 11, 13 };
  const int ASZ = sizeof a / sizeof a[0];
  print(a, a + ASZ, "a", " ");
  int r = accumulate(a, a + ASZ, 0);
  cout << "accumulate 1: " << r << endl;
  // Should produce the same result:
  r = accumulate(a, a + ASZ, 0, plus<int>());
  cout << "accumulate 2: " << r << endl;
  int b[] = { 1, 2, 3, 4, 1, 2, 3, 4, 1, 2 };
  print(b, b + sizeof b / sizeof b[0], "b", " ");
  r = inner_product(a, a + ASZ, b, 0);
  cout << "inner_product 1: " << r << endl;
  // Should produce the same result:
  r = inner_product(a, a + ASZ, b, 0,
    plus<int>(), multiplies<int>());
  cout << "inner_product 2: " << r << endl;
  int* it = partial_sum(a, a + ASZ, b);
  print(b, it, "partial_sum 1", " ");
  // Should produce the same result:
  it = partial_sum(a, a + ASZ, b, plus<int>());
  print(b, it, "partial_sum 2", " ");
  it = adjacent_difference(a, a + ASZ, b);
  print(b, it, "adjacent_difference 1"," ");
  // Should produce the same result:
  it = adjacent_difference(a, a + ASZ, b, minus<int>());
  print(b, it, "adjacent_difference 2"," ");
```

```
} ///:~
```

Note that the return value of **inner_product( )** and **partial_sum( )** is the past-the-end iterator for the resulting sequence, so it is used as the second iterator in the **print( )** function.

Since the second form of each function allows you to provide your own function object, only the first form of the function is purely "numeric." You could conceivably do things that are not intuitively numeric with **inner_product( )**.

General utilities

Finally, here are some basic tools that are used with the other algorithms; you may or may not use them directly yourself.

```
(Templates in the <utility> header)
template<class T1, class T2> struct pair;
template<class T1, class T2> pair<T1, T2>
  make_pair(const T1&, const T2&);
```

These were described and used earlier in this chapter. A **pair** is simply a way to package two objects (which may be of different types) into a single object. This is typically used when you need to return more than one object from a function, but it can also be used to create a container that holds **pair** objects or to pass more than one object as a single argument. You access the elements by saying **p.first** and **p.second**, where **p** is the **pair** object. The function **equal_range( )**, described in this chapter, returns its result as a **pair** of iterators, for example. You can **insert( )** a **pair** directly into a **map** or **multimap**; a **pair** is the **value_type** for those containers.

If you want to create a **pair** "on the fly," you typically use the template function **make_pair( )** rather than explicitly constructing a **pair** object. **make_pair( )** deduces the types of the arguments it receives, relieving you of the typing as well as increasing robustness.

```
(From <iterator>)
difference_type distance(InputIterator first, InputIterator
last);
```

Tells you the number of elements between **first** and **last**. More precisely, it returns an integral value that tells you the number of times **first** must be incremented before it is equal to **last**. No dereferencing of the iterators occurs during this process.

(From <iterator>)
Moves the iterator **i** forward by the value of **n**. (It can also be moved backward for negative values of **n** if the iterator is bidirectional.) This algorithm is aware of the different types of iterators and will use the most efficient approach. For example, random iterators can be incremented directly using ordinary arithmetic (**i+=n**), whereas a bidirectional iterator must be incremented **n** times.

```
(From <iterator>)
back_insert_iterator<Container>
  back_inserter(Container& x);
front_insert_iterator<Container>
  front_inserter(Container& x);
insert_iterator<Container>
  inserter(Container& x, Iterator i);
```

These functions are used to create iterators for the given containers that will insert elements into the container, rather than overwrite the existing elements in the container using **operator=** (which is the default behavior). Each type of iterator uses a different operation for insertion: **back_insert_iterator** uses **push_back( )**, **front_insert_iterator** uses **push_front( )**, and **insert_iterator** uses **insert( )** (and thus it can be used with the associative containers, while the other two can be used with sequence containers). These will be shown in some detail in the next chapter.

```
const LessThanComparable& min(const LessThanComparable& a,
  const LessThanComparable& b);
const T& min(const T& a, const T& b,
  BinaryPredicate binary_pred);
```

Returns the lesser of its two arguments, or returns the first argument if the two are equivalent. The first version performs comparisons using **operator<**, and the second passes both arguments to **binary_pred** to perform the comparison.

```
const LessThanComparable& max(const LessThanComparable& a,
  const LessThanComparable& b);
const T& max(const T& a, const T& b,
  BinaryPredicate binary_pred);
```

Exactly like **min( )**, but returns the greater of its two arguments.

```
void swap(Assignable& a, Assignable& b);
void iter_swap(ForwardIterator1 a, ForwardIterator2 b);
```

Exchanges the values of **a** and **b** using assignment. Note that all container classes use specialized versions of **swap( )** that are typically more efficient than this general version.

The **iter_swap( )** function swaps the values that its two arguments reference.

Creating your own STL–style algorithms

Once you become comfortable with the style of STL algorithms, you can begin to create your own generic algorithms. Because these will conform to the conventions of all the other algorithms in the STL, they're easy to use for programmers who are familiar with the STL, and thus they become a way to "extend the STL vocabulary."

The easiest way to approach the problem is to go to the **<algorithm>** header file, find something similar to what you need, and pattern your code after that.[13] (Virtually all STL implementations provide the code for the templates directly in the header files.)

If you take a close look at the list of algorithms in the Standard C++ library, you might notice a glaring omission: there is no **copy_if( )** algorithm. Although it's true that you can accomplish the same effect with **remove_copy_if( )**, this is not quite as convenient because you have to invert the condition. (Remember, **remove_copy_if( )** only copies those elements that *don't* match its predicate, in effect *removing* those that do.)

---

[13] Without violating any copyright laws, of course.

You might be tempted to write a function object adaptor that negates its predicate before passing it to **remove_copy_if( )**, by including a statement something like this:

```
// Assumes pred is the incoming condition
replace_copy_if(begin, end, not1(pred));
```

This seems reasonable, but when you remember that you want to be able to use predicates that are pointers to raw functions, you see why this won't work—**not1** expects an adaptable function object. The only solution is to write a **copy_if( )** algorithm from scratch. Since you know from inspecting the other copy algorithms that conceptually you need separate iterators for input and output, the following example will do the job:

```
//: C06:copy_if.h
// Create your own STL-style algorithm.
#ifndef COPY_IF_H
#define COPY_IF_H

template<typename ForwardIter,
  typename OutputIter, typename UnaryPred>
OutputIter copy_if(ForwardIter begin, ForwardIter end,
  OutputIter dest, UnaryPred f) {
  while(begin != end) {
    if(f(*begin))
      *dest++ = *begin;
    ++begin;
  }
  return dest;
}
#endif // COPY_IF_H ///:~
```

Notice that the increment of **begin** cannot be integrated into the copy expression.

Summary

The goal of this chapter is to give you a practical understanding of the algorithms in the Standard Template Library. That is, to make you aware of and comfortable enough with the STL that you begin to use it on a regular basis (or, at least, to think of using it so you can come back here and hunt for the appropriate solution). The STL is powerful not only because it's a reasonably complete library of tools, but also because it provides a vocabulary for thinking about problem solutions and it is a framework for creating additional tools.

Although this chapter did show some examples of creating your own tools, we did not go into the full depth of the theory of the STL necessary to completely understand all the STL nooks and crannies. Such understanding will allow you to create tools more sophisticated than those shown here. This omission was in part because of space limitations, but mostly because it is beyond the charter of this book—our goal here is to give you practical understanding that will improve your day-to-day programming skills.

A number of books are dedicated solely to the STL (these are listed in the appendices), but we especially recommend Scott Meyers' *Effective STL* (Addison Wesley, 2002).

Exercises

Solutions to selected exercises can be found in the electronic document *The Thinking in C++ Volume 2 Annotated Solution Guide*, available for a small fee from *www.MindView.net*.

1. Create a generator that returns the current value of **clock( )** (in **<ctime>**). Create a **list<clock_t>**, and fill it with your generator using **generate_n( )**. Remove any duplicates in the list and print it to **cout** using **copy( )**.
2. Using **transform( )** and **toupper( )** (in <cctype>), write a single function call that will convert a string to all uppercase letters.
3. Create a **Sum** function object template that will accumulate all the values in a range when used with **for_each( )**.
4. Write an anagram generator that takes a word as a command-line argument and produces all possible permutations of the letters.
5. Write a "sentence anagram generator" that takes a sentence as a command-line argument and produces all possible permutations of the words in the sentence. (It leaves the words alone and just moves them around.)
6. Create a class hierarchy with a base class **B** and a derived class **D**. Put a **virtual** member function **void f( )** in **B** such that it will print a message indicating that **B**'s **f( )** was called, and redefine this function for **D** to print a different message. Create a **vector<B*>**, and fill it

with **B** and **D** objects. Use **for_each( )** to call **f( )** for each of the objects in your **vector**.

7. Modify **FunctionObjects.cpp** so that it uses **float** instead of **int**.
8. Modify **FunctionObjects.cpp** so that it templatizes the main body of tests so you can choose which type you're going to test. (You'll have to pull most of **main( )** out into a separate template function.)
9. Write a program that takes an integer as a command line argument and finds all of its factors.
10. Write a program that takes as a command-line argument the name of a text file. Open this file and read it a word at a time (hint: use **>>**). Store each word into a **vector<string>**. Force all the words to lowercase, sort them, remove all the duplicates, and print the results.
11. Write a program that finds all the words that are in common between two input files, using **set_intersection( )**. Change it to show the words that are not in common, using **set_symmetric_difference( )**.
12. Create a program that, given an integer on the command line, creates a "factorial table" of all the factorials up to and including the number on the command line. To do this, write a generator to fill a **vector<int>**, and then use **partial_sum( )** with a standard function object.
13. Modify **CalcInventory.cpp** so that it will find all the objects that have a quantity that's less than a certain amount. Provide this amount as a command-line argument, and use **copy_if( )** and **bind2nd( )** to create the collection of values less than the target value.
14. Use **UrandGen( )** to generate 100 numbers. (The size of the numbers does not matter.) Find which numbers in your range are congruent mod 23 (meaning they have the same remainder when divided by 23). Manually pick a random number yourself, and determine whether that number is in your range by dividing each number in the list by your number and checking if the result is 1 instead of just using **find( )** with your value.
15. Fill a **vector<double>** with numbers representing angles in radians. Using function object composition, take the sine of all the elements in your **vector** (see **<cmath>**).
16. Test the speed of your computer. Call **srand(time(0))**, then make an array of random numbers. Call **srand(time(0))** again and generate the same number of random numbers in a second array. Use **equal( )** to see if the arrays are the same. (If your computer is fast enough, **time(0)** will return the same value both times it is called.) If the

arrays are not the same, sort them and use **mismatch( )** to see where they differ. If they are the same, increase the length of your array and try again.

17. Create an STL-style algorithm **transform_if( )** following the first form of **transform( )** that performs transformations only on objects that satisfy a unary predicate. Objects that don't satisfy the predicate are omitted from the result. It needs to return a new "end" iterator.

18. Create an STL-style algorithm that is an overloaded version of **for_each( )** which follows the second form of **transform( )** and takes two input ranges so it can pass the objects of the second input range a to a binary function that it applies to each object of the first range.

19. Create a **Matrix** class template that is made from a **vector<vector<T> >**. Provide it with a friend **ostream& operator<<(ostream&, const Matrix&)** to display the matrix. Create the following binary operations using the STL function objects where possible: **operator+(const Matrix&, const Matrix&)** for matrix addition, **operator*(const Matrix&, const vector<int>&)** for multiplying a matrix by a **vector**, and **operator*(const Matrix&, const Matrix&)** for matrix multiplication. (You might need to look up the mathematical meanings of the matrix operations if you don't remember them.) Test your **Matrix** class template using **int** and **float**.

20. Using the characters
    "~`!@#$%^&*( )_-+=}{[]|\:;'"<.>,?/",
    generate a codebook using an input file given on the command line as a dictionary of words. Don't worry about stripping off the non-alphabetic characters nor worry about case of the words in the dictionary file. Map each permutation of the character string to a word such as the following:
    "=')/%[}]|{*@?!"`,;>&^-~_:$+.#(<\" apple
    "|]\~>#.+%(/-_[`':;=}{*"$^!&?),@<" carrot
    "@=~['].\/<-`>#*)^%+,";&?!_{:|$}(" Carrot
    etc.

    Make sure that no duplicate codes or words exist in your code book. Use **lexicographical_compare( )** to perform a sort on the codes. Use your code book to encode the dictionary file. Decode your encoding of the dictionary file, and make sure you get the same contents back.

21. Using the following names:

Jon Brittle
Jane Brittle
Mike Brittle
Sharon Brittle
George Jensen
Evelyn Jensen
Find all the possible ways to arrange them for a wedding picture.

22. After being separated for one picture, the bride and groom decided they wanted to be together for all of them. Find all the possible ways to arrange the people for the picture if the bride and groom (Jon Brittle and Jane Brittle) are to be next to each other.

23. A travel company wants to find out the average number of days people take to travel from one end of the continent to another. The problem is that in the survey, some people did not take a direct route and took much longer than is needed (such unusual data points are called "outliers"). Using the following generator, generate travel days into a **vector**. Use **remove_if( )** to remove all the outliers in your **vector**. Take the average of the data in the **vector** to find out how long people generally take to travel.

```
int travelTime() {
  // The "outlier"
  if(rand() % 10 == 0)
    return rand() % 100;
  // Regular route
  return rand() % 10 + 10;
}
```

24. Determine how much faster **binary_search( )** is to **find( )** when it comes to searching *sorted* ranges.

25. The army wants to recruit people from its selective service list. They have decided to recruit those that signed up for the service in 1997 starting from the oldest down to the youngest. Generate an arbitrary amount of people (give them data members such as **age** and **yearEnrolled**) into a **vector**. Partition the **vector** so that those who enrolled in 1997 are ordered at the beginning of the list, starting from the youngest to the oldest, and leave the remaining part of the list sorted according to age.

26. Make a **class** called **Town** with population, altitude, and weather data members. Make the weather an **enum** with **{ RAINY, SNOWY,**

CLOUDY, CLEAR }. Make a class that generates **Town** objects. Generate town names (whether they make sense or not it doesn't matter) or pull them off the Internet. Ensure that the whole town name is lower case and there are no duplicate names. For simplicity, we recommend keeping your town names to one word. For the population, altitudes, and weather fields, make a generator that will randomly generate weather conditions, populations within the range [100 to 1,000,000) and altitudes between [0, 8000) feet. Fill a **vector** with your **Town** objects. Rewrite the **vector** out to a new file called **Towns.txt**.

27. There was a baby boom, resulting in a 10% population increase in every town. Update your town data using **transform( )**, rewrite your data back out to file.

28. Find the towns with the highest and lowest population. For this exercise, implement **operator<** for your **Town** class. Also try implementing a function that returns **true** if its first parameter is less than its second. Use it as a predicate to call the algorithm you use.

29. Find all the towns within the altitudes 2500-3500 feet inclusive. Implement equality operators for the **Town** class as needed.

30. We need to place an airport in a certain altitude, but location is not a problem. Organize your list of towns so that there are no duplicate (duplicate meaning that no two altitudes are within the same 100 ft range. Such classes would include [100, 199), [200, 199), etc. altitudes. Sort this list in ascending order in at least two different ways using the function objects in **<functional>**. Do the same for descending order. Implement relational operators for **Town** as needed.

31. Generate an arbitrary number of random numbers in a stack-based array. Use **max_element( )** to find the largest number in array. Swap it with the number at the end of your array. Find the next largest number and place it in the array in the position before the previous number. Continue doing this until all elements have been moved. When the algorithm is complete, you will have a sorted array. (This is a "selection sort".)

32. Write a program that will take phone numbers from a file (that also contains names and other suitable information) and change the numbers that begin with 222 to 863. Be sure to save the old numbers. The file format is as follows:

     222 8945
     756 3920
     222 8432

6: Generic Algorithms   425 etc.

33.   Write a program that, given a last name, will find everyone with that last name with his or her corresponding phone number. Use the algorithms that deal with ranges (**lower_bound**, **upper_bound**, **equal_range**, etc.). Sort with the last name acting as a primary key and the first name acting as a secondary key. Assume that you will read the names and numbers from a file where the format will be as follows. (Be sure to order them so that the last names are ordered, and the first names are ordered within the last names.):

John Doe	345 9483
Nick Bonham	349 2930
Jane Doe	283 2819

34.   Given a file with data similar to the following, pull all the state acronyms from the file and put them in a separate file. (Note that you can't depend on the line number for the type of data. The data is on random lines.)

ALABAMA
AL
AK
ALASKA
ARIZONA
AZ
ARKANSAS
AR
CA
CALIFORNIA
CO
COLORADO
etc.

When complete, you should have a file with all the state acronyms which are:

AL AK AZ AR CA CO CT DE FL GA HI ID IL IN IA KS KY LA ME MD MA MI MN MS MO MT NE NV NH NJ NM NY NC ND OH OK OR PA RI SC SD TN TX UT VT VA WA WV WI WY

35.   Make an **Employee** class with two data members: **hours** and **hourlyPay**. Employee shall also have a **calcSalary( )** function which

returns the pay for that employee. Generate random hourly pay and hours for an arbitrary amount of employees. Keep a **vector<Employee*>**. Find out how much money the company is going to spend for this pay period.

36.   Race **sort( )**, **partial_sort( )**, and **nth_element( )** against each other and find out if it's really worth the time saved to use one of the weaker sorts if they're all that's needed.

7: Generic Containers

Container classes are the solution to a specific kind of code reuse problem. They are building blocks used to create object–oriented programs, and they make the internals of a program much easier to construct.

A container class describes an object that holds other objects. Container classes are so important that they were considered fundamental to early object-oriented languages. In Smalltalk, for example, programmers think of the language as the program translator together with the class library, and a critical part of that library is the set of container classes. It became natural, therefore, for C++ compiler vendors to also include a container class library. You'll note that the **vector** is so useful that it was introduced in its simplest form early in Volume 1 of this book.

Like many other early C++ libraries, early container class libraries followed Smalltalk's *object-based hierarchy*, which worked well for Smalltalk, but turned out to be awkward and difficult to use in C++. Another approach was required.

The C++ approach to containers is based on templates. The containers in the Standard C++ library represent a broad range of data structures designed to work well with the standard algorithms and to meet common software development needs.

Containers and iterators

If you don't know how many objects you're going to need to solve a particular problem, or how long they will last, you also don't know ahead of time how to store those objects. How can you know how much space to create? The answer is you don't—until run time.

The solution to most problems in object-oriented design seems simple; you create another type of object. For the storage problem, the new type of object holds other objects or pointers to objects. This new type of object, which is typically referred to in C++ as a *container* (also called a *collection* in some languages), expands itself whenever necessary to accommodate everything you place inside it. You don't need to know ahead of time how many objects you're going to place in a container; you just create a container object and let it take care of the details.

Fortunately, a good object-oriented programming language comes with a set of containers. In C++, it's the Standard Template Library (STL). In some libraries, a generic container is considered good enough for all needs, and in others (C++ in particular) the library has different types of containers for different needs: a **vector** for efficient access to all elements, and a linked **list** for efficient insertion at all positions, and several more, so you can choose the particular type that fits your needs.

All containers have some way to put things in and get things out. The way you place something into a container is fairly obvious; there's a function called "push" or "add" or a similar name. The way you retrieve things from a container is not always as apparent; if an entity is array-like, such as a **vector**, you might be able to use an indexing operator or function. But in many situations this doesn't make sense. Also, a single-selection function is restrictive. What if you want to manipulate or compare a group of elements in the container?

The solution for flexible element access is the *iterator*, an object whose job is to select the elements within a container and present them to the user of the iterator. As a class, an iterator also provides a level of abstraction, which you can use to separate the details of the container from the code that's accessing that container. The container, via the iterator, is seen as a sequence. The iterator lets you traverse the sequence without worrying about the underlying structure—that is, whether it's a **vector**, a linked **list**, a **set**, or something else. This gives you the flexibility to easily change the underlying data structure without disturbing the code in your program that traverses the container. Separating iteration from the container's control also allows multiple simultaneous iterators.

From a design standpoint, all you really want is a sequence that can be manipulated to solve your problem. If a single type of sequence satisfied all your needs, there would be no reason to have different types. You need a choice of containers for two reasons. First, containers provide different types of interfaces and external behavior. A **stack** has an interface and a behavior that is different from that of a **queue**, which is different from that of a **set** or a **list**. One of these might provide a more flexible solution to your problem than the other, or it might provide a clearer abstraction that conveys your design intent. Second, different containers have different efficiencies for certain operations. Compare a **vector** to a **list**, for example. Both are simple sequences that can have nearly identical interfaces and external behaviors. But certain operations can have radically different costs. Randomly accessing elements in a **vector** is a constant-time operation; it takes the same amount of time regardless of the element you select. However, it is expensive to move through a linked **list** to randomly access an element, and it takes longer to find an element if it is farther down the **list**. On the other hand, if you want to insert an element in the middle of a sequence, it's cheaper with a **list** than with a **vector**. The efficiencies of these and other operations depend on the underlying structure of the sequence. In the design phase, you might start with a **list** and, when tuning for performance, change to a **vector**, or vice-versa. Because of iterators, code that merely traverses sequences is insulated from changes in the underlying sequence implementation.

Remember that a container is only a storage cabinet that holds objects. If that cabinet solves all your needs, it probably doesn't really matter *how* it is implemented. If you're working in a programming environment that has built-in overhead due to other factors, the cost difference between a **vector** and a linked **list** might not matter. You might need only one type of sequence. You can even imagine the "perfect" container abstraction, which can automatically change its underlying implementation according to the way it is used.[1]

STL reference documentation

As in the previous chapter, you will notice that this chapter does not contain exhaustive documentation describing each of the member functions in each STL container. Although we describe the member functions we use, we've left the full descriptions to others. We recommend the online resources available for the Dinkumware, Silicon Graphics, and STLPort STL implementations.[2]

---

[1] This would be an example of the State pattern, described in Chapter 10.
[2] Visit http://www.dinkumware.com, http://www.sgi.com/tech/stl, or http://www.stlport.org.

A first look

Here's an example using the **set** class template, a container modeled after a traditional mathematical set and which does not accept duplicate values. The following **set** was created to work with **int**s:

```
//: C07:Intset.cpp
// Simple use of STL set.
#include <cassert>
#include <set>
using namespace std;

int main() {
  set<int> intset;
  for(int i = 0; i < 25; i++)
    for(int j = 0; j < 10; j++)
      // Try to insert duplicates:
      intset.insert(j);
  assert(intset.size() == 10);
} ///:~
```

The **insert( )** member does all the work: it attempts to insert an element and ignores it if it's already there. Often the only activities involved in using a set are simply insertion and testing to see whether it contains the element. You can also form a union, an intersection, or a difference of sets and test to see if one set is a subset of another. In this example, the values 0–9 are inserted into the set 25 times, but only the 10 unique instances are accepted.

Now consider taking the form of **Intset.cpp** and modifying it to display a list of the words used in a document. The solution becomes remarkably simple.

```
//: C07:WordSet.cpp
#include <fstream>
#include <iostream>
#include <iterator>
#include <set>
#include <string>
#include "../require.h"
using namespace std;

void wordSet(const char* fileName) {
  ifstream source(fileName);
  assure(source, fileName);
```

```
    string word;
    set<string> words;
    while(source >> word)
      words.insert(word);
    copy(words.begin(), words.end(),
      ostream_iterator<string>(cout, "\n"));
    cout << "Number of unique words:"
         << words.size() << endl;
}

int main(int argc, char* argv[]) {
  if(argc > 1)
    wordSet(argv[1]);
  else
    wordSet("WordSet.cpp");
} ///:~
```

The only substantive difference here is that the set holds strings instead of integers. The words are pulled from a file, but the other operations are similar to those in **Intset.cpp**. Not only does the output reveal that duplicates have been ignored, but because of the way **set** is implemented, the words are automatically sorted.

A **set** is an example of an *associative container*, one of the three categories of containers provided by the Standard C++ library. The containers and their categories are summarized in the following table:

Category	Containers
Sequence Containers	**vector**, **list**, **deque**
Container Adaptors	**queue**, **stack**, **priority_queue**
Associative Containers	**set**, **map**, **multiset**, **multimap**

These categories represent different models that are used for different needs. The Sequence Containers simply organize their elements linearly, and are the most fundamental type of containers. For some problems, special properties need to be attached to these sequences, and that's exactly what the Container Adaptors do—they model abstractions such as a queue or stack. The associative containers organize their data based on keys, allowing for fast retrieval of that data.

All the containers in the standard library hold *copies* of the objects you place in them, and expand their resources as needed, so your objects must be *copy-constructible* (have an accessible copy constructor) and *assignable* (have an accessible assignment operator). The key difference between one container and another is the way the objects are stored in memory and what operations are available to the user.

A **vector**, as you already know, is a linear sequence that allows rapid random access to its elements. However, it's expensive to insert an element in the middle of a co-located sequence like a **vector**, just as it is with an array. A **deque** (double-ended-queue, pronounced "deck") also allows random access that's nearly as fast as **vector**, but it's significantly faster when it needs to allocate new storage, and you can easily add new elements at the front as well as the back of the sequence. A **list** is a doubly linked list, so it's expensive to move around randomly but cheap to insert an element anywhere. Thus **list**, **deque** and **vector** are similar in their basic functionality (they all hold linear sequences), but different in the cost of their activities. For your first attempt at a program, you could choose any one and experiment with the others only if you're tuning for efficiency.

Many of the problems you set out to solve will only require a simple linear sequence such as a **vector**, **deque**, or **list**. All three have a member function **push_back( )** that you use to insert a new element at the back of the sequence (**deque** and **list** also have **push_front( )**, which inserts elements at the beginning of the sequence).

But how do you retrieve the elements stored in a sequence container? With a **vector** or **deque**, it is possible to use the indexing **operator[ ]**, but that doesn't work with **list**. You can use iterators on all three sequences to access elements. Each container provides the appropriate type of iterator for accessing its elements.

Even though the containers hold objects by value (that is, they hold copies of whole objects), sometimes you'll want to store pointers so that you can refer to objects from a hierarchy and thus take advantage of the polymorphic behavior of the classes represented. Consider the classic "shape" example where shapes have a set of common operations, and you have different types of shapes. Here's what it looks like using the STL **vector** to hold pointers to various **Shape** types created on the heap:

```
//: C07:Stlshape.cpp
// Simple shapes using the STL.
#include <vector>
#include <iostream>
using namespace std;

class Shape {
public:
  virtual void draw() = 0;
  virtual ~Shape() {};
};

class Circle : public Shape {
public:
  void draw() { cout << "Circle::draw" << endl; }
  ~Circle() { cout << "~Circle" << endl; }
};

class Triangle : public Shape {
public:
  void draw() { cout << "Triangle::draw" << endl; }
  ~Triangle() { cout << "~Triangle" << endl; }
};

class Square : public Shape {
public:
  void draw() { cout << "Square::draw" << endl; }
  ~Square() { cout << "~Square" << endl; }
};

int main() {
  typedef std::vector<Shape*> Container;
  typedef Container::iterator Iter;
  Container shapes;
  shapes.push_back(new Circle);
  shapes.push_back(new Square);
  shapes.push_back(new Triangle);
  for(Iter i = shapes.begin(); i != shapes.end(); i++)
    (*i)->draw();
  // ... Sometime later:
  for(Iter j = shapes.begin(); j != shapes.end(); j++)
    delete *j;
} ///:~
```

The creation of **Shape**, **Circle**, **Square**, and **Triangle** should be fairly familiar. **Shape** is an abstract base class (because of the *pure specifier* **=0**) that defines the interface for all types of **Shapes**. The derived classes override the **virtual** function **draw( )** to perform the appropriate operation. Now we'd like to create a bunch of different types of **Shape** objects, and the natural place to store them is in an STL container. For convenience, this **typedef**:

```
typedef std::vector<Shape*> Container;
```

creates an alias for a **vector** of **Shape***, and this **typedef**:

```
typedef Container::iterator Iter;
```

uses that alias to create another one, for **vector<Shape*>::iterator**. Notice that the container type name must be used to produce the appropriate iterator, which is defined as a nested class. Although there are different types of iterators (forward, bidirectional, random, and so on), they all have the same basic interface: you can increment them with ++, you can dereference them to produce the object they're currently selecting, and you can test them to see if they're at the end of the sequence. That's what you'll want to do 90 percent of the time. And that's what is done in the previous example: after a container is created, it's filled with different types of **Shape** pointers. Notice that the upcast happens as the **Circle**, **Square**, or **Rectangle** pointer is added to the **Shapes** container, which doesn't know about those specific types but instead holds only **Shape***. As soon as the pointer is added to the container, it loses its specific identity and becomes an anonymous **Shape***. This is exactly what we want: toss them all in and let polymorphism sort it out.

The first **for** loop creates an iterator and sets it to the beginning of the sequence by calling the **begin( )** member function for the container. All containers have **begin( )** and **end( )** member functions that produce an iterator selecting, respectively, the beginning of the sequence and one past the end of the sequence. To test to see if you're done, you make sure the iterator is *not equal* to the iterator produced by **end( )**; don't use < or <=. The only tests that work are != and ==, so it's common to write a loop like:

```
for(Iter i = shapes.begin(); i != shapes.end(); i++)
```

This says "take me through every element in the sequence."

What do you do with the iterator to produce the element it's selecting? You dereference it using (what else?) the '*' (which is actually an overloaded operator). What you get back is whatever the container is holding. This container holds **Shape***, so that's what ***i** produces. If you want to call a **Shape** member function, you must do so with the -> operator, so you write the line:

```
(*i)->draw();
```

This calls the **draw( )** function for the **Shape*** the iterator is currently selecting. The parentheses are ugly but necessary to produce the desired operator precedence.

As they are destroyed or in other cases where the pointers are removed, the STL containers *do not* automatically call **delete** for the pointers they contain. If you create an object on the heap with **new** and place its pointer in a container, the container can't tell if that pointer is also placed inside another container, nor if it refers to heap memory in the first place. As always, you are responsible for managing your own heap allocations. The last lines in the program move through and delete every object in the container so that proper cleanup occurs. The easiest and safest way to handle pointers in containers is to use smart pointers. It should be noted that **auto_ptr** can't be used for this purpose, so you will need to look outside of the C++ Standard Library for a suitable smart pointers.[3]

You can change the type of container that this program uses with two lines. Instead of including **<vector>**, you include **<list>**, and in the first **typedef** you say:

```
typedef std::list<Shape*> Container;
```

instead of using a **vector**. Everything else goes untouched. This is possible not because of an interface enforced by inheritance (there is little inheritance in the STL), but because the interface is enforced by a convention adopted by the designers of the STL, precisely so you could perform this kind of interchange. Now you can easily switch between **vector** and **list** or any other

---

[3] This is about to change, as more smart pointer types are about to be added to the next version of the Standard. For a preliminary look at them, see the smart pointers available at www.boost.org.

---

container that supports the same interface (both syntactically and semantically) and see which one works fastest for your needs.

Containers of strings

In the previous example, at the end of **main( )** it was necessary to move through the whole list and **delete** all the **Shape** pointers:

```
for(Iter j = shapes.begin(); j != shapes.end(); j++)
  delete *j;
```

STL containers make sure that each *object* they contain has its destructor called when the container itself is destroyed. Pointers, however, have no destructor, so we have to **delete** them ourselves.

This highlights what could be seen as an oversight in the STL: there's no facility in any of the STL containers to automatically **delete** the pointers they contain, so you must do it manually. It's as if the assumption of the STL designers was that containers of pointers weren't an interesting problem, but that's not the case.

Automatically deleting a pointer turns out to be problematic because of the *multiple membership* problem. If a container holds a pointer to an object, it's not unlikely that pointer could also be in another container. A pointer to an **Aluminum** object in a list of **Trash** pointers could also reside in a list of **Aluminum** pointers. If that happens, which list is responsible for cleaning up that object—that is, which list "owns" the object?

This question is virtually eliminated if the object rather than a pointer resides in the list. Then it seems clear that when the list is destroyed, the objects it contains must also be destroyed. Here, the STL shines, as you can see when creating a container of **string** objects. The following example stores each incoming line as a **string** in a **vector<string>**:

```
//: C07:StringVector.cpp
// A vector of strings.
#include <fstream>
#include <iostream>
#include <iterator>
#include <sstream>
#include <string>
#include <vector>
```

```
#include "../require.h"
using namespace std;

int main(int argc, char* argv[]) {
  const char* fname = "StringVector.cpp";
  if(argc > 1) fname = argv[1];
  ifstream in(fname);
  assure(in, fname);
  vector<string> strings;
  string line;
  while(getline(in, line))
    strings.push_back(line);
  // Do something to the strings...
  int i = 1;
  vector<string>::iterator w;
  for(w = strings.begin(); w != strings.end(); w++) {
    ostringstream ss;
    ss << i++;
    *w = ss.str() + ": " + *w;
  }
  // Now send them out:
  copy(strings.begin(), strings.end(),
    ostream_iterator<string>(cout, "\n"));
  // Since they aren't pointers, string
  // objects clean themselves up!
} ///:~
```

Once the **vector<string>** called **strings** is created, each line in the file is
read into a **string** and put in the **vector**:

```
while(getline(in, line))
  strings.push_back(line);
```

The operation that's being performed on this file is to add line numbers. A
stringstream provides easy conversion from an **int** to a **string** of
characters representing that **int**.

Assembling **string** objects is quite easy, since **operator+** is overloaded.
Sensibly enough, the iterator **w** can be dereferenced to produce a string that
can be used as both an rvalue *and* an lvalue:

```
*w = ss.str() + ": " + *w;
```

You may be surprised that you can assign back into the container via the iterator, but it's a tribute to the careful design of the STL.

Because the **vector<string>** contains the objects, two things are worthy of note. First, as explained before, you don't need to explicitly clean up the **string** objects. Even if you put addresses of the **string** objects as pointers into *other* containers, it's clear that **strings** is the "master list" and maintains ownership of the objects.

Second, you are effectively using dynamic object creation, and yet you never use **new** or **delete**! It's all taken care of for you by the **vector** because it stores *copies* of the objects you give it. Thus your coding is significantly cleaned up.

Inheriting from STL containers

The power of instantly creating a sequence of elements is amazing, and it makes you realize how much time you may have lost in the past solving this particular problem. For example, many utility programs involve reading a file into memory, modifying the file, and writing it back out to disk. You might as well take the functionality in **StringVector.cpp** and package it into a class for later reuse.

Now the question is: do you create a member object of type **vector**, or do you inherit? A general object-oriented design guideline is to prefer composition (member objects) over inheritance, but the standard algorithms expect sequences that implement a particular interface, so inheritance is often necessary.

```
//: C07:FileEditor.h
// A file editor tool.
#ifndef FILEEDITOR_H
#define FILEEDITOR_H
#include <iostream>
#include <string>
#include <vector>

class FileEditor : public std::vector<std::string> {
public:
  void open(const char* filename);
  FileEditor(const char* filename) { open(filename); }
  FileEditor() {};
```

```
    void write(std::ostream& out = std::cout);
};
#endif // FILEEDITOR_H ///:~
```

The constructor opens the file and reads it into the **FileEditor**, and **write( )** puts the **vector** of **string** onto any **ostream**. Notice in **write( )** that you can have a default argument for the reference.

The implementation is quite simple:

```
//: C07:FileEditor.cpp {O}
#include "FileEditor.h"
#include <fstream>
#include "../require.h"
using namespace std;

void FileEditor::open(const char* filename) {
  ifstream in(filename);
  assure(in, filename);
  string line;
  while(getline(in, line))
    push_back(line);
}

// Could also use copy() here:
void FileEditor::write(ostream& out) {
  for(iterator w = begin(); w != end(); w++)
    out << *w << endl;
} ///:~
```

The functions from **StringVector.cpp** are simply repackaged. Often this is the way classes evolve—you start by creating a program to solve a particular application and then discover some commonly used functionality within the program that can be turned into a class.

The line-numbering program can now be rewritten using **FileEditor**:

```
//: C07:FEditTest.cpp
//{L} FileEditor
// Test the FileEditor tool.
#include <sstream>
#include "FileEditor.h"
#include "../require.h"
using namespace std;
```

```
int main(int argc, char* argv[]) {
  FileEditor file;
  if(argc > 1) {
    file.open(argv[1]);
  } else {
    file.open("FEditTest.cpp");
  }
  // Do something to the lines...
  int i = 1;
  FileEditor::iterator w = file.begin();
  while(w != file.end()) {
    ostringstream ss;
    ss << i++;
    *w = ss.str() + ": " + *w;
    ++w;
  }
  // Now send them to cout:
  file.write();
} ///:~
```

Now the operation of reading the file is in the constructor:

```
FileEditor file(argv[1]);
```

(or in the **open( )** member function), and writing happens in the single line (which defaults to sending the output to **cout**):

```
file.write();
```

The bulk of the program is involved with modifying the file in memory.

A plethora of iterators

An iterator is an abstraction for genericity. It works with different types of containers without knowing the underlying structure of those containers. Most containers support iterators,[4] so you can say:

---

[4] The container adaptors, stack, queue, and priority_queue do not support iterators, since they do not behave as sequences from the user's point of view.

```
<ContainerType>::iterator
<ContainerType>::const_iterator
```

to produce the iterator types for a container. Every container has a **begin( )** member function that produces an iterator indicating the beginning of the elements in the container, and an **end( )** member function that produces an iterator which is the *past-the-end* marker of the container. If the container is **const**, **begin( )** and **end( )** produce **const** iterators, which disallow changing the elements pointed to (because the appropriate operators are **const**).

All iterators can advance within their sequence (via **operator++**) and allow == and != comparisons. Thus, to move an iterator **it** forward without running it off the end, you say something like:

```
while(it != pastEnd) {
  // Do something
  ++it;
}
```

where **pastEnd** is the past-the-end marker produced by the container's **end( )** member function.

An iterator can be used to produce the container element that it is currently selecting via the dereferencing operator (**operator***). This can take two forms. If **it** is an iterator traversing a container, and **f( )** is a member function of the type of objects held in the container, you can say either:

```
(*it).f();
```

or

```
it->f();
```

Knowing this, you can create a template that works with any container. Here, the **apply( )** function template calls a member function for every object in the container, using a pointer to member that is passed as an argument:

```
//: C07:Apply.cpp
// Using simple iteration.
#include <iostream>
#include <vector>
#include <iterator>
```

```
using namespace std;

template<class Cont, class PtrMemFun>
void apply(Cont& c, PtrMemFun f) {
  typename Cont::iterator it = c.begin();
  while(it != c.end()) {
    ((*it).*f)(); // Alternate form
    ++it;
  }
}

class Z {
  int i;
public:
  Z(int ii) : i(ii) {}
  void g() { ++i; }
  friend ostream& operator<<(ostream& os, const Z& z) {
    return os << z.i;
  }
};

int main() {
  ostream_iterator<Z> out(cout, " ");
  vector<Z> vz;
  for(int i = 0; i < 10; i++)
    vz.push_back(Z(i));
  copy(vz.begin(), vz.end(), out);
  cout << endl;
  apply(vz, &Z::g);
  copy(vz.begin(), vz.end(), out);
} ///:~
```

You can't use **operator->** here because the resulting statement would be:

```
(it->*f)();
```

which attempts to use the iterator's **operator->***, which is not provided by the iterator classes.[5]

---

[5] It will only work for implementations of **vector** that use a *pointer* (a **T***) as the iterator type, like STLPort does.

It is much easier to use either **for_each( )** or **transform( )** to apply functions to sequences, as you saw in the previous chapter.

Iterators in reversible containers

A container may also be *reversible*, which means that it can produce iterators that move backward from the end, as well as iterators that move forward from the beginning. All standard containers support such bidirectional iteration.

A reversible container has the member functions **rbegin( )** (to produce a **reverse_iterator** selecting the end) and **rend( )** (to produce a **reverse_iterator** indicating "one past the beginning"). If the container is **const**, **rbegin( )** and **rend( )** will produce **const_reverse_iterator**s.

The following example uses **vector** but will work with all containers that support iteration:

```
//: C07:Reversible.cpp
// Using reversible containers.
#include <fstream>
#include <iostream>
#include <string>
#include <vector>
#include "../require.h"
using namespace std;

int main() {
  ifstream in("Reversible.cpp");
  assure(in, "Reversible.cpp");
  string line;
  vector<string> lines;
  while(getline(in, line))
    lines.push_back(line);
  for(vector<string>::reverse_iterator r = lines.rbegin();
      r != lines.rend(); r++)
    cout << *r << endl;
} ///:~
```

You move backward through the container using the same syntax as you do when moving forward through a container with an ordinary iterator.

Iterator categories

The iterators in the Standard C++ library are classified into "categories" that describe their capabilities. The order in which they are generally described moves from the categories with the most restricted behavior to those with the most powerful behavior.

Input: read-only, one pass

The only predefined implementations of input iterators are **istream_iterator** and **istreambuf_iterator**, to read from an **istream**. As you can imagine, an input iterator can only be dereferenced once for each element that's selected, just as you can only read a particular portion of an input stream once. They can only move forward. A special constructor defines the past-the-end value. In summary, you can dereference it for reading (once only for each value) and move it forward.

Output: write-only, one pass

This is the complement of an input iterator, but for writing rather than reading. The only predefined implementations of output iterators are **ostream_iterator** and **ostreambuf_iterator**, to write to an **ostream**, and the less commonly used **raw_storage_iterator**. Again, these can only be dereferenced once for each written value, and they can only move forward. There is no concept of a terminal past-the-end value for an output iterator. Summarizing, you can dereference it for writing (once only for each value) and move it forward.

Forward: multiple read/write

The forward iterator contains all the functionality of both the input iterator and the output iterator, plus you can dereference an iterator location multiple times, so you can read and write to a value multiple times. As the name implies, you can only move forward. There are no predefined iterators that are only forward iterators.

Bidirectional: operator--

The bidirectional iterator has all the functionality of the forward iterator, and in addition it can be moved backward one location at a time using **operator--**. The iterators returned by the **list** container are bidirectional.

Random-access: like a pointer

Finally, the random-access iterator has all the functionality of the bidirectional iterator plus all the functionality of a pointer (a pointer *is* a random-access iterator), except that there is no "null" iterator analogue to a null pointer. Basically, anything you can do with a pointer you can do with a random-access iterator, including indexing with **operator[ ]**, adding integral values to a pointer to move it forward or backward by a number of locations, or comparing one iterator to another with comparison operators.

Is this really important?

Why do you care about this categorization? When you're just using containers in a straightforward way (for example, just hand-coding all the operations you want to perform on the objects in the container), it usually doesn't matter. Things either work or they don't. The iterator categories become important when:

1. You use some of the fancier built-in iterator types that will be demonstrated shortly, or you "graduate" to creating your own iterators (demonstrated later in this chapter).

2. You use the STL algorithms (the subject of the previous chapter). Each of the algorithms places requirements on its iterators. Knowledge of the iterator categories is even more important when you create your own reusable algorithm templates, because the iterator category required by your algorithm determines how flexible the algorithm will be. If you require only the most primitive iterator category (input or output), your algorithm will work with *everything* (**copy( )** is an example of this).

An iterator's category is identified by a hierarchy of iterator tag classes. The class names correspond to the iterator categories, and their derivation reflects the relationship between them:

```
struct input_iterator_tag {};
struct output_iterator_tag {};
struct forward_iterator_tag :
  public input_iterator_tag {};
struct bidirectional_iterator_tag :
  public forward_iterator_tag {};
struct random_access_iterator_tag :
  public bidirectional_iterator_tag {};
```

The class **forward_iterator_tag** derives only from **input_iterator_tag**, not from **output_iterator_tag**, because we need to have past-the-end iterator values in algorithms that use forward iterators, but algorithms that use output iterators always assume that **operator*** can be dereferenced. For this reason, it is important to make sure that a past-the-end value is never passed to an algorithm that expects an output iterator.

For efficiency, certain algorithms provide different implementations for different iterator types, which they infer from the iterator tag defined by the iterator. We will use some of these tag classes later in this chapter when we define our own iterator types.

Predefined iterators

The STL has a predefined set of iterators that can be quite handy. For example, you've already seen the **reverse_iterator** objects produced by calling **rbegin( )** and **rend( )** for all the basic containers.

The *insertion iterators* are necessary because some of the STL algorithms—**copy( )**, for example—use the assignment **operator=** to place objects in the destination container. This is a problem when you're using the algorithm to *fill* the container rather than to overwrite items that are already in the destination container—that is, when the space isn't already there. What the insert iterators do is change the implementation of **operator=** so that instead of doing an assignment, it calls a "push" or "insert" function for that container, thus causing it to allocate new space. The constructors for both **back_insert_iterator** and **front_insert_iterator** take a basic sequence container object (**vector**, **deque** or **list**) as their argument and produce an iterator that calls **push_back( )** or **push_front( )**, respectively, to perform assignment. The helper functions **back_inserter( )** and **front_inserter( )** produce these insert-iterator objects with a little less typing. Since all the basic sequence containers support **push_back( )**, you will probably find yourself using **back_inserter( )** with some regularity.

An **insert_iterator** lets you insert elements in the middle of the sequence, again replacing the meaning of **operator=**, but this time by automatically calling **insert( )** instead of one of the "push" functions. The **insert( )** member function requires an iterator indicating the place to insert before, so the **insert_iterator** requires this iterator in addition to the container object. The shorthand function **inserter( )** produces the same object.

The following example shows the use of the different types of inserters:

```
//: C07:Inserters.cpp
// Different types of iterator inserters.
#include <iostream>
#include <vector>
#include <deque>
#include <list>
#include <iterator>
using namespace std;

int a[] = { 1, 3, 5, 7, 11, 13, 17, 19, 23 };

template<class Cont> void frontInsertion(Cont& ci) {
  copy(a, a + sizeof(a)/sizeof(Cont::value_type),
    front_inserter(ci));
  copy(ci.begin(), ci.end(),
    ostream_iterator<typename Cont::value_type>(
    cout, " "));
  cout << endl;
}

template<class Cont> void backInsertion(Cont& ci) {
  copy(a, a + sizeof(a)/sizeof(Cont::value_type),
    back_inserter(ci));
  copy(ci.begin(), ci.end(),
    ostream_iterator<typename Cont::value_type>(
    cout, " "));
  cout << endl;
}

template<class Cont> void midInsertion(Cont& ci) {
  typename Cont::iterator it = ci.begin();
  ++it; ++it; ++it;
  copy(a, a + sizeof(a)/(sizeof(Cont::value_type) * 2),
    inserter(ci, it));
  copy(ci.begin(), ci.end(),
    ostream_iterator<typename Cont::value_type>(
    cout, " "));
  cout << endl;
}

int main() {
  deque<int> di;
  list<int>  li;
  vector<int> vi;
  // Can't use a front_inserter() with vector
```

```
    frontInsertion(di);
    frontInsertion(li);
    di.clear();
    li.clear();
    backInsertion(vi);
    backInsertion(di);
    backInsertion(li);
    midInsertion(vi);
    midInsertion(di);
    midInsertion(li);
} ///:~
```

Since **vector** does not support **push_front( )**, it cannot produce a
front_insert_iterator. However, you can see that **vector** does support the
other two types of insertions (even though, as you shall see later, **insert( )** is
not an efficient operation for **vector**). Note the use of the nested type
Cont::value_type instead of hard-coding **int**.

More on stream iterators

We introduced the use of the stream iterators **ostream_iterator** (an output
iterator) and **istream_iterator** (an input iterator) in conjunction with
copy( ) in the previous chapter. Remember that an output stream doesn't
have any concept of an "end," since you can always just keep writing more
elements. However, an input stream eventually terminates (for example,
when you reach the end of a file), so you need a way to represent that. An
istream_iterator has two constructors, one that takes an **istream** and
produces the iterator you actually read from, and the other which is the
default constructor and produces an object that is the past-the-end sentinel.
In the following program this object is named **end**:

```
//: C07:StreamIt.cpp
// Iterators for istreams and ostreams.
#include <fstream>
#include <iostream>
#include <iterator>
#include <string>
#include <vector>
#include "../require.h"
using namespace std;

int main() {
  ifstream in("StreamIt.cpp");
  assure(in, "StreamIt.cpp");
```

```
    istream_iterator<string> begin(in), end;
    ostream_iterator<string> out(cout, "\n");
    vector<string> vs;
    copy(begin, end, back_inserter(vs));
    copy(vs.begin(), vs.end(), out);
    *out++ = vs[0];
    *out++ = "That's all, folks!";
} ///:~
```

When **in** runs out of input (in this case when the end of the file is reached), **init** becomes equivalent to **end**, and the **copy( )** terminates.

Because **out** is an **ostream_iterator<string>**, you can simply assign any **string** object to the dereferenced iterator using **operator=**, and that **string** will be placed on the output stream, as seen in the two assignments to **out**. Because **out** is defined with a newline as its second argument, these assignments also insert a newline along with each assignment.

Although it is possible to create an **istream_iterator<char>** and **ostream_iterator<char>**, these actually *parse* the input and thus will, for example, automatically eat whitespace (spaces, tabs, and newlines), which is not desirable if you want to manipulate an exact representation of an **istream**. Instead, you can use the special iterators **istreambuf_iterator** and **ostreambuf_iterator**, which are designed strictly to move characters.[6] Although these are templates, they are meant to be used with template arguments of either **char** or **wchar_t**.[7] The following example lets you compare the behavior of the stream iterators with the streambuf iterators:

```
//: C07:StreambufIterator.cpp
// istreambuf_iterator & ostreambuf_iterator.
#include <algorithm>
#include <fstream>
#include <iostream>
#include <iterator>
```

---

[6] These were actually created to abstract the locale facets away from iostreams so that locale facets could operate on any sequence of characters, not just iostreams. Locales allow iostreams to easily handle culturally–different formatting (such as the representation of money).
[7] You will need to provide a **char_traits** specialization for any other argument type.

```
#include "../require.h"
using namespace std;

int main() {
  ifstream in("StreambufIterator.cpp");
  assure(in, "StreambufIterator.cpp");
  // Exact representation of stream:
  istreambuf_iterator<char> isb(in), end;
  ostreambuf_iterator<char> osb(cout);
  while(isb != end)
    *osb++ = *isb++; // Copy 'in' to cout
  cout << endl;
  ifstream in2("StreambufIterator.cpp");
  // Strips white space:
  istream_iterator<char> is(in2), end2;
  ostream_iterator<char> os(cout);
  while(is != end2)
    *os++ = *is++;
  cout << endl;
} ///:~
```

The stream iterators use the parsing defined by **istream::operator>>**,
which is probably not what you want if you are parsing characters directly—
it's fairly rare that you want all the whitespace stripped out of your character
stream. You'll virtually always want to use a streambuf iterator when using
characters and streams, rather than a stream iterator. In addition,
istream::operator>> adds significant overhead for each operation, so it is
only appropriate for higher-level operations such as parsing numbers.[8]

Manipulating raw storage

The **raw_storage_iterator** is defined in **<memory>** and is an output
iterator. It is provided to enable algorithms to store their results in
uninitialized memory. The interface is quite simple: the constructor takes an
output iterator that is pointing to the raw memory (typically a pointer), and
the **operator=** assigns an object into that raw memory. The template
parameters are the type of the output iterator pointing to the raw storage and
the type of object that will be stored. Here's an example that creates **Noisy**
objects, which print trace statements for their construction, assignment, and
destruction (we'll show the **Noisy** class definition later):

---

[8] We are indebted to Nathan Myers for explaining this.

```
//: C07:RawStorageIterator.cpp {-bor}
// Demonstrate the raw_storage_iterator.
//{L} Noisy
#include <iostream>
#include <iterator>
#include <algorithm>
#include "Noisy.h"
using namespace std;

int main() {
  const int QUANTITY = 10;
  // Create raw storage and cast to desired type:
  Noisy* np = reinterpret_cast<Noisy*>(
    new char[QUANTITY * sizeof(Noisy)]);
  raw_storage_iterator<Noisy*, Noisy> rsi(np);
  for(int i = 0; i < QUANTITY; i++)
    *rsi++ = Noisy(); // Place objects in storage
  cout << endl;
  copy(np, np + QUANTITY,
    ostream_iterator<Noisy>(cout, " "));
  cout << endl;
  // Explicit destructor call for cleanup:
  for(int j = 0; j < QUANTITY; j++)
    (&np[j])->~Noisy();
  // Release raw storage:
  delete reinterpret_cast<char*>(np);
} ///:~
```

To make the **raw_storage_iterator** template happy, the raw storage must
be of the same type as the objects you're creating. That's why the pointer from
the new array of **char** is cast to a **Noisy***. The assignment operator forces the
objects into the raw storage using the copy-constructor. Note that the explicit
destructor call must be made for proper cleanup, and this also allows the
objects to be deleted one at a time during container manipulation. The
expression **delete np** would be invalid anyway since the static type of a
pointer in a **delete** expression must be the same as the type assigned to in
the **new** expression.

The basic sequences: vector, list, deque

Sequences keep objects in whatever order you store them. They differ in the efficiency of their operations, however, so if you are going to manipulate a sequence in a particular fashion, choose the appropriate container for those types of manipulations. So far in this book we've been using **vector** as the container of choice. This is quite often the case in applications. When you start making more sophisticated uses of containers, however, it becomes important to know more about their underlying implementations and behavior so that you can make the right choices.

Basic sequence operations

Using a template, the following example shows the operations supported by all the basic sequences: **vector**, **deque**, and **list**:

```
//: C07:BasicSequenceOperations.cpp
// The operations available for all the
// basic sequence Containers.
#include <deque>
#include <iostream>
#include <list>
#include <vector>
using namespace std;

template<typename Container>
void print(Container& c, char* title = "") {
  cout << title << ':' << endl;
  if(c.empty()) {
    cout << "(empty)" << endl;
    return;
  }
  typename Container::iterator it;
  for(it = c.begin(); it != c.end(); it++)
    cout << *it << " ";
  cout << endl;
  cout << "size() "        << c.size()
       << " max_size() " << c.max_size()
       << " front() "    << c.front()
       << " back() "     << c.back()
       << endl;
```

```
}

template<typename ContainerOfInt> void basicOps(char* s) {
  cout << "------- " << s << " -------" << endl;
  typedef ContainerOfInt Ci;
  Ci c;
  print(c, "c after default constructor");
  Ci c2(10, 1); // 10 elements, values all 1
  print(c2, "c2 after constructor(10,1)");
  int ia[] = { 1, 3, 5, 7, 9 };
  const int IASZ = sizeof(ia)/sizeof(*ia);
  // Initialize with begin & end iterators:
  Ci c3(ia, ia + IASZ);
  print(c3, "c3 after constructor(iter,iter)");
  Ci c4(c2); // Copy-constructor
  print(c4, "c4 after copy-constructor(c2)");
  c = c2; // Assignment operator
  print(c, "c after operator=c2");
  c.assign(10, 2); // 10 elements, values all 2
  print(c, "c after assign(10, 2)");
  // Assign with begin & end iterators:
  c.assign(ia, ia + IASZ);
  print(c, "c after assign(iter, iter)");
  cout << "c using reverse iterators:" << endl;
  typename Ci::reverse_iterator rit = c.rbegin();
  while(rit != c.rend())
    cout << *rit++ << " ";
  cout << endl;
  c.resize(4);
  print(c, "c after resize(4)");
  c.push_back(47);
  print(c, "c after push_back(47)");
  c.pop_back();
  print(c, "c after pop_back()");
  typename Ci::iterator it = c.begin();
  ++it; ++it;
  c.insert(it, 74);
  print(c, "c after insert(it, 74)");
  it = c.begin();
  ++it;
  c.insert(it, 3, 96);
  print(c, "c after insert(it, 3, 96)");
  it = c.begin();
  ++it;
  c.insert(it, c3.begin(), c3.end());
```

```
    print(c, "c after insert("
      "it, c3.begin(), c3.end()))");
    it = c.begin();
    ++it;
    c.erase(it);
    print(c, "c after erase(it)");
    typename Ci::iterator it2 = it = c.begin();
    ++it;
    ++it2; ++it2; ++it2; ++it2; ++it2;
    c.erase(it, it2);
    print(c, "c after erase(it, it2)");
    c.swap(c2);
    print(c, "c after swap(c2)");
    c.clear();
    print(c, "c after clear()");
}

int main() {
  basicOps<vector<int> >("vector");
  basicOps<deque<int> >("deque");
  basicOps<list<int> >("list");
} ///:~
```

The first function template, **print( )**, demonstrates the basic information you can get from any sequence container: whether it's empty, its current size, the size of the largest possible container, the element at the beginning, and the element at the end. You can also see that every container has **begin( )** and **end( )** member functions that return iterators.

The **basicOps( )** function tests everything else (and in turn calls **print( )**), including a variety of constructors: default, copy-constructor, quantity and initial value, and beginning and ending iterators. There are an assignment **operator=** and two kinds of **assign( )** member functions. One takes a quantity and an initial value, and the other takes a beginning and ending iterator.

All the basic sequence containers are reversible containers, as shown by the use of the **rbegin( )** and **rend( )** member functions. A sequence container can be resized, and the entire contents of the container can be removed with **clear( )**. When you call **resize( )** to expand a sequence, the new elements use the default constructor of the type of element in the sequence, or if they are built-in types, they are zero-initialized.

Using an iterator to indicate where you want to start inserting into any sequence container, you can **insert( )** a single element, a number of elements that all have the same value, and a group of elements from another container using the beginning and ending iterators of that group.

To **erase( )** a single element from the middle, use an iterator; to **erase( )** a range of elements, use a pair of iterators. Notice that since a **list** supports only bidirectional iterators, all the iterator motion must be performed with increments and decrements. (If the containers were limited to **vector** and **deque**, which produce random-access iterators, **operator+** and **operator-** could have been used to move the iterators in bigger jumps.)

Although both **list** and **deque** support **push_front( )** and **pop_front( )**, **vector** does not, but **push_back( )** and **pop_back( )** work with all three.

The naming of the member function **swap( )** is a little confusing, since there's also a nonmember **swap( )** algorithm that interchanges the values of any two objects of same type. The member **swap( )** swaps everything in one container for another (if the containers hold the same type), effectively swapping the containers themselves. It does this efficiently by swapping the contents of each container, which consists mostly of pointers. The nonmember **swap( )** algorithm normally uses assignment to interchange its arguments (an expensive operation for an entire container), but it is customized through template specialization to call the member **swap( )** for the standard containers. There is also an **iter_swap** algorithm that uses iterators to interchange two elements in the same container.

The following sections discuss the particulars of each type of sequence container.

vector

The **vector** class template is intentionally made to look like a souped-up array, since it has array-style indexing, but also can expand dynamically. The **vector** class template is so fundamentally useful that it was introduced in a primitive way early in this book and was used regularly in previous examples. This section will give a more in-depth look at **vector**.

To achieve maximally-efficient indexing and iteration, **vector** maintains its storage as a single contiguous array of objects. This is a critical point to observe in understanding the behavior of **vector**. It means that indexing and iteration are lightning-fast, being basically the same as indexing and iterating over an array of objects. But it also means that inserting an object anywhere but at the end (that is, appending) is not really an acceptable operation for a **vector**. In addition, when a **vector** runs out of preallocated storage, to maintain its contiguous array it must allocate a whole new (larger) chunk of storage elsewhere and copy the objects to the new storage. This approach produces a number of unpleasant side-effects.

Cost of overflowing allocated storage

A **vector** starts by grabbing a block of storage, as if it's taking a guess at how many objects you plan to put in it. As long as you don't try to put in more objects than can be held in the initial block of storage, everything proceeds rapidly. (If you *do* know how many objects to expect, you can preallocate storage using **reserve( )**.) But eventually you will put in one too many objects, and the **vector** responds by:

1. Allocating a new, bigger piece of storage.

2. Copying all the objects from the old storage to the new (using the copy-constructor).

3. Destroying all the old objects (the destructor is called for each one).

4. Releasing the old memory.

For complex objects, this copy-construction and destruction can end up being expensive if you often overfill your **vector**, which is why **vector**s (and STL containers in general) are designed for value types (i.e. types that are cheap to copy). This includes pointers.

To see what happens when you're filling a **vector**, here is the **Noisy** class mentioned earlier. It prints information about its creations, destructions, assignments, and copy-constructions:

```
//: C07:Noisy.h
// A class to track various object activities.
#ifndef NOISY_H
#define NOISY_H
#include <iostream>
using std::endl;
using std::cout;
```

```
using std::ostream;

class Noisy {
  static long create, assign, copycons, destroy;
  long id;
public:
  Noisy() : id(create++) {
    cout << "d[" << id << "]" << endl;
  }
  Noisy(const Noisy& rv) : id(rv.id) {
    cout << "c[" << id << "]" << endl;
    ++copycons;
  }
  Noisy& operator=(const Noisy& rv) {
    cout << "(" << id << ")=[" << rv.id << "]" << endl;
    id = rv.id;
    ++assign;
    return *this;
  }
  friend bool operator<(const Noisy& lv, const Noisy& rv) {
    return lv.id < rv.id;
  }
  friend bool operator==(const Noisy& lv,const Noisy& rv) {
    return lv.id == rv.id;
  }
  ~Noisy() {
    cout << "~[" << id << "]" << endl;
    ++destroy;
  }
  friend ostream& operator<<(ostream& os, const Noisy& n) {
    return os << n.id;
  }
  friend class NoisyReport;
};

struct NoisyGen {
  Noisy operator()() { return Noisy(); }
};

// A Singleton. Will automatically report the
// statistics as the program terminates:
class NoisyReport {
  static NoisyReport nr;
  NoisyReport() {} // Private constructor
  NoisyReport & operator=(NoisyReport &);  // Disallowed
```

```
  NoisyReport(const NoisyReport&);          // Disallowed
public:
  ~NoisyReport() {
    cout << "\n------------------\n"
         << "Noisy creations: " << Noisy::create
         << "\nCopy-Constructions: " << Noisy::copycons
         << "\nAssignments: " << Noisy::assign
         << "\nDestructions: " << Noisy::destroy << endl;
  }
};
#endif // NOISY_H ///:~
```

```
//: C07:Noisy.cpp {O}
#include "Noisy.h"
long Noisy::create = 0, Noisy::assign = 0,
  Noisy::copycons = 0, Noisy::destroy = 0;
NoisyReport NoisyReport::nr;
///:~
```

Each **Noisy** object has its own identifier, and **static** variables keep track of all the creations, assignments (using **operator=**), copy-constructions, and destructions. The **id** is initialized using the **create** counter inside the default constructor; the copy-constructor and assignment operator take their **id** values from the rvalue. With **operator=** the lvalue is already an initialized object, so the old value of **id** is printed before it is overwritten with the **id** from the rvalue.

To support certain operations such as sorting and searching (which are used implicitly by some of the containers), **Noisy** must have an **operator<** and **operator==**. These simply compare the **id** values. The **ostream** inserter follows the usual form and simply prints the **id**.

Objects of type **NoisyGen** are function objects (since there is an **operator( )**) that produce **Noisy** objects during testing.

NoisyReport is a Singleton object[9] because we only want one report printed at program termination. It has a **private** constructor so no additional **NoisyReport** objects can be created, it disallows assignment and copy-construction, and it has a single static instance of **NoisyReport** called **nr**.

---

[9] Singleton is a well-known design pattern and is discussed in depth in Chapter 10.

The only executable statements are in the destructor, which is called as the program exits and static destructors are called. This destructor prints the statistics captured by the **static** variables in **Noisy**.

Using **Noisy.h**, the following program shows a **vector** overflowing its allocated storage:

```
//: C07:VectorOverflow.cpp {-bor}
// Shows the copy-construction and destruction
// that occurs when a vector must reallocate.
//{L} Noisy
#include <cstdlib>
#include <iostream>
#include <string>
#include <vector>
#include "Noisy.h"
using namespace std;

int main(int argc, char* argv[]) {
  int size = 1000;
  if(argc >= 2) size = atoi(argv[1]);
  vector<Noisy> vn;
  Noisy n;
  for(int i = 0; i < size; i++)
    vn.push_back(n);
  cout << "\n cleaning up " << endl;
} ///:~
```

You can use the default value of 1000, or you can use your own value by putting it on the command line.

When you run this program, you'll see a single default constructor call (for **n**), then a lot of copy-constructor calls, then some destructor calls, then some more copy-constructor calls, and so on. When the **vector** runs out of space in the linear array of bytes it has allocated, it must (to maintain all the objects in a linear array, which is an essential part of its job) get a bigger piece of storage and move everything over, first copying and then destroying the old objects. You can imagine that if you store a lot of large and complex objects, this process could rapidly become prohibitive.

There are two solutions to this problem. The nicest one requires that you know beforehand how many objects you're going to make. In that case, you can use **reserve( )** to tell the **vector** how much storage to preallocate, thus eliminating all the copies and destructions and making everything very fast (especially random access to the objects with **operator[ ]**). Note that the use of **reserve( )** is different from using the **vector** constructor with an integral first argument; the latter initializes a prescribed number of elements using the element type's default constructor.

Generally you won't know how many objects you'll need. If **vector** reallocations are slowing things down, you can change sequence containers. You could use a **list**, but as you'll see, the **deque** allows speedy insertions at either end of the sequence and never needs to copy or destroy objects as it expands its storage. The **deque** also allows random access with **operator[ ]**, but it's not quite as fast as **vector**'s **operator[ ]**. So if you're creating all your objects in one part of the program and randomly accessing them in another, you may find yourself filling a **deque** and then creating a **vector** from the **deque** and using the **vector** for rapid indexing. You don't want to program this way habitually—just be aware of these issues (that is, avoid premature optimization).

There is a darker side to **vector**'s reallocation of memory, however. Because **vector** keeps its objects in a nice, neat array, the iterators used by **vector** can be simple pointers. This is good—of all the sequence containers, these pointers allow the fastest selection and manipulation. Whether they are simple pointers, or whether they are iterator objects that hold an internal pointer into their container, consider what happens when you add the one additional object that causes the **vector** to reallocate storage and move it elsewhere. The iterator's pointer is now pointing off into nowhere:

```
//: C07:VectorCoreDump.cpp
// Invalidating an iterator.
#include <iterator>
#include <iostream>
#include <vector>
using namespace std;

int main() {
  vector<int> vi(10, 0);
  ostream_iterator<int> out(cout, " ");
  vector<int>::iterator i = vi.begin();
  *i = 47;
  copy(vi.begin(), vi.end(), out);
  cout << endl;
  // Force it to move memory (could also just add
```

```
    // enough objects):
    vi.resize(vi.capacity() + 1);
    // Now i points to wrong memory:
    *i = 48;   // Access violation
    copy(vi.begin(), vi.end(), out); // No change to vi[0]
} ///:~
```

This illustrates the concept of *iterator invalidation*. Certain operations cause internal changes to a container's underlying data, so any iterators in effect before such changes may no longer be valid afterward. If your program is breaking mysteriously, look for places where you hold onto an iterator while adding more objects to a **vector**. You'll need to get a new iterator after adding elements or use **operator[ ]** instead for element selections. If you combine this observation with the awareness of the potential expense of adding new objects to a **vector**, you may conclude that the safest way to use a **vector** is to fill it up all at once (ideally, knowing first how many objects you'll need) and then just use it (without adding more objects) elsewhere in the program. This is the way **vector** has been used in the book up to this point. The Standard C++ library documents the container operations that invalidate iterators.

You may observe that using **vector** as the "basic" container in the earlier chapters of this book might not be the best choice in all cases. This is a fundamental issue in containers and in data structures in general—the "best" choice varies according to the way the container is used. The reason **vector** has been the "best" choice up until now is that it looks a lot like an array and was thus familiar and easy for you to adopt. But from now on it's also worth thinking about other issues when choosing containers.

Inserting and erasing elements

The **vector** is most efficient if:

1.   You **reserve( )** the correct amount of storage at the beginning so the **vector** never has to reallocate.

2.   You only add and remove elements from the back end.

It is possible to insert and erase elements from the middle of a **vector** using an iterator, but the following program demonstrates what a bad idea this is:

```
//: C07:VectorInsertAndErase.cpp {-bor}
// Erasing an element from a vector.
```

```
//{L} Noisy
#include <algorithm>
#include <iostream>
#include <iterator>
#include <vector>
#include "Noisy.h"
using namespace std;

int main() {
  vector<Noisy> v;
  v.reserve(11);
  cout << "11 spaces have been reserved" << endl;
  generate_n(back_inserter(v), 10, NoisyGen());
  ostream_iterator<Noisy> out(cout, " ");
  cout << endl;
  copy(v.begin(), v.end(), out);
  cout << "Inserting an element:" << endl;
  vector<Noisy>::iterator it =
    v.begin() + v.size() / 2; // Middle
  v.insert(it, Noisy());
  cout << endl;
  copy(v.begin(), v.end(), out);
  cout << "\nErasing an element:" << endl;
  // Cannot use the previous value of it:
  it = v.begin() + v.size() / 2;
  v.erase(it);
  cout << endl;
  copy(v.begin(), v.end(), out);
  cout << endl;
} ///:~
```

When you run the program, you'll see that the call to **reserve( )** really does only allocate storage—no constructors are called. The **generate_n( )** call is busy: each call to **NoisyGen::operator( )** results in a construction, a copy-construction (into the **vector**), and a destruction of the temporary. But when an object is inserted into the **vector** in the middle, it must shift everything down to maintain the linear array, and, since there is enough space, it does this with the assignment operator. (If the argument of **reserve( )** is 10 instead of 11, it must reallocate storage.) When an object is erased from the **vector**, the assignment operator is once again used to move everything up to cover the place that is being erased. (Notice that this requires that the assignment operator properly clean up the lvalue.) Last, the object on the end of the array is deleted.

deque

The **deque** container is a basic sequence optimized for adding and removing elements from either end. It also allows for reasonably fast random access—it has an **operator[ ]** like **vector**. However, it does not have **vector**'s constraint of keeping everything in a single sequential block of memory. Instead, a typical implementation of **deque** uses multiple blocks of sequential storage (keeping track of all the blocks and their order in a mapping structure). For this reason, the overhead for a **deque** to add or remove elements at either end is low. In addition, it never needs to copy and destroy contained objects during a new storage allocation (like **vector** does), so it is far more efficient than **vector** if you are adding an unknown quantity of objects at either end. This means that **vector** is the best choice only if you have a good idea of how many objects you need. In addition, many of the programs shown earlier in this book that use **vector** and **push_back( )** might have been more efficient had we used a **deque** instead. The interface to **deque** differs only slightly from **vector** (**deque** has a **push_front( )** and **pop_front( )** while **vector** does not, for example), so converting code from using **vector** to using **deque** is trivial. Consider **StringVector.cpp**, which can be changed to use **deque** by replacing the word "vector" with "deque" everywhere. The following program adds parallel **deque** operations to the **vector** operations in **StringVector.cpp** and performs timing comparisons:

```
//: C07:StringDeque.cpp
// Converted from StringVector.cpp.
#include <cstddef>
#include <ctime>
#include <deque>
#include <fstream>
#include <iostream>
#include <iterator>
#include <sstream>
#include <string>
#include <vector>
#include "../require.h"
using namespace std;

int main(int argc, char* argv[]) {
  char* fname = "StringDeque.cpp";
  if(argc > 1) fname = argv[1];
  ifstream in(fname);
  assure(in, fname);
```

```
vector<string> vstrings;
deque<string> dstrings;
string line;
// Time reading into vector:
clock_t ticks = clock();
while(getline(in, line))
  vstrings.push_back(line);
ticks = clock() - ticks;
cout << "Read into vector: " << ticks << endl;
// Repeat for deque:
ifstream in2(fname);
assure(in2, fname);
ticks = clock();
while(getline(in2, line))
  dstrings.push_back(line);
ticks = clock() - ticks;
cout << "Read into deque: " << ticks << endl;
// Now compare indexing:
ticks = clock();
for(size_t i = 0; i < vstrings.size(); i++) {
  ostringstream ss;
  ss << i;
  vstrings[i] = ss.str() + ": " + vstrings[i];
}
ticks = clock() - ticks;
cout << "Indexing vector: " << ticks << endl;
ticks = clock();
for(size_t j = 0; j < dstrings.size(); j++) {
  ostringstream ss;
  ss << j;
  dstrings[j] = ss.str() + ": " + dstrings[j];
}
ticks = clock() - ticks;
cout << "Indexing deque: " << ticks << endl;
// Compare iteration
ofstream tmp1("tmp1.tmp"), tmp2("tmp2.tmp");
ticks = clock();
copy(vstrings.begin(), vstrings.end(),
  ostream_iterator<string>(tmp1, "\n"));
ticks = clock() - ticks;
cout << "Iterating vector: " << ticks << endl;
ticks = clock();
copy(dstrings.begin(), dstrings.end(),
  ostream_iterator<string>(tmp2, "\n"));
ticks = clock() - ticks;
```

```
    cout << "Iterating deque: " << ticks << endl;
} ///:~
```

Knowing now what you do about the inefficiency of adding things to **vector** because of storage reallocation, you might expect dramatic differences between the two. However, on a 1.7 MB text file, one compiler's program produced the following (measured in platform/compiler specific clock ticks, not seconds):

```
Read into vector: 8350
Read into deque: 7690
Indexing vector: 2360
Indexing deque: 2480
Iterating vector: 2470
Iterating deque: 2410
```

A different compiler and platform roughly agreed with this. It's not so dramatic, is it? This points out some important issues:

1. We (programmers and authors) are typically bad at guessing where inefficiencies occur in our programs.

2. Efficiency comes from a combination of effects. Here, reading the lines in and converting them to strings may dominate over the cost of **vector** vs. **deque**.

3. The **string** class is probably fairly well designed in terms of efficiency.

This doesn't mean you shouldn't use a **deque** rather than a **vector** when you know that an uncertain number of objects will be pushed onto the end of the container. On the contrary, you should—when you're tuning for performance. But also be aware that performance issues are usually not where you think they are, and the only way to know for sure where your bottlenecks are is by testing. Later in this chapter, you'll see a more "pure" comparison of performance between **vector**, **deque**, and **list**.

Converting between sequences

Sometimes you need the behavior or efficiency of one kind of container for one part of your program, and you need a different container's behavior or efficiency in another part of the program. For example, you may need the efficiency of a **deque** when adding objects to the container but the efficiency of a **vector** when indexing them. Each of the basic sequence containers (**vector**, **deque**, and **list**) has a two-iterator constructor (indicating the beginning and ending of the sequence to read from when creating a new object) and an **assign( )** member function to read into an existing container, so you can easily move objects from one sequence container to another.

The following example reads objects into a **deque** and then converts to a **vector**:

```
//: C07:DequeConversion.cpp {-bor}
// Reading into a Deque, converting to a vector.
//{L} Noisy
#include <algorithm>
#include <cstdlib>
#include <deque>
#include <iostream>
#include <iterator>
#include <vector>
#include "Noisy.h"
using namespace std;

int main(int argc, char* argv[]) {
  int size = 25;
  if(argc >= 2) size = atoi(argv[1]);
  deque<Noisy> d;
  generate_n(back_inserter(d), size, NoisyGen());
  cout << "\n Converting to a vector(1)" << endl;
  vector<Noisy> v1(d.begin(), d.end());
  cout << "\n Converting to a vector(2)" << endl;
  vector<Noisy> v2;
  v2.reserve(d.size());
  v2.assign(d.begin(), d.end());
  cout << "\n Cleanup" << endl;
} ///:~
```

You can try various sizes, but note that it makes no difference—the objects are simply copy-constructed into the new **vector**s. What's interesting is that **v1** does not cause multiple allocations while building the **vector**, no matter how many elements you use. You might initially think that you must follow the process used for **v2** and preallocate the storage to prevent messy reallocations, but this is unnecessary because the constructor used for **v1** determines the memory requirement ahead of time.

Cost of overflowing allocated storage

It's illuminating to see what happens with a **deque** when it overflows a block of storage, in contrast with **VectorOverflow.cpp**:

```
//: C07:DequeOverflow.cpp {-bor}
// A deque is much more efficient than a vector when
// pushing back a lot of elements, since it doesn't
// require copying and destroying.
//{L} Noisy
#include <cstdlib>
#include <deque>
#include "Noisy.h"
using namespace std;

int main(int argc, char* argv[]) {
  int size = 1000;
  if(argc >= 2) size = atoi(argv[1]);
  deque<Noisy> dn;
  Noisy n;
  for(int i = 0; i < size; i++)
    dn.push_back(n);
  cout << "\n cleaning up " << endl;
} ///:~
```

Here you will have relatively few (if any) destructors called before the words "cleaning up" appear in the output. Since the **deque** allocates all its storage in blocks instead of a contiguous array like **vector**, it never needs to move existing storage of each of its data blocks. (Thus, no additional copy-constructions and destructions occur.) The **deque** simply allocates a new block. For the same reason, the **deque** can just as efficiently add elements to the *beginning* of the sequence, since if it runs out of storage, it (again) just allocates a new block for the beginning. (The index block that holds the data blocks together may need to be reallocated, however.) Insertions in the middle of a **deque**, however, could be even messier than for **vector** (but not as costly).

Because of **deque**'s clever storage management, an existing iterator is not invalidated after you add new things to either end of a deque, as it was demonstrated to do with **vector** (in **VectorCoreDump.cpp**). If you stick to what **deque** is best at—insertions and removals from either end, reasonably rapid traversals and fairly fast random-access using **operator[ ]**—you'll be in good shape.

Checked random-access

Both **vector** and **deque** provide two random access functions: the indexing operator (**operator[ ]**), which you've seen already, and **at( )**, which checks the boundaries of the container that's being indexed and throws an exception if you go out of bounds. It does cost more to use **at( )**:

```
//: C07:IndexingVsAt.cpp
// Comparing "at()" to operator[].
#include <ctime>
#include <deque>
#include <iostream>
#include <vector>
#include "../require.h"
using namespace std;

int main(int argc, char* argv[]) {
  long count = 1000;
  int sz = 1000;
  if(argc >= 2) count = atoi(argv[1]);
  if(argc >= 3) sz = atoi(argv[2]);
  vector<int> vi(sz);
  clock_t ticks = clock();
  for(int i1 = 0; i1 < count; i1++)
    for(int j = 0; j < sz; j++)
      vi[j];
  cout << "vector[] " << clock() - ticks << endl;
  ticks = clock();
  for(int i2 = 0; i2 < count; i2++)
    for(int j = 0; j < sz; j++)
      vi.at(j);
  cout << "vector::at() " << clock()-ticks <<endl;
  deque<int> di(sz);
  ticks = clock();
  for(int i3 = 0; i3 < count; i3++)
    for(int j = 0; j < sz; j++)
      di[j];
  cout << "deque[] " << clock() - ticks << endl;
  ticks = clock();
  for(int i4 = 0; i4 < count; i4++)
    for(int j = 0; j < sz; j++)
      di.at(j);
  cout << "deque::at() " << clock()-ticks <<endl;
  // Demonstrate at() when you go out of bounds:
```

```
    try {
      di.at(vi.size() + 1);
    } catch(...) {
      cerr << "Exception thrown" << endl;
    }
} ///:~
```

As you saw in Chapter 1, different systems may handle the uncaught exception in different ways, but you'll know one way or another that something went wrong with the program when using **at( )**, whereas it's possible to remain ignorant when using **operator[ ]**.

list

A **list** is implemented as a doubly linked list data structure and is thus designed for rapid insertion and removal of elements *anywhere* in the sequence, whereas for **vector** and **deque** this is a much more costly operation. A list is so slow when randomly accessing elements that it does not have an **operator[ ]**. It's best used when you're traversing a sequence, in order, from beginning to end (or vice-versa), rather than choosing elements randomly from the middle. Even then the traversal can be slower than with a **vector**, but if you aren't doing a lot of traversals, that won't be your bottleneck.

The memory overhead of each link in a **list** requires a forward and backward pointer on top of the storage for the actual object. Thus, a **list** is a better choice when you have larger objects that you'll be inserting and removing from the middle of the **list**.

It's better not to use a **list** if you think you might be traversing it a lot, looking for objects, since the amount of time it takes to get from the beginning of the **list**—which is the only place you can start unless you've already got an iterator to somewhere you know is closer to your destination—to the object of interest is proportional to the number of objects between the beginning and that object.

The objects in a **list** never move after they are created. "Moving" a list element means changing the links, but never copying or assigning the actual objects. This means that iterators aren't invalidated when items are added to the list as it was demonstrated earlier to be the case **vector**. Here's an example using a **list** of **Noisy** objects:

```
//: C07:ListStability.cpp {-bor}
// Things don't move around in lists.
//{L} Noisy
#include <algorithm>
#include <iostream>
#include <iterator>
#include <list>
#include "Noisy.h"
using namespace std;

int main() {
  list<Noisy> l;
  ostream_iterator<Noisy> out(cout, " ");
  generate_n(back_inserter(l), 25, NoisyGen());
  cout << "\n Printing the list:" << endl;
  copy(l.begin(), l.end(), out);
  cout << "\n Reversing the list:" << endl;
  l.reverse();
  copy(l.begin(), l.end(), out);
  cout << "\n Sorting the list:" << endl;
  l.sort();
  copy(l.begin(), l.end(), out);
  cout << "\n Swapping two elements:" << endl;
  list<Noisy>::iterator it1, it2;
  it1 = it2 = l.begin();
  ++it2;
  swap(*it1, *it2);
  cout << endl;
  copy(l.begin(), l.end(), out);
  cout << "\n Using generic reverse(): " << endl;
  reverse(l.begin(), l.end());
  cout << endl;
  copy(l.begin(), l.end(), out);
  cout << "\n Cleanup" << endl;
} ///:~
```

Operations as seemingly radical as reversing and sorting the list require no copying of objects because, instead of moving the objects, the links are simply changed. However, notice that **sort( )** and **reverse( )** are member functions of **list**, so they have special knowledge of the internals of **list** and can rearrange the elements instead of copying them. On the other hand, the **swap( )** function is a generic algorithm and doesn't know about **list** in particular, so it uses the copying approach for swapping two elements. In general, use the member version of an algorithm if that is supplied instead of its generic algorithm equivalent. In particular, use the generic **sort( )** and **reverse( )** algorithms only with arrays, **vector**s, and **deque**s.

If you have large, complex objects, you might want to choose a **list** first, especially if construction, destruction, copy-construction, and assignment are expensive and if you are doing things like sorting the objects or otherwise reordering them a lot.

Special list operations

The **list** has some special built-in operations to make the best use of the structure of the **list**. You've already seen **reverse( )** and **sort( )**. Here are some of the others:

```cpp
//: C07:ListSpecialFunctions.cpp
//{L} Noisy
#include <algorithm>
#include <iostream>
#include <iterator>
#include <list>
#include "Noisy.h"
#include "PrintContainer.h"
using namespace std;

int main() {
  typedef list<Noisy> LN;
  LN l1, l2, l3, l4;
  generate_n(back_inserter(l1), 6, NoisyGen());
  generate_n(back_inserter(l2), 6, NoisyGen());
  generate_n(back_inserter(l3), 6, NoisyGen());
  generate_n(back_inserter(l4), 6, NoisyGen());
  print(l1, "l1", " "); print(l2, "l2", " ");
  print(l3, "l3", " "); print(l4, "l4", " ");
  LN::iterator it1 = l1.begin();
  ++it1; ++it1; ++it1;
  l1.splice(it1, l2);
  print(l1, "l1 after splice(it1, l2)", " ");
  print(l2, "l2 after splice(it1, l2)", " ");
  LN::iterator it2 = l3.begin();
  ++it2; ++it2; ++it2;
  l1.splice(it1, l3, it2);
  print(l1, "l1 after splice(it1, l3, it2)", " ");
  LN::iterator it3 = l4.begin(), it4 = l4.end();
  ++it3; --it4;
```

```
    l1.splice(it1, l4, it3, it4);
    print(l1, "l1 after splice(it1,l4,it3,it4)", " ");
    Noisy n;
    LN l5(3, n);
    generate_n(back_inserter(l5), 4, NoisyGen());
    l5.push_back(n);
    print(l5, "l5 before remove()", " ");
    l5.remove(l5.front());
    print(l5, "l5 after remove()", " ");
    l1.sort(); l5.sort();
    l5.merge(l1);
    print(l5, "l5 after l5.merge(l1)", " ");
    cout << "\n Cleanup" << endl;
} ///:~
```

After filling four **list**s with **Noisy** objects, one list is spliced into another in three ways. In the first, the entire list **l2** is spliced into **l1** at the iterator **it1**. Notice that after the splice, **l2** is empty—splicing means removing the elements from the source list. The second splice inserts elements from **l3** starting at **it2** into **l1** starting at **it1**. The third splice starts at **it1** and uses elements from **l4** starting at **it3** and ending at **it4**. The seemingly redundant mention of the source list is because the elements must be erased from the source list as part of the transfer to the destination list.

The output from the code that demonstrates **remove( )** shows that the list does not have to be sorted in order for all the elements of a particular value to be removed.

Finally, if you **merge( )** one list with another, the merge only works sensibly if the lists have been sorted. What you end up with in that case is a sorted list containing all the elements from both lists (the source list is erased—that is, the elements are *moved* to the destination list).

A **unique( )** member function removes all duplicates, but only if you sort the **list** first:

```
//: C07:UniqueList.cpp
// Testing list's unique() function.
#include <iostream>
#include <iterator>
#include <list>
using namespace std;
```

```
int a[] = { 1, 3, 1, 4, 1, 5, 1, 6, 1 };
const int ASZ = sizeof a / sizeof *a;

int main() {
  // For output:
  ostream_iterator<int> out(cout, " ");
  list<int> li(a, a + ASZ);
  li.unique();
  // Oops! No duplicates removed:
  copy(li.begin(), li.end(), out);
  cout << endl;
  // Must sort it first:
  li.sort();
  copy(li.begin(), li.end(), out);
  cout << endl;
  // Now unique() will have an effect:
  li.unique();
  copy(li.begin(), li.end(), out);
  cout << endl;
} ///:~
```

The **list** constructor used here takes the starting and past-the-end iterator from another container and copies all the elements from that container into itself. Here, the "container" is just an array, and the "iterators" are pointers into that array, but because of the design of the STL, the **list** constructor works with arrays just as easily as with any other container.

The **unique( )** function will remove only *adjacent* duplicate elements, and thus sorting is typically necessary before calling **unique( )**. The exception is when the problem you're trying to solve includes eliminating adjacent duplicates according to the current ordering.

Four additional **list** member functions are not demonstrated here: a **remove_if( )** that takes a predicate, which decides whether an object should be removed; a **unique( )** that takes a binary predicate to perform uniqueness comparisons; a **merge( )** that takes an additional argument which performs comparisons; and a **sort( )** that takes a comparator (to provide a comparison or override the existing one).

list vs. set

Looking at the previous example, you might note that if you want a sorted sequence with no duplicates, you could get that result with a **set**. It's interesting to compare the performance of the two containers:

```
//: C07:ListVsSet.cpp
// Comparing list and set performance.
#include <algorithm>
#include <cstdlib>
#include <ctime>
#include <iostream>
#include <iterator>
#include <list>
#include <set>
#include "PrintContainer.h"
using namespace std;

class Obj {
  int a[20]; // To take up extra space
  int val;
public:
  Obj() : val(rand() % 500) {}
  friend bool
  operator<(const Obj& a, const Obj& b) {
    return a.val < b.val;
  }
  friend bool
  operator==(const Obj& a, const Obj& b) {
    return a.val == b.val;
  }
  friend ostream&
  operator<<(ostream& os, const Obj& a) {
    return os << a.val;
  }
};

struct ObjGen {
  Obj operator()() { return Obj(); }
};

int main() {
  const int SZ = 5000;
  srand(time(0));
  list<Obj> lo;
```

```
    clock_t ticks = clock();
    generate_n(back_inserter(lo), SZ, ObjGen());
    lo.sort();
    lo.unique();
    cout << "list:" << clock() - ticks << endl;
    set<Obj> so;
    ticks = clock();
    generate_n(inserter(so, so.begin()),
      SZ, ObjGen());
    cout << "set:" << clock() - ticks << endl;
    print(lo);
    print(so);
} ///:~
```

When you run the program, you should discover that **set** is much faster than **list**. This is reassuring—after all, it is **set**'s primary job description to hold only unique elements in sorted order!

This example uses the header **PrintContainer.h**, which contains a function template that prints any sequence container to an output stream. **PrintContainer.h** is defined as follows:

```
//: C07:PrintContainer.h
// Prints a sequence container
#ifndef PRINT_CONTAINER_H
#define PRINT_CONTAINER_H
#include "../C06/PrintSequence.h"

template<class Cont>
void print(Cont& c, const char* nm = "",
           const char* sep = "\n",
           std::ostream& os = std::cout) {
  print(c.begin(), c.end(), nm, sep, os);
}
#endif ///:~
```

The **print( )** template defined here just calls the **print( )** function template we defined in the previous chapter in **PrintSequence.h**.

Swapping sequences

We mentioned earlier that all basic sequences have a member function **swap( )** that's designed to switch one sequence with another (but only for sequences of the same type). The member **swap( )** makes use of its knowledge of the internal structure of the particular container in order to be efficient:

```
//: C07:Swapping.cpp {-bor}
// All basic sequence containers can be swapped.
//{L} Noisy
#include <algorithm>
#include <deque>
#include <iostream>
#include <iterator>
#include <list>
#include <vector>
#include "Noisy.h"
#include "PrintContainer.h"
using namespace std;
ostream_iterator<Noisy> out(cout, " ");

template<class Cont> void testSwap(char* cname) {
  Cont c1, c2;
  generate_n(back_inserter(c1), 10, NoisyGen());
  generate_n(back_inserter(c2), 5, NoisyGen());
  cout << endl << cname << ":" << endl;
  print(c1, "c1"); print(c2, "c2");
  cout << "\n Swapping the " << cname << ":" << endl;
  c1.swap(c2);
  print(c1, "c1"); print(c2, "c2");
}

int main() {
  testSwap<vector<Noisy> >("vector");
  testSwap<deque<Noisy> >("deque");
  testSwap<list<Noisy> >("list");
} ///:~
```

When you run this, you'll discover that each type of sequence container can swap one sequence for another without any copying or assignments, even if the sequences are of different sizes. In effect, you're completely swapping the resources of one object for another.

The STL algorithms also contain a **swap( )**, and when this function is applied to two containers of the same type, it uses the member **swap( )** to achieve fast performance. Consequently, if you apply the **sort( )** algorithm to a container of containers, you will find that the performance is very fast—it turns out that fast sorting of a container of containers was a design goal of the STL.

set

The **set** container accepts only one copy of each element. It also sorts the elements. (Sorting isn't intrinsic to the conceptual definition of a set, but the STL **set** stores its elements in a balanced tree data structure to provide rapid lookups, thus producing sorted results when you traverse it.) The first two examples in this chapter used **set**s.

Consider the problem of creating an index for a book. You might like to start with all the words in the book, but you only want one instance of each word, and you want them sorted. A **set** is perfect for this and solves the problem effortlessly. However, there's also the problem of punctuation and any other nonalpha characters, which must be stripped off to generate proper words. One solution to this problem is to use the Standard C library functions **isalpha( )** and **isspace( )** to extract only the characters you want. You can replace all unwanted characters with spaces so that you can easily extract valid words from each line you read:

```
//: C07:WordList.cpp
// Display a list of words used in a document.
#include <algorithm>
#include <cctype>
#include <cstring>
#include <fstream>
#include <iostream>
#include <iterator>
#include <set>
#include <sstream>
#include <string>
#include "../require.h"
using namespace std;

char replaceJunk(char c) {
  // Only keep alphas, space (as a delimiter), and '
  return (isalpha(c) || c == '\'') ? c : ' ';
}
```

```
int main(int argc, char* argv[]) {
  char* fname = "WordList.cpp";
  if(argc > 1) fname = argv[1];
  ifstream in(fname);
  assure(in, fname);
  set<string> wordlist;
  string line;
  while(getline(in, line)) {
    transform(line.begin(), line.end(), line.begin(),
              replaceJunk);
    istringstream is(line);
    string word;
    while(is >> word)
      wordlist.insert(word);
  }
  // Output results:
  copy(wordlist.begin(), wordlist.end(),
       ostream_iterator<string>(cout, "\n"));
} ///:~
```

The call to **transform( )** replaces each character to be ignored with a space. The set container not only ignores duplicate words, but compares the words it keeps according to the function object **less<string>** (the default second template argument for the **set** container), which in turn uses **string::operator<( )**, so the words emerge in alphabetical order.

You don't need to use a **set** just to get a sorted sequence. You can use the **sort( )** function (along with a multitude of other functions in the STL) on different STL containers. However, it's likely that **set** will be faster here. Using a set is particularly handy when you just want to do lookup, since its **find( )** member function has logarithmic complexity and so is much faster than the generic **find( )** algorithm. As you recall, the generic **find( )** algorithm needs to traverse the whole range until it finds the search element (resulting in a worst-case complexity of N, and an average complexity of N/2). However, if you have a sequence container that is already sorted, use **equal_range( )** for logarithmic complexity when finding elements.

The following version shows how to build the list of words with an **istreambuf_iterator** that moves the characters from one place (the input stream) to another (a **string** object), depending on whether the Standard C library function **isalpha( )** returns true:

```
//: C07:WordList2.cpp
// Illustrates istreambuf_iterator and insert iterators.
#include <cstring>
#include <fstream>
#include <iostream>
#include <iterator>
#include <set>
#include <string>
#include "../require.h"
using namespace std;

int main(int argc, char* argv[]) {
  char* fname = "WordList2.cpp";
  if(argc > 1) fname = argv[1];
  ifstream in(fname);
  assure(in, fname);
  istreambuf_iterator<char> p(in), end;
  set<string> wordlist;
  while(p != end) {
    string word;
    insert_iterator<string> ii(word, word.begin());
    // Find the first alpha character:
    while(p != end && !isalpha(*p))
      ++p;
    // Copy until the first non-alpha character:
    while(p != end && isalpha(*p))
      *ii++ = *p++;
    if(word.size() != 0)
      wordlist.insert(word);
  }
  // Output results:
  copy(wordlist.begin(), wordlist.end(),
    ostream_iterator<string>(cout, "\n"));
} ///:~
```

This example was suggested by Nathan Myers, who invented the **istreambuf_iterator** and its relatives. This iterator extracts information character by character from a stream. Although the **istreambuf_iterator** template argument might imply that you could extract, for example, **int**s instead of **char**, that's not the case. The argument must be of some character type—a regular **char** or a wide character.

After the file is open, an **istreambuf_iterator** called **p** is attached to the **istream** so characters can be extracted from it. The **set<string>** called **wordlist** will hold the resulting words.

The **while** loop reads words until it finds the end of the input stream. This is detected using the default constructor for **istreambuf_iterator**, which produces the past-the-end iterator object **end**. Thus, if you want to test to make sure you're not at the end of the stream, you simply say **p != end**.

The second type of iterator that's used here is the **insert_iterator**, which you saw previously. This inserts objects into a container. Here, the "container" is the **string** called **word**, which, for the purposes of **insert_iterator**, behaves like a container. The constructor for **insert_iterator** requires the container and an iterator indicating where it should start inserting the characters. You could also use a **back_insert_iterator**, which requires that the container have a **push_back( )** (**string** does).

After the **while** loop sets everything up, it begins by looking for the first alpha character, incrementing **start** until that character is found. It then copies characters from one iterator to the other, stopping when a nonalpha character is found. Each **word**, assuming it is nonempty, is added to **wordlist**.

A completely reusable tokenizer

The word list examples use different approaches to extract tokens from a stream, neither of which is very flexible. Since the STL containers and algorithms all revolve around iterators, the most flexible solution will itself use an iterator. You could think of the **TokenIterator** as an iterator that wraps itself around any other iterator that can produce characters. Because it is certainly a type of input iterator (the most primitive type of iterator), it can provide input to any STL algorithm. Not only is it a useful tool in itself, the following **TokenIterator** is also a good example of how you can design your own iterators.[10]

---

[10] This is another example coached by Nathan Myers.

The **TokenIterator** class is doubly flexible. First, you can choose the type of iterator that will produce the **char** input. Second, instead of just saying what characters represent the delimiters, **TokenIterator** will use a predicate that is a function object whose **operator( )** takes a **char** and decides whether it should be in the token. Although the two examples given here have a static concept of what characters belong in a token, you could easily design your own function object to change its state as the characters are read, producing a more sophisticated parser.

The following header file contains two basic predicates, **Isalpha** and **Delimiters**, along with the template for **TokenIterator**:

```
//: C07:TokenIterator.h
#ifndef TOKENITERATOR_H
#define TOKENITERATOR_H
#include <algorithm>
#include <cctype>
#include <functional>
#include <iterator>
#include <string>

struct Isalpha : std::unary_function<char, bool> {
  bool operator()(char c) { return std::isalpha(c); }
};

class Delimiters : std::unary_function<char, bool> {
  std::string exclude;
public:
  Delimiters() {}
  Delimiters(const std::string& excl) : exclude(excl) {}
  bool operator()(char c) {
    return exclude.find(c) == std::string::npos;
  }
};

template<class InputIter, class Pred = Isalpha>
class TokenIterator : public std::iterator<
    std::input_iterator_tag, std::string, std::ptrdiff_t> {
  InputIter first;
  InputIter last;
  std::string word;
  Pred predicate;
public:
```

```
TokenIterator(InputIter begin, InputIter end,
  Pred pred = Pred())
  : first(begin), last(end), predicate(pred) {
    ++*this;
}
TokenIterator() {} // End sentinel
// Prefix increment:
TokenIterator& operator++() {
  word.resize(0);
  first = std::find_if(first, last, predicate);
  while(first != last && predicate(*first))
    word += *first++;
  return *this;
}
// Postfix increment
class CaptureState {
  std::string word;
public:
  CaptureState(const std::string& w) : word(w) {}
  std::string operator*() { return word; }
};
CaptureState operator++(int) {
  CaptureState d(word);
  ++*this;
  return d;
}
// Produce the actual value:
std::string operator*() const { return word; }
const std::string* operator->() const { return &word; }
// Compare iterators:
bool operator==(const TokenIterator&) {
  return word.size() == 0 && first == last;
}
bool operator!=(const TokenIterator& rv) {
  return !(*this == rv);
}
};
#endif // TOKENITERATOR_H ///:~
```

The **TokenIterator** class derives from the **std::iterator** template. It might appear that some kind of functionality comes with **std::iterator**, but it is purely a way of tagging an iterator, to tell a container that uses it what it can do. Here, you can see **input_iterator_tag** as the **iterator_category** template argument—this tells anyone who asks that a **TokenIterator** only has the capabilities of an input iterator and cannot be used with algorithms requiring more sophisticated iterators. Apart from the tagging, **std::iterator** doesn't do anything beyond providing several useful type definitions. You must implement all other functionality yourself.

The **TokenIterator** class may look a little strange at first, because the first constructor requires both a "begin" and an "end" iterator as arguments, along with the predicate. Remember, this is a "wrapper" iterator that has no idea how to tell when it's at the end of its input, so the ending iterator is necessary in the first constructor. The reason for the second (default) constructor is that the STL algorithms (and any algorithms you write) need a **TokenIterator** sentinel to be the past-the-end value. Since all the information necessary to see if the **TokenIterator** has reached the end of its input is collected in the first constructor, this second constructor creates a **TokenIterator** that is merely used as a placeholder in algorithms.

The core of the behavior happens in **operator++**. This erases the current value of **word** using **string::resize( )** and then finds the first character that satisfies the predicate (thus discovering the beginning of the new token) using **find_if( )**. The resulting iterator is assigned to **first**, thus moving **first** forward to the beginning of the token. Then, as long as the end of the input is not reached and the predicate is satisfied, input characters are copied into **word**. Finally, the **TokenIterator** object is returned and must be dereferenced to access the new token.

The postfix increment requires an object of type **CaptureState** to hold the value before the increment, so it can be returned. Producing the actual value is a straightforward **operator***. The only other functions to define for an output iterator are the **operator==** and **operator!=** to indicate whether the **TokenIterator** has reached the end of its input. You can see that the argument for **operator==** is ignored—it only cares about whether it has reached its internal **last** iterator. Notice that **operator!=** is defined in terms of **operator==**.

A good test of **TokenIterator** includes a number of different sources of input characters, including a **streambuf_iterator**, a **char***, and a **deque<char>::iterator**. Finally, the original word list problem is solved:

```
//: C07:TokenIteratorTest.cpp {-g++}
#include <fstream>
```

```
#include <iostream>
#include <vector>
#include <deque>
#include <set>
#include "TokenIterator.h"
#include "../require.h"
using namespace std;

int main(int argc, char* argv[]) {
  char* fname = "TokenIteratorTest.cpp";
  if(argc > 1) fname = argv[1];
  ifstream in(fname);
  assure(in, fname);
  ostream_iterator<string> out(cout, "\n");
  typedef istreambuf_iterator<char> IsbIt;
  IsbIt begin(in), isbEnd;
  Delimiters delimiters(" \t\n~;()\"<>:{}[]+-=&*#.,/\\");
  TokenIterator<IsbIt, Delimiters>
    wordIter(begin, isbEnd, delimiters), end;
  vector<string> wordlist;
  copy(wordIter, end, back_inserter(wordlist));
  // Output results:
  copy(wordlist.begin(), wordlist.end(), out);
  *out++ = "---------------------------------";
  // Use a char array as the source:
  char* cp = "typedef std::istreambuf_iterator<char> It";
  TokenIterator<char*, Delimiters>
    charIter(cp, cp + strlen(cp), delimiters), end2;
  vector<string> wordlist2;
  copy(charIter, end2, back_inserter(wordlist2));
  copy(wordlist2.begin(), wordlist2.end(), out);
  *out++ = "---------------------------------";
  // Use a deque<char> as the source:
  ifstream in2("TokenIteratorTest.cpp");
  deque<char> dc;
  copy(IsbIt(in2), IsbIt(), back_inserter(dc));
  TokenIterator<deque<char>::iterator,Delimiters>
    dcIter(dc.begin(), dc.end(), delimiters), end3;
  vector<string> wordlist3;
  copy(dcIter, end3, back_inserter(wordlist3));
  copy(wordlist3.begin(), wordlist3.end(), out);
  *out++ = "---------------------------------";
  // Reproduce the Wordlist.cpp example:
  ifstream in3("TokenIteratorTest.cpp");
  TokenIterator<IsbIt, Delimiters>
```

```
      wordIter2(IsbIt(in3), isbEnd, delimiters);
  set<string> wordlist4;
  while(wordIter2 != end)
    wordlist4.insert(*wordIter2++);
  copy(wordlist4.begin(), wordlist4.end(), out);
} ///:~
```

When using an **istreambuf_iterator**, you create one to attach to the
istream object and one with the default constructor as the past-the-end
marker. Both are used to create the **TokenIterator** that will produce the
tokens; the default constructor produces the faux **TokenIterator** past-the-
end sentinel. (This is just a placeholder and is ignored.) The **TokenIterator**
produces **string**s that are inserted into a container of **string**—here a
vector<string> is used in all cases except the last. (You could also
concatenate the results onto a **string**.) Other than that, a **TokenIterator**
works like any other input iterator.

When defining a bidirectional (and therefore also a random access) iterator,
you can get reverse iterators "for free" by using the **std::reverse_iterator**
adaptor. If you have already defined an iterator for a container with
bidirectional capabilities, you can get a reverse iterator from your forward-
traversing iterator with lines like the following inside your container class:

```
// Assume "iterator" is your nested iterator type
typedef std::reverse_iterator<iterator> reverse_iterator;
reverse_iterator rbegin() {return reverse_iterator(end());
reverse_iterator rend() {return reverse_iterator(begin());
```

The **std::reverse_iterator** adaptor does all the work for you. For example,
if you use the * operator to dereference your reverse iterator, it automatically
decrements a temporary copy of the forward iterator it is holding in order to
return the correct element, since reverse iterators logically point one position
past the element they refer to.

stack

The **stack** container, along with **queue** and **priority_queue**, are classified
as *adaptors*, which means they adapt one of the basic sequence containers to
store their data. This is an unfortunate case of confusing what something
does with the details of its underlying implementation—the fact that these are
called "adaptors" is of primary value only to the creator of the library. When

you use them, you generally don't care that they're adaptors, but instead that they solve your problem. Admittedly it's useful at times to know that you can choose an alternate implementation or build an adaptor from an existing container object, but that's generally one level removed from the adaptor's behavior. So, while you may see it emphasized elsewhere that a particular container is an adaptor, we'll only point out that fact when it's useful. Note that each type of adaptor has a default container that it's built upon, and this default is the most sensible implementation. In most cases you won't need to concern yourself with the underlying implementation.

The following example shows **stack<string>** implemented in the three ways: the default (which uses **deque**), then with a **vector**, and finally with a **list**:

```
//: C07:Stack1.cpp
// Demonstrates the STL stack.
#include <fstream>
#include <iostream>
#include <list>
#include <stack>
#include <string>
#include <vector>
using namespace std;

// Rearrange comments below to use different versions.
typedef stack<string> Stack1; // Default: deque<string>
// typedef stack<string, vector<string> > Stack2;
// typedef stack<string, list<string> > Stack3;

int main() {
  ifstream in("Stack1.cpp");
  Stack1 textlines; // Try the different versions
  // Read file and store lines in the stack:
  string line;
  while(getline(in, line))
    textlines.push(line + "\n");
  // Print lines from the stack and pop them:
  while(!textlines.empty()) {
    cout << textlines.top();
    textlines.pop();
  }
} ///:~
```

The **top( )** and **pop( )** operations will probably seem non-intuitive if you've used other **stack** classes. When you call **pop( )**, it returns **void** rather than the top element that you might have expected. If you want the top element, you get a reference to it with **top( )**. It turns out this is more efficient, since a traditional **pop( )** must return a value rather than a reference and thus invokes the copy-constructor. More important, it is *exception safe*, as we discussed in Chapter 1. If **pop( )** both changed the state of the stack and attempted to return the top element, an exception in the element's copy-constructor could cause the element to be lost. When you're using a **stack** (or a **priority_queue**, described later), you can efficiently refer to **top( )** as many times as you want and then discard the top element explicitly using **pop( )**. (Perhaps if some term other than the familiar "pop" had been used, this would have been a bit clearer.)

The **stack** template has a simple interface—essentially the member functions you saw earlier. Since it only makes sense to access a stack at its top, no iterators are available for traversing it. Nor are there sophisticated forms of initialization, but if you need that, you can use the underlying container upon which the **stack** is implemented. For example, suppose you have a function that expects a **stack** interface, but in the rest of your program you need the objects stored in a **list**. The following program stores each line of a file along with the leading number of spaces in that line. (You might imagine it as a starting point for performing some kind of source-code reformatting.)

```
//: C07:Stack2.cpp
// Converting a list to a stack.
#include <iostream>
#include <fstream>
#include <stack>
#include <list>
#include <string>
#include <cstddef>
using namespace std;

// Expects a stack:
template<class Stk>
void stackOut(Stk& s, ostream& os = cout) {
  while(!s.empty()) {
    os << s.top() << "\n";
    s.pop();
  }
}
```

```
class Line {
  string line; // Without leading spaces
  size_t lspaces; // Number of leading spaces
public:
  Line(string s) : line(s) {
    lspaces = line.find_first_not_of(' ');
    if(lspaces == string::npos)
      lspaces = 0;
    line = line.substr(lspaces);
  }
  friend ostream& operator<<(ostream& os, const Line& l) {
    for(size_t i = 0; i < l.lspaces; i++)
      os << ' ';
    return os << l.line;
  }
  // Other functions here...
};

int main() {
  ifstream in("Stack2.cpp");
  list<Line> lines;
  // Read file and store lines in the list:
  string s;
  while(getline(in, s))
    lines.push_front(s);
  // Turn the list into a stack for printing:
  stack<Line, list<Line> > stk(lines);
  stackOut(stk);
} ///:~
```

The function that requires the **stack** interface just sends each **top( )** object to an **ostream** and then removes it by calling **pop( )**. The **Line** class determines the number of leading spaces and then stores the contents of the line *without* the leading spaces. The **ostream operator<<** re-inserts the leading spaces so the line prints properly, but you can easily change the number of spaces by changing the value of **lspaces**. (The member functions to do this are not shown here.) In **main( )**, the input file is read into a **list<Line>**, and then each line in the list is copied into a **stack** that is sent to **stackOut( )**.

You cannot iterate through a **stack**; this emphasizes that you only want to perform **stack** operations when you create a **stack**. You can get equivalent "stack" functionality using a **vector** and its **back( )**, **push_back( )**, and **pop_back( )** member functions, and then you have all the additional functionality of the **vector**. The program **Stack1.cpp** can be rewritten to show this:

```
//: C07:Stack3.cpp
// Using a vector as a stack; modified Stack1.cpp.
#include <fstream>
#include <iostream>
#include <string>
#include <vector>
using namespace std;

int main() {
  ifstream in("Stack3.cpp");
  vector<string> textlines;
  string line;
  while(getline(in, line))
    textlines.push_back(line + "\n");
  while(!textlines.empty()) {
    cout << textlines.back();
    textlines.pop_back();
  }
} ///:~
```

This produces the same output as **Stack1.cpp**, but you can now perform **vector** operations as well. A **list** can also push things at the front, but it's generally less efficient than using **push_back( )** with **vector**. (In addition, **deque** is usually more efficient than **list** for pushing things at the front.)

queue

The **queue** container is a restricted form of a **deque**—you can only enter elements at one end and pull them off the other end. Functionally, you could use a **deque** anywhere you need a **queue**, and you would then also have the additional functionality of the **deque**. The only reason you need to use a **queue** rather than a **deque**, then, is when you want to emphasize that you will only be performing queue-like behavior.

The **queue** class is an adaptor like **stack**, in that it is built on top of another sequence container. As you might guess, the ideal implementation for a

queue is a **deque**, and that is the default template argument for the **queue**; you'll rarely need a different implementation.

Queues are often used if you want to model a system where some elements are waiting to be served by other elements in the system. A classic example of this is the "bank-teller problem." Customers arrive at random intervals, get into a line, and then are served by a set of tellers. Since the customers arrive randomly and each takes a random amount of time to be served, there's no way to deterministically know how long the line will be at any time. However, it's possible to simulate the situation and see what happens.

In a realistic simulation each customer and teller should be run by a separate thread. What we'd like is a multithreaded environment so that each customer or teller would have his own thread. However, Standard C++ has no support for multithreading. On the other hand, with a little adjustment to the code, it's possible to simulate enough multithreading to provide a satisfactory solution.[11]

In multithreading, multiple threads of control run simultaneously, sharing the same address space. Quite often you have fewer CPUs than you do threads (and often only one CPU). To give the illusion that each thread has its own CPU, a *time-slicing* mechanism says "OK, current thread, you've had enough time. I'm going to stop you and give time to some other thread." This automatic stopping and starting of threads is called *preemptive,* and it means you (the programmer) don't need to manage the threading process.

An alternative approach has each thread voluntarily yield the CPU to the scheduler, which then finds another thread that needs running. Instead, we'll build the "time-slicing" into the classes in the system. Here, it will be the tellers that represent the "threads," (the customers will be passive). Each teller will have an infinite-looping **run( )** member function that will execute for a certain number of "time units" and then simply return. By using the ordinary return mechanism, we eliminate the need for any swapping. The resulting program, although small, provides a remarkably reasonable simulation:

```
//: C07:BankTeller.cpp {RunByHand}
```

---

[11] We revisit multithreading issues in Chapter 11.

```
// Using a queue and simulated multithreading
// to model a bank teller system.
#include <cstdlib>
#include <ctime>
#include <iostream>
#include <iterator>
#include <list>
#include <queue>
using namespace std;

class Customer {
  int serviceTime;
public:
  Customer() : serviceTime(0) {}
  Customer(int tm) : serviceTime(tm) {}
  int getTime() { return serviceTime; }
  void setTime(int newtime) { serviceTime = newtime; }
  friend ostream&
  operator<<(ostream& os, const Customer& c) {
    return os << '[' << c.serviceTime << ']';
  }
};

class Teller {
  queue<Customer>& customers;
  Customer current;
  enum { SLICE = 5 };
  int ttime; // Time left in slice
  bool busy; // Is teller serving a customer?
public:
  Teller(queue<Customer>& cq)
  : customers(cq), ttime(0), busy(false) {}
  Teller& operator=(const Teller& rv) {
    customers = rv.customers;
    current = rv.current;
    ttime = rv.ttime;
    busy = rv.busy;
    return *this;
  }
  bool isBusy() { return busy; }
  void run(bool recursion = false) {
    if(!recursion)
      ttime = SLICE;
    int servtime = current.getTime();
    if(servtime > ttime) {
```

```
        servtime -= ttime;
        current.setTime(servtime);
        busy = true; // Still working on current
        return;
      }
    }
    if(servtime < ttime) {
      ttime -= servtime;
      if(!customers.empty()) {
        current = customers.front();
        customers.pop(); // Remove it
        busy = true;
        run(true); // Recurse
      }
      return;
    }
    if(servtime == ttime) {
      // Done with current, set to empty:
      current = Customer(0);
      busy = false;
      return; // No more time in this slice
    }
  }
};

// Inherit to access protected implementation:
class CustomerQ : public queue<Customer> {
public:
  friend ostream&
  operator<<(ostream& os, const CustomerQ& cd) {
    copy(cd.c.begin(), cd.c.end(),
      ostream_iterator<Customer>(os, ""));
    return os;
  }
};

int main() {
  CustomerQ customers;
  list<Teller> tellers;
  typedef list<Teller>::iterator TellIt;
  tellers.push_back(Teller(customers));
  srand(time(0)); // Seed the random number generator
  clock_t ticks = clock();
  // Run simulation for at least 5 seconds:
  while(clock() < ticks + 5 * CLOCKS_PER_SEC) {
    // Add a random number of customers to the
```

```
    // queue, with random service times:
    for(int i = 0; i < rand() % 5; i++)
      customers.push(Customer(rand() % 15 + 1));
    cout << '{' << tellers.size() << '}'
         << customers << endl;
    // Have the tellers service the queue:
    for(TellIt i = tellers.begin();
      i != tellers.end(); i++)
      (*i).run();
    cout << '{' << tellers.size() << '}'
         << customers << endl;
    // If line is too long, add another teller:
    if(customers.size() / tellers.size() > 2)
      tellers.push_back(Teller(customers));
    // If line is short enough, remove a teller:
    if(tellers.size() > 1 &&
      customers.size() / tellers.size() < 2)
      for(TellIt i = tellers.begin();
        i != tellers.end(); i++)
        if(!(*i).isBusy()) {
          tellers.erase(i);
          break; // Out of for loop
        }
  }
} ///:~
```

Each customer requires a certain amount of service time, which is the number of time units that a teller must spend on the customer to serve that customer's needs. The amount of service time will be different for each customer and will be determined randomly. In addition, you won't know how many customers will be arriving in each interval, so this will also be determined randomly.

The **Customer** objects are kept in a **queue<Customer>**, and each **Teller** object keeps a reference to that queue. When a **Teller** object is finished with its current **Customer** object, that **Teller** will get another **Customer** from the queue and begin working on the new **Customer**, reducing the **Customer**'s service time during each time slice that the **Teller** is allotted. All this logic is in the **run( )** member function, which is basically a three-way **if** statement based on whether the amount of time necessary to serve the customer is less than, greater than, or equal to the amount of time left in the teller's current time slice. Notice that if the **Teller** has more time after finishing with a **Customer**, it gets a new customer and recurses into itself.

Just as with a **stack**, when you use a **queue**, it's only a **queue** and doesn't have any of the other functionality of the basic sequence containers. This includes the ability to get an iterator in order to step through the **stack**. However, the underlying sequence container (that the **queue** is built upon) is held as a **protected** member inside the **queue**, and the identifier for this member is specified in the C++ Standard as '**c**', which means that you can derive from **queue** to access the underlying implementation. The **CustomerQ** class does exactly that, for the sole purpose of defining an **ostream operator<<** that can iterate through the **queue** and display its members.

The driver for the simulation is the **while** loop in **main( )**, which uses processor ticks (defined in **<ctime>**) to determine if the simulation has run for at least 5 seconds. At the beginning of each pass through the loop, a random number of customers is added, with random service times. Both the number of tellers and the queue contents are displayed so you can see the state of the system. After running each teller, the display is repeated. At this point, the system adapts by comparing the number of customers and the number of tellers. If the line is too long, another teller is added, and if it is short enough, a teller can be removed. In this adaptation section of the program you can experiment with policies regarding the optimal addition and removal of tellers. If this is the only section that you're modifying, you might want to encapsulate policies inside different objects.

We'll revisit this example in a multithreaded exercise in Chapter 11.

Priority queues

When you **push( )** an object onto a **priority_queue**, that object is sorted into the queue according to a comparison function or function object. (You can allow the default **less** template to supply this, or you can provide one of your own.) The **priority_queue** ensures that when you look at the **top( )** element, it will be the one with the highest priority. When you're done with it, you call **pop( )** to remove it and bring the next one into place. Thus, the **priority_queue** has nearly the same interface as a **stack**, but it behaves differently.

Like **stack** and **queue**, **priority_queue** is an adaptor that is built on top of one of the basic sequences—the default sequence being **vector**.

It's trivial to make a **priority_queue** that works with **int**s:

```
//: C07:PriorityQueue1.cpp
#include <cstdlib>
#include <ctime>
#include <iostream>
#include <queue>
using namespace std;

int main() {
  priority_queue<int> pqi;
  srand(time(0)); // Seed the random number generator
  for(int i = 0; i < 100; i++)
    pqi.push(rand() % 25);
  while(!pqi.empty()) {
    cout << pqi.top() << ' ';
    pqi.pop();
  }
} ///:~
```

This pushes into the **priority_queue** 100 random values from 0 to 24. When you run this program you'll see that duplicates are allowed, and the highest values appear first. To show how you can change the ordering by providing your own function or function object, the following program gives lower-valued numbers the highest priority:

```
//: C07:PriorityQueue2.cpp
// Changing the priority.
#include <cstdlib>
#include <ctime>
#include <functional>
#include <iostream>
#include <queue>
using namespace std;

int main() {
  priority_queue<int, vector<int>, greater<int> > pqi;
  srand(time(0));
  for(int i = 0; i < 100; i++)
    pqi.push(rand() % 25);
  while(!pqi.empty()) {
    cout << pqi.top() << ' ';
    pqi.pop();
  }
```

```
} ///:~
```

A more interesting problem is a to-do list, where each object contains a
string and a primary and secondary priority value:

```
//: C07:PriorityQueue3.cpp
// A more complex use of priority_queue.
#include <iostream>
#include <queue>
#include <string>
using namespace std;

class ToDoItem {
  char primary;
  int secondary;
  string item;
public:
  ToDoItem(string td, char pri = 'A', int sec = 1)
  : primary(pri), secondary(sec), item(td) {}
  friend bool operator<(
    const ToDoItem& x, const ToDoItem& y) {
    if(x.primary > y.primary)
      return true;
    if(x.primary == y.primary)
      if(x.secondary > y.secondary)
        return true;
    return false;
  }
  friend ostream&
  operator<<(ostream& os, const ToDoItem& td) {
    return os << td.primary << td.secondary
      << ": " << td.item;
  }
};

int main() {
  priority_queue<ToDoItem> toDoList;
  toDoList.push(ToDoItem("Empty trash", 'C', 4));
  toDoList.push(ToDoItem("Feed dog", 'A', 2));
  toDoList.push(ToDoItem("Feed bird", 'B', 7));
  toDoList.push(ToDoItem("Mow lawn", 'C', 3));
  toDoList.push(ToDoItem("Water lawn", 'A', 1));
  toDoList.push(ToDoItem("Feed cat", 'B', 1));
  while(!toDoList.empty()) {
    cout << toDoList.top() << endl;
```

```
      toDoList.pop();
  }
} ///:~
```

The **ToDoItem**'s **operator<** must be a nonmember function for it to work
with **less< >**. Other than that, everything happens automatically. The output
is

```
A1: Water lawn
A2: Feed dog
B1: Feed cat
B7: Feed bird
C3: Mow lawn
C4: Empty trash
```

You cannot iterate through a **priority_queue**, but it's possible to simulate
the behavior of a **priority_queue** using a **vector**, thus allowing you access
to that **vector**. You can do this by looking at the implementation of
priority_queue, which uses **make_heap( )**, **push_heap( )**, and
pop_heap( ). (These are the soul of the **priority_queue**—in fact you could
say that the heap *is* the priority queue and that **priority_queue** is just a
wrapper around it.) This turns out to be reasonably straightforward, but you
might think that a shortcut is possible. Since the container used by
priority_queue is **protected** (and has the identifier, according to the
Standard C++ specification, named **c**), you can inherit a new class that
provides access to the underlying implementation:

```
//: C07:PriorityQueue4.cpp
// Manipulating the underlying implementation.
#include <algorithm>
#include <cstdlib>
#include <ctime>
#include <iostream>
#include <iterator>
#include <queue>
using namespace std;

class PQI : public priority_queue<int> {
public:
  vector<int>& impl() { return c; }
};

int main() {
```

```
  PQI pqi;
  srand(time(0));
  for(int i = 0; i < 100; i++)
    pqi.push(rand() % 25);
  copy(pqi.impl().begin(), pqi.impl().end(),
    ostream_iterator<int>(cout, " "));
  cout << endl;
  while(!pqi.empty()) {
    cout << pqi.top() << ' ';
    pqi.pop();
  }
} ///:~
```

However, if you run this program, you'll discover that the **vector** doesn't contain the items in the descending order that you get when you call **pop( )**, the order that you want from the priority queue. It would seem that if you want to create a **vector** that is a priority queue, you have to do it by hand, like this:

```
//: C07:PriorityQueue5.cpp
// Building your own priority queue.
#include <algorithm>
#include <cstdlib>
#include <ctime>
#include <iostream>
#include <iterator>
#include <queue>
using namespace std;

template<class T, class Compare>
class PQV : public vector<T> {
  Compare comp;
public:
  PQV(Compare cmp = Compare()) : comp(cmp) {
    make_heap(this->begin(),this->end(), comp);
  }
  const T& top() { return this->front(); }
  void push(const T& x) {
    this->push_back(x);
    push_heap(this->begin(),this->end(), comp);
  }
  void pop() {
    pop_heap(this->begin(),this->end(), comp);
    this->pop_back();
```

```
    }
};

int main() {
  PQV< int, less<int> > pqi;
  srand(time(0));
  for(int i = 0; i < 100; i++)
    pqi.push(rand() % 25);
  copy(pqi.begin(), pqi.end(),
    ostream_iterator<int>(cout, " "));
  cout << endl;
  while(!pqi.empty()) {
    cout << pqi.top() << ' ';
    pqi.pop();
  }
} ///:~
```

But this program behaves in the same way as the previous one! What you are seeing in the underlying **vector** is called a *heap*. This heap data structure represents the tree of the priority queue (stored in the linear structure of the **vector**), but when you iterate through it, you do not get a linear priority-queue order. You might think that you can simply call **sort_heap( )**, but that only works once, and then you don't have a heap anymore, but instead a sorted list. This means that to go back to using it as a heap, the user must remember to call **make_heap( )** first. This can be encapsulated into your custom priority queue:

```
//: C07:PriorityQueue6.cpp
#include <algorithm>
#include <cstdlib>
#include <ctime>
#include <iostream>
#include <iterator>
#include <queue>
using namespace std;

template<class T, class Compare>
class PQV : public vector<T> {
  Compare comp;
  bool sorted;
  void assureHeap() {
    if(sorted) {
      // Turn it back into a heap:
      make_heap(this->begin(),this->end(), comp);
```

```
        sorted = false;
      }
    }
  }
public:
  PQV(Compare cmp = Compare()) : comp(cmp) {
    make_heap(this->begin(),this->end(), comp);
    sorted = false;
  }
  const T& top() {
    assureHeap();
    return this->front();
  }
  void push(const T& x) {
    assureHeap();
    this->push_back(x); // Put it at the end
    // Re-adjust the heap:
    push_heap(this->begin(),this->end(), comp);
  }
  void pop() {
    assureHeap();
    // Move the top element to the last position:
    pop_heap(this->begin(),this->end(), comp);
    this->pop_back();// Remove that element
  }
  void sort() {
    if(!sorted) {
      sort_heap(this->begin(),this->end(), comp);
      reverse(this->begin(),this->end());
      sorted = true;
    }
  }
};

int main() {
  PQV< int, less<int> > pqi;
  srand(time(0));
  for(int i = 0; i < 100; i++) {
    pqi.push(rand() % 25);
    copy(pqi.begin(), pqi.end(),
      ostream_iterator<int>(cout, " "));
    cout << "\n-----" << endl;
  }
  pqi.sort();
  copy(pqi.begin(), pqi.end(),
    ostream_iterator<int>(cout, " "));
```

```
    cout << "\n-----" << endl;
    while(!pqi.empty()) {
      cout << pqi.top() << ' ';
      pqi.pop();
    }
} ///:~
```

If **sorted** is true, the **vector** is not organized as a heap but instead as a sorted sequence. The **assureHeap( )** function guarantees that it's put back into heap form before performing any heap operations on it. The first **for** loop in **main( )** now has the additional quality that it displays the heap as it is being built.

In the previous two programs we had to introduce a seemingly extraneous usage of the "**this->**" prefix. Although some compilers do not require it, the standard definition of C++ does. Note that the class **PQV** derives from **vector<T>**, therefore **begin( )** and **end( )**, inherited from **vector<T>**, are dependent names.[12] Compilers can't look up names from dependent base classes in the definition of a template (**vector**, in this case) because for a given instantiation an explicitly specialized version of the template might be used that does not have a given member. The special naming requirement guarantees that you won't end up calling a base class member in some cases and possibly a function from an enclosing scope (such as a global one) in other cases. The compiler has no way of knowing that a call to **begin( )** is dependent, so we must give it a clue with a "**this->**" qualification.[13] This tells the compiler that **begin( )** is in the scope of **PQV**, so it waits until an instance of **PQV** is fully instantiated. If this qualifying prefix is left out, the compiler will attempt an early lookup for the names **begin** and **end** (at template definition time, and will fail to find them because there are no such names declared in enclosing lexical scopes in this example). In the code above, however, the compiler waits until the point of instantiation of **pqi**, and then finds the correct specializations of **begin( )** and **end( )** in **vector<int>**.

---

[12] This means they depend in some way on a template parameter. See Chapter 5 in the section entitled "Name Lookup Issues."
[13] As we explained in Chapter 5, any valid qualification, such as PQV::, will do.

The only drawback to this solution is that the user must remember to call **sort( )** before viewing it as a sorted sequence (although one could conceivably redefine all the member functions that produce iterators so that they guarantee sorting). Another solution is to create a priority queue that is not a **vector**, but will build you a **vector** whenever you want one:

```
//: C07:PriorityQueue7.cpp
// A priority queue that will hand you a vector.
#include <algorithm>
#include <cstdlib>
#include <ctime>
#include <iostream>
#include <iterator>
#include <queue>
#include <vector>
using namespace std;

template<class T, class Compare> class PQV {
  vector<T> v;
  Compare comp;
public:
  // Don't need to call make_heap(); it's empty:
  PQV(Compare cmp = Compare()) : comp(cmp) {}
  void push(const T& x) {
    v.push_back(x); // Put it at the end
    // Re-adjust the heap:
    push_heap(v.begin(), v.end(), comp);
  }
  void pop() {
    // Move the top element to the last position:
    pop_heap(v.begin(), v.end(), comp);
    v.pop_back(); // Remove that element
  }
  const T& top() { return v.front(); }
  bool empty() const { return v.empty(); }
  int size() const { return v.size(); }
  typedef vector<T> TVec;
  TVec getVector() {
    TVec r(v.begin(), v.end());
    // It's already a heap
    sort_heap(r.begin(), r.end(), comp);
    // Put it into priority-queue order:
    reverse(r.begin(), r.end());
    return r;
```

```
    }
};

int main() {
  PQV<int, less<int> > pqi;
  srand(time(0));
  for(int i = 0; i < 100; i++)
    pqi.push(rand() % 25);
  const vector<int>& v = pqi.getVector();
  copy(v.begin(), v.end(),
    ostream_iterator<int>(cout, " "));
  cout << "\n-----------" << endl;
  while(!pqi.empty()) {
    cout << pqi.top() << ' ';
    pqi.pop();
  }
} ///:~
```

The **PQV** class template follows the same form as the STL's
priority_queue, but has the additional member **getVector( )**, which
creates a new **vector** that's a copy of the one in **PQV** (which means that it's
already a heap). It then sorts that copy (leaving **PQV**'s **vector** untouched),
and reverses the order so that traversing the new **vector** produces the same
effect as popping the elements from the priority queue.

You may observe that the approach of deriving from **priority_queue** used
in **PriorityQueue4.cpp** could be used with the above technique to produce
more succinct code:

```
//: C07:PriorityQueue8.cpp
// A more compact version of PriorityQueue7.cpp.
#include <algorithm>
#include <cstdlib>
#include <ctime>
#include <iostream>
#include <iterator>
#include <queue>
using namespace std;

template<class T> class PQV : public priority_queue<T> {
public:
  typedef vector<T> TVec;
  TVec getVector() {
    TVec r(this->c.begin(),this->c.end());
```

```
      // c is already a heap
      sort_heap(r.begin(), r.end(), this->comp);
      // Put it into priority-queue order:
      reverse(r.begin(), r.end());
      return r;
    }
};

int main() {
  PQV<int> pqi;
  srand(time(0));
  for(int i = 0; i < 100; i++)
    pqi.push(rand() % 25);
  const vector<int>& v = pqi.getVector();
  copy(v.begin(), v.end(),
    ostream_iterator<int>(cout, " "));
  cout << "\n-----------" << endl;
  while(!pqi.empty()) {
    cout << pqi.top() << ' ';
    pqi.pop();
  }
} ///:~
```

The brevity of this solution makes it the simplest and most desirable, plus it's guaranteed that the user will not have a **vector** in the unsorted state. The only potential problem is that the **getVector( )** member function returns the **vector<T>** by value, which might cause some overhead issues with complex values of the parameter type **T**.

Holding bits

Because C is a language that purports to be "close to the hardware," many have found it dismaying that there is no native binary representation for numbers. Decimal, of course, and hexadecimal (tolerable only because it's easier to group the bits in your mind), but octal? Ugh. Whenever you read specs for chips you're trying to program, they don't describe the chip registers in octal or even hexadecimal—they use binary. And yet C won't let you say **0b0101101**, which is the obvious solution for a language close to the hardware.

Although there's still no native binary representation in C++, things have improved with the addition of two classes: **bitset** and **vector<bool>**, both of which are designed to manipulate a group of on-off values.[14] The primary differences between these types are:

- Each **bitset** holds a fixed number of bits. You establish the quantity of bits in the **bitset** template argument. The **vector<bool>** can, like a regular **vector**, expand dynamically to hold any number of **bool** values.

- The **bitset** template is explicitly designed for performance when manipulating bits, and is not a "regular" STL container. As such, it has no iterators. The number of bits, being a template parameter, is known at compile time and allows the underlying integral array to be stored on the runtime stack. The **vector<bool>** container, on the other hand, is a specialization of a **vector** and so has all the operations of a normal **vector**—the specialization is just designed to be space efficient for **bool**.

There is no trivial conversion between a **bitset** and a **vector<bool>**, which implies that the two are for very different purposes. Furthermore, neither is a traditional "STL container." The **bitset** template class has an interface for bit-level operations and in no way resembles the STL containers we've discussed up to this point. The **vector<bool>** specialization of **vector** is similar to an STL-like container, but it differs as discussed below.

bitset<n>

The template for **bitset** accepts an unsigned integral template argument that is the number of bits to represent. Thus, **bitset<10>** is a different type than **bitset<20>**, and you cannot perform comparisons, assignments, and so on between the two.

A **bitset** provides the most commonly used bitwise operations in an efficient form. However, each **bitset** is implemented by logically packing bits in an array of integral types (typically **unsigned long**s, which contain at least 32

---

[14] Chuck designed and provided the original reference implementations for **bitset** and also **bitstring**, the precursor to **vector<bool>**, while an active member of the C++ Standards Committee in the early 1990s.

---

bits). In addition, the only conversion from a **bitset** to a numerical value is to an **unsigned long** (via the function **to_ulong( )**).

The following example tests almost all the functionality of the **bitset** (the missing operations are redundant or trivial). You'll see the description of each of the bitset outputs to the right of the output so that the bits all line up and you can compare them to the source values. If you still don't understand bitwise operations, running this program should help.

```cpp
//: C07:BitSet.cpp {-bor}
// Exercising the bitset class.
#include <bitset>
#include <climits>
#include <cstdlib>
#include <ctime>
#include <cstddef>
#include <iostream>
#include <string>
using namespace std;

const int SZ = 32;
typedef bitset<SZ> BS;

template<int bits> bitset<bits> randBitset() {
  bitset<bits> r(rand());
  for(int i = 0; i < bits/16 - 1; i++) {
    r <<= 16;
    // "OR" together with a new lower 16 bits:
    r |= bitset<bits>(rand());
  }
  return r;
}

int main() {
  srand(time(0));
  cout << "sizeof(bitset<16>) = "
       << sizeof(bitset<16>) << endl;
  cout << "sizeof(bitset<32>) = "
       << sizeof(bitset<32>) << endl;
  cout << "sizeof(bitset<48>) = "
       << sizeof(bitset<48>) << endl;
  cout << "sizeof(bitset<64>) = "
       << sizeof(bitset<64>) << endl;
  cout << "sizeof(bitset<65>) = "
```

```
             << sizeof(bitset<65>) << endl;
BS a(randBitset<SZ>()), b(randBitset<SZ>());
// Converting from a bitset:
unsigned long ul = a.to_ulong();
cout << a << endl;
// Converting a string to a bitset:
string cbits("1110110101110111");
cout << "as a string = " << cbits <<endl;
cout << BS(cbits) << " [BS(cbits)]" << endl;
cout << BS(cbits, 2) << " [BS(cbits, 2)]" << endl;
cout << BS(cbits, 2, 11) << " [BS(cbits, 2, 11)]"<< endl;
cout << a << " [a]" << endl;
cout << b << " [b]" << endl;
// Bitwise AND:
cout << (a & b) << " [a & b]" << endl;
cout << (BS(a) &= b) << " [a &= b]" << endl;
// Bitwise OR:
cout << (a | b) << " [a | b]" << endl;
cout << (BS(a) |= b) << " [a |= b]" << endl;
// Exclusive OR:
cout << (a ^ b) << " [a ^ b]" << endl;
cout << (BS(a) ^= b) << " [a ^= b]" << endl;
cout << a << " [a]" << endl; // For reference
// Logical left shift (fill with zeros):
cout << (BS(a) <<= SZ/2) << " [a <<= (SZ/2)]" << endl;
cout << (a << SZ/2) << endl;
cout << a << " [a]" << endl; // For reference
// Logical right shift (fill with zeros):
cout << (BS(a) >>= SZ/2) << " [a >>= (SZ/2)]" << endl;
cout << (a >> SZ/2) << endl;
cout << a << " [a]" << endl; // For reference
cout << BS(a).set() << " [a.set()]" << endl;
for(int i = 0; i < SZ; i++)
  if(!a.test(i)) {
    cout << BS(a).set(i)
         << " [a.set(" << i <<")]" << endl;
    break; // Just do one example of this
  }
cout << BS(a).reset() << " [a.reset()]"<< endl;
for(int j = 0; j < SZ; j++)
  if(a.test(j)) {
    cout << BS(a).reset(j)
         << " [a.reset(" << j <<")]" << endl;
    break; // Just do one example of this
  }
```

```cpp
  cout << BS(a).flip() << " [a.flip()]" << endl;
  cout << ~a << " [~a]" << endl;
  cout << a << " [a]" << endl; // For reference
  cout << BS(a).flip(1) << " [a.flip(1)]"<< endl;
  BS c;
  cout << c << " [c]" << endl;
  cout << "c.count() = " << c.count() << endl;
  cout << "c.any() = "
       << (c.any() ? "true" : "false") << endl;
  cout << "c.none() = "
       << (c.none() ? "true" : "false") << endl;
  c[1].flip(); c[2].flip();
  cout << c << " [c]" << endl;
  cout << "c.count() = " << c.count() << endl;
  cout << "c.any() = "
       << (c.any() ? "true" : "false") << endl;
  cout << "c.none() = "
       << (c.none() ? "true" : "false") << endl;
  // Array indexing operations:
  c.reset();
  for(size_t k = 0; k < c.size(); k++)
    if(k % 2 == 0)
      c[k].flip();
  cout << c << " [c]" << endl;
  c.reset();
  // Assignment to bool:
  for(size_t ii = 0; ii < c.size(); ii++)
    c[ii] = (rand() % 100) < 25;
  cout << c << " [c]" << endl;
  // bool test:
  if(c[1])
    cout << "c[1] == true";
  else
    cout << "c[1] == false" << endl;
} ///:~
```

To generate interesting random **bitset**s, the **randBitset( )** function is
created. This function demonstrates **operator<<=** by shifting each 16
random bits to the left until the **bitset** (which is templatized in this function
for size) is full. The generated number and each new 16 bits are combined
using the **operator|=**.

The **main( )** function first shows the unit size of a **bitset**. If it is less than 32
bits, **sizeof** produces 4 (4 bytes = 32 bits), which is the size of a single **long**

on most implementations. If it's between 32 and 64, it requires two **long**s, greater than 64 requires 3 **long**s, and so on. Thus, you make the best use of space if you use a bit quantity that fits in an integral number of **long**s. However, notice there's no extra overhead for the object—it's as if you were hand-coding for a **long**.

Although there are no other numerical conversions from **bitset** besides **to_ulong( )**, there is a **stream inserter** that produces a **string** containing ones and zeros, and this can be as long as the actual **bitset**.

There's still no primitive format for binary values, but **bitset** supports the next best thing: a **string** of ones and zeros with the least-significant bit (lsb) on the right. The three constructors demonstrated take the entire **string**, the **string** starting at character 2, and the string from character 2 through 11. You can write to an **ostream** from a **bitset** using **operator<<**, and it comes out as ones and zeros. You can also read from an **istream** using **operator>>** (not shown here).

You'll notice that **bitset** only has three nonmember operators: *and* (**&**), *or* (**|**), and *exclusive-or* (**^**). Each of these creates a new **bitset** as its return value. All the member operators opt for the more efficient **&=**, **|=**, and so on, where a temporary is not created. However, these forms change the **bitset**'s value (which is **a** in most of the tests in the above example). To prevent this, we created a temporary to be used as the lvalue by invoking the copy-constructor on **a**; this is why you see the form **BS(a)**. The result of each test is displayed, and occasionally **a** is reprinted so you can easily look at it for reference.

The rest of the example should be self-explanatory when you run it; if not you can find the details in your compiler's documentation or in the other documentation mentioned earlier in this chapter.

vector<bool>

The **vector<bool>** container is a specialization of the **vector** template. A normal **bool** variable requires at least one byte, but since a **bool** only has two states, the ideal implementation of **vector<bool>** is such that each **bool** value only requires one bit. Since typical library implementations pack the bits into integral arrays, the iterator must be specially defined and cannot be a pointer to **bool**.

The bit-manipulation functions for **vector<bool>** are much more limited than those of **bitset**. The only member function that was added to those already in **vector** is **flip( )**, to invert all the bits. There is no **set( )** or **reset( )** as in **bitset**. When you use **operator[ ]**, you get back an object of type **vector<bool>::reference**, which also has a **flip( )** to invert that individual bit.

```
//: C07:VectorOfBool.cpp
// Demonstrate the vector<bool> specialization.
#include <bitset>
#include <cstddef>
#include <iostream>
#include <iterator>
#include <sstream>
#include <vector>
using namespace std;

int main() {
  vector<bool> vb(10, true);
  vector<bool>::iterator it;
  for(it = vb.begin(); it != vb.end(); it++)
    cout << *it;
  cout << endl;
  vb.push_back(false);
  ostream_iterator<bool> out(cout, "");
  copy(vb.begin(), vb.end(), out);
  cout << endl;
  bool ab[] = { true, false, false, true, true,
    true, true, false, false, true };
  // There's a similar constructor:
  vb.assign(ab, ab + sizeof(ab)/sizeof(bool));
  copy(vb.begin(), vb.end(), out);
  cout << endl;
  vb.flip(); // Flip all bits
  copy(vb.begin(), vb.end(), out);
  cout << endl;
  for(size_t i = 0; i < vb.size(); i++)
    vb[i] = 0; // (Equivalent to "false")
  vb[4] = true;
  vb[5] = 1;
  vb[7].flip(); // Invert one bit
  copy(vb.begin(), vb.end(), out);
  cout << endl;
  // Convert to a bitset:
```

```
    ostringstream os;
    copy(vb.begin(), vb.end(),
      ostream_iterator<bool>(os, ""));
    bitset<10> bs(os.str());
    cout << "Bitset:" << endl << bs << endl;
} ///:~
```

The last part of this example takes a **vector<bool>** and converts it to a **bitset** by first turning it into a **string** of ones and zeros. Here, you must know the size of the **bitset** at compile time. You can see that this conversion is not the kind of operation you'll want to do on a regular basis.

The **vector<bool>** specialization is a "crippled" STL container in the sense that certain guarantees that other containers provide are missing. For example, with the other containers the following relationships hold:

```
// Let c be an STL container other than vector<bool>:
T& r = c.front();
T* p = &*c.begin();
```

For all other containers, the **front( )** function yields an lvalue (something you can get a non-const reference to), and **begin( )** must yield something you can dereference and then take the address of. Neither is possible because bits are not addressable. Both **vector<bool>** and **bitset** use a proxy class (the nested **reference** class, mentioned earlier) to read and set bits as necessary.

Associative containers

The **set**, **map**, **multiset**, and **multimap** are called *associative containers* because they associate *keys* with *values*. Well, at least **map**s and **multimap**s associate keys with values, but you can look at a **set** as a **map** that has no values, only keys (and they can in fact be implemented this way), and the same for the relationship between **multiset** and **multimap**. So, because of the structural similarity, **set**s and **multiset**s are lumped in with associative containers.

The most important basic operations with associative containers are putting things in and, in the case of a **set**, seeing if something is in the set. In the case of a **map**, you want to first see if a key is in the **map**, and if it exists, you want the associated value for that key. There are many variations on this theme, but that's the fundamental concept. The following example shows these basics:

```cpp
//: C07:AssociativeBasics.cpp {-bor}
// Basic operations with sets and maps.
//{L} Noisy
#include <cstddef>
#include <iostream>
#include <iterator>
#include <map>
#include <set>
#include "Noisy.h"
using namespace std;

int main() {
  Noisy na[7];
  // Add elements via constructor:
  set<Noisy> ns(na, na + sizeof na/sizeof(Noisy));
  Noisy n;
  ns.insert(n); // Ordinary insertion
  cout << endl;
  // Check for set membership:
  cout << "ns.count(n)= " << ns.count(n) << endl;
  if(ns.find(n) != ns.end())
    cout << "n(" << n << ") found in ns" << endl;
  // Print elements:
  copy(ns.begin(), ns.end(),
    ostream_iterator<Noisy>(cout, " "));
  cout << endl;
  cout << "\n-----------" << endl;
  map<int, Noisy> nm;
  for(int i = 0; i < 10; i++)
    nm[i]; // Automatically makes pairs
  cout << "\n-----------" << endl;
  for(size_t j = 0; j < nm.size(); j++)
    cout << "nm[" << j <<"] = " << nm[j] << endl;
  cout << "\n-----------" << endl;
  nm[10] = n;
  cout << "\n-----------" << endl;
  nm.insert(make_pair(47, n));
  cout << "\n-----------" << endl;
  cout << "\n nm.count(10)= " << nm.count(10) << endl;
  cout << "nm.count(11)= " << nm.count(11) << endl;
  map<int, Noisy>::iterator it = nm.find(6);
```

```
    if(it != nm.end())
      cout << "value:" << (*it).second
           << " found in nm at location 6" << endl;
    for(it = nm.begin(); it != nm.end(); it++)
      cout << (*it).first << ":" << (*it).second << ", ";
    cout << "\n----------" << endl;
} ///:~
```

The **set<Noisy>** object **ns** is created using two iterators into an array of
Noisy objects, but there is also a default constructor and a copy-constructor,
and you can pass in an object that provides an alternate scheme for doing
comparisons. Both **set**s and **map**s have an **insert( )** member function to put
things in, and you can check to see if an object is already in an associative
container in two ways. The **count( )** member function, when given a key, will
tell you how many times that key occurs. (This can only be zero or one in a
set or **map**, but it can be more than one with a **multiset** or **multimap**.)
The **find( )** member function will produce an iterator indicating the first
occurrence (with **set** and **map**, the *only* occurrence) of the key that you give
it or will produce the past-the-end iterator if it can't find the key. The
count( ) and **find( )** member functions exist for all the associative
containers, which makes sense. The associative containers also have member
functions **lower_bound( )**, **upper_bound( )**, and **equal_range( )**,
which only make sense for **multiset** and **multimap**, as you will see. (But
don't try to figure out how they would be useful for **set** and **map**, since they
are designed for dealing with a range of duplicate keys, which those
containers don't allow.)

Designing an **operator[ ]** always presents a bit of a dilemma. Because it's
intended to be treated as an array-indexing operation, people don't tend to
think about performing a test before they use it. But what happens if you
decide to index out of the bounds of the array? One option is to throw an
exception, but with a **map**, "indexing out of the array" could mean that you
want to create a new entry at that location, and that's the way the STL **map**
treats it. The first **for** loop after the creation of the **map<int, Noisy> nm**
just "looks up" objects using the **operator[ ]**, but this is actually creating
new **Noisy** objects! The **map** creates a new key-value pair (using the default
constructor for the value) if you look up a value with **operator[ ]** and it isn't
there. This means that if you really just want to look something up and not
create a new entry, you must use the member functions **count( )** (to see if it's
there) or **find( )** (to get an iterator to it).

A number of problems are associated with the **for** loop that prints the values of the container using **operator[ ]**. First, it requires integral keys (which we happen to have here). Next and worse, if all the keys are not sequential, you'll end up counting from zero to the size of the container, and if some spots don't have key-value pairs, you'll automatically create them and miss some of the higher values of the keys. Finally, if you look at the output from the **for** loop, you'll see that things are *very* busy, and it's quite puzzling at first why there are so many constructions and destructions for what appears to be a simple lookup. The answer only becomes clear when you look at the code in the **map** template for **operator[ ]**, which will be something like this:

```
mapped_type& operator[] (const key_type& k) {
  value_type tmp(k,T());
  return (*((insert(tmp)).first)).second;
}
```

The **map::insert( )** function takes a key-value pair and does nothing if there is already an entry in the map with the given key—otherwise it inserts an entry for the key. In either case, it returns a new key-value pair holding an iterator to the inserted pair as its first element and holding true as the second element if an insertion took place. The members **first** and **second** give the key and value, respectively, because **map::value_type** is really just a **typedef** for a **std::pair**:

```
typedef pair<const Key, T> value_type;
```

You've seen the **std::pair** template before. It's a simple holder for two values of independent types, as you can see by its definition:

```
template<class T1, class T2> struct pair {
  typedef T1 first_type;
  typedef T2 second_type;
  T1 first;
  T2 second;
  pair();
  pair(const T1& x, const T2& y) : first(x), second(y) {}
  // Templatized copy-constructor:
  template<class U, class V> pair(const pair<U, V> &p);
};
```

The **pair** template class is very useful, especially when you want to return two objects from a function (since a **return** statement only takes one object).

There's even a shorthand for creating a pair called **make_pair( )**, which is used in **AssociativeBasics.cpp**.

So to retrace the steps, **map::value_type** is a **pair** of the key and the value of the map—actually, it's a single entry for the map. But notice that **pair** packages its objects by value, which means that copy-constructions are necessary to get the objects into the **pair**. Thus, the creation of **tmp** in **map::operator[ ]** will involve at least a copy-constructor call and destructor call for each object in the **pair**. Here, we're getting off easy because the key is an **int**. But if you want to really see what kind of activity can result from **map::operator[ ]**, try running this:

```
//: C07:NoisyMap.cpp
// Mapping Noisy to Noisy.
//{L} Noisy
#include <map>
#include "Noisy.h"
using namespace std;

int main() {
  map<Noisy, Noisy> mnn;
  Noisy n1, n2;
  cout << "\n--------" << endl;
  mnn[n1] = n2;
  cout << "\n--------" << endl;
  cout << mnn[n1] << endl;
  cout << "\n--------" << endl;
} ///:~
```

You'll see that both the insertion and lookup generate a lot of extra objects, and that's because of the creation of the **tmp** object. If you look back up at **map::operator[ ]**, you'll see that the second line calls **insert( )**, passing it **tmp**—that is, **operator[ ]** does an insertion every time. The return value of **insert( )** is a different kind of **pair**, where **first** is an iterator pointing to the key-value **pair** that was just inserted, and **second** is a **bool** indicating whether the insertion took place. You can see that **operator[ ]** grabs **first** (the iterator), dereferences it to produce the **pair**, and then returns the **second**, which is the value at that location.

So on the upside, **map** has this fancy "make a new entry if one isn't there" behavior, but the downside is that you *always* get a lot of extra object creations and destructions when you use **map::operator[ ]**. Fortunately,

AssociativeBasics.cpp also demonstrates how to reduce the overhead of insertions and deletions, by avoiding **operator[ ]** if you don't need it. The **insert( )** member function is slightly more efficient than **operator[ ]**. With a **set**, you hold only one object, but with a **map**, you hold key-value pairs; so **insert( )** requires a **pair** as its argument. Here's where **make_pair( )** comes in handy, as you can see.

For looking objects up in a **map**, you can use **count( )** to see whether a key is in the map, or you can use **find( )** to produce an iterator pointing directly at the key-value pair. Again, since the **map** contains **pair**s, that's what the iterator produces when you dereference it, so you have to select **first** and **second**. When you run **AssociativeBasics.cpp**, you'll notice that the iterator approach involves no extra object creations or destructions. It's not as easy to write or read, though.

Generators and fillers for associative containers

You've seen how useful the **fill( )**, **fill_n( )**, **generate( )**, and **generate_n( )** function templates in **<algorithm>** have been for filling the sequential containers (**vector**, **list**, and **deque**) with data. However, these are implemented by using **operator=** to assign values into the sequential containers, and the way that you add objects to associative containers is with their respective **insert( )** member functions. Thus, the default "assignment" behavior causes a problem when trying to use the "fill" and "generate" functions with associative containers.

One solution is to duplicate the "fill" and "generate" functions, creating new ones that can be used with associative containers. It turns out that only the **fill_n( )** and **generate_n( )** functions can be duplicated (**fill( )** and **generate( )** copy sequences, which doesn't make sense with associative containers), but the job is fairly easy, since you have the **<algorithm>** header file to work from:

```
//: C07:assocGen.h
// The fill_n() and generate_n() equivalents
// for associative containers.
#ifndef ASSOCGEN_H
#define ASSOCGEN_H

template<class Assoc, class Count, class T>
```

```
void assocFill_n(Assoc& a, Count n, const T& val) {
  while(n-- > 0)
    a.insert(val);
}

template<class Assoc, class Count, class Gen>
void assocGen_n(Assoc& a, Count n, Gen g) {
  while(n-- > 0)
    a.insert(g());
}
#endif // ASSOCGEN_H ///:~
```

You can see that instead of using iterators, the container class itself is passed (by reference, of course).

This code demonstrates two valuable lessons. The first is that if the algorithms don't do what you want, copy the nearest thing and modify it. You have the example at hand in the STL header, so most of the work has already been done.

The second lesson is more pointed: if you look long enough, there's probably a way to do it in the STL *without* inventing anything new. The present problem can instead be solved by using an **insert_iterator** (produced by a call to **inserter( )**), which calls **insert( )** to place items in the container instead of **operator=**. This is *not* simply a variation of **front_insert_iterator** or **back_insert_iterator** because those iterators use **push_front( )** and **push_back( )**, respectively. Each of the insert iterators is different by virtue of the member function it uses for insertion, and **insert( )** is the one we need. Here's a demonstration that shows filling and generating both a **map** and a **set**. (It can also be used with **multimap** and **multiset**.) First, some templatized generators are created. (This may seem like overkill, but you never know when you'll need them. For that reason they're placed in a header file.)

```
//: C07:SimpleGenerators.h
// Generic generators, including one that creates pairs.
#include <iostream>
#include <utility>

// A generator that increments its value:
template<typename T> class IncrGen {
  T i;
```

```
public:
  IncrGen(T ii) : i(ii) {}
  T operator()() { return i++; }
};

// A generator that produces an STL pair<>:
template<typename T1, typename T2> class PairGen {
  T1 i;
  T2 j;
public:
  PairGen(T1 ii, T2 jj) : i(ii), j(jj) {}
  std::pair<T1,T2> operator()() {
    return std::pair<T1,T2>(i++, j++);
  }
};

namespace std {
// A generic global operator<< for printing any STL pair<>:
template<typename F, typename S> ostream&
operator<<(ostream& os, const pair<F,S>& p) {
  return os << p.first << "\t" << p.second << endl;
}
} ///:~
```

Both generators expect that **T** can be incremented, and they simply use **operator++** to generate new values from whatever you used for initialization. **PairGen** creates an STL **pair** object as its return value, and that's what can be placed into a **map** or **multimap** using **insert( )**.

The last function is a generalization of **operator<<** for **ostream**s, so that any **pair** can be printed, assuming each element of the **pair** supports a stream **operator<<**. (It is in namespace **std** for the strange name lookup reasons discussed in Chapter 5, and explained once again after **Thesaurus.cpp** later on in this chapter.) As you can see in the following, this allows the use of **copy( )** to output the **map**:

```
//: C07:AssocInserter.cpp
// Using an insert_iterator so fill_n() and generate_n()
// can be used with associative containers.
#include <iterator>
#include <iostream>
#include <algorithm>
#include <set>
#include <map>
```

```
#include "SimpleGenerators.h"
using namespace std;

int main() {
  set<int> s;
  fill_n(inserter(s, s.begin()), 10, 47);
  generate_n(inserter(s, s.begin()), 10,
    IncrGen<int>(12));
  copy(s.begin(), s.end(),
    ostream_iterator<int>(cout, "\n"));
  map<int, int> m;
  fill_n(inserter(m, m.begin()), 10, make_pair(90,120));
  generate_n(inserter(m, m.begin()), 10,
    PairGen<int, int>(3, 9));
  copy(m.begin(), m.end(),
    ostream_iterator<pair<int,int> >(cout,"\n"));
} ///:~
```

The second argument to **inserter** is an iterator, which is an optimization hint to help the insertion go faster (instead of always starting the search at the root of the underlying tree). Since an **insert_iterator** can be used with many different types of containers, with non-associative containers it is more than a hint—it is required.

Note how the **ostream_iterator** is created to output a **pair**. This won't work if the **operator<<** isn't created. Since it's a template, it is automatically instantiated for **pair<int, int>**.

The magic of maps

An ordinary array uses an integral value to index into a sequential set of elements of some type. A **map** is an *associative array*, which means you associate one object with another in an array-like fashion. Instead of selecting an array element with a number as you do with an ordinary array, you look it up with an object! The example that follows counts the words in a text file, so the index is the **string** object representing the word, and the value being looked up is the object that keeps count of the strings.

In a single-item container such as a **vector** or a **list**, only one thing is being held. But in a **map**, you've got two things: the *key* (what you look up by, as in **mapname[key]**) and the *value* that results from the lookup with the key. If you simply want to move through the entire **map** and list each key-value pair, you use an iterator, which when dereferenced produces a **pair** object containing both the key and the value. You access the members of a **pair** by selecting **first** or **second**.

This same philosophy of packaging two items together is also used to insert elements into the map, but the **pair** is created as part of the instantiated **map** and is called **value_type**, containing the key and the value. So one option for inserting a new element is to create a **value_type** object, loading it with the appropriate objects and then calling the **insert( )** member function for the **map**. Instead, the following example uses the aforementioned special feature of **map**: if you're trying to find an object by passing in a key to **operator[ ]** and that object doesn't exist, **operator[ ]** will automatically insert a new key-value pair for you, using the default constructor for the value object. With that in mind, consider an implementation of a word-counting program:

```
//: C07:WordCount.cpp
// Count occurrences of words using a map.
#include <iostream>
#include <fstream>
#include <map>
#include <string>
#include "../require.h"
using namespace std;

int main(int argc, char* argv[]) {
  typedef map<string, int> WordMap;
  typedef WordMap::iterator WMIter;
  const char* fname = "WordCount.cpp";
  if(argc > 1) fname = argv[1];
  ifstream in(fname);
  assure(in, fname);
  WordMap wordmap;
  string word;
  while(in >> word)
    wordmap[word]++;
  for(WMIter w = wordmap.begin(); w != wordmap.end(); w++)
    cout << w->first << ": " << w->second << endl;
} ///:~
```

This example shows the power of *zero-initialization*. Consider this line of code from the program:

```
wordmap[word]++;
```

This expression increments the **int** associated with **word**. If there isn't such a word in the map, a key-value pair for the word is automatically inserted, with the value initialized to zero by a call to the pseudo-constructor **int( )**, which returns a 0.

Printing the entire list requires traversing it with an iterator. (There's no **copy( )** shortcut for a **map** unless you want to write an **operator<<** for the **pair** in the map.) As previously mentioned, dereferencing this iterator produces a **pair** object, with the **first** member the key and the **second** member the value.

If you want to find the count for a particular word, you can use the array index operator, like this:

```
cout << "the: " << wordmap["the"] << endl;
```

You can see that one of the great advantages of the **map** is the clarity of the syntax; an associative array makes intuitive sense to the reader. (Note, however, that if "the" isn't already in the **wordmap**, a new entry will be created!)

Multimaps and duplicate keys

A **multimap** is a **map** that can contain duplicate keys. At first this may seem like a strange idea, but it can occur surprisingly often. A phone book, for example, can have many entries with the same name.

Suppose you are monitoring wildlife, and you want to keep track of where and when each type of animal is spotted. Thus, you may see many animals of the same kind, all in different locations and at different times. So if the type of animal is the key, you'll need a **multimap**. Here's what it looks like:

```
//: C07:WildLifeMonitor.cpp
#include <algorithm>
#include <cstdlib>
#include <cstddef>
#include <ctime>
#include <iostream>
#include <iterator>
#include <map>
```

```
#include <sstream>
#include <string>
#include <vector>
using namespace std;

class DataPoint {
  int x, y; // Location coordinates
  time_t time; // Time of Sighting
public:
  DataPoint() : x(0), y(0), time(0) {}
  DataPoint(int xx, int yy, time_t tm) :
    x(xx), y(yy), time(tm) {}
  // Synthesized operator=, copy-constructor OK
  int getX() const { return x; }
  int getY() const { return y; }
  const time_t* getTime() const { return &time; }
};

string animal[] = {
  "chipmunk", "beaver", "marmot", "weasel",
  "squirrel", "ptarmigan", "bear", "eagle",
  "hawk", "vole", "deer", "otter", "hummingbird",
};
const int ASZ = sizeof animal/sizeof *animal;
vector<string> animals(animal, animal + ASZ);

// All the information is contained in a
// "Sighting," which can be sent to an ostream:
typedef pair<string, DataPoint> Sighting;

ostream&
operator<<(ostream& os, const Sighting& s) {
  return os << s.first << " sighted at x= "
    << s.second.getX() << ", y= " << s.second.getY()
    << ", time = " << ctime(s.second.getTime());
}

// A generator for Sightings:
class SightingGen {
  vector<string>& animals;
  enum { D = 100 };
public:
  SightingGen(vector<string>& an) : animals(an) {}
  Sighting operator()() {
    Sighting result;
```

```
      int select = rand() % animals.size();
      result.first = animals[select];
      result.second = DataPoint(
        rand() % D, rand() % D, time(0));
      return result;
    }
};

// Display a menu of animals, allow the user to
// select one, return the index value:
int menu() {
  cout << "select an animal or 'q' to quit: ";
  for(size_t i = 0; i < animals.size(); i++)
    cout <<'['<< i <<']'<< animals[i] << ' ';
  cout << endl;
  string reply;
  cin >> reply;
  if(reply.at(0) == 'q') return 0;
  istringstream r(reply);
  int i;
  r >> i; // Converts to int
  i %= animals.size();
  return i;
}

int main() {
  typedef multimap<string, DataPoint> DataMap;
  typedef DataMap::iterator DMIter;
  DataMap sightings;
  srand(time(0));  // Randomize
  generate_n(inserter(sightings, sightings.begin()),
    50, SightingGen(animals));
  // Print everything:
  copy(sightings.begin(), sightings.end(),
    ostream_iterator<Sighting>(cout, ""));
  // Print sightings for selected animal:
  for(int count = 1; count < 10; count++) {
    // Use menu to get selection:
    // int i = menu();
    // Generate randomly (for automated testing):
    int i = rand() % animals.size();
    // Iterators in "range" denote begin, one
    // past end of matching range:
    pair<DMIter, DMIter> range =
      sightings.equal_range(animals[i]);
```

```
        copy(range.first, range.second,
          ostream_iterator<Sighting>(cout, ""));
    }
} ///:~
```

All the data about a sighting is encapsulated into the class **DataPoint**, which is simple enough that it can rely on the synthesized assignment and copy-constructor. It uses the Standard C library time functions to record the time of the sighting.

In the array of **string**, **animal**, notice that the **char*** constructor is automatically used during initialization, which makes initializing an array of **string** quite convenient. Since it's easier to use the animal names in a **vector**, the length of the array is calculated, and a **vector<string>** is initialized using the **vector(iterator, iterator)** constructor.

The key-value pairs that make up a **Sighting** are the **string**, which names the type of animal, and the **DataPoint**, which says where and when it was sighted. The standard **pair** template combines these two types and is typedefed to produce the **Sighting** type. Then an **ostream operator<<** is created for **Sighting**; this will allow you to iterate through a **map** or **multimap** of **Sighting**s and display it.

SightingGen generates random sightings at random data points to use for testing. It has the usual **operator( )** necessary for a function object, but it also has a constructor to capture and store a reference to a **vector<string>**, which is where the aforementioned animal names are stored.

A **DataMap** is a **multimap** of **string-DataPoint** pairs, which means it stores **Sighting**s. It is filled with 50 **Sighting**s using **generate_n( )** and displayed. (Notice that because there is an **operator<<** that takes a **Sighting**, an **ostream_iterator** can be created.) At this point the user is asked to select the animal for which they want to see all the sightings. If you press **q**, the program will quit, but if you select an animal number, the **equal_range( )** member function is invoked. This returns an iterator (**DMIter**) to the beginning of the set of matching pairs and an iterator indicating past-the-end of the set. Since only one object can be returned from a function, **equal_range( )** makes use of **pair**. Since the **range** pair has the beginning and ending iterators of the matching set, those iterators can be used in **copy( )** to print all the sightings for a particular type of animal.

Multisets

You've seen the **set**, which allows only one object of each value to be inserted. The **multiset** is odd by comparison since it allows more than one object of each value to be inserted. This seems to go against the whole idea of "setness," where you can ask, "Is 'it' in this set?" If there can be more than one "it," what does that question mean?

With some thought, you can see that it makes little sense to have more than one object of the same value in a set if those duplicate objects are *exactly* the same (with the possible exception of counting occurrences of objects, but as seen earlier in this chapter that can be handled in an alternative, more elegant fashion). Thus, each duplicate object will have something that makes it "different" from the other duplicates—most likely different state information that is not used in the calculation of the key during the comparison. That is, to the comparison operation, the objects look the same, but they contain some differing internal state.

Like any STL container that must order its elements, the **multiset** template uses the **less** function object by default to determine element ordering. This uses the contained class's **operator<**, but you can always substitute your own comparison function.

Consider a simple class that contains one element that is used in the comparison and another that is not:

```
//: C07:MultiSet1.cpp
// Demonstration of multiset behavior.
#include <algorithm>
#include <cstdlib>
#include <ctime>
#include <iostream>
#include <iterator>
#include <set>
using namespace std;

class X {
  char c; // Used in comparison
  int i; // Not used in comparison
  // Don't need default constructor and operator=
  X();
  X& operator=(const X&);
```

```
  // Usually need a copy-constructor (but the
  // synthesized version works here)
public:
  X(char cc, int ii) : c(cc), i(ii) {}
  // Notice no operator== is required
  friend bool operator<(const X& x, const X& y) {
    return x.c < y.c;
  }
  friend ostream& operator<<(ostream& os, X x) {
    return os << x.c << ":" << x.i;
  }
};

class Xgen {
  static int i;
  // Number of characters to select from:
  enum { SPAN = 6 };
public:
  X operator()() {
    char c = 'A' + rand() % SPAN;
    return X(c, i++);
  }
};

int Xgen::i = 0;

typedef multiset<X> Xmset;
typedef Xmset::const_iterator Xmit;

int main() {
  Xmset mset;
  // Fill it with X's:
  srand(time(0));  // Randomize
  generate_n(inserter(mset, mset.begin()), 25, Xgen());
  // Initialize a regular set from mset:
  set<X> unique(mset.begin(), mset.end());
  copy(unique.begin(), unique.end(),
    ostream_iterator<X>(cout, " "));
  cout << "\n----" << endl;
  // Iterate over the unique values:
  for(set<X>::iterator i = unique.begin();
      i != unique.end(); i++) {
    pair<Xmit, Xmit> p = mset.equal_range(*i);
    copy(p.first,p.second, ostream_iterator<X>(cout, " "));
    cout << endl;
```

```
        }
} ///:~
```

In **X**, all the comparisons are made with the **char c**. The comparison is performed with **operator<**, which is all that is necessary for the **multiset**, since in this example the default **less** comparison object is used. The class **Xgen** randomly generates **X** objects, but the comparison value is restricted to the span from '**A**' to '**E**'. In **main( )**, a **multiset<X>** is created and filled with 25 **X** objects using **Xgen**, guaranteeing that there will be duplicate keys. So that we know what the unique values are, a regular **set<X>** is created from the **multiset** (using the **iterator, iterator** constructor). These values are displayed, and then each one produces the **equal_range( )** in the **multiset** (**equal_range( )** has the same meaning here as it does with **multimap**: all the elements with matching keys). Each set of matching keys is then printed.

As a second example, a (possibly) more elegant version of **WordCount.cpp** can be created using **multiset**:

```
//: C07:MultiSetWordCount.cpp
// Count occurrences of words using a multiset.
#include <fstream>
#include <iostream>
#include <iterator>
#include <set>
#include <string>
#include "../require.h"
using namespace std;

int main(int argc, char* argv[]) {
  const char* fname = "MultiSetWordCount.cpp";
  if(argc > 1) fname = argv[1];
  ifstream in(fname);
  assure(in, fname);
  multiset<string> wordmset;
  string word;
  while(in >> word)
    wordmset.insert(word);
  typedef multiset<string>::iterator MSit;
  MSit it = wordmset.begin();
  while(it != wordmset.end()) {
    pair<MSit, MSit> p = wordmset.equal_range(*it);
    int count = distance(p.first, p.second);
```

```
    cout << *it << ": " << count << endl;
    it = p.second; // Move to the next word
  }
} ///:~
```

The setup in **main( )** is identical to **WordCount.cpp**, but then each word is simply inserted into the **multiset<string>**. An iterator is created and initialized to the beginning of the **multiset**; dereferencing this iterator produces the current word. The **equal_range( )** member function (not generic algorithm) produces the starting and ending iterators of the word that's currently selected, and the algorithm **distance( )** (defined in **<iterator>**) counts the number of elements in that range. The iterator **it** is then moved forward to the end of the range, which puts it at the next word. If you're unfamiliar with the **multiset**, this code can seem more complex. The density of it and the lack of need for supporting classes such as **Count** has a lot of appeal.

In the end, is this really a "set," or should it be called something else? An alternative is the generic "bag" that is defined in some container libraries, since a bag holds anything, without discrimination—including duplicate objects. This is close, but it doesn't quite fit since a bag has no specification about how elements should be ordered. A **multiset** (which requires that all duplicate elements be adjacent to each other) is even more restrictive than the concept of a set. A set implementation might use a hashing function to order its elements, which would not put them in sorted order. Besides, if you want to store a bunch of objects without any special criteria, you will probably just use a **vector**, **deque**, or **list**.

Combining STL containers

When using a thesaurus, you want to know all the words that are similar to a particular word. When you look up a word, then, you want a list of words as the result. Here, the "multi" containers (**multimap** or **multiset**) are not appropriate. The solution is to combine containers, which is easily done using the STL. Here, we need a tool that turns out to be a powerful general concept, which is a **map** that associates a string with a **vector**:

```
//: C07:Thesaurus.cpp
// A map of vectors.
#include <map>
```

```cpp
#include <vector>
#include <string>
#include <iostream>
#include <iterator>
#include <algorithm>
#include <ctime>
#include <cstdlib>
using namespace std;

typedef map<string, vector<string> > Thesaurus;
typedef pair<string, vector<string> > TEntry;
typedef Thesaurus::iterator TIter;

// Name lookup work-around:
namespace std {
ostream& operator<<(ostream& os,const TEntry& t) {
  os << t.first << ": ";
  copy(t.second.begin(), t.second.end(),
    ostream_iterator<string>(os, " "));
  return os;
}
}

// A generator for thesaurus test entries:
class ThesaurusGen {
  static const string letters;
  static int count;
public:
  int maxSize() { return letters.size(); }
  TEntry operator()() {
    TEntry result;
    if(count >= maxSize()) count = 0;
    result.first = letters[count++];
    int entries = (rand() % 5) + 2;
    for(int i = 0; i < entries; i++) {
      int choice = rand() % maxSize();
      char cbuf[2] = { 0 };
      cbuf[0] = letters[choice];
      result.second.push_back(cbuf);
    }
    return result;
  }
};

int ThesaurusGen::count = 0;
```

```cpp
const string ThesaurusGen::letters("ABCDEFGHIJKL"
  "MNOPQRSTUVWXYZabcdefghijklmnopqrstuvwxyz");

// Ask for a "word" to look up:
string menu(Thesaurus& thesaurus) {
  while(true) {
    cout << "Select a \"word\", 0 to quit: ";
    for(TIter it = thesaurus.begin();
        it != thesaurus.end(); it++)
      cout << (*it).first << ' ';
    cout << endl;
    string reply;
    cin >> reply;
    if(reply.at(0) == '0') exit(0); // Quit
    if(thesaurus.find(reply) == thesaurus.end())
      continue; // Not in list, try again
    return reply;
  }
}

int main() {
  srand(time(0)); // Seed the random number generator
  Thesaurus thesaurus;
  // Fill with 10 entries:
  generate_n(inserter(thesaurus, thesaurus.begin()),
    10, ThesaurusGen());
  // Print everything:
  copy(thesaurus.begin(), thesaurus.end(),
    ostream_iterator<TEntry>(cout, "\n"));
  // Create a list of the keys:
  string keys[10];
  int i = 0;
  for(TIter it = thesaurus.begin();
    it != thesaurus.end(); it++)
    keys[i++] = (*it).first;
  for(int count = 0; count < 10; count++) {
    // Enter from the console:
    // string reply = menu(thesaurus);
    // Generate randomly
    string reply = keys[rand() % 10];
    vector<string>& v = thesaurus[reply];
    copy(v.begin(), v.end(),
      ostream_iterator<string>(cout, " "));
    cout << endl;
  }
```

```
} ///:~
```

A **Thesaurus** maps a **string** (the word) to a **vector<string>** (the synonyms). A **TEntry** is a single entry in a **Thesaurus**. By creating an **ostream operator<<** for a **TEntry**, a single entry from the **Thesaurus** can easily be printed (and the whole **Thesaurus** can easily be printed with **copy( )**). Notice the very strange placement of the stream inserter: we put it inside the **std** namespace![15] This **operator<<( )** function is used by **ostream_iterator** in the first call to **copy( )** in **main( )** above. When the compiler instantiates the needed **ostream_iterator** specialization, according to the rules of argument-dependent lookup (ADL) it only looks in **std** because that is where all the arguments to **copy( )** are declared. If we declared our inserter in the global namespace (by removing the namespace block around it), then it would not be found. By placing it in **std** we enable ADL to find it.

The **ThesaurusGen** creates "words" (which are just single letters) and "synonyms" for those words (which are just other randomly chosen single letters) to be used as thesaurus entries. It randomly chooses the number of synonym entries to make, but there must be at least two. All the letters are chosen by indexing into a **static string** that is part of **ThesaurusGen**.

In **main( )**, a **Thesaurus** is created, filled with 10 entries and printed using the **copy( )** algorithm. The **menu( )** function asks the user to choose a "word" to look up by typing the letter of that word. The **find( )** member function discovers whether the entry exists in the **map**. (Remember, you don't want to use **operator[ ]**, which will automatically make a new entry if it doesn't find a match!) If so, **operator[ ]** fetches out the **vector<string>** that is displayed. The selection of the **reply** string is generated randomly, to allow automated testing.

Because templates make the expression of powerful concepts easy, you can take this concept much further, creating a **map** of **vector**s containing **map**s, and so on. For that matter, you can combine any of the STL containers this way.

---

[15] Technically, it is not legal for users to add to the standard namespace, but it is the easiest way to avoid this obscure name lookup problem, and is supported by all the compilers we use.

Cleaning up
containers of pointers

In **Stlshape.cpp**, the pointers did not clean themselves up automatically. It would be convenient to be able to do this easily, rather than writing out the code each time. Here is a function template that will clean up the pointers in any sequence container. Note that it is placed in the book's root directory for easy access:

```
//: :purge.h
// Delete pointers in an STL sequence container.
#ifndef PURGE_H
#define PURGE_H
#include <algorithm>

template<class Seq> void purge(Seq& c) {
  typename Seq::iterator i;
  for(i = c.begin(); i != c.end(); ++i) {
    delete *i;
    *i = 0;
  }
}

// Iterator version:
template<class InpIt> void purge(InpIt begin, InpIt end) {
  while(begin != end) {
    delete *begin;
    *begin = 0;
    ++begin;
  }
}
#endif // PURGE_H ///:~
```

In the first version of **purge( )**, note that **typename** is absolutely necessary. This is exactly the case that keyword was designed to solve: **Seq** is a template argument, and **iterator** is something that is nested within that template. So what does **Seq::iterator** refer to? The **typename** keyword specifies that it refers to a type, and not something else.

Although the container version of **purge( )** must work with an STL-style container, the iterator version of **purge( )** will work with any range, including an array.

Here is a rewrite of **Stlshape.cpp**, modified to use the **purge( )** function:

```
//: C07:Stlshape2.cpp
// Stlshape.cpp with the purge() function.
#include <iostream>
#include <vector>
#include "../purge.h"
using namespace std;

class Shape {
public:
  virtual void draw() = 0;
  virtual ~Shape() {};
};

class Circle : public Shape {
public:
  void draw() { cout << "Circle::draw" << endl; }
  ~Circle() { cout << "~Circle" << endl; }
};

class Triangle : public Shape {
public:
  void draw() { cout << "Triangle::draw" << endl; }
  ~Triangle() { cout << "~Triangle" << endl; }
};

class Square : public Shape {
public:
  void draw() { cout << "Square::draw" << endl; }
  ~Square() { cout << "~Square" << endl; }
};

int main() {
  typedef std::vector<Shape*> Container;
  typedef Container::iterator Iter;
  Container shapes;
  shapes.push_back(new Circle);
  shapes.push_back(new Square);
  shapes.push_back(new Triangle);
  for(Iter i = shapes.begin(); i != shapes.end(); i++)
    (*i)->draw();
  purge(shapes);
} ///:~
```

When using **purge( )**, carefully consider ownership issues. If an object pointer is held in more than one container, be sure not to delete it twice, and you don't want to destroy the object in the first container before the second one is finished with it. Purging the same container twice is not a problem because **purge( )** sets the pointer to zero once it deletes that pointer, and calling **delete** for a zero pointer is a safe operation.

Creating your own containers

With the STL as a foundation, you can create your own containers. Assuming you follow the same model of providing iterators, your new container will behave as if it were a built-in STL container.

Consider the "ring" data structure, which is a circular sequence container. If you reach the end, it just wraps around to the beginning. This can be implemented on top of a **list** as follows:

```
//: C07:Ring.cpp
// Making a "ring" data structure from the STL.
#include <iostream>
#include <iterator>
#include <list>
#include <string>
using namespace std;

template<class T> class Ring {
  list<T> lst;
public:
  // Declaration necessary so the following
  // 'friend' statement sees this 'iterator'
  // instead of std::iterator:
  class iterator;
  friend class iterator;
  class iterator : public std::iterator<
    std::bidirectional_iterator_tag,T,ptrdiff_t>{
    typename list<T>::iterator it;
    list<T>* r;
  public:
    iterator(list<T>& lst,
      const typename list<T>::iterator& i)
      : it(i), r(&lst) {}
    bool operator==(const iterator& x) const {
```

```
      return it == x.it;
    }
    bool operator!=(const iterator& x) const {
      return !(*this == x);
    }
    typename list<T>::reference operator*() const {
      return *it;
    }
    iterator& operator++() {
      ++it;
      if(it == r->end())
        it = r->begin();
      return *this;
    }
    iterator operator++(int) {
      iterator tmp = *this;
      ++*this;
      return tmp;
    }
    iterator& operator--() {
      if(it == r->begin())
        it = r->end();
      --it;
      return *this;
    }
    iterator operator--(int) {
      iterator tmp = *this;
      --*this;
      return tmp;
    }
    iterator insert(const T& x) {
      return iterator(*r, r->insert(it, x));
    }
    iterator erase() {
      return iterator(*r, r->erase(it));
    }
  };
  void push_back(const T& x) { lst.push_back(x); }
  iterator begin() { return iterator(lst, lst.begin()); }
  int size() { return lst.size(); }
};

int main() {
  Ring<string> rs;
  rs.push_back("one");
```

```
    rs.push_back("two");
    rs.push_back("three");
    rs.push_back("four");
    rs.push_back("five");
    Ring<string>::iterator it = rs.begin();
    ++it; ++it;
    it.insert("six");
    it = rs.begin();
    // Twice around the ring:
    for(int i = 0; i < rs.size() * 2; i++)
      cout << *it++ << endl;
} ///:~
```

You can see that most of the coding is in the iterator. The **Ring iterator** must know how to loop back to the beginning, so it must keep a reference to the **list** of its "parent" **Ring** object in order to know if it's at the end and how to get back to the beginning.

You'll notice that the interface for **Ring** is quite limited; in particular, there is no **end( )**, since a ring just keeps looping. This means that you won't be able to use a **Ring** in any STL algorithms that require a past-the-end iterator, which are many. (It turns out that adding this feature is a nontrivial exercise.) Although this can seem limiting, consider **stack**, **queue**, and **priority_queue**, which don't produce any iterators at all!

STL extensions

Although the STL containers may provide all the functionality you'll ever need, they are not complete. For example, the standard implementations of **set** and **map** use trees, and although these are reasonably fast, they may not be fast enough for your needs. In the C++ Standards Committee it was generally agreed that hashed implementations of **set** and **map** should have been included in Standard C++, however, there was not enough time to add these components, and thus they were left out.[16]

Fortunately, alternatives are freely available. One of the nice things about the STL is that it establishes a basic model for creating STL-like classes, so

---

[16] They will likely appear in the next revision of Standard C++.

anything built using the same model is easy to understand if you are already familiar with the STL.

The SGI STL from Silicon Graphics[17] is one of the most robust implementations of the STL and can be used to replace your compiler's STL if that is found wanting. In addition, SGI has added a number of extensions including **hash_set**, **hash_multiset**, **hash_map**, **hash_multimap**, **slist** (a singly linked list), and **rope** (a variant of **string** optimized for very large strings and fast concatenation and substring operations).

Let's consider a performance comparison between a tree-based **map** and the SGI **hash_map**. To keep things simple, the mappings will be from **int** to **int**:

```
//: C07:MapVsHashMap.cpp
// The hash_map header is not part of the Standard C++ STL.
// It is an extension that is only available as part of the
// SGI STL (Included with the dmc distribution).
// You can add the header by hand for all of these:
//{-bor}{-msc}{-g++}{-mwcc}
#include <hash_map>
#include <iostream>
#include <map>
#include <ctime>
using namespace std;

int main() {
  hash_map<int, int> hm;
  map<int, int> m;
  clock_t ticks = clock();
  for(int i = 0; i < 100; i++)
    for(int j = 0; j < 1000; j++)
      m.insert(make_pair(j,j));
  cout << "map insertions: " << clock() - ticks << endl;
  ticks = clock();
  for(int i = 0; i < 100; i++)
    for(int j = 0; j < 1000; j++)
      hm.insert(make_pair(j,j));
  cout << "hash_map insertions: "
       << clock() - ticks << endl;
```

---

[17] Available at http://www.sgi.com/tech/stl.

```
  ticks = clock();
  for(int i = 0; i < 100; i++)
    for(int j = 0; j < 1000; j++)
      m[j];
  cout << "map::operator[] lookups: "
       << clock() - ticks << endl;
  ticks = clock();
  for(int i = 0; i < 100; i++)
    for(int j = 0; j < 1000; j++)
      hm[j];
  cout << "hash_map::operator[] lookups: "
       << clock() - ticks << endl;
  ticks = clock();
  for(int i = 0; i < 100; i++)
    for(int j = 0; j < 1000; j++)
      m.find(j);
  cout << "map::find() lookups: "
       << clock() - ticks << endl;
  ticks = clock();
  for(int i = 0; i < 100; i++)
    for(int j = 0; j < 1000; j++)
      hm.find(j);
  cout << "hash_map::find() lookups: "
       << clock() - ticks << endl;
} ///:~
```

The performance test we ran showed a speed improvement of roughly 4:1 for the **hash_map** over the **map** in all operations (and as expected, **find( )** is slightly faster than **operator[ ]** for lookups for both types of map). If a profiler shows a bottleneck in your **map**, consider a **hash_map**.

Non–STL containers

There are two "non-STL" containers in the standard library: **bitset** and **valarray**.[18] We say "non-STL" because neither of these containers fulfills all the requirements of STL containers. The **bitset** container, which we covered earlier in this chapter, packs bits into integers and does not allow direct addressing of its members. The **valarray** template class is a **vector**-like

---

[18] As we explained earlier, the **vector<bool>** specialization is also a non-STL container to some degree.

container that is optimized for efficient numeric computation. Neither container provides iterators. Although you can instantiate a **valarray** with nonnumeric types, it has mathematical functions that are intended to operate with numeric data, such as **sin**, **cos**, **tan**, and so on.

Here's a tool to print elements in a **valarray**:

```
//: C07:PrintValarray.h
#ifndef PRINTVALARRAY_H
#define PRINTVALARRAY_H
#include <valarray>
#include <iostream>
#include <cstddef>

template<class T>
void print(const char* lbl, const std::valarray<T>& a) {
  std::cout << lbl << ": ";
  for(std::size_t i = 0; i < a.size(); ++i)
    std::cout << a[i] << ' ';
  std::cout << std::endl;
}
#endif // PRINTVALARRAY_H ///:~
```

Most of **valarray**'s functions and operators operate on a **valarray** as a whole, as the following example illustrates:

```
//: C07:Valarray1.cpp {-bor}
// Illustrates basic valarray functionality.
#include "PrintValarray.h"
using namespace std;

double f(double x) { return 2.0 * x - 1.0; }

int main() {
  double n[] = { 1.0, 2.0, 3.0, 4.0 };
  valarray<double> v(n, sizeof n / sizeof n[0]);
  print("v", v);
  valarray<double> sh(v.shift(1));
  print("shift 1", sh);
  valarray<double> acc(v + sh);
  print("sum", acc);
  valarray<double> trig(sin(v) + cos(acc));
  print("trig", trig);
  valarray<double> p(pow(v, 3.0));
```

```
    print("3rd power", p);
    valarray<double> app(v.apply(f));
    print("f(v)", app);
    valarray<bool> eq(v == app);
    print("v == app?", eq);
    double x = v.min();
    double y = v.max();
    double z = v.sum();
    cout << "x = " << x << ", y = " << y
         << ", z = " << z  << endl;
} ///:~
```

The **valarray** class provides a constructor that takes an array of the target type and the count of elements in the array to initialize the new **valarray**. The **shift( )** member function shifts each **valarray** element one position to the left (or to the right, if its argument is negative) and fills in holes with the default value for the type (zero in this case). There is also a **cshift( )** member function that does a circular shift (or "rotate"). All mathematical operators and functions are overloaded to operate on **valarray**s, and binary operators require **valarray** arguments of the same type and size. The **apply( )** member function, like the **transform( )** algorithm, applies a function to each element, but the result is collected into a result **valarray**. The relational operators return suitably-sized instances of **valarray<bool>** that indicate the result of element-by-element comparisons, such as with **eq** above. Most operations return a new result array, but a few, such as **min( )**, **max( )**, and **sum( )**, return a single scalar value, for obvious reasons.

The most interesting thing you can do with **valarray**s is reference subsets of their elements, not only for extracting information, but also for updating it. A subset of a **valarray** is called a *slice*, and certain operators use slices to do their work. The following sample program uses slices:

```
//: C07:Valarray2.cpp {-bor}{-dmc}
// Illustrates slices and masks.
#include "PrintValarray.h"
using namespace std;

int main() {
  int data[] = { 1, 2, 3, 4, 5, 6, 7, 8, 9, 10, 11, 12 };
  valarray<int> v(data, 12);
  valarray<int> r1(v[slice(0, 4, 3)]);
  print("slice(0,4,3)", r1);
  // Extract conditionally
```

```
  valarray<int> r2(v[v > 6]);
  print("elements > 6", r2);
  // Square first column
  v[slice(0, 4, 3)] *= valarray<int>(v[slice(0, 4, 3)]);
  print("after squaring first column", v);
  // Restore it
  int idx[] = { 1, 4, 7, 10 };
  valarray<int> save(idx, 4);
  v[slice(0, 4, 3)] = save;
  print("v restored", v);
  // Extract a 2-d subset: { { 1, 3, 5 }, { 7, 9, 11 } }
  valarray<size_t> siz(2);
  siz[0] = 2;
  siz[1] = 3;
  valarray<size_t> gap(2);
  gap[0] = 6;
  gap[1] = 2;
  valarray<int> r3(v[gslice(0, siz, gap)]);
  print("2-d slice", r3);
  // Extract a subset via a boolean mask (bool elements)
  valarray<bool> mask(false, 5);
  mask[1] = mask[2] = mask[4] = true;
  valarray<int> r4(v[mask]);
  print("v[mask]", r4);
  // Extract a subset via an index mask (size_t elements)
  size_t idx2[] = { 2, 2, 3, 6 };
  valarray<size_t> mask2(idx2, 4);
  valarray<int> r5(v[mask2]);
  print("v[mask2]", r5);
  // Use an index mask in assignment
  valarray<char> text("now is the time", 15);
  valarray<char> caps("NITT", 4);
  valarray<size_t> idx3(4);
  idx3[0] = 0;
  idx3[1] = 4;
  idx3[2] = 7;
  idx3[3] = 11;
  text[idx3] = caps;
  print("capitalized", text);
} ///:~
```

A **slice** object takes three arguments: the starting index, the number of elements to extract, and the "stride," which is the gap between elements of interest. Slices can be used as indexes into an existing **valarray**, and a new

valarray containing the extracted elements is returned. A **valarray** of **bool**, such as is returned by the expression **v > 6**, can be used as an index into another **valarray**; the elements corresponding to the **true** slots are extracted. As you can see, you can also use slices and masks as indexes on the left side of an assignment. A **gslice** object (for "generalized slice") is like a slice, except that the counts and strides are themselves arrays, which means you can interpret a **valarray** as a multidimensional array. The example above extracts a 2 by 3 array from **v**, where the numbers start at zero and the numbers for the first dimension are found six slots apart in **v**, and the others two apart, which effectively extracts the matrix

```
1 3 5
7 9 11
```

Here is the complete output for this program:

```
slice(0,4,3): 1 4 7 10
elements > 6: 7 8 9 10
after squaring v: 1 2 3 16 5 6 49 8 9 100 11 12
v restored: 1 2 3 4 5 6 7 8 9 10 11 12
2-d slice: 1 3 5 7 9 11
v[mask]: 2 3 5
v[mask2]: 3 3 4 7
capitalized: N o w   I s   T h e   T i m e
```

A practical example of slices is found in matrix multiplication. Consider how you would write a function to multiply two matrices of integers with arrays.

```
void matmult(const int a[][MAXCOLS], size_t m, size_t n,
             const int b[][MAXCOLS], size_t p, size_t q,
             int result[][MAXCOLS);
```

This function multiplies the **m**-by-**n** matrix **a** by the **p**-by-**q** matrix **b**, where **n** and **p** are expected to be equal. As you can see, without something like **valarray**, you need to fix the maximum value for the second dimension of each matrix, since locations in arrays are statically determined. It is also difficult to return a result array by value, so the caller usually passes the result array as an argument.

Using **valarray**, you can not only pass any size matrix, but you can also easily process matrices of any type, and return the result by value. Here's how:

```
//: C07:MatrixMultiply.cpp
// Uses valarray to multiply matrices
#include <cassert>
#include <cstddef>
#include <cmath>
#include <iostream>
#include <iomanip>
#include <valarray>
using namespace std;

// Prints a valarray as a square matrix
template<class T>
void printMatrix(const valarray<T>& a, size_t n) {
  size_t siz = n*n;
  assert(siz <= a.size());
  for(size_t i = 0; i < siz; ++i) {
    cout << setw(5) << a[i];
    cout << ((i+1)%n ? ' ' : '\n');
  }
  cout << endl;
}

// Multiplies compatible matrices in valarrays
template<class T>
valarray<T>
matmult(const valarray<T>& a, size_t arows, size_t acols,
        const valarray<T>& b, size_t brows, size_t bcols) {
  assert(acols == brows);
  valarray<T> result(arows * bcols);
  for(size_t i = 0; i < arows; ++i)
    for(size_t j = 0; j < bcols; ++j) {
      // Take dot product of row a[i] and col b[j]
      valarray<T> row = a[slice(acols*i, acols, 1)];
      valarray<T> col = b[slice(j, brows, bcols)];
      result[i*bcols + j] = (row * col).sum();
    }
  return result;
}

int main() {
  const int n = 3;
  int adata[n*n] = {1,0,-1,2,2,-3,3,4,0};
  int bdata[n*n] = {3,4,-1,1,-3,0,-1,1,2};
  valarray<int> a(adata, n*n);
  valarray<int> b(bdata, n*n);
```

```
valarray<int> c(matmult(a, n, n, b, n, n));
printMatrix(c, n);
} ///:~
```

Each entry in the result matrix **c** is the dot product of a row in **a** with a
column in **b**. By taking slices, you can extract these rows and columns as
valarrays and use the global * operator and **sum( )** function provided by
valarray to do the work succinctly. The result **valarray** is computed at
runtime; there's no need to worry about the static limitations of array
dimensions. You do have to compute linear offsets of the position **[i][j]**
yourself (see the formula **i*bcols + j** above), but the size and type freedom is
worth it.

Summary

The goal of this chapter was not just to introduce the STL containers in some
considerable depth. Although every detail could not be covered here, you now
know enough that you can look up further information in the other resources.
Our hope is that this chapter has helped you grasp the power available in the
STL and shown you how much faster and more efficient your programming
activities can be by understanding and using the STL.

Exercises

Solutions to selected exercises can be found in the electronic document *The Thinking in C++ Volume
2 Annotated Solution Guide*, available for a small fee from *www.MindView.net*.

1. Create a **set<char>**, open a file (whose name is provided on the
    command line), and read that file in a **char** at a time, placing each
    char in the set. Print the results, and observe the organization.
    Are there any letters in the alphabet that are not used in that
    particular file?

2. Create three sequences of **Noisy** objects, a **vector**, **deque**, and
    list. Sort them. Now write a function template to receive the
    vector and **deque** sequences as a parameter to sort them and
    record the sorting time. Write a specialized template function to
    do the same for **list** (ensure to call its member **sort( )** instead of
    the generic algorithm). Compare the performance of the different
    sequence types.

3. Write a program to compare the speed of sorting a list using **list::sort( )** vs. using **std::sort( )** (the STL algorithm version of **sort( )**).

4. Create a generator that produces random **int** values between 0 and 20 inclusive, and use it to fill a **multiset<int>**. Count the occurrences of each value, following the example given in **MultiSetWordCount.cpp**.

5. Change **StlShape.cpp** so that it uses a **deque** instead of a **vector**.

6. Modify **Reversible.cpp** so it works with **deque** and **list** instead of **vector**.

7. Use a **stack<int>** and populate it with a Fibonacci sequence. The program's command line should take the number of Fibonacci elements desired, and you should have a loop that looks at the last two elements on the stack and pushes a new one for every pass through the loop.

8. Using only three **stack**s (*source*, *sorted*, and *losers*), sort a random sequence of numbers by first placing the numbers on the *source* stack. Assume the number on the top of the *source* is the largest, and push it on the *sorted* stack. Continue to pop the *source* stack comparing it with the top of the *sorted* stack. Whichever number is the smallest, pop it from its stack and push it onto the on the *losers'* stack. Once the *source* stack is empty, repeat the process using the *losers'* stack as the *source* stack, and use the *source* stack as the *losers'* stack. The algorithm completes when all the numbers have been placed into the *winners'* stack.

9. Open a text file whose name is provided on the command line. Read the file a word at a time, and use a **multiset<string>** to create a word count for each word.

10. Modify **WordCount.cpp** so that it uses **insert( )** instead of **operator[ ]** to insert elements in the map.

11. Create a class that has an **operator<** and an **ostream& operator<<**. The class should contain a priority number. Create a generator for your class that makes a random priority number. Fill a **priority_queue** using your generator, and then pull the elements out to show they are in the proper order.

12. Rewrite **Ring.cpp** so it uses a **deque** instead of a **list** for its underlying implementation.

13. Modify **Ring.cpp** so that the underlying implementation can be chosen using a template argument. (Let that template argument default to **list**.)

14. Create an iterator class called **BitBucket** that just absorbs whatever you send to it without writing it anywhere.

15. Create a kind of "hangman" game. Create a class that contains a **char** and a **bool** to indicate whether that **char** has been guessed yet. Randomly select a word from a file, and read it into a **vector** of your new type. Repeatedly ask the user for a character guess, and after each guess, display the characters in the word that have been guessed, and display underscores for the characters that haven't. Allow a way for the user to guess the whole word. Decrement a value for each guess, and if the user can get the whole word before the value goes to zero, they win.

16. Open a file and read it into a single string. Turn the string into a **stringstream**. Read tokens from the **stringstream** into a **list<string>** using a **TokenIterator**.

17. Compare the performance of **stack** based on whether it is implemented with **vector**, **deque**, or **list**.

18. Create a template that implements a singly-linked list called **SList**. Provide a default constructor and **begin( )** and **end( )** functions (via an appropriate nested iterator), **insert( )**, **erase( )** and a destructor.

19. Generate a sequence of random integers, storing them into an array of **int**. Initialize a **valarray<int>** with its contents. Compute the sum, minimum value, maximum value, average, and median of the integers using **valarray** operations.

20. Create a **valarray<int>** with 12 random values. Create another **valarray<int>** with 20 random values. You will interpret the first **valarray** as a 3 x 4 matrix of **int**s and the second as a 4 x 5 matrix of **int**s, and multiply them by the rules of matrix multiplication. Store the result in a **valarray<int>** of size 15, representing the 3 x 5 result matrix. Use slices to multiply the rows of the first matrix time the columns of the second. Print the result in rectangular matrix form.

Part 3

Special Topics

The mark of a professional appears in his or her attention to the finer points of the craft. In this section of the book we discuss advanced features of C++ along with development techniques used by polished C++ professionals.

Sometimes you may need to depart from the conventional wisdom of sound object-oriented design by inspecting the runtime type of an object. Most of the time you should let virtual functions do that job for you, but when writing special-purpose software tools, such as debuggers, database viewers, or class browsers, you'll need to determine type information at runtime. This is where the runtime type identification (RTTI) mechanism becomes useful. RTTI is the topic of Chapter 8.

Multiple inheritance has taken abuse over the years, and some languages don't even support it. Nonetheless, when used properly, it can be a powerful tool for crafting elegant, efficient code. A number of standard practices involving multiple inheritance have evolved over the years, which we present in Chapter 9.

Perhaps the most notable innovation in software development since object-oriented techniques is the use of design patterns. A design pattern describes solutions for many of the common problems involved in designing software, and can be applied in many situations and implemented in any language. In chapter 10 we describe a selected number of design patterns and implement them in C++.

Chapter 11 explains the benefits and challenges of multithreaded programming. The current version of Standard C++ does not specify support for threads, even though most operating systems provide them. We use a portable, freely available threading library to illustrate how C++ programmers can take advantage of threads to build more usable and responsive applications.

8: Runtime Type Identification

Runtime type identification (RTTI) lets you find the dynamic type of an object when you have only a pointer or a reference to the base type.

This can be thought of as a "secondary" feature in C++, pragmatism to help out when you get into rare difficult situations. Normally, you'll want to intentionally ignore the exact type of an object and let the virtual function mechanism implement the correct behavior for that type. On occasion, however, it's useful to know the exact *runtime* (that is, most derived) type of an object for which you only have a base pointer. With this information, you may perform a special-case operation more efficiently or prevent a base-class interface from becoming ungainly. It happens enough that most class libraries contain virtual functions to produce runtime type information. When exception handling was added to C++, that feature required information about the runtime type of objects, so it became an easy next step to build in access to that information. This chapter explains what RTTI is for and how to use it.

Runtime casts

One way to determine the runtime type of an object through a pointer or reference is to employ a *runtime cast*, which verifies that the attempted conversion is valid. This is useful when you need to cast a base-class pointer to a derived type. Since inheritance hierarchies are typically depicted with base classes above derived classes, such a cast is called a *downcast*.

Consider the following class hierarchy:

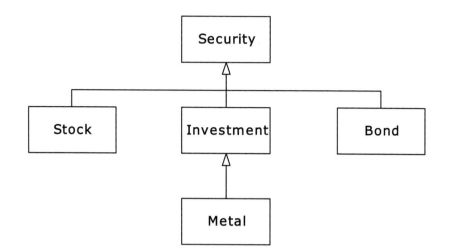

In the code that follows, the **Investment** class has an extra operation that
the other classes do not, so it is important to be able to know at runtime
whether a **Security** pointer refers to a **Investment** object or not. To
implement checked runtime casts, each class keeps an integral identifier to
distinguish it from other classes in the hierarchy.

```
//: C08:CheckedCast.cpp
// Checks casts at runtime.
#include <iostream>
#include <vector>
#include "../purge.h"
using namespace std;

class Security {
protected:
  enum { BASEID = 0 };
public:
  virtual ~Security() {}
  virtual bool isA(int id) { return (id == BASEID); }
};

class Stock : public Security {
  typedef Security Super;
protected:
  enum { OFFSET = 1, TYPEID = BASEID + OFFSET };
public:
  bool isA(int id) {
```

```cpp
    return id == TYPEID || Super::isA(id);
  }
  static Stock* dynacast(Security* s) {
    return (s->isA(TYPEID)) ? static_cast<Stock*>(s) : 0;
  }
};

class Bond : public Security {
  typedef Security Super;
protected:
  enum { OFFSET = 2, TYPEID = BASEID + OFFSET };
public:
  bool isA(int id) {
    return id == TYPEID || Super::isA(id);
  }
  static Bond* dynacast(Security* s) {
    return (s->isA(TYPEID)) ? static_cast<Bond*>(s) : 0;
  }
};

class Investment : public Security {
  typedef Security Super;
protected:
  enum { OFFSET = 3, TYPEID = BASEID + OFFSET };
public:
  bool isA(int id) {
    return id == TYPEID || Super::isA(id);
  }
  static Investment* dynacast(Security* s) {
    return (s->isA(TYPEID)) ?
      static_cast<Investment*>(s) : 0;
  }
  void special() {
    cout << "special Investment function" << endl;
  }
};

class Metal : public Investment {
  typedef Investment Super;
protected:
  enum { OFFSET = 4, TYPEID = BASEID + OFFSET };
public:
  bool isA(int id) {
    return id == TYPEID || Super::isA(id);
  }
```

```
    static Metal* dynacast(Security* s) {
      return (s->isA(TYPEID)) ? static_cast<Metal*>(s) : 0;
    }
};

int main() {
  vector<Security*> portfolio;
  portfolio.push_back(new Metal);
  portfolio.push_back(new Investment);
  portfolio.push_back(new Bond);
  portfolio.push_back(new Stock);
  for(vector<Security*>::iterator it = portfolio.begin();
      it != portfolio.end(); ++it) {
    Investment* cm = Investment::dynacast(*it);
    if(cm)
      cm->special();
    else
      cout << "not an Investment" << endl;
  }
  cout << "cast from intermediate pointer:" << endl;
  Security* sp = new Metal;
  Investment* cp = Investment::dynacast(sp);
  if(cp) cout << "  it's an Investment" << endl;
  Metal* mp = Metal::dynacast(sp);
  if(mp) cout << "  it's a Metal too!" << endl;
  purge(portfolio);
} ///:~
```

The polymorphic **isA( )** function checks to see if its argument is compatible
with its type argument (**id**), which means that either **id** matches the object's
typeID exactly or it matches one of the object's ancestors (hence the call to
Super::isA( ) in that case). The **dynacast( )** function, which is static in
each class, calls **isA( )** for its pointer argument to check if the cast is valid. If
isA( ) returns **true**, the cast is valid, and a suitably cast pointer is returned.
Otherwise, the null pointer is returned, which tells the caller that the cast is
not valid, meaning that the original pointer is not pointing to an object
compatible with (convertible to) the desired type. All this machinery is
necessary to be able to check intermediate casts, such as from a **Security**

pointer that refers to a **Metal** object to a **Investment** pointer in the previous example program.[1]

For most programs downcasting is unnecessary, and is actually discouraged, since everyday polymorphism solves most problems in object-oriented application programs. However, the ability to check a cast to a more derived type is important for utility programs such as debuggers, class browsers, and databases. C++ provides such a checked cast with the **dynamic_cast** operator. The following program is a rewrite of the previous example using **dynamic_cast**:

```
//: C08:Security.h
#ifndef SECURITY_H
#define SECURITY_H
#include <iostream>

class Security {
public:
  virtual ~Security() {}
};

class Stock : public Security {};
class Bond : public Security {};

class Investment : public Security {
public:
  void special() {
    std::cout << "special Investment function" <<std::endl;
  }
};

class Metal : public Investment {};
#endif // SECURITY_H ///:~
```

```
//: C08:CheckedCast2.cpp
// Uses RTTI's dynamic_cast.
#include <vector>
#include "../purge.h"
#include "Security.h"
```

---

[1] With Microsoft's compilers you will have to enable RTTI; it's disabled by default. The command–line option to enable it is **/GR**.

```
using namespace std;

int main() {
  vector<Security*> portfolio;
  portfolio.push_back(new Metal);
  portfolio.push_back(new Investment);
  portfolio.push_back(new Bond);
  portfolio.push_back(new Stock);
  for(vector<Security*>::iterator it =
        portfolio.begin();
        it != portfolio.end(); ++it) {
    Investment* cm = dynamic_cast<Investment*>(*it);
    if(cm)
      cm->special();
    else
      cout << "not a Investment" << endl;
  }
  cout << "cast from intermediate pointer:" << endl;
  Security* sp = new Metal;
  Investment* cp = dynamic_cast<Investment*>(sp);
  if(cp) cout << "  it's an Investment" << endl;
  Metal* mp = dynamic_cast<Metal*>(sp);
  if(mp) cout << "  it's a Metal too!" << endl;
  purge(portfolio);
} ///:~
```

This example is much shorter, since most of the code in the original example was just the overhead for checking the casts. The target type of a **dynamic_cast** is placed in angle brackets, like the other new-style C++ casts (**static_cast**, and so on), and the object to cast appears as the operand. **dynamic_cast** requires that the types you use it with be *polymorphic* if you want safe downcasts.[2] This in turn requires that the class must have at least one virtual function. Fortunately, the **Security** base class has a virtual destructor, so we didn't have to invent an extra function to get the job done. Because **dynamic_cast** does its work at runtime, using the virtual table, it tends to be more expensive than the other new-style casts.

---

[2] Compilers typically insert a pointer to a class's RTTI table inside its virtual function table.

You can also use **dynamic_cast** with references instead of pointers, but since there is no such thing as a null reference, you need another way to know if the cast fails. That "other way" is to catch a **bad_cast** exception, as follows:

```cpp
//: C08:CatchBadCast.cpp
#include <typeinfo>
#include "Security.h"
using namespace std;

int main() {
  Metal m;
  Security& s = m;
  try {
    Investment& c = dynamic_cast<Investment&>(s);
    cout << "It's an Investment" << endl;
  } catch(bad_cast&) {
    cout << "s is not an Investment type" << endl;
  }
  try {
    Bond& b = dynamic_cast<Bond&>(s);
    cout << "It's a Bond" << endl;
  } catch(bad_cast&) {
    cout << "It's not a Bond type" << endl;
  }
} ///:~
```

The **bad_cast** class is defined in the **<typeinfo>** header, and, like most of the standard library, is declared in the **std** namespace.

The typeid operator

The other way to get runtime information for an object is through the **typeid** operator. This operator returns an object of class **type_info**, which yields information about the type of object to which it was applied. If the type is polymorphic, it gives information about the most derived type that applies (the *dynamic type*); otherwise it yields static type information. One use of the **typeid** operator is to get the name of the dynamic type of an object as a **const char***, as you can see in the following example:

```cpp
//: C08:TypeInfo.cpp
// Illustrates the typeid operator.
#include <iostream>
```

```
#include <typeinfo>
using namespace std;

struct PolyBase { virtual ~PolyBase() {} };
struct PolyDer : PolyBase { PolyDer() {} };
struct NonPolyBase {};
struct NonPolyDer : NonPolyBase { NonPolyDer(int) {} };

int main() {
  // Test polymorphic Types
  const PolyDer pd;
  const PolyBase* ppb = &pd;
  cout << typeid(ppb).name() << endl;
  cout << typeid(*ppb).name() << endl;
  cout << boolalpha << (typeid(*ppb) == typeid(pd))
       << endl;
  cout << (typeid(PolyDer) == typeid(const PolyDer))
       << endl;
  // Test non-polymorphic Types
  const NonPolyDer npd(1);
  const NonPolyBase* nppb = &npd;
  cout << typeid(nppb).name() << endl;
  cout << typeid(*nppb).name() << endl;
  cout << (typeid(*nppb) == typeid(npd)) << endl;
  // Test a built-in type
  int i;
  cout << typeid(i).name() << endl;
} ///:~
```

The output from this program using one particular compiler is

```
struct PolyBase const *
struct PolyDer
true
true
struct NonPolyBase const *
struct NonPolyBase
false
int
```

The first output line just echoes the static type of **ppb** because it is a pointer. To get RTTI to kick in, you need to look at the pointer or reference destination object, which is illustrated in the second line. Notice that RTTI ignores top-level **const** and **volatile** qualifiers. With non-polymorphic types, you just get the static type (the type of the pointer itself). As you can see, built-in types are also supported.

It turns out that you can't store the result of a **typeid** operation in a **type_info** object, because there are no accessible constructors and assignment is disallowed. You must use it as we have shown. In addition, the actual string returned by **type_info::name( )** is compiler dependent. For a class named **C**, for example, some compilers return "class C" instead of just "C." Applying **typeid** to an expression that dereferences a null pointer will cause a **bad_typeid** exception (also defined in **<typeinfo>**) to be thrown.

The following example shows that the class name that **type_info::name( )** returns is fully qualified:

```
//: C08:RTTIandNesting.cpp
#include <iostream>
#include <typeinfo>
using namespace std;

class One {
  class Nested {};
  Nested* n;
public:
  One() : n(new Nested) {}
  ~One() { delete n; }
  Nested* nested() { return n; }
};

int main() {
  One o;
  cout << typeid(*o.nested()).name() << endl;
} ///:~
```

Since **Nested** is a member type of the **One** class, the result is **One::Nested**.

You can also ask a **type_info** object if it precedes another **type_info** object in the implementation-defined "collation sequence" (the native ordering rules for text), using **before(type_info&)**, which returns **true** or **false**. When you say,

```
if(typeid(me).before(typeid(you))) // ...
```

you're asking if **me** occurs before **you** in the current collation sequence. This is useful if you use **type_info** objects as keys.

Casting to intermediate levels

As you saw in the earlier program that used the hierarchy of **Security** classes, **dynamic_cast** can detect both exact types and, in an inheritance hierarchy with multiple levels, intermediate types. Here is another example.

```
//: C08:IntermediateCast.cpp
#include <cassert>
#include <typeinfo>
using namespace std;

class B1 {
public:
  virtual ~B1() {}
};

class B2 {
public:
  virtual ~B2() {}
};

class MI : public B1, public B2 {};
class Mi2 : public MI {};

int main() {
  B2* b2 = new Mi2;
  Mi2* mi2 = dynamic_cast<Mi2*>(b2);
  MI* mi = dynamic_cast<MI*>(b2);
  B1* b1 = dynamic_cast<B1*>(b2);
  assert(typeid(b2) != typeid(Mi2*));
  assert(typeid(b2) == typeid(B2*));
  delete b2;
} ///:~
```

This example has the extra complication of multiple inheritance (you'll learn more about multiple inheritance later in this chapter, and in Chapter 9). If you create an **Mi2** and upcast it to the root (in this case, one of the two possible roots is chosen), the **dynamic_cast** back to either of the derived levels **MI** or **Mi2** is successful.

You can even cast from one root to the other:

```
  B1* b1 = dynamic_cast<B1*>(b2);
```

This is successful because **B2** is actually pointing to a **Mi2** object, which contains a subobject of type **B1**.

Casting to intermediate levels brings up an interesting difference between **dynamic_cast** and **typeid**. The **typeid** operator always produces a reference to a static **type_info** object that describes the dynamic type of the object. Thus, it doesn't give you intermediate-level information. In the following expression (which is **true**), **typeid** doesn't see **b2** as a pointer to the derived type, like **dynamic_cast** does:

```
  typeid(b2) != typeid(Mi2*)
```

The type of **b2** is simply the exact type of the pointer:

```
  typeid(b2) == typeid(B2*)
```

void pointers

RTTI only works for complete types, meaning that all class information must be available when **typeid** is used. In particular, it doesn't work with **void** pointers:

```
//: C08:VoidRTTI.cpp
// RTTI & void pointers.
//!#include <iostream>
#include <typeinfo>
using namespace std;

class Stimpy {
public:
  virtual void happy() {}
  virtual void joy() {}
  virtual ~Stimpy() {}
};

int main() {
  void* v = new Stimpy;
  // Error:
//!  Stimpy* s = dynamic_cast<Stimpy*>(v);
```

```
    // Error:
//!  cout << typeid(*v).name() << endl;
} ///:~
```

A **void*** truly means "no type information."[3]

Using RTTI with templates

Class templates work well with RTTI, since all they do is generate classes. As usual, RTTI provides a convenient way to obtain the name of the class you're in. The following example prints the order of constructor and destructor calls:

```
//: C08:ConstructorOrder.cpp
// Order of constructor calls.
#include <iostream>
#include <typeinfo>
using namespace std;

template<int id> class Announce {
public:
  Announce() {
    cout << typeid(*this).name() << " constructor" << endl;
  }
  ~Announce() {
    cout << typeid(*this).name() << " destructor" << endl;
  }
};

class X : public Announce<0> {
  Announce<1> m1;
  Announce<2> m2;
public:
  X() { cout << "X::X()" << endl; }
  ~X() { cout << "X::~X()" << endl; }
};

int main() { X x; } ///:~
```

This template uses a constant **int** to differentiate one class from another, but type arguments would work as well. Inside both the constructor and

---

[3] A **dynamic_cast<void*>** always gives the address of the full object—not a subobject. This will be explained more fully in the next chapter.

---

destructor, RTTI information produces the name of the class to print. The class **X** uses both inheritance and composition to create a class that has an interesting order of constructor and destructor calls. The output is

```
Announce<0> constructor
Announce<1> constructor
Announce<2> constructor
X::X()
X::~X()
Announce<2> destructor
Announce<1> destructor
Announce<0> destructor
```

Of course, you may get different output depending on how your compiler represents its **name( )** information.

Multiple inheritance

The RTTI mechanisms must work properly with all the complexities of multiple inheritance, including **virtual** base classes (discussed in depth in the next chapter—you may want to come back here after reading Chapter 9):

```
//: C08:RTTIandMultipleInheritance.cpp
#include <iostream>
#include <typeinfo>
using namespace std;

class BB {
public:
  virtual void f() {}
  virtual ~BB() {}
};

class B1 : virtual public BB {};
class B2 : virtual public BB {};
class MI : public B1, public B2 {};

int main() {
  BB* bbp = new MI; // Upcast
  // Proper name detection:
  cout << typeid(*bbp).name() << endl;
  // Dynamic_cast works properly:
  MI* mip = dynamic_cast<MI*>(bbp);
```

```
  // Can't force old-style cast:
//! MI* mip2 = (MI*)bbp; // Compile error
} ///:~
```

The **typeid( )** operator properly detects the name of the actual object, even through the **virtual** base class pointer. The **dynamic_cast** also works correctly. But the compiler won't even allow you to try to force a cast the old way:

```
MI* mip = (MI*)bbp; // Compile-time error
```

The compiler knows this is never the right thing to do, so it requires that you use a **dynamic_cast**.

Sensible uses for RTTI

Because you can discover type information from an anonymous polymorphic pointer, RTTI is ripe for misuse by the novice, because RTTI may make sense before virtual functions do. For many people coming from a procedural background, it's difficult not to organize programs into sets of **switch** statements. They could accomplish this with RTTI and thus lose the important value of polymorphism in code development and maintenance. The intent of C++ is that you use virtual functions throughout your code and that you only use RTTI when you must.

However, using virtual functions as they are intended requires that you have control of the base-class definition, because at some point in the extension of your program you may discover the base class doesn't include the virtual function you need. If the base class comes from a library or is otherwise controlled by someone else, one solution to the problem is RTTI; you can derive a new type and add your extra member function. Elsewhere in the code you can detect your particular type and call that member function. This doesn't destroy the polymorphism and extensibility of the program, because adding a new type will not require you to hunt for switch statements. However, when you add new code in the main body that requires your new feature, you'll have to detect your particular type.

Putting a feature in a base class might mean that, for the benefit of one particular class, all the other classes derived from that base require some meaningless stub for a pure virtual function. This makes the interface less clear and annoys those who must override pure virtual functions when they derive from that base class.

Finally, RTTI will sometimes solve efficiency problems. If your code uses polymorphism in a nice way, but it turns out that one of your objects reacts to this general-purpose code in a horribly inefficient way, you can pick that type out using RTTI and write case-specific code to improve the efficiency.

A trash recycler

To further illustrate a practical use of RTTI, the following program simulates a trash recycler. Different kinds of "trash" are inserted into a single container and then later sorted according to their dynamic types.

```
//: C08:Trash.h
// Describing trash.
#ifndef TRASH_H
#define TRASH_H
#include <iostream>

class Trash {
  float _weight;
public:
  Trash(float wt) : _weight(wt) {}
  virtual float value() const = 0;
  float weight() const { return _weight; }
  virtual ~Trash() {
    std::cout << "~Trash()" << std::endl;
  }
};

class Aluminum : public Trash {
  static float val;
public:
  Aluminum(float wt) : Trash(wt) {}
  float value() const { return val; }
  static void value(float newval) {
    val = newval;
  }
};

class Paper : public Trash {
  static float val;
```

```
public:
  Paper(float wt) : Trash(wt) {}
  float value() const { return val; }
  static void value(float newval) {
    val = newval;
  }
};

class Glass : public Trash {
  static float val;
public:
  Glass(float wt) : Trash(wt) {}
  float value() const { return val; }
  static void value(float newval) {
    val = newval;
  }
};
#endif // TRASH_H ///:~
```

The **static** values representing the price per unit of the trash types are defined in the implementation file:

```
//: C08:Trash.cpp {O}
// A Trash Recycler.
#include "Trash.h"

float Aluminum::val = 1.67;
float Paper::val = 0.10;
float Glass::val = 0.23;
///:~
```

The **sumValue( )** template iterates through a container, displaying and calculating results:

```
//: C08:Recycle.cpp
//{L} Trash
// A Trash Recycler.
#include <cstdlib>
#include <ctime>
#include <iostream>
#include <typeinfo>
#include <vector>
#include "Trash.h"
#include "../purge.h"
using namespace std;
```

```
// Sums up the value of the Trash in a bin:
template<class Container>
void sumValue(Container& bin, ostream& os) {
  typename Container::iterator tally = bin.begin();
  float val = 0;
  while(tally != bin.end()) {
    val += (*tally)->weight() * (*tally)->value();
    os << "weight of " << typeid(**tally).name()
       << " = " << (*tally)->weight() << endl;
    ++tally;
  }
  os << "Total value = " << val << endl;
}

int main() {
  srand(time(0)); // Seed the random number generator
  vector<Trash*> bin;
  // Fill up the Trash bin:
  for(int i = 0; i < 30; i++)
    switch(rand() % 3) {
      case 0 :
        bin.push_back(new Aluminum((rand() % 1000)/10.0));
        break;
      case 1 :
        bin.push_back(new Paper((rand() % 1000)/10.0));
        break;
      case 2 :
        bin.push_back(new Glass((rand() % 1000)/10.0));
        break;
    }
  // Note: bins hold exact type of object, not base type:
  vector<Glass*> glassBin;
  vector<Paper*> paperBin;
  vector<Aluminum*> alumBin;
  vector<Trash*>::iterator sorter = bin.begin();
  // Sort the Trash:
  while(sorter != bin.end()) {
    Aluminum* ap = dynamic_cast<Aluminum*>(*sorter);
    Paper* pp = dynamic_cast<Paper*>(*sorter);
    Glass* gp = dynamic_cast<Glass*>(*sorter);
    if(ap) alumBin.push_back(ap);
    else if(pp) paperBin.push_back(pp);
    else if(gp) glassBin.push_back(gp);
    ++sorter;
```

```
    }
    sumValue(alumBin, cout);
    sumValue(paperBin, cout);
    sumValue(glassBin, cout);
    sumValue(bin, cout);
    purge(bin);
} ///:~
```

The trash is thrown unclassified into a single bin, so the specific type information is "lost." But later the specific type information must be recovered to properly sort the trash, and so RTTI is used.

We can improve this solution by using a **map** that associates pointers to **type_info** objects with a **vector** of **Trash** pointers. Since a map requires an ordering predicate, we provide one named **TInfoLess** that calls **type_info::before( )**. As we insert **Trash** pointers into the map, they are automatically associated with their **type_info** key. Notice that **sumValue( )** must be defined differently here:

```
//: C08:Recycle2.cpp
//{L} Trash
// Recyling with a map.
#include <cstdlib>
#include <ctime>
#include <iostream>
#include <map>
#include <typeinfo>
#include <utility>
#include <vector>
#include "Trash.h"
#include "../purge.h"
using namespace std;

// Comparator for type_info pointers
struct TInfoLess {
  bool operator()(const type_info* t1, const type_info* t2)
  const { return t1->before(*t2); }
};

typedef map<const type_info*, vector<Trash*>, TInfoLess>
  TrashMap;

// Sums up the value of the Trash in a bin:
void sumValue(const TrashMap::value_type& p, ostream& os) {
```

```
    vector<Trash*>::const_iterator tally = p.second.begin();
    float val = 0;
    while(tally != p.second.end()) {
      val += (*tally)->weight() * (*tally)->value();
      os << "weight of "
         << p.first->name()  // type_info::name()
         << " = " << (*tally)->weight() << endl;
      ++tally;
    }
    os << "Total value = " << val << endl;
}

int main() {
  srand(time(0)); // Seed the random number generator
  TrashMap bin;
  // Fill up the Trash bin:
  for(int i = 0; i < 30; i++) {
    Trash* tp;
    switch(rand() % 3) {
      case 0 :
        tp = new Aluminum((rand() % 1000)/10.0);
        break;
      case 1 :
        tp = new Paper((rand() % 1000)/10.0);
        break;
      case 2 :
        tp = new Glass((rand() % 1000)/10.0);
        break;
    }
    bin[&typeid(*tp)].push_back(tp);
  }
  // Print sorted results
  for(TrashMap::iterator p = bin.begin();
      p != bin.end(); ++p) {
    sumValue(*p, cout);
    purge(p->second);
  }
} ///:~
```

We've modified **sumValue( )** to call **type_info::name( )** directly, since the **type_info** object is now available as the first member of the **TrashMap::value_type** pair. This avoids the extra call to **typeid** to get the name of the type of **Trash** being processed that was necessary in the previous version of this program.

Mechanism and overhead of RTTI

Typically, RTTI is implemented by placing an additional pointer in a class's virtual function table. This pointer points to the **type_info** structure for that particular type. The effect of a **typeid( )** expression is quite simple: the virtual function table pointer fetches the **type_info** pointer, and a reference to the resulting **type_info** structure is produced. Since this is just a two-pointer dereference operation, it is a constant time operation.

For a **dynamic_cast<destination*>(source_pointer)**, most cases are quite straightforward: **source_pointer**'s RTTI information is retrieved, and RTTI information for the type **destination*** is fetched. A library routine then determines whether **source_pointer**'s type is of type **destination*** or a base class of **destination***. The pointer it returns may be adjusted because of multiple inheritance if the base type isn't the first base of the derived class. The situation is more complicated with multiple inheritance because a base type may appear more than once in an inheritance hierarchy and virtual base classes are used.

Because the library routine used for **dynamic_cast** must check through a list of base classes, the overhead for **dynamic_cast** may be higher than **typeid( )** (but you get different information, which may be essential to your solution), and it may take more time to discover a base class than a derived class. In addition, **dynamic_cast** compares any type to any other type; you aren't restricted to comparing types within the same hierarchy. This adds extra overhead to the library routine used by **dynamic_cast**.

Summary

Although normally you upcast a pointer to a base class and then use the generic interface of that base class (via virtual functions), occasionally you get into a corner where things can be more effective if you know the dynamic type of the object pointed to by a base pointer, and that's what RTTI provides. The most common misuse may come from the programmer who doesn't understand virtual functions and uses RTTI to do type-check coding instead. The philosophy of C++ seems to be to provide you with powerful tools and guard for type violations and integrity, but if you want to deliberately misuse or get around a language feature, there's nothing to stop you. Sometimes a slight burn is the fastest way to gain experience.

Exercises

Solutions to selected exercises can be found in the electronic document *The Thinking in C++ Volume 2 Annotated Solution Guide*, available for a small fee from *www.MindView.net*.

1. Create a **Base** class with a **virtual** destructor and a **Derived** class that inherits from **Base**. Create a **vector** of **Base** pointers that point to **Base** and **Derived** objects randomly. Using the contents your **vector**, fill a second **vector** with all the **Derived** pointers. Compare execution times between **typeid( )** and **dynamic_cast** to see which is faster.

2. Modify **C16:AutoCounter.h** in Volume 1 of this book so that it becomes a useful debugging tool. It will be used as a nested member of each class that you are interested in tracing. Turn **AutoCounter** into a template that takes the class name of the surrounding class as the template argument, and in all the error messages use RTTI to print the name of the class.

3. Use RTTI to assist in program debugging by printing out the exact name of a template using **typeid( )**. Instantiate the template for various types and see what the results are.

4. Modify the **Instrument** hierarchy from Chapter 14 of Volume 1 by first copying **Wind5.cpp** to a new location. Now add a virtual **clearSpitValve( )** function to the **Wind** class, and redefine it for all the classes inherited from **Wind**. Instantiate a **vector** to hold **Instrument** pointers, and fill it with various types of **Instrument** objects created using the **new** operator. Now use RTTI to move through the container looking for objects in class **Wind**, or derived from **Wind**. Call the **clearSpitValve( )** function for these objects. Notice that it would unpleasantly confuse the Instrument base class if it contained a **clearSpitValve( )** function.

5. Modify the previous exercise to place a **prepareInstrument( )** function in the base class, which calls appropriate functions (such as **clearSpitValve( )**, when it fits). Note that **prepareInstrument( )** is a sensible function to place in the base class, and it eliminates the need for RTTI in the previous exercise.

6. Create a **vector** of pointers to 10 random **Shape** objects (at least **Square**s and **Circle**s, for example). The **draw( )** member function should be overridden in each concrete class to print the dimensions of the object being drawn (the length or the radius,

whichever applies). Write a **main( )** program that draws all the **Square**s in your container first, sorted by length, and then draws all **Circle**s, sorted by radius.

7. Create a large **vector** of pointers to random **Shape** objects. Write a non-virtual **draw( )** function in **Shape** that uses RTTI to determine the dynamic type of each object and executes the appropriate code to "draw" the object with a switch statement. Then rewrite your **Shape** hierarchy the "right way," using virtual functions. Compare the code sizes and execution times of the two approaches.

8. Create a hierarchy of **Pet** classes, including **Dog**, **Cat**, and **Horse**. Also create a hierarchy of **Food** classes: **Beef**, **Fish**, and **Oats**. The **Dog** class has a member function, **eat( )**, that takes a **Beef** parameter, likewise, **Cat::eat( )** takes a **Fish** object, and **Oats** objects are passed to **Horse::eat( )**. Create a **vector** of pointers to random **Pet** objects, and visit each **Pet**, passing the correct type of **Food** object to its **eat( )** function.

9. Create a global function named **drawQuad( )** that takes a reference to a **Shape** object. It calls the **draw( )** function of its **Shape** parameter if it has four sides (that is, if it's a **Square** or **Rectangle**). Otherwise, it prints the message "Not a quadrilateral". Traverse a **vector** of pointers to random **Shapes**, calling **drawQuad( )** for each one. Place **Squares**, **Rectangles**, **Circles** and **Triangles** in your **vector**.

10. Sort a **vector** of random **Shape** objects by class name. Use **type_info::before( )** as the comparison function for sorting.

9: Multiple Inheritance

The basic concept of multiple inheritance (MI) sounds simple enough: you create a new type by inheriting from more than one base class. The syntax is exactly what you'd expect, and as long as the inheritance diagrams are simple, MI can be simple as well.

However, MI can introduce a number of ambiguities and strange situations, which are covered in this chapter. But first, it is helpful to get some perspective on the subject.

Perspective

Before C++, the most successful object-oriented language was Smalltalk. Smalltalk was created from the ground up as an object-oriented language. It is often referred to as *pure,* whereas C++ is called a *hybrid* language because it supports multiple programming paradigms, not just the object-oriented paradigm. One of the design decisions made with Smalltalk was that all classes would be derived in a single hierarchy, rooted in a single base class (called **Object**—this is the model for the *object-based hierarchy*).[1] You cannot create a new class in Smalltalk without deriving it from an existing class, which is why it takes a certain amount of time to become productive in Smalltalk: you must learn the class library before you can start making new classes. The Smalltalk class hierarchy is therefore a single monolithic tree.

Classes in Smalltalk usually have a number of things in common, and they always have *some* things in common (the characteristics and behaviors of **Object**), so you don't often run into a situation where you need to inherit from more than one base class. However, with C++ you can create as many distinct inheritance trees as you want. So for logical completeness the language must be able to combine more than one class at a time—thus the need for multiple inheritance.

---

[1] This is also true of Java, and other object–oriented languages.

It was not obvious, however, that programmers required multiple inheritance, and there was (and still is) a lot of disagreement about whether it is essential in C++. MI was added in AT&T **cfront** release 2.0 in 1989 and was the first significant change to the language over version 1.0.[2] Since then, a number of other features have been added to Standard C++ (notably templates) that change the way we think about programming and place MI in a much less important role. You can think of MI as a "minor" language feature that is seldom involved in your daily design decisions.

One of the most pressing arguments for MI involved containers. Suppose you want to create a container that everyone can easily use. One approach is to use **void*** as the type inside the container. The Smalltalk approach, however, is to make a container that holds **Object**s, since **Object** is the base type of the Smalltalk hierarchy. Because everything in Smalltalk is ultimately derived from **Object**, a container that holds **Object**s can hold anything.

Now consider the situation in C++. Suppose vendor **A** creates an object-based hierarchy that includes a useful set of containers including one you want to use called **Holder**. Next you come across vendor **B**'s class hierarchy that contains some other class that is important to you, a **BitImage** class, for example, that holds graphic images. The only way to make a **Holder** of **BitImage**s is to derive a new class from both **Object**, so it can be held in the **Holder**, and **BitImage**:

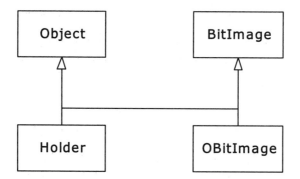

This was seen as an important reason for MI, and a number of class libraries were built on this model. However, as you saw in Chapter 5, the addition of

---

[2] These version numbers are internal AT&T numberings.

templates has changed the way containers are created, so this situation is no longer a driving issue for MI.

The other reason you may need MI is related to design. You can intentionally use MI to make a design more flexible or useful (or at least seemingly so). An example of this is in the original **iostream** library design (which still persists in today's template design, as you saw in Chapter 4):

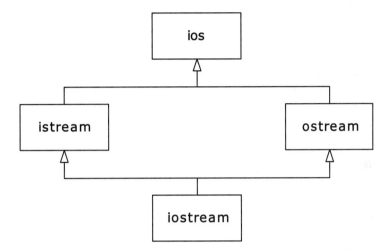

Both **istream** and **ostream** are useful classes by themselves, but they can also be derived from simultaneously by a class that combines both their characteristics and behaviors. The class **ios** provides what is common to all stream classes, and so in this case MI is a code-factoring mechanism.

Regardless of what motivates you to use MI, it's harder to use than it might appear.

Interface inheritance

One use of multiple inheritance that is not controversial pertains to *interface inheritance*. In C++, all inheritance is *implementation inheritance*, because everything in a base class, interface and implementation, becomes part of a derived class. It is not possible to inherit only part of a class (the interface alone, say). As Chapter 14 of Volume 1 explains, private and protected inheritance make it possible to restrict access to members inherited from base classes when used by clients of a derived class object, but this doesn't affect the derived class; it still contains all base class data and can access all non-private base class members.

Interface inheritance, on the other hand, only adds member function *declarations* to a derived class interface and is not directly supported in C++. The usual technique to simulate interface inheritance in C++ is to derive from an *interface class*, which is a class that contains only declarations (no data or function bodies). These declarations will be pure virtual functions, except for the destructor. Here is an example:

```
//: C09:Interfaces.cpp
// Multiple interface inheritance.
#include <iostream>
#include <sstream>
#include <string>
using namespace std;

class Printable {
public:
  virtual ~Printable() {}
  virtual void print(ostream&) const = 0;
};

class Intable {
public:
  virtual ~Intable() {}
  virtual int toInt() const = 0;
};

class Stringable {
public:
  virtual ~Stringable() {}
  virtual string toString() const = 0;
};

class Able : public Printable, public Intable,
             public Stringable {
  int myData;
public:
  Able(int x) { myData = x; }
  void print(ostream& os) const { os << myData; }
  int toInt() const { return myData; }
```

```
    string toString() const {
      ostringstream os;
      os << myData;
      return os.str();
    }
};

void testPrintable(const Printable& p) {
  p.print(cout);
  cout << endl;
}

void testIntable(const Intable& n) {
  cout << n.toInt() + 1 << endl;
}

void testStringable(const Stringable& s) {
  cout << s.toString() + "th" << endl;
}

int main() {
  Able a(7);
  testPrintable(a);
  testIntable(a);
  testStringable(a);
} ///:~
```

The class **Able** "implements" the interfaces **Printable**, **Intable**, and **Stringable** because it provides implementations for the functions they declare. Because **Able** derives from all three classes, **Able** objects have multiple "is-a" relationships. For example, the object **a** can act as a **Printable** object because its class, **Able**, derives publicly from **Printable** and provides an implementation for **print( )**. The test functions have no need to know the most-derived type of their parameter; they just need an object that is substitutable for their parameter's type.

As usual, a template solution is more compact:

```
//: C09:Interfaces2.cpp
// Implicit interface inheritance via templates.
#include <iostream>
#include <sstream>
#include <string>
using namespace std;
```

```
class Able {
  int myData;
public:
  Able(int x) { myData = x; }
  void print(ostream& os) const { os << myData; }
  int toInt() const { return myData; }
  string toString() const {
    ostringstream os;
    os << myData;
    return os.str();
  }
};

template<class Printable>
void testPrintable(const Printable& p) {
  p.print(cout);
  cout << endl;
}

template<class Intable>
void testIntable(const Intable& n) {
  cout << n.toInt() + 1 << endl;
}

template<class Stringable>
void testStringable(const Stringable& s) {
  cout << s.toString() + "th" << endl;
}

int main() {
  Able a(7);
  testPrintable(a);
  testIntable(a);
  testStringable(a);
} ///:~
```

The names **Printable**, **Intable**, and **Stringable** are now just template parameters that assume the existence of the operations indicated in their respective contexts. In other words, the test functions can accept arguments of any type that provides a member function definition with the correct signature and return type; deriving from a common base class in not necessary. Some people are more comfortable with the first version because the type names guarantee by inheritance that the expected interfaces are implemented. Others are content with the fact that if the operations required by the test functions are not satisfied by their template type arguments, the error is still caught at compile time. The latter approach is technically a "weaker" form of type checking than the former (inheritance) approach, but the effect on the programmer (and the program) is the same. This is one form of weak typing that is acceptable to many of today's C++ programmers.

Implementation inheritance

As we stated earlier, C++ provides only implementation inheritance, meaning that you always inherit *everything* from your base classes. This can be good because it frees you from having to implement everything in the derived class, as we had to do with the interface inheritance examples earlier. A common use of multiple inheritance involves using *mixin classes*, which are classes that exist to add capabilities to other classes through inheritance. Mixin classes are not intended to be instantiated by themselves.

As an example, suppose we are clients of a class that supports access to a database. In this scenario, you only have a header file available—part of the point here is that you don't have access to the source code for the implementation. For illustration, assume the following implementation of a **Database** class:

```
//: C09:Database.h
// A prototypical resource class.
#ifndef DATABASE_H
#define DATABASE_H
#include <iostream>
#include <stdexcept>
#include <string>

struct DatabaseError : std::runtime_error {
  DatabaseError(const std::string& msg)
    : std::runtime_error(msg) {}
};

class Database {
  std::string dbid;
public:
  Database(const std::string& dbStr) : dbid(dbStr) {}
  virtual ~Database() {}
```

```
  void open() throw(DatabaseError) {
    std::cout << "Connected to " << dbid << std::endl;
  }
  void close() {
    std::cout << dbid << " closed" << std::endl;
  }
  // Other database functions...
};
#endif // DATABASE_H ///:~
```

We're leaving out actual database functionality (storing, retrieving, and so
on), but that's not important here. Using this class requires a database
connection string and that you call **Database::open( )** to connect and
Database::close( ) to disconnect:

```
//: C09:UseDatabase.cpp
#include "Database.h"

int main() {
  Database db("MyDatabase");
  db.open();
  // Use other db functions...
  db.close();
}
/* Output:
connected to MyDatabase
MyDatabase closed
*/ ///:~
```

In a typical client-server situation, a client will have multiple objects sharing
a connection to a database. It is important that the database eventually be
closed, but only after access to it is no longer required. It is common to
encapsulate this behavior through a class that tracks the number of client
entities using the database connection and to automatically terminate the
connection when that count goes to zero. To add reference counting to the
Database class, we use multiple inheritance to mix a class named
Countable into the **Database** class to create a new class, **DBConnection**.
Here's the **Countable** mixin class:

```
//: C09:Countable.h
// A "mixin" class.
#ifndef COUNTABLE_H
#define COUNTABLE_H
```

```
#include <cassert>

class Countable {
  long count;
protected:
  Countable() { count = 0; }
  virtual ~Countable() { assert(count == 0); }
public:
  long attach() { return ++count; }
  long detach() {
    return (--count > 0) ? count : (delete this, 0);
  }
  long refCount() const { return count; }
};
#endif // COUNTABLE_H ///:~
```

It is evident that this is not a standalone class because its constructor is
protected; it requires a friend or a derived class to use it. It is important that
the destructor is virtual, because it is called only from the **delete this**
statement in **detach( )**, and we want derived objects to be properly
destroyed.[3]

The **DBConnection** class inherits both **Database** and **Countable** and
provides a static **create( )** function that initializes its **Countable** subobject.
This is an example of the Factory Method design pattern, discussed in the
next chapter:

```
//: C09:DBConnection.h
// Uses a "mixin" class.
#ifndef DBCONNECTION_H
#define DBCONNECTION_H
#include <cassert>
#include <string>
#include "Countable.h"
#include "Database.h"
using std::string;

class DBConnection : public Database, public Countable {
  DBConnection(const DBConnection&); // Disallow copy
```

---

[3] Even more importantly, we don't want undefined behavior. It is an error
for a base class not to have a virtual destructor.

```
    DBConnection& operator=(const DBConnection&);
protected:
  DBConnection(const string& dbStr) throw(DatabaseError)
  : Database(dbStr) { open(); }
  ~DBConnection() { close(); }
public:
  static DBConnection*
  create(const string& dbStr) throw(DatabaseError) {
    DBConnection* con = new DBConnection(dbStr);
    con->attach();
    assert(con->refCount() == 1);
    return con;
  }
  // Other added functionality as desired...
};
#endif // DBCONNECTION_H ///:~
```

We now have a reference-counted database connection without modifying the **Database** class, and we can safely assume that it will not be surreptitiously terminated. The opening and closing is done using the Resource Acquisition Is Initialization (RAII) idiom mentioned in Chapter 1 via the **DBConnection** constructor and destructor. This makes the **DBConnection** easy to use:

```
//: C09:UseDatabase2.cpp
// Tests the Countable "mixin" class.
#include <cassert>
#include "DBConnection.h"

class DBClient {
  DBConnection* db;
public:
  DBClient(DBConnection* dbCon) {
    db = dbCon;
    db->attach();
  }
  ~DBClient() { db->detach(); }
  // Other database requests using db…
};

int main() {
  DBConnection* db = DBConnection::create("MyDatabase");
  assert(db->refCount() == 1);
  DBClient c1(db);
  assert(db->refCount() == 2);
```

```
  DBClient c2(db);
  assert(db->refCount() == 3);
  // Use database, then release attach from original create
  db->detach();
  assert(db->refCount() == 2);
} ///:~
```

The call to **DBConnection::create( )** calls **attach( )**, so when we're
finished, we must explicitly call **detach( )** to release the original hold on the
connection. Note that the **DBClient** class also uses RAII to manage its use of
the connection. When the program terminates, the destructors for the two
DBClient objects will decrement the reference count (by calling **detach( )**,
which **DBConnection** inherited from **Countable**), and the database
connection will be closed (because of **Countable**'s virtual destructor) when
the count reaches zero after the object **c1** is destroyed.

A template approach is commonly used for mixin inheritance, allowing the
user to specify at compile time which flavor of mixin is desired. This way you
can use different reference-counting approaches without explicitly defining
DBConnection twice. Here's how it's done:

```
//: C09:DBConnection2.h
// A parameterized mixin.
#ifndef DBCONNECTION2_H
#define DBCONNECTION2_H
#include <cassert>
#include <string>
#include "Database.h"
using std::string;

template<class Counter>
class DBConnection : public Database, public Counter {
  DBConnection(const DBConnection&); // Disallow copy
  DBConnection& operator=(const DBConnection&);
protected:
  DBConnection(const string& dbStr) throw(DatabaseError)
  : Database(dbStr) { open(); }
  ~DBConnection() { close(); }
public:
  static DBConnection* create(const string& dbStr)
  throw(DatabaseError) {
    DBConnection* con = new DBConnection(dbStr);
    con->attach();
```

```
    assert(con->refCount() == 1);
    return con;
  }
  // Other added functionality as desired...
};
#endif // DBCONNECTION2_H ///:~
```

The only change here is the template prefix to the class definition (and renaming **Countable** to **Counter** for clarity). We could also make the database class a template parameter (had we multiple database access classes to choose from), but it is not a mixin since it is a standalone class. The following example uses the original **Countable** as the **Counter** mixin type, but we could use any type that implements the appropriate interface (**attach( )**, **detach( )**, and so on):

```
//: C09:UseDatabase3.cpp
// Tests a parameterized "mixin" class.
#include <cassert>
#include "Countable.h"
#include "DBConnection2.h"

class DBClient {
  DBConnection<Countable>* db;
public:
  DBClient(DBConnection<Countable>* dbCon) {
    db = dbCon;
    db->attach();
  }
  ~DBClient() { db->detach(); }
};

int main() {
  DBConnection<Countable>* db =
    DBConnection<Countable>::create("MyDatabase");
  assert(db->refCount() == 1);
  DBClient c1(db);
  assert(db->refCount() == 2);
  DBClient c2(db);
  assert(db->refCount() == 3);
  db->detach();
  assert(db->refCount() == 2);
} ///:~
```

The general pattern for multiple parameterized mixins is simply

```
template<class Mixin1, class Mixin2, … , class MixinK>
class Subject : public Mixin1,
                public Mixin2,
                …
                public MixinK {…};
```

Duplicate subobjects

When you inherit from a base class, you get a copy of all the data members of
that base class in your derived class. The following program shows how
multiple base subobjects might be laid out in memory:[4]

```
//: C09:Offset.cpp
// Illustrates layout of subobjects with MI.
#include <iostream>
using namespace std;

class A { int x; };
class B { int y; };
class C : public A, public B { int z; };

int main() {
  cout << "sizeof(A) == " << sizeof(A) << endl;
  cout << "sizeof(B) == " << sizeof(B) << endl;
  cout << "sizeof(C) == " << sizeof(C) << endl;
  C c;
  cout << "&c == " << &c << endl;
  A* ap = &c;
  B* bp = &c;
  cout << "ap == " << static_cast<void*>(ap) << endl;
  cout << "bp == " << static_cast<void*>(bp) << endl;
  C* cp = static_cast<C*>(bp);
  cout << "cp == " << static_cast<void*>(cp) << endl;
  cout << "bp == cp? " << boolalpha << (bp == cp) << endl;
  cp = 0;
  bp = cp;
  cout << bp << endl;
}
/* Output:
sizeof(A) == 4
```

---

[4] The actual layout is implementation specific.

```
sizeof(B) == 4
sizeof(C) == 12
&c == 1245052
ap == 1245052
bp == 1245056
cp == 1245052
bp == cp? true
0
*/ ///:~
```

As you can see, the **B** portion of the object **c** is offset 4 bytes from the beginning of the entire object, suggesting the following layout:

The object **c** begins with it's **A** subobject, then the **B** portion, and finally the data from the complete type **C** itself. Since a **C** is-an **A** and is-a **B**, it is possible to upcast to either base type. When upcasting to an **A**, the resulting pointer points to the **A** portion, which happens to be at the beginning of the C object, so the address **ap** is the same as the expression **&c**. When upcasting to a **B**, however, the resulting pointer must point to where the **B** subobject actually resides because class B knows nothing about class **C** (or class **A**, for that matter). In other words, the object pointed to by **bp** must be able to behave as a standalone **B** object (except for any required polymorphic behavior).

When casting **bp** back to a **C***, since the original object was a **C** in the first place, the location where the **B** subobject resides is known, so the pointer is adjusted back to the original address of the complete object. If **bp** had been pointing to a standalone **B** object instead of a **C** object in the first place, the cast would be illegal.[5] Furthermore, in the comparison **bp == cp**, **cp** is implicitly converted to a **B***, since that is the only way to make the comparison meaningful (that is, upcasting is always allowed), hence the **true** result. So when converting back and forth between subobjects and complete types, the appropriate offset is applied.

The null pointer requires special handling, obviously, since blindly subtracting an offset when converting to or from a **B** subobject will result in an invalid address if the pointer was zero to start with. For this reason, when casting to or from a **B***, the compiler generates logic to check first to see if the pointer is zero. If it isn't, it applies the offset; otherwise, it leaves it as zero.

With the syntax we've seen so far, if you have multiple base classes, and those base classes in turn have a common base class, you will have two copies of the top-level base, as you can see in the following example:

```
//: C09:Duplicate.cpp
// Shows duplicate subobjects.
#include <iostream>
using namespace std;

class Top {
  int x;
public:
  Top(int n) { x = n; }
};

class Left : public Top {
  int y;
public:
  Left(int m, int n) : Top(m) { y = n; }
};

class Right : public Top {
  int z;
public:
  Right(int m, int n) : Top(m) { z = n; }
};
```

---

[5] But not detected as an error. **dynamic_cast**, however, can solve this problem. See the previous chapter for details.

```
class Bottom : public Left, public Right {
  int w;
public:
  Bottom(int i, int j, int k, int m)
  : Left(i, k), Right(j, k) { w = m; }
};

int main() {
  Bottom b(1, 2, 3, 4);
  cout << sizeof b << endl; // 20
} ///:~
```

Since the size of **b** is 20 bytes,[6] there are five integers altogether in a complete **Bottom** object. A typical class diagram for this scenario usually appears as:

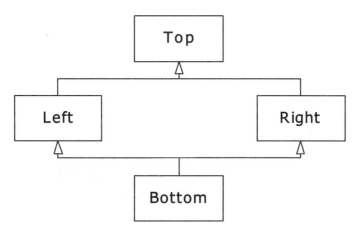

This is the so-called "diamond inheritance", but in this case it would be better rendered as:

---

[6] That is, **5*sizeof(int)**. Compilers can add arbitrary padding, so the size of an object must be at least as large as the sum of its parts, but can be larger.

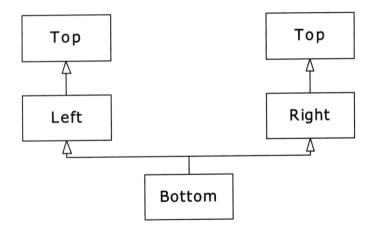

The awkwardness of this design surfaces in the constructor for the **Bottom** class in the previous code. The user thinks that only four integers are required, but which arguments should be passed to the two parameters that **Left** and **Right** require? Although this design is not inherently "wrong," it is usually not what an application needs. It also presents a problem when trying to convert a pointer to a **Bottom** object to a pointer to **Top**. As we showed earlier, the address may need to be adjusted, depending on where the subobject resides within the complete object, but here there are *two* **Top** subobjects to choose from. The compiler doesn't know which to choose, so such an upcast is ambiguous and is not allowed. The same reasoning explains why a **Bottom** object would not be able to call a function that is only defined in **Top**. If such a function **Top::f( )** existed, calling **b.f( )** above would need to refer to a **Top** subobject as an execution context, and there are two to choose from.

Virtual base classes

What we usually want in such cases is *true* diamond inheritance, where a single **Top** object is shared by both **Left** and **Right** subobjects within a complete **Bottom** object, which is what the first class diagram depicts. This is achieved by making **Top** a *virtual base class* of **Left** and **Right**:

```
//: C09:VirtualBase.cpp
// Shows a shared subobject via a virtual base.
#include <iostream>
using namespace std;
```

```
class Top {
protected:
  int x;
public:
  Top(int n) { x = n; }
  virtual ~Top() {}
  friend ostream&
  operator<<(ostream& os, const Top& t) {
    return os << t.x;
  }
};

class Left : virtual public Top {
protected:
  int y;
public:
  Left(int m, int n) : Top(m) { y = n; }
};

class Right : virtual public Top {
protected:
  int z;
public:
  Right(int m, int n) : Top(m) { z = n; }
};

class Bottom : public Left, public Right {
  int w;
public:
  Bottom(int i, int j, int k, int m)
  : Top(i), Left(0, j), Right(0, k) { w = m; }
  friend ostream&
  operator<<(ostream& os, const Bottom& b) {
    return os << b.x << ',' << b.y << ',' << b.z
      << ',' << b.w;
  }
};

int main() {
  Bottom b(1, 2, 3, 4);
  cout << sizeof b << endl;
  cout << b << endl;
  cout << static_cast<void*>(&b) << endl;
  Top* p = static_cast<Top*>(&b);
```

```
    cout << *p << endl;
    cout << static_cast<void*>(p) << endl;
    cout << dynamic_cast<void*>(p) << endl;
} ///:~
```

Each virtual base of a given type refers to the same object, no matter where it appears in the hierarchy.[7] This means that when a **Bottom** object is instantiated, the object layout may look something like this:

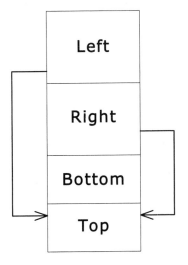

The **Left** and **Right** subobjects each have a pointer (or some conceptual equivalent) to the shared **Top** subobject, and all references to that subobject in **Left** and **Right** member functions will go through those these pointers.[8] Here, there is no ambiguity when upcasting from a **Bottom** to a **Top** object, since there is only one **Top** object to convert to.

The output of the previous program is as follows:

36

---

[7] We use the term *hierarchy* because everyone else does, but the graph representing multiple inheritance relationships is in general a *directed acyclic graph* (DAG), also called a *lattice*, for obvious reasons.
[8] The presence of these pointers explains why the size of **b** is much larger than the size of four integers. This is (part of) the cost of virtual base classes. There is also VPTR overhead due to the virtual destructor.

```
1,2,3,4
1245032
1
1245060
1245032
```

The addresses printed suggest that this particular implementation does indeed store the **Top** subobject at the end of the complete object (although it's not really important where it goes). The result of a **dynamic_cast** to **void*** always resolves to the address of the complete object.

Although it is technically illegal to do so[9], if you remove the virtual destructor (and the **dynamic_cast** statement, so the program will compile), the size of **Bottom** decreases to 24 bytes. That seems to be a decrease equivalent to the size of three pointers. Why?

It's important not to take these numbers too literally. Other compilers we use manage only to increase the size by four bytes when the virtual constructor is added. Not being compiler writers, we can't tell you their secrets. We can tell you, however, that with multiple inheritance, a derived object must behave as if it has multiple VPTRs, one for each of its direct base classes that also have virtual functions. It's as simple as that. Compilers make whatever optimizations their authors invent, but the behavior must be the same.

The strangest thing in the previous code is the initializer for **Top** in the **Bottom** constructor. Normally one doesn't worry about initializing subobjects beyond direct base classes, since all classes take care of initializing their own bases. There are, however, multiple paths from **Bottom** to **Top**, so relying on the intermediate classes **Left** and **Right** to pass along the necessary initialization data results in an ambiguity—who is responsible for performing the initialization? For this reason, the *most derived class* must initialize a virtual base. But what about the expressions in the **Left** and **Right** constructors that also initialize **Top**? They are certainly necessary when creating standalone **Left** or **Right** objects, but must be *ignored* when a **Bottom** object is created (hence the zeros in their initializers in the **Bottom** constructor—any values in those slots are ignored when the **Left** and **Right** constructors execute in the context of a **Bottom** object). The compiler takes

---

[9] Once again, base classes must have virtual destructors, but most compilers will let this experiment compile.

---

care of all this for you, but it's important to understand where the responsibility lies. Always make sure that *all concrete (nonabstract) classes* in a multiple inheritance hierarchy are aware of any virtual bases and initialize them appropriately.

These rules of responsibility apply not only to initialization, but to all operations that span the class hierarchy. Consider the stream inserter in the previous code. We made the data protected so we could "cheat" and access inherited data in **operator<<(ostream&, const Bottom&)**. It usually makes more sense to assign the work of printing each subobject to its corresponding class and have the derived class call its base class functions as needed. What would happen if we tried that with **operator<<( )**, as the following code illustrates?

```cpp
//: C09:VirtualBase2.cpp
// How NOT to implement operator<<.
#include <iostream>
using namespace std;

class Top {
  int x;
public:
  Top(int n) { x = n; }
  virtual ~Top() {}
  friend ostream& operator<<(ostream& os, const Top& t) {
    return os << t.x;
  }
};

class Left : virtual public Top {
  int y;
public:
  Left(int m, int n) : Top(m) { y = n; }
  friend ostream& operator<<(ostream& os, const Left& l) {
    return os << static_cast<const Top&>(l) << ',' << l.y;
  }
};

class Right : virtual public Top {
  int z;
public:
  Right(int m, int n) : Top(m) { z = n; }
  friend ostream& operator<<(ostream& os, const Right& r) {
```

```
    return os << static_cast<const Top&>(r) << ',' << r.z;
  }
};

class Bottom : public Left, public Right {
  int w;
public:
  Bottom(int i, int j, int k, int m)
  : Top(i), Left(0, j), Right(0, k) { w = m; }
  friend ostream& operator<<(ostream& os, const Bottom& b){
    return os << static_cast<const Left&>(b)
      << ',' << static_cast<const Right&>(b)
      << ',' << b.w;
  }
};

int main() {
  Bottom b(1, 2, 3, 4);
  cout << b << endl;  // 1,2,1,3,4
} ///:~
```

You can't just blindly share the responsibility upward in the usual fashion, because the **Left** and **Right** stream inserters each call the **Top** inserter, and again there will be duplication of data. Instead you need to mimic what the compiler does with initialization. One solution is to provide special functions in the classes that know about the virtual base class, which ignore the virtual base when printing (leaving the job to the most derived class):

```
//: C09:VirtualBase3.cpp
// A correct stream inserter.
#include <iostream>
using namespace std;

class Top {
  int x;
public:
  Top(int n) { x = n; }
  virtual ~Top() {}
  friend ostream& operator<<(ostream& os, const Top& t) {
    return os << t.x;
  }
};

class Left : virtual public Top {
```

```
    int y;
protected:
  void specialPrint(ostream& os) const {
    // Only print Left's part
    os << ','<< y;
  }
public:
  Left(int m, int n) : Top(m) { y = n; }
  friend ostream& operator<<(ostream& os, const Left& l) {
    return os << static_cast<const Top&>(l) << ',' << l.y;
  }
};

class Right : virtual public Top {
  int z;
protected:
  void specialPrint(ostream& os) const {
    // Only print Right's part
    os << ','<< z;
  }
public:
  Right(int m, int n) : Top(m) { z = n; }
  friend ostream& operator<<(ostream& os, const Right& r) {
    return os << static_cast<const Top&>(r) << ',' << r.z;
  }
};

class Bottom : public Left, public Right {
  int w;
public:
  Bottom(int i, int j, int k, int m)
    : Top(i), Left(0, j), Right(0, k) { w = m; }
  friend ostream& operator<<(ostream& os, const Bottom& b){
    os << static_cast<const Top&>(b);
    b.Left::specialPrint(os);
    b.Right::specialPrint(os);
    return os << ',' << b.w;
  }
};

int main() {
  Bottom b(1, 2, 3, 4);
  cout << b << endl;  // 1,2,3,4
} ///:~
```

The **specialPrint( )** functions are **protected** since they will be called only by **Bottom**. They print only their own data and ignore their **Top** subobject because the **Bottom** inserter is in control when these functions are called. The **Bottom** inserter must know about the virtual base, just as a **Bottom** constructor needs to. This same reasoning applies to assignment operators in a hierarchy with a virtual base, as well as to any function, member or not, that wants to share the work throughout all classes in the hierarchy.

Having discussed virtual base classes, we can now illustrate the "full story" of object initialization. Since virtual bases give rise to shared subobjects, it makes sense that they should be available before the sharing takes place. So the order of initialization of subobjects follows these rules, recursively:

1.   All virtual base class subobjects are initialized, in top-down, left-to-right order according to where they appear in class definitions.

2.   Non-virtual base classes are then initialized in the usual order.

3.   All member objects are initialized in declaration order.

4.   The complete object's constructor executes.

The following program illustrates this behavior:

```
//: C09:VirtInit.cpp
// Illustrates initialization order with virtual bases.
#include <iostream>
#include <string>
using namespace std;

class M {
public:
  M(const string& s) { cout << "M " << s << endl; }
};

class A {
  M m;
public:
  A(const string& s) : m("in A") {
    cout << "A " << s << endl;
  }
  virtual ~A() {}
};
```

```cpp
class B {
  M m;
public:
  B(const string& s) : m("in B")  {
    cout << "B " << s << endl;
  }
  virtual ~B() {}
};

class C {
  M m;
public:
  C(const string& s) : m("in C")  {
    cout << "C " << s << endl;
  }
  virtual ~C() {}
};

class D {
  M m;
public:
  D(const string& s) : m("in D") {
    cout << "D " << s << endl;
  }
  virtual ~D() {}
};

class E : public A, virtual public B, virtual public C {
  M m;
public:
  E(const string& s) : A("from E"), B("from E"),
  C("from E"), m("in E") {
    cout << "E " << s << endl;
  }
};

class F : virtual public B, virtual public C, public D {
  M m;
public:
  F(const string& s) : B("from F"), C("from F"),
  D("from F"), m("in F") {
    cout << "F " << s << endl;
  }
};
```

```
class G : public E, public F {
  M m;
public:
  G(const string& s) : B("from G"), C("from G"),
  E("from G"),  F("from G"), m("in G") {
    cout << "G " << s << endl;
  }
};

int main() {
  G g("from main");
} ///:~
```

The classes in this code can be represented by the following diagram:

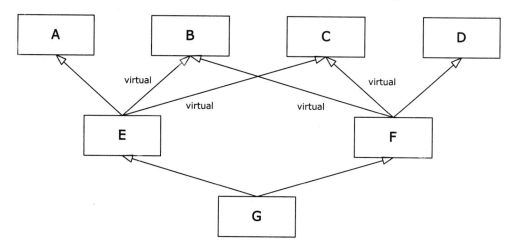

Each class has an embedded member of type **M**. Note that only four derivations are virtual: **E** from **B** and **C**, and **F** from **B** and **C**. The output of this program is:

```
M in B
B from G
M in C
C from G
M in A
A from E
M in E
E from G
M in D
D from F
```

```
M in F
F from G
M in G
G from main
```

The initialization of **g** requires its **E** and **F** part to first be initialized, but the **B** and **C** subobjects are initialized first because they are virtual bases and are initialized from **G**'s initializer, **G** being the most-derived class. The class **B** has no base classes, so according to rule 3, its member object **m** is initialized, then its constructor prints "**B** from **G**", and similarly for the **C** subject of **E**. The **E** subobject requires **A**, **B**, and **C** subobjects. Since **B** and **C** have already been initialized, the **A** subobject of the **E** subobject is initialized next, and then the **E** subobject itself. The same scenario repeats for **g**'s **F** subobject, but without duplicating the initialization of the virtual bases.

Name lookup issues

The ambiguities we have illustrated with subobjects apply to any names, including function names. If a class has multiple direct base classes that share member functions of the same name, and you call one of those member functions, the compiler doesn't know which one to choose. The following sample program would report such an error:

```
//: C09:AmbiguousName.cpp {-xo}

class Top {
public:
  virtual ~Top() {}
};

class Left : virtual public Top {
public:
  void f() {}
};

class Right : virtual public Top {
public:
  void f() {}
};

class Bottom : public Left, public Right {};
```

```
int main() {
  Bottom b;
  b.f(); // Error here
} ///:~
```

The class **Bottom** has inherited two functions of the same name (the signature is irrelevant, since name lookup occurs before overload resolution), and there is no way to choose between them. The usual technique to disambiguate the call is to qualify the function call with the base class name:

```
//: C09:BreakTie.cpp

class Top {
public:
  virtual ~Top() {}
};

class Left : virtual public Top {
public:
  void f() {}
};

class Right : virtual public Top {
public:
  void f() {}
};

class Bottom : public Left, public Right {
public:
  using Left::f;
};

int main() {
  Bottom b;
  b.f(); // Calls Left::f()
} ///:~
```

The name **Left::f** is now found in the scope of **Bottom**, so the name **Right::f** is not even considered. To introduce extra functionality beyond what **Left::f( )** provides, you implement a **Bottom::f( )** function that calls **Left::f( )**.

Functions with the same name occurring in different branches of a hierarchy often conflict. The following hierarchy has no such problem:

```
//: C09:Dominance.cpp

class Top {
public:
  virtual ~Top() {}
  virtual void f() {}
};

class Left : virtual public Top {
public:
  void f() {}
};

class Right : virtual public Top {};

class Bottom : public Left, public Right {};

int main() {
  Bottom b;
  b.f(); // Calls Left::f()
} ///:~
```

Here, there is no explicit **Right::f( )**. Since **Left::f( )** is the most derived, it is chosen. Why? Well, pretend that **Right** did not exist, giving the single-inheritance hierarchy **Top <= Left <= Bottom**. You would certainly expect **Left::f( )** to be the function called by the expression **b.f( )** because of normal scope rules: a derived class is considered a nested scope of a base class. In general, a name **A::f** *dominates* the name **B::f** if **A** derives from **B**, directly or indirectly, or in other words, if **A** is "more derived" in the hierarchy than **B**.[10] Therefore, in choosing between two functions with the same name, the compiler chooses the one that dominates. If there is no dominant name, there is an ambiguity.

The following program further illustrates the dominance principle:

```
//: C09:Dominance2.cpp
#include <iostream>
```

---

[10] Note that virtual inheritance is crucial to this example. If **Top** were not a virtual base class, there would be multiple **Top** subobjects, and the ambiguity would remain. Dominance with multiple inheritance only comes into play with virtual base classes.

```
using namespace std;

class A {
public:
  virtual ~A() {}
  virtual void f() { cout << "A::f\n"; }
};

class B : virtual public A {
public:
  void f() { cout << "B::f\n"; }
};

class C : public B {};
class D : public C, virtual public A {};

int main() {
  B* p = new D;
  p->f(); // Calls B::f()
  delete p;
} ///:~
```

The class diagram for this hierarchy is

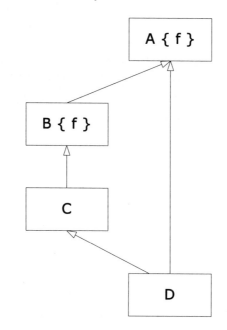

The class **A** is a (direct, in this case) base class for **B**, and so the name **B::f** dominates **A::f**.

Avoiding MI

When the question of whether to use multiple inheritance comes up, ask at least two questions:

1.   Do you need to show the public interfaces of both these classes through your new type? (See instead if one class can be contained within the other, with only some of its interface exposed in the new class.)

2.   Do you need to upcast to both of the base classes? (This also applies when you have more than two base classes.)

If you can answer "no" to either question, you can avoid using MI and should probably do so.

Watch for the situation where one class needs to be upcast only as a function argument. In that case, the class can be embedded and an automatic type conversion function provided in your new class to produce a reference to the embedded object. Any time you use an object of your new class as an argument to a function that expects the embedded object, the type conversion function is used.[11] However, type conversion can't be used for normal polymorphic member function selection; that requires inheritance. Preferring composition over inheritance is a good overall design guideline.

Extending an interface

One of the best uses for multiple inheritance involves code that's out of your control. Suppose you've acquired a library that consists of a header file and compiled member functions, but no source code for member functions. This

---

[11] Jerry Schwarz, the author of iostreams, has remarked to both of us on separate occasions that if he had it to do over again, he would probably remove MI from the design of iostreams and use multiple stream buffers and conversion operators instead.

---

library is a class hierarchy with virtual functions, and it contains some global functions that take pointers to the base class of the library; that is, it uses the library objects polymorphically. Now suppose you build an application around this library and write your own code that uses the base class polymorphically.

Later in the development of the project or sometime during its maintenance, you discover that the base-class interface provided by the vendor doesn't provide what you need: a function may be non-virtual and you need it to be virtual, or a virtual function is completely missing in the interface, but essential to the solution of your problem. Multiple inheritance can be the solution.

For example, here's the header file for a library you acquire:

```
//: C09:Vendor.h
// Vendor-supplied class header
// You only get this & the compiled Vendor.obj.
#ifndef VENDOR_H
#define VENDOR_H

class Vendor {
public:
  virtual void v() const;
  void f() const; // Might want this to be virtual...
  ~Vendor(); // Oops! Not virtual!
};

class Vendor1 : public Vendor {
public:
  void v() const;
  void f() const;
  ~Vendor1();
};

void A(const Vendor&);
void B(const Vendor&);
// Etc.
#endif // VENDOR_H ///:~
```

Assume the library is much bigger, with more derived classes and a larger interface. Notice that it also includes the functions **A( )** and **B( )**, which take a base reference and treat it polymorphically. Here's the implementation file for the library:

```
//: C09:Vendor.cpp {O}
// Assume this is compiled and unavailable to you.
#include "Vendor.h"
#include <iostream>
using namespace std;

void Vendor::v() const { cout << "Vendor::v()" << endl; }

void Vendor::f() const { cout << "Vendor::f()" << endl; }

Vendor::~Vendor() { cout << "~Vendor()" << endl; }

void Vendor1::v() const { cout << "Vendor1::v()" << endl; }

void Vendor1::f() const { cout << "Vendor1::f()" << endl; }

Vendor1::~Vendor1() { cout << "~Vendor1()" << endl; }

void A(const Vendor& v) {
  // ...
  v.v();
  v.f();
  // ...
}

void B(const Vendor& v) {
  // ...
  v.v();
  v.f();
  // ...
} ///:~
```

In your project, this source code is unavailable to you. Instead, you get a compiled file as **Vendor.obj** or **Vendor.lib** (or with the equivalent file suffixes for your system).

The problem occurs in the use of this library. First, the destructor isn't virtual.[12] In addition, **f( )** was not made virtual; we assume the library creator decided it wouldn't need to be. You also discover that the interface to the base class is missing a function essential to the solution of your problem. Also suppose you've already written a fair amount of code using the existing interface (not to mention the functions **A( )** and **B( )**, which are out of your control), and you don't want to change it.

To repair the problem, create your own class interface and multiply inherit a new set of derived classes from your interface and from the existing classes:

```
//: C09:Paste.cpp
//{L} Vendor
// Fixing a mess with MI.
#include <iostream>
#include "Vendor.h"
using namespace std;

class MyBase { // Repair Vendor interface
public:
  virtual void v() const = 0;
  virtual void f() const = 0;
  // New interface function:
  virtual void g() const = 0;
  virtual ~MyBase() { cout << "~MyBase()" << endl; }
};

class Paste1 : public MyBase, public Vendor1 {
public:
  void v() const {
    cout << "Paste1::v()" << endl;
    Vendor1::v();
  }
  void f() const {
    cout << "Paste1::f()" << endl;
    Vendor1::f();
  }
  void g() const { cout << "Paste1::g()" << endl; }
  ~Paste1() { cout << "~Paste1()" << endl; }
```

----

12 We've seen this in commercial C++ libraries, at least in some of the early ones.

```
};

int main() {
  Paste1& p1p = *new Paste1;
  MyBase& mp = p1p; // Upcast
  cout << "calling f()" << endl;
  mp.f();   // Right behavior
  cout << "calling g()" << endl;
  mp.g(); // New behavior
  cout << "calling A(p1p)" << endl;
  A(p1p); // Same old behavior
  cout << "calling B(p1p)" << endl;
  B(p1p);   // Same old behavior
  cout << "delete mp" << endl;
  // Deleting a reference to a heap object:
  delete &mp; // Right behavior
} ///:~
```

In **MyBase** (which does *not* use MI), both **f( )** and the destructor are now virtual, and a new virtual function **g( )** is added to the interface. Now each of the derived classes in the original library must be re-created, mixing in the new interface with MI. The functions **Paste1::v( )** and **Paste1::f( )** need to call only the original base-class versions of their functions. But now, if you upcast to **MyBase** as in **main( )**:

```
MyBase* mp = p1p; // Upcast
```

any function calls made through **mp** will be polymorphic, including **delete**. Also, the new interface function **g( )** can be called through **mp**. Here's the output of the program:

```
calling f()
Paste1::f()
Vendor1::f()
calling g()
Paste1::g()
calling A(p1p)
Paste1::v()
Vendor1::v()
Vendor::f()
calling B(p1p)
Paste1::v()
Vendor1::v()
Vendor::f()
```

```
delete mp
~Paste1()
~Vendor1()
~Vendor()
~MyBase()
```

The original library functions **A( )** and **B( )** still work the same (assuming the new **v( )** calls its base-class version). The destructor is now **virtual** and exhibits the correct behavior.

Although this is a messy example, it does occur in practice, and it's a good demonstration of where multiple inheritance is clearly necessary: You must be able to upcast to both base classes.

Summary

One reason MI exists in C++ is that it is a hybrid language and couldn't enforce a single monolithic class hierarchy the way Smalltalk and Java do. Instead, C++ allows many inheritance trees to be formed, so sometimes you may need to combine the interfaces from two or more trees into a new class.

If no "diamonds" appear in your class hierarchy, MI is fairly simple (although identical function signatures in base classes must still be resolved). If a diamond appears, you may want to eliminate duplicate subobjects by introducing virtual base classes. This not only adds confusion, but the underlying representation becomes more complex and less efficient.

Multiple inheritance has been called the "goto of the '90s."[13] This seems appropriate because, like a goto, MI is best avoided in normal programming, but can occasionally be very useful. It's a "minor" but more advanced feature of C++, designed to solve problems that arise in special situations. If you find yourself using it often, you might want to take a look at your reasoning. Ask yourself, "Must I upcast to all the base classes?" If not, your life will be easier if you embed instances of all the classes you *don't* need to upcast to.

---

[13] A phrase coined by Zack Urlocker.

Exercises

Solutions to selected exercises can be found in the electronic document *The Thinking in C++ Volume 2 Annotated Solution Guide*, available for a small fee from *www.MindView.net*.

1. Create a base class **X** with a single constructor that takes an **int** argument and a member function **f( )**, which takes no arguments and returns **void**. Now derive **Y** and **Z** from **X**, creating constructors for each of them that take a single **int** argument. Next, derive **A** from **Y** and **Z**. Create an object of class **A**, and call **f( )** for that object. Fix the problem with explicit disambiguation.

2. Starting with the results of Exercise 1, create a pointer to an **X** called **px** and assign to it the address of the object of type **A** you created before. Fix the problem using a virtual base class. Now fix **X** so you no longer have to call the constructor for **X** inside **A**.

3. Starting with the results of Exercise 2, remove the explicit disambiguation for **f( )** and see if you can call **f( )** through **px**. Trace it to see which function gets called. Fix the problem so the correct function will be called in a class hierarchy.

4. Make an **Animal** interface class with a **makeNoise( )** function declaration. Make a **SuperHero** interface class with a **savePersonFromFire( )** function declaration. Place a **move( )** function declaration in both interface classes. (Remember to make your interface methods pure virtual.) Now define three separate classes: **SuperlativeMan**, **Amoeba** (a superhero of uncertain gender), and **TarantulaWoman**; **SuperlativeMan** implements the **SuperHero** interface while **Amoeba** and **TarantulaWoman** implement both **Animal** and **SuperHero**. Define two global functions **animalSound(Animal*)** and **saveFromFire(SuperHero*)**. Invoke all the methods that are callable from each interface in both of these functions.

5. Repeat the previous exercise, but use templates instead of inheritance to implement the interfaces, as we did in **Interfaces2.cpp**.

6. Define some concrete mixin classes that represent superhero capabilities (such as **StopTrain**, **BendSteel**, **ClimbBuilding**, etc.). Redo exercise 4 so that your derived **SuperHero** classes derive from these mixins and call their member functions.

7.   Repeat the previous exercise using templates by making your superhero powers mixin template parameters. Use these powers to do some good in the community.

8.   Dropping the **Animal** interface from exercise 4, redefine **Amoeba** to only implement **SuperHero**. Now define a **SuperlativeAmoeba** class that inherits from both **SuperlativeMan** and **Amoeba**. Try to pass a **SuperlativeAmoeba** object to **saveFromFire( )**. What do you have to do to make this legal? How does using virtual inheritance change the size of your objects?

9.   Continuing with the previous exercise, add an integer **strengthFactor** data member to **SuperHero** from exercise 4, along with a constructor to initialize it. Add constructors in the three derived classes to initialize **strengthFactor** as well. What must you do differently in **SuperlativeAmoeba**?

10.   Continuing with the previous exercise, add an **eatFood( )** member function to both **SuperlativeMan** and **Amoeba** (but not **SuperlativeAmoeba**), such that the two versions of **eatFood( )** take different types of food objects (so the signatures of the two functions differ). What must you do in **SuperlativeAmoeba** to call either **eatFood( )** function? Why?

11.   Define a well-behaved output stream inserter and assignment operator for **SuperlativeAmoeba**.

12.   Remove **SuperlativeAmoeba** from your hierarchy and modify **Amoeba** to derive from both **SuperlativeMan** (which still derives from **SuperHero**) and **SuperHero**. Implement a virtual **workout( )** function in both **SuperHero** and **SuperlativeMan** (with identical signatures), and call it with a **Amoeba** object. Which function gets called?

13.   Redefine **SuperlativeAmoeba** to use composition instead of inheritance to act as a **SuperlativeMan** or **Amoeba**. Use conversion operators to provide implicit upcasting. Compare this approach to the inheritance approach.

14.   Suppose you are given a pre-compiled **Person** class (you only have the header and compiled object file). Suppose also that **Person** has a non-virtual **work( )** function. Have **SuperHero** be able to act as a mild-mannered ordinary **Person** by deriving from **Person** and using the implementation of **Person::work( )**, but make **SuperHero::work( )** virtual.

15. Define a reference-counted error logging mixin class, **ErrorLog**, that holds a static file stream to which you can send messages. The class opens the stream when its reference count exceeds 0 and closes the stream when the count returns to 0 (and always appends to the file). Have objects of multiple classes send messages to the static log stream. Watch the stream open and close via trace statements in **ErrorLog**.

16. Modify **BreakTie.cpp** by adding a class named **VeryBottom** that derives (non-virtually) from **Bottom**. **VeryBottom** should look just like **Bottom** except change "Left" to "Right" in the **using** declaration for **f**. Change **main( )** to instantiate a **VeryBottom** instead of a **Bottom** object. Which **f( )** gets called?

10: Design Patterns

"... describe a problem which occurs over and over again in our environment, and then describe the core of the solution to that problem, in such a way that you can use this solution a million times over, without ever doing it the same way twice"—Christopher Alexander

This chapter introduces the important and yet nontraditional "patterns" approach to program design.

The most important recent step forward in object-oriented design is probably the "design patterns" movement, initially chronicled in *Design Patterns*, by Gamma, Helm, Johnson & Vlissides (Addison Wesley, 1995),[1] which is commonly called the "Gang of Four" book (GoF). GoF shows 23 solutions to particular classes of problems. In this chapter, we discuss the basic concepts of design patterns and provide code examples that illustrate selected patterns. This should whet your appetite for reading more about design patterns, a source of what has now become an essential, almost mandatory vocabulary for object-oriented programming.[2]

The pattern concept

Initially, you can think of a pattern as an especially clever and insightful way to solve a particular class of problem. It appears that a team of people have worked out all the angles of a problem and have come up with the most general, flexible solution for that type of problem. This problem could be one that you have seen and solved before, but your solution probably didn't have the kind of completeness you'll see embodied in a pattern. Furthermore, the

---

[1] Conveniently, the examples are in C++; unfortunately, the dialect is pre–Standard C++ which suffers from the lack of more modern language features like STL containers.

[2] Much of this material was derived from *Thinking in Patterns: Problem–Solving Techniques using Java*, available at www.MindView.net.

pattern exists independently of any particular implementation and it can be implemented in a number of ways.

Although they're called "design patterns," they really aren't tied to the realm of design. A pattern seems to stand apart from the traditional way of thinking about analysis, design, and implementation. Instead, a pattern embodies a complete idea within a program, and thus it might also span the analysis phase and high-level design phase. However, because a pattern often has a direct implementation in code, it might not show up until low-level design or implementation (and you might not realize that you need a particular pattern until you get to those phases).

The basic concept of a pattern can also be seen as the basic concept of program design in general: adding layers of abstraction. Whenever you abstract something, you're isolating particular details, and one of the most compelling motivations for this is to *separate things that change from things that stay the same*. Another way to put this is that once you find some part of your program that's likely to change, you'll want to keep those changes from propagating side effects throughout your code. If you achieve this, your code will not only be easier to read and understand, but also easier to maintain—which invariably results in lowered costs over time.

The most difficult part of developing an elegant and maintainable design is often discovering what we call "the vector of change." (Here, "vector" refers to the maximum gradient as understood in the sciences, and not a container class.) This means finding the most important thing that changes in your system or, put another way, discovering where your greatest cost is. Once you discover the vector of change, you have the focal point around which to structure your design.

So the goal of design patterns is to *encapsulate change*. If you look at it this way, you've been seeing some design patterns already in this book. For example, inheritance could be thought of as a design pattern (albeit one implemented by the compiler). It expresses differences in behavior (that's the thing that changes) in objects that all have the same interface (that's what stays the same). Composition could also be considered a pattern, since you can change—dynamically or statically—the objects that implement your class, and thus the way that class works. Normally, however, features that are directly supported by a programming language have not been classified as design patterns.

You've also already seen another pattern that appears in GoF: the *iterator*. This is the fundamental tool used in the design of the STL, described earlier in this book. The iterator hides the particular implementation of the container as you're stepping through and selecting the elements one by one. Iterators allow you to write generic code that performs an operation on all the elements in a range without regard to the container that holds the range. Thus, your generic code can be used with any container that can produce iterators.

Prefer composition to inheritance

The most important contribution of GoF may not be a pattern, but rather a maxim that they introduce in Chapter 1: "Favor object composition over class inheritance." Understanding inheritance and polymorphism is such a challenge that you may begin to assign undue importance to these techniques. We see many over-complicated designs (our own included) that result from "inheritance indulgence"— for example, many multiple inheritance designs evolve by insisting that inheritance be used everywhere.

One of the guidelines in *Extreme Programming* is "Do the simplest thing that could possibly work." A design that seems to want inheritance can often be dramatically simplified by using composition instead, and you will also discover that the result is more flexible, as you will understand by studying some of the design patterns in this chapter. So when pondering a design, ask yourself: "Could this be simpler using composition? Do I really need inheritance here, and what is it buying me?"

Classifying patterns

GoF discusses 23 patterns, classified under three purposes (all of which revolve around the particular aspect that can vary):

1. **Creational**: How an object can be created. This often involves isolating the details of object creation so your code isn't dependent on what types of objects there are and thus doesn't have to be changed when you add a new type of object. This chapter introduces Singleton, Factories, and Builder.

2. **Structural**: These affect the way objects are connected with other objects to ensure that changes in the system don't require changes to

those connections. Structural patterns are often dictated by project constraints. In this chapter you'll see Proxy and Adapter.

3.   **Behavioral**: Objects that handle particular types of actions within a program. These encapsulate processes that you want to perform, such as interpreting a language, fulfilling a request, moving through a sequence (as in an iterator), or implementing an algorithm. This chapter contains examples of Command, Template Method, State, Strategy, Chain of Responsibility, Observer, Multiple Dispatching, and Visitor.

GoF includes a section on each of its 23 patterns along with one or more examples of each, typically in C++ but sometimes in Smalltalk. This book will not repeat the details of the patterns shown in GoF since that book stands on its own and should be studied separately. The description and examples provided here are intended to give you a grasp of the patterns, so you can get a feel for what patterns are about and why they are important.

Features, idioms, patterns

Work continues beyond what is in the GoF book. Since its publication, there are more patterns and a more refined process for defining design patterns.[3] This is important because it is not easy to identify new patterns or to properly describe them. There is some confusion in the popular literature on what a design pattern is, for example. Patterns are not trivial, nor are they typically represented by features that are built into a programming language. Constructors and destructors, for example, could be called the "guaranteed initialization and cleanup design pattern." These are important and essential constructs, but they're routine language features and are not rich enough to be considered design patterns.

Another non-example comes from various forms of aggregation. Aggregation is a completely fundamental principle in object-oriented programming: you make objects out of other objects. Yet sometimes this idea is erroneously classified as a pattern. This is unfortunate because it pollutes the idea of the design pattern and suggests that anything that surprises you the first time you see it should be made into a design pattern.

---

[3] For up-to-date information, visit http://hillside.net/patterns.

The Java language provides another misguided example: The designers of the JavaBeans specification decided to refer to the simple "get/set" naming convention as a design pattern (for example, **getInfo( )** returns an **Info** property and **setInfo( )** changes it). This is just a commonplace naming convention and in no way constitutes a design pattern.

Simplifying Idioms

Before getting into more complex techniques, it's helpful to look at some basic ways to keep code simple and straightforward.

Messenger

The most trivial of these is the messenger,[4] which packages information into an object which is passed around, instead of passing all the pieces around separately. Note that without the messenger, the code for **translate( )** would be much more confusing to read:

```
//: C10:MessengerDemo.cpp
#include <iostream>
#include <string>
using namespace std;

class Point { // A messenger
public:
  int x, y, z; // Since it's just a carrier
  Point(int xi, int yi, int zi) : x(xi), y(yi), z(zi) {}
  Point(const Point& p) :  x(p.x), y(p.y), z(p.z) {}
  Point& operator=(const Point& rhs) {
    x = rhs.x;
    y = rhs.y;
    z = rhs.z;
    return *this;
  }
  friend ostream&
  operator<<(ostream& os, const Point& p) {
    return os << "x=" << p.x << " y=" << p.y
           << " z=" << p.z;
  }
```

---

[4] Bill Venners' name for it; you may see it named differently elsewhere.

```
};

class Vector { // Mathematical vector
public:
  int magnitude, direction;
  Vector(int m, int d) : magnitude(m), direction(d) {}
};

class Space {
public:
  static Point translate(Point p, Vector v) {
    // Copy-constructor prevents modifying the original.
    // A dummy calculation:
    p.x += v.magnitude + v.direction;
    p.y += v.magnitude + v.direction;
    p.z += v.magnitude + v.direction;
    return p;
  }
};

int main() {
  Point p1(1, 2, 3);
  Point p2 = Space::translate(p1, Vector(11, 47));
  cout << "p1: " << p1 << " p2: " << p2 << endl;
} ///:~
```

The code here is trivialized to prevent distractions.

Since the goal of a messenger is only to carry data, that data is made public for easy access. However, you may also have reasons to make the fields private.

Collecting Parameter

Messenger's big brother is the collecting parameter, whose job is to capture information from the function to which it is passed. Generally, this is used when the collecting parameter is passed to multiple functions, so it's like a bee collecting pollen.

A container makes an especially useful collecting parameter, since it is already set up to dynamically add objects:

```
//: C10:CollectingParameterDemo.cpp
#include <iostream>
```

```
#include <string>
#include <vector>
using namespace std;

class CollectingParameter : public vector<string> {};

class Filler {
public:
  void f(CollectingParameter& cp) {
    cp.push_back("accumulating");
  }
  void g(CollectingParameter& cp) {
    cp.push_back("items");
  }
  void h(CollectingParameter& cp) {
    cp.push_back("as we go");
  }
};

int main() {
  Filler filler;
  CollectingParameter cp;
  filler.f(cp);
  filler.g(cp);
  filler.h(cp);
  vector<string>::iterator it = cp.begin();
  while(it != cp.end())
    cout << *it++ << " ";
  cout << endl;
} ///:~
```

The collecting parameter must have some way to set or insert values. Note that by this definition, a messenger could be used as a collecting parameter. The key is that a collecting parameter is passed about and modified by the functions that receive it.

Singleton

Possibly the simplest GoF design pattern is the *Singleton*, which is a way to allow one and only one instance of a class. The following program shows how to implement a Singleton in C++:

```
//: C10:SingletonPattern.cpp
```

```cpp
#include <iostream>
using namespace std;

class Singleton {
  static Singleton s;
  int i;
  Singleton(int x) : i(x) { }
  Singleton& operator=(Singleton&);  // Disallowed
  Singleton(const Singleton&);        // Disallowed
public:
  static Singleton& instance() { return s; }
  int getValue() { return i; }
  void setValue(int x) { i = x; }
};

Singleton Singleton::s(47);

int main() {
  Singleton& s = Singleton::instance();
  cout << s.getValue() << endl;
  Singleton& s2 = Singleton::instance();
  s2.setValue(9);
  cout << s.getValue() << endl;
} ///:~
```

The key to creating a Singleton is to prevent the client programmer from having any control over the lifetime of the object. To do this, declare all constructors **private**, and prevent the compiler from implicitly generating any constructors. Note that the copy constructor and assignment operator (which intentionally have no implementations, since they will never be called) are declared private to prevent any sort of copies being made.

You must also decide how you're going to create the object. Here, it's created statically, but you can also wait until the client programmer asks for one and create it on demand. This is called *lazy initialization*, and it only makes sense if it is expensive to create your object, and if you don't always need it.

If you return a pointer instead of a reference, the user could inadvertently delete the pointer, so the implementation above is considered safest (the destructor can also be declared private or protected to alleviate that problem). In any case, the object should be stored privately.

You provide access through public member functions. Here, **instance( )** produces a reference to the **Singleton** object. The rest of the interface (**getValue( )** and **setValue( )**) is the regular class interface.

Note that you aren't restricted to creating only one object. This technique also supports the creation of a limited pool of objects. In that case, however, you can be confronted with the problem of sharing objects in the pool. If this is an issue, you can create a solution involving a check-out and check-in of the shared objects.

Variations on Singleton

Any **static** member object inside a class is an expression of Singleton: one and only one will be made. So in a sense, the language has direct support for the idea; we certainly use it on a regular basis. However, there's a problem with **static** objects (member or not): the order of initialization, as described in Volume 1 of this book. If one **static** object depends on another, it's important that the objects are initialized in the correct order.

In Volume 1, you were shown how to control initialization order by defining a static object inside a function. This delays the initialization of the object until the first time the function is called. If the function returns a reference to the static object, it gives you the effect of a Singleton while removing much of the worry of static initialization. For example, suppose you want to create a log file upon the first call to a function that returns a reference to that log file. This header file will do the trick:

```
//: C10:LogFile.h
#ifndef LOGFILE_H
#define LOGFILE_H
#include <fstream>
std::ofstream& logfile();
#endif // LOGFILE_H ///:~
```

The implementation *must not be inlined* because that would mean that the whole function, including the static object definition within, could be duplicated in any translation unit where it's included, which violates C++'s one-definition rule.[5] This would most certainly foil the attempts to control the order of initialization (but potentially in a subtle and hard-to-detect fashion). So the implementation must be separate:

```
//: C10:LogFile.cpp {O}
#include "LogFile.h"
std::ofstream& logfile() {
  static std::ofstream log("Logfile.log");
  return log;
} ///:~
```

Now the **log** object will not be initialized until the first time **logfile( )** is called. So if you create a function:

```
//: C10:UseLog1.h
#ifndef USELOG1_H
#define USELOG1_H
void f();
#endif // USELOG1_H ///:~
```

that uses **logfile( )** in its implementation:

```
//: C10:UseLog1.cpp {O}
#include "UseLog1.h"
#include "LogFile.h"
void f() {
  logfile() << __FILE__ << std::endl;
} ///:~
```

And you use **logfile( )** again in another file:

```
//: C10:UseLog2.cpp
//{L} LogFile UseLog1
#include "UseLog1.h"
#include "LogFile.h"
using namespace std;
void g() {
  logfile() << __FILE__ << endl;
```

---

[5] The C++ Standard states: "No translation unit shall contain more than one definition of any variable, function, class type, enumeration type or template... Every program shall contain exactly one definition of every non–inline function or object that is used in that program."

```
}

int main() {
  f();
  g();
} ///:~
```

the **log** object doesn't get created until the first call to **f( )**.

You can easily combine the creation of the static object inside a member function with the Singleton class. **SingletonPattern.cpp** can be modified to use this approach:[6]

```
//: C10:SingletonPattern2.cpp
// Meyers' Singleton.
#include <iostream>
using namespace std;

class Singleton {
  int i;
  Singleton(int x) : i(x) { }
  void operator=(Singleton&);
  Singleton(const Singleton&);
public:
  static Singleton& instance() {
    static Singleton s(47);
    return s;
  }
  int getValue() { return i; }
  void setValue(int x) { i = x; }
};

int main() {
  Singleton& s = Singleton::instance();
  cout << s.getValue() << endl;
  Singleton& s2 = Singleton::instance();
  s2.setValue(9);
  cout << s.getValue() << endl;
} ///:~
```

---

6 This is known as Meyers' Singleton, after its creator, Scott Meyers.

An especially interesting case occurs if two Singletons depend on each other, like this:

```
//: C10:FunctionStaticSingleton.cpp

class Singleton1 {
  Singleton1() {}
public:
  static Singleton1& ref() {
    static Singleton1 single;
    return single;
  }
};

class Singleton2 {
  Singleton1& s1;
  Singleton2(Singleton1& s) : s1(s) {}
public:
  static Singleton2& ref() {
    static Singleton2 single(Singleton1::ref());
    return single;
  }
  Singleton1& f() { return s1; }
};

int main() {
  Singleton1& s1 = Singleton2::ref().f();
} ///:~
```

When **Singleton2::ref( )** is called, it causes its sole **Singleton2** object to be created. In the process of this creation, **Singleton1::ref( )** is called, and that causes the sole **Singleton1** object to be created. Because this technique doesn't rely on the order of linking or loading, the programmer has much better control over initialization, leading to fewer problems.

Yet another variation on Singleton separates the "Singleton-ness" of an object from its implementation. This is achieved using the Curiously Recurring Template Pattern mentioned in Chapter 5:

```
//: C10:CuriousSingleton.cpp
// Separates a class from its Singleton-ness (almost).
#include <iostream>
using namespace std;
```

```
template<class T> class Singleton {
  Singleton(const Singleton&);
  Singleton& operator=(const Singleton&);
protected:
  Singleton() {}
  virtual ~Singleton() {}
public:
  static T& instance() {
    static T theInstance;
    return theInstance;
  }
};

// A sample class to be made into a Singleton
class MyClass : public Singleton<MyClass> {
  int x;
protected:
  friend class Singleton<MyClass>;
  MyClass() { x = 0; }
public:
  void setValue(int n) { x = n; }
  int getValue() const { return x; }
};

int main() {
  MyClass& m = MyClass::instance();
  cout << m.getValue() << endl;
  m.setValue(1);
  cout << m.getValue() << endl;
} ///:~
```

MyClass is made a Singleton by:

1. Making its constructor private or protected.

2. Making **Singleton<MyClass>** a friend.

3. Deriving **MyClass** from **Singleton<MyClass>**.

The self-referencing in step 3 may sound implausible, but as we explained in Chapter 5, it works because there is only a static dependency on the template argument in the **Singleton** template. In other words, the code for the class **Singleton<MyClass>** can be instantiated by the compiler because it is not dependent on the size of **MyClass**. It's only later, when

---

Singleton\<MyClass\>::instance( ) is first called, that the size of **MyClass** is needed, and by then **MyClass** has been compiled and its size is known.[7]

It's interesting how intricate such a simple pattern as Singleton can be, and we haven't even addressed issues of thread safety. Finally, Singleton should be used sparingly. True Singleton objects arise rarely, and the last thing a Singleton should be used for is to replace a global variable.[8]

Command: choosing the operation

The Command pattern is structurally very simple, but can have an important impact on decoupling—and thus cleaning up—your code.

In *Advanced C++: Programming Styles And Idioms (Addison Wesley, 1992)*, Jim Coplien coins the term *functor* which is an object whose sole purpose is to encapsulate a function (since "functor" has a meaning in mathematics, we shall use the more explicit term *function object*). The point is to decouple the choice of function to be called from the site where that function is called.

This term is mentioned but not used in GoF. However, the theme of the function object is repeated in a number of patterns in that book.

A Command is a function object in its purest sense: a function that's an object. By wrapping a function in an object, you can pass it to other functions or objects as a parameter, to tell them to perform this particular operation in the process of fulfilling your request. You could say that a *Command* is a Messenger that carries behavior.

```
//: C10:CommandPattern.cpp
#include <iostream>
#include <vector>
using namespace std;

class Command {
```

---

[7] Andrei Alexandrescu develops a superior, policy-based solution to implementing the Singleton pattern in *Modern C++ Design*.
[8] For more information, see the article "Once is Not Enough" by Hyslop and Sutter in the March 2003 issue of *CUJ*.

```cpp
public:
  virtual void execute() = 0;
};

class Hello : public Command {
public:
  void execute() { cout << "Hello "; }
};

class World : public Command {
public:
  void execute() { cout << "World! "; }
};

class IAm : public Command {
public:
  void execute() { cout << "I'm the command pattern!"; }
};

// An object that holds commands:
class Macro {
  vector<Command*> commands;
public:
  void add(Command* c) { commands.push_back(c); }
  void run() {
    vector<Command*>::iterator it = commands.begin();
    while(it != commands.end())
      (*it++)->execute();
  }
};

int main() {
  Macro macro;
  macro.add(new Hello);
  macro.add(new World);
  macro.add(new IAm);
  macro.run();
} ///:~
```

The primary point of Command is to allow you to hand a desired action to a function or object. In the above example, this provides a way to queue a set of actions to be performed collectively. Here, you can dynamically create new behavior, something you can normally only do by writing new code but in the above example could be done by interpreting a script (see the Interpreter pattern if what you need to do gets very complex).

GoF says that "Commands are an object-oriented replacement for callbacks."[9] However, we think that the word "back" is an essential part of the concept of callbacks—a callback reaches back to the creator of the callback. On the other hand, with a Command object you typically just create it and hand it to some function or object, and you are not otherwise connected over time to the Command object.

A common example of Command is the implementation of "undo" functionality in an application. Each time the user performs an operation, the corresponding "undo" Command object is placed into a queue. Each Command object that is executed backs up the state of the program by one step.

Decoupling event handling with Command

As you shall see in the next chapter, one of the reasons for employing *concurrency* techniques is to more easily manage *event-driven programming*, where the events can appear unpredictably in your program. For example, a user pressing a "quit" button while you're performing an operation expects the program to respond quickly.

An argument for using concurrency is that it prevents coupling across the pieces of your code. That is, if you're running a separate thread to watch the quit button, your program's "normal" operations don't need to know about the quit button or any of the other operations that need to be watched.

However, once you understand that coupling is the issue, you can avoid it using the Command pattern. Each "normal" operation must periodically call a function to check the state of the events, but with the Command pattern these normal operations don't need to know anything about what they are checking, and thus are decoupled from the event-handling code:

```
//: C10:MulticastCommand.cpp {RunByHand}
// Decoupling event management with the Command pattern.
#include <iostream>
```

---

[9] Page 235.

```cpp
#include <vector>
#include <string>
#include <ctime>
#include <cstdlib>
using namespace std;

// Framework for running tasks:
class Task {
public:
  virtual void operation() = 0;
};

class TaskRunner {
  static vector<Task*> tasks;
  TaskRunner() {} // Make it a Singleton
  TaskRunner& operator=(TaskRunner&); // Disallowed
  TaskRunner(const TaskRunner&); // Disallowed
  static TaskRunner tr;
public:
  static void add(Task& t) { tasks.push_back(&t); }
  static void run() {
    vector<Task*>::iterator it = tasks.begin();
    while(it != tasks.end())
      (*it++)->operation();
  }
};

TaskRunner TaskRunner::tr;
vector<Task*> TaskRunner::tasks;

class EventSimulator {
  clock_t creation;
  clock_t delay;
public:
  EventSimulator() : creation(clock()) {
    delay = CLOCKS_PER_SEC/4 * (rand() % 20 + 1);
    cout << "delay = " << delay << endl;
  }
  bool fired() {
    return clock() > creation + delay;
  }
};

// Something that can produce asynchronous events:
class Button {
```

```
    bool pressed;
    string id;
    EventSimulator e; // For demonstration
public:
    Button(string name) : pressed(false), id(name) {}
    void press() { pressed = true; }
    bool isPressed() {
        if(e.fired()) press(); // Simulate the event
        return pressed;
    }
    friend ostream&
    operator<<(ostream& os, const Button& b) {
        return os << b.id;
    }
};

// The Command object
class CheckButton : public Task {
    Button& button;
    bool handled;
public:
    CheckButton(Button & b) : button(b), handled(false) {}
    void operation() {
        if(button.isPressed() && !handled) {
            cout << button << " pressed" << endl;
            handled = true;
        }
    }
};

// The procedures that perform the main processing. These
// need to be occasionally "interrupted" in order to
// check the state of the buttons or other events:
void procedure1() {
    // Perform procedure1 operations here.
    // ...
    TaskRunner::run(); // Check all events
}

void procedure2() {
    // Perform procedure2 operations here.
    // ...
    TaskRunner::run(); // Check all events
}
```

```
void procedure3() {
  // Perform procedure3 operations here.
  // ...
  TaskRunner::run(); // Check all events
}

int main() {
  srand(time(0)); // Randomize
  Button b1("Button 1"), b2("Button 2"), b3("Button 3");
  CheckButton cb1(b1), cb2(b2), cb3(b3);
  TaskRunner::add(cb1);
  TaskRunner::add(cb2);
  TaskRunner::add(cb3);
  cout << "Control-C to exit" << endl;
  while(true) {
    procedure1();
    procedure2();
    procedure3();
  }
} ///:~
```

Here, the Command object is represented by **Task**s executed by the Singleton **TaskRunner**. **EventSimulator** creates a random delay time, so if you periodically call **fired( )** the result will change from **false** to **true** at some random time. **EventSimulator** objects are used inside **Button**s to simulate the act of a user event occurring at some unpredictable time. **CheckButton** is the implementation of the **Task** that is periodically checked by all the "normal" code in the program—you can see this happening at the end of **procedure1( )**, **procedure2( )** and **procedure3( )**.

Although this requires a little bit of extra thought to set up, you'll see in Chapter 11 that threading requires a *lot* of thought and care to prevent the various difficulties inherent to concurrent programming, so the simpler solution may be preferable. You can also create a very simple threading scheme by moving the **TaskRunner::run( )** calls into a multithreaded "timer" object. By doing this, you eliminate all coupling between the "normal operations" (procedures, in the above example) and the event code.

Object decoupling

Both Proxy and State provide a surrogate class. Your code talks to this surrogate class, and the real class that does the work is hidden behind this

---

surrogate class. When you call a function in the surrogate, it simply turns around and calls the function in the implementing class. These two patterns are so similar that, structurally, Proxy is simply a special case of State. One is tempted to just lump the two together into a pattern called Surrogate, but the *intent* of the two patterns is different. It can be easy to fall into the trap of thinking that if the structure is the same, the patterns are the same. You must always look to the intent of the pattern in order to be clear about what it does.

The basic idea is simple: from a base class, the surrogate is derived along with the class or classes that provide the actual implementation:

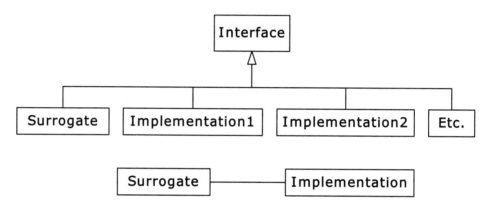

When a surrogate object is created, it is given an implementation to which it sends the function calls.

Structurally, the difference between Proxy and State is simple: a Proxy has only one implementation, while State has more than one. The application of the patterns is considered (in GoF) to be distinct: Proxy controls access to its implementation, while State changes the implementation dynamically. However, if you expand your notion of "controlling access to implementation" then the two seem to be part of a continuum.

Proxy: fronting for another object

If we implement Proxy using the above diagram, it looks like this:

```
//: C10:ProxyDemo.cpp
// Simple demonstration of the Proxy pattern.
#include <iostream>
using namespace std;
```

```
class ProxyBase {
public:
  virtual void f() = 0;
  virtual void g() = 0;
  virtual void h() = 0;
  virtual ~ProxyBase() {}
};

class Implementation : public ProxyBase {
public:
  void f() { cout << "Implementation.f()" << endl; }
  void g() { cout << "Implementation.g()" << endl; }
  void h() { cout << "Implementation.h()" << endl; }
};

class Proxy : public ProxyBase {
  ProxyBase* implementation;
public:
  Proxy() { implementation = new Implementation(); }
  ~Proxy() { delete implementation; }
  // Forward calls to the implementation:
  void f() { implementation->f(); }
  void g() { implementation->g(); }
  void h() { implementation->h(); }
};

int main()  {
  Proxy p;
  p.f();
  p.g();
  p.h();
} ///:~
```

In some cases, **Implementation** doesn't need the same interface as
Proxy—as long as **Proxy** is somehow "speaking for" the **Implementation**
class and referring function calls to it, then the basic idea is satisfied (note
that this statement is at odds with the definition for Proxy in GoF). However,
with a common interface you are able to do a drop-in replacement of the
proxy into the client code—the client code is written to talk to the original
object, and it doesn't need to be changed in order to accept the proxy (This is
probably the key issue with Proxy). In addition, **Implementation** is forced,
through the common interface, to fulfill all the functions that **Proxy** needs to
call.

The difference between Proxy and State is in the problems that are solved. The common uses for Proxy as described in GoF are:

1. **Remote proxy**. This proxies for an object in a different address space. This is implemented by some remote object technologies.

2. **Virtual proxy**. This provides "lazy initialization" to create expensive objects on demand.

3. **Protection proxy**. Used when you don't want the client programmer to have full access to the proxied object.

4. **Smart reference**. To add additional actions when the proxied object is accessed. *Reference counting* is an example: this keeps track of the number of references that are held for a particular object, in order to implement the *copy-on-write* idiom and prevent object aliasing.[10] A simpler example is counting the calls to a particular function.

State: changing object behavior

The State pattern produces an object that appears to change its class, and is useful when you discover that you have conditional code in most or all functions. Like Proxy, State is created by having a front-end object that uses a back-end implementation object to fulfill its duties. However, the State pattern switches from one implementation to another during the lifetime of the front-end object, in order to produce different behavior for the same function call(s). It's a way to improve the implementation of your code when you seem to be doing a lot of testing inside each of your functions before deciding what to do for that function. For example, the fairy tale of the frog-prince contains an object (the creature) that behaves differently depending on what state it's in. You could implement this by testing a **bool**:

```
//: C10:KissingPrincess.cpp
#include <iostream>
using namespace std;

class Creature {
  bool isFrog;
```

---

[10] See *Thinking in C++, Volume 1* for more details about reference counting.

```
public:
  Creature() : isFrog(true) {}
  void greet() {
    if(isFrog)
      cout << "Ribbet!" << endl;
    else
      cout << "Darling!" << endl;
  }
  void kiss() { isFrog = false; }
};

int main() {
  Creature creature;
  creature.greet();
  creature.kiss();
  creature.greet();
} ///:~
```

However, the **greet( )** function, and any other functions that must test **isFrog** before they perform their operations, end up with awkward code, especially if you find yourself adding additional states to the system. By delegating the operations to a State object that can be changed, this code is simplified.

```
//: C10:KissingPrincess2.cpp
// The State pattern.
#include <iostream>
#include <string>
using namespace std;

class Creature {
  class State {
  public:
    virtual string response() = 0;
  };
  class Frog : public State {
  public:
    string response() { return "Ribbet!"; }
  };
  class Prince : public State {
  public:
    string response() { return "Darling!"; }
  };
  State* state;
```

```
public:
  Creature() : state(new Frog()) {}
  void greet() {
    cout << state->response() << endl;
  }
  void kiss() {
    delete state;
    state = new Prince();
  }
};

int main() {
  Creature creature;
  creature.greet();
  creature.kiss();
  creature.greet();
} ///:~
```

It is not necessary to make the implementing classes nested or private, but if you can it creates cleaner code.

Note that changes to the State classes are automatically propagated throughout your code, rather than requiring an edit across the classes in order to effect changes.

Adapter

Adapter takes one type and produces an interface to some other type. This is useful when you're given a library or piece of code that has a particular interface, and you've got a second library or piece of code that uses the same basic ideas as the first piece, but expresses itself differently. If you adapt the forms of expression to each other, you can rapidly produce a solution.

Suppose you have a generator class that produces Fibonacci numbers:

```
//: C10:FibonacciGenerator.h
#ifndef FIBONACCIGENERATOR_H
#define FIBONACCIGENERATOR_H

class FibonacciGenerator {
  int n;
  int val[2];
public:
```

```
    FibonacciGenerator() : n(0) { val[0] = val[1] = 0; }
    int operator()() {
      int result = n > 2 ? val[0] + val[1] : n > 0 ? 1 : 0;
      ++n;
      val[0] = val[1];
      val[1] = result;
      return result;
    }
    int count() { return n; }
};
#endif // FIBONACCIGENERATOR_H ///:~
```

Since it's a generator, you use it by calling the **operator( )**, like this:

```
//: C10:FibonacciGeneratorTest.cpp
#include <iostream>
#include "FibonacciGenerator.h"
using namespace std;

int main() {
  FibonacciGenerator f;
  for(int i =0; i < 20; i++)
    cout << f.count() << ": " << f() << endl;
} ///:~
```

Perhaps you would like to take this generator and perform STL numeric algorithm operations with it. Unfortunately, the STL algorithms only work with iterators, so you have an interface mismatch. The solution is to create an adapter that will take the **FibonacciGenerator** and produce an iterator for the STL algorithms to use. Since the numeric algorithms only require an input iterator, the Adapter is fairly straightforward (for something that produces an STL iterator, that is):

```
//: C10:FibonacciAdapter.cpp
// Adapting an interface to something you already have.
#include <iostream>
#include <numeric>
#include "FibonacciGenerator.h"
#include "../C06/PrintSequence.h"
using namespace std;

class FibonacciAdapter { // Produce an iterator
  FibonacciGenerator f;
  int length;
```

```
public:
  FibonacciAdapter(int size) : length(size) {}
  class iterator;
  friend class iterator;
  class iterator : public std::iterator<
    std::input_iterator_tag, FibonacciAdapter, ptrdiff_t> {
    FibonacciAdapter& ap;
  public:
    typedef int value_type;
    iterator(FibonacciAdapter& a) : ap(a) {}
    bool operator==(const iterator&) const {
      return ap.f.count() == ap.length;
    }
    bool operator!=(const iterator& x) const {
      return !(*this == x);
    }
    int operator*() const { return ap.f(); }
    iterator& operator++() { return *this; }
    iterator operator++(int) { return *this; }
  };
  iterator begin() { return iterator(*this); }
  iterator end() { return iterator(*this); }
};

int main() {
  const int SZ = 20;
  FibonacciAdapter a1(SZ);
  cout << "accumulate: "
    << accumulate(a1.begin(), a1.end(), 0) << endl;
  FibonacciAdapter a2(SZ), a3(SZ);
  cout << "inner product: "
    << inner_product(a2.begin(), a2.end(), a3.begin(), 0)
    << endl;
  FibonacciAdapter a4(SZ);
  int r1[SZ] = {0};
  int* end = partial_sum(a4.begin(), a4.end(), r1);
  print(r1, end, "partial_sum", " ");
  FibonacciAdapter a5(SZ);
  int r2[SZ] = {0};
  end = adjacent_difference(a5.begin(), a5.end(), r2);
  print(r2, end, "adjacent_difference", " ");
} ///:~
```

You initialize a **FibonacciAdapter** by telling it how long the Fibonacci
sequence can be. When an **iterator** is created, it simply captures a reference

to the containing **FibonacciAdapter** so that it can access the
FibonacciGenerator and **length**. Note that the equivalence comparison
ignores the right-hand value because the only important issue is whether the
generator has reached its length. In addition, the **operator++( )** doesn't
modify the iterator; the only operation that changes the state of the
FibonacciAdapter is calling the generator function **operator( )** on the
FibonacciGenerator. We can get away with this extremely simple version
of the iterator because the constraints on an Input Iterator are so strong; in
particular, you can only read each value in the sequence once.

In **main( )**, you can see that all four different types of numeric algorithms
are successfully tested with the **FibonacciAdapter**.

Template Method

An application framework allows you to inherit from a class or set of classes
and create a new application, reusing most of the code in the existing classes
and overriding one or more functions in order to customize the application to
your needs. A fundamental concept in the application framework is the
Template Method, which is typically hidden beneath the covers and drives the
application by calling the various functions in the base class (some of which
you have overridden in order to create the application).

An important characteristic of the Template Method is that it is defined in the
base class (sometimes as a private member function) and cannot be
changed—the Template Method is the "thing that stays the same." It calls
other base-class functions (the ones you override) in order to do its job, but
the client programmer isn't necessarily able to call it directly, as you can see
here:

```
//: C10:TemplateMethod.cpp
// Simple demonstration of Template Method.
#include <iostream>
using namespace std;

class ApplicationFramework {
protected:
  virtual void customize1() = 0;
  virtual void customize2() = 0;
public:
  void templateMethod() {
```

```
    for(int i = 0; i < 5; i++) {
      customize1();
      customize2();
    }
  }
};

// Create a new "application":
class MyApp : public ApplicationFramework {
protected:
  void customize1() { cout << "Hello "; }
  void customize2() { cout << "World!" << endl; }
};

int main() {
  MyApp app;
  app.templateMethod();
} ///:~
```

The "engine" that runs the application is the Template Method. In a GUI application, this "engine" would be the main event loop. The client programmer simply provides definitions for **customize1( )** and **customize2( )** and the "application" is ready to run.

Strategy: choosing the algorithm at runtime

Note that the Template Method is the "code that stays the same," and the functions that you override are the "code that changes." However, this change is fixed at compile time via inheritance. Following the maxim of "prefer composition to inheritance," we can use composition to approach the problem of separating code that changes from code that stays the same, and produce the Strategy pattern. This approach has a distinct benefit: at runtime, you can plug in the code that changes. Strategy also adds a "Context" which can be a surrogate class that controls the selection and use of the particular strategy object—just like State!

"Strategy" means just that: you can solve a problem in a number of ways. Consider the situation where you've forgotten someone's name. Here are the different ways you can cope:

```
//: C10:Strategy.cpp
// The Strategy design pattern.
#include <iostream>
using namespace std;

class NameStrategy {
public:
  virtual void greet() = 0;
};

class SayHi : public NameStrategy {
public:
  void greet() {
    cout << "Hi! How's it going?" << endl;
  }
};

class Ignore : public NameStrategy {
public:
  void greet() {
    cout << "(Pretend I don't see you)" << endl;
  }
};

class Admission : public NameStrategy {
public:
  void greet() {
    cout << "I'm sorry. I forgot your name." << endl;
  }
};

// The "Context" controls the strategy:
class Context {
  NameStrategy& strategy;
public:
  Context(NameStrategy& strat) : strategy(strat) {}
  void greet() { strategy.greet(); }
};

int main() {
  SayHi sayhi;
  Ignore ignore;
  Admission admission;
  Context c1(sayhi), c2(ignore), c3(admission);
  c1.greet();
```

```
    c2.greet();
    c3.greet();
} ///:~
```

Context::greet( ) would normally be more complex; it's the analog of the Template Method because it contains the code that doesn't change. But you can see in **main( )** that the choice of strategy can be made at runtime. If you go one step further you can combine this with the State pattern and change the Strategy during the lifetime of the **Context** object.

Chain of Responsibility: trying a sequence of strategies

Chain of Responsibility might be thought of as a "dynamic generalization of recursion" using Strategy objects. You make a call, and each Strategy in a linked sequence tries to satisfy the call. The process ends when one of the strategies is successful or the chain ends. In recursion, one function calls itself over and over until a termination condition is reached; with Chain of Responsibility, a function calls itself, which (by moving down the chain of Strategies) calls a different implementation of the function, etc., until a termination condition is reached. The termination condition is either that the bottom of the chain is reached (this returns a default object; you may or may not be able to provide a default result so you must be able to determine the success or failure of the chain) or one of the Strategies is successful.

Instead of calling a single function to satisfy a request, multiple functions in the chain have a chance to satisfy the request, so it has the flavor of an expert system. Since the chain is effectively a list, it can be dynamically created, so you could also think of it as a more general, dynamically-built **switch** statement.

In GoF, there's a fair amount of discussion of how to create the chain of responsibility as a linked list. However, when you look at the pattern it really shouldn't matter how the chain is created; that's an implementation detail. Since GoF was written before the STL containers were available in most C++ compilers, the reason for this is most likely (1) there was no built-in list and thus they had to create one and (2) data structures are often taught as a fundamental skill in academia, and the idea that data structures should be standard tools available with the programming language may not have occurred to the GoF authors. We maintain that the details of the container used to implement Chain of Responsibility as a chain (in GoF, a linked list) adds nothing to the solution and can just as easily be implemented using an STL container, as shown below.

Here you can see Chain of Responsibility automatically finding a solution using a mechanism to automatically recurse through each Strategy in the chain:

```
//: C10:ChainOfReponsibility.cpp
// The approach of the five-year-old.
#include <iostream>
#include <vector>
#include "../purge.h"
using namespace std;

enum Answer { NO, YES };

class GimmeStrategy {
public:
  virtual Answer canIHave() = 0;
  virtual ~GimmeStrategy() {}
};

class AskMom : public GimmeStrategy {
public:
  Answer canIHave() {
    cout << "Mooom? Can I have this?" << endl;
    return NO;
  }
};

class AskDad : public GimmeStrategy {
public:
  Answer canIHave() {
    cout << "Dad, I really need this!" << endl;
    return NO;
  }
};

class AskGrandpa : public GimmeStrategy {
public:
  Answer canIHave() {
    cout << "Grandpa, is it my birthday yet?" << endl;
```

```
      return NO;
    }
};

class AskGrandma : public GimmeStrategy {
public:
  Answer canIHave() {
    cout << "Grandma, I really love you!" << endl;
    return YES;
  }
};

class Gimme : public GimmeStrategy {
  vector<GimmeStrategy*> chain;
public:
  Gimme() {
    chain.push_back(new AskMom());
    chain.push_back(new AskDad());
    chain.push_back(new AskGrandpa());
    chain.push_back(new AskGrandma());
  }
  Answer canIHave() {
    vector<GimmeStrategy*>::iterator it = chain.begin();
    while(it != chain.end())
      if((*it++)->canIHave() == YES)
        return YES;
    // Reached end without success...
    cout << "Whiiiiinnne!" << endl;
    return NO;
  }
  ~Gimme() { purge(chain); }
};

int main() {
  Gimme chain;
  chain.canIHave();
} ///:~
```

Notice that the "Context" class **Gimme** and all the Strategy classes are all derived from the same base class, **GimmeStrategy**.

If you study the section on Chain of Responsibility in GoF, you'll find that the structure differs significantly from the one above because they focus on creating their own linked list. However, if you keep in mind that the essence of Chain of Responsibility is to try a number of solutions until you find one that works, you'll realize that the implementation of the sequencing mechanism is not an essential part of the pattern.

Factories: encapsulating object creation

When you discover that you need to add new types to a system, the most sensible first step is to use polymorphism to create a common interface to those new types. This separates the rest of the code in your system from the knowledge of the specific types that you are adding. New types can be added without disturbing existing code ... or so it seems. At first it would appear that you need to change the code only in the place where you inherit a new type, but this is not quite true. You must still create an object of your new type, and at the point of creation you must specify the exact constructor to use. Thus, if the code that creates objects is distributed throughout your application, you have the same problem when adding new types—you must still chase down all the points of your code where type matters. It is the *creation* of the type that matters here, rather than the *use* of the type (which is taken care of by polymorphism), but the effect is the same: adding a new type can cause problems.

The solution is to force the creation of objects to occur through a common *factory* rather than to allow the creational code to be spread throughout your system. If all the code in your program must go to this factory whenever it needs to create one of your objects, all you must do when you add a new object is modify the factory. This design is a variation of the pattern commonly known as Factory Method. Since every object-oriented program creates objects, and since it's likely you will extend your program by adding new types, factories may be the most useful of all design patterns.

As an example, consider the commonly-used **Shape** example. One approach to implementing a factory is to define a **static** member function in the base class:

```
//: C10:ShapeFactory1.cpp
#include <iostream>
#include <stdexcept>
#include <cstddef>
#include <string>
#include <vector>
```

```
#include "../purge.h"
using namespace std;

class Shape {
public:
  virtual void draw() = 0;
  virtual void erase() = 0;
  virtual ~Shape() {}
  class BadShapeCreation : public logic_error {
  public:
    BadShapeCreation(string type)
    : logic_error("Cannot create type " + type) {}
  };
  static Shape* factory(const string& type)
    throw(BadShapeCreation);
};

class Circle : public Shape {
  Circle() {} // Private constructor
  friend class Shape;
public:
  void draw() { cout << "Circle::draw" << endl; }
  void erase() { cout << "Circle::erase" << endl; }
  ~Circle() { cout << "Circle::~Circle" << endl; }
};

class Square : public Shape {
  Square() {}
  friend class Shape;
public:
  void draw() { cout << "Square::draw" << endl; }
  void erase() { cout << "Square::erase" << endl; }
  ~Square() { cout << "Square::~Square" << endl; }
};

Shape* Shape::factory(const string& type)
  throw(Shape::BadShapeCreation) {
  if(type == "Circle") return new Circle;
  if(type == "Square") return new Square;
  throw BadShapeCreation(type);
}

char* sl[] = { "Circle", "Square", "Square",
  "Circle", "Circle", "Circle", "Square" };
```

```
int main() {
  vector<Shape*> shapes;
  try {
    for(size_t i = 0; i < sizeof sl / sizeof sl[0]; i++)
      shapes.push_back(Shape::factory(sl[i]));
  } catch(Shape::BadShapeCreation e) {
    cout << e.what() << endl;
    purge(shapes);
    return EXIT_FAILURE;
  }
  for(size_t i = 0; i < shapes.size(); i++) {
    shapes[i]->draw();
    shapes[i]->erase();
  }
  purge(shapes);
} ///:~
```

The **factory( )** function takes an argument that allows it to determine what type of **Shape** to create. Here, the argument is a **string**, but it could be any set of data. The **factory( )** is now the only other code in the system that needs to be changed when a new type of **Shape** is added. (The initialization data for the objects will presumably come from somewhere outside the system and will not be a hard-coded array as in this example.)

To ensure that the creation can only happen in the **factory( )**, the constructors for the specific types of **Shape** are made **private**, and **Shape** is declared a **friend** so that **factory( )** has access to the constructors. (You could also declare only **Shape::factory( )** to be a **friend**, but it seems reasonably harmless to declare the entire base class as a **friend**.) There is another important implication of this design—the base class, **Shape**, must now know the details about every derived class—a property that object-oriented designs try to avoid. For frameworks or any class library that should support extension, this can quickly become unwieldy, as the base class must be updated as soon as a new type is added to the hierarchy. Polymorphic factories, described in the next subsection, can be used to avoid this unfortunate circular dependency.

Polymorphic factories

The **static factory( )** member function in the previous example forces all the creation operations to be focused in one spot, so that's the only place you need to change the code. This is certainly a reasonable solution, as it nicely encapsulates the process of creating objects. However, GoF emphasizes that the reason for the Factory Method pattern is so that different types of factories can be derived from the basic factory. Factory Method is in fact a special type of polymorphic factory. Here is **ShapeFactory1.cpp** modified so the Factory Methods are in a separate class as virtual functions:

```
//: C10:ShapeFactory2.cpp
// Polymorphic Factory Methods.
#include <iostream>
#include <map>
#include <string>
#include <vector>
#include <stdexcept>
#include <cstddef>
#include "../purge.h"
using namespace std;

class Shape {
public:
  virtual void draw() = 0;
  virtual void erase() = 0;
  virtual ~Shape() {}
};

class ShapeFactory {
  virtual Shape* create() = 0;
  static map<string, ShapeFactory*> factories;
public:
  virtual ~ShapeFactory() {}
  friend class ShapeFactoryInitializer;
  class BadShapeCreation : public logic_error {
  public:
    BadShapeCreation(string type)
    : logic_error("Cannot create type " + type) {}
  };
  static Shape*
  createShape(const string& id) throw(BadShapeCreation) {
    if(factories.find(id) != factories.end())
      return factories[id]->create();
    else
      throw BadShapeCreation(id);
  }
};
```

```
// Define the static object:
map<string, ShapeFactory*> ShapeFactory::factories;

class Circle : public Shape {
  Circle() {} // Private constructor
  friend class ShapeFactoryInitializer;
  class Factory;
  friend class Factory;
  class Factory : public ShapeFactory {
  public:
    Shape* create() { return new Circle; }
    friend class ShapeFactoryInitializer;
  };
public:
  void draw() { cout << "Circle::draw" << endl; }
  void erase() { cout << "Circle::erase" << endl; }
  ~Circle() { cout << "Circle::~Circle" << endl; }
};

class Square : public Shape {
  Square() {}
  friend class ShapeFactoryInitializer;
  class Factory;
  friend class Factory;
  class Factory : public ShapeFactory {
  public:
    Shape* create() { return new Square; }
    friend class ShapeFactoryInitializer;
  };
public:
  void draw() { cout << "Square::draw" << endl; }
  void erase() { cout << "Square::erase" << endl; }
  ~Square() { cout << "Square::~Square" << endl; }
};

// Singleton to initialize the ShapeFactory:
class ShapeFactoryInitializer {
  static ShapeFactoryInitializer si;
  ShapeFactoryInitializer() {
    ShapeFactory::factories["Circle"]= new Circle::Factory;
    ShapeFactory::factories["Square"]= new Square::Factory;
  }
  ~ShapeFactoryInitializer() {
    map<string, ShapeFactory*>::iterator it =
      ShapeFactory::factories.begin();
```

```
      while(it != ShapeFactory::factories.end())
        delete it++->second;
    }
};

// Static member definition:
ShapeFactoryInitializer ShapeFactoryInitializer::si;

char* sl[] = { "Circle", "Square", "Square",
  "Circle", "Circle", "Circle", "Square" };

int main() {
  vector<Shape*> shapes;
  try {
    for(size_t i = 0; i < sizeof sl / sizeof sl[0]; i++)
      shapes.push_back(ShapeFactory::createShape(sl[i]));
  } catch(ShapeFactory::BadShapeCreation e) {
    cout << e.what() << endl;
    return EXIT_FAILURE;
  }
  for(size_t i = 0; i < shapes.size(); i++) {
    shapes[i]->draw();
    shapes[i]->erase();
  }
  purge(shapes);
} ///:~
```

Now the Factory Method appears in its own class, **ShapeFactory**, as **virtual create( )**. This is a private member function, which means it cannot be called directly but can be overridden. The subclasses of **Shape** must each create their own subclasses of **ShapeFactory** and override the **create( )** member function to create an object of their own type. These factories are private, so that they are only accessible from the main Factory Method. This way, all client code must go through the Factory Method in order to create objects.

The actual creation of shapes is performed by calling **ShapeFactory::createShape( )**, which is a static member function that uses the **map** in **ShapeFactory** to find the appropriate factory object based on an identifier that you pass it. The factory creates the shape object directly, but you could imagine a more complex problem where the appropriate factory object is returned and then used by the caller to create an object in a more sophisticated way. However, it seems that much of the time you don't need the intricacies of the polymorphic Factory Method, and a single static member function in the base class (as shown in **ShapeFactory1.cpp**) will work fine.

Notice that the **ShapeFactory** must be initialized by loading its **map** with factory objects, which takes place in the Singleton **ShapeFactoryInitializer**. So to add a new type to this design you must define the type, create a factory, and modify **ShapeFactoryInitializer** so that an instance of your factory is inserted in the map. This extra complexity again suggests the use of a **static** Factory Method if you don't need to create individual factory objects.

Abstract factories

The Abstract Factory pattern looks like the factories we've seen previously, but with several Factory Methods. Each of the Factory Methods creates a different kind of object. When you create the factory object, you decide how all the objects created by that factory will be used. The example in GoF implements portability across various graphical user interfaces (GUIs): you create a factory object appropriate to the GUI that you're working with, and from then on when you ask it for a menu, a button, a slider, and so on, it will automatically create the appropriate version of that item for the GUI. Thus, you're able to isolate, in one place, the effect of changing from one GUI to another.

As another example, suppose you are creating a general-purpose gaming environment and you want to be able to support different types of games. Here's how it might look using an Abstract Factory:

```
//: C10:AbstractFactory.cpp
// A gaming environment.
#include <iostream>
using namespace std;

class Obstacle {
public:
  virtual void action() = 0;
};

class Player {
public:
  virtual void interactWith(Obstacle*) = 0;
```

```
};

class Kitty: public Player {
  virtual void interactWith(Obstacle* ob) {
    cout << "Kitty has encountered a ";
    ob->action();
  }
};

class KungFuGuy: public Player {
  virtual void interactWith(Obstacle* ob) {
    cout << "KungFuGuy now battles against a ";
    ob->action();
  }
};

class Puzzle: public Obstacle {
public:
  void action() { cout << "Puzzle" << endl; }
};

class NastyWeapon: public Obstacle {
public:
  void action() { cout << "NastyWeapon" << endl; }
};

// The abstract factory:
class GameElementFactory {
public:
  virtual Player* makePlayer() = 0;
  virtual Obstacle* makeObstacle() = 0;
};

// Concrete factories:
class KittiesAndPuzzles : public GameElementFactory {
public:
  virtual Player* makePlayer() { return new Kitty; }
  virtual Obstacle* makeObstacle() { return new Puzzle; }
};

class KillAndDismember : public GameElementFactory {
public:
  virtual Player* makePlayer() { return new KungFuGuy; }
  virtual Obstacle* makeObstacle() {
    return new NastyWeapon;
```

```
    }
};

class GameEnvironment {
  GameElementFactory* gef;
  Player* p;
  Obstacle* ob;
public:
  GameEnvironment(GameElementFactory* factory)
  : gef(factory), p(factory->makePlayer()),
    ob(factory->makeObstacle()) {}
  void play() { p->interactWith(ob); }
  ~GameEnvironment() {
    delete p;
    delete ob;
    delete gef;
  }
};

int main() {
  GameEnvironment
    g1(new KittiesAndPuzzles),
    g2(new KillAndDismember);
  g1.play();
  g2.play();
}
/* Output:
Kitty has encountered a Puzzle
KungFuGuy now battles against a NastyWeapon */ ///:~
```

In this environment, **Player** objects interact with **Obstacle** objects, but the types of players and obstacles depend on the game. You determine the kind of game by choosing a particular **GameElementFactory**, and then the **GameEnvironment** controls the setup and play of the game. In this example, the setup and play are simple, but those activities (the *initial conditions* and the *state change*) can determine much of the game's outcome. Here, **GameEnvironment** is not designed to be inherited, although it could possibly make sense to do that.

This example also illustrates *double dispatching*, which will be explained later.

Virtual constructors

One of the primary goals of using a factory is to organize your code so you don't need to select the exact constructor type when creating an object. That is, you can tell a factory: "I don't know precisely what kind of object I need, but here's the information. Create the appropriate type."

In addition, during a constructor call the virtual mechanism does not operate (early binding occurs). Sometimes this is awkward. For example, in the **Shape** program it seems logical that inside the constructor for a **Shape** object, you would want to set everything up and then **draw( )** the **Shape**. The **draw( )** function should be a virtual function, a message to the **Shape** that it should draw itself appropriately, depending on whether it is a **Circle**, a **Square**, a **Line**, and so on. However, this doesn't work inside the constructor because virtual functions resolve to the "local" function bodies when called in constructors.

If you want to be able to call a virtual function inside the constructor and have it do the right thing, you must use a technique to *simulate* a virtual constructor. This is a conundrum. Remember, the idea of a virtual function is that you send a message to an object and let the object figure out the right thing to do. But a constructor builds an object. So a virtual constructor would be like saying, "I don't know exactly what kind of object you are, but build the right type anyway." In an ordinary constructor, the compiler must know which VTABLE address to bind to the VPTR, and even if it existed, a virtual constructor couldn't do this because it doesn't know all the type information at compile time. It makes sense that a constructor can't be virtual because it is the one function that absolutely must know everything about the type of the object.

And yet there are times when you want something approximating the behavior of a virtual constructor.

In the **Shape** example, it would be nice to hand the **Shape** constructor some specific information in the argument list and let the constructor create a specific type of **Shape** (a **Circle** or a **Square**) with no further intervention. Ordinarily, you'd have to make an explicit call to the **Circle** or **Square** constructor yourself.

Coplien[11] calls his solution to this problem "envelope and letter classes." The "envelope" class is the base class, a shell that contains a pointer to an object, also of the base class type. The constructor for the "envelope" determines (at runtime, when the constructor is called, not at compile time, when the type checking is normally done) what specific type to make, creates an object of that specific type (on the heap), and then assigns the object to its pointer. All the function calls are then handled by the base class through its pointer. It's really just a slight variation of the State pattern, where the base class is acting as a surrogate for the derived class, and the derived class provides the variation in behavior:

```cpp
//: C10:VirtualConstructor.cpp
#include <iostream>
#include <string>
#include <stdexcept>
#include <stdexcept>
#include <cstddef>
#include <vector>
#include "../purge.h"
using namespace std;

class Shape {
  Shape* s;
  // Prevent copy-construction & operator=
  Shape(Shape&);
  Shape operator=(Shape&);
protected:
  Shape() { s = 0; }
public:
  virtual void draw() { s->draw(); }
  virtual void erase() { s->erase(); }
  virtual void test() { s->test(); }
  virtual ~Shape() {
    cout << "~Shape" << endl;
    if(s) {
      cout << "Making virtual call: ";
      s->erase(); // Virtual call
    }
    cout << "delete s: ";
```

[11]James O. Coplien, *Advanced C++ Programming Styles and Idioms,* Addison Wesley, 1992.

```
    delete s; // The polymorphic deletion
    // (delete 0 is legal; it produces a no-op)
  }
  class BadShapeCreation : public logic_error {
  public:
    BadShapeCreation(string type)
    : logic_error("Cannot create type " + type) {}
  };
  Shape(string type) throw(BadShapeCreation);
};

class Circle : public Shape {
  Circle(Circle&);
  Circle operator=(Circle&);
  Circle() {} // Private constructor
  friend class Shape;
public:
  void draw() { cout << "Circle::draw" << endl; }
  void erase() { cout << "Circle::erase" << endl; }
  void test() { draw(); }
  ~Circle() { cout << "Circle::~Circle" << endl; }
};

class Square : public Shape {
  Square(Square&);
  Square operator=(Square&);
  Square() {}
  friend class Shape;
public:
  void draw() { cout << "Square::draw" << endl; }
  void erase() { cout << "Square::erase" << endl; }
  void test() { draw(); }
  ~Square() { cout << "Square::~Square" << endl; }
};

Shape::Shape(string type) throw(Shape::BadShapeCreation) {
  if(type == "Circle")
    s = new Circle;
  else if(type == "Square")
    s = new Square;
  else throw BadShapeCreation(type);
  draw();  // Virtual call in the constructor
}

char* sl[] = { "Circle", "Square", "Square",
```

```
    "Circle", "Circle", "Circle", "Square" };

int main() {
  vector<Shape*> shapes;
  cout << "virtual constructor calls:" << endl;
  try {
    for(size_t i = 0; i < sizeof sl / sizeof sl[0]; i++)
      shapes.push_back(new Shape(sl[i]));
  } catch(Shape::BadShapeCreation e) {
    cout << e.what() << endl;
    purge(shapes);
    return EXIT_FAILURE;
  }
  for(size_t i = 0; i < shapes.size(); i++) {
    shapes[i]->draw();
    cout << "test" << endl;
    shapes[i]->test();
    cout << "end test" << endl;
    shapes[i]->erase();
  }
  Shape c("Circle"); // Create on the stack
  cout << "destructor calls:" << endl;
  purge(shapes);
} ///:~
```

The base class **Shape** contains a pointer to an object of type **Shape** as its only data member. (When you create a "virtual constructor" scheme, exercise special care to ensure this pointer is always initialized to a live object.) This base class is effectively a proxy because it is the only thing the client code sees and interacts with.

Each time you derive a new subtype from **Shape**, you must go back and add the creation for that type in one place, inside the "virtual constructor" in the **Shape** base class. This is not too onerous a task, but the disadvantage is you now have a dependency between the **Shape** class and all classes derived from it.

In this example, the information you must hand the virtual constructor about what type to create is explicit: it's a **string** that names the type. However, your scheme can use other information—for example, in a parser the output of the scanner can be handed to the virtual constructor, which then uses that information to determine which token to create.

The virtual constructor **Shape(type)** cannot be defined until after all the derived classes have been declared. However, the default constructor can be defined inside **class Shape**, but it should be made **protected** so temporary **Shape** objects cannot be created. This default constructor is only called by the constructors of derived-class objects. You are forced to explicitly create a default constructor because the compiler will create one for you automatically only if there are *no* constructors defined. Because you must define **Shape(type)**, you must also define **Shape( )**.

The default constructor in this scheme has at least one important chore—it must set the value of the **s** pointer to zero. This may sound strange at first, but remember that the default constructor will be called as part of the construction of the *actual object*—in Coplien's terms, the "letter," not the "envelope." However, the "letter" is derived from the "envelope," so it also inherits the data member **s**. In the "envelope," **s** is important because it points to the actual object, but in the "letter," **s** is simply excess baggage. Even excess baggage should be initialized, however, and if **s** is not set to zero by the default constructor called for the "letter," bad things happen (as you'll see later).

The virtual constructor takes as its argument information that completely determines the type of the object. Notice, though, that this type information isn't read and acted upon until runtime, whereas normally the compiler must know the exact type at compile time (one other reason this system effectively imitates virtual constructors).

The virtual constructor uses its argument to select the actual ("letter") object to construct, which is then assigned to the pointer inside the "envelope." At that point, the construction of the "letter" has been completed, so any virtual calls will be properly redirected.

As an example, consider the call to **draw( )** inside the virtual constructor. If you trace this call (either by hand or with a debugger), you can see that it starts in the **draw( )** function in the base class, **Shape**. This function calls **draw( )** for the "envelope" **s** pointer to its "letter." All types derived from **Shape** share the same interface, so this virtual call is properly executed, even though it seems to be in the constructor. (Actually, the constructor for the "letter" has already completed.) As long as all virtual calls in the base class simply make calls to identical virtual functions through the pointer to the "letter," the system operates properly.

To understand how it works, consider the code in **main( )**. To fill the **vector shapes**, "virtual constructor" calls are made to **Shape**. Ordinarily in a situation like this, you would call the constructor for the actual type, and the VPTR for that type would be installed in the object. Here, however, the VPTR used in each case is the one for **Shape**, not the one for the specific **Circle**, **Square**, or **Triangle**.

In the **for** loop where the **draw( )** and **erase( )** functions are called for each **Shape**, the virtual function call resolves, through the VPTR, to the corresponding type. However, this is **Shape** in each case. In fact, you might wonder why **draw( )** and **erase( )** were made **virtual**. The reason shows up in the next step: the base-class version of **draw( )** makes a call, through the "letter" pointer **s**, to the **virtual** function **draw( )** for the "letter." This time the call resolves to the actual type of the object, not just the base class **Shape**. Thus, the runtime cost of using virtual constructors is one extra virtual indirection every time you make a virtual function call.

To create any function that is overridden, such as **draw( )**, **erase( )**, or **test( )**, you must forward all calls to the **s** pointer in the base class implementation, as shown earlier. This is because, when the call is made, the call to the envelope's member function will resolve as being to **Shape**, and not to a derived type of **Shape**. Only when you forward the call to **s** will the virtual behavior take place. In **main( )**, you can see that everything works correctly, even when calls are made inside constructors and destructors.

Destructor operation
The activities of destruction in this scheme are also tricky. To understand, let's verbally walk through what happens when you call **delete** for a pointer to a **Shape** object—specifically, a **Square**—created on the heap. (This is more complicated than an object created on the stack.) This will be a **delete** through the polymorphic interface, and will happen via the call to **purge( )**.

The type of any pointer in **shapes** is of the base class **Shape**, so the compiler makes the call through **Shape**. Normally, you might say that it's a virtual call, so **Square**'s destructor will be called. But with the virtual constructor scheme, the compiler is creating actual **Shape** objects, even though the constructor initializes the letter pointer to a specific type of **Shape**. The virtual mechanism *is* used, but the VPTR inside the **Shape** object is **Shape**'s VPTR, not **Square**'s. This resolves to **Shape**'s destructor, which calls **delete** for the letter pointer **s**, which actually points to a **Square** object. This is again a virtual call, but this time it resolves to **Square**'s destructor.

C++ guarantees, via the compiler, that all destructors in the hierarchy are called. **Square**'s destructor is called first, followed by any intermediate destructors, in order, until finally the base-class destructor is called. This base-class destructor contains code that says **delete s**. When this destructor was called originally, it was for the "envelope" **s**, but now it's for the "letter" **s**, which is there because the "letter" was inherited from the "envelope," and not because it contains anything. So *this* call to **delete** should do nothing.

The solution to the problem is to make the "letter" **s** pointer zero. Then when the "letter" base-class destructor is called, you get **delete 0**, which by definition does nothing. Because the default constructor is protected, it will be called *only* during the construction of a "letter," so that's the only situation where **s** is set to zero.

Although it's interesting, you can see this is a complex approach, and the most common tool for hiding construction will generally be ordinary Factory Methods rather than something like this "virtual constructor" scheme.

Builder: creating complex objects

The goal of Builder (which is a Creational pattern, like the Factories we've just looked at) is to separate the construction of an object from its "representation." This means that the construction process stays the same, but the resulting object has different possible representations. GoF points out that the main difference between Builder and Abstract Factory is that a Builder creates the object step-by-step, so the fact that the creation process is spread out in time seems to be important. In addition, the "director" gets a stream of pieces that it passes to the Builder, and each piece is used to perform one of the steps in the build process.

The following example models a bicycle that can have a choice of parts, according to its type (mountain bike, touring bike, or racing bike). A Builder class is associated with each type of bicycle, and each Builder implements the interface specified in the abstract class **BicycleBuilder**. A separate class, **BicycleTechnician**, represents the "director" object described in GoF, and uses a concrete **BicycleBuilder** object to construct a **Bicycle** object.

```
//: C10:Bicycle.h
// Defines classes to build bicycles;
// Illustrates the Builder design pattern.
#ifndef BICYCLE_H
#define BICYCLE_H
#include <iostream>
#include <string>
#include <vector>
#include <cstddef>
#include "../purge.h"
using std::size_t;

class BicyclePart {
public:
  enum BPart { FRAME, WHEEL, SEAT, DERAILLEUR,
    HANDLEBAR, SPROCKET, RACK, SHOCK, NPARTS };
private:
  BPart id;
  static std::string names[NPARTS];
public:
  BicyclePart(BPart bp) { id = bp; }
  friend std::ostream&
  operator<<(std::ostream& os, const BicyclePart& bp) {
    return os << bp.names[bp.id];
  }
};

class Bicycle {
  std::vector<BicyclePart*> parts;
public:
  ~Bicycle() { purge(parts); }
  void addPart(BicyclePart* bp) { parts.push_back(bp); }
  friend std::ostream&
  operator<<(std::ostream& os, const Bicycle& b) {
    os << "{ ";
    for(size_t i = 0; i < b.parts.size(); ++i)
      os << *b.parts[i] << ' ';
    return os << '}';
  }
};

class BicycleBuilder {
protected:
  Bicycle* product;
public:
```

```
BicycleBuilder() { product = 0; }
void createProduct() { product = new Bicycle; }
virtual void buildFrame() = 0;
virtual void buildWheel() = 0;
virtual void buildSeat() = 0;
virtual void buildDerailleur() = 0;
virtual void buildHandlebar() = 0;
virtual void buildSprocket() = 0;
virtual void buildRack() = 0;
virtual void buildShock() = 0;
virtual std::string getBikeName() const = 0;
Bicycle* getProduct() {
  Bicycle* temp = product;
  product = 0;  // Relinquish product
  return temp;
}
};

class MountainBikeBuilder : public BicycleBuilder {
public:
  void buildFrame();
  void buildWheel();
  void buildSeat();
  void buildDerailleur();
  void buildHandlebar();
  void buildSprocket();
  void buildRack();
  void buildShock();
  std::string getBikeName() const { return "MountainBike";}
};

class TouringBikeBuilder : public BicycleBuilder {
public:
  void buildFrame();
  void buildWheel();
  void buildSeat();
  void buildDerailleur();
  void buildHandlebar();
  void buildSprocket();
  void buildRack();
  void buildShock();
  std::string getBikeName() const { return "TouringBike"; }
};

class RacingBikeBuilder : public BicycleBuilder {
```

```
public:
  void buildFrame();
  void buildWheel();
  void buildSeat();
  void buildDerailleur();
  void buildHandlebar();
  void buildSprocket();
  void buildRack();
  void buildShock();
  std::string getBikeName() const { return "RacingBike"; }
};

class BicycleTechnician {
  BicycleBuilder* builder;
public:
  BicycleTechnician() { builder = 0; }
  void setBuilder(BicycleBuilder* b) { builder = b; }
  void construct();
};
#endif // BICYCLE_H ///:~
```

A **Bicycle** holds a **vector** of pointers to **BicyclePart**, representing the parts used to construct the bicycle. To initiate the construction of a bicycle, a **BicycleTechnician** (the "director" in this example) calls **BicycleBuilder::createproduct( )** on a derived **BicycleBuilder** object. The **BicycleTechnician::construct( )** function calls all the functions in the **BicycleBuilder** interface (since it doesn't know what type of concrete builder it has). The concrete builder classes omit (via empty function bodies) those actions that do not apply to the type of bicycle they build, as you can see in the following implementation file:

```
//: C10:Bicycle.cpp {O} {-mwcc}
#include "Bicycle.h"
#include <cassert>
#include <cstddef>
using namespace std;

std::string BicyclePart::names[NPARTS] = {
  "Frame", "Wheel", "Seat", "Derailleur",
  "Handlebar", "Sprocket", "Rack", "Shock" };

// MountainBikeBuilder implementation
void MountainBikeBuilder::buildFrame() {
  product->addPart(new BicyclePart(BicyclePart::FRAME));
```

```
}
void MountainBikeBuilder::buildWheel() {
  product->addPart(new BicyclePart(BicyclePart::WHEEL));
}
void MountainBikeBuilder::buildSeat() {
  product->addPart(new BicyclePart(BicyclePart::SEAT));
}
void MountainBikeBuilder::buildDerailleur() {
  product->addPart(
    new BicyclePart(BicyclePart::DERAILLEUR));
}
void MountainBikeBuilder::buildHandlebar() {
  product->addPart(
    new BicyclePart(BicyclePart::HANDLEBAR));
}
void MountainBikeBuilder::buildSprocket() {
  product->addPart(new BicyclePart(BicyclePart::SPROCKET));
}
void MountainBikeBuilder::buildRack() {}
void MountainBikeBuilder::buildShock() {
  product->addPart(new BicyclePart(BicyclePart::SHOCK));
}

// TouringBikeBuilder implementation
void TouringBikeBuilder::buildFrame() {
  product->addPart(new BicyclePart(BicyclePart::FRAME));
}
void TouringBikeBuilder::buildWheel() {
  product->addPart(new BicyclePart(BicyclePart::WHEEL));
}
void TouringBikeBuilder::buildSeat() {
  product->addPart(new BicyclePart(BicyclePart::SEAT));
}
void TouringBikeBuilder::buildDerailleur() {
  product->addPart(
    new BicyclePart(BicyclePart::DERAILLEUR));
}
void TouringBikeBuilder::buildHandlebar() {
  product->addPart(
    new BicyclePart(BicyclePart::HANDLEBAR));
}
void TouringBikeBuilder::buildSprocket() {
  product->addPart(new BicyclePart(BicyclePart::SPROCKET));
}
void TouringBikeBuilder::buildRack() {
```

```
    product->addPart(new BicyclePart(BicyclePart::RACK));
}
void TouringBikeBuilder::buildShock() {}

// RacingBikeBuilder implementation
void RacingBikeBuilder::buildFrame() {
  product->addPart(new BicyclePart(BicyclePart::FRAME));
}
void RacingBikeBuilder::buildWheel() {
  product->addPart(new BicyclePart(BicyclePart::WHEEL));
}
void RacingBikeBuilder::buildSeat() {
  product->addPart(new BicyclePart(BicyclePart::SEAT));
}
void RacingBikeBuilder::buildDerailleur() {}
void RacingBikeBuilder::buildHandlebar() {
  product->addPart(
    new BicyclePart(BicyclePart::HANDLEBAR));
}
void RacingBikeBuilder::buildSprocket() {
  product->addPart(new BicyclePart(BicyclePart::SPROCKET));
}
void RacingBikeBuilder::buildRack() {}
void RacingBikeBuilder::buildShock() {}

// BicycleTechnician implementation
void BicycleTechnician::construct() {
  assert(builder);
  builder->createProduct();
  builder->buildFrame();
  builder->buildWheel();
  builder->buildSeat();
  builder->buildDerailleur();
  builder->buildHandlebar();
  builder->buildSprocket();
  builder->buildRack();
  builder->buildShock();
} ///:~
```

The **Bicycle** stream inserter calls the corresponding inserter for each
BicyclePart, and that prints its type name so that you can see what a
Bicycle contains. Here is a sample program:

```
//: C10:BuildBicycles.cpp
```

```
//{L} Bicycle
// The Builder design pattern.
#include <cstddef>
#include <iostream>
#include <map>
#include <vector>
#include "Bicycle.h"
#include "../purge.h"
using namespace std;

// Constructs a bike via a concrete builder
Bicycle* buildMeABike(
  BicycleTechnician& t, BicycleBuilder* builder) {
  t.setBuilder(builder);
  t.construct();
  Bicycle* b = builder->getProduct();
  cout << "Built a " << builder->getBikeName() << endl;
  return b;
}

int main() {
  // Create an order for some bicycles
  map <string, size_t> order;
  order["mountain"] = 2;
  order["touring"] = 1;
  order["racing"] = 3;

  // Build bikes
  vector<Bicycle*> bikes;
  BicycleBuilder* m = new MountainBikeBuilder;
  BicycleBuilder* t = new TouringBikeBuilder;
  BicycleBuilder* r = new RacingBikeBuilder;
  BicycleTechnician tech;
  map<string, size_t>::iterator it = order.begin();
  while(it != order.end()) {
    BicycleBuilder* builder;
    if(it->first == "mountain")
      builder = m;
    else if(it->first == "touring")
      builder = t;
    else if(it->first == "racing")
      builder = r;
    for(size_t i = 0; i < it->second; ++i)
      bikes.push_back(buildMeABike(tech, builder));
    ++it;
```

```
  }
  delete m;
  delete t;
  delete r;

  // Display inventory
  for(size_t i = 0; i < bikes.size(); ++i)
    cout << "Bicycle: " << *bikes[i] << endl;
  purge(bikes);
}

/* Output:
Built a MountainBike
Built a MountainBike
Built a RacingBike
Built a RacingBike
Built a RacingBike
Built a TouringBike
Bicycle: {
  Frame Wheel Seat Derailleur Handlebar Sprocket Shock }
Bicycle: {
  Frame Wheel Seat Derailleur Handlebar Sprocket Shock }
Bicycle: { Frame Wheel Seat Handlebar Sprocket }
Bicycle: { Frame Wheel Seat Handlebar Sprocket }
Bicycle: { Frame Wheel Seat Handlebar Sprocket }
Bicycle: {
  Frame Wheel Seat Derailleur Handlebar Sprocket Rack }
*/ ///:~
```

The power of this pattern is that it separates the algorithm for assembling parts into a complete product from the parts themselves and allows different algorithms for different products via different implementations of a common interface.

Observer

The Observer pattern solves a fairly common problem: what if a group of objects needs to update themselves when some other object changes state? This can be seen in the "model-view" aspect of Smalltalk's MVC (model-view-controller) or the almost-equivalent "Document-View Architecture." Suppose that you have some data (the "document") and two views: a plot view and a textual view. When you change the data, the views must be told to update themselves, and that's what the observer facilitates.

Two types of objects are used to implement the observer pattern in the following code. The **Observable** class keeps track of the objects that want to be informed when a change happens. The **Observable** class calls the **notifyObservers( )** member function for each observer on the list. The **notifyObservers( )** member function is part of the base class **Observable**.

There are *two* "things that change" in the observer pattern: the quantity of observing objects and the way an update occurs. That is, the observer pattern allows you to modify both of these without affecting the surrounding code.

You can implement the observer pattern in a number of ways, but the code shown here will create a framework from which you can build your own observer code, by following the example. First, this interface describes what an observer looks like:

```
//: C10:Observer.h
// The Observer interface.
#ifndef OBSERVER_H
#define OBSERVER_H

class Observable;
class Argument {};

class Observer {
public:
  // Called by the observed object, whenever
  // the observed object is changed:
  virtual void update(Observable* o, Argument* arg) = 0;
  virtual ~Observer() {}
};
#endif // OBSERVER_H ///:~
```

Since **Observer** interacts with **Observable** in this approach, **Observable** must be declared first. In addition, the **Argument** class is empty and only acts as a base class for any type of argument you want to pass during an update. If you want, you can simply pass the extra argument as a **void***. You'll have to downcast in either case.

The **Observer** type is an "interface" class that only has one member function, **update( )**. This function is called by the object that's being observed, when that object decides it's time to update all its observers. The arguments are optional; you could have an **update( )** with no arguments, and that would still fit the observer pattern. However this is more general—it allows the observed object to pass the object that caused the update (since an **Observer** may be registered with more than one observed object) and any extra information if that's helpful, rather than forcing the **Observer** object to hunt around to see who is updating and to fetch any other information it needs.

The "observed object" will be of type **Observable**:

```
//: C10:Observable.h
// The Observable class.
#ifndef OBSERVABLE_H
#define OBSERVABLE_H
#include <set>
#include "Observer.h"

class Observable {
  bool changed;
  std::set<Observer*> observers;
protected:
  virtual void setChanged() { changed = true; }
  virtual void clearChanged() { changed = false; }
public:
  virtual void addObserver(Observer& o) {
    observers.insert(&o);
  }
  virtual void deleteObserver(Observer& o) {
    observers.erase(&o);
  }
  virtual void deleteObservers() {
    observers.clear();
  }
  virtual int countObservers() {
    return observers.size();
  }
  virtual bool hasChanged() { return changed; }
  // If this object has changed, notify all
  // of its observers:
  virtual void notifyObservers(Argument* arg = 0) {
```

```
    if(!hasChanged()) return;
    clearChanged(); // Not "changed" anymore
    std::set<Observer*>::iterator it;
    for(it = observers.begin();it != observers.end(); it++)
      (*it)->update(this, arg);
  }
  virtual ~Observable() {}
};
#endif // OBSERVABLE_H ///:~
```

Again, the design here is more elaborate than is necessary. As long as there's a way to register an **Observer** with an **Observable** and a way for the **Observable** to update its **Observer**s, the set of member functions doesn't matter. However, this design is intended to be reusable. (It was lifted from the design used in the Java standard library.)[12]

The **Observable** object has a flag to indicate whether it's been changed. In a simpler design, there would be no flag; if something happened, everyone would be notified. Notice, however, that the control of the flag's state is **protected** so that only an inheritor can decide what constitutes a change, and not the end user of the resulting derived **Observer** class.

The collection of **Observer** objects is kept in a **set<Observer*>** to prevent duplicates; the **set insert( )**, **erase( )**, **clear( )**, and **size( )** functions are exposed to allow **Observer**s to be added and removed at any time, thus providing runtime flexibility.

Most of the work is done in **notifyObservers( )**. If the **changed** flag has not been set, this does nothing. Otherwise, it first clears the **changed** flag so that repeated calls to **notifyObservers( )** won't waste time. This is done before notifying the observers in case the calls to **update( )** do anything that causes a change back to this **Observable** object. It then moves through the **set** and calls back to the **update( )** member function of each **Observer**.

At first it may appear that you can use an ordinary **Observable** object to manage the updates. But this doesn't work; to get any effect, you *must* derive from **Observable** and somewhere in your derived-class code call

---

[12] It differs from Java in that **java.util.Observable.notifyObservers( )** doesn't call **clearChanged( )** until after notifying all the observers

setChanged( ). This is the member function that sets the "changed" flag, which means that when you call **notifyObservers( )** all the observers will, in fact, get notified. *Where* you call **setChanged( )** depends on the logic of your program.

Now we encounter a dilemma. Objects that are being observed may have more than one such item of interest. For example, if you're dealing with a GUI item—a button, say—the items of interest might be the mouse clicked the button, the mouse moved over the button, and (for some reason) the button changed its color. So we'd like to be able to report all these events to different observers, each of which is interested in a different type of event.

The problem is that we would normally reach for multiple inheritance in such a situation: "I'll inherit from **Observable** to deal with mouse clicks, and I'll ... er ... inherit from **Observable** to deal with mouse-overs, and, well, ... hmm, that doesn't work."

The "inner class" idiom

Here's a situation where we must (in effect) upcast to more than one type, but in this case we need to provide several *different* implementations of the same base type. The solution is something we've lifted from Java, which takes C++'s nested class one step further. Java has a built-in feature called an *inner class*, which is like a nested class in C++, but it has access to the nonstatic data of its containing class by implicitly using the "this" pointer of the class object it was created within.[13]

To implement the inner class idiom in C++, we must obtain and use a pointer to the containing object explicitly. Here's an example:

```
//: C10:InnerClassIdiom.cpp
// Example of the "inner class" idiom.
#include <iostream>
#include <string>
using namespace std;
```

---

[13] There is some similarity between inner classes and *subroutine closures*, which save the reference environment of a function call so it can be reproduced later.

```
class Poingable {
public:
  virtual void poing() = 0;
};

void callPoing(Poingable& p) {
  p.poing();
}

class Bingable {
public:
  virtual void bing() = 0;
};

void callBing(Bingable& b) {
  b.bing();
}

class Outer {
  string name;
  // Define one inner class:
  class Inner1;
  friend class Outer::Inner1;
  class Inner1 : public Poingable {
    Outer* parent;
  public:
    Inner1(Outer* p) : parent(p) {}
    void poing() {
      cout << "poing called for "
        << parent->name << endl;
      // Accesses data in the outer class object
    }
  } inner1;
  // Define a second inner class:
  class Inner2;
  friend class Outer::Inner2;
  class Inner2 : public Bingable {
    Outer* parent;
  public:
    Inner2(Outer* p) : parent(p) {}
    void bing() {
      cout << "bing called for "
        << parent->name << endl;
    }
  } inner2;
```

```
public:
  Outer(const string& nm)
  : name(nm), inner1(this), inner2(this) {}
  // Return reference to interfaces
  // implemented by the inner classes:
  operator Poingable&() { return inner1; }
  operator Bingable&() { return inner2; }
};

int main() {
  Outer x("Ping Pong");
  // Like upcasting to multiple base types!:
  callPoing(x);
  callBing(x);
} ///:~
```

The example (intended to show the simplest syntax for the idiom; you'll see a real use shortly) begins with the **Poingable** and **Bingable** interfaces, each containing a single member function. The services provided by **callPoing( )** and **callBing( )** require that the object they receive implements the **Poingable** and **Bingable** interfaces, respectively, but they put no other requirements on that object so as to maximize the flexibility of using **callPoing( )** and **callBing( )**. Note the lack of **virtual** destructors in either interface—the intent is that you never perform object destruction via the interface.

The **Outer** constructor contains some private data (**name**), and it wants to provide both a **Poingable** interface and a **Bingable** interface so it can be used with **callPoing( )** and **callBing( )**. (In this situation we *could* simply use multiple inheritance, but it is kept simple for clarity.) To provide a **Poingable** object without deriving **Outer** from **Poingable**, the inner class idiom is used. First, the declaration **class Inner** says that, somewhere, there is a nested class of this name. This allows the **friend** declaration for the class, which follows. Finally, now that the nested class has been granted access to all the private elements of **Outer**, the class can be defined. Notice that it keeps a pointer to the **Outer** which created it, and this pointer must be initialized in the constructor. Finally, the **poing( )** function from **Poingable** is implemented. The same process occurs for the second inner class which implements **Bingable**. Each inner class has a single **private** instance created, which is initialized in the **Outer** constructor. By creating the member objects and returning references to them, issues of object lifetime are eliminated.

Notice that both inner class definitions are **private**, and in fact the client code doesn't have any access to details of the implementation, since the two access functions **operator Poingable&( )** and **operator Bingable&( )** only return a reference to the upcast interface, not to the object that implements it. In fact, since the two inner classes are **private**, the client code cannot even downcast to the implementation classes, thus providing complete isolation between interface and implementation.

We've taken the extra liberty here of defining the automatic type conversion functions **operator Poingable&( )** and **operator Bingable&( )**. In **main( )**, you can see that these allow a syntax that looks as if **Outer** multiply inherits from **Poingable** and **Bingable**. The difference is that the "casts" in this case are one-way. You can get the effect of an upcast to **Poingable** or **Bingable**, but you cannot downcast back to an **Outer**. In the following example of **observer**, you'll see the more typical approach: you provide access to the inner class objects using ordinary member functions, not automatic type conversion functions.

The observer example

Armed with the **Observer** and **Observable** header files and the inner class idiom, we can look at an example of the Observer pattern:

```
//: C10:ObservedFlower.cpp
// Demonstration of "observer" pattern.
#include <algorithm>
#include <iostream>
#include <string>
#include <vector>
#include "Observable.h"
using namespace std;

class Flower {
  bool isOpen;
public:
  Flower() : isOpen(false),
    openNotifier(this), closeNotifier(this) {}
  void open() { // Opens its petals
    isOpen = true;
    openNotifier.notifyObservers();
    closeNotifier.open();
  }
```

```
  void close() { // Closes its petals
    isOpen = false;
    closeNotifier.notifyObservers();
    openNotifier.close();
  }
  // Using the "inner class" idiom:
  class OpenNotifier;
  friend class Flower::OpenNotifier;
  class OpenNotifier : public Observable {
    Flower* parent;
    bool alreadyOpen;
  public:
    OpenNotifier(Flower* f) : parent(f),
      alreadyOpen(false) {}
    void notifyObservers(Argument* arg = 0) {
      if(parent->isOpen && !alreadyOpen) {
        setChanged();
        Observable::notifyObservers();
        alreadyOpen = true;
      }
    }
    void close() { alreadyOpen = false; }
  } openNotifier;
  class CloseNotifier;
  friend class Flower::CloseNotifier;
  class CloseNotifier : public Observable {
    Flower* parent;
    bool alreadyClosed;
  public:
    CloseNotifier(Flower* f) : parent(f),
      alreadyClosed(false) {}
    void notifyObservers(Argument* arg = 0) {
      if(!parent->isOpen && !alreadyClosed) {
        setChanged();
        Observable::notifyObservers();
        alreadyClosed = true;
      }
    }
    void open() { alreadyClosed = false; }
  } closeNotifier;
};

class Bee {
  string name;
  // An "inner class" for observing openings:
```

```
      class OpenObserver;
      friend class Bee::OpenObserver;
      class OpenObserver : public Observer {
        Bee* parent;
      public:
        OpenObserver(Bee* b) : parent(b) {}
        void update(Observable*, Argument *) {
          cout << "Bee " << parent->name
            << "'s breakfast time!" << endl;
        }
      } openObsrv;
      // Another "inner class" for closings:
      class CloseObserver;
      friend class Bee::CloseObserver;
      class CloseObserver : public Observer {
        Bee* parent;
      public:
        CloseObserver(Bee* b) : parent(b) {}
        void update(Observable*, Argument *) {
          cout << "Bee " << parent->name
            << "'s bed time!" << endl;
        }
      } closeObsrv;
    public:
      Bee(string nm) : name(nm),
        openObsrv(this), closeObsrv(this) {}
      Observer& openObserver() { return openObsrv; }
      Observer& closeObserver() { return closeObsrv;}
    };

    class Hummingbird {
      string name;
      class OpenObserver;
      friend class Hummingbird::OpenObserver;
      class OpenObserver : public Observer {
        Hummingbird* parent;
      public:
        OpenObserver(Hummingbird* h) : parent(h) {}
        void update(Observable*, Argument *) {
          cout << "Hummingbird " << parent->name
            << "'s breakfast time!" << endl;
        }
      } openObsrv;
      class CloseObserver;
      friend class Hummingbird::CloseObserver;
```

```
    class CloseObserver : public Observer {
      Hummingbird* parent;
    public:
      CloseObserver(Hummingbird* h) : parent(h) {}
      void update(Observable*, Argument *) {
        cout << "Hummingbird " << parent->name
          << "'s bed time!" << endl;
      }
    } closeObsrv;
public:
  Hummingbird(string nm) : name(nm),
    openObsrv(this), closeObsrv(this) {}
  Observer& openObserver() { return openObsrv; }
  Observer& closeObserver() { return closeObsrv;}
};

int main() {
  Flower f;
  Bee ba("A"), bb("B");
  Hummingbird ha("A"), hb("B");
  f.openNotifier.addObserver(ha.openObserver());
  f.openNotifier.addObserver(hb.openObserver());
  f.openNotifier.addObserver(ba.openObserver());
  f.openNotifier.addObserver(bb.openObserver());
  f.closeNotifier.addObserver(ha.closeObserver());
  f.closeNotifier.addObserver(hb.closeObserver());
  f.closeNotifier.addObserver(ba.closeObserver());
  f.closeNotifier.addObserver(bb.closeObserver());
  // Hummingbird B decides to sleep in:
  f.openNotifier.deleteObserver(hb.openObserver());
  // Something changes that interests observers:
  f.open();
  f.open(); // It's already open, no change.
  // Bee A doesn't want to go to bed:
  f.closeNotifier.deleteObserver(
    ba.closeObserver());
  f.close();
  f.close(); // It's already closed; no change
  f.openNotifier.deleteObservers();
  f.open();
  f.close();
} ///:~
```

The events of interest are that a **Flower** can open or close. Because of the use of the inner class idiom, both these events can be separately observable

---

phenomena. The **OpenNotifier** and **CloseNotifier** classes both derive from **Observable**, so they have access to **setChanged( )** and can be handed to anything that needs an **Observable**. You'll notice that, contrary to **InnerClassIdiom.cpp**, the **Observable** descendants are **public**. This is because some of their member functions must be available to the client programmer. There's nothing that says that an inner class must be **private**; in **InnerClassIdiom.cpp** we were simply following the design guideline "make things as private as possible." You could make the classes **private** and expose the appropriate member functions by proxy in **Flower**, but it wouldn't gain much.

The inner class idiom also comes in handy to define more than one kind of **Observer** in **Bee** and **Hummingbird**, since both those classes may want to independently observe **Flower** openings and closings. Notice how the inner class idiom provides something that has most of the benefits of inheritance (the ability to access the private data in the outer class, for example).

In **main( )**, you can see one of the primary benefits of the Observer pattern: the ability to change behavior at runtime by dynamically registering and unregistering **Observer**s with **Observable**s. This flexibility is achieved at the cost of significant additional code—you will often see this kind of tradeoff in design patterns: more complexity in one place in exchange for increased flexibility and/or lowered complexity in another place.

If you study the previous example, you'll see that **OpenNotifier** and **CloseNotifier** use the basic **Observable** interface. This means that you could derive from other completely different **Observer** classes; the only connection the **Observer**s have with **Flower**s is the **Observer** interface.

Another way to accomplish this fine granularity of observable phenomena is to use some form of tags for the phenomena, for example empty classes, strings, or enumerations that denote different types of observable behavior. This approach can be implemented using aggregation rather than inheritance, and the differences are mainly tradeoffs between time and space efficiency. For the client, the differences are negligible.

Multiple dispatching

When dealing with multiple interacting types, a program can get particularly messy. For example, consider a system that parses and executes mathematical expressions. You want to be able to say **Number + Number**, **Number * Number**, and so on, where **Number** is the base class for a family of numerical objects. But when you say **a + b**, and you don't know the exact type of either **a** or **b**, how can you get them to interact properly?

The answer starts with something you probably don't think about: C++ performs only single dispatching. That is, if you are performing an operation on more than one object whose type is unknown, C++ can invoke the dynamic binding mechanism on only one of those types. This doesn't solve the problem described here, so you end up detecting some types manually and effectively producing your own dynamic binding behavior.

The solution is called *multiple dispatching* (described in GoF in the context of the Visitor pattern, shown in the next section). Here, there will be only two dispatches, which is referred to as *double dispatching*. Remember that polymorphism can occur only via virtual function calls, so if you want multiple dispatching to occur, there must be a virtual function call to determine each unknown type. Thus, if you are working with two different type hierarchies that are interacting, you'll need a virtual call in each hierarchy. Generally, you'll set up a configuration such that a single member function call generates more than one virtual member function call and thus determines more than one type in the process: you'll need a virtual function call for each dispatch. The virtual functions in the following example are called **compete( )** and **eval( )** and are both members of the same type (this is not a requirement for multiple dispatching):[14]

```
//: C10:PaperScissorsRock.cpp
// Demonstration of multiple dispatching.
#include <algorithm>
#include <iostream>
#include <iterator>
#include <vector>
```

---

[14] This example existed for a number of years in both C++ and Java on www.MindView.net before it appeared, without attribution, in a recent book by other authors.

```
#include <ctime>
#include <cstdlib>
#include "../purge.h"
using namespace std;

class Paper;
class Scissors;
class Rock;

enum Outcome { WIN, LOSE, DRAW };

ostream& operator<<(ostream& os, const Outcome out) {
  switch(out) {
    default:
    case WIN: return os << "win";
    case LOSE: return os << "lose";
    case DRAW: return os << "draw";
  }
}

class Item {
public:
  virtual Outcome compete(const Item*) = 0;
  virtual Outcome eval(const Paper*) const = 0;
  virtual Outcome eval(const Scissors*) const= 0;
  virtual Outcome eval(const Rock*) const = 0;
  virtual ostream& print(ostream& os) const = 0;
  virtual ~Item() {}
  friend ostream& operator<<(ostream& os, const Item* it) {
    return it->print(os);
  }
};

class Paper : public Item {
public:
  Outcome compete(const Item* it) { return it->eval(this);}
  Outcome eval(const Paper*) const { return DRAW; }
  Outcome eval(const Scissors*) const { return WIN; }
  Outcome eval(const Rock*) const { return LOSE; }
  ostream& print(ostream& os) const {
    return os << "Paper    ";
  }
};

class Scissors : public Item {
```

```cpp
public:
  Outcome compete(const Item* it) { return it->eval(this);}
  Outcome eval(const Paper*) const { return LOSE; }
  Outcome eval(const Scissors*) const { return DRAW; }
  Outcome eval(const Rock*) const { return WIN; }
  ostream& print(ostream& os) const {
    return os << "Scissors";
  }
};

class Rock : public Item {
public:
  Outcome compete(const Item* it) { return it->eval(this);}
  Outcome eval(const Paper*) const { return WIN; }
  Outcome eval(const Scissors*) const { return LOSE; }
  Outcome eval(const Rock*) const { return DRAW; }
  ostream& print(ostream& os) const {
    return os << "Rock    ";
  }
};

struct ItemGen {
  Item* operator()() {
    switch(rand() % 3) {
      default:
      case 0: return new Scissors;
      case 1: return new Paper;
      case 2: return new Rock;
    }
  }
};

struct Compete {
  Outcome operator()(Item* a, Item* b) {
    cout << a << "\t" << b << "\t";
    return a->compete(b);
  }
};

int main() {
  srand(time(0)); // Seed the random number generator
  const int sz = 20;
  vector<Item*> v(sz*2);
  generate(v.begin(), v.end(), ItemGen());
  transform(v.begin(), v.begin() + sz,
```

```
        v.begin() + sz,
        ostream_iterator<Outcome>(cout, "\n"),
        Compete());
    purge(v);
} ///:~
```

Outcome categorizes the different possible results of a **compete( )**, and the **operator<<** simplifies the process of displaying a particular **Outcome**.

Item is the base class for the types that will be multiply-dispatched. **Compete::operator( )** takes two **Item*** (the exact type of both are unknown) and begins the double-dispatching process by calling the **virtual Item::compete( )** function. The virtual mechanism determines the type **a**, so it wakes up inside the **compete( )** function of **a**'s concrete type. The **compete( )** function performs the second dispatch by calling **eval( )** on the remaining type. Passing itself (**this**) as an argument to **eval( )** produces a call to the overloaded **eval( )** function, thus preserving the type information of the first dispatch. When the second dispatch is completed, you know the exact types of both **Item** objects.

In **main( )**, the STL algorithm **generate( )** populates the **vector v**, then **transform( )** applies **Compete::operator( )** to the two ranges. This version of **transform( )** takes the start and end point of the first range (containing the left-hand **Item**s used in the double dispatch); the starting point of the second range, which holds the right-hand **Item**s; the destination iterator, which in this case is standard output; and the function object (a temporary of type **Compete**) to call for each object.

It requires a lot of ceremony to set up multiple dispatching, but keep in mind that the benefit is the syntactic elegance achieved when making the call— instead of writing awkward code to determine the type of one or more objects during a call, you simply say: "You two! I don't care what types you are, interact properly with each other!" Make sure this kind of elegance is important to you before embarking on multiple dispatching, however.

Note that multiple dispatching is, in effect, performing a table lookup. Here, the lookup is performed using virtual functions, but you could instead perform a literal table lookup. With more than a few dispatches (and if you are prone to making additions and changes), a table lookup may be a better solution to the problem.

Multiple dispatching with Visitor

The goal of Visitor (the final, and arguably most complex, pattern in GoF) is to separate the operations on a class hierarchy from the hierarchy itself. This is quite an odd motivation because most of what we do in object-oriented programming is to combine data and operations into objects, and to use polymorphism to automatically select the correct variation of an operation, depending on the exact type of an object.

With Visitor you extract the operations from inside your class hierarchy into a separate, external hierarchy. The "main" hierarchy then contains a **visit( )** function that accepts any object from your hierarchy of operations. As a result, you get two class hierarchies instead of one. In addition, you'll see that your "main" hierarchy becomes very brittle—if you add a new class, you will force changes throughout the second hierarchy. GoF says that the main hierarchy should thus "rarely change." This constraint is very limiting, and it further reduces the applicability of this pattern.

For the sake of argument, then, assume that you have a primary class hierarchy that is fixed; perhaps it's from another vendor and you can't make changes to that hierarchy. If you had the source code for the library, you could add new virtual functions in the base class, but this is, for some reason, not feasible. A more likely scenario is that adding new virtual functions is somehow awkward, ugly or otherwise difficult to maintain. GoF argues that "distributing all these operations across the various node classes leads to a system that's hard to understand, maintain, and change." (As you'll see, Visitor can be much harder to understand, maintain and change.) Another GoF argument is that you want to avoid "polluting" the interface of the main hierarchy with too many operations (but if your interface is too "fat," you might ask whether the object is trying to do too many things).

The library creator must have foreseen, however, that you will want to add new operations to that hierarchy, so that they can know to include the **visit( )** function.

So (assuming you really need to do this) the dilemma is that you need to add member functions to the base class, but for some reason you can't touch the base class. How do you get around this?

Visitor builds on the double-dispatching scheme shown in the previous section. The Visitor pattern allows you to effectively extend the interface of the primary type by creating a separate class hierarchy of type **Visitor** to "virtualize" the operations performed on the primary type. The objects of the primary type simply "accept" the visitor and then call the visitor's dynamically bound member function. Thus, you create a visitor, pass it into the primary hierarchy, and you get the effect of a virtual function. Here's a simple example:

```
//: C10:BeeAndFlowers.cpp
// Demonstration of "visitor" pattern.
#include <algorithm>
#include <iostream>
#include <string>
#include <vector>
#include <ctime>
#include <cstdlib>
#include "../purge.h"
using namespace std;

class Gladiolus;
class Renuculus;
class Chrysanthemum;

class Visitor {
public:
  virtual void visit(Gladiolus* f) = 0;
  virtual void visit(Renuculus* f) = 0;
  virtual void visit(Chrysanthemum* f) = 0;
  virtual ~Visitor() {}
};

class Flower {
public:
  virtual void accept(Visitor&) = 0;
  virtual ~Flower() {}
};

class Gladiolus : public Flower {
public:
  virtual void accept(Visitor& v) {
    v.visit(this);
  }
};

class Renuculus : public Flower {
```

```
public:
  virtual void accept(Visitor& v) {
    v.visit(this);
  }
};

class Chrysanthemum : public Flower {
public:
  virtual void accept(Visitor& v) {
    v.visit(this);
  }
};

// Add the ability to produce a string:
class StringVal : public Visitor {
  string s;
public:
  operator const string&() { return s; }
  virtual void visit(Gladiolus*) {
    s = "Gladiolus";
  }
  virtual void visit(Renuculus*) {
    s = "Renuculus";
  }
  virtual void visit(Chrysanthemum*) {
    s = "Chrysanthemum";
  }
};

// Add the ability to do "Bee" activities:
class Bee : public Visitor {
public:
  virtual void visit(Gladiolus*) {
    cout << "Bee and Gladiolus" << endl;
  }
  virtual void visit(Renuculus*) {
    cout << "Bee and Renuculus" << endl;
  }
  virtual void visit(Chrysanthemum*) {
    cout << "Bee and Chrysanthemum" << endl;
  }
};

struct FlowerGen {
  Flower* operator()() {
```

```
      switch(rand() % 3) {
        default:
        case 0: return new Gladiolus;
        case 1: return new Renuculus;
        case 2: return new Chrysanthemum;
      }
    }
};

int main() {
  srand(time(0)); // Seed the random number generator
  vector<Flower*> v(10);
  generate(v.begin(), v.end(), FlowerGen());
  vector<Flower*>::iterator it;
  // It's almost as if I added a virtual function
  // to produce a Flower string representation:
  StringVal sval;
  for(it = v.begin(); it != v.end(); it++) {
    (*it)->accept(sval);
    cout << string(sval) << endl;
  }
  // Perform "Bee" operation on all Flowers:
  Bee bee;
  for(it = v.begin(); it != v.end(); it++)
    (*it)->accept(bee);
  purge(v);
} ///:~
```

Flower is the primary hierarchy, and each subtype of **Flower** can **accept( )** a **Visitor**. The **Flower** hierarchy has no operations other than **accept( )**, so all the functionality of the **Flower** hierarchy is contained in the **Visitor** hierarchy. Note that the **Visitor** classes must know about all the specific types of **Flower**, and if you add a new type of **Flower** the entire **Visitor** hierarchy must be reworked.

The **accept( )** function in each **Flower** begins a double dispatch as described in the previous section. The first dispatch determines the exact type of **Flower** and the second determines the exact type of **Visitor**. Once you know the exact types you can perform an operation appropriate to both.

It's very unlikely that you'll use Visitor because its motivation is unusual and its constraints are stultifying. The GoF examples are not convincing—the first is a compiler (not many people write compilers, and it seems quite rare that

Visitor is used within these compilers), and they apologize for the other examples, saying you wouldn't actually use Visitor for anything like this. You would need a stronger compulsion than that presented in GoF to abandon an ordinary OO structure for Visitor—what benefit does it really buy you in exchange for much greater complexity and constraint? Why can't you simply add more virtual functions in the base class when you discover you need them? Or, if you really need to paste new functions into an existing hierarchy and you are unable to modify that hierarchy, why not try multiple inheritance first? (Even then, the likelihood of "saving" the existing hierarchy this way is slim). Consider also that, to use Visitor, the existing hierarchy must incorporate a **visit( )** function from the beginning, because to add it later would mean that you had permission to modify the hierarchy, so you could just add ordinary virtual functions as you need them. No, Visitor must be part of the architecture from the beginning, and to use it requires a motivation greater than that in GoF.[15]

We present Visitor here because we have seen it used when it shouldn't be, just as multiple inheritance and any number of other approaches have been used inappropriately. If you find yourself using Visitor, ask why. Are you *really* unable to add new virtual functions in the base class? Do you *really* want to be restricted from adding new types in your primary hierarchy?

Summary

The point of design patterns, like the point of any abstraction, is to make your life easier. Usually something in your system is changing—this could be code during the lifetime of the project, or objects during the lifetime of one program execution. Discover what is changing, and a design pattern may help you encapsulate that change, and thus bring it under control.

It's easy to get infatuated with a particular design, and to create trouble for yourself by applying it just because you know how. What's hard, ironically, is to follow the XP maxim of "do the simplest thing that could possibly work." But by doing the simplest thing, you not only get a design that's faster to

---

[15] The motivation for including Visitor in GoF was probably excessive cleverness. At a workshop, one of the GoF authors told one of us that "Visitor was his favorite pattern."

---

implement, but also easier to maintain. And if the simplest thing doesn't do the job, you'll find out a lot sooner than if you spend the time implementing something complex, and then find out *that* doesn't work.

Exercises

Solutions to selected exercises can be found in the electronic document *The Thinking in C++ Volume 2 Annotated Solution Guide*, available for a small fee from *www.MindView.net*.

1. Create a variation of **SingletonPattern.cpp** where all functions are static. Is the **instance( )** function still necessary in this case?

2. Starting with **SingletonPattern.cpp**, create a class that provides a connection to a service that stores and retrieves data from a configuration file.

3. Using **SingletonPattern.cpp** as a starting point, create a class that manages a fixed number of its own objects. Assume the objects are database connections and you only have a license to use a fixed quantity of these at any one time.

4. Modify **KissingPrincess2.cpp** by adding another state to the system, so that each kiss cycles the creature to the next state.

5. Find **C16:TStack.h** from *Thinking in C++, Volume 1, 2nd Edition* (downloadable from www. BruceEckel.com). Create an Adapter for this class such that you can apply the STL algorithm **for_each( )** to the elements of the **TStack**, using your adapter. Create a **TStack** of **string**, fill it with strings and use **for_each( )** to count all the letters in all the strings in the **TStack**.

6. Create a framework (that is, use the Template Method pattern) that takes a list of file names on the command line. It opens each file except the last for reading, and the last file it opens for writing. The framework will process each input file using an undetermined policy and write the output to the last file. Inherit to customize this framework to create two separate applications:
   1) Converts all the letters in each file to uppercase.
   2) Searches the files for words given in the first file.

7. Modify Exercise 6 to use Strategy instead of Template Method.

8. Modify **Strategy.cpp** to include State behavior, so that the Strategy can be changed during the lifetime of the **Context** object.

9. Modify **Strategy.cpp** to use a Chain of Responsibility approach, where you keep trying different ways to get someone to say their name without admitting you've forgotten it.

10. Add a class **Triangle** to **ShapeFactory1.cpp**.
11. Add a class **Triangle** to **ShapeFactory2.cpp**.
12. Add a new type of **GameEnvironment** called **GnomesAndFairies** to **AbstractFactory.cpp**.
13. Modify **ShapeFactory2.cpp** so that it uses an Abstract Factory to create different sets of shapes (for example, one particular type of factory object creates "thick shapes," another creates "thin shapes," but each factory object can create all the shapes: circles, squares, triangles, and so on).
14. Modify **VirtualConstructor.cpp** to use a **map** instead of **if-else** statements inside **Shape::Shape(string type)**.
15. Break a text file up into an input stream of words (keep it simple: just break the input stream on white space). Create one Builder that puts the words into a **set**, and another that produces a **map** containing words and occurrences of those words (that is, it does a word count).
16. Create a minimal Observer-Observable design in two classes, without base classes and without the extra arguments in **Observer.h** and the member functions in **Observable.h**. Just create the bare minimum in the two classes, and then demonstrate your design by creating one **Observable** and many **Observers** and cause the **Observable** to update the **Observers**.
17. Change **InnerClassIdiom.cpp** so that **Outer** uses multiple inheritance instead of the inner class idiom.
18. Modify **PaperScissorsRock.java** to replace the double dispatch with a table lookup. The easiest way to do this is to create a **map** of **map**s, with the key of each **map** the **typeid(obj).name( )** information of each object. Then you can do the lookup by saying: **map[typeid(obj1).name( )][typeid(obj2).name( )]**. Notice how much easier it is to reconfigure the system. When is it more appropriate to use this approach vs. hard-coding the dynamic dispatches? Can you create a system that has the syntactic simplicity of use of the dynamic dispatch but uses a table lookup?
19. Create a business-modeling environment with three types of **Inhabitant**: **Dwarf** (for engineers), **Elf** (for marketers), and **Troll** (for managers). Now create a class called **Project** that instantiates the different inhabitants and causes them to **interact( )** with each other using multiple dispatching.
20. Modify the previous exercise to make the interactions more detailed. Each **Inhabitant** can randomly produce a **Weapon** using **getWeapon( )**: a **Dwarf** uses **Jargon** or **Play**, an **Elf** uses

InventFeature or **SellImaginaryProduct**, and a **Troll** uses **Edict** and **Schedule**. You decide which weapons "win" and "lose" in each interaction (as in **PaperScissorsRock.cpp**). Add a **battle( )** member function to **Project** that takes two **Inhabitant**s and matches them against each other. Now create a **meeting( )** member function for **Project** that creates groups of **Dwarf**, **Elf**, and **Manager** and battles the groups against each other until only members of one group are left standing. These are the "winners."

21.   Add a **Hummingbird Visitor** to **BeeAndFlowers.cpp**.

22.   Add a **Sunflower** type to **BeeAndFlowers.cpp** and notice what you need to change to accommodate this new type.

23.   Modify **BeeAndFlowers.cpp** so that it does *not* use Visitor, but "reverts" to a regular class hierarchy instead. Turn **Bee** into a collecting parameter.

11: Concurrency

Objects provide a way to divide a program into independent sections. Often, you also need to partition a program into separate, independently running subtasks.

Using *multithreading*, each of these independent subtasks is driven by a *thread of execution*, and you program as if each thread has the CPU to itself. An underlying mechanism is dividing up the CPU time for you, but in general, you don't need to think about it, which helps to simplify programming with multiple threads.

A *process* is a self-contained program running within its own address space. A *multitasking* operating system can run more than one process (program) at a time, while making it look as if each one is chugging along on its own, by periodically switching the CPU from one task to another. A *thread* is a single sequential flow of control *within* a process. A single process can thus have multiple concurrently executing threads. Since the threads run within a single process, they share memory and other resources. The fundamental difficulty in writing multithreaded programs is coordinating the use of those resources between different threads.

There are many possible uses for multithreading, but you'll most often want to use it when you have some part of your program tied to a particular event or resource. To keep from holding up the rest of your program, you create a thread associated with that event or resource and let it run independently of the main program.

Concurrent programming is like stepping into an entirely new world and learning a new programming language, or at least a new set of language concepts. With the appearance of thread support in most microcomputer operating systems, extensions for threads have also been appearing in programming languages or libraries. In all cases, thread programming:

1. Seems mysterious and requires a shift in the way you think about programming.

2. Looks similar to thread support in other languages. When you understand threads, you understand a common tongue.

Understanding concurrent programming is on the same order of difficulty as understanding polymorphism. If you apply some effort, you can fathom the basic mechanism, but it generally takes deep study and understanding to develop a true grasp of the subject. The goal of this chapter is to give you a solid foundation in the basics of concurrency so that you can understand the concepts and write reasonable multithreaded programs. Be aware that you can easily become overconfident. If you are writing anything complex, you will need to study dedicated books on the topic.

Motivation

One of the most compelling reasons for using concurrency is to produce a responsive user interface. Consider a program that performs some CPU-intensive operation and thus ends up ignoring user input and being unresponsive. The program needs to continue performing its operations, and at the same time it needs to return control to the user interface so that the program can respond to the user. If you have a "quit" button, you don't want to be forced to poll it in every piece of code you write in your program. (This would couple your quit button across the program and be a maintenance headache.) Yet you want the quit button to be responsive, as if you *were* checking it regularly.

A conventional function cannot continue performing its operations and at the same time return control to the rest of the program. In fact, this sounds like an impossibility, as if the CPU must be in two places at once, but this is precisely the illusion that concurrency provides (in the case of multiprocessor systems, this may be more than an illusion).

You can also use concurrency to optimize throughput. For example, you might be able to do important work while you're stuck waiting for input to arrive on an I/O port. Without threading, the only reasonable solution is to poll the I/O port, which is awkward and can be difficult.

If you have a multiprocessor machine, multiple threads can be distributed across multiple processors, which can dramatically improve throughput. This is often the case with powerful multiprocessor web servers, which can distribute large numbers of user requests across CPUs in a program that allocates one thread per request.

A program that uses threads on a single-CPU machine is still just doing one thing at a time, so it must be theoretically possible to write the same program without using any threads. However, multithreading provides an important organizational benefit: The design of your program can be greatly simplified. Some types of problems, such as simulation—a video game, for example—are difficult to solve without support for concurrency.

The threading model is a programming convenience to simplify juggling several operations at the same time within a single program: The CPU will pop around and give each thread some of its time.[1] Each thread has the consciousness of constantly having the CPU to itself, but the CPU's time is actually sliced among all the threads. The exception is a program that is running on multiple CPU. But one of the great things about threading is that you are abstracted away from this layer, so your code does not need to know whether it is running on a single CPU or many.[2] Thus, using threads is a way to create transparently scalable programs—if a program is running too slowly, you can easily speed it up by adding CPUs to your computer. Multitasking and multithreading tend to be the most reasonable ways to utilize multiprocessor systems.

Threading can reduce computing efficiency somewhat, but the net improvement in program design, resource balancing, and user convenience is often quite valuable. In general, threads enable you to create a more loosely coupled design; otherwise, parts of your code would be forced to pay explicit attention to tasks that would normally be handled by threads.

---

[1] This is true when the system uses time slicing (Windows, for example). Solaris uses a FIFO concurrency model: unless a higher priority thread is awakened the current thread runs until it blocks or terminates. That means that other threads with the same priority don't run until the current one gives up the processor.

[2] Assuming you've designed it for multiple CPUs. Otherwise, code that seems to work fine on a time-sliced single processor system can fail when moved to multiple-CPU system, since the additional CPUs can reveal problems that a one-CPU system does not.

Concurrency in C++

When the C++ Standards Committee was creating the initial C++ Standard, a concurrency mechanism was explicitly excluded because C didn't have one and also because there were a number of competing approaches to implementing concurrency. It seemed too much of a constraint to force programmers to use only one of these.

The alternative turned out to be worse, however. To use concurrency, you had to find and learn a library and deal with its idiosyncrasies and the uncertainties of working with a particular vendor. In addition, there was no guarantee that such a library would work on different compilers or across different platforms. Also, since concurrency was not part of the standard language, it was more difficult to find C++ programmers who also understood concurrent programming.

Another influence may have been the Java language, which included concurrency in the core language. Although multithreading is still complicated, Java programmers tend to start learning and using it from the beginning.

The C++ Standards Committee is considering the addition of concurrency support to the next iteration of C++, but at the time of this writing it is unclear what the library will look like. We decided to use the ZThread library as the basis for this chapter. We preferred the design, and it is open-source and freely available at *http://zthread.sourceforge.net*. Eric Crahen of IBM, the author of the ZThread library, was instrumental in creating this chapter.[3]

This chapter uses only a subset of the ZThread library, in order to convey the fundamental ideas of threading. The ZThread library contains significantly more sophisticated thread support than is shown here, and you should study that library further in order to fully understand its capabilities.

---

[3] Much of this chapter began as a translation from the *Concurrency* chapter in *Thinking in Java, 3rd edition*, Prentice Hall 2003, although it has changed very significantly in the process.

Installing ZThreads

Please note that the ZThread library is an independent project and is not supported by the authors of this book; we are simply using the library in this chapter and cannot provide technical support for installation issues. See the ZThread web site for installation support and error reports.

The ZThread library is distributed as source code. After downloading it (version 2.3 or greater) from the ZThread web site, you must first compile the library, and then configure your project to use the library.

The preferred method for compiling ZThreads for most flavors of UNIX (Linux, SunOS, Cygwin, etc.) is to use the configure script. After unpacking the files (using **tar**), simply execute:

```
./configure && make install
```

from the main directory of the ZThreads archive to compile and install a copy of the library in the */usr/local* directory. You can customize a number of options when using this script, including the locations of files. For details, use this command:

```
./configure -help
```

The ZThreads code is structured to simplify compilation for other platforms and compilers (such as Borland, Microsoft, and Metrowerks). To do this, create a new project and add all the *.cxx* files in the *src* directory of the ZThreads archive to the list of files to be compiled. Also, be sure to include the *include* directory of the archive in the header search path for your project. The exact details will vary from compiler to compiler so you'll need to be somewhat familiar with your toolset to be able to use this option.

Once the compilation has succeeded, the next step is to create a project that uses the newly compiled library. First, let the compiler know where the headers are located so that your **#include** statements will work properly. Typically, you will add an option such as the following to your project:

```
-I/path/to/installation/include
```

If you used the *configure* script, the installation path will be whatever you selected for the prefix (which defaults to */usr/local*). If you used one of the

---

project files in the *build* directory, the installation path would simply be the path to the main directory of the ZThreads archive.

Next, you'll need to add an option to your project that will let the linker know where to find the library. If you used the configure script, this will look like:

```
-L/path/to/installation/lib -lZThread
```

If you used one of the project files provided, this will look like:

```
-L/path/to/installation/Debug ZThread.lib
```

Again, if you used the *configure* script, the installation path will be whatever you selected for the prefix. If you used a provided project file, the path will be the path to the main directory of the ZThreads archive.

Note that if you're using Linux, or if you are using Cygwin (www.cygwin.com) under Windows, you may not need to modify your include or library path; the installation process and defaults will often take care of everything for you.

Under Linux, you will probably need to add the following to your **.bashrc** so that the runtime system can find the shared library file **LibZThread-x.x.so.O** when it executes the programs in this chapter:

export LD_LIBRARY_PATH=/usr/local/lib:${LD_LIBRARY_PATH}

(Assuming you used the default installation process and the shared library ended up in /user/local/lib; otherwise, change the path to your location).

Defining Tasks

A thread carries out a task, so you need a way to describe that task. The **Runnable** class provides a common interface to execute any arbitrary task. Here is the core of the ZThread **Runnable** class, which you will find in **Runnable.h** in the *include* directory, after installing the ZThread library:

```
class Runnable {
public:
  virtual void run() = 0;
  virtual ~Runnable() {}
};
```

By making this an abstract base class, **Runnable** is easily combinable with a base class and other classes.

To define a task, simply inherit from the **Runnable** class and override **run( )** to make the task do your bidding.

For example, the following **LiftOff** task displays the countdown before liftoff:

```
//: C11:LiftOff.h
// Demonstration of the Runnable interface.
#ifndef LIFTOFF_H
#define LIFTOFF_H
#include <iostream>
#include "zthread/Runnable.h"

class LiftOff : public ZThread::Runnable {
  int countDown;
  int id;
public:
  LiftOff(int count, int ident = 0) :
    countDown(count), id(ident) {}
  ~LiftOff() {
    std::cout << id << " completed" << std::endl;
  }
  void run() {
    while(countDown--)
      std::cout << id << ":" << countDown << std::endl;
    std::cout << "Liftoff!" << std::endl;
  }
};
#endif // LIFTOFF_H ///:~
```

The identifier **id** distinguishes between multiple instances of the task. If you only make a single instance, you can use the default value for **ident**. The destructor will allow you to see that a task is properly destroyed.

In the following example, the task's **run( )** is not driven by a separate thread; it is simply called directly in **main( )**:

```
//: C11:NoThread.cpp
#include "LiftOff.h"

int main() {
  LiftOff launch(10);
```

```
    launch.run();
} ///:~
```

When a class is derived from **Runnable**, it must have a **run( )** function, but that's nothing special—it doesn't produce any innate threading abilities.

To achieve threading behavior, you must use the **Thread** class.

Using Threads

To drive a **Runnable** object with a thread, you create a separate **Thread** object and hand a **Runnable** pointer to the **Thread**'s constructor. This performs the thread initialization and then calls the **Runnable**'s **run( )** as an interruptible thread. By driving **LiftOff** with a **Thread**, the example below shows how any task can be run in the context of another thread:

```
//: C11:BasicThreads.cpp
// The most basic use of the Thread class.
//{L} ZThread
#include <iostream>
#include "LiftOff.h"
#include "zthread/Thread.h"
using namespace ZThread;
using namespace std;

int main() {
  try {
    Thread t(new LiftOff(10));
    cout << "Waiting for LiftOff" << endl;
  } catch(Synchronization_Exception& e) {
    cerr << e.what() << endl;
  }
} ///:~
```

Synchronization_Exception is part of the ZThread library and is the base class for all ZThread exceptions. It will be thrown if there is an error starting or using a thread.

A **Thread** constructor only needs a pointer to a **Runnable** object. Creating a **Thread** object will perform the necessary initialization for the thread and then call that **Runnable**'s **run( )** member function to start the task. Even though the **Thread** constructor is, in effect, making a call to a long-running function, that constructor quickly returns. In effect, you have made a member function call to **LiftOff::run( )**, and that function has not yet finished, but because **LiftOff::run( )** is being executed by a different thread, you can still perform other operations in the **main( )** thread. (This ability is not restricted to the **main( )** thread—any thread can start another thread.) You can see this by running the program. Even though **LiftOff::run( )** has been called, the "Waiting for LiftOff" message will appear before the countdown has completed. Thus, the program is running two functions at once— **LiftOff::run( )** and **main( )**.

You can easily add more threads to drive more tasks. Here, you can see how all the threads run in concert with one another:

```
//: C11:MoreBasicThreads.cpp
// Adding more threads.
//{L} ZThread
#include <iostream>
#include "LiftOff.h"
#include "zthread/Thread.h"
using namespace ZThread;
using namespace std;

int main() {
  const int SZ = 5;
  try {
    for(int i = 0; i < SZ; i++)
      Thread t(new LiftOff(10, i));
    cout << "Waiting for LiftOff" << endl;
  } catch(Synchronization_Exception& e) {
    cerr << e.what() << endl;
  }
} ///:~
```

The second argument for the **LiftOff** constructor identifies each task. When you run the program, you'll see that the execution of the different tasks is mixed together as the threads are swapped in and out. This swapping is automatically controlled by the thread scheduler. If you have multiple processors on your machine, the thread scheduler will quietly distribute the threads among the processors.

The **for** loop can seem a little strange at first because **t** is being created locally inside the **for** loop and then immediately goes out of scope and is destroyed.

This makes it appear that the thread itself might be immediately lost, but you can see from the output that the threads are indeed running to conclusion. When you create a **Thread** object, the associated thread is registered with the threading system, which keeps it alive. Even though the stack-based **Thread** object is lost, the thread itself lives on until its associated task completes. Although this may be counterintuitive from a C++ standpoint, the concept of threads is a departure from the norm: a thread creates a separate thread of execution that persists after the function call ends. This departure is reflected in the persistence of the underlying thread after the object vanishes.

Creating responsive user interfaces

As stated earlier, one of the motivations for using threading is to create a responsive user interface. Although we don't cover *graphical* user interfaces in this book, you can still see a simple example of a console-based user interface.

The following example reads lines from a file and prints them to the console, *sleeping* (suspending the current thread) for a second after each line is displayed. (You'll learn more about sleeping later in the chapter.) During this process, the program doesn't look for user input, so the UI is unresponsive:

```
//: C11:UnresponsiveUI.cpp {RunByHand}
// Lack of threading produces an unresponsive UI.
//{L} ZThread
#include <iostream>
#include <fstream>
#include <string>
#include "zthread/Thread.h"
using namespace std;
using namespace ZThread;

int main() {
  cout << "Press <Enter> to quit:" << endl;
  ifstream file("UnresponsiveUI.cpp");
  string line;
  while(getline(file, line)) {
    cout << line << endl;
    Thread::sleep(1000); // Time in milliseconds
  }
  // Read input from the console
  cin.get();
```

```
  cout << "Shutting down..." << endl;
} ///:~
```

To make the program responsive, you can execute a task that displays the file in a separate thread. The main thread can then watch for user input so the program becomes responsive:

```
//: C11:ResponsiveUI.cpp {RunByHand}
// Threading for a responsive user interface.
//{L} ZThread
#include <iostream>
#include <fstream>
#include <string>
#include "zthread/Thread.h"
using namespace ZThread;
using namespace std;

class DisplayTask : public Runnable {
  ifstream in;
  string line;
  bool quitFlag;
public:
  DisplayTask(const string& file) : quitFlag(false) {
    in.open(file.c_str());
  }
  ~DisplayTask() { in.close(); }
  void run() {
    while(getline(in, line) && !quitFlag) {
      cout << line << endl;
      Thread::sleep(1000);
    }
  }
  void quit() { quitFlag = true; }
};

int main() {
  try {
    cout << "Press <Enter> to quit:" << endl;
    DisplayTask* dt = new DisplayTask("ResponsiveUI.cpp");
    Thread t(dt);
    cin.get();
    dt->quit();
  } catch(Synchronization_Exception& e) {
    cerr << e.what() << endl;
  }
```

```
    cout << "Shutting down..." << endl;
} ///:~
```

Now the **main( )** thread can respond immediately when you press <Return> and call **quit( )** on the **DisplayTask**.

This example also shows the need for communication between tasks—the task in the **main( )** thread needs to tell the **DisplayTask** to shut down. Since we have a pointer to the **DisplayTask**, you might think of just calling **delete** on that pointer to kill the task, but this produces unreliable programs. The problem is that the task could be in the middle of something important when you destroy it, and so you are likely to put the program in an unstable state. Here, the task itself decides when it's safe to shut down. The easiest way to do this is by simply notifying the task that you'd like it to stop by setting a Boolean flag. When the task gets to a stable point it can check that flag and do whatever is necessary to clean up before returning from **run( )**. When the task returns from **run( )**, the **Thread** knows that the task has completed.

Although this program is simple enough that it should not have any problems, there are some small flaws regarding inter-task communication. This is an important topic that will be covered later in this chapter.

Simplifying with Executors

You can simplify your coding overhead by using ZThread *Executors*. Executors provide a layer of indirection between a client and the execution of a task; instead of a client executing a task directly, an intermediate object executes the task.

We can show this by using an **Executor** instead of explicitly creating **Thread** objects in **MoreBasicThreads.cpp**. A **LiftOff** object knows how to run a specific task; like the Command Pattern, it exposes a single function to be executed. An **Executor** object knows how build the appropriate context to execute **Runnable** objects. In the following example, the **ThreadedExecutor** creates one thread per task:

```
//: c11:ThreadedExecutor.cpp
//{L} ZThread
#include <iostream>
#include "zthread/ThreadedExecutor.h"
#include "LiftOff.h"
using namespace ZThread;
```

```
using namespace std;

int main() {
  try {
    ThreadedExecutor executor;
    for(int i = 0; i < 5; i++)
      executor.execute(new LiftOff(10, i));
  } catch(Synchronization_Exception& e) {
    cerr << e.what() << endl;
  }
} ///:~
```

Note that in some cases a single **Executor** can be used to create and manage all the threads in your system. You must still place the threading code inside a **try** block because an **Executor**'s **execute( )** function may throw a **Synchronization_Exception** if something goes wrong. This is true for any function that involves changing the state of a synchronization object (starting threads, acquiring mutexes, waiting on conditions, etc.), as you will learn later in this chapter.

The program will exit as soon as all the tasks in the **Executor** complete.

In the previous example, the **ThreadedExecutor** creates a thread for each task that you want to run, but you can easily change the way these tasks are executed by replacing the **ThreadedExecutor** with a different type of **Executor**. In this chapter, using a **ThreadedExecutor** is fine, but in production code it might result in excessive costs from the creation of too many threads. In that case, you can replace it with a **PoolExecutor**, which will use a limited set of threads to execute the submitted tasks in parallel:

```
//: C11:PoolExecutor.cpp
//{L} ZThread
#include <iostream>
#include "zthread/PoolExecutor.h"
#include "LiftOff.h"
using namespace ZThread;
using namespace std;

int main() {
  try {
    // Constructor argument is minimum number of threads:
    PoolExecutor executor(5);
    for(int i = 0; i < 5; i++)
```

```
      executor.execute(new LiftOff(10, i));
  } catch(Synchronization_Exception& e) {
    cerr << e.what() << endl;
  }
} ///:~
```

With the **PoolExecutor**, you do expensive thread allocation once, up front, and the threads are reused when possible. This saves time because you aren't constantly paying for thread creation overhead for every single task. Also, in an event-driven system, events that require threads to handle them can be generated as quickly as you want by simply fetching them from the pool. You don't overrun the available resources because the **PoolExecutor** uses a bounded number of **Thread** objects. Thus, although this book will use **ThreadedExecutor**s, consider using **PoolExecutor**s in production code.

A **ConcurrentExecutor** is like a **PoolExecutor** with a fixed size of one thread. This is useful for anything you want to run in another thread continually (a long-lived task), such as a task that listens to incoming socket connections. It is also handy for short tasks that you want to run in a thread, for example, small tasks that update a local or remote log, or for an event-dispatching thread.

If more than one task is submitted to a **ConcurrentExecutor**, each task will run to completion before the next task is begun, all using the same thread. In the following example, you'll see each task completed, in the order that it was submitted, before the next one is begun. Thus, a **ConcurrentExecutor** serializes the tasks that are submitted to it.

```
//: C11:ConcurrentExecutor.cpp
//{L} ZThread
#include <iostream>
#include "zthread/ConcurrentExecutor.h"
#include "LiftOff.h"
using namespace ZThread;
using namespace std;

int main() {
  try {
    ConcurrentExecutor executor;
    for(int i = 0; i < 5; i++)
      executor.execute(new LiftOff(10, i));
  } catch(Synchronization_Exception& e) {
```

```
      cerr << e.what() << endl;
  }
} ///:~
```

Like a **ConcurrentExecutor**, a **SynchronousExecutor** is used when you
want only one task at a time to run, serially instead of concurrently. Unlike
ConcurrentExecutor, a **SynchronousExecutor** doesn't create or
manage threads on it own. It uses the thread that submits the task and thus
only acts as a focal point for synchronization. If you have **n** threads
submitting tasks to a **SynchronousExecutor**, no two tasks are ever run at
once. Instead, each one is run to completion, then the next one in the queue is
begun.

For example, suppose you have a number of threads running tasks that use
the file system, but you are writing portable code so you don't want to use
flock( ) or another OS-specific call to lock a file. You can run these tasks with
a **SynchronousExecutor** to ensure that only one task at a time is running
from any thread. This way, you don't need to deal with synchronizing on the
shared resource (and you won't clobber the file system in the meantime). A
better solution is to synchronize on the resource (which you'll learn about
later in this chapter), but a **SynchronousExecutor** lets you skip the trouble
of getting coordinated properly just to prototype something.

```
//: C11:SynchronousExecutor.cpp
//{L} ZThread
#include <iostream>
#include "zthread/SynchronousExecutor.h"
#include "LiftOff.h"
using namespace ZThread;
using namespace std;

int main() {
  try {
    SynchronousExecutor executor;
    for(int i = 0; i < 5; i++)
      executor.execute(new LiftOff(10, i));
  } catch(Synchronization_Exception& e) {
    cerr << e.what() << endl;
  }
} ///:~
```

When you run the program, you'll see that the tasks are executed in the order
they are submitted, and each task runs to completion before the next one

---

starts. What you don't see is that no new threads are created—the **main( )** thread is used for each task, since in this example, that's the thread that submits all the tasks. Because **SynchronousExecutor** is primarily for prototyping, you may not use it much in production code.

Yielding

If you know that you've accomplished what you need to during one pass through a loop in your **run( )** function (most **run( )** functions involve a long-running loop), you can give a hint to the thread scheduling mechanism that you've done enough and that some other thread might as well have the CPU. This hint (and it *is* a hint—there's no guarantee your implementation will listen to it) takes the form of the **yield( )** function.

We can make a modified version of the **LiftOff** examples by yielding after each loop:

```
//: C11:YieldingTask.cpp
// Suggesting when to switch threads with yield().
//{L} ZThread
#include <iostream>
#include "zthread/Thread.h"
#include "zthread/ThreadedExecutor.h"
using namespace ZThread;
using namespace std;

class YieldingTask : public Runnable {
  int countDown;
  int id;
public:
  YieldingTask(int ident = 0) : countDown(5), id(ident) {}
  ~YieldingTask() {
    cout << id << " completed" << endl;
  }
  friend ostream&
  operator<<(ostream& os, const YieldingTask& yt) {
    return os << "#" << yt.id << ": " << yt.countDown;
  }
  void run() {
    while(true) {
      cout << *this << endl;
      if(--countDown == 0) return;
      Thread::yield();
```

```
      }
    }
};

int main() {
  try {
    ThreadedExecutor executor;
    for(int i = 0; i < 5; i++)
      executor.execute(new YieldingTask(i));
  } catch(Synchronization_Exception& e) {
    cerr << e.what() << endl;
  }
} ///:~
```

You can see that the task's **run( )** member function consists entirely of an infinite loop. By using **yield( )**, the output is evened up quite a bit over that without yielding. Try commenting out the call to **Thread::yield( )** to see the difference. In general, however, **yield( )** is useful only in rare situations, and you can't rely on it to do any serious tuning of your application.

Sleeping

Another way you can control the behavior of your threads is by calling **sleep( )** to cease execution of a thread for a given number of milliseconds. In the preceding example, if you replace the call to **yield( )** with a call to **sleep( )**, you get the following:

```
//: C11:SleepingTask.cpp
// Calling sleep() to pause for awhile.
//{L} ZThread
#include <iostream>
#include "zthread/Thread.h"
#include "zthread/ThreadedExecutor.h"
using namespace ZThread;
using namespace std;

class SleepingTask : public Runnable {
  int countDown;
  int id;
public:
  SleepingTask(int ident = 0) : countDown(5), id(ident) {}
  ~SleepingTask() {
    cout << id << " completed" << endl;
  }
```

```
    friend ostream&
    operator<<(ostream& os, const SleepingTask& st) {
      return os << "#" << st.id << ": " << st.countDown;
    }
    void run() {
      while(true) {
        try {
          cout << *this << endl;
          if(--countDown == 0) return;
          Thread::sleep(100);
        } catch(Interrupted_Exception& e) {
          cerr << e.what() << endl;
        }
      }
    }
};

int main() {
  try {
    ThreadedExecutor executor;
    for(int i = 0; i < 5; i++)
      executor.execute(new SleepingTask(i));
  } catch(Synchronization_Exception& e) {
    cerr << e.what() << endl;
  }
} ///:~
```

Thread::sleep( ) can throw an **Interrupted_Exception** (you'll learn about interrupts later), and you can see that this is caught in **run( )**. But the task is created and executed inside a **try** block in **main( )** that catches **Synchronization_Exception** (the base class for all ZThread exceptions), so wouldn't it be possible to just ignore the exception in **run( )** and assume that it will propagate to the handler in **main( )**? This won't work because exceptions won't propagate across threads back to **main( )**. Thus, you must handle any exceptions locally that may arise within a task.

You'll notice that the threads tend to run in any order, which means that **sleep( )** is also not a way for you to control the order of thread execution. It just stops the execution of the thread for awhile. The only guarantee that you have is that the thread will sleep at least 100 milliseconds (in this example), but it may take longer before the thread resumes execution because the thread scheduler still has to get back to it after the sleep interval expires.

If you must control the order of execution of threads, your best bet is to use synchronization controls (described later) or, in some cases, not to use threads at all, but instead to write your own cooperative routines that hand control to each other in a specified order.

Priority

The *priority* of a thread conveys the importance of a thread to the scheduler. Although the order that the CPU runs a set of threads is indeterminate, the scheduler will *lean* toward running the waiting thread with the highest priority first. However, this doesn't mean that threads with lower priority aren't run (that is, you can't get deadlocked because of priorities). Lower priority threads just tend to run less often.

Here's **MoreBasicThreads.cpp** modified so that the priority levels are demonstrated. The priorities are adjusting by using **Thread**'s **setPriority( )** function.

```cpp
//: C11:SimplePriorities.cpp
// Shows the use of thread priorities.
//{L} ZThread
#include <iostream>
#include "zthread/Thread.h"
using namespace ZThread;
using namespace std;

const double pi = 3.14159265358979323846;
const double e = 2.7182818284590452354;

class SimplePriorities : public Runnable {
  int countDown;
  volatile double d; // No optimization
  int id;
public:
  SimplePriorities(int ident=0): countDown(5), id(ident) {}
  ~SimplePriorities() {
    cout << id << " completed" << endl;
  }
  friend ostream&
  operator<<(ostream& os, const SimplePriorities& sp) {
    return os << "#" << sp.id << " priority: "
      << Thread().getPriority()
      << " count: "<< sp.countDown;
```

```
    }
  void run() {
    while(true) {
      // An expensive, interruptable operation:
      for(int i = 1; i < 100000; i++)
        d = d + (pi + e) / double(i);
      cout << *this << endl;
      if(--countDown == 0) return;
    }
  }
};

int main() {
  try {
    Thread high(new SimplePriorities);
    high.setPriority(High);
    for(int i = 0; i < 5; i++) {
      Thread low(new SimplePriorities(i));
      low.setPriority(Low);
    }
  } catch(Synchronization_Exception& e) {
    cerr << e.what() << endl;
  }
} ///:~
```

Here, **operator<<( )** is overridden to display the identifier, priority, and
countDown value of the task.

You can see that the priority level of thread **high** is at the highest level, and
all the rest of the threads are at the lowest level. We are not using an
Executor in this example because we need direct access to the threads in
order to set their priorities.

Inside **SimplePriorities::run( )**, 100,000 repetitions of a rather expensive
floating-point calculation are performed, involving **double** addition and
division. The variable **d** is **volatile** to try to ensure that no compilers
optimizations are performed. Without this calculation, you don't see the
effect of setting the priority levels. (Try it: comment out the **for** loop
containing the **double** calculations.) With the calculation, you see that
thread **high** is given a higher preference by the thread scheduler. (At least,
this was the behavior on a Windows machine.) The calculation takes long
enough that the thread scheduling mechanism jumps in, changes threads,
and pays attention to the priorities so that thread **high** gets preference.

You can also read the priority of an existing thread with **getPriority( )** and change it at any time (not just before the thread is run, as in **SimplePriorities.cpp**) with **setPriority( )**.

Mapping priorities to operating systems is problematic. For example, Windows 2000 has seven priority levels, while Sun's Solaris has 2^{31} levels. The only portable approach is to stick to very large priority granulations, such as the **Low**, **Medium**, and **High** used in the ZThread library.

Sharing limited resources

You can think of a single-threaded program as one lonely entity moving around through your problem space and doing one thing at a time. Because there's only one entity, you never have to think about the problem of two entities trying to use the same resource at the same time: problems such as two people trying to park in the same space, walk through a door at the same time, or even talk at the same time.

With multithreading things aren't lonely anymore, but you now have the possibility of two or more threads trying to use the same resource at once. This can cause two different kinds of problems. The first is that the necessary resources may not exist. In C++, the programmer has complete control over the lifetime of objects, and it's easy to create threads that try to use objects that get destroyed before those threads complete.

The second problem is that two or more threads may collide when they try to access the same resource at the same time. If you don't prevent such a collision, you'll have two threads trying to access the same bank account at the same time, print to the same printer, adjust the same valve, and so on.

This section introduces the problem of objects that vanish while tasks are still using them and the problem of tasks colliding over shared resources. You'll learn about the tools that are used to solve these problems.

Ensuring the existence of objects

Memory and resource management are major concerns in C++. When you create any C++ program, you have the option of creating objects on the stack or on the heap (using **new**). In a single-threaded program, it's usually easy to

---

keep track of object lifetimes so that you don't try to use objects that are already destroyed.

The examples shown in this chapter create **Runnable** objects on the heap using **new**, but you'll notice that these objects are never *explicitly* deleted. However, you can see from the output when you run the programs that the thread library keeps track of each task and eventually deletes it, because the destructors for the tasks are called. This happens when the **Runnable::run( )** member function completes—returning from **run( )** indicates that the task is finished.

Burdening the thread with deleting a task is a problem. That thread doesn't necessarily know if another thread still needs to make a reference to that **Runnable**, and so the **Runnable** may be prematurely destroyed. To deal with this problem, tasks in ZThreads are automatically reference-counted by the ZThread library mechanism. A task is maintained until the reference count for that task goes to zero, at which point the task is deleted. This means that tasks must always be deleted dynamically, and so they cannot be created on the stack. Instead, tasks must always be created using **new**, as you see in all the examples in this chapter.

Often you must also ensure that non-task objects stay alive as long as tasks need them. Otherwise, it's easy for objects that are used by tasks to go out of scope before those tasks are completed. If this happens, the tasks will try to access illegal storage and will cause program faults. Here's a simple example:

```
//: C11:Incrementer.cpp {RunByHand}
// Destroying objects while threads are still
// running will cause serious problems.
//{L} ZThread
#include <iostream>
#include "zthread/Thread.h"
#include "zthread/ThreadedExecutor.h"
using namespace ZThread;
using namespace std;

class Count {
  enum { SZ = 100 };
  int n[SZ];
public:
  void increment() {
    for(int i = 0; i < SZ; i++)
```

```
        n[i]++;
    }
};

class Incrementer : public Runnable {
  Count* count;
public:
  Incrementer(Count* c) : count(c) {}
  void run() {
    for(int n = 100; n > 0; n--) {
      Thread::sleep(250);
      count->increment();
    }
  }
};

int main() {
  cout << "This will cause a segmentation fault!" << endl;
  Count count;
  try {
    Thread t0(new Incrementer(&count));
    Thread t1(new Incrementer(&count));
  } catch(Synchronization_Exception& e) {
    cerr << e.what() << endl;
  }
} ///:~
```

The **Count** class may seem like overkill at first, but if **n** is only a single **int** (rather than an array), the compiler can put it into a register and that storage will still be available (albeit technically illegal) after the **Count** object goes out of scope. It's difficult to detect the memory violation in that case. Your results may vary depending on your compiler and operating system, but try making it **n** a single **int** and see what happens. In any event, if **Count** contains an array of **int**s as above, the compiler is forced to put it on the stack and not in a register.

Incrementer is a simple task that uses a **Count** object. In **main( )**, you can see that the **Incrementer** tasks are running for long enough that the **Count** object will go out of scope, and so the tasks try to access an object that no longer exists. This produces a program fault.

To fix the problem, we must guarantee that any objects shared between tasks will be around as long as those tasks need them. (If the objects were not

---

11: Concurrency
713

shared, they could be composed directly into the task's class and thus tie their lifetime to that task.) Since we don't want the static program scope to control the lifetime of the object, we put the object on the heap. And to make sure that the object is not destroyed until there are no other objects (tasks, in this case) using it, we use reference counting.

Reference counting was explained thoroughly in volume one of this book and further revisited in this volume. The ZThread library includes a template called **CountedPtr** that automatically performs reference counting and **delete**s an object when the reference count goes to zero. Here's the above program modified to use **CountedPtr** to prevent the fault:

```
//: C11:ReferenceCounting.cpp
// A CountedPtr prevents too-early destruction.
//{L} ZThread
#include <iostream>
#include "zthread/Thread.h"
#include "zthread/CountedPtr.h"
using namespace ZThread;
using namespace std;

class Count {
  enum { SZ = 100 };
  int n[SZ];
public:
  void increment() {
    for(int i = 0; i < SZ; i++)
      n[i]++;
  }
};

class Incrementer : public Runnable {
  CountedPtr<Count> count;
public:
  Incrementer(const CountedPtr<Count>& c ) : count(c) {}
  void run() {
    for(int n = 100; n > 0; n--) {
      Thread::sleep(250);
      count->increment();
    }
  }
};
```

```
int main() {
  CountedPtr<Count> count(new Count);
  try {
    Thread t0(new Incrementer(count));
    Thread t1(new Incrementer(count));
  } catch(Synchronization_Exception& e) {
    cerr << e.what() << endl;
  }
} ///:~
```

Incrementer now contains a **CountedPtr** object, which manages a **Count**.
In **main( )**, the **CountedPtr** objects are passed into the two **Incrementer**
objects by value, so the copy-constructor is called, increasing the reference
count. As long as the tasks are still running, the reference count will be
nonzero, and so the **Count** object managed by the **CountedPtr** will not be
destroyed. Only when all the tasks using the **Count** are completed will
delete be called (automatically) on the **Count** object by the **CountedPtr**.

Whenever you have objects that are used by more than one task, you'll almost
always need to manage those objects using the **CountedPtr** template in
order to prevent problems arising from object lifetime issues.

Improperly accessing resources

Consider the following example where one task generates even numbers and
other tasks consume those numbers. Here, the only job of the consumer
threads is to check the validity of the even numbers.

We'll first define **EvenChecker**, the consumer thread, since it will be reused
in all the subsequent examples. To decouple **EvenChecker** from the various
types of generators that we will experiment with, we'll create an interface
called **Generator**, which contains the minimum necessary functions that
EvenChecker must know about: that it has a **nextValue( )** function and
that it can be canceled.

```
//: C11:EvenChecker.h
#ifndef EVENCHECKER_H
#define EVENCHECKER_H
#include <iostream>
#include "zthread/CountedPtr.h"
#include "zthread/Thread.h"
#include "zthread/Cancelable.h"
```

```cpp
#include "zthread/ThreadedExecutor.h"

class Generator : public ZThread::Cancelable {
  bool canceled;
public:
  Generator() : canceled(false) {}
  virtual int nextValue() = 0;
  void cancel() { canceled = true; }
  bool isCanceled() { return canceled; }
};

class EvenChecker : public ZThread::Runnable {
  ZThread::CountedPtr<Generator> generator;
  int id;
public:
  EvenChecker(ZThread::CountedPtr<Generator>& g, int ident)
  : generator(g), id(ident) {}
  ~EvenChecker() {
    std::cout << "~EvenChecker " << id << std::endl;
  }
  void run() {
    while(!generator->isCanceled()) {
      int val = generator->nextValue();
      if(val % 2 != 0) {
        std::cout << val << " not even!" << std::endl;
        generator->cancel(); // Cancels all EvenCheckers
      }
    }
  }
  // Test any type of generator:
  template<typename GenType> static void test(int n = 10) {
    std::cout << "Press Control-C to exit" << std::endl;
    try {
      ZThread::ThreadedExecutor executor;
      ZThread::CountedPtr<Generator> gp(new GenType);
      for(int i = 0; i < n; i++)
        executor.execute(new EvenChecker(gp, i));
    } catch(ZThread::Synchronization_Exception& e) {
      std::cerr << e.what() << std::endl;
    }
  }
};
#endif // EVENCHECKER_H ///:~
```

The **Generator** class introduces the abstract **Cancelable** class, which is part of the ZThread library. The goal of **Cancelable** is to provide a consistent interface to change the state of an object via the **cancel( )** function and to see whether the object has been canceled with the **isCanceled( )** function. Here, we use the simple approach of a **bool** canceled flag, similar to the **quitFlag** previously seen in **ResponsiveUI.cpp**. Note that in this example the class that is **Cancelable** is not **Runnable**. Instead, all the **EvenChecker** tasks that depend on the **Cancelable** object (the **Generator**) test it to see if it's been canceled, as you can see in **run( )**. This way, the tasks that share the common resource (the **Cancelable Generator**) watch that resource for the signal to terminate. This eliminates the so-called *race condition*, where two or more tasks race to respond to a condition and thus collide or otherwise produce inconsistent results. You must be careful to think about and protect against all the possible ways a concurrent system can fail. For example, a task cannot depend on another task because task shutdown order is not guaranteed. Here, by making tasks depend on non-task objects (which are reference counted using **CountedPtr**) we eliminate the potential race condition.

In later sections, you'll see that the ZThread library contains more general mechanisms for termination of threads.

Since multiple **EvenChecker** objects may end up sharing a **Generator**, the **CountedPtr** template is used to reference count the **Generator** objects.

The last member function in **EvenChecker** is a **static** member template that sets up and performs a test of any type of **Generator** by creating one inside a **CountedPtr** and then starting a number of **EvenChecker**s that use that **Generator**. If the **Generator** causes a failure, **test( )** will report it and return; otherwise, you must press Control-C to terminate it.

EvenChecker tasks constantly read and test the values from their associated **Generator**. Note that if **generator->isCanceled( )** is true, **run( )** returns, which tells the **Executor** in **EvenChecker::test( )** that the task is complete. Any **EvenChecker** task can call **cancel( )** on its associated **Generator**, which will cause all other **EvenChecker**s using that **Generator** to gracefully shut down.

The **EvenGenerator** is simple—**nextValue( )** produces the next even value:

```
//: C11:EvenGenerator.cpp
// When threads collide.
//{L} ZThread
#include <iostream>
#include "EvenChecker.h"
#include "zthread/ThreadedExecutor.h"
using namespace ZThread;
using namespace std;

class EvenGenerator : public Generator {
  unsigned int currentEvenValue; // Unsigned can't overflow
public:
  EvenGenerator() { currentEvenValue = 0; }
  ~EvenGenerator() { cout << "~EvenGenerator" << endl; }
  int nextValue() {
    ++currentEvenValue; // Danger point here!
    ++currentEvenValue;
    return currentEvenValue;
  }
};

int main() {
  EvenChecker::test<EvenGenerator>();
} ///:~
```

It's possible for one thread to call **nextValue( )** after the first increment of **currentEvenValue** and before the second (at the place in the code commented "Danger point here!"), which puts the value into an "incorrect" state. To prove that this can happen, **EvenChecker::test( )** creates a group of **EvenChecker** objects to continually read the output of an **EvenGenerator** and test to see if each one is even. If not, the error is reported and the program is shut down.

This program may not detect the problem until the **EvenGenerator** has completed many cycles, depending on the particulars of your operating system and other implementation details. If you want to see it fail much faster, try putting a call to **yield( )** between the first and second increments. In any event, it *will* eventually fail because the **EvenChecker** threads are able to access the information in **EvenGenerator** while it's in an "incorrect" state.

Controlling access

The previous example shows a fundamental problem when using threads: You never know when a thread might be run. Imagine sitting at a table with a fork, about to spear the last piece of food on a platter, and as your fork reaches for it, the food suddenly vanishes (because your thread was suspended and another diner came in and ate the food). That's the problem you're dealing with when writing concurrent programs.

Occasionally you don't care if a resource is being accessed at the same time you're trying to use it. But in most cases you do care, and for multithreading to work, you need some way to prevent two threads from accessing the same resource, at least during critical periods.

Preventing this kind of collision is simply a matter of putting a lock on a resource when one thread is using it. The first thread that accesses a resource locks it, and then the other threads cannot access that resource until it is unlocked, at which time another thread locks and uses it, and so on. If the front seat of the car is the limited resource, the child who shouts "Dibs!" acquires the lock.

Thus, we need to be able to prevent any other tasks from accessing the storage when that storage is not in a proper state. That is, we need to have a mechanism that *excludes* a second task from accessing the storage when a first task is already using it. This idea is fundamental to all multithreading systems and is called *mutual exclusion*; the mechanism used abbreviates this to *mutex*. The ZThread library contains a mutex mechanism declared in the header **Mutex.h**.

To solve the problem in the above program, we identify the *critical sections* where mutual exclusion must apply; then we *acquire* the mutex before entering the critical section and *release* it at the end of the critical section. Only one thread can acquire the mutex at any time, so mutual exclusion is achieved:

```
//: C11:MutexEvenGenerator.cpp {RunByHand}
// Preventing thread collisions with mutexes.
//{L} ZThread
#include <iostream>
#include "EvenChecker.h"
#include "zthread/ThreadedExecutor.h"
```

```
#include "zthread/Mutex.h"
using namespace ZThread;
using namespace std;

class MutexEvenGenerator : public Generator {
  unsigned int currentEvenValue;
  Mutex lock;
public:
  MutexEvenGenerator() { currentEvenValue = 0; }
  ~MutexEvenGenerator() {
    cout << "~MutexEvenGenerator" << endl;
  }
  int nextValue() {
    lock.acquire();
    ++currentEvenValue;
    Thread::yield(); // Cause failure faster
    ++currentEvenValue;
    int rval = currentEvenValue;
    lock.release();
    return rval;
  }
};

int main() {
  EvenChecker::test<MutexEvenGenerator>();
} ///:~
```

MutexEvenGenerator adds a **Mutex** called **lock** and uses **acquire( )** and
release( ) to create a critical section within **nextValue( )**. In addition, a call
to **Thread::yield( )** is inserted between the two increments, to raise the
likelihood of a context switch while **currentEvenValue** is in an odd state.
Because the mutex prevents more than one thread at a time in the critical
section, this will not produce a failure, but calling **yield( )** is a helpful way to
promote a failure if it's going to happen.

Note that **nextValue( )** must capture the return value inside the critical
section because if you return from inside the critical section, you won't
release the lock and will thus prevent it from being acquired again. (This
usually leads to *deadlock*, which you'll learn about at the end of this chapter.)

The first thread that enters **nextValue( )** acquires the lock, and any further
threads that try to acquire the lock are blocked from doing so until the first
thread releases the lock. At that point, the scheduling mechanism selects

another thread that is waiting on the lock. This way, only one thread at a time can pass through the code that is guarded by the mutex.

Simplified coding with Guards

The use of mutexes rapidly becomes complicated when exceptions are introduced. To make sure that the mutex is always released, you must ensure that each possible exception path includes a call to **release( )**. In addition, any function that has multiple return paths must carefully ensure that it calls **release( )** at the appropriate points.

These problems can be easily solved by using the fact that a stack-based (auto) object has a destructor that is always called regardless of how you exit from a function scope. In the ZThread library, this is implemented as the **Guard** template. The **Guard** template creates objects that **acquire( )** a **Lockable** object when constructed and **release( )** that lock when destroyed. **Guard** objects created on the local stack will automatically be destroyed regardless of how the function exits and will always unlock the **Lockable** object. Here's the above example reimplemented using **Guard**s:

```
//: C11:GuardedEvenGenerator.cpp {RunByHand}
// Simplifying mutexes with the Guard template.
//{L} ZThread
#include <iostream>
#include "EvenChecker.h"
#include "zthread/ThreadedExecutor.h"
#include "zthread/Mutex.h"
#include "zthread/Guard.h"
using namespace ZThread;
using namespace std;

class GuardedEvenGenerator : public Generator {
  unsigned int currentEvenValue;
  Mutex lock;
public:
  GuardedEvenGenerator() { currentEvenValue = 0; }
  ~GuardedEvenGenerator() {
    cout << "~GuardedEvenGenerator" << endl;
  }
  int nextValue() {
    Guard<Mutex> g(lock);
    ++currentEvenValue;
    Thread::yield();
```

```
    ++currentEvenValue;
    return currentEvenValue;
  }
};

int main() {
  EvenChecker::test<GuardedEvenGenerator>();
} ///:~
```

Note that the temporary return value is no longer necessary in **nextValue( )**.
In general, there is less code to write, and the opportunity for user error is
greatly reduced.

An interesting feature of the **Guard** template is that it can be used to
manipulate other guards safely. For example, a second **Guard** can be used to
temporarily unlock a guard:

```
//: C11:TemporaryUnlocking.cpp
// Temporarily unlocking another guard.
//{L} ZThread
#include "zthread/Thread.h"
#include "zthread/Mutex.h"
#include "zthread/Guard.h"
using namespace ZThread;

class TemporaryUnlocking {
  Mutex lock;
public:
  void f() {
    Guard<Mutex> g(lock);
    // lock is acquired
    // ...
    {
      Guard<Mutex, UnlockedScope> h(g);
      // lock is released
      // ...
      // lock is acquired
    }
    // ...
    // lock is released
  }
};

int main() {
```

```
    TemporaryUnlocking t;
    t.f();
} ///:~
```

A Guard can also be used to try to acquire a lock for a certain amount of time and then give up:

```
//: C11:TimedLocking.cpp
// Limited time locking.
//{L} ZThread
#include "zthread/Thread.h"
#include "zthread/Mutex.h"
#include "zthread/Guard.h"
using namespace ZThread;

class TimedLocking {
  Mutex lock;
public:
  void f() {
    Guard<Mutex, TimedLockedScope<500> > g(lock);
    // ...
  }
};

int main() {
  TimedLocking t;
  t.f();
} ///:~
```

In this example, a **Timeout_Exception** will be thrown if the lock cannot be acquired within 500 milliseconds.

Synchronizing entire classes

The ZThread library also provides a **GuardedClass** template to automatically create a synchronized wrapper for an entire class. This means that every member function in the class will automatically be guarded:

```
//: C11:SynchronizedClass.cpp {-dmc}
//{L} ZThread
#include "zthread/GuardedClass.h"
using namespace ZThread;

class MyClass {
public:
```

```
    void func1() {}
    void func2() {}
};

int main() {
  MyClass a;
  a.func1(); // Not synchronized
  a.func2(); // Not synchronized
  GuardedClass<MyClass> b(new MyClass);
  // Synchronized calls, only one thread at a time allowed:
  b->func1();
  b->func2();
} ///:~
```

Object **a** is a not synchronized, so **func1( )** and **func2( )** can be called at any time by any number of threads. Object **b** is protected by the **GuardedClass** wrapper, so each member function is automatically synchronized and only one function per object can be called any time.

The wrapper locks at a class level of granularity, which may affect performance.[4] If a class contains some unrelated functions, it may be better to synchronize those functions internally with two different locks. However, if you find yourself doing this, it means that one class contains groups of data that may not be strongly associated. Consider breaking the class into two classes.

Guarding all member functions of a class with a mutex does not automatically make that class thread-safe. You must carefully consider all threading issues in order to guarantee thread safety.

Thread local storage

A second way to eliminate the problem of tasks colliding over shared resources is to eliminate the sharing of variables, which can be done by creating different storage for the same variable, for each different thread that uses an object. Thus, if you have five threads using an object with a variable **x**, *thread local storage* automatically generates five different pieces of storage

---

[4] This can be significant. Usually only a small part of a function needs to be guarded. Putting the guard at the function entry point can often make the critical section longer than it needs to be.

for **x**. Fortunately, the creation and management of thread local storage is taken care of automatically by ZThread's **ThreadLocal** template, as seen here:

```
//: C11:ThreadLocalVariables.cpp {RunByHand}
// Automatically giving each thread its own storage.
//{L} ZThread
#include <iostream>
#include "zthread/Thread.h"
#include "zthread/Mutex.h"
#include "zthread/Guard.h"
#include "zthread/ThreadedExecutor.h"
#include "zthread/Cancelable.h"
#include "zthread/ThreadLocal.h"
#include "zthread/CountedPtr.h"
using namespace ZThread;
using namespace std;

class ThreadLocalVariables : public Cancelable {
  ThreadLocal<int> value;
  bool canceled;
  Mutex lock;
public:
  ThreadLocalVariables() : canceled(false) {
    value.set(0);
  }
  void increment() { value.set(value.get() + 1); }
  int get() { return value.get(); }
  void cancel() {
    Guard<Mutex> g(lock);
    canceled = true;
  }
  bool isCanceled() {
    Guard<Mutex> g(lock);
    return canceled;
  }
};

class Accessor : public Runnable {
  int id;
  CountedPtr<ThreadLocalVariables> tlv;
public:
  Accessor(CountedPtr<ThreadLocalVariables>& tl, int idn)
  : id(idn), tlv(tl) {}
```

```
    void run() {
      while(!tlv->isCanceled()) {
        tlv->increment();
        cout << *this << endl;
      }
    }
    friend ostream&
      operator<<(ostream& os, Accessor& a) {
      return os << "#" << a.id << ": " << a.tlv->get();
    }
};

int main() {
  cout << "Press <Enter> to quit" << endl;
  try {
    CountedPtr<ThreadLocalVariables>
      tlv(new ThreadLocalVariables);
    const int SZ = 5;
    ThreadedExecutor executor;
    for(int i = 0; i < SZ; i++)
      executor.execute(new Accessor(tlv, i));
    cin.get();
    tlv->cancel(); // All Accessors will quit
  } catch(Synchronization_Exception& e) {
    cerr << e.what() << endl;
  }
} ///:~
```

When you create a **ThreadLocal** object by instantiating the template, you are only able to access the contents of the object using the **get( )** and **set( )** member functions. The **get( )** function returns a copy of the object that is associated with that thread, and **set( )** inserts its argument into the object stored for that thread, returning the old object that was in storage. You can see this is use in **increment( )** and **get( )** in **ThreadLocalVariables**.

Since **tlv** is shared by multiple **Accessor** objects, it is written as **Cancelable** so that the **Accessors** can be signaled when we want to shut the system down.

When you run this program, you'll see evidence that the individual threads are each allocated their own storage.

Terminating tasks

In previous examples, we have seen the use of a "quit flag" or the **Cancelable** interface in order to terminate a task. This is a reasonable approach to the problem. However, in some situations the task must be terminated more abruptly. In this section, you'll learn about the issues and problems of such termination.

First, let's look at an example that not only demonstrates the termination problem but is also an additional example of resource sharing. To present this example, we'll first need to solve the problem of iostream collision

Preventing iostream collision

You may have noticed in previous examples that the output is sometimes garbled. C++ iostreams were not created with threading in mind, so there's nothing to keep one thread's output from interfering with another thread's output. Thus, you must write your applications so that they synchronize the use of iostreams.

To solve the problem, we need to create the entire output packet first and then explicitly decide when to try to send it to the console. One simple solution is to write the information to an **ostringstream** and then use a single object with a mutex as the point of output among all threads, to prevent more than one thread from writing at the same time:

```
//: C11:Display.h
// Prevents ostream collisions.
#ifndef DISPLAY_H
#define DISPLAY_H
#include <iostream>
#include <sstream>
#include "zthread/Mutex.h"
#include "zthread/Guard.h"

class Display { // Share one of these among all threads
  ZThread::Mutex iolock;
public:
  void output(std::ostringstream& os) {
    ZThread::Guard<ZThread::Mutex> g(iolock);
    std::cout << os.str();
  }
```

```
          {
            ostringstream os;
            os << *this << " Total: "
               << count->increment() << endl;
            display->output(os);
          }
          Thread::sleep(100);
        }
        waitingForCancel = true;
        while(!count->isCanceled()) // Hold here...
          Thread::sleep(100);
        ostringstream os;
        os << "Terminating " << *this << endl;
        display->output(os);
      }
      int getValue() {
        while(count->isPaused() && !waitingForCancel)
          Thread::sleep(100);
        return number;
      }
      friend ostream&
      operator<<(ostream& os, const Entrance& e) {
        return os << "Entrance " << e.id << ": " << e.number;
      }
};

int main() {
  srand(time(0)); // Seed the random number generator
  cout << "Press <ENTER> to quit" << endl;
  CountedPtr<Count> count(new Count);
  vector<Entrance*> v;
  CountedPtr<Display> display(new Display);
  const int SZ = 5;
  try {
    ThreadedExecutor executor;
    for(int i = 0; i < SZ; i++) {
      Entrance* task = new Entrance(count, display, i);
      executor.execute(task);
      // Save the pointer to the task:
      v.push_back(task);
    }
    cin.get(); // Wait for user to press <Enter>
    count->pause(); // Causes tasks to stop counting
    int sum = 0;
    vector<Entrance*>::iterator it = v.begin();
```

```
    while(it != v.end()) {
      sum += (*it)->getValue();
      ++it;
    }
    ostringstream os;
    os << "Total: " << count->value() << endl
       << "Sum of Entrances: " << sum << endl;
    display->output(os);
    count->cancel(); // Causes threads to quit
  } catch(Synchronization_Exception& e) {
    cerr << e.what() << endl;
  }
} ///:~
```

Count is the class that keeps the master count of garden visitors. The single **Count** object defined in **main( )** as **count** is held as a **CountedPtr** in **Entrance** and thus is shared by all **Entrance** objects. A **FastMutex** called **lock** is used in this example instead of an ordinary **Mutex** because a **FastMutex** uses the native operating system mutex and will thus yield more interesting results.

A **Guard** is used with **lock** in **increment( )** to synchronize access to **count**. This function uses **rand( )** to cause a **yield( )** roughly half the time, in between fetching **count** into **temp** and incrementing and storing **temp** back into **count**. Because of this, if you comment out the **Guard** object definition, you will rapidly see the program break because multiple threads will be accessing and modifying **count** simultaneously.

The **Entrance** class also keeps a local **number** with the number of visitors that have passed through this particular entrance. This provides a double-check against the **count** object to make sure that the proper number of visitors is being recorded. **Entrance::run( )** simply increments **number** and the **count** object and sleeps for 100 milliseconds.

In main, a **vector<Entrance*>** is loaded with each **Entrance** that is created. After the user presses **<Enter>**, this **vector** is used to iterate over all the individual **Entrance** values and total them.

This program goes to quite a bit of extra trouble to shut everything down in a stable fashion. Part of the reason for this is to show just how careful you must be when terminating a multithreaded program, and part of the reason is to demonstrate the value of **interrupt( )**, which you will learn about shortly.

All the communication between the **Entrance** objects takes place through the single **Count** object. When the user presses <Enter>, **main( )** sends the **pause( )** message to **count**. Since each **Entrance::run( )** is watching the **count** object to see whether it is paused, this causes each **Entrance** to move into the **waitingForCancel** state, where it is no longer counting, but it is still alive. This is essential because **main( )** must still be able to safely iterate over the objects in the **vector<Entrance*>**. Note that because there is a slight possibility that the iteration might occur before an **Entrance** has finished counting and moved into the **waitingForCancel** state, the **getValue( )** function cycles through calls to **sleep( )** until the object moves into **waitingForCancel**. (This is one form of what is called a *busy wait*, which is undesirable. You'll see the preferred approach of using **wait( )** later in the chapter.) Once **main( )** completes its iteration through the **vector<Entrance*>**, the **cancel( )** message is sent to the **count** object, and once again all the **Entrance** objects are watching for this state change. At this point, they print a termination message and exit from **run( )**, which causes each task to be destroyed by the threading mechanism.

As this program runs, you will see the total count and the count at each entrance displayed as people walk through a turnstile. If you comment out the **Guard** object in **Count::increment( )**, you'll notice that the total number of people is not what you expect it to be. The number of people counted by each turnstile will be different from the value in **count**. As long as the **Mutex** is there to synchronize access to the **Counter**, things work correctly. Keep in mind that **Count::increment( )** exaggerates the potential for failure by using **temp** and **yield( )**. In real threading problems, the possibility for failure may be statistically small, so you can easily fall into the trap of believing that things are working correctly. Just as in the example above, there are likely to be hidden problems that haven't occurred to you, so be exceptionally diligent when reviewing concurrent code.

Atomic operations
Note that **Count::value( )** returns the value of **count** using a **Guard** object for synchronization. This brings up an interesting point because this code will *probably* work fine with most compilers and systems without synchronization. The reason is that, in general, a simple operation such as returning an **int** will be an *atomic operation*, which means that it will probably happen in a single microprocessor instruction that will not get interrupted. (The multithreading mechanism is unable to stop a thread in the middle of a microprocessor instruction.) That is, atomic operations are not

interruptible by the threading mechanism and thus do not need to be guarded.[5] In fact, if we removed the fetch of **count** into **temp** and removed the **yield( )**, and instead simply incremented **count** directly, we probably wouldn't need a lock because the increment operation is *usually* atomic, as well.[6]

The problem is that the C++ Standard doesn't guarantee atomicity for any of these operations. Although operations such as returning an **int** and incrementing an **int** are almost certainly atomic on most machines, there's no guarantee. And because there's no guarantee, you have to assume the worst. Sometimes you might investigate the atomicity behavior on a particular machine (usually by looking at assembly language) and write code based on those assumptions. That's always dangerous and ill-advised. It's too easy for that information to be lost or hidden, and the next person that comes along may assume that this code can be ported to another machine and then go mad tracking down the occasional glitch caused by thread collisions.

So, while removing the guard on **Count::value( )** seems to work, it's not airtight, and thus on some machines you may see aberrant behavior.

Terminating when blocked

Entrance::run( ) in the previous example includes a call to **sleep( )** in the main loop. We know that **sleep( )** will eventually wake up and the task will

---

[5] This is an oversimplification. Sometimes even when it seems like an atomic operation should be safe, it may not be, so you must be very careful when deciding that you can get away without synchronization. Removing synchronization is often a sign of premature optimization— things that can cause you a lot of trouble without gaining much. Or anything.

[6] Atomicity isn't the only issue. On multiprocessor systems visibility is much more of an issue than on single processor systems. Changes made by one thread, even if they're atomic in the sense of not being interruptible, might not be visible to other threads (the changes might be temporarily stored in a local processor cache, for example), so different threads will have a different view of the application's state. The synchronization mechanism forces changes by one thread on a multiprocessor system to be visible across the application, whereas without synchronization it's indeterminate when changes become visible.

---

reach the top of the loop where it has an opportunity to break out of that loop by checking the **isPaused( )** status. However, **sleep( )** is just one situation where a thread is *blocked* from executing, and sometimes you must terminate a task that's blocked.

Thread states

A thread can be in any one of four states:

1. *New*: A thread remains in this state only momentarily, as it is being created. It allocates any necessary system resources and performs initialization. At this point it becomes eligible to receive CPU time. The scheduler will then transition this thread to the *runnable* or *blocked* state.

2. *Runnable*: This means that a thread *can* be run when the time-slicing mechanism has CPU cycles available for the thread. Thus, the thread might or might not be running at any moment, but there's nothing to prevent it from being run if the scheduler can arrange it; it's not dead or blocked.

3. *Blocked*: The thread could be run, but something prevents it. (It might be waiting for I/O to complete, for example.) While a thread is in the blocked state, the scheduler will simply skip it and not give it any CPU time. Until a thread reenters the *runnable* state, it won't perform any operations.

4. *Dead*: A thread in the dead state is no longer schedulable and will not receive any CPU time. Its task is completed, and it is no longer *runnable*. The normal way for a thread to die is by returning from its **run( )** function.

Becoming blocked

A thread is blocked when it cannot continue running. A thread can become blocked for the following reasons:

- You've put the thread to sleep by calling **sleep(milliseconds)**, in which case it will not be run for the specified time.

- You've suspended the execution of the thread with **wait( )**. It will not become runnable again until the thread gets the **signal( )** or **broadcast( )** message. We'll examine these in a later section.

- The thread is waiting for some I/O to complete.

- The thread is trying to enter a block of code that is guarded by a mutex, and that mutex has already been acquired by another thread.

The problem we need to look at now is this: sometimes you want to terminate a thread that is in a blocked state. If you can't wait for it to get to a point in the code where it can check a state value and decide to terminate on its own, you have to force the thread out of its blocked state.

Interruption

As you might imagine, it's much messier to break out of the middle of a **Runnable::run( )** function than it is to wait for that function to get to a test of **isCanceled( )** (or some other place where the programmer is ready to leave the function). When you break out of a blocked task, you might need to destroy objects and clean up resources. Because of this, breaking out of the middle of a task's **run( )** is more like throwing an exception than anything else, so in ZThreads, exceptions are used for this kind of abort. (This walks the fine edge of being an inappropriate use of exceptions, because it means you are often using them for control flow.)[7] To return to a known good state when terminating a task this way, carefully consider the execution paths of your code and properly clean up everything inside the **catch** clause. We'll look at these issues in this section.

To terminate a blocked thread, the ZThread library provides the **Thread**::**interrupt( )** function. This sets the *interrupted status* for that thread. A thread with its interrupted status set will throw an **Interrupted_Exception** if it is already blocked or it attempts a blocking operation. The interrupted status will be reset when the exception is thrown or if the task calls **Thread::interrupted( )**. As you'll see, **Thread::interrupted( )** provides a second way to leave your **run( )** loop, without throwing an exception.

Here's an example that shows the basics of **interrupt( )**:

---

[7] However, exceptions are never delivered asynchronously in ZThreads. Thus, there is no danger of something aborting mid-instruction/function call. And as long as you use the **Guard** template to acquire mutexes, the mutexes will be automatically released if an exception is thrown.

```
//: C11:Interrupting.cpp
// Interrupting a blocked thread.
//{L} ZThread
#include <iostream>
#include "zthread/Thread.h"
using namespace ZThread;
using namespace std;

class Blocked : public Runnable {
public:
  void run() {
    try {
      Thread::sleep(1000);
      cout << "Waiting for get() in run():";
      cin.get();
    } catch(Interrupted_Exception&) {
      cout << "Caught Interrupted_Exception" << endl;
      // Exit the task
    }
  }
};

int main(int argc, char* argv[]) {
  try {
    Thread t(new Blocked);
    if(argc > 1)
      Thread::sleep(1100);
    t.interrupt();
  } catch(Synchronization_Exception& e) {
    cerr << e.what() << endl;
  }
} ///:~
```

You can see that, in addition to the insertion into **cout**, **run( )** contains two other points where blocking can occur: the call to **Thread::sleep(1000)** and the call to **cin.get( )**. By giving the program any command-line argument, you tell **main( )** to sleep long enough that the task will finish its **sleep( )** and call **cin.get( )**.[8] If you don't give the program an argument, the **sleep( )** in **main( )** is skipped. Here, the call to **interrupt( )** will occur

---

[8] Actually, **sleep( )** only provides a minimum delay, not a guaranteed delay, so it's possible (although improbable) that the **sleep(1100)** will wake up before the **sleep(1000)**.

---

while the task is sleeping, and you'll see that this will cause
Interrupted_Exception to be thrown. If you give the program a
command-line argument, you'll discover that a task cannot be interrupted if it
is blocked on IO. That is, you can interrupt out of any blocking operation
except IO.[9]

This is a little disconcerting if you're creating a thread that performs IO
because it means that I/O has the potential of locking your multithreaded
program. The problem is that, again, C++ was not designed with threading in
mind; quite the opposite, it effectively pretends that threading doesn't exist.
Thus, the iostream library is not thread-friendly. If the new C++ Standard
decides to add thread support, the iostream library may need to be
reconsidered in the process.

Blocked by a mutex

If you try to call a function whose mutex has already been acquired, the
calling task will be suspended until the mutex becomes available. The
following example tests whether this kind of blocking is interruptible:

```
//: C11:Interrupting2.cpp
// Interrupting a thread blocked
// with a synchronization guard.
//{L} ZThread
#include <iostream>
#include "zthread/Thread.h"
#include "zthread/Mutex.h"
#include "zthread/Guard.h"
using namespace ZThread;
using namespace std;

class BlockedMutex {
  Mutex lock;
public:
  BlockedMutex() {
    lock.acquire();
  }
  void f() {
```

---

[9] There is nothing in the C++ Standard that says that interruptions can't
occur during IO operations. However, most implementations don't support
it.

```
      Guard<Mutex> g(lock);
      // This will never be available
  }
};

class Blocked2 : public Runnable {
  BlockedMutex blocked;
public:
  void run() {
    try {
      cout << "Waiting for f() in BlockedMutex" << endl;
      blocked.f();
    } catch(Interrupted_Exception& e) {
      cerr << e.what() << endl;
      // Exit the task
    }
  }
};

int main(int argc, char* argv[]) {
  try {
    Thread t(new Blocked2);
    t.interrupt();
  } catch(Synchronization_Exception& e) {
    cerr << e.what() << endl;
  }
} ///:~
```

The class **BlockedMutex** has a constructor that acquires the object's own **Mutex** and never releases it. For that reason, if you try to call **f( )**, you will always be blocked because the **Mutex** cannot be acquired. In **Blocked2**, the **run( )** function will be stopped at the call to **blocked.f( )**. When you run the program you'll see that, unlike the iostream call, **interrupt( )** can break out of a call that's blocked by a mutex.[10]

Checking for an interrupt
Note that when you call **interrupt( )** on a thread, the only time that the interrupt occurs is when the task enters, or is already inside, a blocking operation (except, as you've seen, in the case of IO, where you're just stuck).

---

[10] Note that, although it's unlikely, the call to **t.interrupt( )** could actually happen before the call to **blocked.f( )**.

But what if you've written code that may or may not make such a blocking call, depending on the conditions in which it is run? If you can only exit by throwing an exception on a blocking call, you won't always be able to leave the **run( )** loop. Thus, if you call **interrupt( )** to stop a task, your task needs a *second* opportunity to exit in the event that your **run( )** loop doesn't happen to be making any blocking calls.

This opportunity is presented by the *interrupted status*, which is set by the call to **interrupt( )**. You check for the interrupted status by calling **interrupted( )**. This not only tells you whether **interrupt( )** has been called, it also clears the interrupted status. Clearing the interrupted status ensures that the framework will not notify you twice about a task being interrupted. You will be notified via either a single **Interrupted_Exception**, or a single successful **Thread::interrupted( )** test. If you want to check again to see whether you were interrupted, you can store the result when you call **Thread::interrupted( )**.

The following example shows the typical idiom that you should use in your **run( )** function to handle both blocked and non-blocked possibilities when the interrupted status is set:

```
//: C11:Interrupting3.cpp {RunByHand}
// General idiom for interrupting a task.
//{L} ZThread
#include <iostream>
#include "zthread/Thread.h"
using namespace ZThread;
using namespace std;

const double PI = 3.14159265358979323846;
const double E = 2.7182818284590452354;

class NeedsCleanup {
  int id;
public:
  NeedsCleanup(int ident) : id(ident) {
    cout << "NeedsCleanup " << id << endl;
  }
  ~NeedsCleanup() {
    cout << "~NeedsCleanup " << id << endl;
  }
};
```

```
class Blocked3 : public Runnable {
  volatile double d;
public:
  Blocked3() : d(0.0) {}
  void run() {
    try {
      while(!Thread::interrupted()) {
        point1:
        NeedsCleanup n1(1);
        cout << "Sleeping" << endl;
        Thread::sleep(1000);
        point2:
        NeedsCleanup n2(2);
        cout << "Calculating" << endl;
        // A time-consuming, non-blocking operation:
        for(int i = 1; i < 100000; i++)
          d = d + (PI + E) / (double)i;
      }
      cout << "Exiting via while() test" << endl;
    } catch(Interrupted_Exception&) {
      cout << "Exiting via Interrupted_Exception" << endl;
    }
  }
};

int main(int argc, char* argv[]) {
  if(argc != 2) {
    cerr << "usage: " << argv[0]
      << " delay-in-milliseconds" << endl;
    exit(1);
  }
  int delay = atoi(argv[1]);
  try {
    Thread t(new Blocked3);
    Thread::sleep(delay);
    t.interrupt();
  } catch(Synchronization_Exception& e) {
    cerr << e.what() << endl;
  }
} ///:~
```

The **NeedsCleanup** class emphasizes the necessity of proper resource cleanup if you leave the loop via an exception. Note that no pointers are defined in **Blocked3::run( )** because, for exception safety, all resources must be enclosed in stack-based objects so that the exception handler can automatically clean them up by calling the destructor.

You must give the program a command-line argument which is the delay time in milliseconds before it calls **interrupt( )**. By using different delays, you can exit **Blocked3::run( )** at different points in the loop: in the blocking **sleep( )** call, and in the non-blocking mathematical calculation. You'll see that if **interrupt( )** is called after the label **point2** (during the non-blocking operation), first the loop is completed, then all the local objects are destructed, and finally the loop is exited at the top via the **while** statement. However, if **interrupt( )** is called between **point1** and **point2** (after the **while** statement but before or during the blocking operation **sleep( )**), the task exits via the **Interrupted_Exception**. In that case, only the stack objects that have been created up to the point where the exception is thrown are cleaned up, and you have the opportunity to perform any other cleanup in the **catch** clause.

A class designed to respond to an **interrupt( )** must establish a policy that ensures it will remain in a consistent state. This generally means that all resource acquisition should be wrapped inside stack-based objects so that the destructors will be called regardless of how the **run( )** loop exits. Correctly done, code like this can be elegant. Components can be created that completely encapsulate their synchronization mechanisms but are still responsive to an external stimulus (via **interrupt( )**) without adding any special functions to an object's interface.

Cooperation between threads

As you've seen, when you use threads to run more than one task at a time, you can keep one task from interfering with another task's resources by using a mutex to synchronize the behavior of the two tasks. That is, if two tasks are stepping on each other over a shared resource (usually memory), you use a mutex to allow only one task at a time to access that resource.

With that problem solved, you can move on to the issue of getting threads to cooperate, so that multiple threads can work together to solve a problem. Now the issue is not about interfering with one another, but rather about working in unison, since portions of such problems must be solved before other portions can be solved. It's much like project planning: the footings for the house must be dug first, but the steel can be laid and the concrete forms can be built in parallel, and both of those tasks must be finished before the concrete foundation can be poured. The plumbing must be in place before the concrete slab can be poured, the concrete slab must be in place before you start framing, and so on. Some of these tasks can be done in parallel, but certain steps require all tasks to be completed before you can move ahead.

The key issue when tasks are cooperating is handshaking between those tasks. To accomplish this handshaking, we use the same foundation: the mutex, which in this case guarantees that only one task can respond to a signal. This eliminates any possible race conditions. On top of the mutex, we add a way for a task to suspend itself until some external state changes ("the plumbing is now in place"), indicating that it's time for that task to move forward. In this section, we'll look at the issues of handshaking between tasks, the problems that can arise, and their solutions.

Wait and signal

In ZThreads, the basic class that uses a mutex and allows task suspension is the **Condition**, and you can suspend a task by calling **wait( )** on a **Condition**. When external state changes take place that might mean that a task should continue processing, you notify the task by calling **signal( )**, to wake up one task, or **broadcast( )**, to wake up all tasks that have suspended themselves on that **Condition** object.

There are two forms of **wait( )**. The first form takes an argument in milliseconds that has the same meaning as in **sleep( )**: "pause for this period of time." The second form takes no arguments; this version is more commonly used. Both forms of **wait( )** release the **Mutex** that is controlled by the **Condition** object and suspends the thread until that **Condition** object receives a **signal( )** or **broadcast( )**. The first form may also terminate if it times out before a **signal( )** or **broadcast( )** is received.

Because **wait( )** releases the **Mutex**, it means that the **Mutex** can be acquired by another thread. Thus, when you call **wait( )** you're saying "I've done all I can right now so I'm going to wait right here, but I want to allow other synchronized operations to take place if they can."

Typically, you use **wait( )** when you're waiting for some condition to change that is under the control of forces outside the current function. (Often, this condition will be changed by another thread.) You don't want to idly loop while testing the condition inside your thread; this is called a "busy wait," and it's usually a bad use of CPU cycles. Thus, **wait( )** suspends the thread while waiting for the world to change, and only when a **signal( )** or **broadcast( )** occurs (suggesting that something of interest may have happened), does the thread wake up and check for changes. So **wait( )** provides a way to synchronize activities between threads.

Let's look at a simple example. **WaxOMatic.cpp** has two processes: one to apply wax to a **Car** and one to polish it. The polishing process cannot do its job until the application process is finished, and the application process must wait until the polishing process is finished before it can put on another coat of wax. Both **WaxOn** and **WaxOff** use the **Car** object, which contains a **Condition** that it uses to suspend a thread inside **waitForWaxing( )** or **waitForBuffing( )**:

```cpp
//: C11:WaxOMatic.cpp {RunByHand}
// Basic thread cooperation.
//{L} ZThread
#include <iostream>
#include <string>
#include "zthread/Thread.h"
#include "zthread/Mutex.h"
#include "zthread/Guard.h"
#include "zthread/Condition.h"
#include "zthread/ThreadedExecutor.h"
using namespace ZThread;
using namespace std;

class Car {
  Mutex lock;
  Condition condition;
  bool waxOn;
public:
  Car() : condition(lock), waxOn(false) {}
  void waxed() {
    Guard<Mutex> g(lock);
    waxOn = true; // Ready to buff
    condition.signal();
  }
  void buffed() {
```

```
      Guard<Mutex> g(lock);
      waxOn = false; // Ready for another coat of wax
      condition.signal();
    }
    void waitForWaxing() {
      Guard<Mutex> g(lock);
      while(waxOn == false)
        condition.wait();
    }
    void waitForBuffing() {
      Guard<Mutex> g(lock);
      while(waxOn == true)
        condition.wait();
    }
};

class WaxOn : public Runnable {
  CountedPtr<Car> car;
public:
  WaxOn(CountedPtr<Car>& c) : car(c) {}
  void run() {
    try {
      while(!Thread::interrupted()) {
        cout << "Wax On!" << endl;
        Thread::sleep(200);
        car->waxed();
        car->waitForBuffing();
      }
    } catch(Interrupted_Exception&) { /* Exit */ }
    cout << "Ending Wax On process" << endl;
  }
};

class WaxOff : public Runnable {
  CountedPtr<Car> car;
public:
  WaxOff(CountedPtr<Car>& c) : car(c) {}
  void run() {
    try {
      while(!Thread::interrupted()) {
        car->waitForWaxing();
        cout << "Wax Off!" << endl;
        Thread::sleep(200);
        car->buffed();
      }
```

```
      } catch(Interrupted_Exception&) { /* Exit */ }
      cout << "Ending Wax Off process" << endl;
  }
};

int main() {
  cout << "Press <Enter> to quit" << endl;
  try {
    CountedPtr<Car> car(new Car);
    ThreadedExecutor executor;
    executor.execute(new WaxOff(car));
    executor.execute(new WaxOn(car));
    cin.get();
    executor.interrupt();
  } catch(Synchronization_Exception& e) {
    cerr << e.what() << endl;
  }
} ///:~
```

In **Car**'s constructor, a single **Mutex** is wrapped in a **Condition** object so that it can be used to manage inter-task communication. However, the **Condition** object contains no information about the state of your process, so you need to manage additional information to indicate process state. Here, **Car** has a single **bool waxOn**, which indicates the state of the waxing-polishing process.

In **waitForWaxing( )**, the **waxOn** flag is checked, and if it is **false**, the calling thread is suspended by calling **wait( )** on the **Condition** object. It's important that this occur inside a guarded clause, where the thread has acquired the lock (here, by creating a **Guard** object). When you call **wait( )**, the thread is suspended and *the lock is released*. It is essential that the lock be released because, to safely change the state of the object (for example, to change **waxOn** to **true**, which must happen if the suspended thread is to ever continue), that lock must be available to be acquired by some other task. In this example, when another thread calls **waxed( )** to tell it that it's time to do something, the mutex must be acquired in order to change **waxOn** to **true**. Afterward, **waxed( )** sends a **signal( )** to the **Condition** object, which wakes up the thread suspended in the call to **wait( )**. Although **signal( )** may be called inside a guarded clause—as it is here—you are not required to do this.[11]

In order for a thread to wake up from a **wait( )**, it must first reacquire the mutex that it released when it entered the **wait( )**. The thread will not wake up until that mutex becomes available.

The call to **wait( )** is placed inside a **while** loop that checks the condition of interest. This is important for two reasons:[12]

- It is possible that when the thread gets a **signal( )**, some other condition has changed that is not associated with the reason that we called **wait( )** here. If that is the case, this thread should be suspended again until its condition of interest changes.

- By the time this thread awakens from its **wait( )**, it's possible that some other task has changed things such that this thread is unable or uninterested in performing its operation at this time. Again, it should be re-suspended by calling **wait( )** again.

Because these two reasons are always present when you are calling **wait( )**, always write your call to **wait( )** inside a **while** loop that tests for your condition(s) of interest.

---

[11] This is in contrast to Java, where you must hold the lock in order to call **notify( )** (Java's version of **signal( )**). Although Posix threads, on which the ZThread library is loosely based, do not require that you hold the lock in order to call **signal( )** or **broadcast( )**, it is often recommended.

[12] On some platforms there's a third way to come out of a **wait( )**, the so-called *spurious wakeup*. A spurious wakeup essentially means that a thread may prematurely stop blocking (while waiting on a condition variable or semaphore) without being prompted by a **signal( )** or **broadcast( )**. The thread just wakes up, seemingly by itself. Spurious wakeups exist because implementing POSIX threads, or the equivalent, isn't always as straightforward as it should be on some platforms. By allowing spurious wakeups the job of building a library like pthreads is easier for those platforms. Spurious wakeups do not occur in ZThreads, because the library compensates for and hides these issues from the user.

WaxOn::run( ) represents the first step in the process of waxing the car, so it performs its operation (a call to **sleep( )** to simulate the time necessary for waxing). It then tells the car that waxing is complete, and calls **waitForBuffing( )**, which suspends this thread with a **wait( )** until the **WaxOff** process calls **buffed( )** for the car, changing the state and calling **notify( )**. **WaxOff::run( )**, on the other hand, immediately moves into **waitForWaxing( )** and is thus suspended until the wax has been applied by **WaxOn** and **waxed( )** is called. When you run this program, you can watch this two-step process repeat itself as control is handed back and forth between the two threads. When you press the <Enter> key, **interrupt( )** halts both threads—when you call **interrupt( )** for an **Executor**, it calls **interrupt( )** for all the threads it is controlling.

Producer–consumer relationships

A common situation in threading problems is the *producer-consumer* relationship, where one task is creating objects and other tasks are consuming them. In such a situation, make sure that (among other things) the consuming tasks do not accidentally skip any of the produced objects.

To show this problem, consider a machine that has three tasks: one to make toast, one to butter the toast, and one to put jam on the buttered toast.

```
//: C11:ToastOMatic.cpp {RunByHand}
// Problems with thread cooperation.
//{L} ZThread
#include <iostream>
#include <cstdlib>
#include <ctime>
#include "zthread/Thread.h"
#include "zthread/Mutex.h"
#include "zthread/Guard.h"
#include "zthread/Condition.h"
#include "zthread/ThreadedExecutor.h"
using namespace ZThread;
using namespace std;

// Apply jam to buttered toast:
class Jammer : public Runnable {
  Mutex lock;
  Condition butteredToastReady;
  bool gotButteredToast;
```

```
    int jammed;
public:
  Jammer() : butteredToastReady(lock) {
    gotButteredToast = false;
    jammed = 0;
  }
  void moreButteredToastReady() {
    Guard<Mutex> g(lock);
    gotButteredToast = true;
    butteredToastReady.signal();
  }
  void run() {
    try {
      while(!Thread::interrupted()) {
        {
          Guard<Mutex> g(lock);
          while(!gotButteredToast)
            butteredToastReady.wait();
          ++jammed;
        }
        cout << "Putting jam on toast " << jammed << endl;
        {
          Guard<Mutex> g(lock);
          gotButteredToast = false;
        }
      }
    } catch(Interrupted_Exception&) { /* Exit */ }
    cout << "Jammer off" << endl;
  }
};

// Apply butter to toast:
class Butterer : public Runnable {
  Mutex lock;
  Condition toastReady;
  CountedPtr<Jammer> jammer;
  bool gotToast;
  int buttered;
public:
  Butterer(CountedPtr<Jammer>& j)
  : toastReady(lock), jammer(j) {
    gotToast = false;
    buttered = 0;
  }
  void moreToastReady() {
```

```
      Guard<Mutex> g(lock);
      gotToast = true;
      toastReady.signal();
  }
  void run() {
    try {
      while(!Thread::interrupted()) {
        {
          Guard<Mutex> g(lock);
          while(!gotToast)
            toastReady.wait();
          ++buttered;
        }
        cout << "Buttering toast " << buttered << endl;
        jammer->moreButteredToastReady();
        {
          Guard<Mutex> g(lock);
          gotToast = false;
        }
      }
    } catch(Interrupted_Exception&) { /* Exit */ }
    cout << "Butterer off" << endl;
  }
};

class Toaster : public Runnable {
  CountedPtr<Butterer> butterer;
  int toasted;
public:
  Toaster(CountedPtr<Butterer>& b) : butterer(b) {
    toasted = 0;
  }
  void run() {
    try {
      while(!Thread::interrupted()) {
        Thread::sleep(rand()/(RAND_MAX/5)*100);
        // ...
        // Create new toast
        // ...
        cout << "New toast " << ++toasted << endl;
        butterer->moreToastReady();
      }
    } catch(Interrupted_Exception&) { /* Exit */ }
    cout << "Toaster off" << endl;
  }
```

```
    };

    int main() {
      srand(time(0)); // Seed the random number generator
      try {
        cout << "Press <Return> to quit" << endl;
        CountedPtr<Jammer> jammer(new Jammer);
        CountedPtr<Butterer> butterer(new Butterer(jammer));
        ThreadedExecutor executor;
        executor.execute(new Toaster(butterer));
        executor.execute(butterer);
        executor.execute(jammer);
        cin.get();
        executor.interrupt();
      } catch(Synchronization_Exception& e) {
        cerr << e.what() << endl;
      }
    } ///:~
```

The classes are defined in the reverse order that they operate to simplify
forward-referencing issues.

Jammer and **Butterer** both contain a **Mutex**, a **Condition**, and some
kind of internal state information that changes to indicate that the process
should suspend or resume. (**Toaster** doesn't need these since it is the
producer and doesn't have to wait on anything.) The two **run( )** functions
perform an operation, set a state flag, and then call **wait( )** to suspend the
task. The **moreToastReady( )** and **moreButteredToastReady( )**
functions change their respective state flags to indicate that something has
changed and the process should consider resuming and then call **signal( )** to
wake up the thread.

The difference between this example and the previous one is that, at least
conceptually, something is being produced here: toast. The rate of toast
production is randomized a bit, to add some uncertainty. And you'll see that
when you run the program, things aren't going right because many pieces of
toast appear to be getting dropped on the floor—not buttered, not jammed.

Solving threading problems with queues

Often, threading problems are based on the need for tasks to be serialized—
that is, to take care of things in order. **ToastOMatic.cpp** must not only take

care of things in order, it must be able to work on one piece of toast without worrying that toast is falling on the floor in the meantime. You can solve many threading problems by using a queue that synchronizes access to the elements within:

```
//: C11:TQueue.h
#ifndef TQUEUE_H
#define TQUEUE_H
#include <deque>
#include "zthread/Thread.h"
#include "zthread/Condition.h"
#include "zthread/Mutex.h"
#include "zthread/Guard.h"

template<class T> class TQueue {
  ZThread::Mutex lock;
  ZThread::Condition cond;
  std::deque<T> data;
public:
  TQueue() : cond(lock) {}
  void put(T item) {
    ZThread::Guard<ZThread::Mutex> g(lock);
    data.push_back(item);
    cond.signal();
  }
  T get() {
    ZThread::Guard<ZThread::Mutex> g(lock);
    while(data.empty())
      cond.wait();
    T returnVal = data.front();
    data.pop_front();
    return returnVal;
  }
};
#endif // TQUEUE_H ///:~
```

This builds on the Standard C++ Library **deque** by adding:

1. Synchronization to ensure that no two threads add objects at the same time.

2. **wait( )** and **signal( )** so that a consumer thread will automatically suspend if the queue is empty, and resume when more elements become available.

This relatively small amount of code can solve a remarkable number of problems.[13]

Here's a simple test that serializes the execution of **LiftOff** objects. The consumer is **LiftOffRunner**, which pulls each **LiftOff** object off the **TQueue** and runs it directly. (That is, it uses its own thread by calling **run( )** explicitly rather than starting up a new thread for each task.)

```
//: C11:TestTQueue.cpp {RunByHand}
//{L} ZThread
#include <string>
#include <iostream>
#include "TQueue.h"
#include "zthread/Thread.h"
#include "LiftOff.h"
using namespace ZThread;
using namespace std;

class LiftOffRunner : public Runnable {
  TQueue<LiftOff*> rockets;
public:
  void add(LiftOff* lo) { rockets.put(lo); }
  void run() {
    try {
      while(!Thread::interrupted()) {
        LiftOff* rocket = rockets.get();
        rocket->run();
      }
    } catch(Interrupted_Exception&) { /* Exit */ }
    cout << "Exiting LiftOffRunner" << endl;
  }
};

int main() {
  try {
    LiftOffRunner* lor = new LiftOffRunner;
    Thread t(lor);
```

---

[13] Note that if the readers stop for some reason, the writers will keep on writing until the system runs out of memory. If this is an issue with your program you can add a maximum allowable element count, and writers should then block if the queue is full.

```
      for(int i = 0; i < 5; i++)
        lor->add(new LiftOff(10, i));
      cin.get();
      lor->add(new LiftOff(10, 99));
      cin.get();
      t.interrupt();
  } catch(Synchronization_Exception& e) {
    cerr << e.what() << endl;
  }
} ///:~
```

The tasks are placed on the **TQueue** by **main( )** and are taken off the **TQueue** by the **LiftOffRunner**. Notice that **LiftOffRunner** can ignore the synchronization issues because they are solved by the **TQueue**.

Proper toasting

To solve the **ToastOMatic.cpp** problem, we can run the toast through **TQueue**s between processes. And to do this, we will need actual toast objects, which maintain and display their state:

```
//: C11:ToastOMaticMarkII.cpp {RunByHand}
// Solving the problems using TQueues.
//{L} ZThread
#include <iostream>
#include <string>
#include <cstdlib>
#include <ctime>
#include "zthread/Thread.h"
#include "zthread/Mutex.h"
#include "zthread/Guard.h"
#include "zthread/Condition.h"
#include "zthread/ThreadedExecutor.h"
#include "TQueue.h"
using namespace ZThread;
using namespace std;

class Toast {
  enum Status { DRY, BUTTERED, JAMMED };
  Status status;
  int id;
public:
  Toast(int idn) : status(DRY), id(idn) {}
  #ifdef __DMC__ // Incorrectly requires default
  Toast() { assert(0); } // Should never be called
```

```
    #endif
    void butter() { status = BUTTERED; }
    void jam() { status = JAMMED; }
    string getStatus() const {
      switch(status) {
        case DRY: return "dry";
        case BUTTERED: return "buttered";
        case JAMMED: return "jammed";
        default: return "error";
      }
    }
    int getId() { return id; }
    friend ostream& operator<<(ostream& os, const Toast& t) {
      return os << "Toast " << t.id << ": " << t.getStatus();
    }
};

typedef CountedPtr< TQueue<Toast> > ToastQueue;

class Toaster : public Runnable {
  ToastQueue toastQueue;
  int count;
public:
  Toaster(ToastQueue& tq) : toastQueue(tq), count(0) {}
  void run() {
    try {
      while(!Thread::interrupted()) {
        int delay = rand()/(RAND_MAX/5)*100;
        Thread::sleep(delay);
        // Make toast
        Toast t(count++);
        cout << t << endl;
        // Insert into queue
        toastQueue->put(t);
      }
    } catch(Interrupted_Exception&) { /* Exit */ }
    cout << "Toaster off" << endl;
  }
};

// Apply butter to toast:
class Butterer : public Runnable {
  ToastQueue dryQueue, butteredQueue;
public:
  Butterer(ToastQueue& dry, ToastQueue& buttered)
```

```
    : dryQueue(dry), butteredQueue(buttered) {}
  void run() {
    try {
      while(!Thread::interrupted()) {
        // Blocks until next piece of toast is available:
        Toast t = dryQueue->get();
        t.butter();
        cout << t << endl;
        butteredQueue->put(t);
      }
    } catch(Interrupted_Exception&) { /* Exit */ }
    cout << "Butterer off" << endl;
  }
};

// Apply jam to buttered toast:
class Jammer : public Runnable {
  ToastQueue butteredQueue, finishedQueue;
public:
  Jammer(ToastQueue& buttered, ToastQueue& finished)
  : butteredQueue(buttered), finishedQueue(finished) {}
  void run() {
    try {
      while(!Thread::interrupted()) {
        // Blocks until next piece of toast is available:
        Toast t = butteredQueue->get();
        t.jam();
        cout << t << endl;
        finishedQueue->put(t);
      }
    } catch(Interrupted_Exception&) { /* Exit */ }
    cout << "Jammer off" << endl;
  }
};

// Consume the toast:
class Eater : public Runnable {
  ToastQueue finishedQueue;
  int counter;
public:
  Eater(ToastQueue& finished)
  : finishedQueue(finished), counter(0) {}
  void run() {
    try {
      while(!Thread::interrupted()) {
```

```
        // Blocks until next piece of toast is available:
        Toast t = finishedQueue->get();
        // Verify that the toast is coming in order,
        // and that all pieces are getting jammed:
        if(t.getId() != counter++ ||
           t.getStatus() != "jammed") {
          cout << ">>>> Error: " << t << endl;
          exit(1);
        } else
          cout << "Chomp! " << t << endl;
      }
    } catch(Interrupted_Exception&) { /* Exit */ }
    cout << "Eater off" << endl;
  }
};

int main() {
  srand(time(0)); // Seed the random number generator
  try {
    ToastQueue dryQueue(new TQueue<Toast>),
              butteredQueue(new TQueue<Toast>),
              finishedQueue(new TQueue<Toast>);
    cout << "Press <Return> to quit" << endl;
    ThreadedExecutor executor;
    executor.execute(new Toaster(dryQueue));
    executor.execute(new Butterer(dryQueue,butteredQueue));
    executor.execute(
      new Jammer(butteredQueue, finishedQueue));
    executor.execute(new Eater(finishedQueue));
    cin.get();
    executor.interrupt();
  } catch(Synchronization_Exception& e) {
    cerr << e.what() << endl;
  }
} ///:~
```

Two things are immediately apparent in this solution: first, the amount and complexity of code within each **Runnable** class is dramatically reduced by the use of the **TQueue** because the guarding, communication, and **wait( )/signal( )** operations are now taken care of by the **TQueue**. The **Runnable** classes don't have **Mutex**es or **Condition** objects anymore. Second, the coupling between the classes is eliminated because each class communicates only with its **TQueue**s. Notice that the definition order of the classes is now independent. Less code and less coupling are always good things, which suggests that the use of the **TQueue** has a positive effect here, as it does on most problems.

Broadcast

The **signal( )** function wakes up one thread that is waiting on a **Condition** object. However, multiple threads may be waiting on the same condition object, and in that case you might want to wake them all up using **broadcast( )** instead of **signal( )**.

As an example that brings together many of the concepts in this chapter, consider a hypothetical robotic assembly line for automobiles. Each **Car** will be built in several stages, and in this example we'll look at a single stage: after the chassis has been created, at the time when the engine, drive train, and wheels are attached. The **Car**s are transported from one place to another via a **CarQueue**, which is a type of **TQueue**. A **Director** takes each **Car** (as a raw chassis) from the incoming **CarQueue** and places it in a **Cradle**, which is where all the work is done. At this point, the **Director** tells all the waiting robots (using **broadcast( )**) that the **Car** is in the **Cradle** ready for the robots to work on it. The three types of robots go to work, sending a message to the **Cradle** when they finish their tasks. The **Director** waits until all the tasks are complete and then puts the **Car** onto the outgoing **CarQueue** to be transported to the next operation. Here, the consumer of the outgoing **CarQueue** is a **Reporter** object, which just prints the **Car** to show that the tasks have been properly completed.

```
//: C11:CarBuilder.cpp {RunByHand}
// How broadcast() works.
//{L} ZThread
#include <iostream>
#include <string>
#include "zthread/Thread.h"
#include "zthread/Mutex.h"
#include "zthread/Guard.h"
#include "zthread/Condition.h"
#include "zthread/ThreadedExecutor.h"
#include "TQueue.h"
using namespace ZThread;
using namespace std;

class Car {
  int id;
```

```
    bool engine, driveTrain, wheels;
public:
  Car(int idn) : id(idn), engine(false),
  driveTrain(false), wheels(false) {}
  // Empty Car object:
  Car() : id(-1), engine(false),
  driveTrain(false), wheels(false) {}
  // Unsynchronized -- assumes atomic bool operations:
  int getId() { return id; }
  void addEngine() { engine = true; }
  bool engineInstalled() { return engine; }
  void addDriveTrain() { driveTrain = true; }
  bool driveTrainInstalled() { return driveTrain; }
  void addWheels() { wheels = true; }
  bool wheelsInstalled() { return wheels; }
  friend ostream& operator<<(ostream& os, const Car& c) {
    return os << "Car " << c.id << " ["
      << " engine: " << c.engine
      << " driveTrain: " << c.driveTrain
      << " wheels: " << c.wheels << " ]";
  }
};

typedef CountedPtr< TQueue<Car> > CarQueue;

class ChassisBuilder : public Runnable {
  CarQueue carQueue;
  int counter;
public:
  ChassisBuilder(CarQueue& cq) : carQueue(cq),counter(0) {}
  void run() {
    try {
      while(!Thread::interrupted()) {
        Thread::sleep(1000);
        // Make chassis:
        Car c(counter++);
        cout << c << endl;
        // Insert into queue
        carQueue->put(c);
      }
    } catch(Interrupted_Exception&) { /* Exit */ }
    cout << "ChassisBuilder off" << endl;
  }
};
```

```
class Cradle {
  Car c; // Holds current car being worked on
  bool occupied;
  Mutex workLock, readyLock;
  Condition workCondition, readyCondition;
  bool engineBotHired, wheelBotHired, driveTrainBotHired;
public:
  Cradle()
  : workCondition(workLock), readyCondition(readyLock) {
    occupied = false;
    engineBotHired = true;
    wheelBotHired = true;
    driveTrainBotHired = true;
  }
  void insertCar(Car chassis) {
    c = chassis;
    occupied = true;
  }
  Car getCar() { // Can only extract car once
    if(!occupied) {
      cerr << "No Car in Cradle for getCar()" << endl;
      return Car(); // "Null" Car object
    }
    occupied = false;
    return c;
  }
  // Access car while in cradle:
  Car* operator->() { return &c; }
  // Allow robots to offer services to this cradle:
  void offerEngineBotServices() {
    Guard<Mutex> g(workLock);
    while(engineBotHired)
      workCondition.wait();
    engineBotHired = true; // Accept the job
  }
  void offerWheelBotServices() {
    Guard<Mutex> g(workLock);
    while(wheelBotHired)
      workCondition.wait();
    wheelBotHired = true; // Accept the job
  }
  void offerDriveTrainBotServices() {
    Guard<Mutex> g(workLock);
    while(driveTrainBotHired)
      workCondition.wait();
```

```
      driveTrainBotHired = true; // Accept the job
    }
    // Tell waiting robots that work is ready:
    void startWork() {
      Guard<Mutex> g(workLock);
      engineBotHired = false;
      wheelBotHired = false;
      driveTrainBotHired = false;
      workCondition.broadcast();
    }
    // Each robot reports when their job is done:
    void taskFinished() {
      Guard<Mutex> g(readyLock);
      readyCondition.signal();
    }
    // Director waits until all jobs are done:
    void waitUntilWorkFinished() {
      Guard<Mutex> g(readyLock);
      while(!(c.engineInstalled() && c.driveTrainInstalled()
              && c.wheelsInstalled()))
        readyCondition.wait();
    }
};

typedef CountedPtr<Cradle> CradlePtr;

class Director : public Runnable {
  CarQueue chassisQueue, finishingQueue;
  CradlePtr cradle;
public:
  Director(CarQueue& cq, CarQueue& fq, CradlePtr cr)
  : chassisQueue(cq), finishingQueue(fq), cradle(cr) {}
  void run() {
    try {
      while(!Thread::interrupted()) {
        // Blocks until chassis is available:
        cradle->insertCar(chassisQueue->get());
        // Notify robots car is ready for work
        cradle->startWork();
        // Wait until work completes
        cradle->waitUntilWorkFinished();
        // Put car into queue for further work
        finishingQueue->put(cradle->getCar());
      }
    } catch(Interrupted_Exception&) { /* Exit */ }
```

```
        cout << "Director off" << endl;
    }
};

class EngineRobot : public Runnable {
  CradlePtr cradle;
public:
  EngineRobot(CradlePtr cr) : cradle(cr) {}
  void run() {
    try {
      while(!Thread::interrupted()) {
        // Blocks until job is offered/accepted:
        cradle->offerEngineBotServices();
        cout << "Installing engine" << endl;
        (*cradle)->addEngine();
        cradle->taskFinished();
      }
    } catch(Interrupted_Exception&) { /* Exit */ }
    cout << "EngineRobot off" << endl;
  }
};

class DriveTrainRobot : public Runnable {
  CradlePtr cradle;
public:
  DriveTrainRobot(CradlePtr cr) : cradle(cr) {}
  void run() {
    try {
      while(!Thread::interrupted()) {
        // Blocks until job is offered/accepted:
        cradle->offerDriveTrainBotServices();
        cout << "Installing DriveTrain" << endl;
        (*cradle)->addDriveTrain();
        cradle->taskFinished();
      }
    } catch(Interrupted_Exception&) { /* Exit */ }
    cout << "DriveTrainRobot off" << endl;
  }
};

class WheelRobot : public Runnable {
  CradlePtr cradle;
public:
  WheelRobot(CradlePtr cr) : cradle(cr) {}
  void run() {
```

```
      try {
        while(!Thread::interrupted()) {
          // Blocks until job is offered/accepted:
          cradle->offerWheelBotServices();
          cout << "Installing Wheels" << endl;
          (*cradle)->addWheels();
          cradle->taskFinished();
        }
      } catch(Interrupted_Exception&) { /* Exit */ }
      cout << "WheelRobot off" << endl;
    }
};

class Reporter : public Runnable {
  CarQueue carQueue;
public:
  Reporter(CarQueue& cq) : carQueue(cq) {}
  void run() {
    try {
      while(!Thread::interrupted()) {
        cout << carQueue->get() << endl;
      }
    } catch(Interrupted_Exception&) { /* Exit */ }
    cout << "Reporter off" << endl;
  }
};

int main() {
  cout << "Press <Enter> to quit" << endl;
  try {
    CarQueue chassisQueue(new TQueue<Car>),
             finishingQueue(new TQueue<Car>);
    CradlePtr cradle(new Cradle);
    ThreadedExecutor assemblyLine;
    assemblyLine.execute(new EngineRobot(cradle));
    assemblyLine.execute(new DriveTrainRobot(cradle));
    assemblyLine.execute(new WheelRobot(cradle));
    assemblyLine.execute(
      new Director(chassisQueue, finishingQueue, cradle));
    assemblyLine.execute(new Reporter(finishingQueue));
    // Start everything running by producing chassis:
    assemblyLine.execute(new ChassisBuilder(chassisQueue));
    cin.get();
    assemblyLine.interrupt();
  } catch(Synchronization_Exception& e) {
```

```
        cerr << e.what() << endl;
    }
} ///:~
```

You'll notice that **Car** takes a shortcut: it assumes that **bool** operations are atomic, which, as previously discussed, is sometimes a safe assumption but requires careful thought.[14] Each **Car** begins as an unadorned chassis, and different robots will attach different parts to it, calling the appropriate "add" function when they do.

A **ChassisBuilder** simply creates a new **Car** every second and places it into the **chassisQueue**. A **Director** manages the build process by taking the next **Car** off the **chassisQueue**, putting it into the **Cradle**, telling all the robots to **startWork( )**, and suspending itself by calling **waitUntilWorkFinished( )**. When the work is done, the **Director** takes the **Car** out of the **Cradle** and puts in into the **finishingQueue**.

The **Cradle** is the crux of the signaling operations. A **Mutex** and a **Condition** object control both the working of the robots and indicate whether all the operations are finished. A particular type of robot can offer its services to the **Cradle** by calling the "offer" function appropriate to its type. At this point, that robot thread is suspended until the **Director** calls **startWork( )**, which changes the hiring flags and calls **broadcast( )** to tell all the robots to show up for work. Although this system allows any number of robots to offer their services, each one of those robots has its thread suspended by doing so. You could imagine a more sophisticated system where the robots register themselves with many different **Cradle**s without being suspended by that registration process and then reside in a pool waiting for the first **Cradle** that needs a task completed.

After each robot finishes its task (changing the state of the **Car** in the process), it calls **taskFinished( )**, which sends a **signal( )** to the **readyCondition**, which is what the **Director** is waiting on in **waitUntilWorkFinished( )**. Each time the director thread awakens, the state of the **Car** is checked, and if it still isn't finished, that thread is suspended again.

---

[14] In particular, refer to the earlier footnote in this chapter on multiprocessors and visibility.

When the **Director** inserts a **Car** into the **Cradle**, you can perform operations on that **Car** via the **operator->( )**. To prevent multiple extractions of the same car, a flag causes an error report to be generated. (Exceptions don't propagate across threads in the ZThread library.)

In **main( )**, all the necessary objects are created and the tasks are initialized, with the **ChassisBuilder** begun last to start the process. (However, because of the behavior of the **TQueue**, it wouldn't matter if it were started first.) Note that this program follows all the guidelines regarding object and task lifetime presented in this chapter, and so the shutdown process is safe.

Deadlock

Because threads can become blocked *and* because objects can have mutexes that prevent threads from accessing that object until the mutex is released, it's possible for one thread to get stuck waiting for another thread, which in turn waits for another thread, and so on, until the chain leads back to a thread waiting on the first one. You get a continuous loop of threads waiting on each other, and no one can move. This is called *deadlock*.

If you try running a program and it deadlocks right away, you immediately know you have a problem, and you can track it down. The real problem is when your program seems to be working fine but has the hidden potential to deadlock. In this case, you may get no indication that deadlocking is a possibility, so it will be latent in your program until it unexpectedly happens to a customer. (And you probably won't be able to easily reproduce it.) Thus, preventing deadlock through careful program design is a critical part of developing concurrent programs.

Let's look at the classic demonstration of deadlock, invented by Edsger Dijkstra: the *dining philosophers* problem. The basic description specifies five philosophers (but the example shown here will allow any number). These philosophers spend part of their time thinking and part of their time eating. While they are thinking, they don't need any shared resources, but they eat using a limited number of utensils. In the original problem description, the utensils are forks, and two forks are required to get spaghetti from a bowl in the middle of the table, but it seems to make more sense to say that the utensils are chopsticks. Clearly, each philosopher will require two chopsticks in order to eat.

A difficulty is introduced into the problem: as philosophers, they have very little money, so they can only afford five chopsticks. These are spaced around the table between them. When a philosopher wants to eat, they must pick up the chopstick to the left and the one to the right. If the philosopher on either side is using a desired chopstick, our philosopher must wait until the necessary chopsticks become available.

```cpp
//: C11:DiningPhilosophers.h
// Classes for Dining Philosophers.
#ifndef DININGPHILOSOPHERS_H
#define DININGPHILOSOPHERS_H
#include <string>
#include <iostream>
#include <cstdlib>
#include "zthread/Condition.h"
#include "zthread/Guard.h"
#include "zthread/Mutex.h"
#include "zthread/Thread.h"
#include "Display.h"

class Chopstick {
  ZThread::Mutex lock;
  ZThread::Condition notTaken;
  bool taken;
public:
  Chopstick() : notTaken(lock), taken(false) {}
  void take() {
    ZThread::Guard<ZThread::Mutex> g(lock);
    while(taken)
      notTaken.wait();
    taken = true;
  }
  void drop() {
    ZThread::Guard<ZThread::Mutex> g(lock);
    taken = false;
    notTaken.signal();
  }
};

class Philosopher : public ZThread::Runnable {
  Chopstick& left;
  Chopstick& right;
  int id;
  int ponderFactor;
```

```
  ZThread::CountedPtr<Display> display;
  int randSleepTime() {
    if(ponderFactor == 0) return 0;
    return rand()/(RAND_MAX/ponderFactor) * 250;
  }
  void output(std::string s) {
    std::ostringstream os;
    os << *this << " " << s << std::endl;
    display->output(os);
  }
public:
  Philosopher(Chopstick& l, Chopstick& r,
  ZThread::CountedPtr<Display>& disp, int ident,int ponder)
  : left(l), right(r), id(ident), ponderFactor(ponder),
    display(disp) {}
  virtual void run() {
    try {
      while(!ZThread::Thread::interrupted()) {
        output("thinking");
        ZThread::Thread::sleep(randSleepTime());
        // Hungry
        output("grabbing right");
        right.take();
        output("grabbing left");
        left.take();
        output("eating");
        ZThread::Thread::sleep(randSleepTime());
        right.drop();
        left.drop();
      }
    } catch(ZThread::Synchronization_Exception& e) {
      output(e.what());
    }
  }
  friend std::ostream&
  operator<<(std::ostream& os, const Philosopher& p) {
    return os << "Philosopher " << p.id;
  }
};
#endif // DININGPHILOSOPHERS_H ///:~
```

No two **Philosopher**s can **take( )** a **Chopstick** at the same time, since
take( ) is synchronized with a **Mutex**. In addition, if the chopstick has
already been taken by one **Philosopher**, another can **wait( )** on the

available Condition until the **Chopstick** becomes available when the current holder calls **drop( )** (which must also be synchronized to prevent race conditions and ensure memory visibility in multiprocessor systems).

Each **Philosopher** holds references to their left and right **Chopstick** so they can attempt to pick those up. The goal of the **Philosopher** is to think part of the time and eat part of the time, and this is expressed in **main( )**. However, you will observe that if the **Philosopher**s spend very little time thinking, they will all be competing for the **Chopstick**s while they try to eat, and deadlock will happen much more quickly. So you can experiment with this, the **ponderFactor** weights the length of time that a **Philosopher** tends to spend thinking and eating. A smaller **ponderFactor** will increase the probability of deadlock.

In **Philosopher::run( )**, each **Philosopher** just thinks and eats continuously. You see the **Philosopher** thinking for a randomized amount of time, then trying to **take( )** the **right** and then the **left Chopstick**, eating for a randomized amount of time, and then doing it again. Output to the console is synchronized as seen earlier in this chapter.

This problem is interesting because it demonstrates that a program can appear to run correctly but actually be deadlock prone. To show this, the command-line argument adjusts a factor to affect the amount of time each philosopher spends thinking. If you have lots of philosophers or they spend a lot of time thinking, you may never see the deadlock even though it remains a possibility. A command-line argument of zero tends to make it deadlock fairly quickly:[15]

```
//: C11:DeadlockingDiningPhilosophers.cpp {RunByHand}
// Dining Philosophers with Deadlock.
//{L} ZThread
#include <ctime>
#include "DiningPhilosophers.h"
#include "zthread/ThreadedExecutor.h"
```

---

[15] At the time of this writing, Cygwin (www.cygwin.com) was undergoing changes and improvements to its threading support, but we were still unable to observe deadlocking behavior with this program under the available version of Cygwin. The program deadlocked quickly under, for example, Linux.

```
using namespace ZThread;
using namespace std;

int main(int argc, char* argv[]) {
  srand(time(0)); // Seed the random number generator
  int ponder = argc > 1 ? atoi(argv[1]) : 5;
  cout << "Press <ENTER> to quit" << endl;
  enum { SZ = 5 };
  try {
    CountedPtr<Display> d(new Display);
    ThreadedExecutor executor;
    Chopstick c[SZ];
    for(int i = 0; i < SZ; i++) {
      executor.execute(
        new Philosopher(c[i], c[(i+1) % SZ], d, i,ponder));
    }
    cin.get();
    executor.interrupt();
    executor.wait();
  } catch(Synchronization_Exception& e) {
    cerr << e.what() << endl;
  }
} ///:~
```

Note that the **Chopstick** objects do not need internal identifiers; they are identified by their position in the array **c**. Each **Philosopher** is given a reference to a left and right **Chopstick** object when constructed; these are the utensils that must be picked up before that **Philosopher** can eat. Every **Philosopher** except the last one is initialized by situating that **Philosopher** between the next pair of **Chopstick** objects. The last **Philosopher** is given the zeroth **Chopstick** for its right **Chopstick**, so the round table is completed. That's because the last **Philosopher** is sitting right next to the first one, and they both share that zeroth chopstick. With this arrangement, it's possible at some point for all the philosophers to be trying to eat and waiting on the philosopher next to them to put down their chopstick, and the program will deadlock.

If your threads (philosophers) are spending more time on other tasks (thinking) than eating, then they have a much lower probability of requiring the shared resources (chopsticks), and thus you can convince yourself that the program is deadlock free (using a nonzero **ponder** value), even though it isn't.

To repair the problem, you must understand that deadlock can occur if four conditions are simultaneously met:

1. Mutual exclusion. At least one resource used by the threads must not be shareable. In this case, a chopstick can be used by only one philosopher at a time.

2. At least one process must be holding a resource and waiting to acquire a resource currently held by another process. That is, for deadlock to occur, a philosopher must be holding one chopstick and waiting for another one.

3. A resource cannot be preemptively taken away from a process. Processes only release resources as a normal event. Our philosophers are polite and they don't grab chopsticks from other philosophers.

4. A circular wait can happen, whereby a process waits on a resource held by another process, which in turn is waiting on a resource held by another process, and so on, until one of the processes is waiting on a resource held by the first process, thus gridlocking everything. In **DeadlockingDiningPhilosophers.cpp**, the circular wait happens because each philosopher tries to get the right chopstick first and then the left.

Because all these conditions must be met to cause deadlock, you need to stop only one of them from occurring to prevent deadlock. In this program, the easiest way to prevent deadlock is to break condition four. This condition happens because each philosopher is trying to pick up their chopsticks in a particular sequence: first right, then left. Because of that, it's possible to get into a situation where each of them is holding their right chopstick and waiting to get the left, causing the circular wait condition. However, if the last philosopher is initialized to try to get the left chopstick first and then the right, that philosopher will never prevent the philosopher on the immediate right from picking up their left chopstick. In this case, the circular wait is prevented. This is only one solution to the problem, but you could also solve it by preventing one of the other conditions (see advanced threading books for more details):

```
//: C11:FixedDiningPhilosophers.cpp {RunByHand}
// Dining Philosophers without Deadlock.
//{L} ZThread
#include <ctime>
```

```
#include "DiningPhilosophers.h"
#include "zthread/ThreadedExecutor.h"
using namespace ZThread;
using namespace std;

int main(int argc, char* argv[]) {
  srand(time(0)); // Seed the random number generator
  int ponder = argc > 1 ? atoi(argv[1]) : 5;
  cout << "Press <ENTER> to quit" << endl;
  enum { SZ = 5 };
  try {
    CountedPtr<Display> d(new Display);
    ThreadedExecutor executor;
    Chopstick c[SZ];
    for(int i = 0; i < SZ; i++) {
      if(i < (SZ-1))
        executor.execute(
          new Philosopher(c[i], c[i + 1], d, i, ponder));
      else
        executor.execute(
          new Philosopher(c[0], c[i], d, i, ponder));
    }
    cin.get();
    executor.interrupt();
    executor.wait();
  } catch(Synchronization_Exception& e) {
    cerr << e.what() << endl;
  }
} ///:~
```

By ensuring that the last philosopher picks up and puts down their left chopstick before their right, the deadlock is removed, and the program will run smoothly.

There is no language support to help prevent deadlock; it's up to you to avoid it by careful design. These are not comforting words to the person who's trying to debug a deadlocking program.

Summary

The goal of this chapter was to give you the foundations of concurrent programming with threads:

1. You can run multiple independent tasks.

2. You must consider all the possible problems when these tasks shut down. Objects or other tasks may disappear before tasks are finished with them.

3. Tasks can collide with each other over shared resources. The mutex is the basic tool used to prevent these collisions.

4. Tasks can deadlock if they are not carefully designed.

However, there are multiple additional facets of threading and tools to help you solve threading problems. The ZThreads library contains a number of these tools, such as *semaphores* and special types of queues, similar to the one you saw in this chapter. Explore that library as well as other resources on threading to gain more in-depth knowledge.

It is vital to learn when to use concurrency and when to avoid it. The main reasons to use it are:

- To manage a number of tasks whose intermingling use the computer more efficiently (including the ability to transparently distribute the tasks across multiple CPUs).

- To allow better code organization.

- To be more convenient for the user.

The classic example of resource balancing is to use the CPU during I/O waits. The classic example of user convenience is to monitor a "stop" button during long downloads.

An additional advantage to threads is that they provide "light" execution context switches (on the order of 100 instructions) rather than "heavy" process context switches (thousands of instructions). Since all threads in a given process share the same memory space, a light context switch changes only program execution and local variables. A process change—the heavy context switch—must exchange the full memory space.

The main drawbacks to multithreading are:

- Slowdown occurs while waiting for shared resources.

- Additional CPU overhead is required to manage threads.

- Unrewarded complexity arises from poor design decisions.

- Opportunities are created for pathologies such as starving, racing, deadlock, and livelock.

- Inconsistencies occur across platforms. When developing the original material (in Java) for this chapter, we discovered race conditions that quickly appeared on some computers but wouldn't appear on others. The C++ examples in this chapter behaved differently (but usually acceptably) under different operating systems. If you develop a program on a computer and things seem to work right, you might get an unwelcome surprise when you distribute it.

One of the biggest difficulties with threads occurs because more than one thread might be sharing a resource—such as the memory in an object—and you must make sure that multiple threads don't try to read and change that resource at the same time. This requires judicious use of synchronization tools, which must be thoroughly understood because they can quietly introduce deadlock situations.

In addition, there's a certain art to the application of threads. C++ is designed to allow you to create as many objects as you need to solve your problem—at least in theory. (Creating millions of objects for an engineering finite-element analysis, for example, might not be practical.) However, there is usually an upper bound to the number of threads you'll want to create, because at some number, threads may become balky. This critical point can be difficult to detect and will often depend on the OS and thread library; it could be fewer than a hundred or in the thousands. As you often create only a handful of threads to solve a problem, this is typically not much of a limit; but in a more general design it becomes a constraint.

Regardless of how simple threading can seem using a particular language or library, consider it a black art. There's always something you haven't considered that can bite you when you least expect it. (For example, note that because the dining philosophers problem can be adjusted so that deadlock rarely happens, you can get the impression that everything is OK.) An appropriate quote comes from Guido van Rossum, creator of the Python programming language:

> *In any project that is multithreaded, most bugs will come from threading issues. This is regardless of programming language—it's a deep, as yet un-understood property of threads.*

For more advanced discussions of threading, see *Parallel and Distributed Programming Using C++,* by Cameron Hughes and Tracey Hughes, Addison Wesley 2004.

Exercises

Solutions to selected exercises can be found in the electronic document *The Thinking in C++ Volume 2 Annotated Solution Guide*, available for a small fee from *www.MindView.net*.

1.   Inherit a class from **Runnable** and override the **run( )** function. Inside **run( )**, print a message, and then call **sleep( )**. Repeat this three times, and then return from **run( )**. Put a start-up message in the constructor and a shut-down message when the task terminates. Make several thread objects of this type, and run them to see what happens.

2.   Modify **BasicThreads.cpp** to make **LiftOff** threads start other **LiftOff** threads.

3.   Modify **ResponsiveUI.cpp** to eliminate any possible race conditions. (Assume **bool** operations are not atomic.)

4.   In **Incrementer.cpp**, modify the **Count** class to use a single **int** instead of an array of **int**. Explain the resulting behavior.

5.   In **EvenChecker.h**, correct the potential problem in the **Generator** class. (Assume **bool** operations are not atomic.)

6.   Modify **EvenGenerator.cpp** to use **interrupt( )** instead of quit flags.

7.   In **MutexEvenGenerator.cpp**, change the code in **MutexEvenGenerator::nextValue( )** so that the return expression precedes the **release( )** statement and explain what happens.

8.   Modify **ResponsiveUI.cpp** to use **interrupt( )** instead of the **quitFlag** approach.

9.   Look up the **Singleton** documentation in the ZThreads library. Modify **OrnamentalGarden.cpp** so that the **Display** object is

controlled by a **Singleton** to prevent more than one **Display** from being accidentally created.

10. In **OrnamentalGarden.cpp**, change the **Count::increment( )** function so that it does a direct increment of **count** (that is, it just does a **count++**). Now remove the guard and see if that causes a failure. Is this safe and reliable?

11. Modify **OrnamentalGarden.cpp** so that it uses **interrupt( )** instead of the **pause( )** mechanism. Make sure that your solution doesn't prematurely destroy objects.

12. Modify **WaxOMatic.cpp** by adding more instances of the **Process** class so that it applies and polishes three coats of wax instead of just one.

13. Create two **Runnable** subclasses, one with a **run( )** that starts and calls **wait( )**. The other class's **run( )** should capture the reference of the first **Runnable** object. Its **run( )** should call **signal( )** for the first thread after some number of seconds have passed so that first thread can print a message.

14. Create an example of a "busy wait." One thread sleeps for awhile and then sets a flag to **true**. The second thread watches that flag inside a **while** loop (this is the "busy wait") and, when the flag becomes **true**, sets it back to **false** and reports the change to the console. Note how much wasted time the program spends inside the "busy wait," and create a second version of the program that uses **wait( )** instead of the "busy wait." Extra: run a profiler to show the time used by the CPU in each case.

15. Modify **TQueue.h** to add a maximum allowable element count. If the count is reached, further writes should be blocked until the count drops below the maximum. Write code to test this behavior.

16. Modify **ToastOMaticMarkII.cpp** to create peanut-butter and jelly on toast sandwiches using two separate assembly lines and an output **TQueue** for the finished sandwiches. Use a **Reporter** object as in **CarBuilder.cpp** to display the results.

17. Rewrite **C07:BankTeller.cpp** to use real threading instead of simulated threading.

18. Modify **CarBuilder.cpp** to give identifiers to the robots, and add more instances of the different kinds of robots. Note whether all robots get utilized.

19. Modify **CarBuilder.cpp** to add another stage to the car-building process, whereby you add the exhaust system, body, and fenders.

As with the first stage, assume these processes can be performed simultaneously by robots.

20.   Modify **CarBuilder.cpp** so that **Car** has synchronized access to all the **bool** variables. Because **Mutex**es cannot be copied, this will require significant changes throughout the program.

21.   Using the approach in **CarBuilder.cpp**, model the house-building story that was given in this chapter.

22.   Create a **Timer** class with two options: (1) a one-shot timer that only goes off once (2) a timer that goes off at regular intervals. Use this class with **C10:MulticastCommand.cpp** to move the calls to **TaskRunner::run( )** from the procedures into the timer.

23.   Change both of the dining philosophers examples so that the number of **Philosopher**s is controlled on the command line, in addition to the ponder time. Try different values and explain the results.

24.   Change **DiningPhilosophers.cpp** so that the **Philosopher**s just pick the next available chopstick. (When a **Philosopher** is done with their chopsticks, they drop them into a bin. When a **Philosopher** wants to eat, they take the next two available chopsticks from the bin.) Does this eliminate the possibility of deadlock? Can you reintroduce deadlock by simply reducing the number of available chopsticks?

A: Recommended Reading

General C++

The C++ Programming Language, 3rd edition, by Bjarne Stroustrup (Addison Wesley 1997). To some degree, the goal of the book that you're currently holding is to allow you to use Bjarne's book as a reference. Since his book contains the description of the language by the author of that language, it's typically the place where you'll go to resolve any uncertainties about what C++ is or isn't supposed to do. When you get the knack of the language and are ready to get serious, you'll need it.

C++ Primer, 3rd Edition, by Stanley Lippman and Josee Lajoie (Addison Wesley 1998). Not that much of a primer anymore; it's evolved into a thick book filled with lots of detail, and the one that I reach for along with Stroustrup's when trying to resolve an issue. *Thinking in C++* should provide a basis for understanding the *C++ Primer* as well as Stroustrup's book.

Accelerated C++, by Andrew Koenig and Barbara Moo (Addison Wesley, 2000). Takes you through C++ by programming topic instead of language feature. Excellent introductory book.

The C++ Standard Library, by Nicolai Josuttis (Addison Wesley, 1999). Readable tutorial and reference for the entire C++ library, including STL. Assumes familiarity with language concepts.

STL Tutorial and Reference Guide, 2nd Edition, by David R. Musser et al (Addison Wesley, 2001). Gentle but thorough introduction to the concepts underlying STL. Contains an STL reference manual.

The C++ ANSI/ISO Standard. This is *not* free, unfortunately (I certainly didn't get paid for my time and effort on the Standards Committee—in fact, it cost me a lot of money). But at least you can buy the electronic form in PDF for only $18 at http://www.ncits.org/cplusplus.htm.

Bruce's books

Listed in order of publication. Not all these are currently available.

Computer Interfacing with Pascal & C, (Self-published via the Eisys imprint, 1988. Only available via *www.MindView.net*). An introduction to electronics from back when CP/M was still king and DOS was an upstart. I used high-level languages and often the parallel port of the computer to drive various electronic projects. Adapted from my columns in the first and best magazine I wrote for, *Micro Cornucopia*. (To paraphrase Larry O'Brien, long-time editor of *Software Development Magazine*: The best computer magazine ever published—they even had plans for building a robot in a flower pot!) Alas, Micro C became lost long before the Internet appeared. Creating this book was an extremely satisfying publishing experience.

Using C++, (Osborne/McGraw-Hill, 1989). One of the first books out on C++. This is out of print and replaced by its second edition, the renamed *C++ Inside & Out*.

C++ Inside & Out, (Osborne/McGraw-Hill, 1993). As noted, this is actually the second edition of **Using C++**. The C++ in this book is reasonably accurate, but it's circa 1992 and *Thinking in C++* is intended to replace it. You can find out more about this book and download the source code at *www.MindView.net*.

Thinking in C++, 1ˢᵗ Edition, (Prentice Hall, 1995). Winner of the *Software Development Magazine Jolt Award* for best book of 1995.

Thinking in C++, 2ⁿᵈ Edition, Volume 1, (Prentice Hall, 2000). Downloadable from *www.MindView.net*.

Black Belt C++: the Master's Collection, Bruce Eckel, editor (M&T Books, 1994). Out of print (often available through out-of-print services on the Web). A collection of chapters by various C++ luminaries based on their presentations in the C++ track at the Software Development Conference, which I chaired. The cover on this book stimulated me to gain control over all future cover designs.

Thinking in Java, 1ˢᵗ Edition, (Prentice Hall, 1998). The first edition of this book won the *Software Development Magazine Productivity Award*, the *Java Developer's Journal* Editor's Choice Award, and the *JavaWorld Reader's Choice Award for best book*. On the CD ROM in the back of this book, and downloadable from *www.MindView.net*.

Thinking in Java, 2ⁿᵈ Edition, (Prentice Hall, 2000). This edition won the *JavaWorld Editor's Choice Award for best book*. On the CD ROM in the back of this book, and downloadable from *www.MindView.net*.

Thinking in Java, 3ʳᵈ Edition, (Prentice Hall, 2002). This edition won the *Software Development Magazine Jolt Award* for best book of 2002, and the *Java Developer's Journal* Editor's Choice Award. The new CD ROM in the back of this book now includes the first seven lectures from the 2ⁿᵈ edition of the *Hands-On Java CD ROM*.

The Hands-On Java CD ROM, 3ʳᵈ edition (MindView, 2004). Over 15 hours of Bruce's lectures and slides covering the basics of the Java language, based on *Thinking in Java, 3ʳᵈ Edition*. Available only at www.MindView.net.

Chuck's books

C & C++ Code Capsules, by Chuck Allison (Prentice-Hall, 1998). An in-the-trenches guide for practical C and C++ programming. Thoroughly covers the 1998 ISO C++ standard, especially library features, and serves as a bridge to more advanced topics. Based on Chuck's well-known column in the C/C++ Users Journal.

Thinking in C: Foundations for Java & C++, by Chuck Allison (*not a book*, but a MindView, Inc. Seminar on CD ROM, 1999, bundled with *Thinking in Java* and *Thinking in C++, Volume 1*). A multimedia course including lectures and slides in the foundations of the C Language, to prepare you to learn Java or C++. This is not an exhaustive course in C; only the necessities for moving on to the other languages are included. An extra section covering features for the C++ programmer is included. Prerequisite: experience with a high-level programming language, such as Pascal, BASIC, FORTRAN, or LISP.

In-depth C++

Books that go more deeply into topics of the language, and help you avoid the typical pitfalls inherent in developing C++ programs.

Large-Scale C++ Software Design, by John Lakos (Addison Wesley, 1996). Motivates and presents in-the-trenches techniques for large C++ projects.

B: Etc

This appendix contains files that are required to build the
examples in Volume 2.

```cpp
//: :require.h
// Test for error conditions in programs.
#ifndef REQUIRE_H
#define REQUIRE_H
#include <cstdio>
#include <cstdlib>
#include <fstream>

inline void require(bool requirement,
  const char* msg = "Requirement failed") {
  // Local "using namespace std" for old compilers:
  using namespace std;
  if(!requirement) {
    fputs(msg, stderr);
    fputs("\n", stderr);
    exit(EXIT_FAILURE);
  }
}

inline void requireArgs(int argc, int args,
  const char* msg = "Must use %d arguments") {
  using namespace std;
  if(argc != args + 1) {
    fprintf(stderr, msg, args);
    fputs("\n", stderr);
    exit(EXIT_FAILURE);
  }
}

inline void requireMinArgs(int argc, int minArgs,
  const char* msg = "Must use at least %d arguments") {
  using namespace std;
  if(argc < minArgs + 1) {
    fprintf(stderr, msg, minArgs);
    fputs("\n", stderr);
    exit(EXIT_FAILURE);
  }
```

```
   }

   inline void assure(std::ifstream& in,
     const char* filename = "") {
     using namespace std;
     if(!in) {
       fprintf(stderr, "Could not open file %s\n", filename);
       exit(EXIT_FAILURE);
     }
   }

   inline void assure(std::ofstream& in,
     const char* filename = "") {
     using namespace std;
     if(!in) {
       fprintf(stderr, "Could not open file %s\n", filename);
       exit(EXIT_FAILURE);
     }
   }

   inline void assure(std::fstream& in,
     const char* filename = "") {
     using namespace std;
     if(!in) {
       fprintf(stderr, "Could not open file %s\n", filename);
       exit(EXIT_FAILURE);
     }
   }
#endif // REQUIRE_H ///:~

//: C0B:Dummy.cpp
// To give the makefile at least
// one target for this directory.
int main() {} ///:~
```

The **Date** class files:

```
//: C02:Date.h
#ifndef DATE_H
#define DATE_H
#include <string>
#include <stdexcept>
#include <iosfwd>

class Date {
```

```
    int year, month, day;
    int compare(const Date&) const;
    static int daysInPrevMonth(int year, int mon);
public:
  // A class for date calculations
  struct Duration {
    int years, months, days;
    Duration(int y, int m, int d)
    : years(y), months(m) ,days(d) {}
  };
  // An exception class
  struct DateError : public std::logic_error {
    DateError(const std::string& msg = "")
    : std::logic_error(msg) {}
  };
  Date();
  Date(int, int, int) throw(DateError);
  Date(const std::string&) throw(DateError);
  int getYear() const;
  int getMonth() const;
  int getDay() const;
  std::string toString() const;
  friend Duration duration(const Date&, const Date&);
  friend bool operator<(const Date&, const Date&);
  friend bool operator<=(const Date&, const Date&);
  friend bool operator>(const Date&, const Date&);
  friend bool operator>=(const Date&, const Date&);
  friend bool operator==(const Date&, const Date&);
  friend bool operator!=(const Date&, const Date&);
  friend std::ostream& operator<<(std::ostream&,
                                  const Date&);
  friend std::istream& operator>>(std::istream&, Date&);
};
#endif // DATE_H ///:~

//: C02:Date.cpp {O}
#include "Date.h"
#include <iostream>
#include <sstream>
#include <cstdlib>
#include <string>
#include <algorithm> // For swap()
#include <ctime>
#include <cassert>
#include <iomanip>
```

```
using namespace std;

namespace {
  const int daysInMonth[][13] = {
    { 0, 31, 28, 31, 30, 31, 30, 31, 31, 30, 31, 30, 31 },
    { 0, 31, 29, 31, 30, 31, 30, 31, 31, 30, 31, 30, 31 }
  };
  inline bool isleap(int y) {
    return y%4 == 0 && y%100 != 0 || y%400 == 0;
  }
}

Date::Date() {
  // Get current date
  time_t tval = time(0);
  struct tm *now = localtime(&tval);
  year = now->tm_year + 1900;
  month = now->tm_mon + 1;
  day = now->tm_mday;
}

Date::Date(int yr,int mon,int dy) throw(Date::DateError) {
  if(!(1 <= mon && mon <= 12))
    throw DateError("Bad month in Date ctor");
  if(!(1 <= dy && dy <= daysInMonth[isleap(year)][mon]))
    throw DateError("Bad day in Date ctor");
  year = yr;
  month = mon;
  day = dy;
}

Date::Date(const std::string& s) throw(Date::DateError) {
  // Assume YYYYMMDD format
  if(!(s.size() == 8))
    throw DateError("Bad string in Date ctor");
  for(int n = 8; --n >= 0;)
    if(!isdigit(s[n]))
      throw DateError("Bad string in Date ctor");
  string buf = s.substr(0, 4);
  year = atoi(buf.c_str());
  buf = s.substr(4, 2);
  month = atoi(buf.c_str());
  buf = s.substr(6, 2);
  day = atoi(buf.c_str());
  if(!(1 <= month && month <= 12))
```

```cpp
      throw DateError("Bad month in Date ctor");
  if(!(1 <= day && day <=
    daysInMonth[isleap(year)][month]))
      throw DateError("Bad day in Date ctor");
}

int Date::getYear() const { return year; }

int Date::getMonth() const { return month; }

int Date::getDay() const { return day; }

string Date::toString() const {
  ostringstream os;
  os.fill('0');
  os << setw(4) << year
     << setw(2) << month
     << setw(2) << day;
  return os.str();
}

int Date::compare(const Date& d2) const {
  int result = year - d2.year;
  if(result == 0) {
    result = month - d2.month;
    if(result == 0)
      result = day - d2.day;
  }
  return result;
}

int Date::daysInPrevMonth(int year, int month) {
  if(month == 1) {
    --year;
    month = 12;
  }
  else
    --month;
  return daysInMonth[isleap(year)][month];
}

bool operator<(const Date& d1, const Date& d2) {
  return d1.compare(d2) < 0;
}
bool operator<=(const Date& d1, const Date& d2) {
```

```cpp
    return d1 < d2 || d1 == d2;
}
bool operator>(const Date& d1, const Date& d2) {
    return !(d1 < d2) && !(d1 == d2);
}
bool operator>=(const Date& d1, const Date& d2) {
    return !(d1 < d2);
}
bool operator==(const Date& d1, const Date& d2) {
    return d1.compare(d2) == 0;
}
bool operator!=(const Date& d1, const Date& d2) {
    return !(d1 == d2);
}

Date::Duration
duration(const Date& date1, const Date& date2) {
    int y1 = date1.year;
    int y2 = date2.year;
    int m1 = date1.month;
    int m2 = date2.month;
    int d1 = date1.day;
    int d2 = date2.day;

    // Compute the compare
    int order = date1.compare(date2);
    if(order == 0)
        return Date::Duration(0,0,0);
    else if(order > 0) {
        // Make date1 precede date2 locally
        using std::swap;
        swap(y1, y2);
        swap(m1, m2);
        swap(d1, d2);
    }

    int years = y2 - y1;
    int months = m2 - m1;
    int days = d2 - d1;
    assert(years > 0 ||
        years == 0 && months > 0 ||
        years == 0 && months == 0 && days > 0);

    // Do the obvious corrections (must adjust days
    // before months!) - This is a loop in case the
```

```
  // previous month is February, and days < -28.
  int lastMonth = m2;
  int lastYear = y2;
  while(days < 0) {
    // Borrow from month
    assert(months > 0);
    days += Date::daysInPrevMonth(
      lastYear, lastMonth--);
    --months;
  }

  if(months < 0) {
    // Borrow from year
    assert(years > 0);
    months += 12;
    --years;
  }
  return Date::Duration(years, months, days);
}

ostream& operator<<(ostream& os, const Date& d) {
  char fillc = os.fill('0');
  os << setw(2) << d.getMonth() << '-'
     << setw(2) << d.getDay() << '-'
     << setw(4) << setfill(fillc) << d.getYear();
  return os;
}

istream& operator>>(istream& is, Date& d) {
  is >> d.month;
  char dash;
  is >> dash;
  if(dash != '-')
    is.setstate(ios::failbit);
  is >> d.day;
  is >> dash;
  if(dash != '-')
    is.setstate(ios::failbit);
  is >> d.year;
  return is;
} ///:~
```

The file test.txt used in Chapter 6:

```
//: C06:Test.txt
```

```
f a f d A  G f d F a A F h f A d f f a a
/ / / :~
```

Index

remove_if · 389; removing elements · 389; **replace** · 380; **replace_copy** · 380; **replace_copy_if** · 330, 380; **replace_if** · 330, 380; **reverse** · 372; **reverse_copy** · 372; **rotate** · 373; **rotate_copy** · 373; **search** · 379; **search_n** · 379; searching and replacing · 377; **set** operations · 400; **set_difference** · 401; **set_intersection** · 401; **set_symmetric_difference** · 402; **set_union** · 401; **sort** · 366, 393; **sort_heap** · 404; sorting · 393; **stable_partition** · 374; **stable_sort** · 366, 393; **swap** · 419; **swap_ranges** · 373; **transform** · 347, 349, 355, 405; **unique** · 390; **unique_copy** · 390; **upper_bound** · 395; utilities · 417

ANSI/ISO C++ Committee · 9

applicator algorithms · 405

applicator, iostreams manipulator · 200

applying a function to a container · 255

argument_type · 342

argument-dependent lookup · 274, 278; disabling · 275

assert macro · 66

assertion · 66; side effects in an · 67

Assignable · 337

associative container · 433, 513

atof( ) · 181

atoi( ) · 181

atomic operation · 732

auto_ptr · 35; not for containers · 437

automated testing · 71

automatic type conversion, and exception handling · 23

C

D

E

effectors · 201

efficiency: runtime type identification · 565; threads and · 693

Eisenecker, Ulrich · 300

ellipses, with exception handling · 25

endl · 195

envelope, and letter classes · 655

eofbit · 166

epsilon( ) · 181

equal algorithm · 327, 385

equal_range algorithm · 396

equal_to function object · 339, 341

EqualityComparable · 337

errno · 16

error: handling · 15; handling, in C · 16; recovery · 15; reporting errors in book · 10

event-driven programming, and the Command pattern · 628

exception class · 38; **what( )** · 38

exception handling · 15; asynchronous events · 53; atomic allocations for safety · 32; automatic type conversions · 23; **bad_cast** exception class · 40, 557; **bad_exception** class · 44; **bad_typeid** exception class · 40, 559; catching an exception · 20; catching any exception · 25, 26; catching by reference · 23; catching via accessible base · 25; class hierarchies · 24; cleaning up the stack during a throw · 28; constructors · 29, 30, 57; destructors · 28, 36, 57; **domain_error** exception class · 40; ellipses · 25; **exception** class · 38; **exception** class, **what( )** · 38; exception handler · 20; exception hierarchies · 56; exception matching · 23; exception neutral · 52; exception

safety · 48; exception specifications · 40; **exception** type · 39; incomplete objects · 29; inheritance · 24; **invalid_argument** exception class · 40, **length_error** exception class · 40; **logic_error** class · 38; memory leaks · 29; multiple inheritance · 56; naked pointers · 30; object slicing and · 23; **out_of_range** exception class · 40; overhead of · 58; programming guidelines · 52; references · 34, 56; resource management · 30; rethrowing an exception · 26, 52; **runtime_error** class · 38; **set_terminate( )** · 27; **set_unexpected( )** · 41; specifications, and inheritance · 46; specifications, covariance of · 47; specifications, when not to use · 47; stack unwinding · 19; Standard C++ library exceptions · 38; **terminate( )** · 44; termination vs. resumption · 22; testing · 79; throwing & catching pointers · 57; throwing an exception · 18, 19; typical uses of exceptions · 54; uncaught exceptions · 26, 28; **unexpected( )** · 41; when to avoid · 52; zero-cost model · 60; ZThreads (Concurrency) · 708

exception specifications · 40; covariance of · 47; inheritance · 46; when not to use · 47

exclusion, mutual, in threads · 719

Executors, ZThread (Concurrency) · 702

explicit instantiation, of templates · 316

export keyword · 319

exported templates · 319

expression templates · 308

extractor, stream · 158

Extreme Programming (XP) · 71, 615

F

G

generate_n algorithm · 369

generator · 337, 369

generic algorithms · 325

get pointer · 177

get( ) · 170; overloaded versions · 165

getline( ) · 164, 171

getline( ), for strings · 129

getPriority( ) · 711

GoF, Gang of Four · 613

goodbit · 166

greater function object · 338, 341, 371

greater_equal function object · 341

Guard template, ZThread (concurrency) · 721

H

handler, exception · 20

handshaking, between concurrent tasks · 742

hash_map non-standard container · 539

hash_multimap non-standard container · 539

hash_multiset non-standard container · 539

hash_set non-standard container · 539

heap operations · 403

hex · 187

hierarchy, object-based · 573

I

I/O: console · 162; interactive · 162; raw · 165; threads, blocking · 737

i18n, see *internationalization* · 216

ifstream · 156, 168, 174

ignore( ) · 170

imbue( ) · 220

implementation inheritance · 579

includes algorithm · 400

inclusion model, of template compilation · 315

incomplete type · 163

in-core formatting · 179

inheritance: design patterns · 614; diamond · 588; hierarchies · 573; implementation · 579; interface · 575

inheritance, multiple · 573, 673; avoiding · 603; dominance · 601; name lookup · 599; runtime type identification · 560, 563, 570

initialization: controlling initialization order · 621; lazy · 620; object · 596; Resource Acquisition Is Initialization (RAII) · 32, 36, 582; zero initialization · 522

inner class idiom, adapted from Java · 671

inner_product algorithm · 414

inplace_merge algorithm · 399

input iterator · 446

input_iterator_tag · 447

InputIterator · 363

insert( ) · 448

insert_iterator · 372, 448, 482

inserter( ) · 372, 418, 448

inserter, stream · 158

instantiation, template · 260

interactive I/O · 162

interface: class · 576; command-line · 162; extending an · 603; inheritance · 575; repairing an interface with multiple inheritance · 603; responsive user · 700

internationalization · 216

interrupt( ), threading · 735

interrupted status, threading · 739

Interrupted_Exception, threading · 739

invalid_argument exception class · 40

invalidation, iterator · 463

J

K

King, Jamie · 10
Koenig, Andrew · 274
Kreft, Klaus · 314, 780

L

Lajoie, Josee · 60
Langer, Angelika · 314, 780
lazy initialization · 620, 634
length_error exception class · 40
less function object · 341
less_equal function object · 341
LessThanComparable · 337
letter, envelope and letter classes · 655
lexicographical_compare algorithm · 385
library: documentation · 101; maintaining class source · 204
line input · 162
linear search · 377
Linux, and ZThreads · 696
list · 434, 471; **merge( )** · 474; **remove( )** · 474; **reverse( )** · 472; **sort( )** · 472; **unique( )** · 474; vs. **set** · 476
locale · 216, 218; **collate** category · 219; **ctype** category · 219; facet · 220; iostreams · 216; **messages** category · 219; **monetary** category · 219; **money_get** facet · 220; **money_punct** facet · 220; **money_put** facet · 220; **numeric** category · 219; **time** category · 219; **time_get** facet · 220; **time_put** facet · 220
localtime( ) · 213
logic_error class · 38
logical_and function object · 341

logical_not function object · 341
logical_or function object · 341
longjmp( ) · 16
loop: invariant · 64; unrolling · 301
lower_bound algorithm · 395

M

machine epsilon · 181
maintaining class library source · 204
make_heap algorithm · 404, 499
make_pair( ) · 417
manipulating sequences · 372
manipulators · 160; creating · 199; iostreams formatting · 194; with arguments · 196
map · 521; keys and values · 521
max algorithm · 419
max_element algorithm · 380
mem_fun member pointer adaptor · 355
mem_fun_ref member pointer adaptor · 355
member templates · 242; vs. **virtual** · 245
memory leaks · 90
memory management, and threads · 711
merge algorithm · 399
merging algorithms · 398
Messenger design pattern (idiom) · 617
metaprogramming · 297; compile-time assertions · 304; compile-time looping · 299; compile-time selection · 303; loop unrolling · 301; Turing completeness of · 298
Meyer, Bertrand · 68
Meyers, Scott · 60, 623
min algorithm · 418
min_element algorithm · 379
minus function object · 340
mismatch algorithm · 386

mixin: class · 579; parameterized · 583

model-view-controller (MVC) · 667

modulus function object · 341

money_get · 220

money_punct · 220

money_put · 220

multimap · 523

Multiple Dispatching design pattern · 679

multiple inheritance · 573, 673; avoiding · 603; dominance · 601; duplicate subobjects · 585; exception handling · 56; name lookup · 599; repairing an interface · 603; runtime type identification · 560, 563, 570

multiplies function object · 341

multiprocessor machine, and threading · 692

multiset · 527; **equal_range( )** · 529

multitasking · 691

multithreading · 691; drawbacks · 771; ZThread library for C++ · 694

mutex: simplifying with the Guard template · 721; threading · 742; ZThread **FastMutex** · 731

mutual exclusion, in threads · 719

Myers, Nathan · 11, 251, 285, 452, 481, 482

N

naked pointers, and exception handling · 30

name lookup, and multiple inheritance · 599

name( ), RTTI function · 559

narrow streams · 216

narrow( ) · 218

negate function object · 341

new, placement · 91

newline, differences between DOS and Unix · 172

next_permutation algorithm · 373

not_equal_to function object · 341

not1 function object adaptor · 339, 352

nth_element algorithm · 394

numeric algorithms · 413

numeric_limits · 203, 285

O

object: initialization · 596; object-based hierarchy · 573; slicing, and exception handling · 23

Observable · 668

Observer design pattern · 667

oct · 187

ofstream · 156, 168

one-definition rule · 622

open modes, iostreams · 171

operator new( ) · 90

operator void*( ), for streams · 167

operator( ) · 229, 335, 339

operator++( ) · 234

optimization, throughput, with threading · 692

order: controlling initialization · 621; of constructor and destructor calls · 562

ordering: algorithms · 393; strict weak · 337

ostream · 156; **fill( )** · 160; manipulators · 160; **seekp( )** · 176; **setfill( )** · 160; **setw( )** · 160; **tellp** · 176; **write( )** · 165

ostream_iterator · 332, 365, 446, 451

ostreambuf_iterator · 446, 451

ostringstream · 156, 179; **str( )** · 182

out_of_range exception class · 40

output: iterator · 446; stream formatting · 186

raw_storage_iterator · 446, 452

rbegin( ) · 445, 448

rdbuf( ) · 174

read( ) · 165

refactoring · 70

reference counting · 582, 634; ZThreads (Concurrency) · 712

references: **bad_cast** · 557; exception handling · 34, 56

remove algorithm · 389

remove_copy algorithm · 389

remove_copy_if algorithm · 329, 339, 350, 390

remove_if algorithm · 389

removing elements, algorithm · 389

rend( ) · 445, 448

reordering, stable and unstable · 366

replace algorithm · 380

replace_copy algorithm · 380

replace_copy_if algorithm · 330, 380

replace_if algorithm · 330, 380

reporting errors in book · 10

requirements · 70

reserve( ) · 458

resize( ) · 456

Resource Acquisition Is Initialization (RAII) · 32, 36, 582

responsive user interfaces · 700

result_type · 342

resumption, vs. termination, exception handling · 22

rethrow, exception · 26, 52

reverse algorithm · 372

reverse_copy algorithm · 372

reverse_iterator · 445, 448, 487

reversible container · 445

rope non-standard string class · 539

rotate algorithm · 373

rotate_copy algorithm · 373

Runnable · 696

runtime cast · 551

runtime stack · 228

runtime type identification · 551; casting to intermediate levels · 560; **const** and **volatile** and · 558; difference between **dynamic_cast** and **typeid** · 561; efficiency · 565; mechanism & overhead · 570; misuse · 564; multiple inheritance · 560, 563, 570; templates and · 562; **type_info** · 570; **type_info** class · 557; **type_info::before( )** · 559; **type_info::name( )** · 559; **typeid** operator · 557; void pointers · 561; VTABLE · 570; when to use it · 564

runtime_error class · 38

S

Saks, Dan · 282

Schwarz, Jerry · 201

search algorithm · 379

search_n algorithm · 379

searching and replacing algorithms · 377

second_argument_type · 342

seekg( ) · 176

seeking in iostreams · 175

seekp( ) · 176

separation model, of template compilation · 319

sequence: **at( )** · 470; container · 433; converting between sequences · 467; **deque** · 465; **erase( )** · 457; expanding with **resize( )** · 456; **insert( )** · 457; **list** · 471; operations · 454; **operator[ ]** · 471; random-access · 470; **swap( )** · 457; swapping sequences · 477; **vector** · 457

serialization: object · 215; thread · 750

U

V

W

X

Y

Z

DID THE BOOK YOU'RE HOLDING GET YOU THINKING? THEN TRY...

BRUCE ECKEL

THINKING IN JAVA

3RD EDITION

THE DEFINITIVE INTRODUCTION TO OBJECT-ORIENTED PROGRAMMING
IN THE LANGUAGE OF THE WORLD-WIDE WEB

FULL TEXT, UPDATES AND CODE AT HTTP://WWW.BRUCEECKEL.COM

WINNER:

Software Development
Magazine Jolt Award for
Best book of 2002

JavaWorld Editor's Choice
Award for Best Book, 2001

JavaWorld Reader's Choice
Award for Best Book, 2001

Software Development
Magazine Productivity
Award, 1999

Java Developer's Journal
Editor's Choice Award for
Best Book, 1998, 2003